"With a sensational ensemble, compelling storytelling, and beautiful design, this play is something very special."
—*Broadway World*

"Colleen Murphy's remarkable play is making an ecological statement . . . it radiates genuine heart when it comes to environmental matters. It is an intensely human play tinged at the end with a melancholy that is palpable. We're conscious that we are witnessing a work of epic proportions."
—Jamie Portman,
Capital Critics Circle / Le cercle des critiques de la capitale

"There are plenty of plays that tell of climate change. This may be the first to find a way of showing it . . . What *Warhorse* did for horses, this does for bears."
—Robert Cushman, *National Post*

THE BREATHING HOLE

AGLU

ᐊᒡᓗ

ALSO BY COLLEEN MURPHY

Armstrong's War
The December Man (L'homme de décembre)
The Goodnight Bird
Pig Girl

ALSO BY JANET TAMALIK MCGRATH

The Qaggiq Model: Toward a Theory of Inuktut Knowledge Renewal
"Sila" in *An Ecotopian Lexicon*

THE BREATHING HOLE

AGLU

ᐊᒡᓗ

BY COLLEEN MURPHY

WITH SIOBHAN ARNATSIAQ-MURPHY

NATTILINGMIUTUT TRANSLATION
BY JANET TAMALIK MCGRATH

PLAYWRIGHTS CANADA PRESS
TORONTO

For professional or amateur production rights, please contact:
Michael Petrasek, Kensington Literary Representation
34 St. Andrew Street, Toronto, ON M5T 1K6
416.848.9648, kensingtonlit@rogers.com

LIBRARY AND ARCHIVES CANADA CATALOGUING IN PUBLICATION
Title: The breathing hole = Aglu / Colleen Murphy with Siobhan Arnatsiaq-Murphy ; Nattilingmiutut translation by Janet Tamalik McGrath.
Other titles: Aglu
Names: Murphy, Colleen, author. | Arnatsiaq-Murphy, Siobhan, Inuk dramaturg and cultural consultant. | McGrath, Janet Tamalik, translator.
Description: First edition. | Title includes some text in Nattilingmiutut syllabics. | Text in original English and Nattilingmiutut translation.
Identifiers: Canadiana (print) 20200301802 | Canadiana (ebook) 20200301845 | ISBN 9780369101105 (softcover) | ISBN 9780369101112 (PDF) | ISBN 9780369101129 (EPUB) | ISBN 9780369101136 (Kindle)
Subjects: LCGFT: Drama.
Classification: LCC PS8576.U615 B74 2020 | DDC C812/.54—dc23

Playwrights Canada Press operates on Mississaugas of the Credit, Wendat, Anishinaabe, Métis, and Haudenosaunee land. It always was and always will be Indigenous land.

We acknowledge the financial support of the Canada Council for the Arts—which last year invested $153 million to bring the arts to Canadians throughout the country—the Ontario Arts Council (OAC), Ontario Creates, and the Government of Canada for our publishing activities.

Canada Council for the Arts | Conseil des arts du Canada

ONTARIO ARTS COUNCIL
CONSEIL DES ARTS DE L'ONTARIO
an Ontario government agency
un organisme du gouvernement de l'Ontario

Canada

ONTARIO CREATES | ONTARIO CRÉATIF

This play is dedicated to Aaron Gervais.

A CONFLUENCE OF CULTURES AND SOULS

BY KENN HARPER

Colleen Murphy's play begins with an epigraph from an Inuk shaman: "The greatest peril of life lies in the fact that human food consists entirely of souls. All the creatures that we have to kill and eat, all those that we have to strike down and destroy to make clothes for ourselves, have souls, like we have, souls that do not perish with the body, and which must therefore be propitiated lest they should avenge themselves on us for taking away their bodies."

That shaman was Aua, a man from the western shores of Foxe Basin in farthest northern Hudson Bay. This was but one piece of the wisdom that he imparted to Knud Rasmussen, the Danish ethnologist and adventurer, himself part Inuit, who had arrived in Aua's land in 1921. Rasmussen was intent on collecting the traditional tales of Inuit before they disappeared in a confusion of cultures brought on by the arrival of missionaries, traders, police—the triumvirate of the *Qallunaat* advance force that would shortly overwhelm Inuit beliefs.

"We explain nothing, we believe nothing," Aua claimed. "We fear the weather spirit of earth, that we must fight against to wrest our food from land and sea. We fear *Sila*."

Sila—now there's a word that packs a wealth of meaning. Ubiquitous in Inuit culture, it encompasses the weather, the outside, the environment, and—in a different sense—intelligence, knowledge, wisdom. The modern-day Nunavut Arctic College, in the bilingual world of today's north, uses Sila as the root of its Inuktut name, *Nunavummi Silatuqsarvik*. Rasmussen, on the basis of what he learned from Aua and other shamans, called Sila a great and dangerous spirit that threatened mankind through the powers of nature.

Yet Sila was but an agent, an embodiment of something greater. Aua told the explorer, "We fear *Takannakapsaaluk*, the great woman down at the bottom of the sea, that rules over all the beasts of the sea." Elsewhere she was known as *Nuliajuq*, a being well beloved of Inuit carvers and art collectors. Sila was the force that she unleashed when angry, to bring inclement weather to punish mankind for its transgressions of the rules that circumscribed their lives.

"We fear the souls of dead human beings and of the animals we have killed."

Aua tells us melted water had to be dripped into the mouth of a freshly caught seal to quench the seal's thirst so that the animal's soul might appear again in another seal and offer itself to mankind.

And how are these seals—this lifeblood of the Inuit—caught? For most of the year, Inuit hunt using the technique of *mauliqtuq*—hunting at the breathing hole. The farther one ventures into the deepest recesses of the Arctic, the more long-lasting becomes the ice cover, and the longer the mauliqtuq technique is used. It has come to epitomize the Inuit seal hunt. But one shouldn't sentimentalize it. Although a difficult and technologically sophisticated method, it was a tough way to feed one's family. Charles Francis Hall wrote about the Inuk hunter Kudlago waiting patiently over a breathing hole for two days and two nights before he achieved what passed for success—a single seal to feed his family and dogs.

Colleen Murphy's play is set in the harsh landscape of the central Canadian Arctic. It comes as a shock to most Canadians, who live in a thin line just north of the American border, to learn that this isolated area near the Northwest Passage is barely north of the geographic centre of our peculiarly shaped country. Here an Inuk woman uncharacteristically risks her life to save Angu'řuaq, a polar bear cub, and teaches him to be calm and helpful, against the advice of the hunter Nukilik that "none of us can go against our nature."

Three centuries later, Sir John Franklin and his desperate crew share this same unchanged geography with the descendants of the Inuit who rescued Angu'řuaq, and with the bear itself, now three hundred years old. The Qallunaat—white men—couldn't have chosen a worse time or place. Science hasn't yet given the name "Little Ice Age" to the frigid period in which they make their unfortunate attempt on the Northwest Passage. Having failed to adopt Inuit clothing and travel techniques, they perish, to a man, over a hundred of them. The search for Franklin, seemingly never-ending due to the single-mindedness of his wife, the indomitable Lady Jane, results in the charting of the final stretches of this man-killing coast. But the men and the ships are never found, not until the summers of 2015 and 2016 when first the *Erebus* and then the *Terror* were discovered almost intact, preserved in warming waters, the last one more or less where Inuit had predicted it would be found.

Sir John remains, his resting place unknown, his legacy uncertain; Margaret Atwood called him a "dope," but one Inuk researcher has recently proclaimed him "a good guy."

Almost two centuries pass. The modern machinery of an oil platform throbs incessantly. The ice is deteriorating. Now, in the heart of winter, cruise ships ply the waters that were once impenetrable ice even in summer. The anthropomorphic polar bear, old and tired now, is not what the tourists expected; zoomorphic humans in costume prove more reliable and appealing to the paying passengers.

Angu'řuaq lived at the intersection of land—or in winter, *sinaaq*, the ice edge—and sea. For Inuit, a complex set of taboos governed their relationship with *nanuq*, this beast both feared and sought, whose soul remained with its corpse for three days after it gave its life to a hunter. Like the playwright, Indigenous peoples anthropomorphized the polar bear in their legends—it hunts at the same breathing holes as they do. Climate change threatens this iconic predator now, as it does nanuq's own hunter, the Inuit. In the future as imagined by Murphy, Angu'řuaq succumbs to a world made worse by man—not the men of his experience, the Inuit, nor even the first wave of invaders, the British explorers, but modern, acquisitive man.

Reneltta Arluk, director of the world premiere, inhabits an intersection too, the juncture of several Indigenous cultures. I first encountered her in Iqaluit when she performed in Christopher Morris's play, *Night*. Reneltta brings to her craft a deep understanding of Indigenous culture and a strong awareness of the fragility of her northern environment.

A hunter—is it a man or a bear?—stands over a breathing hole, hostage to Sila. The great woman at the bottom of the sea withholds her largesse. She is angry.

Kenn Harper is a writer and historian who lived for fifty years in the Arctic. He is the author of Minik, the New York Eskimo *(formerly* Give Me My Father's Body: The Life of Minik, the New York Eskimo*);* Thou Shalt Do No Murder: Inuit, Injustice, and the Canadian Arctic*; and the series* In Those Days: Collected Writings on Arctic History*. He is a Fellow of the Royal Geographical Society and the Royal Canadian Geographical Society, and a Knight of the Order of Dannebrog (Denmark).*

COLLEEN MURPHY'S STATEMENT

As a dramatist and as a mother, I felt compelled to write a play about the climate emergency—factually grounding it in science and history, yet rooting it in emotional reality . . . but the subject is so vast and complex that I was not sure how to create an epic journey that could touch people's hearts.

Years ago, I had read a very moving children's story about an old woman in the Arctic who adopted a bear cub and raised him. Inspired by the essence of that story—a special bond and a profound connection between human and animal worlds—I developed the play around a mythical polar bear who lives through five hundred years of history. It begins in 1535 when a Nattilingmiut woman named Hummiktuq takes in the little cub and names him Angu'řuaq. The bond between mother and son is so powerful that it continues to grow through time. Angu'řuaq interacts with all kinds of people in the play, but mostly he interacts with the twenty-first century, because he represents all of us in our lives . . . and in our deaths.

My deepest gratitude to Aaron Gervais for helping me work through the original outline; to Siobhan Arnatsiaq-Murphy, who generously shared her extensive traditional knowledge and her artistry to help shape the specificity and behaviour of all the Inuit characters; to Janet Tamalik McGrath, who vividly and precisely translated this play into the Nattilingmiut dialect, and who kindly allowed us to incorporate some of her Nattilingmiut-back-to-English retranslations that now enrich the play; and, finally, to Nilaulaaq Aglukkaq, an Elder from Gjoa Haven, who carries within her soul the original story of the old woman and the polar bear. Life is a circle.

SIOBHAN ARNATSIAQ-MURPHY'S STATEMENT

I met Colleen, a fellow Murphy, in the fall of 2016 at Qaggiavuut, our northern artist collective in Iqaluit. Myself and a team of Inuit artists provided cultural insight and authenticity to her proposed work of art.

In the spring of 2018, I worked in earnest with Colleen both critiquing and writing the play. In turn she mentored me on how to write a play. She did this the Inuit way by allowing me to see her rewrites and not by overt instruction but through modelling.

It has been such a joy to work with Colleen and a highlight of my past few years.

JANET TAMALIK MCGRATH'S STATEMENT

This book was both challenging and delightful to translate. It really required getting inside each character, exchange, and scene to understand how to bridge the story to a Nattilingmiut audience in Inuktut (the Inuit language). My goal was to convey the range of feelings that the masterfully crafted English text inspired in me as a reader. However, Nattilingmiut oral tradition relies more on context and shared reference for written material. Literary forms are newly adopted and can be sometimes awkward, especially when it is translated material. For first-language readers a work written as a transcription of an oral piece would be easiest to read. With translated works a reader always needs much more contextual information. As such, a number of adaptations were made in the translation to provide that.

It was truly a joy to work closely with my childhood Inuktut teacher, Nilaulaaq Aglukkaq of Gjoa Haven, Nunavut. She is a gifted storyteller and she connected to the play easily, provided archaic words, named the English characters in Inuktut, and also worked through questions the writers wanted to explore. She supports this adaptation of the traditional Nattilingmiut legend "The One Who Adopted a Polar Bear" for an international English audience and affirms that the essence of the original story was well understood and preserved by the authors. I thank Nilaulaaq as well as the Uluulaaq and Arviq families, and the community of Taloyoak for graciously including me in their lives and homes as a child—without which I would not speak their isolated dialect. The success of this translation is owing to their teaching and support. Any weaknesses or mishaps are embraced as my own.

I also thank Samantha MacDonald, producer for Indigenous Theatre at the National Arts Centre, who created a pathway for this kind of work where there was none before. She keenly understood both the complexities of the work and the need to see Indigenous language translation as different from French and other modern languages. As a result, this project has been a great boost for other Nattilingmiutut revitalization work, and this book is the longest manuscript in the Nattilingmiutut dialect and syllabic font set to date.

As well, Nilaulaaq plans to use her original version for an all-Inuktut first-language production in her home community, with the aim of engaging youth in language immersion and stage production. The text of her oral version is featured in full as part of this publication. Samantha has most certainly established a precedent at Canada's national level for supporting art, language, and culture in Indigenous contexts.

For further details about the translation process, with reflection and commentary, see my blog at www.tamalik.com. For more information on Nattilingmiutut dialect preservation, revitalization, and literacy work efforts by Hadlari Consulting and the Ikajuqtigiit Society of Cambridge Bay, Nunavut, see https://hadlariconsulting.com/ikajuqtigiit. They developed and distributed the first generation of Nattilik fonts, which are used throughout this translation.

ᐃᓄᒃᑑᖅᑕᐅᓂᖓ ᐱ'ᓗᒍ ᑎᑎᕋᐅᔮᑦᓗ ᐱ'ᓗᒋᑦ

ᐅᑯᐊᑦ ᖁᓐᖏᐊᓚᒃᓯᓕᐅᖅᑕᐅᔨᒪᔪᑦ ᓴᓇᔭᐅᒐᓗᐊ'ᒪᑕ ᑎᑎᕋᖅᑕᐅᖄᖅᑐᑎᒃ ᖃᑉᓗᓈᑐᑦ, ᒥᒃᓴᐅᑦᑎ'ᓗᑎᒃ ᐃᓄᐃᑦ ᓇᑦᑎᓕᖕᒥᐅᑕᐃᑦ ᐅᓂᑉᑳᖅᑐᐊᑐᖃᐃᑦ ᐅᖃᐅᔨᖃᕐᒪᑕ ᓇᓄᓐᓄᐊᕐᒥᒃ ᑎᒍᐊᖅᑐᕕᓂᕐᒥᒃ. ᐃᓄᒃᑑᓕᖅᑕᐅᕐᑯᔭᐅᓕ'ᒪᑕᓗ ᖃᔾᔨᐊᕘᑦᑯ'ᓂᑦ ᐊᐱᕆᔭᐅᓚᓚ ᐊᖏᖅᐸᖓ. ᓂᓚᐅᑖᖅ ᐅᖅᓱᖅᑑᕐᒥᐅᑕᖅ ᑖᑉᓱᒥᖓ ᐅᓂᑉᑳᖅᑐᐊᕐᒥᒃ ᖃᐅᔨᒪᑦᑎᐊ'ᒪᑦ ᐊᐱᕆᔭᕋ ᖃᑉᓗᓈᑐᑦ ᑎᑎᕋᖅᔨᒪᔪᖅ ᐃᓄᒃᑑᓕᖅᑕᐅᓚᐅᖅᐸᑦ ᖃᓄᖅ ᐃᔪᒪᔮᒃᓴ. ᐅᓂᑉᑳᖅᑐᐊᑐᖃᕐᒥᒃ ᒪᓕᒪᓂᖖᒋᑦᑲᓗᐊᖅᐳᓂ ᐊᑐᖅᑕᐅᒃᐸᑦ ᖃᓄᓂᖖᒋᑖ ᖁᓐᖏᐊᓚᒃᓯᓕᐅᖅᑕᐅᓗᓂ ᖃᑉᓗᓈᓄᑦ.

ᐃᓄᒃᑐᖅᔨᒪᑎ'ᓗᒍᓗ ᑯᑕᐃᔾᔪᑎᓂᒃ ᐊᑐᕐᓗᖓᒎᖅ ᓇᑦᑎᓕᖕᒥᐅᑐᑦ ᑎᑎᕋᐅᔫᑦ ᐊᑐᖅᑕᐅᕐᑯ'ᓗᓂᒋᑦ ᑕᑯᔭᐅᕐᑯ'ᓗᒋᑦ ᔨᒥᑐᐃᓐᓇᖅ ᐃᓕᑕᕆᔭᐅᓂᐊ'ᒪᑕ. ᓂᓚᐅᑖᕐᓗ ᓇ'ᒥᓂᖅ ᓴᓇᔨᒪᔪᕆ'ᓗᓂ ᖁᓐᖏᐊᖅᑕᐅᔪᒃᓯᒥᒃ ᒪᓕᑦᑎᐊᖅᑐᒥᒃ ᐅᓂᑉᑳᖅᑐᐊᒻᒪᕆᖕᒥᒃ, ᐅᖅᓱᖅᑑᕐᒥ ᐃᓅᔪᒃᑐᑦ ᓴᓇᔭᒃᓯᐃ'ᓂᒃ ᐃᓕᑦᐹᓪᓕᕈᑎᒃᓯᐃ'ᓂᒡᓗ ᐅᖃᐅᔨᖅᑲᓂᒃ, ᐃᓄᒃᑐᓪᓗ ᐅᖃᒪᑦᑎᐊᕐᓂᕐᒥᒃ. ᑕᐃᒪᓗ ᓂᓚᐅᑖᖅ ᓂᐱᓕᐅᖅᑕᕋᓗᐊᕋ ᐅᓂᑉᑳᖅᑐᐊᖅ ᑎᑎᕋᖅᐳᒍ ᐊᑐᕐᓂᐊ'ᒪᒍ ᓇ'ᒥᓂᖅ (ᐆᒪ ᐅᖃᓖᒪᐅᑉ ᐃᔨᐊᓃᑦᑐᖅ ᑕᐃᒪ). ᑕᔾᔫᖓ ᐃᓕᔭᐅᖃᑕᐅᕐᑯ'ᓗᓂᐅᒃ ᓇᑦᑎᓕᖕᒥᐅᑕᐃᑦ ᐱᒻᒪᕆᐊᑦ ᖃᐅᔨᒪᔭᐅᓂᐊ'ᒪᑦ.

ᐅᖃᓖᒪᒋᒥᒃ ᑕᓴᑉᓱᒥᖓᑦ ᓴᓇ'ᓗᖓ ᐃᓄᒃᑑᓕᖅᑕᖃ ᐊᑐᖅᐸᖓ ᑎᑎᕋᐅᔨᓂᒃ ᑯᑕᐃᔾᔪᑎᓂᒃ ᑕᐃᔭᐅᔪᓂᒃ ᐊᑐᖅᑕᐅᕙᑦᑐᐊᓕᓵᓕᕿᓗᐊᖅᑎ'ᓗᒋᑦ ᓵᑦᑭᐅᒪᕙᑦᑐᐊᓕᓵᖅᐳᑎᓪᓗ ᓇᓗᓇᐃᑯᑕᒻᒪᕆᐅ'ᒪᑕ ᒪᓕᒃᐳᑎᒃ ᓇᑦᑎᓕᖕᒥᐅᑕᐃᑦ ᐅᖃᐅᔫ'ᓂᒃ ᐃᐳᐊᕆᔭᐅᕙᒃᐳᑎᓪᓗ ᐃᓕᓴᐃᔨᓂᑦ. ᐅᓇᖕᒥᓇᐃᒥᔾᖄᖅᐳᒋᑦ ᐃᓛ'ᓂᒃᑯᓪᓗ ᐅᕈᓗᒋ'ᓗᒋᑦ ᑭᔨᐊᓂᒃ ᐊᑐᖅᐸᓪᓕᐊ'ᓗᒋᑦ ᐅᓇᖕᒥᓕᖅᐳᒋᓪᓗ

ᐃᓱᐊᓇᓕᖅᓱᒋᓪᓗ. ᑕᐃᑉᓱᒪᓂ ᑕᓗᕐᓯᐊᓂ ᓄᑕᕋᐅ’ᑐᖕᒐ ᐃᓄᒃᑐᑦ ᐃᓕᓴᖅᓯᒪᓕᕋᒪ ᓈᓂᖃᑦᑎᐊᖖᒋᒻᒪᒃᑐᓂᒃ ᑕ’ᓇᐃᑦᑐᓂᒃ ᐊᑐᖅᓱᑕ ᓈᓂᖃᖖᒋᑦᑐᓂᒃ ᑎᑎᖅᑲᑦ ᑐᑭᓯᓐᓇᖁᓗᐊᖅᓱᑎᒃ ᑕᐃᑉᓱᒪᓂ ᖃᐸᓗᓇᐅᔭᖅᑐᖃᑦᑎᐊᖖᒋᑦᑲᓱᐊ’ᒪᑦ. ᒫ’ᓇᐅᓕᖅᑐᕐᓗ ᐃᓅᓯᒃᑐᑦ ᓇᓗᖁᖖᒋ’ᓗᒋᑦ ᑯᑕᐃᔾᔭᑎᓂᒃ ᐱᑦᖁᔭᐅᓂᖅᓴᐅᓕ’ᒪᑕ ᑎᑎᕋᕐᓂᒃᑯᑦ ᐃᑲᔪᕐᓂᖃ’ᒪᑕᔫᖅ ᐅᖃᓇᐅᖅᓴᑦᑎᐊᕐᓂᒃᑯᑦ ᖃᐸᓗᓇᐅᔭᕐᓂᖅᓴᐅᓕᖅᑎ’ᓗᒋᑦ ᓄᑕᖅᑲᑦ ᐃᓅᓯᒃᑐᓪᓗ.

ᑎᑎᕋᐅᓯᑦ ᑯᑕᐃᔾᔭᑎᑦ ᑕᓴᑉᑯᐊᑦ ᓇᑦᑎᓕᖕᒥᐅᑕᐃᑦ ᐅᖃᐅᓰ’ᓂᒃ ᐃᓚᐃ’ᓂᑦ ᐊᑐᖅᑕᐅ’ᑐᑎᒃ ᐃᓚᐃ’ᓂᓗ ᐊᑐᖅᑕᐅᖖᒋᑦᑐᑦ. ᑭᓯᐊᓂᒃ ᐃᓕᓴᐃᔮᓂ ᐃᓱᐊᓇᔭᐅᓂᖕᒋ’ᓄᑦ ᓄᑕᖅᑲᓄᑦ ᐃᓕᓴᑦᑎᐊᕐᓂᕐᒍᑦᑐ ᐃᑲᔫᑎᖃ’ᒪᑕ. ᑕᓴᑉᑯᓂᖕᒍᑦ ᐊᑐᕋᓯᐊᓕᖅᑐᖕᒐ ᑎᑎᕋᕐᓂᒃᑯᑦ ᐃᓕᓴᐅᑎᒃᓴᓕᐅᓂᒃᑯᓪᓗ ᐅᖃᓕᒫᒐᒃᓴᓕᐅᓂᒃᑯᓪᓗ ᐅᖃᐅᓯᑦ ᑕᐃᑦᑎᐊᕈᑎᒃᓴᐃ’ᓂᒃ ᓇᑐᓇᐃᑉᑯᑕᒻᒪᓇᐅ’ᒪᑕ ᐃᓱᐊᖅᓱᑎᒃ. ᓯᕗᓂᒃᓴᒍᑦ ᐅᑯᐊᑦ ᐅᖃᓕᒫᒐᒃᓴᑦ ᐊᑐᕈᒪᔭᖃᓗᐊᖅᑯᑦ ᐅᖃᓕᒫᓇᐅᖅᓴᔾᔭᑎᓕᐅᕐᓂᕐᒍᑦ ᐃᓕᓴᐅᑎᒃᓴᓕᐅᖅᑕᐅᓗᑎᒃ.

ᐅᖃᓕᒫᒐᖅ ᑖᒻᓇ ᑕᒫᑦ ᑕᑭᔭᐸᓇᓘ’ᒪᑦ ᑕᒻᒪᖅᓯᒪᔭᖃᕐᓂᖅᐸᑦ ᒪᒥᐊᓇᖅ, ᓴᓇᑦᑎᐊᕋᓯᐊᕋᓗᐊᖅᓱᒍ, ᓇᓗᓇᖖᒋᑦᑐᖅ ᓯᓕ ᑕᒻᒪᖅᓯᒪᓐᓄᐊᖅᑐᖃᖅᑐᒃᓴᐅ’ᒥ’ᒪᑕ ᐊᔪᕐᓇ’ᒪᑦ.

ᖁᔭᓐᓇᒦᕐᓗᐊᖅᑕᕋ ᓂᓚᐅᑖᖅ ᐅᖃᐅᔫᑦ ᐅᖃᐅᔪᑐᖅᑲᑦᑐ ᒥᒃᓴᓄᑦ ᐊᐱᕆᕝᒃᑲᓗᐊᕋᑉᑯ ᐆᒥᖕᒐᑦ ᐅᖃᓕᒫᒐᒃᓴᒥᒃ ᓴᓇᑎ’ᓱᖕᒐ. ᑕᐃᒪ’ᖕᒐᓂᑐᖃᕐᓗ ᐃᓄᒃᑐᑦ ᐃᓕᓴᐃᔮᒋᓯᒪᓚᐅᑉᑯ ᓄᑕᕋᐅᓂᒻᓂᑦ ᑕᓗᕐᓯᐊᓂ ᐃᓕᓴᐃᔭᐅ’ᑐᓂ ᐃᓄᒃᑐᑦ. ᐃᓕᓴᖅᓯᒪ’ᑐᖕᒐᓗ ᐃᓄᒃᑐᑦ ᐅᖃᒪᓂᕐᒥᒃ ᐅᓘᓰᑦᑯ’ᓂ ᐊᕐᕕᑦᑯ’ᓂᓗ ᑖᑦᓕᕐᑦᑯ’ᓂ ᑕᓗᕐᓯᐊᓃᑎ’ᓗᒋᑦ. ᐊᕐᓇᖃᕐᕕᖕᒥᓗ ᑕᓗᕐᓯᐊᕐᒥᐅᑕᓂᑦᓗ ᐃᑲᔪᖅᑕᐅᑦᑎᐊᖅᓯᒪᓖᓪᓚ ᖁᔭᓕᑦᓗᐊᖅᑐᖕᒐ ᐅᑉᓗᒥᐅᓯᒧᑦ ᑭᓯᒥᐅᓗᖕᒐ ᐊᔪᕐᓂᐊᕋᓗᐊᕋᒪ ᐃᓕᓴᑦᑎᐊᖅᑐᕕᓂᐅᒐᒪ ᐃᓚᒋᓴᐅᖃᑕᐅ’ᓗᖕᒐ ᓄᑕᕋᐅ’ᓗᖕᒐ. ~ᖃᐸᓗᓈᓐᓄᐊᖅ ᑕᒪᓕᒃ.

PRONUNCIATION GUIDE

This pronunciation guide is intended to help readers and performers phonetically pronounce some of the Nattilingmiutut names and words found throughout. This guide is not meant to be a replacement for Nattilingmiutut actors or language coaches. The phonetic guide uses **bold** to indicate word/syllable stress. If there is no bold present, then there is no stress in the word/syllable and all syllables are to be treated equally.

Aglu	ug-loo
Hummiktuq	ho**m-mic**k-tok (like "who," but *short*)
Maniilaq	moneyy**yy**-luck
Nukilik	noo-key-lick
Higguk	he**g-g**ook
Ibřuq	eb-ruck
Avin'ngaq	ah-ve**n**-gnawk
Qiluniq	qhay-lu-nehk
Atugauq	atu-gaok
Qaakšaattiaq	kawk-shr**aa-ch**eck
Angu'řuaq	uh-ngoot-rock
Ukuannuaq	ook-wahn-noak

Aluruti (Wickers's nickname, meaning a warming layer inside a skin boot, a humorous piece of clothing that bunches and creeps up.)	uh-low-rhooti (French r sound)
Piniq (Bean, based on the sound of his name. It pairs with Aluruti, because it's the inner slipper that gives an extra layer, humorous in how it doesn't always stay in place either.)	pin-neck
Aqutirřuaq (Franklin, "the great driver.")	uckoo-tech-rock
Hanguřinaluk (Holloway, using "H" from his name, it also refers to his role, "the great steering one")	hungoo-rhee-nah-luk
Katuut (Carter, based on the sound of his name, but it also means the short stubby handle used to beat the frame of the drum.)	cah-toot
Ařgiaq	ud-gyakh
Paningajak	pah-nee-ngaw-yuck
Nauttiqtuqti (Morshead, meaning "the one who oversees and guides the wayfaring.")	now-**ch**eck-took-tee
Hanaři (worker, whether crew or steward)	hanad-rhee (similar to English r sound)
Maphakaaq (Matson, from the sound of her name.)	mup-**fh**a-k**aa**wk
Qi'ngaqtuq	kheyt-ngawk-tok

Tuutalik	too-ta-leek
Roy, Larkin, Rivera, Griffith-Thomson, Lee, Hayden, Dufort, Ainsworth	Names pronounced as they are in English, reflecting the times, except Mr. Griffith-Thomson is Angutautqiřaq Gee-Tee and Mrs. Griffith-Thomson is Arnautqiřaq Gee-Tee (meaning male one of a couple and female one of a couple, reference to the terms Mr. and Mrs.)
Kaapitaija (A Nattilingmiut word historically borrowed from the English word "captian," and still used today.)	copy-tey-yah
Lucy	loo-see
Marinnuaq (Marriane, literally "little" or "dear Mary.")	mah-ree-nnoak

NOTES

The whole play takes place by a breathing hole in the eastern portion of the Kitikmeot Region of Nunavut, traditional homelands of the Nattilik Inuit (Nattilingmiut). Nunavut makes up 20% of Canada's land mass and 60% of its coastline. If it were a country on its own, Nunavut would be the fifteenth largest country in the world.

When the bears are on stage it is important for the audience to hear their breathing, grunts, and yelps. The sound of their breathing should fill the theatre.

Throughout Act II, when Ağgiaq and Paningajak speak to each other, they speak in English, and when they speak to the British characters, they speak in Nattilingmiutut.

Also in Act II, Franklin mangles all the Inuit language he tries to speak, while Morshead's pronunciation, although poor, is much better than Franklin's.

The text at the end of Act III, Scene One can be used fully or partially to help cover the set change into Scene Two. It is also entirely unnecessary.

The Breathing Hole was first produced by the Stratford Festival at the Studio Theatre in Stratford, Ontario, from July 30 to October 6, 2017, with the following cast and creative team. In this updated publication, some character names have been changed from the original cast list below, some characters have been eliminated, and the spelling of some names have changed.

Randy Hughson: Sir John Franklin and Mr. Griffith-Thomson
Jani Lauzon: Huumittuq, Panik (female bear), and Marianne
Thomas Mitchell Barnet: Bean and Steward #1
Jimmy Blais: Paningajak and Félix Bonnière
Yolanda Bonnell: Iprug and Atugauq
Miali Buscemi: Mannilaq and Qi'ngatuq
Jaun Chioran: Oliver Morshead and Rivera
Jim Codrington: Holloway and Shen Young
Sarah Dodd: Matson Day
Victor Ertmanis: Franklin Crew #1 and Captain Matias
Ujarneg Fleischer: Avinngaq, Ajjiaq, and Steward #2
Angelina Foster del Mundo: Young Atuguaq and Atugauq's daughter
Deidre Gillard-Rowlings: Panik (female bear), Larkin, and Mrs. Griffith-Thomson
Bruce Hunter: Angu'řuaq (the bear)
Johnny Issaluk: Nukilik and Totalik
Evan Kearns: Qiluniq's son
Clara Kittmer: Lucy
Jamie Mac: Young Angu'řuaq, Wickers, and Roy
Katelyn McCulloch: Melody and Lee
Zlatomir Moldovanski: Carter and Ainsworth
Nick Nahwegahbow: Qiluniq and Dufort
Hunter Smalley: Young Qiluniq
Gordon Patrick White: Higguk, Franklin Crew #2, and Hayden

Director: Reneltta Arluk
Assistant Director: Zack Russell
Dramaturge: Bob White
Inuit Dramaturgy and Cultural Consultation: Siobhan Arnatsiaq-Murphy, Laakkuluk Williamson Bathory, Miali Buscemi, Mary Itorcheak, Vinnie Karetak, Alika Komangapik, and Annabella Piugattuk
Inuktut Consultation and Translation: Kevin Eetoolook and Arnaoyok Alookee
Set Design: Daniela Masellis
Inuit Props Consultant: Koomuatuk Curley
Costume Design: Joanna Yu
Inuit Costume Consultant: Beatrice Deer
Inuit Makeup Consultant: Lucy Tulugarjuk
Assistant Costume Designers: Francesca Callow and Mary-Jo Carter Dodd
Lighting Design: Itai Erdal
Assistant Lighting Design: C.J. Astronomo
Composer and Sound Design: Carmen Braden
Movement Director: Brad Cook
Fight Director: John Stead
Associate Fight Director: Anita Nittoly
Stage Manager: Maxwell T. Wilson
Assistant Stage Managers: Jackie Brabazon and Zeph Williams
Production Stage Manager: Meghan Callan
Production Assistant: Troy Taylor
Technical Director: Robbin Cheesman
Associate Technical Director: Eleanor Creelman

CHARACTERS

ACT I

Hummiktuq
forty-five, widow

Maniilaq
thirty-five, wife of Nukilik

Nukilik
thirty, husband of Maniilaq

Higguk
thirty, husband of Ibřuq

Ibřuq
thirty-five, wife of Higguk

Avinngaq
thirty, *angakkut [shaman]*

Qiluniq
ten, son of Maniilaq and Nukilik

Atugauq
eight, daughter of Ibřuq and Higguk

Qaakšaattiaq
Qiluniq and Atugauq's young daughter

ᔨᓚᓇᙳᐊᖅᑐᑦ

ᖁᓐᖕᒋᐊᖅᑕᐅᔪᒃᓯᒥ ᓱᕗᓪᓘᑦᑐᒥ

ᔨᒻᒥᒃᑐᖅ
ᐃᓂᕐᓂᖅ, ᐊ'ᓚᐃᕈᕐᓂᐅᔪᖅ

ᒪᓃᓚᖅ
ᐃᓅᔨᒃᑐᖅ, ᓄᑭᓚᐅᑉ ᓄᓚᐊᖕᒐ

ᓄᑭᓚᒃ
ᐃᓅᔨᒃᑐᖅ, ᒪᓃᓚᐅᑉ ᐅᐃᖕᒐ

ᓱᒡᒍᒃ
ᐃᓅᔨᒃᑐᖅ, ᐃᑉᔩᑉ ᐅᐃᖕᒐ

ᐃᑉᔪᖅ
ᐃᓅᔨᒃᑐᖅ, ᓱᒡᒎᑉ ᓄᓚᐊᖕᒐ

ᐊᕕᓐᖕᒐᖅ
ᐃᓅᔨᒃᑐᖅ, ᐊᖕᒐᑦᖁᖅ

ᕿᓗᓂᖅ
ᐃᓅᔨᒃᑐᐊᕐᔪᙳᔮᖅᑐᖅ, ᒪᓃᓚᐅᑉ ᓄᑭᓚᐅᑉᓗ ᐃᕐᓃᖕᒋᒃ

ᐊᑐᒐᐅᖅ
ᓂᕕᐊᖅᓵᖅ, ᐃᑉᔩᑉ ᓱᒡᒎᑉᓗ ᐸᓃᖕᒋᒃ

ᖄᒃᓵᑦᑎᐊᖅ
ᕿᓗᓂᐅᑉ ᐊᑐᒐᐅᑉᓗ ᐸᕐᓃᖕᒋᒃ

Angu'řuaq
polar bear

Ukuannuaq
polar bear, Angu'řuaq's wife

ACT II

Wickers
twenties, midshipman

Bean
twenties, midshipman's mate

Sir John Franklin
fifty-nine, expedition commander

James Holloway
twenties, second commander of the *Erebus*

Carter
twenties, boatswain

Ařgiaq
twenties, hunter

Paningajak
thirties, hunter

Oliver Morshead
fifty, chief engineer and ice master

Crew #1 and #2
of the *Erebus*

Angu'řuaq
polar bear

Ukuannuaq
polar bear, Angu'řuaq's wife

ᐊᖑ’ᔪᐊᖅ
ᓇᓅᔪᖅ

ᐅᑯᐊᓐᓄᐊᖅ
ᓇᓅᔪᖅ, ᐊᖑ’ᔪᐊᑉ ᓄᓕᐊᖓ

ᖅᑯᓐᖏᐊᖅᑕᐅᔪᒃᓴᒥ ᑐᓪᓚᐅᔪᒥ

ᐊᓗᕈᑎ
ᐃᓂᓚᓵᖅ ᐃᓅᓱᒃᑐᖅ, ᐅᒥᐊᖅᑐᖅᑎ

ᐱᓂᖅ
ᐃᓂᓚᓵᖅ ᐃᓅᓱᒃᑐᖅ, ᐅᒥᐊᖅᑐᖅᑎᐅᑉ ᐃᑲᔪᖅᑎᐊ

ᐊᖁᑎᖅᔪᐊᖅ
ᐃᓂᖅᓂᖅ, ᐅᒥᐊᖅᔪᐊᖅᑐᖅᑐᑦ ᖅᑭᓂᖅᑎᑦ ᐊᑕᓂᐊᑦ

ᓴᖑᔨᓇᓗᒃ
ᐃᓂᓚᓵᖅ ᐃᓅᓱᒃᑐᖅ, ᖅᑲᒪᔨ ᐃᐅᕋᐸᔅᒥ ᐅᒥᐊᖅᔪᐊᖅᒥ

ᑲᑑᑦ
ᐃᓂᓚᓵᖅ ᐃᓅᓱᒃᑐᖅ, ᐅᒥᐊᖅᔪᐊᖅᒥᒃ ᐅᒥᐊᖅᑐᖅᑎᓂᒡᓗ ᑲᒪᔨᐅᖅᑕᐅᔪᖅ

ᐊᕐᒋᐊᖅ
ᐃᓂᓚᓵᖅ ᐃᓅᓱᒃᑐᖅ, ᐊᖑᓇᓱᐊᖅᑎ

ᐸᓂᖕᒐᔭᒃ
ᐃᓅᓱᒃᑐᖅ, ᐊᖑᓇᓱᐊᖅᑎ

ᓇᐅᑦᑎᖅᑐᖅᑎ
ᐃᓂᖅᓂᖅ, ᐃᖕᒋᕐᕋᕐᔪᑎᓂᒃ ᑲᒪᔨᐅᔪᖅ ᓱᑯᓕᕆᔨᓗ

ᓴᓇᖅᑯᓗᒃᑎᒃ ᒪᕐᕈᒃ
ᐃᐅᕋᐸᔅ-ᒥ ᐅᒥᐊᖅᔪᐊᖅᒥ

ᐊᖑ’ᔪᐊᖅ
ᓇᓅᔪᖅ

ᐅᑯᐊᓐᓄᐊᖅ
ᓇᓅᔪᖅ, ᐊᖑ’ᔪᐊᑉ ᓄᓕᐊᖓ

ACT III

Matson Day
thirties, entrepreneur, Oceanus Adventures

Qi'ngaqtuq Donoghue
thirties, biologist

Tuutalik
thirties, security guard at Circumpolar Oil

Roy
twenties, ad agency professional

Larkin
twenties, ad agency professional

Rivera Garcia
sixties, entrepreneur, Oceanus Adventures

Mr. Ryan Griffith-Thomson
forties, entrepreneur, Oceanus Adventures

Mrs. Lori Griffith-Thomson
forties, entrepreneur, Oceanus Adventures

Lee
thirties, entrepreneur, Oceanus Adventures

Dufort Bonnière
thirties, entrepreneur, Oceanus Adventures

Ainsworth
forties, entrepreneur, Oceanus Adventures

Captain Matias
captain of the *Aurora Borealis*

Steward
on the *Aurora Borealis*

ᖁᓐᓂᐊᖅᑕᐅᔪᒃᓴᒥ ᑭᖑᓪᓖᑦᑐᒥ

ᒪᑉᓴᑳᖅ
ᐃᓅᔪᒃᑐᖅ, ᐳᓚᕋᖅᑎᓂ ᑎᒥᐅᔪᓂ ᐃᓚᒋᔭᐅᔪᖅ

ᕿ’ᖕᒐᖅᑐᖅ ᑖᓇᔪᐅ
ᐃᓅᔪᒃᑐᖅ, ᐆᒪᔪᓕᕆᔨᐅᔪᖅ

ᑑᑕᓕᒃ
ᐃᓅᔪᒃᑐᖅ, ᐅᖅᓱᕐᔪᐊᓕᕆᔨᓂ ᓴᐳᓐᓇᔪᐊᑎᐅᔪᖅ

ᕈᐃ
ᐃᓂᓕᓵᖅ ᐃᓅᔪᒃᑐᖅ, ᑐᓴᒐᒃᓴᓕᐅᖅᑎ ᖃᐅᔨᑉᑲᐃᔪᓕᕆᔨᓂ

ᓖᑭᓐ
ᐃᓂᓕᓵᖅ ᐃᓅᔪᒃᑐᖅ, ᑐᓴᒐᒃᓴᓕᐅᖅᑎ ᖃᐅᔨᑉᑲᐃᔪᓕᕆᔨᓂ

ᓇᕕᐊᕋ ᒑᒍᓴ
ᐃᓂᕐᓂᖅ, ᐳᓚᕋᖅᑎᓂ ᑎᒥᐅᔪᓂ ᐃᓚᒋᔭᐅᔪᖅ

ᐊᖑᑕᐅᑦᕿᔭᖅ ᒍᓇᕕᔅ-ᑖᒻᓴᓐ
ᐃᓂᕐᓂᖅ, ᐳᓚᕋᖅᑎᓂ ᑎᒥᐅᔪᓂ ᐃᓚᒋᔭᐅᔪᖅ

ᐊᕐᓇᐅᑦᕿᔭᖅ ᒍᓇᕕᔅ-ᑖᒻᓴᓐ
ᐃᓂᕐᓂᖅ, ᐳᓚᕋᖅᑎᓂ ᑎᒥᐅᔪᓂ ᐃᓚᒋᔭᐅᔪᖅ

ᓛ
ᐃᓅᔪᒃᑐᖅ, ᐳᓚᕋᖅᑎᓂ ᑎᒥᐅᔪᓂ ᐃᓚᒋᔭᐅᔪᖅ

ᑑᕗᐊᖅᑦ ᐸᓐᓯᓇ
ᐃᓅᔪᒃᑐᖅ, ᐳᓚᕋᖅᑎᓂ ᑎᒥᐅᔪᓂ ᐃᓚᒋᔭᐅᔪᖅ

ᐊᐃᓐᓯᕗᐊᑦ
ᐃᓂᕐᓂᖅ, ᐳᓚᕋᖅᑎᓂ ᑎᒥᐅᔪᓂ ᐃᓚᒋᔭᐅᔪᖅ

ᑳᐱᑕᐃᓴ
ᑳᐱᑕᐃᓴᒋᔭᐅᔪᖅ ᐅᒥᐊᖅᔪᐊᖅᒥ ᑕᐃᔭᐅᔪᒥ ᐊᖅᓱᖅᓂᖅᒥᒃ

ᓴᓇᔨ
ᐅᒥᐊᖅᔪᐊᖅᒥ ᑕᐃᔭᐅᔪᒥ ᐊᖅᓱᖅᓂᖅᒥᒃ

Lucy
Larkin's nine-year-old daughter

Marianne
forty, Lucy's grandmother

Angu'řuaq
polar bear

ᓘᓯ
ᓂᕕᐊᖅᓯᐊᖅ, ᓛᑭᓐᓂᐅᑉ ᐸᓂᐊ

ᒪᓇᓐᓄᐊᖅ
ᐃᓂᖅᓂᖅ, ᓘᓯᐅᑉ ᓂᖕᒋᐅᖕᒐ

ᐊᖕᑌ’ᔭᐊᖅ
ᓇᓅᔭᖅ

1535

SOULS

The greatest peril of life lies in the fact that human food consists entirely of souls. All the creatures that we have to kill and eat, all those that we have to strike down and destroy to make clothes for ourselves, have souls, like we have, souls that do not perish with the body, and which must therefore be propitiated lest they should avenge themselves on us for taking away their bodies.

—Knud Rasmussen (1879–1933) was a Danish–Inuit explorer and anthropologist, and the first European to cross the Northwest Passage via dogsled

1534-ᖑᑎ'ᓗᒍ

ᑕᕐᓂᑦ

ᐊᑦᕐᑐᓇᕐᓇᕐᓂᖅᓴᐃᑦᑑᕗᖅ ᐃᓅᓯᕐᒥ ᐃᓄᐃᑦ ᑕᕐᓃᓐᓇᕐᓂᒃ ᓂᖅᑲᐅᑎᕐᑲ'ᒪᑕ. ᓴᑉᑯᐊᑦ ᐊᓐᖑᑎᒃᓴᖅᑯᑦ ᓂᖅᑲᐅᑎᒃᓴᖅᑯᑦ, ᓴᑉᑯᐊᕌᓗᐃᑦ ᐊᖑᕙᒃᑕᖅᑯᑦ ᑐᕐᑯᓴᖅᐸᒃᑕᖅᑯᑦ ᐊ'ᓄᕌᕐᑲᕐᑯ'ᓗᑕ, ᑕᕐᓂᕐᑲ'ᒪᑕ, ᐅᕙᑉᑐᑦ, ᑕᕐᓂᖕᒋᑦ ᑐᕐᑯᕙᖖᒋ'ᒪᑕ ᑎᒥᖕᒋᑦ ᑐᕐᑯᒐᓗᐊᖅᑎ'ᓗᒋᑦ, ᑕ'ᓇᐃ'ᒪᓪᓗ ᓴᑐᕆᐊᕐᑲᖅᑕᕗᑦ ᐊᑭᓇᕉᐊᕐᑯᖖᒋ'ᓗᒋᑦ ᐅᕙᑉᑎ'ᓂᒃ ᑎᒦ'ᓂᒃ ᐊᑐᕋᑉᑕ.

—ᑯᓅᑎ ᕋᔅᒧᔅᓐ (1879–1933) ᕿᓂᖅᑎᑕᐅᕐᑲᑕᐅᓯᒪᓂ'ᒪᑦ ᐊᑯᑭᑦᑐᒥᐅᑕᖅ ᐃᓄᖕᒥᒃ ᐊᓈᓇᓂᒃ ᑕᐃᓂᓯᒥᒃ ᐊᑖᑕᕐᑲᖅᑰᓂ, ᐊᑭᐊᓂ'ᖕᓚᖅᑐᓂᒃ ᓯᕗᓪᓕᑦᑑᓯᒪᓂᖅᑰᓂ ᕿᒧᒃᓯᒃᑯᑦ ᐅᑭᐅᖅᑕᖅᑑᑉ ᐊᑉᕐᑯᑎᐊᔫᖅᑐᓂᒃ.

ACT I

SCENE ONE

It is May 1535, and light sparkles along the ridge of a glacial hill in the distance. Cold water, heavy with drift ice, flanks one side of the shore.

The land is alive with sounds rumbling from deep inside the ice. The wind blows softly, birds squawk, and the barking and whining of the huskies can be heard when they pick up the smell of meat.

HUMMIKTUQ stands by the edge of a breathing hole, clutching a soapstone pot and staring intently down at the water.

Enter MANIILAQ carrying a baby in the hood of her amauti.

MANIILAQ: Why are you standing there doing nothing useful?

No response.

Did you rinse the pot?

HUMMIKTUQ: What colour is this water?

MANIILAQ: It's just water.

HUMMIKTUQ: It's black, look . . .

MANIILAQ moves closer to look at the water.

MANIILAQ: No it isn't.

ᖁᓐᖏᐊᖅᑕᐅᔪᒃᓴ ᓯᕗᓪᓖᑦᑐᖅ

ᖃᓄᓕᑦᑑᓂᐊ ᐱᒋᐊᕐᓂᐊᓂ

ᐅᐱᓐᖕᒑᖑ'ᒪᑦ ᖃᕘᕝᕕᖕᒥ 1535-ᖑᑎ'ᓗᒍ, ᐅᖕᒐᓯᒃᑐᒥ ᐊᐅᔭᐃᑦᑐᒥ ᓯᕿᓐᓂᖅᓗᓂ ᑕᑯᖃᓐᓂᖅᑐᖅ. ᐆᓇᐅᑦᑐᐊᓗᒃ ᐃᒪᖅ, ᓯᑯᖃᖅᓗᓂ ᓯᑳᓂ.

ᓄᓇ ᐆᒻᒪᑦᖂᒻᒪᓇᒃᓗᓂ ᑐᓴᕐᓇᖅᓗᓂ ᓯᑯ. ᐊᓄᕌᓐᓄᐊᖅᑐᖅ, ᑎᖕᒥᐊᑦ ᑐᓴᕐᓇᖅᑐᑦ ᕿ'ᒦᓪᓗ ᕿᓗᒃᓗᑎᒃ ᕿᓄᔭᑦ ᓇᐃᒪᒐᒥᒃ ᐆᔭᖅᔭᖕᓃᑦᑐᒥᒃ.

ᔮᒻᒥᒃᑐᖅ ᐊᒡᒍᑉ ᖃᓂᐊᓃᑦᑐᖅ ᑎᒍᒥᐊᖅᓗᓂ ᐅᑦᑯᓯᖕᒥᒃ, ᑕᐅᑐᒡᒍᐊᖅᑐᖅᑐ ᐃᒪᕐᒍᑦ.

ᒪᓃᓚᖅ ᐃᔪᖅᓗᓂ ᐊᒫᖅᑐᖅ ᓄᑕᕋᓐᓄᐊᕐᒥᒃ.

ᒪᓃᓚᖅ: ᔮ'ᒪᑦ ᔮᓚᖕᖏᒻᒪᓇᒃᑐᑎᑦ?

ᑭᐅᖕᖏᑦᑐᖅ.

ᒪᓃᓚᖅ: ᐅᑦᑯᓯᒃ ᐃᔅᓱᕋᓗᐊᖅᐱᐅᒃ?

ᔮᒻᒥᒃᑐᖅ: ᐃᒪᖅ ᑕᓴᒻᒪ ᑕᖅᓯ ᖃᓄᓕᑦᑑᕙ?

ᒪᓃᓚᖅ: ᐃᒪᐃᓐᓇᔅᓗᒃ.

ᔮᒻᒥᒃᑐᖅ: ᑕᒃᑰᒃ, ᕿᕐᓇᓕᒃᑐᖅ . . .

ᒪᓃᓚᖅ ᖃᒡᓚᒋᐊᕋᓐᓂᖅᑐᖅ ᐃᒪᕐᒍᑦ ᑕᑯᑦᑎᐊᖅᐹᓪᓚᕋᔮᐊᖅᓗᓂᐅᒃ.

ᒪᓃᓚᖅ: ᐄᕿᔅᓗᒃ ᕿᕐᓇᓕᖕᖏᑦᑐᓈᓗᒃ.

HUMMIKTUQ: Through my eyes it appears quite black.

MANIILAQ: If you make yourself sunblind from too much sun then objects appear black.

*HUMMIKTUQ quickly puts on her sun goggles—*iřgak, *made of bone—and looks down at the water, then removes the goggles.*

HUMMIKTUQ: No, it's not from the sun—it's remnants from my dream last night. As I walked through my dream, everywhere I looked the water was black.

MANIILAQ: Maybe the souls of your forebearers are darkening the water in your dream, or maybe the souls of the animals make it dark with their shadows.

HUMMIKTUQ: I didn't see any animal souls or human souls, only black water but—eeee, I did see something injured . . . a white creature struggling in the black water, its foreleg reaching to me. I heard it call out to me, not out loud but in here *(points to her head)* and in here *(points to her heart)* I heard it calling to me.

MANIILAQ: Maybe the dream is about you being alone because you didn't see any souls.

HUMMIKTUQ: . . . yes . . . maybe, but still this black water—

MANIILAQ: This water's *not* black, *Arnarvik [Maternal Aunt]*. It has no colour. Look at it . . . *(scoops up some water with her hand)* Water: simple, ordinary water.

HUMMIKTUQ: Yes . . . I see now that it has no colour.

Sounds can be heard . . . dogs barking and perhaps voices.

MANIILAQ: Did you rinse the pot? We need to boil the meat.

HUMMIKTUQ: Yes, here . . . *(gives MANIILAQ the soapstone pot)* Don't tell your husband I saw black water in my dream, as he might tease me about it.

MANIILAQ: He's a big teaser, that one.

ᖬᒻᒥᒃᑯᖅ: ᐃᖬᑉᑯᑦ ᖃᕐᓇᕆᑦᕐᑰ'ᒪᑦ.

ᒪᓃᓚᖅ: ᖮᕐᑭᓂᕐᒍᕐᔫᖭᖅᑐᖅ. ᐃᓪᓗᑦᑎᓕᕐᕙᑦ ᖬᓇᕚᓗᐃᑦ ᕐᑭᕐᓇᕆᑦᕐᑰᓕᖅᑦᑕ'ᒪᑕ.

ᖬᒻᒥᒃᑯᖅ ᐊᑐᓕᖅᑯᓂᐅᒃ ᐃᔅᒐᓂ—ᔅᐅᓂᕐᒍᑦ ᔅᓇᖮᒪᖬᖅ—ᐃᒪᕐᒍᑦ ᑕᑯᑉᔅᖅᑯᓂ ᐃᔅᒐᓂᓗ ᐊᖮᕙᖅᑯᔪ.

ᖬᒻᒥᒃᑯᖅ: ᐃᕐᑭᔅᑯᒃ ᖮᕐᑭᓂᕐᔫᖕᖏᑦᑐᔅᑯᒃ—ᐅᕙᓪᓂᖕᖖᖅᑐᖯᖅᑐᖅ ᐅᓐᓄᒃᑯᑦ ᖮᓐᓇᖅᑐᕆᔅᓪᓂᑦ. ᐱᖬᒃᑯᖕᒐ ᖬᒥᑐᐃᓐᓇᖅ ᐃᒪᓐᓇᓗᒃ ᕐᑭᕐᓇᕆᒃᑐᐃᓐᓇᓇᔫ'ᒪᑦ.

ᒪᓃᓚᖅ: ᖮᕖᓪᓕᕙᓂᖅᐱᑦ ᑕᕐᓂᖕᖏᑦ ᑖᖅᑎᑦᑎᖬᔅ'ᒪᑕ ᐃᒪᕐᒥᒃ, ᐆᒪᖬᓇᓗᐃᓪᔫᓐᓃᑦ ᑕᕐᓂᖕᖏᑦ ᑖᖅᑎᑦᑎ'ᔅ'ᒪᑕ ᑕᕐᕋᐃᑎᒍᑦ.

ᖬᒻᒥᒃᑯᖅ: ᑕᑯᖕᖏᒻᒪᕆᒃᑐᖕᒐ ᐆᒪᖬᑦ ᑕᕐᓃ'ᓂᒃ ᐃᓄᐃᓪᔫᓐᓃᑦ, ᐃᒪᖅ ᕐᑭᕐᓇᕆᒃᖮᓐᓇᖅᑐᖅ ᑭᖮᐊᓂᒃ—ᐄ ᖬᓇᒥᒃ ᑕᑯᖬᖕᒐ . . . ᐋ'ᓂᖅᖮᒪᑦᕐᑰᖅᑐᒥᒃ ᐊᑦᕐᑯᓇᖅᑐᒥᒃ, ᖃᑯᖅᑕᓐᓄᐊᖅ ᐃᒪᕐᒥ ᕐᑭᕐᓇᕆᒃᑐᒥ, ᐃᔄᑦᕐᑰᖅᑯᓂᖕᒐ. ᑐᖅᑯᓚ'ᓘᓂᖕᒐᓗ, ᓂᐱᖃᖕᖏᑦᑐᑦᑯᑦ ᐅᖄᓇ *(ᑎᑦᑯᐊᖅᑯᔪ ᓂᐊᕐᑯᓂ)* ᐅᖄᓇᓗ *(ᑎᑦᑯᐊᖅᑯᔪ ᐆᒪᑎᓂ).* ᑐᔄᖭᕐᓗᐊᕐ ᑐᖅᑯᓚ'ᓘᓂᖕᒐ.

ᒪᓃᓚᖅ: ᐊᖮᖃᖕᖏᓃ'ᓄᑦ ᖮᓐᓇᒃᑑᒪᒐᕙᑦ ᑕ'ᓇ ᑕᕐᓂᕐᓂᒃ ᑕᑯᖕᖏᑦᑲᓗᐊᕐᓂᖅᑯᑎᑦ.

ᖬᒻᒥᒃᑯᖅ: . . . ᐄᒃᓴᐅᖬᖅ . . . ᑭᖮᐊᓂᒃ ᕐᑭᕐᓇᕆᒃᑐᓇᓗᒃ ᐃᒪᓇᓗᒃ—

ᒪᓃᓚᖅ: ᐃᒪᖅ ᑕᔅᓪᒪ ᕐᑭᕐᓇᕆᖕᖏᑦᑐᓇᓗᒃ, ᐊᕐᓇᕐᕙᒐ. ᑕᖅᓴᖅᑲᖕᖏᒻᒪᕆᒃᑐᕐᓕ. ᑕᒃᑰᒃ . . . *(ᐊᔅᒐᖕᒥᔪᑦ ᖃᓗᕋᖅᑯᓂ ᐃᒪᕐᒥᒃ)* . . . ᐃᒪᑐᐃᓐᓇᓇᓗᒃ ᑕᔅᒪ.

ᖬᒻᒥᒃᑯᖅ: ᖬᖬᓇᓗᒃ . . . ᐄ, ᐊᖮᐅᔅᑯᒃ ᑕᖅᓴᖅᑲᖕᖏᔅᑯᓂ'ᒪᑦ.

ᑐᔅᕐᓇᖅᑐᖅᑲᓕᖅᑯᓂ . . . ᕐᑭ'ᒦᑦ ᕐᑭᓗᒃᑐᑦ, ᖬᓇᓪᓗ ᑐᔅᖅᔅᐅ'ᓗᑎᒃ ᐃᓄᐃᑦ ᐅᕐᑲᒪᖬᑦ.

ᒪᓃᓚᖅ: ᐅᑦᑯᖮᒃ ᐃᔅᕈᕋᓗᐊᖅᐱᐅᒃ? ᐆᖬᓕᐅᕆᐊᕐᑲᓕᖅᑐᔪᒃ.

ᖬᒻᒥᒃᑯᖅ: ᐄ, ᐅᕝᕙ . . . *(ᐅᑦᑯᖮᒃ ᑐᓂ'ᓗᓂᐅᒃ ᒪᓃᓚᕐᒧᑦ)*
. . . ᐅᐃᑦ ᐃᓪᓇ ᐊᒃᐱᐅᑎᑦᑕᐃᓕ'ᔅᕙᑦ ᕐᑭᕐᓇᕆᒃᑐᒥᒃ ᐃᒪᕐᒥᒃ ᑕᑯᒐᒪ ᖮᓐᓇᒃᑐᕆᔅᓪᓂ ᐱᔅᕆᓂᐊᕙ'ᒪᖕᒐ.

HUMMIKTUQ: Please do not tell him. Oh look . . .

HUMMIKTUQ picks up a feather and hands it to MANIILAQ, who takes it.

. . . give this to your son. That little one loves feathers so much.

MANIILAQ: We are starving, and we'll starve even longer waiting for you—I'll boil the meat myself.

HUMMIKTUQ: I'll melt snow for the water.

MANIILAQ: No—you always take too long.

HUMMIKTUQ: I can help with your newborn baby.

MANIILAQ: She's sleeping.

MANIILAQ exits.

HUMMIKTUQ: *(softly wails)* AAAAHHH . . .

HUMMIKTUQ looks down at the water again and cups some in her hand. It is not black. She shakes off the water.

NUKILIK and HIGGUK enter. Between them they carry a rack laid out with the hide of a freshly killed polar bear. Following behind are MANIILAQ and IBŘUQ, one carrying a pot with broth and the other carrying a pot with chunks of boiled meat. Behind them are NUKILIK's son, QILUNIQ, and HIGGUK's daughter, ATUGAUQ. Finally, AVINNGAQ enters carrying a small skin drum. He is an angakkut—a shaman—and has many amulets attached to his intricately designed clothing.

NUKILIK and HIGGUK set up the rack. The women set the boiled meat down. HUMMIKTUQ sits apart from the group and watches as the bowl is passed around and everyone sips a bit of broth. MANIILAQ gives the bowl to QILUNIQ.

MANIILAQ: Give it to Hummiktuq.

QILUNIQ takes the bowl to HUMMIKTUQ and she drinks with relish.

ᒪᓃᓚᖅ: ᐱᔮᕆᑐᖤᓇᓗᒃ ᑕᐃᒻᓇ.

ᖤᒻᒥᒃᑐᖅ: ᐊᒃᐱᐅᑎᑦᑕᐃᓕᐅᒃ . . . ᐄᖅ ᑕᒃᑰᒃ . . .

ᖤᒻᒥᒃᑐᖅ ᖤᓗᖕᒥᒃ ᓇᓪᓖᕋᒥ ᑐᓂ'ᓗᓂᐅᒃ ᒪᓃᓚᕐᒧᑦ.

ᖤᒻᒥᒃᑐᖅ: ᐃᕐᓂ'ᖁᑦ ᑐᓂ'ᓴᕗᑦ. ᖤᓗᖕᓂᒃ ᐱᑦᑕᐅᒍᖤᓪᓗᐊᖅᑐᓐᖁᐊᖅ.

ᒪᓃᓚᖅ: ᑳᖅᑐᒍᓪᓕ ᐱᕐᓕᓕᕋᑉᑕ ᖤᒃᑲᐃᑉᐸᓪᓛᕋᕕᑦ—ᐅᕙᒻᓂᒃ ᑲᒪᑎᓂᐊᖅᐸᕋ ᐆᖤᒃᓴᖅ.

ᖤᒻᒥᒃᑐᖅ: ᐊᓂᐅᓕᕐᓗᒍ ᐃᒻᒥᐅᕐᓂᐊᖅᐸᕋ.

ᒪᓃᓚᖅ: ᐄᕐᑭ—ᖤᕖᑐᐃᑦᑐᓇᓘᒐᕕᑦ.

ᖤᒻᒥᒃᑐᖅ: ᓄᑕᕋᓐᓄᐃᑦ ᐃᓅᓕᖣᓐᓄᐊᖅ ᐅᓇ ᑲᒪᑎᓚᒍ.

ᒪᓃᓚᖅ: ᖠᓂᒃᑐᑦ.

ᒪᓃᓚᖅ ᐊᓂ'ᓗᓂ.

ᖤᒻᒥᒃᑐᖅ: (ᑐᖢᕐᓇᓕᖅᑐᖅ) ᐋᐊᐊ'ᐋ . . .

ᖤᒻᒥᒃᑐᖅ ᑕᑯᑎᐊᖅᔪᓂᐅᒃ ᐃᒪᖅ ᖃᓗᕋᖅᔪᒍ ᐊᕝᓛᒍᑦ. ᖁᕐᓂᖕᒋᑦᑐᖅ. ᖃᑉᑰ'ᓗᓂᐅᒃ.

ᓄᑭᓕᓪᓗ ᖠᓪᒍᓪᓗ ᐃᖠᖅᖠᖥᒃ ᓇᓄᕋᕐᒥᒃ. ᐃᖠᖅᑲᑕᐅᖥᒃ ᒪᓃᓚᕐᓗ ᐃᑉᖤᕐᓗ, ᐊᐃᑉᐹ ᖅᑲᑦᑕᖅᑲᖅᔪᓂ ᖅᑲᔪᕐᒥᒃ ᐊᐃᑉᐹᓗ ᖅᑲᑦᑕᖅᑲᖅᔪᓂ ᐆᖤᕐᒥᒃ. ᒪᓕᒃᑑᒃ ᓄᑭᓕᐅᑉ ᐃᕐᓂᐊ ᖅᑭᓗᓂᖅ, ᖠᓪᒎᑉᓗ ᐸᓂᐊ ᐊᑐᒐᐅᖅ. ᑭᖕᒍᑦᓖᑦᑑ'ᓗᓂ ᐊᕕᓐᖕᒐᖅ ᐃᖠᕐᓚᖑᔭᖅᑯᖅ ᑎᒍᒥᐊᖅᔪᓂ ᖅᑭᓚᐅᑎᓐᓄᐊᕐᒥᒃ ᐊᒥᕐᓄᑦ ᖤᓇᖠᒪᖤᖅ. ᐊᖕᒐᑦᑰᖤᖅ ᑖᒻᓇ ᐋᓐᖑᐊᖅᑲᐅᖅᔪᓂ ᐊ'ᓄᕌᕐᒥᓄᑦ ᒥᖅᓱᖅᖠᒪᖤᑦ.

ᓄᑭᓕᓪᓗ ᖠᓪᒍᓪᓗ ᐃᓐᓂᖅᕕᒃᓴᐅᓂᐊᖅᑐᒥᒃ ᐃᑦᑐᐊᖤᐃ'ᓗᑎᒃ. ᐊᕐᓈᒃ ᐆᒐᖕᒋᖅᖠ'ᓗᑎᒃ ᖥᕕ'ᓗᑎᑦ ᖠᓪᖣᕐᒍᑦ ᑕᐅᓄᖕᒐ. ᖤᒻᒥᒃᑐᖅ ᐃᓚᐅᖕᒋ'ᓗᓂ ᑕᐅᑐᒃᖠᓐᓇᖅᑐᖅ ᖅᑲᔪᖅᑐᖅᑎ'ᓗᑎᑦ ᐊᒥᖅᑳᖅᔪᑎᒃ. ᒪᓃᓚᖅ ᖅᑲᔪᖅ ᑐᓂ'ᒪᒍ ᖅᑭᓗᓂᕐᒧᑦ.

ᒪᓃᓚᖅ: ᖤᒻᒥᒃᑐᕐᒧᑦ ᑐᓂᓪᒎᒃ.

Finally, AVINNGAQ speaks.

AVINNGAQ: We are grateful to the polar bear for allowing itself to be caught. Its life means that we are no longer hungry. We are thankful to you that you are the means of our life. Your strength on land and in the sky is felt by us, so if your spirit returns and you are a polar bear again, let it be that we may hunt you, as we are good humans. We thank you and we respect you.

AVINNGAQ picks up the heart of the bear . . .

Nanuq's heart . . .

. . . and bites off a small piece, then, following the direction of the sun, hands it to the person to their left, and they do the same until it goes around to each person—HIGGUK, QILUNIQ, IBŘUQ, MANIILAQ, ATUGAUQ, and NUKILIK.

Then NUKILIK begins to hand out pieces of the meat, but he will forget—purposefully or not—to give a piece to HUMMIKTUQ.

NUKILIK: *(to AVINNGAQ)* The choicest part of the chest meat for the one who changes shape. *(turns to HIGGUK)* Some with lots of fat for a good hunter . . .

HIGGUK takes the piece and mightily resists the urge to tear into the meat.

(to QILUNIQ) . . . very nice tongue, good meat for my son.

AVINNGAQ: Slowly, Higguk. Eat slowly.

Starving, everyone struggles to eat slowly, trying to take small bites.

QILUNIQ: *(eating too fast)* It's tasty, very tasty.

IBŘUQ: *(to QILUNIQ)* Slowly, or you'll start to shake.

NUKILIK: This bear has saved us.

HIGGUK: Nukilik chanced upon our survival prey and for this we are profoundly grateful.

ᕿᓗᓂᖅ ᔓᒻᒥᒃᑐᕐᒧᑦ ᑐᓂ'ᒪᒍ ᓂᐅᖅᔑᕝᕕᓕ'ᓇᒥᐅᒃ
ᒪᒪᕈᔓᒡᓗᐊᖅᑐᖅ.

ᐊᕕᓐᖓᖅ ᐅᖃᒪᓕᑕᐃᓐᓇᓕᖅᓱᓂ.

ᐊᕕᓐᖓᖅ: ᔕᑐᕐᓗᐊᖅᑐᒍᑦ ᓇᓄᕐᒧᑦ ᐊᖑᔕᐅᔪᖕᓇ'ᒪᑦ. ᐆᒪᒐᓗᐊᕐᓂᖓᓄᑦ ᑳᒡᒍᐃᖅᑐᒍᑦ. ᖁᔭᓕᕗᒍᑦ ᐃᓕ'ᓄᑦ ᐆᒪᔥᔕᑎᓕᒐᑉᑎᓕᑦ. ᔕᓐᖏᓂᕆᔐᐃᑦ ᓄᓇᒥ ᕿᓚᖓᒥᓗ ᐃᒃᐱᕆᒐᑉᑎᒍᑦ ᐊᓂᕐᓃᑦ ᐅᑎᕐᒥᒃᐸᑦ ᓇᓅᑉᔕᐊ'ᔭᒍᑎᑦ, ᐊᖑᔪᖕᓇᔥᔕ'ᔭᕙᑉᑎᓕᑦ ᐱᑦᑎᐊᕐᐸᑕ ᐃᓅ'ᓗᑕ ᐃᔓᒪᓕᕙᑉᑎᓕᑦ ᐱᓂᕐᓗᒃᑕᐃᓕᒪᒐᑉᑕ.

ᐊᕕᓐᖓᖅ ᑎᒍᔐ'ᓗᓂ ᓇᓅᑉ ᐆᒪᑖᓂ . . .

ᐊᕕᓐᖓᖅ: ᓇᓅᑉ ᐆᒪᑖ . . .

. . . ᓂᕆ'ᓗᓂ ᒥᑭᔐᒥᒃ ᑐᓂ'ᓗᓂᐅᒃ ᔕᐅᒥᐊᓃᑦᑐᒧᑦ ᔐᕿᓂᖅ
ᒪᓕᒃᓱᒍ ᐊᒥᖅᑳᓕᖅᓱᑎᒃ—ᔐᒡᒍᒃ, ᕿᓗᓂᖅ, ᐃᑉᔓᖅ, ᒪᓃᓚᖅ,
ᐊᑐᒐᐅᖅ, ᓄᑭᓕᒡᓗ.

ᓄᑭᓕᒃ ᑕᐃᒪ ᑐᓂᐅᖅᑲᐃᓕᖅᓱᓂ ᐆᔓᕐᓂᒃ—ᖄᖕᒥᐅᑎᓐᓂᖅᓱᒍ
ᔓᒻᒥᒃᑐᑦ ᔓ'ᒪᑦᑭᐊᖅ ᑐᓂᖖᒥᓐᓂ'ᒪᒍ.

ᓄᑭᓕᒃ: (ᐊᕕᓐᖓᕐᒧᑦ) ᔕᑦᖄᑕ ᐱᑦᑕᐅᓂᖓ ᐃᑭᐊᖕᒥᓐᓇᒃᑯᑦ ᐃᓕᒻᒪᖅᑐᕈᖕᓇᖅᑐᒧᑦ (ᔖ'ᓗᒍᓗ ᔐᒡᒍᒃ) ᐅᖅᓱᖅᑲᑦᑎᐊᖅᑐᒥᒃ ᓇᓚᐅᑦᑎᔐᒧᑦ . . .

ᔐᒡᒍᒃ ᑎᒍ'ᓗᓂᐅᒃ ᐃᒃᓰᑭᒐᒥᐅᒃ ᑭᒐᐃᖓ'ᓗᓂ
ᓂᕆᓐᓄᐊᕋᔕᐊᖅᔓᓐᓇᖅᑐᖅ ᐊᕿᐊᕈᐊᖅᑕᐃᓕᓇᔥᔕᐊᖅᓱᓂ
ᓂᕆᖖᒥᒃᔖᐸᑦᓛ'ᒪᑕ.

ᓄᑭᓕᒃ: (ᕿᓗᓂᕐᒧᑦ) . . . ᐅᖃᑦᑎᐊᕙᓇᓗᒃ ᓂᕿᑦᑎᐊᕙᒃ ᐃᕐᓂᒻᓄᑦ.

ᐊᕕᓐᖓᖅ: ᑭᒐᐃᖓᓗᑎᑦ ᔐᒡᒍᒃ. ᑕᒧᐊᑦᑎᐊᖅᓗᒍ.

ᑳᒃᔐᒪᔐᑐᖅᑲᐅ'ᓗᑎᒃ, ᑕᒪᐃᑕ ᑭᒐᐃᖓ'ᓗᑎᒃ
ᐊᕿᐊᕈᐊᖅᑕᐃᓕᓇᔓᐊᖅᑐᑦ ᑕᒧᐊᓐᓄᐊᕋᔕᐊᖅᓱᑎᒃ.

ᕿᓗᓂᖅ: (ᓂᕆᔐᐊᓗᒃ). ᒪᒪᖅᑐᖅ ᒪᒪᖅᑐᐊᓗᒃ.

ᐃᑉᔓᖅ: (ᕿᓗᓂᕐᒧᑦ) ᑭᒐᐃᖓᓗᑎᑦ ᔕᔪᓕᖅᓂᐊᕕᒃᑲᕕᑦ.

NUKILIK: Don't speak so loud. I fear invisible retribution.

HIGGUK: *(whispers)* The tiny one chanced upon our survival prey for—

AVINNGAQ: *(to HIGGUK) Taima'na*—stop, else you'll arouse the wrath of the child snatcher.

MANIILAQ gives the feather to QILUNIQ.

MANIILAQ: This is for you, son.

QILUNIQ: A snow goose feather . . . *(hands it to ATUGAUQ)* Here.

ATUGAUQ takes the feather and tickles QILUNIQ, who laughs.

IBŘUQ: We give great thanks to Nuliajuq today.

QILUNIQ: *(to NUKILIK)* How did you hunt the bear, *Ataataa [Father]*?

NUKILIK: We could hardly lift our legs. I was dizzy. My stomach was screaming from hunger . . . then we saw fresh tracks. We followed them wondering, "Why is this polar bear here?" With summer coming they usually roam farther north to permanent ice places. I whispered, "Higguk, walk faster, walk faster," but we all know how fast my cousin, my *idlunnuaq [dearest cousin]* walks, even when his food might be up ahead.

HIGGUK: I have short legs.

NUKILIK: You have no legs at all.

HIGGUK: I have *two* legs!

IBŘUQ: He has *three* legs!

Laughter.

NUKILIK: *(to IBŘUQ)* You're a good woman.

IBŘUQ: A good woman makes a man happy.

ᓄᑭᓕᒃ: ᓇᓐᓄᒃᑐᖅᑲᕋᓗᐊ’ᒪᑦ ᐊᓐᓇᒃᑑᑎᒋᕙᕗᑦ ᓂᕆᔭᖕᓇᖅᓯᔪᒍᑦ.

ᔪᒡᒍᒃ: ᓄᑭᓕᒃ ᐊᓐᖑᑎᒃᓴᒥᒃ ᓇᓚᐅᑦᑎᔮᖓ ᖁᔭᓇᖅᑐᕌᓗᒃ.

ᓄᑭᓕᒃ: ᓂᐱᑐᕆᓪᓛᖖᒋᓗᑎᑦ. ᓇᓐᖓᖅᑕᐅᔪᒪᖖᒋ’ᓇᒪ.

ᔪᒡᒍᒃ: *(ᐃᔨᑉᔨᒃᑐᖅ)* ᓇᓚᐅᑦᑎᔨᓐᓄᐊᓇᓗᕐᖢᒃ—

ᐊᕙᓐᖓᖅ: *(ᔪᒡᒍᖕᒧᑦ)* ᑕᐃᒪ’ᓇ—ᓄᑕᖅᑲᓂᒃ ᐊᖅᖄᖅᑎᓇᓗᒃ ᓂᖖᒐᒃᖄᕆᓂᐊᕙᒃᑲᕙᐅᒃ.

ᑕᐃᒪᓗ ᒪᓃᓚᖅ ᔨᓗᒃ ᑐᓂ’ᓗᓂᐅᒃ ᕿᓗᓂᖅᒧᑦ.

ᒪᓃᓚᖅ: ᐅᕝᕙ ᐱᒃᓴᑦ, ᐅᑕᕌ.

ᕿᓗᓂᖅ: ᑲᖕᒎᑉ ᐱᐊ . . . *(ᑐᓂ’ᓗᓂᐅᒃ ᐊᑐᒐᐅᖅᒧᑦ)* ᐅᕝᕙ.

ᐊᑐᒐᐅᖅ ᑎᒍ’ᓗᓂᐅᒃ ᕿᓗᓂᖅᒥᒃ ᖁᐃᓇᒃᓵᖅᔪ’ᒪᑦ ᐃᓪᓚᖅᖢᓂ.

ᐃᑉᔨᖅ: ᓄᓕᐊᔪᒃ ᐅᑉᓗᒥ ᓴᑐᖅᓇᖅᑐᕌᓗᒃ.

ᕿᓗᓂᖅ: *(ᓄᑭᓕᖕᒧᑦ)* ᖅᑲᓄᖅ ᐊᖑᕕᐅᒃ ᐊᑖᑖ?

ᓄᑭᓕᒃ: ᓂᐅᕗᑦ ᐃᒃᑕᓇᓪᓚᔨᓐᓇ’ᒪᑕ ᐱᔮᓚᐃ’ᓗᓄᓪᓗ. ᐅᐃᑉᔮᖖᒍᓕᕋᒪ. ᐊᖅᑭᐊᕈᕋᓗ ᐃᖢᐃᑦᑐᕌᓘᓕ’ᒪᑦ . . . ᑕᑯᓕᖅᖢᓄᒃ ᑐᒥᖕᓂᒃ ᓄᑖᓇᓗᖕᓂᒃ ᑐᑉᔭᖅᔪᓕᖅᖢᓄᒃ. ᐃᔨᒪ’ᓗᓄᓪᓗ ᔨ’ᒪᓇᓗᒃ ᓇᓄᖅ ᑕᔭᒧᖕᖓᖅᑲᑉ? ᐊᐅᔭᐅᕙᓪᓕᐊᓕᕐᖓᑦ ᔪᑯᐃᓚᐃᑦᑐᒧᖕᖓᐅᕙ’ᒪᑕ ᔪᑯᐃᖅᔭᓇᑐᔨᒧᑦ. ᐃᔨᑉᔨᓕᖅᓱᖓ ᔪᒡᒍᖕᒧᑦ, ᑐᐊᕕᑲᐃᑦ, ᐊᑕᐃ, ᑭᔨᐊᓂᒃ ᐅᓇ ᐃᓪᓗᓐᓄᐊᕈ ᔨᕖᑐᐃᑦᑐᓇᓘ’ᒪᑦ, ᓂᖅᑭᒃᓵ ᑕᕝᕙᐅᓚᓗᐊᖅᑎ’ᓗᒍ.

ᔪᒡᒍᒃ: ᓂᐅᕐᖣᒃᑲᒃ ᓇᐃᑦᑐᓇᓘ’ᒪᓂᒃ.

ᓄᑭᓕᒃ: ᓂᐅᖅᑲᖅᑰᖖᒋᒻᒪᓇᑦᑐᑎᓪᓕ.

ᔪᒡᒍᒃ: ᒪᕝᕘᖕᓂᒃ ᓂᐅᖅᑲᕈᓗᐊᖅᑐᖓ!

ᐃᑉᔨᖅ: ᐱᖓᔨᓇᓗᖕᓂᒃ!

ᐃᓪᓚᖅᑐᑦ.

HIGGUK: *(to* IBŘUQ*) Nuliaq [my wife]*, today I am happy.

IBŘUQ: I am happy, also.

MANIILAQ: *(to* IBŘUQ*)* I am very happy.

NUKILIK: I am very very happy.

QILUNIQ: I'm happier than my aṭaata and my *anaana [mother]*.

ATUGAUQ: I'm happier than my anaana and my ataata.

HUMMIKTUQ: I'm sad—completely and utterly sad because I am alone.

ATUGAUQ: *(to* HUMMIKTUQ*)* Why are you sad when Nanuq is right here?

NUKILIK: Hummiktuq is always sad and alone, leave her be.

HUMMIKTUQ: *(to* ATUGAUQ*)* I have no companion in my life. *(begins to wail)* AAAAAHHHHHHHHH . . .

NUKILIK: *(to* HUMMIKTUQ*)* You always make us aware of how alone you are—we're more aware of you being alone than we are of a seal's breath.

HUMMIKTUQ: Being alone and being *hungry* is my lot in life.

IBŘUQ: *(to* HUMMIKTUQ*)* Where's your portion of food?

HUMMIKTUQ: I am waiting.

AVINNGAQ: *(to* NUKILIK*)* Nukilik, you are camp leader—give her a bit of meat.

NUKILIK: I'm giving her a bit.

HUMMIKTUQ: *(to* NUKILIK*)* You always make me wait.

IBŘUQ: *(to* HUMMIKTUQ*)* Eat! Quit yabbering.

NUKILIK: She does not work hard like the rest of us.

ᓄᑭᓚᒃ: *(ᐃᑉᔕᖅᒧᑦ)* ᐊᖅᓇᑦᑎᐊᕋᐅᓚᕈᑦ.

ᐃᑉᔕᖅ: ᐊᖅᓇᑦᑎᐊᕋᐃᑦ ᐊᖑᑎᒥ'ᓂᒃ ᑲᒪᑦᑎᐊᖅᐸ'ᒪᑕ.

ᔑᒡᒍᒃ: *(ᐃᑉᔕᖅᒧᑦ)* ᓄᓚᐊᖅ, ᐅᑉᓗᒥ ᖁᕕᐊᔓᒃᑐᖕᒐ.

ᐃᑉᔕᖅ: ᖁᕕᐊᔓᒃᑕᖕᒐᑉᑕᐅᖅ.

ᒪᓃᓚᖅ: *(ᐃᑉᔕᖅᒧᑦ)* ᖁᕕᐊᔓᒃᑐᓇᓘᔕᖕᒐ.

ᓄᑭᓚᒃ: ᖁᕕᐊᔓᒃᑐᐸᓇᓗᓘᔕᖕᒐᓗ.

ᖁᔪᓂᖅ: ᖁᕕᐊᔓᑦᖁᔨᐅᔕᖕᒐ ᐊᑖᑕᒻᓂᐅᖕᒐᓂᑦ ᐊᓈᓇᒻᓂᐅᖕᒐᓂᓪᓗ.

ᐊᑐᒐᐅᖅ: ᐅᕙᖕᒐ ᖁᕕᐊᔓᑦᖁᔨᐅᔕᖕᒐ ᐊᑖᑕᒻᓂᐅᖕᒐᓂᑦ ᐊᓈᓇᒻᓂᐅᖕᒐᓂᓪᓗ.

ᔑᒻᒥᒃᑐᖅ: ᖁᕕᐊᔓᖕᖏᑦᑐᖕᒐᓚ—ᖁᕕᐊᓇᐃᓪᓗᐊᖅᑐᖅ ᐃᓅ'ᓗᓂ.

ᐊᑐᒐᐅᖅ: *(ᔑᒻᒥᒃᑐᖅᒧᑦ)* ᔑ'ᒪᑦ ᖁᕕᐊᔓᖕᖏᑦᑐᑎᑦ ᓇᓄᖅ ᑕᔾᕙᐅᒐᓗᐊᖅᑎ'ᓗᒍ?

ᓄᑭᓚᒃ: ᔑᒻᒥᒃᑐᖅ ᖁᕕᐊᔓᖕᖏᓐᓇᔑᐊᖅᔨᓐᓇᖅᑐᖅ ᑲᒪᖏᖕᖏᓗᒍ.

ᔑᒻᒥᒃᑐᖅ: *(ᐊᑐᒐᐅᖅᒧᑦ)* ᐊᔨᖅᑲᖕᖏ'ᓇᒪ ᐃᓅᔨᒻᓂ. *(ᖁᐊᓚᖅᓘᓂ)*
ᐋᐊᐊᐊᐊᐊᐊ . . .

ᓄᑭᓚᒃ: *(ᔑᒻᒥᒃᑐᖅᒧᑦ)* ᐅᖅᑲᒪᐃᓐᓇᖅᑐᑎᑦ ᐊᔨᖅᑲᖕᖏᑦᑐᓐ'ᓗᑎᑦ—ᓇᑦᑎᐅᑉ ᐊᓂᖅᔖᖅᓂᐊᓂᑦ ᐅᕝᔦᖅᓇᑦᖁᔨᐅᕙᑎᑦ.

ᔑᒻᒥᒃᑐᖅ: ᐃᓅᔨᒻᓂ ᐊᔨᖅᑲᖕᖐᓐᓇᖅᑐᖅ ᑳᖕᖏᓐᓇᖅᓘᖅᒐᓗ.

ᐃᑉᔕᖅ: *(ᔑᒻᒥᒃᑐᖅᒧᑦ)* ᓇᐅᓚ ᓂᖅᑭᒃᔕᑦ?

ᔑᒻᒥᒃᑐᖅ: ᐅᑕᖅᑭᔕᔅᓘᔕᖕᒐ.

ᐊᕕᓐᖕᒐᖅ: *(ᓄᑭᓚᖕᒧᑦ)* ᐊᖑᓇᔑᐊᖅᑎᐅᒐᕈᑦ ᐊᑕᐃ, ᓂᖅᑭᓐᓄᐊᖅᒥᒃ ᐊᐃᑦᑐᖅᓗᒍ.

ᓄᑭᓚᒃ: ᐊᐃᑦᑐᓚᖅᐸᖅ.

ᔑᒻᒥᒃᑐᖅ: *(ᓄᑭᓚᖕᒧᑦ)* ᐅᑕᖅᑰᓐᓇᖅᑎ'ᓇ'ᒪ.

HIGGUK: Maybe she still feels the loss of her family.

NUKILIK picks up small chunk of meat and hands it to HUMMIKTUQ. She takes it.

NUKILIK: (*to HUMMIKTUQ*) Your husband was a good hunter, but he didn't pay close attention to his dogs.

IBŘUQ: We can never know what happened on the ice that day.

NUKILIK: Something brought it on. Maybe someone was harbouring a secret.

HUMMIKTUQ: I have never harboured secrets.

HUMMIKTUQ moves away from the group.

AVINNGAQ: I know who harbours them and who does not.

IBŘUQ: (*to NUKILIK*) Get on with your story.

NUKILIK: I kept walking, and from her tracks I saw she was very big. I whispered, "We must be cautious," but my *idluq [cousin]* was not beside me anymore. I turned my head, and even with three legs he's woefully lagging behind and being pursued by a great polar bear . . . so I scream out, "BEHIND YOU, BEHIND YOU!"

HIGGUK: I turned and saw her and oh—I didn't even know she was behind me!

AVINNGAQ raises his arms over his head, mimicking the bear.

AVINNGAQ: I'm watching you two.

HIGGUK: (*to AVINNGAQ, the bear*) Great Hunter, always searching, do you smell our starvation?

AVINNGAQ: (*as the bear*) Do you smell my hunger? I have nothing but air left inside my stomach.

HIGGUK: I was afraid I'd soon be inside her stomach to remove the air. When she opened her mouth, I put my arm up like this to avoid getting swallowed

ᐃᑉᓯᖅ: *(ᓴᒻᒥᒃᑯᕐᒍᑦ)* ᓂᕆᒡᒍᐃᑦ ᐅᕐᑲᓕᑕᓵᖕᒋᓗᑎᑦ.

ᓄᑭᓕᒃ: ᓴᑦᓗᐊᖅᐸᖕᒋ'ᒪᑦ ᐅᕙᑉᑐᑦ ᐅᓇ.

ᓱᒡᒍᒃ: ᐃᓚᐃᕋᒥᓕ ᓂᑲᑦᓗᖕᑲᑦᓗᐊᖅᑐᖅ ᐃᓐᖑᒪᓴᐊᓗᒃ.

ᓄᑭᓕᒃ ᓂᕐᑭᓐᓄᐊᕐᒥᒃ ᑎᒍᓱ'ᓗᓂ ᑐᓂᓵ ᓴᒻᒥᒃᑯᕐᒍᑦ.

ᓄᑭᓕᒃ: *(ᓴᒻᒥᒃᑯᕐᒍᑦ)* ᐅᐃᑦ ᐊᖑᓇᓴᕐᕋᖅᑐᕕᓂᐅᑲᓗᐊᖅ ᑭᓱᐊᓂᒃ ᐅᔅᓴᓇᑦᑎᐊᖕᒋ'ᓇᒥᒋᑦ ᕐᑭ'ᒥᓂ.

ᐃᑉᓯᖅ: ᕐᑲᐅᓴᒪᓚᐃᑦᑐᒍᑦ ᕐᑲᓄᕐᓕᐅᖅᑐᕐᑲᓇᐊᒃᓰ'ᓂᒃ ᑕᐃᑉᓴᒪᓂ ᓱᑯᒥ.

ᓄᑭᓕᒃ: ᐱᔅᓯᑎᓕᓇᓘᓚᓗᐊᖅ. ᐊᓐᖏᐊᕆᓴᖅᑲᖅᑐᖅᑲᖅᑑ'ᔭ'ᒪᑦ.

ᓴᒻᒥᒃᑯᖅ: ᐊᓐᖏᐊᕆᓴᖅᑲᓚᐃᑦᑐᖓ.

ᓴᒻᒥᒃᑯᖅ ᐊᕗᖓ ᐃᓄᖅᑲᖕᒋᓐᓂᖑᖕᖓᖅᓗᓂ.

ᐊᕕᓐᖓᖅ: ᕐᑲᐅᓵᒪᓴᖕᖓ ᓴᓇᑦ ᐊᓐᖏᐊᕆᓴᖅᑲᕆᐊᒃᓯᐃᑕ ᓴᓇᑦᓗ
ᐊᓐᖏᐊᕆᓴᖅᑲᖕᒋᑦᑐᓂᒃ.

ᐃᑉᓯᖅ: *(ᓄᑭᓕᖕᒍᑦ)* ᐅᖅᑲᕋᓴᐅᑎᒋᓴᕋᓗᐃᑦ ᐅᖅᑲᐅᓯᓇᑉᓯᐊᓕᕈᒃ.

ᓄᑭᓕᒃ: ᐱᓴᐃᓐᓇᕋᓴᐊᖅᓗᖓ ᑐᒦ'ᓂᑦ ᕐᑲᐅᓵ'ᓗᖓ ᐊᖕᒋᓯᐊᓘ'ᒪᑦ.
ᐃᓱᑉᓴᒃᓗᖓ "ᐅᔅᓴᖅᑐᑦᑎᐊᕆᐊᖅᑲᖅᑐᒍᒃ" ᑭᓱᐊᓂᒃ ᐃᑦᓗᔅᓗ
ᓴᓂᑉᕐᑲᒻᓃᑦᑐᐃ'ᒪᑦ—ᓵᕖᑐᐃ'ᒪᑦ ᐱᖕᖓᓴᓂᒃ ᓂᐅᓕᔅᓘᓚᓗᐊᖅ—ᕐᑭᕕᐊᕋᒪ
ᑭᖑᓂᒻᓃᑦᑐᖅ ᑕᑯᔅᓗᒃᓗᒍ, ᒪᓕᒃᑕᐅᓕᖅᑐᐊᓘᓐᓂᖅ ᓇᓄᓇᓗᖕᒥᑦ
. . . ᐃᕆᐊᑖᓕᖅᓗᖓ, "ᑐᓄ'ᓂ, ᑐᓄ'ᓂ."

ᓱᒡᒍᒃ: ᑐᓄ'ᓗᖓ ᑕᑯ'ᓗᒍ—ᑭᖑᒻᓃᑐᕐᑲᓇᐊᒃᓯᖅ ᕐᑲᐅᓵᖕᒋᒻᒪᓇᑦᑲᓗᐊᕋᒪ!

ᐊᕕᓐᖓᖅ ᓇᓅᖕᖑᐊᖅᓗᓂ ᐃᓵᒃᑐᐊᓗᒃ.

ᐊᕕᓐᖓᖅ: ᑕᐅᑐᒃᐸᑉᓱᒃ.

ᓱᒡᒍᒃ: *(ᐊᕕᓐᖓᕐᒍᑦ, ᓇᓅᖕᖑᐊᖅᑐᒧᑦ)* ᐊᖑᓇᓴᐊᑎᓇᓗᒃ, ᕐᑭᓃᓐᓇᖅᑐᖅ,
ᑳᕕᒡᓱᐊᕐᓂᑉᑎ'ᓂᒃ ᓇᐃᒪᕕᑦ?

and preventing a jaw latch . . . *(holds his forearm perpendicular to* AVINNGAQ*'s mouth)* Frightened, I turned and saw my idlunnuaq running toward me—"Harpoon," I hollered to him. "HARPOON."

NUKILIK and HIGGUK encircle AVINNGAQ.

NUKILIK: I ran, gripping my harpoon, the whalebone edge sharp, but she was uncertain of giving her life and she was fast! Before I could throw my harpoon, she smacked me with her paw and I fell. *(falls down)* Then she stood over me, her big paw on my stomach. We stared deeply into each other's eyes. *(to AVINNGAQ, the bear)* "Nanuq," I intervened and whispered. "Let me live. I have many relatives and am the only food provider."

HIGGUK: No no, it was I who intervened. *(to AVINNGAQ, the bear)* "Nanuq," I whispered quite loudly. "Let my idlunnuaq live."

NUKILIK: *(to HIGGUK)* I heard myself intervening in a very loud whisper, "Nanuq, I have families to feed."

HIGGUK: *(to NUKILIK)* I heard myself shouting in very whispered tones, "Nanuq, let my idlunnuaq live."

IBŘUQ: *(to NUKILIK and HIGGUK)* Get on with the story, you two!

MANIILAQ: They need time to make more things up.

HIGGUK: *(to IBŘUQ)* Every word we speak is the truth!

IBŘUQ: Yes, your story is true, but you keep on trying to add more to it—so go on, what happened?

AVINNGAQ: *(to HIGGUK)* Continue your report, as I know what is true and what is untrue.

NUKILIK: *(to AVINNGAQ)* We respect your powers. *(continues the story)* I heard myself speak— *(to AVINNGAQ, the bear)* "Nanuq, I have families to feed."

AVINNGAQ: *(as the bear)* Will you respect my soul?

ᐊᕙᓐᖓᖅ: (ᓇᓅᔾᔪᓂ) ᑳᖕᓂᕋᑦᑕᐅᖅ ᓇᐃᒪᕙᔑᐅᒃ? ᐊᕐᑭᐊᕈᕋ
ᔨᑕᕐᑲᖕᒋᒻᒪᓇ'ᒪᑦ ᔑᓚᐃᓐᓇᕐᔪᒃ ᐃᔪᐊᓂ.

ᔑᓪᒍᒃ: ᐊᕐᑭᐊᕈᐊᓃᓂᐊᓇᐊᒃᓴᓪᓂᒃ ᐃᔨᒫᔪᓕᕋᒪ ᔑᓚᕐᑲᐅᑎᓂ
ᐊᔑᕙᕈᒪ'ᒪᒍ, ᐊᐃᑦᑕ'ᒪᓪᔪ ᑕᓕᕋ ᐃᒪ'ᓇᐃᓕ'ᔪᒍ ᐄᔭᐅᑦᑕᐃᓕᓇᔨᐊᖅᔪᖕᖓ
ᑭᖕᒪᓚᐃᖅᑎᓐᓇᔨᐊᖅᔪᒍ . . . (ᑕᓕᓂ ᐆᒃᑐᕋᐅᑎᒋ'ᔪᒍ ᐊᕙᓐᖓᐅᑉ
ᔑᓪᒍᖕᖑᐊᖕᖓᓄᑦ) ᐃᖅᔑ'ᔪᖕᖓ ᑐᓄ'ᔪᖕᖓ ᐃᓪᔪᓐᓄᐊᕋ ᐅ'ᓚᒃᔪᓂ ᖃᐃᔨᖅ,
"ᐅᓈᕐᓕ" ᐃᓇᐊᓪᓚᓪᕙᒋ'ᔪᒍ, "ᐅᓈᕐᓕ."

ᓄᑭᓕᓪᔪ ᔑᓪᒍᓪᔪ ᐊᖑᖕᖑᐊᓕᖅᔪᔾᔨᒃ ᐊᕙᓐᖓᖅ.

ᓄᑭᓕᒃ: ᐅ'ᓚᒃᔪᖕᖓ, ᐅᓈᕋ ᑎᒍᒻᒥ'ᔪᒍ, ᐃᐱᒃᑐᓇᔫᖓᔪᐊᖅ, ᑭᔑᐊᓂᒃ
ᐊᖑᔭᐅᔦᒪᔮᒃᔮ'ᓂ ᕐᑯᓚᒃᑲᒥ ᔨᑲᔨᕍᔪᒃ! ᓇᐅᑦᑭᐊᕈᖕᓇᖅᑎ'ᓇᖕᖓ
ᐸᑎ'ᓇᒥᖕᖓ ᓂᕙᖅᔪᖕᖓ. (ᐃᔨᒃᑲᖕᖑᐊᖅᑯᖅ) ᕐᑭᒥᔾᕈᓕᖅᔪᓂᖕᖓ ᐃᔑᓛᑕ
ᔑᕗᐊ ᓈᒻᓃᓕᖅᔪᓂ. ᐃᔾᔖᑦᑯᑎᔨᐊᔫᔨᒍᒃ. (ᐊᕙᓐᖓᕐᒍᑦ, ᓇᓅᖕᖑᐊᖅᑐᒍᑦ)
"ᓇᓅᓚ'ᔪᒍ, ᐃᓅᓚᖕᖓ ᐃᓚᕐᑲᐅᕋᒪ ᓂᕐᑭᒃᓴᖅᔑᐅᖅᑎᐱᑐᐊᕐᔫᖓᒪ."

ᔑᓪᒍᒃ: ᐄᕐᑭᕐᔪᒃ ᑕ'ᓇᐅᖕᖏᑦᑐᖅ, ᐅᕗᖕᖓᕗᓪᔪᕐᔪᒃ ᐊᒃᐱᐅᑎᖓᑉᑯ
(ᐅᕐᑲᖅᔪᓂ ᐊᕙᓐᖓᕐᒍᑦ, ᓇᓅᖕᖑᐊᖅᑐᒍᑦ), ᓂᐱᑮᓇᖅᑕᐃᓕ'ᔪᖕᖓ
ᐃᒪ'ᓇᐃᓕᐅᕋᒪ, "ᓇᓄᖅ, ᐃᓪᔪᓐᓄᐊᕋ ᐃᓅᔦᖕᓇᖅᑎᒍᒃ."

ᓄᑭᓕᒃ: (ᔑᓪᒍᖕᒍᑦ) ᐅᕗᖕᖓᕐᔪᒃ ᐃᒪ'ᓇᐃᓕᐅᕋᒪ,
"ᓂᕐᑭᒃᓴᖅᔑᐅᖅᑎᐱᑐᐊᕐᔫᖓᒪ."

ᔑᓪᒍᒃ: (ᓄᑭᓕᖕᒍᑦ) ᐅᕗᖕᖓᕐᔪᓪᓕ ᓂᐱᑮᓇᖅᑕᐃᓕ'ᔪᖕᖓ ᐃᒪ'ᓇᐃᓕᐅᕋᒪ,
"ᐃᓪᔪᓐᓄᐊᕋ ᐃᓅᔦᖕᓇᖅᑎᒍᒃ."

ᐃᐸᔨᖅ: (ᓄᑭᓕᖕᒍᑦ ᔑᓪᒍᖕᒍᓪᔪ) ᐅᕐᑲᕋᕓᐅᑎᒋᓕᖅᔑᐅᒃ!

ᒫᓂᓚᖅ: ᐊᐃᕗᐅᑎᒃᓴᒥ'ᓂᒃ ᐃᔨᒪᓇᔨᐊᓇᐊᓕᕐᔫᒃ ᐅᑯᐊᒃ.

ᔑᓪᒍᒃ: (ᐃᐸᔨᕐᒍᑦ) ᔨᓕᑦᑎᐊᖅᑐᒥᒃ ᐅᕐᑲᒪᔨᒍᒃ!

ᐃᐸᔨᖅ: ᐄ ᐅᕐᑲᕋᕓᐅᑎᒋᔭᖅᔑ ᔨᓕᔨᖅ ᑭᔑᐊᓂᒃ
ᐃᓚᕘᓪᓕᕋᔨᐊᖅᐸᑖᕋᐸᔑᐅᒃ—ᐊᑕᐃ ᔨᕗᔾᔫᖅ.

ᐊᕙᓐᖓᖅ: (ᔑᓪᒍᖕᒍᑦ) ᐅᕐᑲᕋᕓᐅᑎᒋᑦᑎᐊᓕᖅᔑᐅᒃ ᕐᑲᐅᔭᒪᓚᓚ ᔨᓕᔨᓂᒃ
ᔨᓕᖕᒋᑦᑐᓂᓪᔪ.

NUKILIK: *(to* AVINNGAQ, *the bear)* "We'll respect your soul. You'll have no reason to avenge us." Then the Great Yellow One stood to her full height. How magnificent she was as she raised her arms over her head and whispered . . . "I want to be caught for sustenance" . . .

AVINNGAQ: *(as the bear, raising his arms)* "Do not disrespect me."

> *NUKILIK puts his hand near to AVINNGAQ's heart and AVINNGAQ slumps over.*

NUKILIK: I was quick . . . and when I pulled my harpoon from her heart . . . she laid down gently as if falling asleep . . .

> *NUKILIK lifts AVINNGAQ up in his arms and turns slowly in circles, then NUKILIK puts AVINNGAQ down . . .*

> *. . . then AVINNGAQ picks up the drum and begins drumming. Everyone kneels in a semicircle.*

AVINNGAQ: And now we must express our gratitude to the polar bear and have a celebration as it allowed us to live forward. We will catch up to our future. Let my song be sung . . .

> *IBŘUQ starts to sing. Everyone joins in except HUMMIKTUQ. At some point they begin to dance.*

IBŘUQ: *(sings)* I'm going to live to see tomorrow,
To walk upon our lands again,
To dance upon the ice and the sea, *a jaa jaa*

ALL: *(sing)* I'm going to see my children grow,
To hunt more seal and whale and walrus,
To welcome all Nuliajuq brings, *a jaa jaa*

HIGGUK: Tonight we'll sleep with our bellies full.

IBŘUQ: We'll sleep after laughing all together.

NUKILIK: Yes, my many stories are hilarious.

ᓄᑭᓕᒃ: (ᐊᕙᓐᖕᒐᕐᒧᑦ) ᐃᔨᒪᒋᑦᑎᐊᖅᐸᑉᑎᒋᑦ. (ᐅᖅᑲᖃᓕᕆ'ᓗᓂ) ᐅᕙᒻᓂᒃ ᑐᓵᔪᖓ, (ᖁᕕᐊᖅᓱᒍ ᐊᕙᓐᖕᒐᖅ, ᓇᓅ'ᓗᓂ) "ᓇᓄᖅ, ᐃᓚᖅᑲᐅᖃᒪ ᓂᖅᑭᒃᓴᖅᔭᐅᖅᑎᐱᑐᐊᕐᓘᓚᒪ."

ᐊᕙᓐᖕᒐᖅ: (ᓇᓅ'ᓗᓂ) ᑕᕐᓂᖃ ᐱᑦᑎᐊᕐᓂᐊᖅᓴᖄᓗᐃᑦ.

ᓄᑭᓕᒃ: (ᐊᕙᓐᖕᒐᕐᒧᑦ, ᓇᓄᕐᒧᑦ) "ᐱᑦᑎᐊᕐᓂᐊᖅᐸᑉᑎᒋᑦ. ᐊᑭᒋᐊᖅᑲᓚᐃᑕᑉᑎᒍᑦ." ᑕᐃᒪᓗ ᖁᖅᓱᖅᑐᕐᔪᐊᖑᓗᒃ ᖁ'ᒧᑦ ᐃᓵᒃᔭᒫ'ᓗᓂ ᑕᑯᖃᓐᓂᖅᑐᐸᓇᓗᒃ ᐃᔭᑉᔪᓕᖅᑯᖅ ᐅᖄᓪᓚᒃᓱᓂ ᐊᓐᖑᑕᕆᔮᐅᔪᒪ'ᓗᓂ . . .

ᐊᕙᓐᖕᒐᖅ: (ᓇᓅ'ᓗᓂ ᐃᓵᒃᓱᓂ) "ᐱᓂᕐᓗᒃᑕᐃᓕᓗᑉᔪᖕᖓ."

ᓄᑭᓕᒃ ᐊᕙᓐᖕᒐᐅᑉ ᐆᒪᑖᓂᒃ ᐊᒃᑐᖅᔪ'ᓗᓂ ᐊᕙᓐᖕᒐᖅ ᐅᑯ'ᓗᓂ.

ᓄᑭᓕᒃ: ᔨᑲᔪᒥᒃ ᐅᓈᖅ ᓄᔨᒃᓱᒍ ᐅᒪᑖᓂᑦ ᓇᓪᓕᖅᓱᓂ ᔫᖅᓗ ᔪᓂᒃᑐᑐᑦ. . . .

ᓄᑭᓕᐅᑉ ᖃᖓᑦᑕᖅᑎᑖ ᐊᕙᓐᖕᒐᖅ ᑲᐃᕗ'ᓗᓂ ᔨᒃᑲᐃᑦᑐᒥ ᐃᓕ'ᓗᓂᐅᒃ ᒪᓂᖅᑲᒍᑦ . . .

. . . ᐊᕙᓐᖕᒐᖅ ᑕᐃᒪ ᑎᒍ'ᓗᓂᐅᒃ ᕿᓚᐅᑎ ᔨᖁᓚᓕᖅᓱᑎᒃ
. . . ᐃᖁᑦᖃ'ᓗᑎᒃ ᓴᓂᓕᓅᒃᓱᑎᒃ.

ᐊᕙᓐᖕᒐᖅ: ᑕᓭ ᓴᑐᓇᐊᖅᑲᓕᖅᑕᖅᑯᑦ ᓇᓄᖅ ᑕᐃᒪ, ᖁᕕᐊᔩᑎᖅᑲᖅᓗᑕ ᐃᓅᔪᖕᓇᖅᔭᔭᒪᓕ'ᒪᑎᒍᑦ ᔭᕗᓂᒃᓴᖅᑯᑦ ᐊᓐᖑᑎᓂᐊᖅᓗᒍ. ᐱᔭᖃ ᐊᑐᖅᑕᐅᓕᖅᓕ . . .

ᐃᐸᔫᖅ ᐃᖕᒋᐅᓕᖅᓱᓂ. ᑕᒪᖅᒥᒃ ᐃᖕᒋᐅᖅᑲᑕᐅᓕᖅᓱᑎᒃ ᑭᔭᐊᓂᒃ ᔨᒻᒥᒃᑐᖅ ᐱᙵᕆᑦᑐᖅ. ᒧᒥᓕᖅᓱᑎᓗ.

ᐃᐸᔫᖅ: (ᐃᖕᒋᐅᖅᓱᓂ) ᐃᓅᓂᐊᖃᒪ ᔭᕗᓂᒃᓴᖃ ᐊᓐᖑᑎᓂᐊᖅᓗᒍ.
ᓄᓇᒃᑯᑦ ᐱᔨᕕᒋᕓᖕᓂᐊᕆ'ᓗᒋᑦ,
ᑐᕓᖅᒥ ᒧᒥᖅᓗᖕᓚ ᑐᕝᕓᒥ, ᐊ ᔮ ᔮ

ᑕᒪᖅᒥᒃ: (ᐃᖕᒋᐅᖅᓱᑎᒃ) ᓄᑕᖃᑦᑲ ᐊᓪᓚᕓᓪᓚᐊᓗᑎᒃ.
ᐊᓐᖑᑎᒃᓴᖅᔭᐅᖅᓗᑕ ᓇᑦᑎᖅᓂᒃ, ᖁᓇᓗᒃᑲᓂᒃ, ᐊᐃᕕᖅᓂᒃ.
ᑐᓐᖓᓴᒃᑎᑦᑎᐊᖅᓗᕆᑦ ᓄᓕᐊᔩᑉ ᖃᐃᑕᐃᑦ ᐊ ᔮ ᔮ

IBŘUQ: Mine are even more hilarious!

HIGGUK: I am happy now.

MANIILAQ: Look . . . the sea is calm.

AVINNGAQ: The sky is bright.

NUKILIK: Tonight Nanuq sleeps inside the tent with us.

NUKILIK and HIGGUK take hold of the rack and the hunters carry it. IBŘUQ and MANIILAQ pick up the uneaten meat.

IBŘUQ: The meat gives me strength. I can fly like an *ařgiq [long-tailed duck]*.

ATUGAUQ: Me too.
A'a ahangiq, A'a ahangiq, A'a ahangiq . . .

QILUNIQ and ATUGAUQ stretch out their arms like wings and swirl around, pretending to be birds. ATUGAUQ is so caught up in this that she leaves the feather behind.

All but HUMMIKTUQ exit, who waits until the rest are out of earshot . . .

HUMMIKTUQ: Secrets—what secrets? I have never withheld anything from anyone, not about my blood, not about my jealousies or my desires, or about the depth of my grief . . .

(wails) AAAAAAAAAHHHHHHHHHHHHHHH . . . my sprirt-breath is weak, my voice barely a whisper.

Nuliajuq, Mother of the Sea Mamamals, you took my husband and my two children. I do not blame you, but I have been left with nothing . . . and so, in desperation, I beseech you—you who have power over all the mammals of the sea, the power to release them to us, or to withhold them—help me.

There is no one left to hunt and fish for me and I have no one left to care for. I have no more purpose in my life . . . my spirit-breath is dying. Help me.

ᖨᒃᒍᒃ: ᐅᓐᓄᒃ ᖨᓂᑦᑎᐊᕐᓂᐊᖅᑐᒍᑦ ᐊᕐᑭᐊᑐᑦᑎᐊᕋᑉᑕ.

ᐃᑉᔪ̵ᖅ: ᖨᓂᖕᓂᐊᑐᒍᑦ ᐃᒡᓚᒪᖅᑲᑎᕇᑦᑎᐊᖅᑳᕐᓗᑕ.

ᓄᑭᓕᒃ: ᐄ, ᑎᑉᖨᓇᖅᑐᕌᓗᐃᑦ ᐅᕐᑲᕋᔭᐅᑎᒃᓯᕌᓗᑦᑲ.

ᐃᑉᔪ̵ᖅ: ᐅᕙᖕᒐᕙᓪᓛᕐᓕ!

ᖨᒃᒍᒃ: ᔭᐃᒻᒪᓕᖅᑯᖕᒐ.

ᒪᓃᓚᖅ: ᑕᒃᑰᒃ . . . ᑕᕆᐅᖅ ᐅᖅᓱᐊᖅᑐᓇᓗᒃ.

ᐊᕕᓐᖕᒐᖅ: ᕿᓚᒃ ᖃᐅᒪ’ᓗᓂ.

ᓄᑭᓕᒃ: ᐅᓐᓄᖅ ᓇᓄᖅ ᑖᓐᓇ ᖨᓂᖅᑲᑎᕆᕖᑎᒍᑦ ᑐᐱᕐᒥ ᖩᕐᓗ.

ᓄᑭᓕᒃᓗ ᖨᒃᒍᒃᓗ ᐃᖕᓂᖅᑕᐅᔪ̵ᒥᒃ ᑎᒍᒥᐊᖅᓱᑎᒃ ᐊᖑᓇᖬᐊᑎᑦ ᐊᒃᔮᖅᓱᔾᔪ̵ᒃ. ᐃᑉᔪ̵ᕐᓗ ᒪᓃᓚᕐᓗ ᓂᕐᑭᓂᒃ ᐊᓄᐅᕐᓂᑯᓂᒃ ᖃᑎᑦᑎ’ᓱᑎᒃ.

ᐃᑉᔪ̵ᖅ: ᓂᕐᑭ ᐆᒻᒪᕖᑦᓕᕈᑎᕆᕙᕋ. ᑎᕐᕆᔪ̵ᕐᓇᖅᖨᔪ̵ᖕᓚ ᐊᔾᕆᖅᑐᑦ.

ᐊᑐᒐᐅᖅ: ᐅᕙᖕᒐᓗ.
ᐊ’ᐋ ᐋᔭᖕᒋᖅ, ᐊ’ᐋ ᐋᔭᖕᒋᖅ, ᐊ’ᐋ ᐋᔭᖕᒋᖅ . . .

ᕿᓗᓂᕐᓗ ᐊᑐᒐᐅᕐᓗ ᐃᔮᒃᓱᑎᒃ ᑎᖕᒋᙳᐊᖅᑐᒃ ᑲᐃᕕᓕᖅᓱᑎᒃ ᑎᖕᒥᐊᖑᙳᐊᖅᓱᑎᒃ. ᐊᑐᒐᐅᖅ ᐱᕙᓪᓛᖅᓱᓂ ᖬᓗᓂ ᕿᒪᐃᓪᓚᒃᖨᓐᓇᖅᑯᖅ.

ᑕᒪᐃᑕ ᐊᓂ’ᓱᑎᒃ ᑭᖨᐊᓂᒃ ᖬᒻᒥᒃᑐᖅ, ᐅᑕᖅᑭ’ᓱᓂ ᖬᖅᑲᕈᐃᕐᓃ’ᓄᑦ ᑕᐃᒪᓗ . . .

ᖬᒻᒥᒃᑐᖅ: ᑲᓐᖑᒋᔾᖃᖅᑐᑦ—ᖬᓇᓕ? ᐊᓐᖏᐊᓇᔾᖃᖅᐸᙱ’ᓇᒪ ᖬᓇᓂᒃ ᐊᐅᓪᓂ, ᑐᖬᒋᔾᒪ ᐱᔪ̵ᒪᔾᒪᓗ ᒥᒃᓵᒍᑦ, ᕿᒃᔮᕐᓂᕋᓘᓐᓃᑦ ᑲᓐᖑᒋᙳᒋᑕᕋ . . .

(ᐃᓗᖕᒋᖅᑐᕐᓗᐊᓕᖅᓱᓂ) ᐋᐊᐊᐊᐊᐊᐊᐊᐊᐊᐊᐊᐊ . . . ᐊᓂᕐᓂᕋ ᔭᖖᕇᑦᑐᓇᓗᒃ, ᓂᐱᖓ ᐃᖨᑉᔪ̵ᒃᑐᑦ.

ᓄᓕᐊᖬᒃ, ᐊᓈᓇᒋᔾᐅᔪ̵ᖅ ᐸᐃᖭᓄᑦ, ᑎᒍᔾᐃᑦ ᐅᐃᒐ ᓄᑕᕋᑦᑲᓗ ᒪᔾᑰᒃ. ᐸᖨᖕᒋᒃᑲᓗᐊᖅᐸᒋᑦ ᑭᖨᐊᓂᒃ ᑕᒃᑰᒃ ᐊᖨᖅᑲᖕᒋᑦᑐᖕᒐ

I have nothing. Where is my purpose? Why do I see the things I see? Nuliajuq, do I even have a place among these people? Or do I have no place?

She waits for a moment then begins to walk away, but something catches her eye and she stops when she sees . . . a shape coming into view. Sitting on a small ice floe and bobbing closer and closer to shore is a polar bear cub.

. . . Who is this? *(calls to the cub)* Who is this?

ATUGAUQ enters to pick up her forgotten snow goose feather.

ATUGAUQ: Where did I drop that goose feather . . .

HUMMIKTUQ gets her foot or hands on the ice floe to stop it from floating away.

HUMMIKTUQ: *(to the cub)* I am here, little one . . . come, dear, come to me.

ATUGAUQ sees HUMMIKTUQ and is suddenly afraid.

ATUGAUQ: *(calls to the others)* HUMITTUQ IS TRYING TO GO INTO THE OCEAN, TRYING TO DROWN HERSELF!

HUMMIKTUQ: I'm not trying to drown myself. I'm just stepping into it.

HUMMIKTUQ steps on the floe and scoops up the little cub.

HUMMIKTUQ: *(to the cub)* Little one, I will take care of you.

ATUGAUQ: Mmm, it would be delicious, its meat so tender. Look, one of its ears is missing.

HUMMIKTUQ: Will you teach him the ways of a child?

ATUGAUQ: No—it's a polar bear, not a child.

MANIILAQ enters.

. . . ᐊᑦᑯᓇᖅᐸᑦᑖᓕᖁᒪ, ᑐᒃᖤᖅᑐᖅᕕᒋᕙᒋᑦ, ᐊᑕᓂᓇᖦᐅᓚᕕᑦ ᐳᐃᖥᓂᑦ, ᓵᐸᑯᑦᑐᖕᓇᖅᑕᑎᑦ ᐅᕝᐸᑎ’ᓄᑦ, ᑎᒍᒥᐊᕈᖕᓇᖅᓱᕆᑦ . . . ᐃᑲᔪᖖᒐ.

ᐊᖕᒍᓇᖠᐊᖅᑎᒃᓴᖅᑲᕈᐃᖁᒪ ᑲᒪᒋᖤᒃᓴᖅᑲᕈᐃᖁᒪ. ᐱᖦᖤᑎᖅᑲᕈᐃᖁᒪ ᐃᓅᖤᒻᓂ . . . ᐊᓂᖅᓂᖁ ᑐᖅᑯᑕᖅᑐᖅ. ᐃᑲᔪᖖᒐ.

ᖠᓇᖅᑲᖖᒋ’ᓇᒪ. ᓇᐅᓪᓚ ᐱᖦᖤᑎᒃᓴᖁ? ᖠ’ᒪᑦ ᑕᐅᑐᒃᑕᑦᑲ ᑕᐅᑐᒃᐸᒃᐸᑦᑲ? ᓄᓚᐊᔪᒃ, ᐃᓂᖅᑲᖁᓗᐊᖅᑯᖕᒐ ᐅᑯᓇᓂ? ᐃᓂᒃᓴᖅᑲᖖᒋᒻᒪᓇᒃᑲᓗᐊᕈᒪᓘᓐᓃᑦ ᖠᒥᑐᐃᓐᓇᖅ?

ᐅᑕᖅᑭᖦᖀᖅᓱᓂ ᐱᖠᓚᓇᐊᖅᓱᓂ ᖠᓇᒥᒃ ᑕᐅᑐᓚᖅᓱᓂ ᐅᖕᒐᖤᕝᔭᒃᑐᒥ. ᖠᓇᐅᕝᕗ ᖤᑯᒥ ᐳᒃᑖᒥ ᓇᓄᐊᓐᓄᐊᖅ ᐃᒃᖤᕙᖥᖅ ᖅᑲᓪᓚᕗᓪᓚᐊ’ᓗᓂ ᖤᓈᒧᑦ.

ᖠᒻᒥᒃᑐᖅ: . . . ᖠᓇᑦᑕᐅᖅ ᐅᓇ? (ᓂ’ᓚᖅᕕᒋᕚ) ᖠᓇᑦᑕᐅᖅ ᐅᓇ?

ᐊᑐᒐᐅᖅ ᐃᖤᖅᓱᓂ ᖅᑭᓂᖁᒥᐅᒃ ᑲᑕᐃᖦᓂ ᖠᓗᓐᓄᐊᖅ ᑲᖖᒎᑉ.

ᐊᑐᒐᐅᖅ: ᖠᒥᔅᓱᑭᐊᖅ ᑲᑕᐃᖦᓇᓗᒐ . . .

ᖠᒻᒥᒃᑐᖅ ᖤᑯᒥᒃ ᐳᒃᑖᒥ ᓄᑦᖅᑲᖖᒐᑎᑦᑎᓇᖠᐊᖅᓱᓂ ᐃᖤᓛᒍᑦ ᐊᖦᓛᒍᓪᓘᓐᓃᑦ.

ᖠᒻᒥᒃᑐᖅ: (ᐊᑎᖅᑕᓐᓄᐊᖅᒎᑦ) ᑕᖦᕗᐅᖑᖖᒐ ᐅᓇᓐᓄᐊᖅ . . . ᖅᑲᐃᑲᐃᑦ, ᖅᑲᐃᓪᒍᐃᑦ.

ᐊᑐᒐᐅᖅ ᖠᒻᒥᒃᑐᖅᒥᒃ ᑕᖅᑯᒐᒥ ᐃᖅᖤᓚᖅᑐᖅ.

ᐊᑐᒐᐅᖅ: (ᑐᖅᓱᓚ’ᓱᓂ ᐊᖤᒥ’ᓄᑦ) ᖠᒻᒥᒃᑐᖅ ᐅᓇ ᑕᓇᐅᖅᒎᖖᒐᐅᓇᖠᐊᖅᑐᖅ ᐃᒫᖅᑎᓐᓇᖠᐊᖅᑐᓇᓗᒃ!

ᖠᒻᒥᒃᑐᖅ: ᐃᒫᖅᑎᓐᓇᖠᐊᖖᒋᑦᑐᖖᒐ ᐃᐱᖁᖅᖤᓐᓇᖅᑐᖖᒐ.

ᖠᒻᒥᒃᑐᖅ ᑐᑎ’ᓱᓂ ᐳᒃᑕᖥᒎᑦ ᑎᒍ’ᓱᒍ ᓇᓄᐊᓐᓄᐊᖅ.

ᖠᒻᒥᒃᑐᖅ: (ᓇᓄᐊᓐᓄᐊᖅᒎᑦ) ᒥᑭᖥᓐᓅᖥᑎᑦ, ᑲᒪᒋᓂᐊᖅᐸᒋᑦ.

ᐊᑐᒐᐅᖅ: ᓇᓄᐊᓐᓄᐊᖅ—ᒪᒪᕈᒥᓇᖅᑐᖅ ᓂᖅᑭᐊ ᐊᖅᑭᑦᑐᒃᓴᐅᖑᖅ. ᑕᒃᑰᒃ ᐊᐃᑉᐹ’ᓂᒃ ᖤᐅᑎᖅᑲᖖᒋᑦᑐᓐᓄᐊᖅ.

MANIILAQ: *(to HUMMIKTUQ)* What's all this commotion—why are you trying to drown in the ocean and spoil our celebration?

HUMMIKTUQ: I appreciate with my whole heart that this cub came to me, otherwise it would die.

MANIILAQ: First "black water" and now—what are you talking about, Arnarvik? Where did this little polar bear come from?

HUMMIKTUQ: He came to me on a small ice floe. Atugauq, you can teach him to dance and Qiluniq can teach him to hunt.

ATUGAUQ: *(to MANIILAQ)* Why is she talking strangely?

MANIILAQ: Maybe a malicious spirit has taken her mind.

HUMMIKTUQ: Nothing has taken my mind, but this dear little one has taken my heart.

NUKILIK: *(off stage)* DID HUMMIKTUQ GO DOWN UNDER THE OCEAN?

IBŘUQ: *(off stage)* DON'T GO DOWN UNDER THE OCEAN!

QILUNIQ, NUKILIK, IBŘUQ, HIGGUK, and AVINNGAQ enter to answer ATUGAUQ's call for assistance.

NUKILIK: *(to HUMMIKTUQ)* I thought you drowned in the ocean!

HUMMIKTUQ: I didn't drown!

HIGGUK: *(to HUMMIKTUQ)* Where did this cub come from?

HUMMIKTUQ: He came to me on a small ice floe.

QILUNIQ: Mmm, meat so tender—

HUMMIKTUQ: *(to QILUNIQ)* He is my child now.

NUKILIK: *(to HUMMIKTUQ)* Polar bears are not children.

ᖠᒻᒥᒃᑯᖅ: ᐃᓕᓴᖅᑎ’ᓲᕙᑦ ᓄᑕᕋᖅᖢᐅᑎᓂᒃ.

ᐊᑐᒐᐅᖅ: ᐋᕐᑭᔅᓱᒃ—ᓇᓅ’ᒪᑦ ᓄᑕᕋᐅᙳᕆᑦᑐᕐᓚ.

ᒪᓃᓚᖅ ᐃᖢᖅᓱᓂ

ᒪᓃᓚᖅ: *(ᖠᒻᒥᒃᑯᕐᒧᑦ)* ᖠᖤᓇᓘᖤᖢ—ᖠ’ᒪᔅᑐ ᑕᓇᐅᕐᒧᑦ ᐊᑦᖅᑲᕋᖠᐊᖅᐱᑦ ᖁᕕᐊᓇᐃᑦᑐᖅᖢᐅᖅᑎᑦᓚᔅᖣᓱᒃᑎᓐᓇᖠᐊᖅᐱᑎᒍᑦ?

ᖠᒻᒥᒃᑯᖅ: ᓴᑐᕐᓱᐊᖅᑕᓐᓄᐊᕋ ᐅᓇ ᑐᕐᑯᓐᓂᐊᕋᓱᐊ’ᒪᑦ ᐅᕙᒻᒧᙳᐅᕙᔅᓱᖅᓱᓂ.

ᒪᓃᓚᖅ: ᐃᒪᖅ ᕿᕐᓂᖅᑐᓇᑦᖄᐸᖠᔅᓱᒃᓱᒍ ᑕᕝᕙᓚ ᖃᓄᕐᓚᐅᖅᑐᓇᓘᖤᑎᑦ, ᐊᕐᓇᕐᕕᒃ? ᖠᒥ’ᙳᓛᖅᑐᖅ ᐅᓇ ᓇᓄᐊᓐᓄᐊᖅ?

ᖠᒻᒥᒃᑯᖅ: ᐅᕙᒻᒧᙳᐅᖤᖅ ᖢᑯᒥᑦ. ᐊᑐᒐᐅᖅ ᒧᒥᖅᑎᖤᖕᓇᓲ’ᕙᑦ ᕿᓗᓂᖅ ᐊᖖᒍᓇᖠᐊᖅᑎᖤᖕᓇ’ᓲᕙᔅᑐ.

ᐊᑐᒐᐅᖅ: *(ᒪᓃᓚᕐᒧᑦ)* ᖠ’ᒪᑦ ᐅᓇ ᑐᑮᓕᖅᑐᖅ?

ᒪᓃᓚᖅ: ᐱᑦᑕᐅᙳᕆᑦᑐᒧᑦ ᐃᖠᒫ ᐱᔭᐅ’ᒪᔅᓘᓐᓃᑦ.

ᖠᒻᒥᒃᑯᖅ: ᐃᖠᒪᒐ ᐱᔭᐅᙳᕆᑦᑐᖅ, ᐅᓇᓐᓅᑉ ᐆᒪᑎᒪ ᐱᔭᓇᓗᐊ.

ᓄᑭᓕᒃ: *(ᐊᕙ’ᖕᒐᑦ)* ᖠᒻᒥᒃᑯᖅ ᑕᓇᐅᕐᒧᙳᒐᐅᒐᓗᐊᖅᐸ ᐃᒫᖅᑎᓐᓇᖠᐊᖅᓱᓂ?

ᐃᐸᖤᖅ: *(ᐊᕙ’ᖕᒐᑦ)* ᑕᓇᐅᕐᒥ ᐃᒫᖅᑎᓐᓇᖠᐊᖅᑕᐃᓛᑦ!

ᐃᖢᖅᑐᑦ ᕿᓗᓂᖅ, ᓄᑭᓕᒃ, ᐃᐸᖤᖅ, ᖢᒃᒍᒃ, ᐊᕕᓐᖕᒐᕐᓗ ᐃᑲᔪᓚᐊᖅᑐᖅᓱᑎᒃ ᐊᑐᒐᐅᕐᒥᒃ ᐃᓚᐊᓛᕋᓗᐊ’ᒪᑦ.

ᓄᑭᓕᒃ: *(ᖠᒻᒥᒃᑯᕐᒧᑦ)* ᐃᒫᕋᖠᕆ’ᓗᑎᑦ ᑕᓇᐅᕐᒥ!

ᖠᒻᒥᒃᑯᖅ: ᐃᒫᖅᑎᓐᓇᖠᐊᙳᕆᑦᑐᖕᒐᓚ!

ᖢᒃᒍᒃ: *(ᖠᒻᒥᒃᑯᕐᒧᑦ)* ᓇᓄᐊᓐᓄᐊᖅ ᐅᓇ ᖠᒥ’ᙳᓛᖅᐸ?

ᖠᒻᒥᒃᑯᖅ: ᑕᓇᐅᕐᒥ’ᙳᓛᖅᑐᖅ ᐳᒃᑖᒦᑦᑲᓗᐊ’ᒪᑦ ᐅᕙᒻᒧᙳᐅᖤᖅ.

ᕿᓗᓂᖅ: ᒪᒪᖅ . . . ᓂᕿᐊ ᐊᕐᑭᑦᑐᑦᑎᐊᕙᒃ—

HUMMIKTUQ: I'm keeping him and taking care of him.

NUKILIK: He'll grow too big for you to keep—let him go.

HIGGUK: Yes, polar bears grow quite big.

AVINNGAQ: You'll put us in danger if you keep him.

HUMMIKTUQ: No, he'll grow up to become helpful to us.

IBŘUQ: He'll grow to become ferocious.

NUKILIK: Yes, ferocious and harmful.

HUMMIKTUQ: I'll teach him to behave.

NUKILIK: None of us can be taught to act against our nature—let him go.

HUMMIKTUQ: *(to NUKILIK)* He won't survive.

NUKILIK: His life is not our responsibility.

HUMMIKTUQ: He's lost!

IBŘUQ: Let him go so he can find his mother.

HUMMIKTUQ: She's dead. I'm his mother now.

NUKILIK: *(to AVINNGAQ)* What's gotten into her— *(to HUMMIKTUQ)* This is a *bear*!

IBŘUQ: You cannot be a mother to a bear.

HUMMIKTUQ: Yes I can, Ibřuq.

NUKILIK: You must think you're very special.

HUMMIKTUQ: I'm not special, but this bear is special.

ᕃᒻᒥᒃᑯᖅ: (ᕿᓗᓂᕐᒧᑦ) ᓄᑕᕋᓇᓕᖅᑕᕋᓕ.

ᓄᑭᑕᒃ: (ᕃᒻᒥᒃᑯᕐᒧᑦ) ᓇᓄᐃᑦ ᓄᑕᕋᐅᙱᑦᑐᑦ.

ᕃᒻᒥᒃᑯᖅ: ᐱᔦᒪᓂᐊᖅᑕᕋ. ᐸᒥᖅᓴᓕᖅᑕᕋ.

ᓄᑭᑕᒃ: ᐊᖏᕙᓪᓛᓕᕈᒫ'ᒪᑦ—ᑲᒪᒋᕃᐃᕈᒃ.

ᔦᒡᒍᒃ: ᐄ, ᐊᒡᓕᖅᑲᑦᑕᖅᑐᕐᑰᒐᓗᐊᑦ ᓇᓄᐃᑦ.

ᐊᕕᓐᖓᒐᖅ: ᐅᓗᓇᐊᓇᕐᓂᐊᕕ'ᒪᑦ ᐅᕙᑉᑎ'ᓄᑦ ᐱᔦᒪᒍᕕᐅᒃ.

ᕃᒻᒥᒃᑯᖅ: ᐄᕿ, ᐱᕈᕐᓂᐊᓇᓗᒃ ᐃᑲᔪᕈᒫᖅᓱᓂᑎᒍᑦ.

ᐃᐸᕃᖅ: ᐱᕈᕐᓂᐊᓇᓗᒃ ᐃᖅᔦᓇᕐᓗᓂ.

ᓄᑭᑕᒃ: ᐄ, ᐃᖅᔦᓇᕐᓗᓂ ᐋ'ᓂᖅᔦᓗᓂᓗ.

ᕃᒻᒥᒃᑯᖅ: ᐃᓂᖅᑎᓇᑦᑎᐊᕐᓂᐊᖅᐸᕋ ᐱᑦᑎᐊᕐᓂᐊ'ᒪᑦ.

ᓄᑭᑕᒃ: ᐃᓕᑦᕐᑯᔦᑉᑎ'ᓂᒃ ᓴᓇᒪᓂᑉᑎ'ᓂᒃ ᑕᒪᑉᑕ ᐊᔦᐊᒎᓚᐃᑦᑐᒍᑦ—ᑲᒪᒋᕃᐃᕈᒃ.

ᕃᒻᒥᒃᑯᖅ: (ᓄᑭᑕᖕᒧᑦ) ᐊᓐᓇᐅᒪᓚᐃᑦᑐᖅ.

ᓄᑭᑕᒃ: ᐆᒪᓂᖓ ᐅᕙᑉᑎ'ᓂᙶᙱ'ᒪᑦ.

ᕃᒻᒥᒃᑯᖅ: ᐊᔦᐅᕃᖅ!

ᐃᐸᕃᖅ: ᑲᒪᒋᕃᐃᕈᒃ ᐊᓈᓇᒥᓄᙵᐅᓂᐊ'ᒪᑦ.

ᕃᒻᒥᒃᑯᖅ: ᑐᕐᑯᕃᕐᓕ. ᐊᓈᓇᒋᓕᖅᐹᖓ.

ᓄᑭᑕᒃ: (ᐊᕕᓐᖓᒐᕐᒧᑦ) ᕃᕃᓇᓗᒃᑕᐅᖅ ᐅᓇ— (ᕃᒻᒥᒃᑯᕐᒧᑦ) ᓇᓄᕐᕗᒃ!

ᐃᐸᕃᖅ: ᐊᓈᓇᒋᓭᐅᓚᐃᑦᑐᑎᑦ ᓇᓄᕐᒧᑦ.

ᕃᒻᒥᒃᑯᖅ: ᐄ ᐱᔦᖕᓇᖅᑐᖓ, ᐃᐸᕃᖅ.

ᓄᑭᑕᒃ: ᓴᓇᒪᕃᒃᑲᕕᑦ.

NUKILIK: Stop yabbering. This bear won't survive without his mother, so we must kill him now.

NUKILIK reaches out to take the cub from HUMMIKTUQ and it becomes a tug of war.

Clutching the cub, HUMMIKTUQ begins to wail.

HUMMIKTUQ: . . . AAAAHHHHHH . . .

HIGGUK: Oh no, here comes the wailing again.

HUMMIKTUQ: *(wails)* AAAAHHHHHH . . . AAAAHHHHHHH . . .

IBŘUQ: *(to HUMMIKTUQ)* When you cry so loud it hurts my ears.

HIGGUK: She'll keep us up all night.

HUMMIKTUQ: *(wails)* AAAAHHHHHH . . .

NUKILIK: Give the cub to me.

HUMMIKTUQ: *(wails)* AAAAHHHHHH.

NUKILIK: Hummiktuq!

MANIILAQ: *(to HUMMIKTUQ)* Arnarvik, never mind this cub—you can mother my son—Qiluniq.

MANIILAQ indicates to QILUNIQ to go over to HUMMIKTUQ.

Looking after Qiluniq will bring you comfort, and you won't feel so sad and alone.

HUMMIKTUQ: *(wails)* AAAAHHHHHHH.

HUMMIKTUQ manages to pull the little cub free of NUKILIK's grasp.

IBŘUQ: *(to HUMMIKTUQ)* When my baby is born you can carry it in your *amauti [parka with infant pouch]*.

ᓭᒻᒥᒃᑰᖅ: ᓭᓇᒪᓭᙵᒋᑦᑐᖕᒐ, ᐅᓇᓐᓄᐊᖅ ᐱᓐᓇᓇᓭᐅᔦᒃᓴᓐᓄᐊᖅ.

ᓄᑭᓚᒃ: ᐅᕐᑲᒪᕋᓗᒍᐃᓇᑦ. ᐊᓈᓇᖅᑲᕈᐃᕋᒥ ᐊᓐᓇᐅᒪᓚᐃᑦᑐᖅ—ᑐᕐᑯᓭᕐᓗᒍ ᑭᔦᐊᓂᒃ.

ᓄᑭᓚᒃ ᑖᒪ ᓭᒻᒥᒃᑰᕐᒥᑦ ᐱᓇᓭᐊᓚᖅᓱᓂᐅᒃ ᓇᓄᐊᓐᓄᐊᖅ ᓄᓭᑎᒋᓭᐅᓚᖅᓱᓂ.

ᑕᐃᒪᓗ ᓭᒻᒥᒃᑰᖅ ᐃᕿ'ᓗᓂᐅᒃ ᓇᓄᐊᓐᓄᐊᖅ, ᕿᐊᓚᖅᓱᓂ.

ᓭᒻᒥᒃᑰᖅ: . . . ᐋᐊᐊᐊᐊ . . .

ᔦᒡᒍᒃ: ᓭᔦᕐᓱᒃ, ᕿᐊᓚᓇᖁᖅ.

ᓭᒻᒥᒃᑰᖅ: *(ᕿᐊ'ᓗᓂ)* ᐋᐊᐊᐊᐊᐊ . . . ᐋᐊᐊᐊᐊᐊ . . .

ᐃᐸᔦᖅ: *(ᓭᒻᒥᒃᑰᕐᒧᑦ)* ᕐᑯᑭᕐᓇ'ᒪᑦ ᕿᐊᓃᑦ ᔦᐅᑏᒃᑲ ᐋ'ᓂᖅᑑᒃ.

ᔦᒡᒍᒃ: ᐱᓘᖅᑎᕐᑲᑦᑕᖅᑎᓐᓂᐊᕚᒃᑖᑎᒍᑦ ᕿᐊᕙᑦᑖᕐᓱᒃᓱᓂ.

ᓭᒻᒥᒃᑰᖅ: *(ᕿᐊ'ᓗᓂ)* ᐋᐊᐊᐊᐊᐊ . . .

ᓄᑭᓚᒃ: ᓇᓄᐊᓐᓄᐊᖅ ᐊᑕᐃ ᖃᐃᒡᒎᒃ.

ᓭᒻᒥᒃᑰᖅ: *(ᕿᐊ'ᓗᓂ)* ᐋᐊᐊᐊᐊᐊ.

ᓄᑭᓚᒃ: ᓭᒻᒥᒃᑰᖅ!

ᒪᓃᓚᖅ: *(ᓭᒻᒥᒃᑰᕐᒧᑦ)* ᐊᕐᓇᕐᕖᒃ, ᑲᒪᒋᓭᐃᕈᒃ—ᑎᒍᐊᕈᒪᒍᕖᑦ, ᐊᓈᓇᒋᓚᕐᓛᑎᑦ ᐃᕐᓂᕐᒪ ᕿᓗᓂᐅᑉ.

ᒪᓃᓚᖅ ᐃᕐᓂᓂ ᓭᒻᒥᒃᑰᕐᒧᙵᕐᑯᔦ'ᓗᓂ.

ᒪᓃᓚᖅ: ᑲᒪᒋᓂᐊᕋ'ᓂ ᕿᓗᓂᖅ ᓭᐃᒻᒪᖕᓂᐊᖅᑯᑎᑦ ᓂᒃᑦᑐᙱᑐᑎᑦ ᐊᔦᕐᑲᙱᑉᐸᓛᙱᑐᑎᑦ.

ᓭᒻᒥᒃᑰᖅ: *(ᕿᐊ'ᓗᓂ)* ᐋᐊᐊᐊᐊᐊ.

ᓭᒻᒥᒃᑰᖅ ᐋᖅᓵᖅᓱᓂᐅᒃ ᓇᓄᐊᓐᓄᐊᖅ ᓄᑭᓚᖕᒥᑦ.

HUMMIKTUQ: I'll carry this little bear in my amauti.

HIGGUK: Oh I can't wait to see you carrying a polar bear cub in your amauti!

IBŘUQ: With your poor vision you couldn't see if she was carrying a caribou in her amauti.

AVINNGAQ: Hummiktuq, a cub is not a child.

HUMMIKTUQ: Avinngaq, I received this bear as a gift.

AVINNGAQ realizes what she means.

AVINNGAQ: You received it as a gift?

HUMMIKTUQ: Yes, I received it as a gift.

AVINNGAQ: *(to the group)* Enough now. What harm is there to allow this woman, who has lost all her family, to care for a cub?

NUKILIK: She's too old to look after a polar bear.

HUMMIKTUQ: I'm not too old.

AVINNGAQ: *(to the group)* Do we all agree that Hummiktuq can look after this bear for a little while?

MANIILAQ: Yes. For a little while.

NUKILIK: How long is a little while?

AVINNGAQ: When he grows too big to carry in your amauti you must let him go.

HUMMIKTUQ: Yes, when he grows too big to carry in my amauti I will let him go. *(holding the bear close)* Now I am happy, too.

AVINNGAQ: But only for a little while, Hummiktuq.

HUMMIKTUQ: Yes, only for a little while.

ᐃᐸᔦᖅ: (ᓭᒻᒥᒃᑐᕐᒧᑦ) ᓄᑕᕋᒃᓴᕋ ᐅᓇ ᐃᓅᓕᖅᐸᑦ ᐊᒫᖅᑲᑦᑕᕈᓐᓇᖅᑕᑦ.

ᓭᒻᒥᒃᑐᖅ: ᓇᓄᐊᓐᓄᐊᖅ ᐅᓇ ᐊᒫᖅᑲᑦᑕᕈᓐᓇᖅᑕᕋ.

ᔦᒡᒍᒃ: ᖃᓄᓂᑦᑰᖅᔮᓗᒡᓗᓂᓕᑭᐊᖅ ᐊᒪᕐᓗᓂ ᓇᓄᕐᒥᒃ ᐊᒪᐅᑎᒥᓂ?

ᐃᐸᔦᖅ: ᑕᒃᐲᑦᑐᓇᓘᒐᕕᑦ ᐊᒪᕋᓗᐊᖅᐸᑦ ᓭᓇᒥᒡᓘᓐᓃᑦ ᑐᒃᑐᒥᒃ
ᑕᑯᓇᔭᖏᒻᒪᓂᒃᑕᑦ.

ᐊᕕᓐᖓᖅ: ᓭᒻᒥᒃᑐᖅ, ᓇᓄᐊᓐᓄᐊᖅ ᓄᑕᕋᐅᖏ'ᒪᓪᓕ.

ᓭᒻᒥᒃᑐᖅ: ᐊᕕᓐᖓᖅ, ᑕᒃᑰᒃ ᑐᓂᔾᕙᔦᐊᓂᔦᒪᓭᕋ.

ᐊᕕᓐᖓᖅ ᑐᑭᔦᓕᕋᒥ ᖃᓄᖅ ᐅᖅᑲᕋᓭᐊᓂᐊᒃᓵ.

ᐊᕕᓐᖓᖅ: ᑐᓂᔾᕙᔦᐊᓂᓭᑦ?

ᓭᒻᒥᒃᑐᖅ: ᐄ, ᑐᓂᔾᕙᔦᐊᓂᕋ.

ᐊᕕᓐᖓᖅ: (ᐃᓄᖕᓄᑦ) ᑕᐃ'ᓇᐃ'ᒪᑦ, ᖃᓄᓂᓕᐃᑦᑰᖅᑐᖅ ᐊᕐᓇᖅ ᐅᓇ,
ᐃᓕᐃᖅᑐᓐᓄᐊᖅ ᑲᒪᒋᒃᐸᒍ ᓇᓄᐊᓐᓄᐊᖅ. ᖃᓄᓂᓕᐃᑦᑐᖅ.

ᓄᑭᓕᒃ: ᐊᕐᓇᑦᖁᐊᖅᓵᖑ'ᒪᑦ ᓇᓄᕐᒥᒃ ᑲᒪᑦᑎᐊᓕᐃᑦᖁ'ᒪᑦ.

ᓭᒻᒥᒃᑐᖅ: ᐊᕐᓇᑦᖁᐊᖅᓵᖑᖏᑦᑐᖓ.

ᐊᕕᓐᖓᖅ: (ᐃᓄᖕᓄᑦ) ᐊᖕᒥᖅᑲᖅᑮᒃᐱᑕ ᓭᒻᒥᒃᑐᖅ ᐅᓇ
ᑲᒪᒋᒃᑲᓐᓄᐊᕈᖕᓇ'ᒪᒍ ᓇᓄᐊᓐᓄᐊᔾᔪᒃ?

ᒪᓃᓕᖅ: ᐄ. ᔦᕕᑐᖕᖏᑦᑐᒥᒃ.

ᓄᑭᓕᒃ: ᔦᕕᑭᑦᑐᒥᐅᓂᐊᖅᐸᑦ ᖃᓄᖅ ᔦᕕᑐᑎᒋᓂᐊᖅᐸ?

ᐊᕕᓐᖓᖅ: ᐊᒪᐅᑎᒋᔦ'ᓂ ᐊᖕᒋᕙᓪᓘᓕᕈᓂ ᑲᒪᒋᓭᐃᕈᒫᖅᑕᑦ.

ᓭᒻᒥᒃᑐᖅ: ᐄ, ᐊᒪᐅᑎᒋᔦᒻᓂ ᐊᖕᒋᕙᓪᓘᓕᕈᓂ ᑲᒪᒋᓭᐃᕈᒫᖅᑕᕋ.
(ᐃᕿ'ᓗᓂᐅᒃ ᓇᓄᐊᓐᓄᐊᖅ) ᖁᕕᐊᓭᖅᑕᐅᓕᖅᑯᖕᖑᓕ.

ᐊᕕᓐᖓᖅ: ᓭᒻᒥᒃᑐᖅ, ᔦᕕᑭᑦᑑᓂᐊᕋᓗᐊᖅᑐᒥᒃ ᐱᔦᒪᓂᐊᖅᑕᑦ.

HIGGUK: Now that the bear has been sorted out, let's return to the tent and to our celebration.

IBŘUQ: Yes, celebrations are too rare to waste. *(to ATUGAUQ)* Come, ataataa; come, husband.

ATUGAUQ is referred as husband here through kinship naming.

NUKILIK: *(to HIGGUK)* We'll keep an eye on him, and when the time comes, he'll make a very tasty meal.

HIGGUK: Yes . . . *(to IBŘUQ)* But tonight I cannot think about anything except tonight.

IBŘUQ laughs.

IBŘUQ: You crazy man.

NUKILIK: *(to HUMMIKTUQ, harshly)* Sleep over there with the stupid cub.

All exit but HUMMIKTUQ.

HUMMIKTUQ: You are very tiny, so I'll name you Angu'řuaq, which means "the big man" . . . but do not grow too big, too fast.

HUMMIKTUQ pets the cub and he raises his foreleg. She touches his foreleg.

(to the cub) My name is Hummiktuq. My grandmother's name is my name and she comes through me now.

She hugs him, so happy.

I will be your anaana, your mother . . . your human mother.

ᖁᒻᒥᒃᑐᖅ: ᐃ, ᔪᕕᑭᑦᑐᒥᐅᒐᓗᐊᖅ ᐊᔪᐅ.

ᔪᒡᒍᒃ: ᓇᓄᐊᓐᓄᐊᕐᓗ ᑲᒪᑭᑖᕋᑉᑎᒍᑦ, ᐅᑎᓕᖅᑕ ᑐᐱᕐᒧᑦ ᕐᑯᕕᐊᖁᖅᑲᑎᒌ’ᒥᑕ.

ᐃᑉᖁᖅ: ᐃ, ᕐᑯᕕᐊᖁᖅᑲᑎᒌᖕᓂᕗᑦ ᔪᕕᑭᑦᕐᑰᖅᑲᑦᑕ’ᒥ’ᒪᑦ. (ᐊᑐᒐᐅᕐᒧᑦ) ᖃᐃᓗᑎᑦ ᐊᑖᑕ, ᖃᐃᒡᒍᐃᑦ ᐅᐃ.

ᐊᑐᒐᐅᖅ ᐅᐃᓈᖅᑕᐅᖃᑦᑕᖅᑐᖅ ᐊᑎᕐᒥᒍᑦ.

ᓄᑭᓕᒃ: (ᔪᒡᒍᖕᒧᑦ) ᑕᑯᖃᑦᑕᕐᓂᐊᖅᐸᕗᑦ ᓈᒻᒪᒃᔪᒍᓂᓗ ᓂᓇᔾᔭᒃᓴᑦᑎᐊᕙᐅᔪᒫᖅᑯᖅ.

ᔪᒡᒍᒃ: ᐄᖑᒐᓗᐊᖅ . . . (ᐃᑉᖁᕐᒧᑦ) ᑕᔾᕙ ᐅᓐᓄᒃ ᐃᖁᒪᑭᔾᕐᑲᑦᑎᐊᓚᐃ’ᓇᒪ ᐊᔪᐊᓂ.

ᐃᑉᖁᖅ ᐃᒡᓕᖅᓘᓂ.

ᐃᑉᖁᖅ: ᖁᕐᑯᑕᐅᙵᑭᑦᑐᑉᑲᓇᓇᓗᕐᓘᒃ ᐅᓇ.

ᓄᑭᓕᒃ: (ᖁᒻᒥᒃᑐᕐᒧᑦ ᓂᙵᒐᒃᓘᓂ) ᐊᕗᙵᒐᕋᓐᓂᑲᐃᑦ ᔪᓂᖅᑲᑎᑭᓗᒍ ᓇᓄᕐᓘᒃ.

ᑕᒪᕐᒥᒃ ᐊᓂᖁᑦ ᖁᒻᒥᒃᑐᖅ ᐃᓄᑑᓕᖅᓘᓂ.

ᖁᒻᒥᒃᑐᖅ: ᒥᑭᖁᓐᓅᒐᕕᑦ ᐊᖑ’ᖁᐊᕐᒥᒃ ᐊᑎᖅᑲᖅᑎᓂᐊᖅᐸᑭᑦ ᐊᖑ’ᖁᐊᖑᔭᒫᕋᕕᑦ . . . ᑭᔪᐊᓂᒃ ᐊᒡᓕᔫᑦᕐᑯᔾᔭᑭᑦ.

ᖁᒻᒥᒃᑑᑉ ᐊᒃᑐ’ᒪᒍ ᐃᔾᔭᓕᖅᑐᓐᓄᐊᖅ. ᖁᒻᒥᒃᑐᖅ ᐊᒃᑐᖅᔪ’ᓗᓂ ᓇᓄᐊᓐᓄᐊᑉ ᐃᔪᓖᓂ.

ᖁᒻᒥᒃᑐᖅ: (ᓇᓄᐊᓐᓄᐊᕐᒧᑦ) ᐊᑎᕋ ᖁᒻᒥᒃᑐᖅ. ᓂᖕᑭᐅᕐᒪ ᐊᑎᐊ’ᓂ ᐊᑎᖅᑲᕋᒪ ᐅᕙᑉᑰᓕᖅᑐᖅ.

ᐃᖁ’ᓗᓂᐅᒃ, ᕐᑯᕕᐊᖁᑦᑎᐊᖅᓘᓂ

ᖁᒻᒥᒃᑐᖅ: ᐊᓈᓇᑭᓂᐊᖅᑕ’ᒪ . . . ᐃᓄᖕᒥᒃ ᐊᓈᓐᖃᕐᓂᐊᕋᕕᑦ.

SCENE TWO

Nine years later. It is January and a storm is coming. The land is white and frozen with the glacial hill in the distance. The wind—erratic, strong—builds throughout the scene.

In utter silence, HIGGUK *waits by a breathing hole, his harpoon at the ready. A little distance away,* NUKILIK *waits by another breathing hole with his harpoon. With grizzled skin and white hair they are tired, hungry, impatient, and cold.*

ANGU'ŘUAQ *enters, and he is huge. He lumbers over to* HIGGUK *and, after a moment,* HIGGUK *surrenders the hole to the bear and goes over to join* NUKILIK. ANGU'ŘUAQ *remains absolutely still, all his attention focused on the smell of seals swimming beneath the ice. He waits for one to come up for air.*

NUKILIK: *(whispers)* No seals for us and another storm coming.

HIGGUK: *(whispers)* The spirits do not help those who are anxious.

NUKILIK: *(whispers)* I live carefully, follow the taboos, and I care for my relatives.

HIGGUK: *(whispers)* Patience.

NUKILIK: *(whispers)* For once I'd like to catch a seal before that damn bear does. Just once.

HIGGUK: *(whispers)* Patience.

ᖃᓄᕆᑦᑑᓂᖕᒐᐊ ᑭᖕᒍᐊᒍᑦ

ᐅᑭᐅᑦ ᖁᓚᐅᕐᒥᓐᓄᐊᖅᑐᑦ ᓈᓯᒪᓕ’ᒪᑕ. ᑕᑦᕿᐊ ᓯᕿᓐᓇᐅᑕᐅ’ᓗᓂ ᐅᑭᐅᒃᑯᑦ ᐱᖅᓯᖅᐸᓪᓕᐊᓕᖅᓱᓂ. ᐊᓄᕐᕋᒃᐸᓪᓕᐊᔪᖅ ᓴᕐᒥᔪᖅ ᓴᕐᒥᒡᓕᓪᓕᐊ’ᓗᓂ.

ᓂᐸᐃᑦᑎᐊᓱᓂ, ᓯᒡᒍᒃ ᐊᒡᓗᒥ ᓂᒃᐸᖅᑐᖅ, ᐅᓈᓂ ᑐᒍᒻᒥ’ᓗᒍ. ᐊᕙᓂᑦᑕᐅᖅ ᓄᑭᓕᒃ ᑕᐅᑐᖕᓇᖅᑐᖅ ᓂᒃᐸᖅᑐᖅᑕᐅᖅ ᐊᒡᓗᒥ ᐅᓈᖅᑲᖅᓱᓂ. ᑮᓇᐃᑦ ᐃᒧᑦᑐᖅᑲᓕᖅᓱᑎᒃ ᓄᔭᐃᑦ ᖀᖅᑲᓕᖅᓱᑎᒃ, ᑕᖅᑲᕗᑦ, ᑳᒃᑐᑦ, ᐃᓱᐃᒍᔭᒃᑐᑦ, ᐆᓇᐃᔭᒃᓱᑎᒃ.

ᐃᓯᖅᓱᓂ ᐊᖕᒍ’ᔪᐊᖅ, ᐊᖕᒋᔪᐊᓘ’ᓗᓂ. ᓯᒡᒍᖕᒧᕐᒐᐅ’ᒪᑦ ᐊᒡᓗᐊ ᐱ’ᓗᓂᐅᒃ ᓯᒡᒍᒃ ᓄᑭᓕᖕᒧᕐᒐᐅᕙᓪᓗᓕᖅᓱᓂ. ᐊᖕᒍ’ᔪᐊᖅ ᓄᑦᖃᖕᒐᑦᑎᐊᒻᒪᕆ’ᒪᑦ ᓇᐃᒪᓇᔭᐊᖅᓱᓂ ᓇᑦᑎᕐᓂᒃ ᓯᑰᑉ ᐊᑖᓃᑦᑐᓂᒃ. ᐅᑕᖅᑭᔪᖅ ᐳᐃᓐᓇᔭᐊᖅᑐᒥᒃ.

ᓄᑭᓕᒃ: (ᐃᓯᑉᔭᒃᓱᓂ) ᓇᑦᑎᖅᑲᓚᐃᑦᑐᕐᓱᒃ ᐱᖅᓯᖅᓂᐊᓕᕐᕌᓗᒃᓱᓂᓗ.

ᓯᒡᒍᒃ: (ᐃᓯᑉᔭᒃᓱᓂ) ᐃᑲᔪᖅᑎᑦ ᐃᑲᔪᖅᐸᕐᒥ’ᒪᑕ ᐃᔭᒫᓗᒐᔭᐊᖅᑐᓂᒃ.

ᓄᑭᓕᒃ: (ᐃᓯᑉᔭᒃᓱᓂ) ᐱᑦᑎᐊᖅᑐᕐᒐᓕ, ᑎᓕᒋᓭᐅᔭᓂᒃ ᒪᓕᒃᐸᒃᑲᒪ ᐃᓚᑦᑲᓗ ᑲᒪᒋᑦᑎᐊᖅᓱᒋᑦ.

ᓯᒡᒍᒃ: (ᐃᓯᑉᔭᒃᓱᓂ) ᓴᐃᒻᒪᖅᓴᕋᔭᐊᑲᐃᑦ.

ᓄᑭᓕᒃ: (ᐃᓯᑉᔭᒃᓱᓂ) ᓇᑦᑎᖅᑳᕈᒪᔪᖕᒐ ᓇᑦᑎᕐᒥᓐᓂᐊᓂ ᓇᓄᕐᓱᒃ, ᔭᔮᓇᓗᒃ.

ᓯᒡᒍᒃ: (ᐃᓯᑉᔭᒃᓱᓂ) ᕿᓄᕐᒋᓗᑎᑦ.

A seal's nose appears in the breathing hole beneath ANGU'ŘUAQ *and he grabs it, shakes it, kills it, then puts it in his mouth and carries it off towards the iglu.*

His swiftness always amazes me . . . *(calls)* HUMMIKTUQ.

HUMMIKTUQ enters with MANIILAQ and ATUGAUQ, who is very pregnant. The bear offers the seal to HUMMIKTUQ. She takes it, lays it down, then she puts her hand on the bear's head. He raises his foreleg to her and she takes it.

HUMMIKTUQ: *(to ANGU'ŘUAQ)* My son, you are kind. With all my heart I wish for you to have a wife in the future.

MANIILAQ: Atugauq, give a little water to the seal to please its soul.

MANIILAQ watches ATUGAUQ put a bit of snow in her mouth to melt it, then she puts it in the mouth of the seal.

(to ATUGAUQ) Dear daughter-in-law, you are so much like your mother, Ibřuq, you bring me comfort.

The women help ATUGAUQ drag the seal off towards the iglu.

HUMMIKTUQ, MANIILAQ, and ATUGAUQ exit with the dead seal.

HIGGUK: He always brings a seal to her.

NUKILIK: Lucky her.

HIGGUK: She's generous with the seals.

NUKILIK: She likes her generosity—it makes her feel powerful. She sees things in the future, but it seems like foolishness.

ANGU'ŘUAQ takes his place at the same breathing hole again.

HIGGUK: She still sees black water in her dreams.

ᓇᑦᑎᖅ ᐳᐃ'ᒪᑦ ᕿᖓᒑ ᑕᐅᑐᖕᓇᓕᖅᑯᖅ ᐊᖑ'ᔦᐊᑉ ᑰ'ᓗᒍ
ᔪᑦᖁᐊᒍᑦ ᐊᒧ'ᓗᓂᐅᒃ ᑐᖁᓴᓕᖅᓗᓂᐅᒃ ᑰᔪᒫ'ᓗᒍ ᐊᖕᔭᖅᑖ
ᐃᒡᓗᒧᑦ.

ᔪᒡᒍᒃ: ᔦᑲᔦᕌᓗᕐᓗᒃ ᑖᒻᓇ ᐊᔪᒐᐃᑦᑐᓇᓗᒃ . . . (ᑐᖅᓗᑖ'ᓗᓂᓗ)
ᔦᒻᒥᒃᑐᖅ.

ᔦᒻᒥᒃᑐᕐᓗ ᒫᓂᓚᕐᓗ ᐃᔪᖅᓗᑎᒃ ᐊᑐᒐᐅᕐᓗ ᓈᖅᑯᖅᑐᔦ'ᓗᓂ ᔪᖓᒐᐃᒐᒥ.
ᓇᓄᖅ ᓇᑦᑎᕐᒥᒃ ᑐᓂᔪ'ᓗᓂ ᑎᒍᐊᖅᔪᒥᓄᑦ. ᑎᒍᐊᖅᔪᐊᑕᓗ
ᑎᒍ'ᓗᓂᐅᒃ, ᐃᓕ'ᓗᓂᐅᒃ ᐊᔅᒐᓂ ᐃᓕᕖ ᓇᓅᑉ ᓂᐊᖁᐊᓄᑦ.
ᐃᔪᓘᑕᓗ ᔪᕗᓂᐊ ᐃᓴᒃᓗᒍ ᑎᒍᐊᖅᔪᐊᑕ ᑎᒍᕖ.

ᔦᒻᒥᒃᑐᖅ: (ᐊᖑ'ᔦᐊᖁᑦ) ᐃᖅᓂᖃ ᐱᑦᑎᐊᖅᑐᑎᑦ. ᓄᓕᐊᖅᑖᖁᒐᓗᐊᖅᓗᑎᑦ
ᖃᑯᒍ.

ᒫᓂᓚᖅ: ᐊᑐᒐᐅᖅ, ᐃᒻᒥᖅᑎᓪᓚᕐᓴᕿᒃ ᓇᑦᑎᖅ, ᑕᖅᓂᐊ ᐃᓗᖅᓇᓂᐊ'ᒪᑦ.

ᒫᓂᓚᖅ ᑕᐅᑐᒃᑐᖅ ᐊᑐᒐᐅᖅᒥᒃ ᐊᐳ'ᒥᒃ ᐅᖁᒻᒥᖅᓗᓂ ᐊᐅᒃᑎ'ᓇᒥᐅᒃ
ᓇᑦᑎᐅᑉ ᑲᓂᐊᓄᑦ ᐃᓕᕙᑦᓕᐊ'ᓗᒍ ᐃᒥᕈᖁᖖᕆ'ᓗᕆᑦ.

ᒫᓂᓚᖅ: (ᐊᑐᒐᐅᖑᑦ) ᐅᑯᐊᓐᓄᐊᖃ, ᐊᓈᓇᒃᓱᖅᑐᐸᓇᓘᔦᑎᑦ ᐃᑉᔦᖅᑐᑦ.
ᓴᐃᒻᒪᐅᑎᕆᕖᕆᑦ.

ᐊᖅᓈᒃ ᐊᑐᒐᐅᖅᒥᒃ ᐃᑲᔪᖅᑰᒃ ᐅᓂᐊᖅᓗᔦᒃ ᓇᑦᑎᖅ ᐃᒡᓗᒧᑦ.

ᐊᓂ'ᓗᑎᒃ ᔦᒻᒥᒃᑐᖅ, ᒫᓂᓚᖅ ᐊᑐᒐᐅᕐᓗ ᓇᑦᑎᖅ ᐱ'ᓗᓂᕆᑦ.

ᔪᒡᒍᒃ: ᓇᑦᑎᖅᓂᒃ ᐊᖕᔭᖅᔪᕕᕖ'ᒪᒍ.

ᓄᑭᓕᒃ: ᐊᑕᓕ.

ᔪᒡᒍᒃ: ᓴᑐᖅᓈᖅᑐᕌᓗᒡᓕ ᐊᖅᓇᑦᖁᐊᖅᓰᖅ ᐸᔪᒃᑕᐅᖅᑲᑦᑕ'ᒪᑦ.

ᓄᑭᓕᒃ: ᐱᑦᑕᐅᕆᔮᐅᓇᔦᐊ'ᒪᑦ ᓴᓇᒪᔦᓐᓄᐊᓪᓚᕐᓴ. ᑕᐅᑐᙱᐊᖅᑐᓇᕖ'ᒪᑦ
ᔪᕗᓂᖑᑦ ᑭᔪᐊᓂᒃ ᔦᓕᖅᑰᙱᑦᑐᕐᓗᒃ.

ᐊᖑ'ᔦᐊᖅ ᑕᐃᑯᖓ ᐅᑎᖅᓗᓂ ᓂᒃᐸᓕᓇ'ᓗᓂ.

ᔪᒡᒍᒃ: ᔦᓕ ᖄᖅᓇᓇᒃᑐᒥᒃ ᔪᓐᓇᒃᑑᒪᕆᔮᖅᑲᖅᑲᑦᑕᖅᑐᖅ.

NUKILIK: Every single day . . . *(mimicking HUMMIKTUQ) "I seeee blaaack waaater, everywhere is blaaack,"* but I don't argue with her anymore just in case she has the ability to do me harm. She thinks she is a shaman.

HIGGUK: Perhaps you could be a shaman.

NUKILIK: *(lowering his voice)* No. Avinngaq is the only shaman. I am just a simple hunter.

HIGGUK: Angu'řuaq is the greatest hunter. He taught me to hunt like a bear, to think like a bear. I think of Hummiktuq as foolish too, but I am grateful that she raised a polar bear.

NUKILIK does not roll his eyes at this, but that is the feeling.

NUKILIK: If she could see the future, she would have helped her husband and he would have not lost his life and there would be no Angu'řuaq gobbling up the seals!

HIGGUK: He only eats what he needs and always gives us meat. Nukilik, even if Hummiktuq had warned her husband, he would still have gone on the ice by dog team with his children so they'd forget their hunger for a while.

NUKILIK: True, but he might have listened to his dogs when they wanted to run faster. Dogs run faster when they feel the shifting of the ice through their paws—he knew that—everybody knows that.

HIGGUK: Maybe he saw something up ahead—a great storm approaching.

NUKILIK: The time we told Hummiktuq we found her children dead her black hair turned white like snow.

HIGGUK: Ibřuq had to sing her to sleep night after night.

A moment.

Nukilik . . . sometimes I hear Ibřuq's voice in the wind singing to me.

ᓄᑭᓕᒃ: ᐅᐸᓗᖅᑕᒫᕐᓕ . . . (ᐱᔫᓇ'ᓗᓂᐅᒃ ᖤᒻᒥᒃᑯᖅ) "ᐃᒪᕐᒥᒃ ᕿᕐᓇᓇᒃᑐᒥᒃ ᑕᑯᒐᒪ, ᖤᒥᑐᐃᓐᓇᖅ ᕿᕐᓇᓇᒃᑐᖅ," ᑲᒪᑎᖤᐃᓕᖅᑕᕋᓕ ᐊᑭᓂᐊᕙ'ᒪᖓ. ᐊᖓᑦᑰᓇᖤᑎ'ᒪᑦ.

ᖢᒡᒍᒃ: ᐃᔾᕙᕚᓪᓗᖅ ᐊᖓᑦᑰᒃᓴᐅᖠᑎᑦ.

ᓄᑭᓕᒃ: (ᖃᑎᑐᕆᐊᖅᓱᒍ ᓂᐱᓂ) ᐄᕿᔅᓱᒃ. ᐊᕚᓐᖓᖅ ᐊᖓᑦᑐᐱᑐᐊᔅᓱᒃ. ᐊᖑᓇᖤᐊᖅᑎᑐᐃᓐᓇᐅᖠᖓᓕ.

ᖢᒡᒍᒃ: ᐊᖑ'ᖠᐊᖅ ᐊᖑᓇᖤᐊᖅᑎᓂᒃ ᐊᖢᓚᐃᓛᖑᖠᖅ ᖤᒥᑐᐃᓐᓇᖅ. ᐃᓕᓴᖅᑎᑖᖓ ᐊᖑᓂᕐᒥᒃ ᓇᓄᖅᑐᑦ, ᐃᖤᒪᕐᑲᕐᓗᖓ ᓇᓄᖅᑐᑦ. ᖤᓕᖕᖏᓐᓇᖤᑎᔭᕋ ᖤᒻᒥᒃᑯᖅ ᑭᖠᐊᓂᒃ ᓴᑐᕐᓗᐊᖅᐸᕋ ᓇᓄᕐᒥᒃ ᐸᒥᖅᓯ'ᒪᑦ.

ᓄᑭᓕᒃ ᐃᓱᐊᑎᖡᔮ'ᒪᒍ ᐅᖃᐅᖢᐊ.

ᓄᑭᓕᒃ: ᖢᕗᓂᕐᒧᑦ ᑕᐅᑐᒍᓐᓇᖅᐸᑦ ᐅᐃᒥᓂᒃ ᐃᑲᔪᕐᓂᐊᕋᓗᐊ'ᒪᑦ ᑐᕐᑯᓇᓴᙱᓗᓂ ᐊᖑ'ᖠᐊᖅᑕᕐᑲᕐᓂᐊᙱᒃᑲᓗᐊᖅᓱᓂᓗ ᓂᓇᒪᐃᓐᓇᖅᑐᒥᒃ ᓇᑦᑎᕐᓂᒃ!

ᖢᒡᒍᒃ: ᓂᓇᕆᐊᖃᖅᑕᒥᓐᓇᖅ ᓂᓇᕗ'ᒪᑦ ᑐᓂ'ᓗᓂᑎᒍᑦ ᓂᕿᓂᒃ. ᓄᑭᓕᒃ, ᖤᒻᒥᒃᑯᖅ ᐃᒻᓇ ᖃᐅᖣᑎᓚᓗᐊᖅᐸᒍ ᐅᐃᓂ, ᖤᓕ ᖢᑯᒧᓐᓚᐅᓇᔭᕋᓗᐊᖅᑐᖅ ᕿᒧᒃᖢᒃᑯᑦ ᓄᑕᖀᕆᒃ ᐳᐃᒍᑲᓐᓄᐊᕐᓂᐊ'ᒪᑕ ᑳᖕᓂᕐᒥ'ᓂᒃ.

ᓄᑭᓕᒃ: ᐄᓴᐅᓚᓗᐊᕐᓕ, ᑐᓵᓇᓯᕋᓗᐊᖅᑐᖅ ᕿ'ᒥᖕᒋᑦ ᖤᑲᔪᓕᖅᑐᕐᓵᓗᓕᖅᑎ'ᓗᕆᑦ. ᑕ'ᓇᐃᓕᐅᖅᑲᑦᑕ'ᒪᑕ ᐃᒃᐱᕆᔅᖄᖓᒥᕆᑦ ᐃᖢᓚᐃᑎᒍᑦ ᖢᑯ ᖢᕐᑯᒥᓕᖅᑎ'ᓗᒍ—ᖃᐅᖣᒪᓚᓗᐊ'ᒪᑦ—ᑕᒪᐃᓐᓂᑦ ᑕᓴᒻᒪ ᖃᐅᖣᒪᔮᐅᖠᖅ.

ᖢᒡᒍᒃ: ᑕᑯᓚᓗᐊ'ᒪᓪᓘᓐᓃᑦ ᖢᕗᓂᕐᒥᓂ ᖤᓇᒥᒃ—ᐱᖅᖢᕐᖠᐊᖅᑐᒃᓴᒥᒡᓘᓐᓃᑦ ᑕᑯ'ᔭᓚᒥ.

ᓄᑭᓕᒃ: ᑕᐃᑉᖤᒪᓂ ᖤᒻᒥᒃᑯᖅ ᐊᒃᐱᐅᑎᓚᑉᑎᒍᑦ ᓄᑕᕋᐃ'ᓂᒃ ᓇᓂᖢᓚᑉᑕ ᑐᕐᑯᖓᒐ'ᓗᑎᒃ, ᓄᔭᐃᑦ ᕿᕐᓇᖅᓇᒃᑐᑦ ᖃᑯᖅᖢᖢᒪᖠᑦ ᐊᐳᑎᑐᑦ.

ᖢᒡᒍᒃ: ᐃᑉᖠᕐᓗ ᑕᐃᑉᖤᒪᓂ ᐃᖕᒋᐅᕐᓗᓂ ᑭᖢᐊᓂᒃ ᖢᓐᓇᒃᓴᐃ'ᓗᓂᐅᒃ ᐅᓐᓄᒃ ᑕᒫᑦ.

ᓂᐸᐃᑲᓐᓄᐊᖅᓱᓂ.

ᖢᒡᒍᒃ: ᓄᑭᓕᒃ . . . ᐃᓛ'ᓂᑦᑯᑦ ᐊᓄᓇᒥ ᑐᕐᖃᑦᑕᖅᑕᕋ ᐃᑉᖠᖅ ᐃᖕᒋᐅᖅᓱᓂ ᐅᕙᒻᒪᑦ.

NUKILIK: Expressing grief and moving past it can make a human being wise, like you, my idlunnuaq—but that woman is so damn unpredictable. I even offered to take her as a second wife, but she refused me—imagine—she refused *me*!

HIGGUK: She refused *me* too—imagine.

NUKILIK: . . . And now she's running around with that bear. I'm no longer a strong hunter because we don't need to hunt as much—that damn bear has become our hunter! *(abruptly gets to his feet and points to the bear)* He's the reason why Nukilik—the once great hunter—is losing his greatness—

HIGGUK: Shut up, the seals can hear.

NUKILIK: He has compromised our skills!

HIGGUK: Angu'řuaq helps us, too.

NUKILIK: He helps us become useless!

HIGGUK: We're not useless—we're *old*. Your son and your grandchildren will become great hunters, but you and me, idlunnuaq, our lives have an ending.

NUKILIK: No . . . I have lots to keep hunting for!

HIGGUK: Then hunt quietly.

They are silent as they concentrate, harpoons at the ready.

NUKILIK: *(lowering his voice)* In my dreams I am still a good hunter . . . but I am losing my strength—the same way you are losing your eyesight.

HIGGUK: I am *not* losing my eyesight—I have perfect vision.

Suddenly ANGU'ŘUAQ *lunges and grabs another seal out of the hole.*

NUKILIK: That old woman doesn't need to have *two* seals!

HIGGUK: It's for him—it's his dinner.

ᓄᑭᓕᒃ: ᐃᓗᕐᕆᖅᑐᖅᓗᓂ ᐊᓂᒍᐃᖅᓗᒍ ᓯᓚᑦᑐᖅᐹᓪᓕᖅᓇ’ᒥᓴᖅ, ᐃᕝᕙᑐᑦ, ᐃᓪᓗᓐᓄᐊᕋ—ᑕᐃᒻᓇᓕ ᓱᒻᒥᒃᑐᖅ ᐃᓱᒪ’ᓇᐃᑦᑐᖒᓗᖅᔪᒃ. ᐊᒃᐱᐅᑎᕗᕋᓗᐊᕋ ᓄᓕᐊᖅᑖᕆᔭᖕᓇᖅᔪᒍ ᒪᖅᕈᕋᖅᑲᖅᓗᖕᒐ ᖅᑭᐱᓗᒃᔪᓂᖕᒐ—ᓱᖅᑯᑕᐅᙱᑦᑐᑉᑲᓇᓇᓗᒃ—ᖅᑭᐱᓗ’ᒪᖕᒐ!

ᓯᒡᒍᒃ: ᖅᑭᐱᓗ’ᒥᔮᖕᒐ—ᓱᖅᑯᑕᐅᙱᑦᑐᖅᔪᒃ.

ᓄᑭᓕᒃ: . . . ᓇᓄᖅᑲᓕᕋᓗᐊᖅᔪᓂᓗ ᑎᒍᐊᓐᓄᐊᖅᔪᖕᒥᒃ. ᐊᖑᓇᓱᐊᖅᑎᓇᓘᓱᐃᖅᑐᖕᒐ ᐊᖑᓇᓱᐊᖅᐸᓪᓛᕈᐃᕋᑉᑕ ᓇᓄᖅᔪ ᐊᖑᓇᓱᐊᖅᑎᒋᕙᓪᓗᖅᔪᒍ! (ᓇᖕᒋᖅᔪᓂ ᑎᑦᑯᐊᖅᑐᖅ ᓇᓄᖅᒎᑦ) ᐅᓇᖅᔪᒃ ᐱᕝᓴᑕᐅᕗᖅ ᐅᕙᒻᓄᑦ ᓄᑭᓕᖕᒍᑦ—ᐊᔭᒐᐃᑦᑐᓇᓘᔪᒪᓕᖅᑐᖕᒐᓕ ᐊᔭᖅᐸᓪᓕᐊᓕᕋᒪ—

ᓯᒡᒍᒃ: ᓂᐱᖅᑲᕈᐃᓇᑦ ᓇᑦᑎᑦ ᑐᓵᔭᑦ.

ᓄᑭᓕᒃ: ᐊᔭᓕᖅᑎᓯᒪᔮᑎᒍᑦ!

ᓯᒡᒍᒃ: ᐊᖑ’ᔮᐊᖅᓕ ᐃᑲᔭᖅᑖᑎᒍᑦᑕᐅᖅ.

ᓄᑭᓕᒃ: ᐃᑲᔭᖅᑖᑎᒍᑦ ᐃᖅᑭᐊᓱᓕᖅᑯ’ᓗᑕ!

ᓯᒡᒍᒃ: ᐃᖅᑭᐊᓱᙱᑦᑐᒍᒃ—ᐃᓄᑐᖅᑲᐅᔮᒍᒃ. ᐃᖅᓃᓪᓗ ᐃᓐᖑᑕᑎᓪᓗ ᐊᖑᓇᓱᐊᖅᑎᐸᓇᓘᓂᐊᖅᑐᑦ, ᐅᕙᒍᓪᓕ ᐃᓪᓗᓐᓄᐊᖅ ᐃᓅᓯᒃᓴᖅᑯᑦ ᐃᓱᓕᓕ’ᒪᑦ.

ᓄᑭᓕᒃ: ᐄᖅᑭ . . . ᐊᖑᓇᓱᐊᖅᑕᒃᓴᖅᑲᐅᖅᑐᖕᒐ!

ᓯᒡᒍᒃ: ᓂᐱᑭᓗᑎᑦ ᐊᑕᐃ ᐊᖑᓇᓱᐊᓕᑦᑭᑦ.

ᓂᐸᐃ’ᓗᑎᒃ ᐅᑕᖅᑭᔮᒃ, ᐅᓈᖅᑎᒃ ᑎᒍᒥᐊᖅᔪᕝᔮᒃ.

ᓄᑭᓕᒃ: (ᖅᑲᑎᑐᒋᐊᖅᔪᒍ ᓂᐱᓂ) ᓯᓐᓇᒃᑑᒪ’ᓗᖕᒐ ᓱᓕ ᐊᖑᓇᓱᐊᖅᑎᑦᑎᐊᕙᐅᔮᖕᒐ . . . ᑭᓯᐊᓂᒃ ᐃᑦᖅᑯᒪᑎ’ᓗᖕᒐ ᖅᑲᐅᔨᕙᒃᑲᒪ ᔭᙱᑦᑐᓇᓘᓕᕋᒪ—ᓲᖅᑐ ᐃᕝᕙᑦ ᑕᒃᐲᓕᕋᕙᑦ.

ᓯᒡᒍᒃ: ᑕᒃᐲᙱᒻᒪᓇᒃᑐᖕᒐᓕ—ᑕᒃᐱᑦᑎᐊᖅᑐᓇᓘᔮᖕᒐ.

ᐊᖑ’ᔮᐊᖅ ᓇᑦᑎᖅᓴᖕᖑᔭᓇ’ᓗᓂ.

NUKILIK: He had one this morning!

HIGGUK: He's big.

NUKILIK: He's greedy!

HIGGUK: He's not greedy. See, he's taking it to Hummiktuq . . . wait, no—ahh, he's keeping that one for himself.

NUKILIK: *(calls to the bear)* Angu'řuaq! *(to HIGGUK)* Where's that damn bear going?

Curious, the hunters follow the bear, but suddenly they jump back.

UKUANNUAQ, a smaller polar bear, enters. The men watch ANGU'ŘUAQ give her the seal.

See, SEE! He *is* taking more than his share—and behind our backs!

HIGGUK: He's found a mate!

NUKILIK: He already gobbles up the seals, and now his wife needs some, too! And when they have offspring, they too will gobble up even more seals—we have to put these two down now!

HIGGUK: You're getting old and crazy, idluq.

NUKILIK: I am getting old and wise. *(calls)* Qiluniq, Atugauq, Maniilaq . . .

MANIILAQ, QILUNIQ, ATUGAUQ, and her young daughter, QAAQŠAATTIAQ, enter.

Is your arnarvik in the iglu?

MANIILAQ: Yes, she's butchering the seal—

NUKILIK: Don't call her. Be quiet—this is very important. *(points to the bears)* Look, Angu'řuaq has a wife and this poses a grave threat.

QILUNIQ: You're right, father. This is dangerous.

ᓄᑭᓕᒃ: ᐊᕐᓇᑦᑯᐊᖅᓵᔅᓱᒃ ᑕᐃᒻᓇ ᒪᕝᕈᓇᓗᖕᓂᒃ ᓇᑦᑎᖅᑲᖅᑐᒃᓴᐅᙱᑦᑐᖅ!

ᔨᒡᒍᒃ: ᐃᖕᒥᓂᒃ—ᓇ'ᒥᓂᖅ ᓂᖅᑲᐅᑎᒃᓵ.

ᓄᑭᓕᒃ: ᐅᑉᓛᖅ ᐱᒐᓗᐊ'ᒪᑦ.

ᔨᒡᒍᒃ: ᐊᖕᒋᔭᓇᓗᒃ.

ᓄᑭᓕᒃ: ᐸᓚᐃᑦᑐᖅ!

ᔨᒡᒍᒃ: ᐄᖅᑭ, ᐸᓚᐃᙱᓪᒪᓇᒃᑐᖅ. ᑕᒃᑰᒃ ᔭᓪᒥᒃᑐᖅᒍᑦ ᐊᒡᔭᓚᖅᐹ . . . ᐄᖅᑭᔅᓱᒃ—ᔭᓇᐅᕝᕙ ᐃᖕᒥᓄᐃᓐᓇᖅ.

ᓄᑭᓕᒃ: (ᓇᓄᕐᒧᑦ) ᐊᖑ'ᔭᐊᖅ! (ᔨᒡᒍᖕᒧᑦ) ᔭᒧᙵᒐᐅᔭᔅᓱᒃ ᐃᒻᓇ?

ᑕᑯᔭᒫ'ᓱᑎᒃ ᓇᓄᕐᒥᒃ ᒪᓕᓕᖅᑑᒃ, ᖁᒃᓴᓪᓚᒃᓱᑎᒃ.

ᐃᔨᖅᑐᖅ ᑖᒻᓇ ᓇᓄᖅ ᐊᑎᖅᑲᖅᓱᓂ ᐅᑯᐊᓐᓄᐊᕐᒥᒃ, ᒥᑭᕝᔭᒃᑐᖅ. ᐊᖑᑏᒃ ᑕᐅᑐᒃᓱᑎᒃ ᐊᖑ'ᔭᐊᖅ ᓂᕐᑭᒥᒃ ᑐᓂ'ᒪᒍ.

ᓄᑭᓕᒃ: ᑕᒃᑰᒃ! ᐃᕝᕈᒥᐊᖅᐸ'ᒪᑦ ᐱᒃᓴᒥᓃᓐᓇᔅᓱᖕᓂᒃ ᐱᓇᔭᐊᖅᐸᒃᑐᔅᓲ'ᒪᑦ.

ᔨᒡᒍᒃ: ᓄᓕᐊᖅᑲᓕᕐᓂ'ᒪᑦ!

ᓄᑭᓕᒃ: ᓇᑦᑎᑐᕈᒻᒪᖅᑑᓇᓗᒃ, ᓄᓕᐊᖕᒐᓗ ᑕᕝᕙ ᐱᔫᖅᑲᖅᑯᖅ! ᕿᑐᓐᖏᐅᕈᓂᓗ ᓇᑦᑎᖅᑐᕈᒫᖅᑐᓇᓗᐃᑦᑕᐅᖅ—ᐊᖑᒋᐊᖅᑲᖅᑕᒃᑯᑦ ᐅᑯᐊᒃ!

ᔨᒡᒍᒃ: ᔭᖅᑯᑕᐅᙱᑦᑐᑉᑲᓇᔅᓲᔭᑎᑦ, ᐃᑦᓲᖅ.

ᓄᑭᓕᒃ: ᐃᓐᓇᒃᓴᕈᓕᑫᒪ ᔨᓚᑦᑐᖅᐹᑦᓕᖅᑯᖕᒐ. (ᑐᖅᓱᓛ'ᓱᓂᒋᑦ) ᕿᓗᓂᖅ, ᐊᑐᒐᐅᖅ, ᒪᓃᓚᖅ . . .

ᐃᔨᖅᓱᑎᒃ ᒪᓃᓚᖅ, ᕿᓗᓂᖅ, ᐊᑐᒐᐅᕐᓗ ᐸᓂᓐᓄᐊᓂᓗ ᖄᒃᓵᑦᑎᐊᖅ.

ᓄᑭᓕᒃ: ᐊᕐᓇᕐᕚᑦ ᐃᓪᓗᒦᑦᐸ?

ᒪᓃᓚᖅ: ᐄ, ᐱᓚᒃᑐᐃᔭᖅ ᓇᑦᑎᕐᒥᒃ—

HIGGUK: But Angu'řuaq shares the seals he catches with us.

NUKILIK: Yes, but someday when there are fewer seals and he begins to starve . . . then what will he eat?

ATUGAUQ: He has never harmed my children—never.

NUKILIK: *(to ATUGAUQ) Ukuaq [daughter-in-law]*, he can become different, and when his wife has cubs, she'll protect them because she must do what she must do, and we must do what we must do.

MANIILAQ: *(to ATUGAUQ)* Your *hakik [parent-in-law]* is telling the truth.

ATUGAUQ: Then what must we do?

NUKILIK: *(lowering his voice)* Slaughter Angu'řuaq and his wife.

ATUGAUQ: No.

NUKILIK: He'll never leave of his own volition.

HIGGUK: No, please—

NUKILIK: We'll do it fast. He won't feel a thing.

ATUGAUQ: I grew up thinking he was my relative, like my real blood . . . but now I have children of my own to care for.

NUKILIK: I blame myself for not sending the bear away in the beginning, but Hummiktuq always refused to let him go.

MANIILAQ: *(to NUKILIK)* I blame myself for urging you to give in to Hummiktuq's demands.

HIGGUK: I blame myself for . . . everything.

NUKILIK: We're all culpable, even Avinngaq, for he agreed to Hummiktuq keeping him when he was small. So we must all do something about it.

ATUGAUQ: She will not be happy.

ᓄᑭᓕᒃ: ᑐᖅᓱᓚᖕᒋᓗᒍ. ᓂᐱᑭᑦᓗᓯ—ᐱᕕᒡᔪᐊᓇᓗᒃ. *(ᑎᑦᑯᐊᖅᓱᓗᓂ ᓇᓄᕐᓄᑦ)* ᑕᒃᑰᒃ ᐊᖑ'ᔪᐊᖅ ᓄᓕᐊᕐᑲᓕ'ᒪᑦ ᓵᓚᒋᔭᐅᓂᐊᖅᑐᓇᓘᔪᒍᑦ.

ᕿᑐᓂᖅ: ᐊᑖᑖ ᓯᓚᔪᑎᑦ. ᐅᓗᕆᐊᓇᖅᓯᕗᖅ.

ᓯᒡᒍᒃ: ᐊᖑ'ᔪᐊᕐᓕ ᓇᑦᑎᑕᕆᔭᒥᓂᒃ ᐊᐃᑦᑐᐃᖏᒃᑐᒐᓗᐊᖅ.

ᓄᑭᓕᒃ: ᐄᖑᒐᓗᐊᖅ, ᓇᑦᑎᖅᑲᑦᑎᐊᕈᐃᖅᐸᑦᓗ ᑳᓕᕈᓂ ᐃᓱᕐᓇᖏᐃᕐᓗᓂ ᖃᓄᖅ ᐱᓂᐊ'ᒪᑦ?

ᐊᑐᒐᐅᖅ: ᓄᑕᕋᒻᓂᒃ ᐋ'ᓂᖅᓯᒪᓕᖕᒋᑦᑎᐊᖅᑐᕐᓕ.

ᓄᑭᓕᒃ: *(ᐊᑐᒐᐅᕐᒧᑦ)* ᐅᑯᐊᖅ, ᐋ'ᓚᖑᖅᑐᒃᓴᕐᓱᒃ, ᓄᓕᐊᖕᒐᓗ ᕿᑐᓐᖕᒋᐅᕈᓂ ᓵᐳᑎᓂᐊ'ᒥᔮᖕᒋᑦ. ᑕᐃ'ᓇᐃᑦᑐᒫ'ᒪᑦ ᐅᕙᒍᑦᑕ ᐃᒪ'ᓇᐃ'ᓇᑉᑕ.

ᒪᓃᓚᖅ: *(ᐊᑐᒐᐅᕐᒧᑦ)* ᔭᑮᑦ ᓯᓚᔪᖅ.

ᐊᑐᒐᐅᖅ: ᖃᓄᕐᓕᐅᕐᓗᑕᓕ?

ᓄᑭᓕᒃ: *(ᓂᐱᑭ'ᓗᓂ)* ᑐᕐᑯᓴᕐᓗᒋᒃ ᐊᖑ'ᔪᐊᕐᓗ ᓄᓕᐊᓂᓗ.

ᐊᑐᒐᐅᖅ: ᐄᕐᑭ.

ᓄᑭᓕᒃ: ᐃᖕᒥᓂᒃ ᓇ'ᒥᓂᖅ ᐊᐅᓪᓚᖅᓯᓐᓇᓚᐃᑦᑐᖅ.

ᓯᒡᒍᒃ: ᐄᕐᑭᕐᓱᒃ—

ᓄᑭᓕᒃ: ᔭᑲᓇᔭᐊᕐᓗᑕ ᐋ'ᓂᓚᐃᑦᑐᖅ ᐃᒃᐱᒋᓂᐊᖕᒋᑖ.

ᐊᑐᒐᐅᖅ: ᐱᕈᕐᒪᓕ ᐃᓚᒋᓇᔭᒋ'ᓗᒍ ᐃᓚᒻᒪᓇᒃᑐᑦ ᐱᒐᑉᑯ, ᐊᐅᕐᑲᕐᑲᑎᒋᓇᔭᒋ'ᓗᒍᓘᓐᓃᑦ . . .ᓇ'ᒥᓂᕐᓗ ᓄᑕᕐᑲᓕᕐᒪ ᑲᒪᒋᔭᒻᓂᒃ.

ᓄᑭᓕᒃ: ᐅᕙᖕᒐᑉᔭᕐᓱᒃ ᐸᓯᔮᒃᓴᐅᕐᕉᕐᕋᒪ ᐊᐅᓪᓚᖅᑎᖕᒋᕐᓱᒃᑲᑉᑎᒍᑦ ᓯᕗᓪᓕᕐᒥ, ᓯᒻᒥᒃᑐᕐᓗ ᐊᐅᓪᓚᕐᑯᖕᒋᕐᓱᒃᓱᓂᐅᒃ.

ᒪᓃᓚᖅ: *(ᓄᑭᓕᖕᒧᑦ)* ᐅᕙᖕᒐᑉᔭᕐᓱᒃ ᐸᓯᔮᒃᓴᐅᕐᕉᕐᕋᒪᓕ ᓯᒻᒥᒃᑐᕐᒥᒃ ᓈᓚᕐᑯᒐᓗᐊᖅᓱᓯ.

ᓯᒡᒍᒃ: ᐅᕙᖕᒐᓕ ᐸᓯᔮᒃᓴᐅᔪᖕᒐ . . .ᑕᒪᐃ'ᓄᑦ.

MANIILAQ: *(to NUKILIK)* Go tell Arnarvik why we have to kill him now.

NUKILIK: No—if I tell Hummiktuq she'll do something unpredictable.

HIGGUK: I don't know if I can live through her being all alone again as before.

NUKILIK: *(to MANIILAQ)* Keep her in the iglu and don't tell her anything.

MANIILAQ: We must not keep secrets.

NUKILIK: I know, but what else can we do?

HIGGUK: Avinngaq will be furious.

NUKILIK: He's on the ice . . . when he returns, we say that Angu'řuaq tried to maul Qaaqšaattiaq, so we had to kill him.

ATUGAUQ: A lie on top of a secret, Father. Not good.

MANIILAQ: Yes, not good, and Hummiktuq will wail when she finds the bear dead.

NUKILIK: You will both wail when our grandchild comes between a mother bear and her cubs and gets mauled!

QILUNIQ: We must act fast. It's beginning to get windy and the blizzard is approaching.

NUKILIK: Let's sharpen our harpoons. We'll be swift and respect the bears . . . *(in HIGGUK's direction)* then we'll have meat to last until spring.

NUKILIK, HIGGUK, and QILUNIQ exit.

The storm is threatening now—the wind roars.

ATUGAUQ goes towards the bear . . . MANIILAQ watches her.

ATUGAUQ: *(to ANGU'ŘUAQ)* I am going to miss you so much. You are like my own brother.

ᓄᑭᓕᒃ: ᑕᒪᑉᑕᓕ ᐸᔪᔮᒃᓴᐅᔨᒍᑦ ᐊᕙᓐᖓᕐᓘᓐᓂᑦ, ᐊᖏᕋᓗᐊ'ᒪᑦ ᔪᒻᒥᒃᑐᖅ ᐱᔪᒪᔪᓐᓇᖅᑐᓇ'ᓗᓂᐅᒃ ᒥᑭ'ᓗᓂ. ᒫ'ᓇᕐᖢᒃ ᔪᓐᓇᔪᐊᓇᐊᖅᑲᓕᖅᑐᒍᑦ.

ᐊᑐᓚᐅᖅ: ᖁᕙᐊᔪᖕᓂᐊᖕᖏᑦᑐᖅ.

ᒪᓃᓚᖅ: *(ᓄᑭᓕᖑᑦ)* ᐊᕐᓇᕐᕖᑦ ᐊᒃᐱᐅᑎᔅᖅᑐᓕᕈᒃ ᔪ'ᒪᑦ ᑐᕐᑯᔅᐃᓇᔪᐊᕐᓂᐊᓇᐊᒃᓴᑉᑎ'ᓂᒃ ᑎᒍᐊᖓᓂᒃ.

ᓄᑭᓕᒃ: ᐄᕐᑭᕐᖢᒃ—ᐊᒃᐱᐅᑎᒍᑉᑯ ᔪᒻᒥᒃᑐᖅ ᓇᓗᓇᕐᓂᐊ'ᒥᔦᓇᓗᒃ.

ᔪᒡᒍᒃ: ᖃᓄᓇᓗᒃᑕᐅᖅ ᐊᔪᖅᑲᕈᐃᖅᐸᓪᓖᓕ'ᒥᒍᓂᓕ.

ᓄᑭᓕᒃ: *(ᒪᓃᓚᕐᔫᑦ)* ᐃᒡᓗᒥᑦ ᐊᓂᑎᑦᑕᐃᓕᒍᒃ ᐊᒃᐱᐅᑎᙱᓗᒍᓗ.

ᒪᓃᓚᖅ: ᔭᒡᓗᕆᐊᖅᑲᖏ'ᓇᑉᑕ ᐊᓐᖏᐊᓇᔮᖅᑲᓇᐊᖅᑲᖏᑦᑐᒍᑦ.

ᓄᑭᓕᒃ: ᐄᖑᒐᓗᐊᖅ, ᖃᓄᕐᓕ?

ᔪᒡᒍᒃ: ᐊᕙᓐᖓᖅ ᓂᖕᒐᐅᒪᓂᐊᓇᓗᒃ.

ᓄᑭᓕᒃ: ᔪᑯᒦ'ᒪᑦ . . .ᐅᑎᖅᐸᑦ ᐊᒃᐱᐅᑎᓂᐊᖅᐸᕗᑦ ᐊᖑ'ᔪᐊᕿᖅ ᐅᕆᐊᕋᔪᐊᕋᓗᐊ'ᒪᑦ ᖄᒃᓵᑦᑎᐊᕐᒥᒃ ᑐᕐᑯᕆᐊᖅᑲᖅᖢᑎᒍᑦ.

ᐊᑐᓚᐅᖅ: ᔭᒡᓗᕿᑕᐃᓗᔪ ᐊᓐᖏᐊᓇᔮᖅᑲᕐᓗᔪᓗ, ᐊᑖᑖ, ᐱᑦᑕᐅᙱ'ᒪᑦ.

ᒪᓃᓚᖅ: ᐄ, ᐱᑦᑕᐅᙱ'ᒪᑦ, ᔪᒻᒥᒃᑐᕐᓗ ᐃᓗᖏᖅᑐᕐᓗᐊᕐᓂᐊᖅᑐᖅ ᑕᑯᒍᓂᐅᒃ ᓇᓄᖅ ᑐᕐᑯᑕᐅᑎ'ᓗᒍ.

ᓄᑭᓕᒃ: ᑕᒪᑎᒃ ᐃᓗᖏᖅᑐᒃᓴᕈᖅᑐᔪᒃ ᐃᓐᖑᑕᕗᑦ ᓇᓄᕐᓗ ᕿᑐᓐᖓᐃᑕᓗ ᐊᑯᓂᖓ'ᓅᙵᕐᓂᖅᐸᑦ ᐅᕆᐊᖅᑕᐅᓗᓂ!

ᕿᓗᓂᖅ: ᑐᐊᕙᐅᓇᐊᖅᑲᖅᑐᒍᑦ. ᐊᓄᖅᓯᐅᒪᓕ'ᒪᑦ ᐱᖅᔪᖅᑐᒃᓴᕈᓕ'ᒪᑦ.

ᓄᑭᓕᒃ: ᐃᐱᒃᔭᓕᕐᓚᕗᒃ ᐅᓈᕗᒃ. ᐱᓂᕐᓗᙱᓗᒍ ᐱᑦᑎᐊᕐᓂᐊᖅᐸᕗᒃ ᓇᓅᒃ . . . *(ᔪᒡᒍᒃ ᕿᕙᐊᖅᓗᒍ)* ᓂᖅᑲᐅᑎᒃᓴᕗᑦ ᓈᒻᒪᖕᓂᐊ'ᒪᑦ ᐅᐱᓐᖓᓖᕐᔫᑦ.

ᐊᔪᐊᓄᙵᖅᓗᑎᒃ ᓄᑭᓕᒃ, ᔪᒡᒍᒃ, ᕿᓗᓂᕐᓗ.

ᐱᖅᑑᒪᓕ'ᒪᑦ ᐊᓄᖅᓯᐅᒪᔪᐊᓘ'ᓗᓂ.

MANIILAQ: *(to ATUGAUQ)* Call Hummiktuq to come here now.

ATUGAUQ: But *hakinnuaq [dear in-law]*, we are not supposed to say anything to her.

MANIILAQ: *(calls to HUMMIKTUQ)* Arnarvik, come here.

HUMMIKTUQ enters, her hands bloody.

HUMMIKTUQ: I'm done with the seal meat.

MANIILAQ: Look, Angu'řuaq has a wife now.

HUMMIKTUQ: Oh, so much gratitude. I wished for him to have a wife. Let her name be Ukuannuaq, because she is my beloved daughter-in-law, my *ukuannuaq*!

QAAKŠAATTIAQ plays with UKUANNUAQ.

MANIILAQ: It'll be too dangerous for the grandchildren when she has offspring.

HUMMIKTUQ: They are good. Look, they don't even take notice of Qaaqšaattiaq.

ATUGAUQ: Come, dear Qaaqšaattiaq . . . quickly.

HUMMIKTUQ: *(to ATUGAUQ)* They would never hurt Qaaqšaattiaq.

MANIILAQ: Listen with your ears, not your heart: my husband wants to kill the two bears.

HUMMIKTUQ: He's speaking foolishness—he's just teasing.

MANIILAQ: The two will become dangerous when they have cubs—why don't you believe me when you know how they can be dangerous?

HUMMIKTUQ: Because Angu'řuaq is my child.

MANIILAQ: You can look after my daughter-in-law's children.

ATUGAUQ places her hand on her large stomach.

ᐊᑐᒐᐅᖅ ᓇᓄᕐᒍᖖᒐᐅ’ᓗᓂ . . . ᒫᓂᓚᐅᑉ ᑕᐅᑐᒃᓱᓂᐅᒃ.

ᐊᑐᒐᐅᖅ: *(ᐊᖑ’ᕗᐊᕐᒧᑦ)* ᐅᖓᒋᓂᐊᖅᑕᐸᓇᓗᒋᕙᒋᑦ ᐊᓂᒋᕘᕙᒻᒪᓇᒃᑲᑉᑭᓪᓕ ᓇ’ᒥᓂᖅᑐᑦ.

ᒫᓂᓚᖅ: *(ᐊᑐᒐᐅᕐᒧᑦ)* ᕗᒻᒥᒃᑐᖅ ᖃᐃᑦᕐᑯᓕᕈᒃ ᑕᓴᒧᖓ.

ᐊᑐᒐᐅᖅ: ᓴᑭᓐᓄᐊᖅ, ᐅᕐᑲᕐᑯᕙᐅᙱᑦᑲᓗᐊᕐᑉᑕ.

ᒫᓂᓚᖅ: *(ᑐᖅᓱᓚ’ᓗᓂ ᕗᒻᒥᒃᑐᕐᒧᑦ)* ᐊᕐᓇᒃᕚᒃ ᖃᐃᑲᐃᑦ.

ᕗᒻᒥᒃᑐᖅ ᐃᕙᖅᓱᓂ ᐱᓚᒃᑐᐃᑖᒥ ᐊᐅᖏᓐᓇᐅ’ᓗᓂ ᐊᕚᒃᑯᑦ.

ᕗᒻᒥᒃᑐᖅ: ᓂᕐᑭᓕᓇᑖᖅᑯᖓᓕ ᓇᑦᑎᕐᒥᒃ.

ᒫᓂᓚᖅ: ᑕᒃᑰᒃ ᐊᖑ’ᕗᐊᖅ ᓄᓕᐊᒃᓵᖅᑲᓕ’ᒪᑦ.

ᕗᒻᒥᒃᑐᖅ: ᕐᑯᔭᓇᖅᑐᕐᕿᓗᒃ. ᓄᓕᐊᖅᑖᕐᑯᕙᒪᓕᕐᑉᑯ. ᐊᑎᕐᑲᓕᕐᓕ ᐅᑯᐊᓐᓄᐊᕐᒥᒃ ᐅᑯᐊᓂᓂᐊᕐᑉᑯ!

ᕐᑳᒃᓵᑦᑎᐊᖅ ᐅᓚᑉᕐᑭᕐᑲᑎᒋ’ᓗᒍ ᐅᑯᐊᓐᓄᐊᖅ.

ᒫᓂᓚᖅ: ᕐᑭᑐᓐᖓᕐᑲᓕᕈᓂ ᐅᓗᓂᐊᓇᕐᓂᐊᖅᑐᖅ ᐃᓐᖑᑕᑉᑎ’ᓄᑦ.

ᕗᒻᒥᒃᑐᖅ: ᐱᑦᑎᐊᖅᑐᑦ. ᑕᒃᑰᒃ ᕐᑳᒃᓵᑦᑎᐊᖅ ᑲᒪᒋᙱᒻᒪᓇᒃᑕᐃᑦ.

ᐊᑐᒐᐅᖅ: ᖃᐃᑲᐃᑦ ᕐᑳᒃᓵᑦᑎᐊᖅ . . . ᑐᐊᕚ.

ᕗᒻᒥᒃᑐᖅ: *(ᐊᑐᒐᐅᕐᒧᑦ)* ᐊ’ᓂᓚᐃᑕᓇᓗᐊ ᐅᓇ ᕐᑳᒃᓵᑦᑎᐊᖅ.

ᒫᓂᓚᖅ: ᕙᐅᑎᒃᑯᑦ ᑐᓴᙵ ᐅᐃᒪᙱᓗᑎᑦ: ᐅᐃᒪ ᑐᕐᑯᓴᓇᐊᕈᒪᕖᒋᒃ ᐅᑯᐊᒃ ᓇᓅᒃ.

ᕗᒻᒥᒃᑐᖅ: ᐅᕐᑲᒪᙳᐊᖅᕙᓐᓇᖅᑐᕐᓱᒃ—ᓴᒡᓗᕗᕐᓱᒃ ᐱᔮᓇᕗᕐᓕ.

ᒫᓂᓚᖅ: ᓴᒡᓗᙱᑦᑐᖅ. ᐅᓗᓇᐊᓇᖅᕙᕚᒫ’ᒪᓂᒃ ᓇᓅᒃ ᕐᑭᑐᓐᖏᐅᓕᖅᐸᓂᒃ—ᕗ’ᒪᑦ ᐅᒃᐱᓇᙱᒋᑕ’ᒪ ᖃᐅᕚᒪᑎ’ᓗᑎᑦ ᐅᓗᓇᐊᓇᖅᐸ’ᒪᑕ?

ᕗᒻᒥᒃᑐᖅ: ᐊᖑ’ᕗᐊᖅ ᑖᒻᓇ ᓄᑕᕐᑲᓇᒐᑉᑯ.

ATUGAUQ: I will have another baby coming along soon—

HUMMIKTUQ: But Angu'řuaq *is* my family.

MANIILAQ: The men will be returning soon. Go say goodbye to Angu'řuaq, then go into the iglu. Be quick about it, Arnarvik.

MANIILAQ, ATUGAUQ, and QAAQŠAATTIAQ exit.

HUMMIKTUQ: *(to ANGU'ŘUAQ)* My son, when I first saw you on the ice, I felt in your eyes what it means to breathe . . . if I never see you again, my life will be shattered . . . I cannot speak. Go to another place. Leave.

ANGU'ŘUAQ does not move but raises his foreleg. She holds it then puts it down.

Be wise. Be wiser than Nukilik—go away now with my ukuannuaq.

ANGU'ŘUAQ does not move. The sounds of the men can be heard coming closer.

Get moving— Go . . . *(pushing him)* No one wants you here anymore. Qiluniq and Atugauq have their own children to play with now—they do not want you, go—GO!

ANGU'ŘUAQ still does not move.

MANIILAQ: *(off stage, from the iglu)* I HEAR THE MEN—COME INSIDE, ARNARVIK—HURRY!

HUMMIKTUQ: *(to ANGU'ŘUAQ)* Follow me.

She starts walking and ANGU'ŘUAQ follows her. UKUANNUAQ follows ANGU'ŘUAQ.

You're so damn stubborn, making me run like this. If I go with you a ways, then you must never return.

HUMMIKTUQ, ANGU'ŘUAQ, and UKUANNUAQ exit as a big wind roars through.

ᒪᓃᓚᕐᒃ: ᐅᑯᐊᓐᓄᐊᕐᒪ ᓄᑕᕋᐃᑦ ᑲᒪᒋᔪᖕᓇᕐᒃᓯᔭᑎᑦ.

ᐊᑐᒐᐅᕐᒃ ᓈᓂ ᐸᑎᖕᒥᔮ.

ᐊᑐᒐᐅᕐᒃ: ᓄᑕᕋᕐᒃᑖᕐᓂᐊᕋᒪ ᕐᑲᓂᒃᑐᒃᑯᑦ—

ᔫᒥᒃᑐᕐᒃ: ᐊᖑ'ᔦᐊᕐᓕ ᐃᓚᒋᒐᑉᑯ.

ᒪᓃᓚᕐᒃ: ᐊᖑᑎᑦ ᐅᑎᔫᖕᒐᕐᓂᐊ'ᒪᓂᒃ—ᐊᖑ'ᔦᐊᕐᒃ ᑕᑯᕐᒃᑳᕐᓗᒍ ᐃᒡᓗᒍᖖᒐᕐᓗᑎᑦ. ᑐᐊᕗᑲᐃᑦ ᐊᕐᓇᕐᕗᒃ.

ᐊᔪᐊᓄᖖᒐᐅᔦᑦ ᒪᓃᓚᕐᒃ, ᐊᑐᒐᐅᕐᒃ, ᕐᑳᒃᔩᑦᑎᐊᕐᓗ.

ᔫᒥᒃᑐᕐᒃ: *(ᐊᖑ'ᔦᐊᕐᔪᑦ)* ᐃᕐᓂᕋ, ᑕᑯᓐᖕᒐᕋᑉᑭᑦ ᔪᑯᒥ ᐃᔮ'ᓂᑦ ᐃᒃᐱᒋᔪᒪᓕᕋᒪ ᔫᕐᓗ ᐊᓂᕐᒃᔭᕐᒃᑐᑦᑎᐊᕐᓂᕐᒥᒃ . . . ᑕᑯᓚᐃᓕᕐᓂᐊᕈᑉᑭᑦ ᐃᓅᔪᕋ ᔪᕐᑯᒥᖕᓂᐊᕐᒃᑐᕐᒃ . . . ᐅᕐᑲᓚᐃᑦᑐᖕᒐ. ᐊᑕᐃ ᐊᔪᐊᓄᖖᒐᓇᑦ ᐊᐅᓪᓚᓇ.

ᐊᖑ'ᔦᐊᕐᒃ ᔫᖖᒋᑦᑐᕐᒃ ᐃᖑᖖᒋᑦᑐᕐᒃ ᑭᔪᐊᓂᒃ ᐃᔪᒐᓂ ᐃᔭᒃᓗᒍ ᑎᒎᑎᕚ ᔭᑉᑯ'ᓗᓂᐅᒡᓗ.

ᔫᒥᒃᑐᕐᒃ: ᔪᓚᑐᓗᑎᑦ. ᓄᑭᓕᖕᒥᐅᖕᒐᓂᑦ ᔪᓚᑐᑦᕐᑭᔭᐅᓗᑎᑦ—ᐊᐅᓪᓚᕐᑲᑎᒋᓕᕈᒃ ᐅᑯᐊᓐᓄᐊᕋ.

ᐊᖑ'ᔦᐊᕐᒃ ᐃᖑᖖᒋᑦᑐᕐᒃ. ᑐᔭᕐᓇᓕᕐᒃᓗᑎᒃ ᐊᖑᑏᒃ ᕐᑲᐃᓕᕐᒃᑑᒃ ᕐᑲᒡᓕᕚᓪᓕᐊᔩᒃ.

ᔫᒥᒃᑐᕐᒃ: ᐊᐅᓪᓚᓕᓇᑦ ᐊᑕᐃ . . . *(ᐊᓯᒃᓗᓂᐅᒃ)* ᐅᕚᓃᕐᑯᔭᐅᔫᐃᕐᒃᑐᑎᑦ. ᕐᑭᓗᓂᕐᓗ ᐊᑐᒐᐅᕐᓗ ᓇ'ᒥᓂᕐᒃ ᓄᑕᕋᕐᑲᓕ'ᒪᓂᒃ ᐅᓚᑉᕐᑭᕐᑲᑎᒃᓴᓂᒃ. ᐃᓕ'ᓂᒃ ᐱᔦᒪᖖᒋᑦᑑᒃ—ᐊᑕᐃ!

ᐊᖑ'ᔦᐊᕐᒃ ᐃᖑᖖᒋᒻᒪᓇᒃᑐᕐᒃ.

ᒪᓃᓚᕐᒃ: *(ᐊᕙ'ᖓᑦ ᐃᒡᓗᒥᑦ)* ᑐᖅᓕᕐᒃᐸᑦᑲ ᐊᖑᑏᒃ—ᐃᔪᕐᓗᑎᑦ, ᐊᕐᓇᕐᕗᒃ ᑐᐊᕗᑲᐃᑦ.

ᔫᒥᒃᑐᕐᒃ: *(ᐊᖑ'ᔦᐊᕐᔪᑦ)* ᒪᓕᖖᒐ.

ᐱᔫᓕᕐᒃᓗᓂ ᐊᖑ'ᔦᐊᕐᒃ ᒪᓕᓕᕐᒃᓗᓂᐅᒃ ᐅᑯᐊᓐᓄᐊᕐᒃ, ᐅᐃᒥᓂᒃ ᒪᓕᓕᕐᒃᓗᓂ.

MANIILAQ enters, thinking HUMMIKTUQ has finished saying goodbye to the bears.

MANIILAQ: Hummiktuq, nothing you can say to my husband will make a difference—Nukilik never changes his mind, so come with me to the iglu while the men kill the . . . *(sees that HUMMIKTUQ is gone)* Hummiktuq? Where are you? *(calls towards the iglu)* Atugauq, come.

ATUGAUQ enters, followed by QAAQŠAATTIAQ.

Where has Arnarvik gone to?

ATUGAUQ: . . . it's too windy now . . . I cannot see.

MANIILAQ: I didn't see the bears either.

ATUGAUQ: *(to QAAQŠAATTIAQ)* Hold on to me—come closer!

MANIILAQ: *(calls)* Arnarvik.

HIGGUK: *(off stage)* Whoa, the weather changed all of a sudden.

NUKILIK, HIGGUK, and QILUNIQ enter carrying harpoons.

NUKILIK: The two polar bears were right over there . . . I saw them. They were eating a seal—eating a seal that I should have caught! *(calling the bear)* Angu'řuaq? *(to MANIILAQ)* Where's that rascally bear?

MANIILAQ: Gone. Hummiktuq's gone, too.

NUKILIK: Gone where?

MANIILAQ: I don't know. I told her what we're planning to do.

NUKILIK: Why did you tell her?

MANIILAQ: It's better that way, then she can say goodbye to the bear.

NUKILIK: I told you not to say anything to her!

ᔕᒻᒥᒃᑯᖅ: ᔕᕐᑯᑕᐅᖖᒋᑦᑐᓲᕗᑎᑦ ᐅ'ᓚᑎ'ᓇ'ᒪ ᐃᒪ'ᓇ. ᐊᐅᓚᖃᑎᒋᕝᕿᐱᑉᑭᑦ ᐅᑎᖅᑕᐃᓚᑦᑎᐊᕐᓂᖅᑯᑎᑦ.

ᐊᔑᐊᓄᖖᒐᐅᖬᑦ ᔕᒻᒥᒃᑯᖅ, ᐊᖕᒍ'ᖬᐊᖅ, ᐅᑯᐊᓐᓄᐊᕐᓗ ᐊᓄᓇᖬᐊᓘᓚᖅᓱᓂ.

ᐃᔑᖅᓱᓂ ᒪᓃᓚᖅ. ᔕᒻᒥᒃᑯᖅ ᐃᔑᕐᓂᐊᕋᔕᕆ'ᓗᓂᐅᒃ ᓇᓄᕐᓃᔮᒃᓛ'ᓂ ᐃᔕᒪᖖᒋ'ᒪᑦ.

ᒪᓃᓚᖅ: ᖃᓄᕐᓕᐅᕋᓗᐊᕐᓗᑎᑦ ᐅᐃᒐ ᐊ'ᓚᖖᒍᓚᐃᑦᑐᖅ ᐃᔑᒪᓚᐅᓚᖀᖕᒐᒥ ᐱᓂᐊᖅᑕᒥᓂᒃ ᐱᖃᑦᑕ'ᒪᑦ, ᐊᑕᐃ ᐃᒡᓗᒧᖖᒐᖃᑎᒥᖖᒐ ᑐᕐᑯᖬᕋᔑᐊ . . . (ᖃᐅᖬᒐᒥ ᔕᒻᒥᒃᑯᖅ ᔕᖃᕈᐃ'ᒪᑦ) ᔕᒻᒥᒃᑯᖅ? ᔕᒦᑦᐱᑦ? (ᐃᒡᓗᒧᑦ ᖀ'ᓗᓂ ᑐᖅᓱᓚ'ᓗᓂ) ᐊᑐᒐᐅᖅ ᖃᐃᓗᑎᑦ.

ᐊᑐᒐᐅᖅ ᖬᑦᕿ'ᓗᓂ ᒪᓚᒃᑕᐅ'ᓗᓂ ᖀᒃᖬᑦᑎᐊᕐᒥᑦ.

ᒪᓃᓚᖅ: ᔕᒧᖖᒐᐅᒐᓗᐊ'ᒪᑦᑭᐊᖅ ᐊᕐᓇᕐᕙᒐ?

ᐊᑐᒐᐅᖅ: . . . ᐊᓄᖅᓯᐅᒪᖓᓛ'ᒪᑦ . . . ᑕᐅᑐᑦᑎᐊᖖᒋᑦᑐᖕᒐ.

ᒪᓃᓚᖅ: ᓇᓅᒃ ᑕᑯᖖᒋ'ᒥᒐᑉᑭᒃ.

ᐊᑐᒐᐅᖅ: (ᖀᒃᖬᑦᑎᐊᕐᒍᑦ) ᑎᒍᖖᒐ—ᖃᒡᓚᒐᓐᓂᕐᓗᑎᑦ!

ᒪᓃᓚᖅ: (ᑐᖅᓱᓚ'ᓗᓂ) ᐊᕐᓇᕐᕙᒃ.

ᖬᒡᒍᒃ: (ᐊᕙ'ᖕᒐᑦ) ᖀᖬᓇᓗᒃ, ᖬᓚ ᐊ'ᓚᖖᒍᑲᖅᑑᓐᓂᖅ.

ᐃᔑᖅᓱᑎᒃ ᓄᑭᓚᒃ, ᖬᒡᒍᒃ, ᕿᓗᓂᕐᓗ ᐅᓈᓚᖬᖅᓱᑎᒃ.

ᓄᑭᓚᒃ: ᓇᓅᒃ ᐅᕙᓃᖄᕋᓗᐊ'ᒪᓂᒃ . . . ᑕᑯᖬᕋᓗᐊᑦᑲᓚ. ᓇᑦᑎᖅᑐᕋᓗᐊ'ᒪᓂᒃ—ᓇᑦᑎᖅᑕᕆᓂᐊᖅᑕᕋᓗᐊᒻᓂᒃ ᓂᕆᖬᔅᔫ'ᓗᑎᒃ! (ᑐᖅᓱᓚ'ᓗᓂ) ᐊᖕᒍ'ᖬᐊᖅ? (ᒪᓃᓚᕐᒍᑦ) ᔕᒦᑦᑐᑭᐊᖅ ᐃᒻᓇ ᓇᓄᔅᓱᒃ?

ᒪᓃᓚᖅ: ᔕᖃᕈᐃᖅᑐᖅ. ᔕᒻᒥᒃᑯᕐᔫᓐᓃᑦ ᔕᖃᕈᐃ'ᒥᖬᖅ.

ᓄᑭᓚᒃ: ᔕᒧᖖᒐᐅᖬᕐᓚ?

ᒪᓃᓚᖅ: ᔕᒧᑦᑭᐊᖅ. ᐊᒃᐱᐅᑎᖬᕋᓗᐊᕋ ᖃᓄᕐᓕᐅᕋᔕᐊᕐᓂᑉᑎ'ᓂᒃ.

MANIILAQ: I didn't think that she'd go away, too.

NUKILIK: She's an Elder and can sense things, but now she'll get lost and die. If she dies we will be to blame—you of course being the cause.

MANIILAQ: You should have told her that you were going to kill the two bears instead of keeping it a secret.

A big wind sweeps through.

QILUNIQ: Father, we have to look for them before the blizzard takes over or we'll all be lost in the storm.

NUKILIK: *(to QILUNIQ)* I have walked through many a blizzard.

QILUNIQ: Your plan to secretly kill the bears has put us all in danger.

HIGGUK: *(to NUKILIK)* Your son here is wise. You were too quick to act, too urgent in trying to deal with it. We should have spoken to Hummiktuq about it.

QILUNIQ: The breathing holes will be covered over in the snow, so she won't know how to step safely. Okay now, follow me.

NUKILIK: No, follow me instead. I have walked through many, many blizzards.

HIGGUK: Me also, I have walked through many, many blizzards.

NUKILIK exits, running ahead, followed by QILUNIQ and HIGGUK.

QAAKŠAATTIAQ: Where are Angu'ř̌uaq and Ukuannuaq?

MANIILAQ: Hummiktuq went away with them.

QAAKŠAATTIAQ pulls on MANIILAQ's arm.

QAAKŠAATTIAQ: Please, *Ningiuq [Grandmother]*, please tell them to return.

MANIILAQ: If only Hummiktuq hadn't lost her family. I still think of them sinking into the freezing water.

ᓄᑭᓕᒃ: ᖃ'ᒪᑦ ᐊᒃᐱᐅᑎᒐᓗᐊᖅᐱᐅᒡᓕ?

ᒪᓃᓚᖅ: ᐃᓗᐊᑦᕿᔮᐅ'ᒪᑦ ᑕᑯᖅᑳᕐᑯᒐᓗᐊᖅᓘᒍ ᑎᒍᐊᕐᓘᖕᒥᓂᒃ.

ᓄᑭᓕᒃ: ᐊᒃᐱᐅᑎᑦᑎᐊᖅᑕᕋᓗᐊᑉᑭᑦ ᐅᕐᑲᕐᑯᙱ'ᓇᑉᑭᑦ.

ᒪᓃᓚᖅ: ᐃᖃᙳᕆᒃᑲᓗᐊᕋᒪ ᐊᐅᓚᕐᓂᐊᕆᐊᒃᓵ'ᓂᒃ.

ᓄᑭᓕᒃ: ᐃᓄᑐᕐᑲᐅ'ᒪᑦ ᓇᓗᓇᐃᖅᓯᕙᖕᓇᖅᑐᖅ ᖅᑲᐅᔾᒪᒐᒥ ᐊᓐᖏᐊᕆᔮᖅᑲᓕᕌᖕᒐᑉᑕ. ᑕᔾᕙᓕ ᐊᓯᐅᓕᕐᓂᐊᖅᓘᓂ ᑐᕐᑯᓗᓂᓗ, ᑐᕐᑯᒃᐸᓪᓗ ᐸᓯᔾᒃᓴᐅᓂᐊᖅᓘᑕ ᐃᔾᕚᑦ ᐱᔾᖃᑕᐅ'ᓗᑎᑦ.

ᒪᓃᓚᖅ: ᐊᒃᐱᐅᑎᓇᔭᕋᓗᐊᕋ'ᓂ ᓇᓅᖕᓂᒃ ᑐᕐᑯᔅᐃᓂᐊᖅᑐᕆᓗᑎᑦ ᐊᓐᖏᐊᕆᔮᖅᑲᕋᖃᐊᙱᓗᑎᑦ.

ᐊᓄᕗᕐᖃᐊᓕᖅᑐᖅ

ᖁᓗᓂᖅ: ᐊᑖᑖ, ᕿᓂᕆᐊᖅᑲᖅᑕᕗᑦ ᐱᖅᓯᖅᐸᓪᓛᙱᓂᐊ'ᓂᒃ ᐊᓯᐅᓂᐊᕙᒃᑲᑉᑕ ᐱᖅᑐᔪᑦ.

ᓄᑭᓕᒃ: *(ᖁᓗᓂᕐᔪᑦ)* ᐱᖃᒃᓯᒪᖅᖓ ᐊᒥᖃᓂᒃ ᐱᖅᑐᒃᑯᑦ.

ᖁᓗᓂᖅ: ᐃᔾᕚᑦ ᐊᓐᖏᐊᕆᔮᖅᑲᖅᓘᑎᒃ ᑐᕐᑯᔅᑲᖃᐊᕐᓂᐊᑲᓗᐊᑲᕚᒋᒃ ᓇᓅᒃ ᐅᓗᕆᐊᓇᖅᑐᖅᓯᐅᖅᑎᒃᐸᑉᑎᒍᑦ.

ᓯᒡᒍᒃ: *(ᓄᑭᓕᖕᔪᑦ)*. ᐃᕐᓃᑦ ᐅᓇ ᓯᓚᑐᖅᖓ. ᑐᐊᕙᖅᐸᓪᓛᖅᑰᖅᓘᓯ ᐊᑦᕐᑯᓇᖅᓘᓯ ᐃᓗᐊᖅᓴᕋᖃᐊᖅᐸᓪᓚᕋᑉᓯ. ᖃᒻᒥᒃᑐᕐᒥᒃ ᐅᕐᑲᕐᑲᑎᕐᑲᖅᐸᖀᖅᑐᒃᓴᐅᒐᓗᐊᖅᑐᒍᓪᓕ.

ᖁᓗᓂᖅ: ᐊᒡᓗᐃᑦ ᑕᐅᑐᖕᓇᕈᐃᖅᐸᑕ ᐊᐳ'ᔪᑦ, ᖃᒻᒥᒃᑐᖅ ᖃᔪᑦ ᐱᖃᕆᐊᒃᓴᖅ ᓇᓗᓂᐊ'ᒥᖓᖅ. ᐊᑕᐃ—ᒪᓕᒃᑕᐅᓚᖕᒐ.

ᓄᑭᓕᒃ: ᐄᖅᑭ ᐅᕙᖕᒐᕙᓪᓗᖅ ᒪᓕᒃᑕᐅᓚᖕᒐ. ᐱᖅᑐᑦᑯᑦ ᐊᒥᖃᑎᒍᑦ ᐱᖃᒃᓯᒪᓕᕋᒪ.

ᓯᒡᒍᒃ: ᐅᕙᖕᒐᓘᒐᓗᐊᖅ . . . ᐱᖅᑐᒃᑰᖅᓯᒪᓕᕋᒪᓕ ᐊᒥᔾᕋᖅᑐᓇᓗᖕᓂᒃ.

ᓄᑭᓕᒃ ᐅ'ᓚᒃᓘᓂ ᖁᓗᓂᖅ ᓯᒡᒍᒡᓗ ᒪᓕᒃᓘᔾᖓᒃ.

ᖄᒃᓵᑦᑎᐊᖅ: ᓇᐅᒡᓕ ᐊᖑ'ᖓᐊᕐᓗ ᐅᑯᐊᓐᓄᐊᕐᓗ?

ATUGAUQ: Try not to think of them now, anaanaa.

MANIILAQ: Maybe Nuliajuq herself looked up from the ocean and, seeing the children drowning and sinking and losing their breath, and their big father and his sledge sinking into the water, and their dogs scampering like they were still on the ice . . . I like to believe that Nuliajuq took pity and sent beluga to escort the children down . . . then with her mighty power she turned the children into belugas, and now they live below the ice and rise to breathe, and even today they can come close to where we are—

ATUGAUQ: Mother . . . Hummiktuq's children were not turned into belugas . . . Hummiktuq's children are polar bears.

A moment.

MANIILAQ: Yes, Atugauq. You are wise. Her children *are* polar bears, so we must call them back . . . *(calls)* Arnarvik . . . Hummiktuq . . . HUMMIKTUQ . . .

QAAKŠAATTIAQ: *(calls)* ANGU'ŘUAQ . . .

ATUGAUQ: *(calls)* HUMMIKTUQ . . . ANGU'ŘUAQ . . .

QAAKŠAATTIAQ: *(calls)* ANGU'ŘUAQ, ANGU'ŘUAQ . . . HUMMIKTUQ . . .

HUMMIKTUQ enters.

HUMMIKTUQ: Stop your shouting or you'll scare all the sea mammals away!

MANIILAQ: I'm so happy you returned.

ATUGAUQ: I'm happy you returned, Hummiktuq.

HUMMIKTUQ is surprised by the attention.

HUMMIKTUQ: I'm not used to being welcomed.

MANIILAQ: *(to HUMMIKTUQ)* Where are your children?

HUMMIKTUQ: I was trying to guide them to another place, but we got separated by the blizzard. I could hear the hunters—I called and called to

ᒪᓃᓚᖅ: ᔪᒻᒥᒃᑯᕐᓕ ᐊᐅᓪᓚᕐᑲᑎᒋᔭᐃᑦ.

ᖃᒃᑮᑦᑎᐊᖅ ᓄᔪᒃᓱᓂᐅᒃ ᒪᓃᓚᐅᑉ ᑕᓕᐊ.

ᖃᒃᑮᑦᑎᐊᖅ: ᐊᑕᐃ ᓂᖏᐅᖅ, ᖃᐃᑦᖁᓕᑦᑭᑦ ᐅᑎᖁᓕᑦᑭᑦ.

ᒪᓃᓚᖅ: ᔪᒻᒥᒃᑯᖅ ᐃᓚᐃᖅᑯᕕᓂᐅᖖᒋᑦᑲᓗᐊᖅᐸᓪᓕ. ᐃᔪᒪᒋᕚᒃᐸᑦᑲ ᔪᓕ ᐃᓖᖅᑎ’ᓱᒋᑦ ᐃᒪᓇᓱᖕᒍᑦ ᐆᓇᐃᑦᑑᑎ’ᓱᒍ.

ᐊᑯᓚᐅᖅ: ᐃᔪᒪᒋᓇᔪᐊᖖᒋᓱᒋᑦ, ᐊᓅᓅ.

ᒪᓃᓚᖅ: ᓄᓕᐊᔪᒡᔫᓐᓃᑦ ᑕᕆᐅᕐᒥᑦ ᑕᐅᑯᒃᑲᓗᐊᖅᐸᖏᒃ ᓄᑕᖀᒃ ᐅᖁᐊᒃ ᐃᓛᓕᖅᑯᒃ ᑭᕙᓕᖅᑯᒃ ᑕᐅᓄᖕᒐ ᐊᓂᕐᓂᖅᑳᐃᓕᖅᓱᑎᒃ ᐊᑖᑕᖏᓪᓗ ᐊᖏᔪᐊᓗᒃ ᖃᒧᑎᒃᑯᑦ ᑭᕙ’ᓱᓂ ᐃᒪᓇᓱᖕᒍᑦ ᕿ’ᒥᖏᑦᓗ ᔪᑯᒦᓇᔪᒋ’ᓱᑎᒃ ᔪᓕ ᐸᖓᓕᒃᑑᔭᖅᓱᑎᒃ ᐃᒪᒃᑯᓕᕐᓗᐊᖅᑎ’ᓱᑦ . . . ᐃᔪᒪᓇᔪᐊᖅᐸᒃᑲᓗᐊᖅᑯᖓ ᓄᓕᐊᔪᒃ ᓇᓪᓕᒋ’ᓱᓂᒋᒃ ᕿᓇᓗᒃᑲᓂᒃ ᐊᐃᒃᓴᖅᑎᑦᑎᔫᖅ ᓄᑕᖀᒃ ᑕᐅᓄᖖᒐᐅᕐᑯ’ᓱᒋᒃ ᑭᓇᓗᐅᖅᑕᐅᓕᕐᓗᑎᒃ, ᐊᔨᖖᒋ’ᓇᒥ ᓄᓕᐊᔪᒃ, ᔪᑯᑉ ᐊᑖᓃᓂᐊ’ᒪᓂᒃ ᐸᐃᖃᑦᑕᕐᓗᑎᒃ ᐅᑉᓗᒥᔫᓐᓃᑦ ᖃᓂᒋᔭᑉᑎ’ᓄᖖᒐᐅᔪᖕᓇᖅᓱᑎᒃ ᑕᐃᒪ’ᓇ—

ᐊᑯᓚᐅᖅ: ᐊᓅᓅ ᔪᒻᒥᒃᑰᑉ ᓄᑕᖀᒥᒃ ᕿᓇᓗᖖᒍᖅᑎᑕᐅᖖᒋᑦᑯᒃ . . . ᓄᑕᖀᒥᒃ ᑕᐃᑉᑯᐊᒃ ᓇᓅᓕᖅᑰᒃ.

ᓂᐸᐃᖅᑳᖅᓱᓂ, ᑕᐃᒪᓗ.

ᒪᓃᓚᖅ: ᐄ ᐊᑯᓚᐅᖅ. ᔪᓕᔦᑎᑦ. ᓄᑕᖀᒃ ᓇᓅ’ᒪᓂᒃ ᖃᐃᑦᖁᒋᐊᖅᑲᖅᑕᕗᒃ . . . (ᑯᖅᓱᓚ’ᓱᓂ) ᐊᕐᓇᕐᕚᒃ . . . ᔪᒻᒥᒃᑯᖅ . . . ᔪᒻᒥᒃᑯᖅ . . .

ᖃᒃᑮᑦᑎᐊᖅ: (ᑯᖅᓱᓚ’ᓱᓂ) ᐊᖑ’ᔦᐊᖅ . . .

ᐊᑯᓚᐅᖅ: (ᑯᖅᓱᓚ’ᓱᓂ) ᔪᒻᒥᒃᑯᖅ: . . . ᐊᖑ’ᔦᐊᖅ . . .

ᖃᒃᑮᑦᑎᐊᖅ: (ᑯᖅᓱᓚ’ᓱᓂ) ᐊᖑ’ᔦᐊᖅ . . . ᐊᖑ’ᔦᐊᖅ . . . ᔪᒻᒥᒃᑯᖅ . . .

ᔪᒻᒥᒃᑯᖅ ᐃᔨᖅᓱᓂ.

ᔪᒻᒥᒃᑯᖅ: ᐃᓇᐊᓛᖅᐸᓪᓛᓯᐃᓇᑦᑎ ᐸᐃᔫᑦ ᑕᒪᐃᑕ ᐃᖅᔪᓕᖅᑎᓂᐊᕚᒃᑲᕚᒋᑦ!

Angu'ȓuaq . . . but there was no response, so I hurried back here hoping they might have returned but . . . *(close to a wail)* they are gone . . . *(wails)* AAAAHHHHHH . . .

HIGGUK: *(off stage)* I FOUND HER!

QILUNIQ: *(off stage)* You *stepped* on me!

HIGGUK enters, stumbling blindly in the wind, pulling QILUNIQ.

HIGGUK: Hummiktuq, if I hadn't stepped on you, I wouldn't have found you.

MANIILAQ: She is well. *Hummiktuq* is with us.

HIGGUK: *(to QILUNIQ)* Then who are you?

QILUNIQ pulls off his hood.

QILUNIQ: Qiluniq.

HIGGUK: Sorry—so much wind against my eyes I could hardly see.

QILUNIQ: I think we were walking around in circles.

MANIILAQ: *(to HUMMIKTUQ)* My husband will surely tease you for running off during a blizzard.

HUMMIKTUQ: I'll tease him for running after me during a blizzard.

MANIILAQ: *(to HUMMIKTUQ)* Let's both tease him.

HUMMIKTUQ: Where is he?

MANIILAQ: He's with Higguk.

HIGGUK: . . . is he? *(looks around himself)* No. He's not with me.

MANIILAQ: Where's my husband?

ᒪᓃᓚᖅ: ᖁᕕᐊᓱᑦᑎᐊᖅᑐᖓ ᐅᑎᕋᕕᑦ.

ᐊᑐᒐᐅᖅ: ᖁᕕᐊᓱᒃᑐᖓ ᐅᑎᕋᕕᑦ, ᓱᒻᒥᒃᑐᖅ.

ᓱᒻᒥᒃᑐᖅ ᐃᕿᑕᐅᔮᒥᓂᒃ ᑲᙳᓱᓕ'ᒪᑦ.

ᓱᒻᒥᒃᑐᖅ: ᑐᙵᓱᒃᑎᑕᐅᕙᙱ'ᓇᒪᓕ.

ᒪᓃᓚᖅ: *(ᓱᒻᒥᒃᑐᖅᒧᑦ)* ᓇᐅᓪᓕ ᓄᑕᖀᒃᑭᒃ?

ᓱᒻᒥᒃᑐᖅ: ᐊᓯᐊᓄᙵᖅᑎᑦᑎᓇᓱᐊᕋᓗᐊᖅᖢᒥᒃ ᐊᕕᒃᑐᒍᑦ ᐱᖅᑐᒧᑦ. ᑐᓴᕐᓇᓕ'ᒪᓂᓪᓗ ᐊᖑᓇᓱᐊᖅᑎᒃ—ᑐᖅᖢᓚᐃᓐᓇᓕᖅᖢᒍ ᐊᖑ'ᓴᐊᖅ . . . ᑭᐅᙱ'ᒪᑦ ᐅᑎᖅᓯᓐᓇᖅᑐᖓ ᐅᑎᕋᓱᒋᒐᓗᐊᖅᖢᒋᒃ ᑭᓯᐊᓂᒃ . . . *(ᐃᓗᕐᒋᖅᑐᓕᖅᖢᓂ)* ᓯᖃᕈᐃᖅᖣᒃ . . . ᐋᐊᐊᐊᐊᐊ . . .

ᓯᓪᒧᒃ: *(ᐊᕙ'ᖓᑦ)* ᓇᓂᕙᕋ!

ᕿᓗᓂᖅ: *(ᐊᕙ'ᖓᑦ)* ᑐᑎᕝᕕᕆᔭ'ᒪ.

ᓯᓪᒧᒃ ᐃᓯᔅᓴᖑᓴᖅᖢᓂ, ᐊᓄᕆᒧᑦ ᐅᕐᕈᑦᑕᐃᓕᓇᓱᐊᖅᖢᓂ ᑕᓯᐅᖅᑐᒧᑦ ᕿᓗᓂᖅ.

ᓯᓪᒧᒃ: ᓱᒻᒥᒃᑐᖅ, ᑐᑎᕝᕕᕆᙱ'ᓄᑉᑭᓪᓕ ᓱᒦᑦᑖᒃᓴ'ᓂᒃ ᓇᓗᓇᔭᕋᓗᐊᕋᒪ.

ᒪᓃᓚᖅ: ᓈᒻᒪᒃᑐᖅ. ᓱᒻᒥᒃᑐᖅ ᐅᕙᑉᑎ'ᓃᑦᑐᖅ.

ᓯᓪᒧᒃ: *(ᕿᓗᓂᒧᑦ)* ᓱᓇᐅᓯᑎᑦᓕ?

ᕿᓗᓂᖅ ᓇᔅᐃᖅᖢᓂ.

ᕿᓗᓂᖅ: ᕿᓗᓂᐅᓯᖓ.

ᓯᓪᒧᒃ: ᖄ—ᐊᓄᕆᒧᑦ ᑕᐅᑐᑦᑎᐊᙱ'ᓇᒪ.

ᕿᓗᓂᖅ: ᑐ'ᔮᐱᒃᑲᓗᐊᕋᑉᑕ ᓂᑉᑕᐃᑦᑐᒧᑦ ᑕᒻᒫᒐᑉᑕ ᐱᒋᐊᕐᕕᒋᔭᑉᑎ'ᓄᑦ ᐅᑏᓐᓇᖅᖢᑕ.

ᒪᓃᓚᖅ: *(ᓱᒻᒥᒃᑐᖅᒧᑦ)* ᐅᐃᒪ ᐱᔮᕆᓂᐊᖅᑕᓇᓗᒋᕚᑎᑦ ᐊᐅᓪᓚᕋᓱᐊᕋᕕᑦ ᐱᖅᓯᓕᖅᑎ'ᓗᒍ.

HIGGUK: He was leading and we were following when he started to run very fast . . . maybe towards his son.

QILUNIQ: No, he didn't go to me. You were right behind him.

HIGGUK: Yes, I was right behind him, but I lost sight of him. *(calls)* NUKILIK!

MANIILAQ: *(calls) Uinnuara [my dear little husband]*. Where are you?

ATUGAUQ: The wind may have turned him around, but he'll find his direction again.

MANIILAQ: Yes, he will.

HIGGUK: He's very, very knowledgeable and very capable and very smart.

MANIILAQ: I believe in my husband's skills on the land.

HIGGUK: He is a great hunter . . .

Silence as worry begins to set in. It builds and builds until . . .

AVINNGAQ enters, stumbling.

MANIILAQ: Nukilik?

AVINNGAQ pulls off his hood.

AVINNGAQ: I was on the ice, but it got too windy . . .

He sees that everyone is looking at him.

. . . Something is different now, what is going on?

MANIILAQ: Avinngaq, when you were away, we saw that Angu'ř̌uaq has a wife. We tried to kill them as they will never leave on their own, but we didn't speak to Hummiktuq first. When we did speak to her, she ran off with the bears. Nukilik, Higguk, and Qiluniq all went to look for Hummiktuq, but then she returned on her own. Nukilik has not returned.

ᔨᒻᒥᒃᑐᖅ: ᐱᔫᓇᓂᐊᖅᑕᕋ ᒪᓕᒐᔨᐊ'ᒪᖓ ᐱᖅᑐᒥ.

ᒫᓂᓚᖅ: (ᔨᒻᒥᒃᑐᕐᒧᑦ) ᑕᒪᒻᓄᒡᓕ ᐱᔫᓇᓚᕗᒃ.

ᔨᒻᒥᒃᑐᖅ: ᔨᒦᑦᐸᓕ?

ᒫᓂᓚᖅ: ᔪᒡᒍᖕᒦᑦᑐᖅ.

ᔪᒡᒍᒃ: . . . ᖀᖃᓇᓗᒃ (ᖃᓂᒥᓂ ᑕᑯ'ᓗᓂ) ᐅᕙᒻᓃᖖᒋᒻᒪᓇᒃᑐᖅ.

ᒫᓂᓚᖅ: ᐅᐃᒐ ᓇᐅᒃ?

ᔪᒡᒍᒃ: ᒪᓕᒃᑲᓗᐊᕋᑉᑕ ᐅ'ᓚᓕᕐᖄᓗᓕ'ᒪᑦ . . . ᐃᕐᓂᕐᒥᓄᖖᒐᐅ'ᓴᒐᒥ.

ᕿᓗᓂᖅ: ᐄᕿ, ᐅᕙᒻᓄᖖᒐᐅᖖᒋᑦᑐᕐᓕ. ᑭᖑᑦᑎᐊᖓᓃᑦᑲᓗᐊᖅᑐᑎᓪᓕ.

ᔪᒡᒍᒃ: ᐄ, ᑭᖑᑦᑎᐊᖓᓃᑦᑲᓗᐊᖅᑐᖓ ᑭᔪᐊᓂᒃ ᔨᖅᑲᕈᐃᖅᖢᓂ.
(ᑐᖅᖢᓚ'ᓗᓂ) ᓄᑭᓛᒃ!

ᒫᓂᓚᖅ: (ᑐᖅᖢᓚ'ᓗᓂ) ᐅᐃᓐᓄᐊᕋ, ᔨᒦᑦᐱᑦ?

ᐊᑐᒐᐅᖅ: ᐊᓄᓇᒧᕐᖣᖃᖅᑐᖅ ᖃᖑᑎᑕᐅ'ᒪᑦ ᐃᖢᕐᓇᓂᐊᖅᑐᒃᓴᐅᒐᓗᐊᖅ
ᑐᕌᒃᑕᒃᓵ'ᓂᒃ ᐃᓕᑕᖅᔪ'ᒥᓗᓂ.

ᒫᓂᓚᖅ: ᐄ ᑕᐃ'ᓇᐃᑦᑐᒫᖅᑯᖅ.

ᔪᒡᒍᒃ: ᐊᔪᒐᐃ'ᒪᑦ ᖃᐅᔮᒪ'ᒪᑦ ᐱᔪᖕᓇᖅᑐᖅ ᐱᕐᖃᓇᒃᑐᓇᓗᒃ.

ᒫᓂᓚᖅ: ᐅᒃᐱᓇᕙᕋ ᐅᐃᒐ ᐊᔪᒐᐃᑦᑐᖅ ᓄᓇᒥ.

ᔪᒡᒍᒃ: ᐊᖑᓇᔨᐊᖅᑎᐸᓇᓘ'ᒪᑦ.

ᓂᐸᐃᓕᒃᑐᖅᑐᑦ ᑕᒪᕐᒥᒃ ᐃᔨᒫᓗᒃᐸᓪᓕᐊᓕ'ᒪᑕ.
ᓂᐸᐃᓕᒃᑐᕐᓂᕐᒥ'ᓂᒃ ᐃᖢᐃᒍᔨᓕᖅᖢᑎᒃ ᑕᕝᕙ . . .

ᐊᕕᓐᖓᖅ ᐃᔪᕐᖃᖑᔮᖅᖢᓂ ᐅᖅᕈᑎᑦᖃᓴᓪᓚᕐᖄᒃᖢᓂ.

ᒫᓂᓚᖅ: ᓄᑭᓕᒃ?

ᐊᕕᓐᖓᖅ ᓇᖃᐃᖅᖢᓂ.

AVINNGAQ: Keeping secrets causes disaster.

HIGGUK: Yes, I feel so terrible.

AVINNGAQ: We must stay together and go look for Nukilik.

They begin to move when they hear moaning.

NUKILIK enters, wet, crawling on his hands and knees, trembling, his shoulder and neck bloody.

QILUNIQ: . . . Father. What happened to you?

NUKILIK catches his breath. MANIILAQ, QILUNIQ, and everyone helps him as he struggles to get to his feet.

MANIILAQ: There's ice in your hair.

HIGGUK: *(to NUKILIK)* Idlunnuaq, I saw you in front of me . . . then you disappeared.

NUKILIK: Well, I . . . I saw Angu'řuaq, so I snuck up behind him, trying to harpoon him. He turned around and slapped the harpoon out of my hands, but I picked it up and went after him—and then I slipped . . . and the next thing I knew, there's a seal swimming around my head. I was under the ice and couldn't breathe, couldn't find the breathing hole—then I had no more breath . . . and I saw Angu'řuaq's black nose and teeth and suddenly I'm flying through the air like a bird and landed on the hard ice . . . *(in pain)* "*A-aa-naluk.*"

HIGGUK: *(to NUKILIK)* You're lucky he didn't eat you.

NUKILIK: I think I was too quick in my decision to kill him.

HUMMIKTUQ: *(to NUKILIK)* I am no longer speaking to you—and you should no longer be camp leader!

AVINNGAQ: *(to HUMMIKTUQ)* Do not harbour contempt.

ᐊᕙᓐᖓᖅ: ᓯᑯᒦᑦᑲᓗᐊᕋᒪ ᑭᓯᐊᓂᒃ ᐊᓄᖅᓱᐃᒪᔫᕐᓗᐊᓕ’ᒪᑦ . . .

ᑕᒪᐃ’ᓂᑦ ᑕᐅᑦᑕᐅ’ᒪᑦ.

ᐊᕙᓐᖓᖅ: ᐊ’ᓚᙵᖅᑐᖅᑲᖅᑑᔭᖅᑐᖅ ᑕᓴᓂ, ᓴᕗᐅᕙᓗᐊᕐᓕ.

ᒫᓂᓚᖅ: ᐊᕙᓐᖓᖅ, ᐊᐅᓪᓚᖅᓯᒪᑎ’ᓗᑎᑦ ᐊᖑ’ᓴᐊᕐᒥᒃ ᑕᑯᓴᒍᑦ ᓄᓕᐊᕐᑲᖅᑐᓂᓗ. ᑐᕐᑯᓴᕋᓴᐊᕈᒪᓕᖅᑐᑎᒍᒃ ᐃᖕᒥᓂ ᐊᐅᓚᓚᐃ’ᒪᓂᒃ, ᑭᓯᐊᓂᒃ ᓴᓪᒥᒃᑐᖅ ᐊᒃᐱᐅᑎᑦᕐᑳᙱ’ᓇᑉᑎᒍᑦ. ᐊᒃᐱᐅᑎᓕᖅᑐᒍ ᐊᐅᓚᕐᑲᑎᒋᓕᖅᑐᒋᒃ ᓇᓅᒃ. ᓄᑭᓕᒡᓗ, ᓯᒡᒍᒡᓗ ᕿᓗᓂᕐᓗ ᓴᓪᒥᒃᑐᕐᒥᒃ ᕿᓂᕆᐊᓕᖅᑐᑎᒃ. ᓴᓪᒥᒃᑐᖅ ᐃᖕᒥᓂᒃ ᐅᑎᕋᓗᐊᖅᑐᓂ ᑭᓯᐊᓂᒃ ᓄᑭᓕᒃ ᐅᑎᙱᑦᑐᖅ ᓴᓕ.

ᐊᕙᓐᖓᖅ: ᐊᓐᖏᐊᓇᔭᕐᑲᕐᓗᓂ ᐃᓗᐃᓪᓕᖅᑎᑦᑎᓇ’ᒪᑦ.

ᓯᒡᒍᒃ: ᐄ, ᐅᒡᒍᐊᕐᓗᐊᖅᑐᖕᒐ.

ᐊᕙᓐᖓᖅ: ᑲᑎᙵᑦᑎᐊᓇᐊᕐᑲᖅᑐᒍᑦ ᓄᑭᓕᒃ ᕿᓂᓇᐊᕐᓗᒍ.

ᐱᓴᓕᖁᓗᐊᖅᑎ’ᓗᒋᑦ ᑐᕋᕐᓇᖅᑐᕐᑲᓕᖅᑐᓂ ᕿᐊᓵᔭᖅᑐᒥᒃ.

ᓄᑭᓕᒃ ᐃᓯᖅᑐᓂ, ᖃᐅᓯᖅᑐᖅ, ᐹᓪᓚᖑᖅᑐᓂ ᓴᔪᒃᑐᖅ ᐋᓇᐊᖓᓗ ᖁᖑᓯᐊᓗ ᐊᐅᖕᒋᓐᓇᐅ’ᓗᑎᒃ.

ᕿᓗᓂᖅ: . . . ᐊᑖᑖ ᓴᒐᕕᑦ?

ᐊᓂᖅᓵᕋᓴᐊᖅᑐᓂ. ᒫᓂᓚᕐᓗ ᕿᓗᓂᕐᓗ ᑕᒪᐃᑕᓗ ᐃᑲᔪᓕᖅᑐᒍ ᒪᑭᑦᖁ’ᓗᒍ.

ᒫᓂᓚᖅ: ᓄᔭᑎᑦ ᐸᑐᒃᑐᑦ.

ᓯᒡᒍᒃ: (ᓄᑭᓕᖑᑦ) ᐃᓪᓗᓄᐊᖅ, ᓵᓪᓂ ᑕᑯᒐᓗᐊᕋᑉᑭᑦ . . . ᓴᖅᑲᕈᐃᖅᑐᑎᓪᓗ.

ᓄᑭᓕᒃ: ᐲ . . . ᐲ . . . ᐊᖑ’ᓴᐊᖅ ᑕᑯᑉᑯ ᑎᕐᓕᐊᖅᑐᒍ, ᓇᐅᓕᒐᓴᐊᖅᑐᒍ, ᓴᖑ’ᓗᓂ ᐸᑎᒃᑕᓇᓗᒋ’ᓗᓂᐅᒃ ᐅᓈᕐᓗᒃ ᓴᑉᑯ’ᓗᒍ, ᑎᒍᑉᓯᐊᖅᑐᒍ ᐱᒋᐊᓕᕆ’ᓗᒍ ᖁᐊᔭᕿ’ᓇᒪ . . . ᖃᐅᓯᒪᓴᐃᖅᑳᖅᑐᖕᒐ ᓇᑦᑎᓇᓗᒃ ᑕᑯᖅᑰᖅᑐᒍ ᓂᐊᖁᒻᓃᑦᑐᖅ. ᓯᑰᑉ ᐊᑖᓃᑦᑲᓗᐊᕋᒪ ᐊᓂᖅᓵᓚᐃ’ᓗᖓ ᐊᓪᓗ ᕿᓂᕋᓗᐊᖅᑐᒍ ᓇᓂᓚᐃ’ᓗᒍ. ᐊᓂᕐᓂᖅᑲᕈᐃᕋᒪ ᐊᔪᓕᕋᒪ ᑕᑯ’ᓗᒍ ᐊᖑ’ᓴᐊᑉ ᕿᖓᖓ ᕿᕐᓇᓇᒃᑐᖅ ᑭᒍᑎᖕᒋᓪᓗ,

NUKILIK: *(to HUMMIKTUQ)* We were mistaken . . . I was mistaken for not speaking to you first. The bear could have killed me or let me drown, but instead he helped me and pulled me out of the breathing hole.

AVINNGAQ: Nukilik, you now have to correct this and put the two bears back out in the wilderness.

HUMMIKTUQ: I already sent them away. *(a tiny wail begins)* AAAAAHHHH . . .

QAAKŠAATTIAQ points.

QAAKŠAATTIAQ: LOOK!

ANGU'ŘUAQ enters sporting a wound and carrying NUKILIK's harpoon between his teeth. UKUANNUAQ follows. The bear drops the harpoon near NUKILIK. NUKILIK gives ANGU'ŘUAQ a sign of respect.

HUMMIKTUQ: *(to ANGU'ŘUAQ)* My son, you do not harbour resentment towards Nukilik. I taught you well . . . and now you teach me.

HUMMIKTUQ reaches for NUKILIK's hand to help him up—a gesture of peace that NUKILIK might acknowledge in some way.

NUKILIK: Avinngaq, can Angu'řuaq stay with us for a while . . . until his wife gets ready to make a den?

AVINNGAQ: No. He did well and didn't try to avenge you . . . instead he helped to save your life, but I was mistaken to let him stay for so long. For the good of our lives they must leave.

ANGU'ŘUAQ looks at HUMMIKTUQ.

HUMMIKTUQ: Angu'řuaq, it's time for you to go away—and live your life.

NUKILIK: He can stay—

MANIILAQ: *(to NUKILIK) Iiqi*—no.

HUMMIKTUQ: *(to QAAQŠAATTIAQ)* Give your parting words to him.

ᑎᖕᒋᓕᖅᔪᖕᒐ ᑎᖕᒥᐊᖅᑐᑦ ᒥ'ᓇᒪᑐ ᖁᑯᒧᑦ . . . *(ᐊ'ᓂᕈᖃᒃᑐᖅ)*
ᐊ'ᐋᓇᑐᒃ.

ᖁᒡᒍᒃ: *(ᓄᑭᓕᖕᒍᑦ)* ᓂᕆᖖᒋᑕᓇᑐᒋᕖᑎᑦ.

ᓄᑭᓕᒃ: ᑐᖅᑯᓴᕈᒪᓪᓗᐊᖅᔪᒍ ᑐᐊᕕᖅᐸᓪᓛᔾᔪᖕᓂᕋᒪ.

ᖃᒻᒥᒃᑐᖅ: *(ᓄᑭᓕᖕᒍᑦ)* ᐅᖅᑲᒪᖅᑲᑎᒋᓚᐃᒻᒪᓇᒃᐸᒋᑦ—ᐃᓅᖅᑲᑎᒌᒃᑐᓂᒃ
ᓴᒪᓂ ᐊᑕᓂᐅᖃᐃᖅᑐᒃᓴᐅᕗᑎᑦ!

ᐊᕕᓐᖕᒐᖅ: *(ᖃᒻᒥᒃᑐᖕᒍᑦ)* ᐅᕈᑐᒋᙱᒋᑐᒍ.

ᓄᑭᓕᒃ: *(ᖃᒻᒥᒃᑐᖕᒍᑦ)* ᑕᒻᒪᖅᑐᒍᑦ . . . ᑕᒻᒪᖅᑐᖕᖓᓕ
. . . ᐊᒃᐱᐅᑎᕙᒌᙱᑕᑉᑎᒋᑦ. ᓇᓄᖅ ᑐᖅᑯᓴᕈᖕᓇᕋᓗᐊ'ᒪᖕᖓ
ᐃᒫᖅᑎᓗᖕᖓᓘᓐᓃᑦ, ᑭᖁᐊᓂᒃ ᐃᑲᔪ'ᒪᖕᖓ ᐊᒧ'ᒪᖕᖓ ᑕᐃᑳ'ᖕᖓᑦ ᐊᒡᓗᒥᑦ.

ᐊᕕᓐᖕᒐᖅ: ᓄᑭᓕᒃ ᑕᓴᒻᒪ ᐃᔪᐊᖅᖁᒋᐊᖅᑲᓕᖅᑕᑦ ᐅᑎᖅᑎᑦᑎᐊᕆᐊᖅᑐᒋᑦ
ᓇᓅᒃ ᐃᓄᐃᓪᓚᒧᑦ.

ᖃᒻᒥᒃᑐᖅ: ᐊᐅᓪᓚᖅᑎᑖᖅᑕᕋᓗᐊᑦᑲᓪᓚ. *(ᕿᐊᑦᑕᐃᓚᓇᖃᐊᖅᔪᓂ)* ᐋᐊᐊᐊ

ᖄᒃᓵᑦᑎᐊᖅ ᑎᑦᑯᐊᖅᔪᓂ.

ᖄᒃᓵᑦᑎᐊᖅ: ᑕᒃᑰᒃ!

*ᐃᖁᖅᔪᓂ ᐊᖕᒎ'ᖃᐊᖅ ᑭᓕᖅᓂᖅᑲᖅᔪᓂ ᖁᒡᒍᖕᒥᐅᑕᓇ'ᑐᒍ ᓄᑭᓕᐅᑉ
ᐅᓈᖕᒐ. ᐅᑯᐊᓐᓄᐊᖅ ᒪᓕᒃᔪᓂ. ᓇᓄᖅ ᐅᓈᖅ ᐃᓕ'ᑐᓂᐅᒃ
ᓇᑎᖑᑦ ᓄᑭᓕᐅᑉ ᖅᑲᓂᒋᓵᓄᑦ. ᓄᑭᓕᒃ ᖅᑯᓯᒋᕖ ᐊᖕᒎ'ᖃ'ᐊᖅ.*

ᖃᒻᒥᒃᑐᖅ: *(ᐊᖕᒎ'ᖃᐊᖑᑦ)* ᐃᖅᓃᒃ ᒪᒥᐊᒋᙱᒋᑐᒍ ᓄᑭᓕᒃ.
ᐃᓕᓴᖅᑎᑦᑎᐊᖅᐸᑭᑦ . . . ᑕᔅᕙᑐ ᐃᓕᓴᖅᑎᓕᖅᐸ'ᒪ ᐃᓅᖁᒃᓴᒻᓂᒃ.

*ᖃᒻᒥᒃᑐᖅ ᐃᓵᒃᔪᓂ ᓄᑭᓕᖕᒧᑦ ᐃᑲᔪᕋᖁᐊᖅᔪᒍ ᒪᑭᓐᓂᐊ'ᒪᑦ—
ᖅᑲᐅᖁᒪᓂᐊ'ᒪᓪᓗ ᒪᒥᐊᒋᔭᐅᙱ'ᒪᑦ.*

ᓄᑭᓕᒃ: ᐊᕕᓐᖕᒐᖅ, ᐅᓇ ᐊᖕᒎ'ᖃᐊᖅ ᐅᕙᑉᑎ'ᓃᑲᓐᓄᐊᕈᖕᓇᖅᐸ
. . . ᐊᐅᓪᓚᖅᑐᑎᒃ ᓄᓚᐊᖕᒐ ᖁᑎᖅᑲᓕᖅᓂᐊᓵᖅᑎ'ᑐᒍᓚ?

ᐊᕕᓐᖕᒐᖅ: ᐃᓯᑲᒃ. ᐱᑦᑎᐊᖅᑑᒐᑐᐊᖅ ᐊᑭᓇᖃᐊᖕᒋ'ᒪᑦ,
ᐃᑲᔪᖅᔪᓂᑎᑦᑑᓐᓃᑦ, ᑭᖁᐊᓂᒃ ᑕᒻᒪᕋᒪ ᐊᑯᓂᕖᑦᓵᖅ

QAAQŠAATTIAQ, ATUGAUQ, and QILUNIQ go up to the bear—their sibling—and feel the shock of time freezing. They have no words, but feel the profound connection that is about to end . . . then HUMMIKTUQ goes to ANGU'ŘUAQ.

HUMMIKTUQ: *(to ANGU'ŘUAQ)* In your travels across the snow and ice, always return to this place where you were brought up and loved for so long, and if you ever get lost or find yourself in difficulty, try and hear my voice in the wind. You will be able to hear it. I will call your name—Angu'řuaq. Go away now.

For a moment ANGU'ŘUAQ is reluctant to leave . . . then he moves away.

ANGU'ŘUAQ and UKUANNUAQ exit.

QAAKŠAATTIAQ: I'm feeling sad.

HUMMIKTUQ: I'm feeling sad too, but it is clear they will flourish, and my son will live a long life. For this I am happy.

HIGGUK: Me too—I'm happy.

MANIILAQ: I am happier than either of you because my dear husband is alive.

HIGGUK: *(sings)* I'm going to live to see tomorrow
To walk upon our lands again
To dance upon the ice and—

AVINNGAQ points at something out in the sea.

AVINNGAQ: Look . . . LOOK!

They all turn to stare out, but only AVINNGAQ and HUMMIKTUQ can see something coming into view.

I have never seen such an unusual thing before.

HUMMIKTUQ: Ahhh . . . it looks like a very large narwhal.

QILUNIQ: Where? *(raises his harpoon)* Where . . . where is it?

ᖃᒪᓃᔭᐅᖅᑎᑦᑐᖕᓇᕋᑉᑯ. ᐃᓅᑦᑎᐊᕐᓂᐊᕋᑉᑕᕋ
ᐊᐅᓪᓚᕆᐊᖅᑲᒻᒪᕆᒃᑰᒃ ᐅᑯᐊᒃ.

ᐊᖓ'ᔪᐊᖅ ᑕᐅᑐᕋᖅᓱᓂ ᔨᒻᒥᒃᑐᖅᒥᒃ.

ᔨᒻᒥᒃᑐᖅ: ᐊᖓ'ᔪᐊᖅ ᐊᐅᓪᓚᕆᐊᖅᑲᕋᖅᑐᑎᑦ—ᐆᒪᓇᔨᐊᕐᓗᑎᑦ ᔨᒥᑐᐃᓐᓇᖅ.

ᓄᑭᕋᒃ: ᖃᒪᓃᑦᑐᖕᓇᖅᑐᖅ—

ᒪᓂᓚᖅ: *(ᓄᑭᕋᖕᒧᑦ)* ᐄᖅᑭ.

ᔨᒻᒥᒃᑐᖅ: *(ᖄᒃᓵᑦᑎᐊᕐᒧᑦ)* ᑖᕝᕙᐅᕗᑏᖅᓗᒍ.

ᖄᒃᓵᑦᑎᐊᖅᓗ ᐊᑐᒐᐅᖅᓗ ᖁᓗᓂᖅᓗ ᓇᓄᖅᒧᙱᒐᐅᔨᑦ ᐃᓚᒻᒪᕆᒃᑐᑦ ᐱ'ᒪᒋᑦ—ᐃᓱᐃᑦᑐᖄᓗᒃ ᓂᐸᐃᓚᒃᑐᓚᖅᓱᑎᒃ. ᐅᖅᑲᐅᔭᒃᓴᖅᑲᖅᑲᓯᐃᑦᑑ'ᒪᑕ ᐃᒃᐱᒍᔪᒃᑲᒥᒃ ᑕᑯ'ᓯᐃᒪᓇᖕᓂᐊ'ᒪᒋᑦ ᐃᓚᓐᓄᐊᖅᑎᒃ . . . ᔨᒻᒥᒃᑐᖅᓗ ᑕᐃᒪ ᐊᖓ'ᔪᐊᖅᒧᙱᒐᐅᔨᖅ.

ᔨᒻᒥᒃᑐᖅ: *(ᐊᖓ'ᔪᐊᕐᒧᑦ)* ᔨᒧᙱᒐᐅᒐᓗᐊᖄᙱᒐᕕᑦ, ᖃᒧᙱ ᐅᑎᖅᑲᑦᑕ'ᓴᕗᑎᑦ, ᐸᒥᖅᓴᖅᑕᐅᒐᕕᑦ ᑕᖃᒪᓂ, ᐊᔭᐅᒍᕕᖕᑐ ᐊᑦᖅᑯᓇᖅᓇᖅᑐᒃᑰᕈᕕᑦᓘᓐᓃᑦ ᑐᖕᓇᔨᐊᖅᓗᑎᑦ ᓂᐱᓪᓂᒃ ᐊᓄᓇᑦᑯᑦ ᑐᖕᔨᖕᓇᖅᓂᐊᖅᑕᑦ, ᐊᑎ'ᓂᒃ ᑐᖅᓱᓚᓱᖕᒐ ᑐᖕᓂᐊᖅᑕ'ᒪ, ᐊᖓ'ᔪᐊᖅ. ᐊᑕᐃ ᐊᐅᓪᓚᓚᕆᑦ.

ᐊᖓ'ᔪᐊ ᐊᐅᓪᓚᕿᒪᖕᒋᑦᑲᓗᐊᖅᓱᓂ . . . ᐱᔭᕋᖅᓱᓂ ᑖᕚᓇ.

ᐊᖓ'ᔪᐊᖅ ᐅᑯᐊᓐᓄᐊᖅ ᐊᔭᐊᓄᒧᙱᒐᐅ'ᑐᑎᒃ.

ᖄᒃᓵᑦᑎᐊᖅ: ᓂᑲᓪᓗᑕᕋᒪ.

ᔨᒻᒥᒃᑐᖅ: ᖁᕕᐊᓇᐃᑦᑑᒐᓗᐊᖅ ᑭᔭᐊᓂᒃ ᓇᓗᓇᙱᑦᑎ'ᒪᑦ
ᔭᒃᓯᓂᖅᑲᑦᑎᐊ'ᒪᓂ ᐃᖅᓯᖃᕆ ᐊᑯᓂ ᐆᒪᓂᐊ'ᒪᑦ. ᑕᖃᒪ ᖁᕕᐊᔨᑎᒋᔭᖅ.

ᔭᒡᒍᒃ: ᐅᕙᖓᓗ—ᖁᕕᐊᓲᑎᒋᕙᑉᑲᑦᑕᐅᖅ.

ᒪᓂᓚᖅ: ᖁᕕᐊᓲᓂᖅᖃᐃᑦᑑᔪᖓᓚ ᐅᐃᓐᓄᐊᖅ ᐃᓅ'ᒪᑦ.

ᔭᒡᒍᒃ: *(ᐃᖏᐅᖅᓱᓂ)* ᐃᓅᓂᐊᕋᒪ ᔭᕗᓂᖅᑲᖅᓂᐊᕋᒪ
ᐱᔨᖅᑭᒥᑐᒥᑦ ᓄᓇᒃᑯᑦ
ᒧᒥᖅᑐᖓ ᑐᕚᒥ ᑕᐃᒪᑐ—

HIGGUK: I don't see anything. *(to NUKILIK)* Do you?

NUKILIK: There's nothing out there.

QILUNIQ moves towards the sea.

QILUNIQ: Point to it and I'll hunt it.

AVINNGAQ: No, don't go, Qiluniq—it's not a narwhal.

HUMMIKTUQ: Its huge white wings are flapping.

NUKILIK: What are the wings . . . where, Hummiktuq?

AVINNGAQ: I'll call on my helping spirits to travel through the layers so I can see what it is.

MANIILAQ: . . . EEEEEEE . . . I'm afraid.

HUMMIKTUQ: So am I. This creature makes me afraid, for it heralds the beginning of the end and the end of the beginning.

NUKILIK: Hummiktuq, what is it you see out there?

HUMMIKTUQ: Time . . . not in the shape of a circle, but in the shape of a line.

ATUGAUQ suddenly bends over, holding her pregnant belly.

QILUNIQ: Dear wife—*Nuliannuaq*.

ATUGAUQ: I'm in labour.

MANIILAQ: Breathe in and out. Breathe.

AVINNGAQ: It has disappeared . . . no longer in sight.

HUMMIKTUQ: It was a glimpse of the future.

AVINNGAQ: I hope it does not return.

ᐊᕙᓐᖓᖅ ᑎᑦᑯᐊᖅᖢᓂ ᓯᓇᒥᒃ ᑕᕆᐅᕐᒦᑦᑐᒥᒃ.

ᐊᕙᓐᖓᖅ: ᑕᒃᑰᒃ . . . ᑕᒃᑰᒃ!

ᑕᒪᐃᑕ ᑕᑯᓇᓯᐊᖅᖢᑎᑦ ᑭᓴᐊᓂᒃ ᐊᕙᓐᖓᕐᓗ ᓯᒻᒥᒃᑐᕐᓗ ᑕᐅᑐᒃᑕᖃᖅᑐᐱᑐᐊᒃ.

ᐊᕙᓐᖓᖅ: ᑕ'ᓇᐃᑦᑐᓇᓗᖕᒥᒃ ᑕᑯᑉᖃᓕᖕᖏᒻᒪᕆᒃᑲᒪᓕ.

ᓯᒻᒥᒃᑐᖅ: ᐋᐊᐊ . . . ᑑᒑᓕᓪᓴᐊᖑᓵᖅᑐᖅ.

ᕿᓗᓂᖅ: ᓯᒥ? (ᐅᓈᓂ ᖃᖓᑦᑕᖅᖢᒍ) ᓯᒥ . . . ᓯᒦᑦᐸ?

ᓴᒡᒍᒃ: ᑕᑯᖕᖏᒻᒪᕆᒃᑐᖓᓕ. (ᓄᑭᓕᖑᑦ) ᐃᔾᕙᓪᓕ?

ᓄᑭᓕᒃ: ᓯᓇᖃᖕᖏᑦᑐᕐᖢᒃ.

ᕿᓗᓂᖅ ᑕᕆᐅᕐᒍᖕᖓᐅᓇᓯᐊᖅᖢᓂ.

ᕿᓗᓂᖅ: ᓯᒦᑦᑖᒃᓯ ᑎᑦᑯᐊᕐᓗᒍ ᐊᖑᑦᓕᕐᓵᓗᖕᓂᐊᕐᑉᑯ.

ᐊᕙᓐᖓᖅ: ᐄᕿ, ᐱᖕᖏᓗᑎᑦ, ᕿᓗᓂᖅ—ᑑᒑᓕᐅᖕᖏᑦᑐᖅ.

ᓯᒻᒥᒃᑐᖅ: ᐃᔾᔨᑖᒥᒃ ᖃᑯᖅᑑᒃ ᐊᖕᑎᓴᐊᓘᒃ ᐊᐅᓕᓵᒃ.

ᓄᑭᓕᒃ: ᓇᐅᒃ ᐃᔾᔨᑕᐃᑦ . . . ᓯᒥ, ᓯᒻᒥᒃᑐᖅ?

ᐊᕙᓐᖓᖅ: ᖃᐃᑦᖁᓂᐊᖅᐸᑦᑲᑦ ᐃᑲᔪᖅᑎᑦᑲᑦ
ᐃᓕᒻᒪᖅᑐᕐᓂᐊᕐᒪ ᑕᑯᔭᖅᑐᕐᓂᐊᕐᑉᑯ ᓯᓇᐅᔮᒃᓯ.

ᒪᓃᓚᖅ: . . . ᐃᐃᐃᐃᐃᐃᐃ . . . ᐃᖅᓯᔭᖓ.

ᓯᒻᒥᒃᑐᖅ: ᐅᕙᖓᓗ. ᐃᓯᔭᐊᓗᓘᔭᖓ ᐃᓯᓕᒃᑐᖅᑲᕐᓂ'ᒪᑦ
ᐊ'ᓕᖕᖑᕐᓗᐊᖅᑐᒃᓯᐅᓕᖅᑯᒍᑦᓕ ᐃᓅᓯᖅᑯᑦ
ᖃᓄᕆᑦᑐᒫᖅᑐᓇᓘᒐᓗᐊ'ᒪᑦᑭᐊᖅ.

ᓄᑭᓕᒃ: ᓯᒻᒥᒃᑐᖅ, ᓯᓇᒥᒡᓕ ᑕᑯᒐᕙᑦ ᑖᕙᓂ.

ᓯᒻᒥᒃᑐᖅ: ᑕᑯᖅᑰᖅᑐᖓ ᓴᕗᓂᒃᓯᐸᑎ'ᓂ ᐊᖕᒪᓗᖅᑰᖅᑐᖅ ᓯᑕᖃᔨᐃᓕ'ᒪᑦ
ᐊ'ᓕᖕᖑᖅᑐᒃᓯᓵᓗᒃ ᖃᓄᕆᑦᑑᓕᖅᐸᑭᐊᖅ ᓇᓗᔭᕐ.

HUMMIKTUQ still stares out at the sea.

HUMMIKTUQ: It will return, Avinngaq, but not for a long, long time.

MANIILAQ: Hummiktuq, we will need your help.

HUMMIKTUQ: Yes, I will help.

HUMMIKTUQ turns and helps MANIILAQ with ATUGAUQ as the group vanishes into the mists of time.

What HUMMIKTUQ and AVINNGAQ actually glimpsed in the turbulent mash of sea ice and sky was not a narwhal or a strange winged creature, but the mid-nineteenth century ushering in the mast, spars, and sails of Sir John FRANKLIN's ship, the HMS Erebus.

We hear the click clack of two pairs of leather boot heels marching on the ice, transitioning into the nineteenth century . . . click clack, click clack . . .

ᐊᑐᒐᐅᖅ ᐅᑯ’ᓗᓂ, ᐃᕐᓂᔨᓚᖃᒥ ᓈᕐᒥᓂᒃ ᑎᒍᒻᒥᔪᖅ.

ᕿᓗᓂᖅ: ᓄᓚᐊᓐᓄᐊᖅ.

ᐊᑐᒐᐅᖅ: ᐃᕐᓂᔨᓚᖃᒪ.

ᒪᓃᓚᖅ: ᐊᓂᖅᖂᖅᑐᓇᑦ. ᐊᓂᖅᖂᖅᑐᕐᓗᑎᑦ.

ᐊᕙᓐᖓᖅ: ᔨᖅᑲᕆᐃᖅᑐᕐᓲᓐᓂᖅ . . . ᑕᐅᑐᖕᓇᕆᐃᖅᑐᖅ.

ᔨᒻᒥᒃᑐᖅ: ᑕᐅᑐᒃᑲᓗᐊᖃᕙᑦ ᔭᕗᓂᕐᔪᑦ ᖅᑲᓄᓇᑦᑐᒫᖅᑐᔪᑦ.

ᐊᕙᓐᖓᖅ: ᐅᑎᕐᑯᖖᒋᓚᑕᖃ ᑕᐃᒻᓇ.

ᔨᒻᒥᒃᑐᖅ ᔨᓚ ᑕᐅᑐᒃᑐᖅ ᑕᐅᓄᖓ ᑕᓇᐅᕐᔪᑦ.

ᔨᒻᒥᒃᑐᖅ: ᐅᑎᕆᒫᖅᑑᒐᓗᐊᖅ, ᐊᕙᓐᖓᖅ, ᖅᑲᑯᒍᑭᐊᖅ
ᐊᑯᓂᓇᓘᓂᐊᖅᑐᒃᓴᐅᕗᖅ.

ᒪᓃᓚᖅ: ᐊᕐᓇᕐᕙᒃ, ᐃᓚ’ᓂᑦ ᐃᑲᔪᖅᑕᐅᒋᐊᖅᑲᕐᓂᐊᖅᑐᒍᑦ.

ᔨᒻᒥᒃᑐᖅ: ᐄ, ᐃᑲᔪᕐᓂᐊᖅᑯᖓ.

ᔨᒻᒥᒃᑐᖅ ᓴᖑ’ᓗᓂ ᐃᑲᔪᓚᖅᐸᐃᑦ ᒪᓃᓚᕐᓗ ᐊᑐᒐᐅᕐᓗ ᐊᔫᑕᓗ ᔨᖅᑲᕆᐃᖅᑐᐃᓐᓇᐅ’ᓗᑎᒃ ᑕᒃᔭᖅᑐᒥ ᐅᖓᔭᒃᔭᔾᕉᖅᓱᑎᒃ.

ᔨᓇᐅᐤᕙᓚ ᔨᒻᒥᒃᑐᕐᓗ ᐊᕙᓐᖓᕐᓗ ᑕᑯᖃᐃᑦ ᔪᑯᒥ ᑑᓛᓚᐅᖖᒋᑦᑐᖅ, ᑑᓐᖓᐅᖖᒋᑦᑐᖅ ᔨᓇᐅᐤᕙ ᐅᒥᐊᕐᔪᐊᖑᓐᓂᖅᓱᓂ ᖅᑲᐃᓛᖅᑐᒥᒃ 1800 ᐊᑐᓕᖅᐸᑕ ᐃᖃᕆᑕᐃ’ᓂᒃ ᓇᐸᕆᑖ’ᓂᓪᓗ ᑕᑯᒐᒥᒃ ᐅᒥᐊᕐᔪᐊᖅ ᐃᖃᐸᔅ-ᒥᒃ ᑕᐃᖃᐅᔪᖅ ᕿᓂᖅᑎᑦ ᐱᖕᒋᑦ.

ᑐᖃᕐᓇᖅᑐᖅᑲᖅᓱᓂ ᖅᑲᑉᑐᓈᑦ ᒪᔾᕆᒃ ᑲᒫᓘᒋᒃ ᑭ’ᒥᖕᒋᑦ ᔪᑎ’ᒪᑕ ᑐᖃᕐᓇᖅᑐᑦ ᔪᑯᒃᑯᑦ. ᑕᒃ-ᑕᒃ-ᑕᒃ-ᑕᒃ . . .

1845

BODIES

At a later date the same season, but previous to the disruption of the ice, the bodies of some thirty persons and some Graves were discovered on the continent, and five dead bodies on an Island near it, about a long day's journey to the north west of a large stream, which can be no other than Great Fish River (named by the Esquimaux Ool-koo-i-hi-ca-lik), as its description and that of the low shore in the neighborhood of Point Ogle and Montreal Island agree exactly with that of Sir George Back. Some of the bodies had been buried (probably those of the first victims of famine); some were in tents; others under the boat, which had been turned over to form a shelter, and several lay scattered about in different directions. Of those found on the Island one was supposed to have been an Officer, as he had a telescope strapped over his shoulders and his double-barrel gun lay beneath him. From the mutilated state of many of the bodies and the contents of the kettles, it is evident that our wretched Countrymen had been driven to the last dread alternative—cannibalism—as a means of prolonging existence.

—Dr. John Rae's Report to the British Admiralty, 1854

1845-ᖑᑎ’ᓗᒍ

ᑎᒥᓇᓗᐃᑦ

ᓯᑯᐃᖅᑎ’ᓇᒍ ᑕᐃᑉᓱᒪᓂ ᑐᖁᖓᔪᑦ ᐊᕙᑎᑦ ᖁᓕᓪᓗ ᓇᓂᔭᐅ’ᒪᑕ ᓄᓇᒥ ᐃᓚᐃᓪᓗ ᐃᓗᕕᖅᓯᒪ’ᓗᑎᒃ, ᕿᑭᖅᑕᒥᓗ ᑕᓪᓕᒪᐃᑦᑕᐅᖅ ᓇᓂᔭᐅ’ᒪᑕ, ᐅᑦᑯᓱᒃᓴᓕᐅᑉ ᑰᑉ ᐅᖓᑖᓂ ᕿᓂᖅᑎᓂ [ᖃᑉᓗᓈᑐᑦ] ᑕᐃᔭᐅᔪᓂᒃ ᓄᕗ-ᐆᓚᑦ-ᒥᒃ ᒫᓐᓇᐊᓕᐅᑉᓗ ᕿᑭᖅᑖᓂᓗ ᑖᑉᑯᐊᒃ ᖃᓂᕆᔭᐃ’ᓂ ᑐᖁᖅᑳᖅᑐᕕᓃᑦ ᐃᓗᕕᖅᑕᐅ’ᒪᑕ (ᑳᖕᓂᕐᒍᒃᓴᐅᔪᖅ); ᐃᓚᐃᓪᓗ ᑎᒦᑦ ᑐᐱᕐᒦᑦᑐᑦ ᐃᓚᐃᓪᓗ ᐅᒥᐊᕐᓂ ᐳᔪᖓᔪᓂ, ᐅᒥᐊᕐᒥᒃ ᐃᒡᓗᖃᕋᓱᐊᕐᓂ’ᒪᑕ ᐃᓚᐃᑦ, ᐃᓚᐃᓪᓗ ᑎᒦᑦ ᓯᒥᑐᐃᓐᓇᖅ ᓱᐊᒻᒪᒃᓱᒪᔪᑦ ᓄᓇᒥ. ᐊᑕᐅᓯᖅ ᓯᕗᓕᖅᑎᕆᔭᐅᖅᑯ’ᒪᑦ ᕿᓐᖑᑎᖅᑲᖅᖢᓂ ᐋᕆᐊᕐᒥᓄᑦ ᑭᓚᒃᓯᒪᔪᒥᒃ ᓯᖅᑯᖅᑎᔾᔪᑖᓗ ᒪᔾᕈᓕᒃ ᑎᒥᐊᑕ ᐊᑖᓃ’ᓗᓂ. ᑎᒥᖕᒥᑦ ᑕᑯ’ᓗᒥᑦ ᐱᓚᒃᑐᖅᑕᐅᓯᒪᔪᑦ ᑕᑯ’ᓗᒥᓪᓗ ᐅᑦᑯᓲᑕ ᐃᓗᐊᓃᑦᑐᑦ, ᔮᓇᐅᕝᕙ ᓄᓇᖅᑲᑎᒥ’ᓂᒃ ᓂᕆᔭᕕᓂᓇᓗᐃᑦ ᑳᑉᐸᓪᓛᖅᖢᑎᒃ ᐃᓅᓇᓱᐊᖅᖢᑎᒃ.

—ᐃᖢᐊᖅᓴᐃᔨᑉ ᔫᓐ ᕋᐃ ᐅᓂᑉᑳᖅᑖ ᖃᑉᓗᓈᑦ ᐊᑖᓃ’ᓄᑦ ᑕᓇᐅᑉ ᐊᑭᐊᓂ, 1854-ᒥ

ACT II

SCENE ONE

It is late October 1845, almost midnight. The ridge of the glacial hill is barely seen in the distance. Nearby is the bow of the HMS Erebus, *its lanterns ablaze. The land is pure ice. There are hints of auroras dancing in the dark sky.* WICKERS *and* BEAN *enter, both in full uniform.* BEAN *carries a folded British flag and a wooden box;* WICKERS *carries a gold-tipped flagstaff with ropes and hoist.*

BEAN: Feels some good to walk on land again, Wickers—to stand on something that's not bloody moving or floating or near capsizing.

*He slips and falls—*WICKERS *helps him up.*

WICKERS: This isn't land, Bean—this is ice, and look up . . . aurora borealis.

BEAN *looks up.*

BEAN: Those lights—are they God?

WICKERS: God mixed with the interaction of solar wind and Earth's magnetosphere, but we're going to unlock the secret of the earth's magnetism.

BEAN: We are?

WICKERS: Yes. The captain will settle this compass business once and for all. *(pulls out his compass)* Look—the needle keeps pointing to the magnetic north pole, not to the geographic North Pole, and the closer we get to the geographic North Pole, the more useless these things will become.

ᖁᓐᖏᐊᖅᑕᐅᖬᒃᓴᖅ ᑐᒡᓚᐅᖬᖅ

ᖃᓄᕆᑦᑑᓂᐊ ᐱᕆᐊᕐᓂᐊᓂ

ᐅᑭᐊᒃᓵᒃᑯᑦ ᑕᑦᕿᐊᓂ ᐊᒥᕋᐃᕐᕕᖕᒥ ᑎᕿᑐᖅᑲᓄᑦ 1845-ᖑᑎ’ᑐᒍ. ᐅᓐᓄᒻᒪᓇᓕᖅᑎ’ᑐᒍ. ᐊᐃᔦᐃᑦᑐᖅ ᐅᖕᒐᖪᒃᑐᒥ ᑕᐅᑐᖕᓇᓐᓄᐊᖅᑐᖅ. ᖃᓂᕆᓰᓂ ᐅᒥᐊᕐᖬᐊᑉ ᖪᕗᓂᐊ ᑕᐅᑐᖕᓇᖅᑐᖅ ᐃᑯᒪᖕᕆᓪᓗ ᖃᐅᒪ’ᑐᑎᒃ. ᑕᓴᒻᒪ ᖪᑯᐃᓐᓇᑦᑎᐊᖑ’ᒪᑦ. ᑕᐅᑐᖕᓇᖅᑐᓪᓗ ᐊᖅᓴᕐᓃᑦ ᑕᑦᐹᓂ ᑖᖅᑐᒥ. ᐊᓗᕈᑎᓗ ᐱᓂᕐᓗ, ᐊ’ᓄᕌᖅᓯᒪᑦᑎᐊᖅᓗᑎᒃ ᖃᑉᓗᓈᖅᑕᕐᓂᒃ. ᐱᓂᖅ ᑎᒍᒥᐊᖅᑐᖅ ᖃᑉᓗᓈᑦ ᑯᐃᓐ ᓄᓈᑕ ᓴᐃᒪᑕᐃ’ᓂᒃ ᕿᖬᕐᑯᑎᓐᓄᐊᕐᒥᒡᓗ; ᐊᓗᕈᑎᓗ ᑎᒍᒥᐊᖅᑐᖅ ᓴᐃᒪᑎᑉ ᓇᐸᕈᑖ’ᓂᒃ ᕿᑉᓚᖅᑐᓇᓗᒃ ᐊᒃᓗᓈᒃᓴᓂᒡᓗ.

ᐱᓂᖅ: ᐃᓗᐊᖅᑐᕌᓗᒃ ᐱᖪᕆᐊᒃᓴᖅ ᓄᓇᒻᒪᓇᒃᑎᒍᑦ—ᒪᑭᒪᓗᓂ ᓇᖕᕆᕐᓗᓂ ᐊᐅᓚᖖᕆᑦᑐᒥ, ᐳᒃᑕᖖᕆᑦᑐᒥ, ᖃᔭᐅᖪᓐᖑᓇᖖᕆᑦᑐᒥ, ᐊᖪᐅ, ᐊᓗᕈᑎ.

ᖁᐊᔭᑭ’ᑐᓂ ᑕᐅᓄᖓ—ᐊᓗᕈᑎᑉ ᐃᑲᔦᓚᖅᐹ.

ᐊᓗᕈᑎ: ᑕᓴᒻᒪ ᓄᓇᐅᖖᕆᑦᑐᖅ, ᐱᓂᖅ—ᖪᑯ ᑕᓴᒻᒪ, ᑕᑦᐱᑦᑯᐊᑦ ᑕᒃᑰᒃ . . . ᐊᖅᓴᕐᓂᑦ.

ᐱᓂᖅ ᖁ’ᒍᑦ ᑕᑯᓴᓕᖅᓗᓂ.

ᐱᓂᖅ: ᐃᑯᒪᑦ ᑕᓴᑉᑯᐊᑦ—ᒎᑎᐅᕙᑦ?

ᐊᓗᕈᑎ: ᒎᑎᐅᖬᓪᓗ ᖪᕿᓂᐅᑉ ᐊᐅᓚᓂᐊᓗ ᓄᓇᐅᑉ ᐊᓂᕐᓂᐊᓗ, ᑭᖪᐊᓂᒃ ᑕᒃᑰᒃ ᖪᓚᕐᖬᐊᕐᒥ ᖬᒥᑐᐃᓐᓇᖅ ᖃᐅᖪᒪᖬᐅᖖᕆᑦᑐᓂᒃ ᖃᐅᖪᓂᐊᖅᑐᒍᒃ ᓄᓇᐅᑉ ᐱᐊ’ᓂᒃ ᐊᓂᕐᓂᐊ’ᓂᒃ.

ᐱᓂᖅ: ᖬᓚᖬᓇᓘ’ᖬᒐᕕᑦ.

BEAN looks at his own compass.

BEAN: Mine's already pretty useless.

WICKERS: The scuttlebutt is that he'll be setting up portable shore observatories and we'll all be asked to collect oceanographic, ornithological, and botanical specimens.

BEAN: I thought we're supposed to complete the Northwest Passage.

WICKERS: That too, I suppose—in our spare time.

BEAN: It'll be a frosty Friday morning I find me a specimen that's still alive in this bloody freezing cold.

WICKERS: You'll see a *Bubo scandiacus*—that's a snowy owl—and imagine, Bean, imagine seeing a real live *Ursus maritimus*.

BEAN: A what?

WICKERS: A sea bear! They're ever so regal—wait till you see one—they're fantastically white and have black noses.

BEAN: Black noses?

VOICES: *(off stage)* GANGWAY, GANGWAY.

The click clack of many more boots on the ice can be heard.

WICKERS: Where do I plant this?

BEAN: Try here.

WICKERS smashes the ice with the bottom of the flagstaff.

WICKERS: It's frozen solid.

BEAN: Chip away at it.

WICKERS: Chip away—easy for you to say, mate.

ᐊᓗᕈᑎ: ᓵᓕᕚᖓ. ᑳᐱᑕᐃᔭ ᓇᓗᓇᐃᑦᑎᐊᕐᓂᐊᖅᐹ. (ᑕᒻᒪᓃᒃᑯᑎᓂ ᔭᑦᕐᑯᒻᒥᖅᓱᒍ). ᑕᒃᑰᒃ ᑎᑦᑯᐊᕈᑖ ᐊᑕᐅᔫᓐᓇᒻᒪᓇᖑᑦ ᑎᑦᑯᐊᕐᑲᑦᑕᖅᑑᓐᓂᖅ, ᐅᑭᐅᖅᑕᖅᑐᒥ ᐅᑯᐊ ᑕᒻᒪᓅᑦᑯᑎᑦ ᐊᔪᖅᑐᓇᓗᕐᓱᐃᑦ.

ᐱᓂᖅ ᑕᒻᒪᓅᑦᑯᑎᓂᑦᑕᐅᖅ ᑕᑯ'ᓗᒍ.

ᐱᓂᖅ: ᐱᕐᓱᖓ ᐅᓇ ᐊᔪᖅᐸᕆᖅᑐᕐᓱᒃ.

ᐊᓗᕈᑎ: ᐅᖃᐅ'ᔮᐅᒐᑉᑕ ᐊᑕᓂᖅᑯᑦ ᐱᕐᑯᔾᔨᓂᐊ'ᒪᓐᖑᖅ ᔫᓈᒍᑦ ᖃᐅᔾᔭᕐᕚᓐᓄᐊᕐᓂᒃ ᓇᑉᐸᐃᑦᕐᑯᔮᐅᓗᑕ, ᖃᐅᔾᔭᕐᓗᕆᑦ ᑕᓇᐅᖅ, ᑎᖕᒥᐊᑦ, ᐱᕈᖅᑐᓪᓗ.

ᐱᓂᖅ: ᐃᖕᕆᔻᕙᒃᓵᖅᔫᐅᕙᓵᕆᓇᖅᑯᒍᓪᓚ.

ᐊᓗᕈᑎ: ᐃᙳᒐᓗᐊᖅᑕᐅᖅ—ᓵᓚᔮᒃᓵᖃᕈᐃᓪᓚᕐᔮᓗᖏᖓᑉᑕᐅ'ᔭᕚᖅ.

ᐱᓂᖅ: ᐆᓇᐃᑉᐸᓪᓛᕐᔮᓗᒃᐸ'ᒪᑦ ᑕᔭᒻᒪ ᓄᓇ ᐆᒪᕚᓐᓄᐊᕐᑲᓚᐃᑦᑰᒻᒪᓇᒃᑐᖅ ᓵᓇᕐᑲᓚᐃᑦᑐᕐᓱᒃ.

ᐊᓗᕈᑎ: ᑕᑯᔫᒪᖅᑐᑎᑦ ᐅᒃᐱᒡᕙᐊᑦᑎᐊᓇᓗᖕᒥᒃ, ᐊᔪᐅᓇᓗᒃ ᐱᓂᖅ, ᑕᑯᔫᒪ'ᒥᕚᑎᑦ ᕐᑯᖅᓯᖅᑐᕐᕚᐊᕞᓗᖕᒥᒃᑕᐅᖅ.

ᐱᓂᖅ: ᓵᓇᒥᒃ?

ᐊᓗᕈᑎ: ᑕᓇᐅᕐᒥᐅᑕᑦ ᐊᖅᓴᐅᔮᑦ! ᑕᑯᕙᓐᓂᖅᑐᐸᓇᓗᐃᑦ—ᐊᙵᕆᕚᕞᓗᐃᑦ ᕐᑯᖅᓵᕝᔮᒃᓱᑎᒃ ᕿᓇᓇᒃᑐᐸᓇᓗᖕᒥᒃ ᕿᖓᕐᑲᖅᓱᑎᒃ.

ᐱᓂᖅ: ᕿᖓᖕᕆᑦ ᕿᓇᓇᒃᑐᑦ?

ᑐᔭᕐᓇᖅᑐᕐᑲᓕ'ᒪᕐ: (ᐊᕚ'ᖓᑦ) ᐊᕗᙵᕙᓐᓂᑲᓇᑦᑎ, ᐊᕗᙵᕙᓐᓂᑲᓇᑦᑎ.

ᐱᓵᒃᑐᑦ ᑲᒫᓗᓛᑦ ᐊᒥᔾᕙᖅᓱᑎᒃ ᑐᔭᕐᓇᖅᑐᑦ.

ᐊᓗᕈᑎ: ᐅᓇ ᓵᒍᑦ ᐃᓕᓂᐊᖅᑕᕙ?

ᐱᓂᖅ: ᐅᕗᖓᓚ.

ᐊᓗᕈᑎ ᔭᐃᒪᑎᐅᑉ ᓈᐸᕈᑖ ᑑᓇᓇᓵᐊᓕᖅᓱᒍ ᔫᑯᐃᕙᓵᐊᖅᓱᓂᐅᒃ.

ᐊᓗᕈᑎ: ᕿᕿᕚᓇᓗᕐᓱᒃ.

BEAN helps WICKERS smash hard into the ice with the flagstaff.

(*to the flagstaff*) Oh God . . . go in!

The flagstaff breaks through the ice of the breathing hole.

Grab it, GRAB IT . . .

WICKERS plunges his mitted hands into the frigid water and grabs for the sinking flagstaff. BEAN reaches out to help WICKERS, inadvertently letting go the folded flag, and it too falls into the hole.

BEAN: Bollocks, BOLLOCKS!

BEAN plunges his mitted hands in and manages to yank the flag out of the wet as WICKERS pulls up the flagstaff. BEAN tries to ring out the soaking-wet flag.

We're right pooched now.

Sir John FRANKLIN and Commander HOLLOWAY enter, both in full Royal Navy regalia, complete with gold epaulettes, followed by CARTER and CREW #1 and #2 carrying a trunk. FRANKLIN checks his pocket chronometer, something he does compulsively.

FRANKLIN: The magnetic deviation is reduced as we move away from the ship's iron.

HOLLOWAY: The deviation will likely increase with the influence of the aurora.

FRANKLIN: Make a note, Holloway.

HOLLOWAY spits into his ink bottle.

HOLLOWAY: Yes, sir.

FRANKLIN: Wickers and Bean—get that flagstaff up!

WICKERS: Yes, sir.

ᐱᓂᖅ: ᑑᕐᓗᒍ.

ᐊᓗᕈᑎ: ᑑᕐᑯᔭᔪᓇᓗᕐᔪᒃ ᐅᓇ ᖃᓇᕐᑲᑎᒐ.

ᐱᓂᖅ ᐊᓗᕈᑎᒥᒃ ᐃᑲᔦᖅᑐᓕᖅᔪᓂ ᔨᑯᐃᕋᔪᐊᖅᔪᒍ ᓇᐸᕈᑕᕐᒍᑦ.

ᐊᓗᕈᑎ: (ᐅᕐᑲᖅᔪᓂ ᓇᐸᕈᑕᕐᒍᑦ) ᐊᑕᐃ . . . ᐃᓗᐊᓄᙳᓇᑦ!

ᔪᓇᐅᖕᖏ ᐊᒡᓗᓘᓐᓂᖅ ᔨᑯᐃᖅᑎᑕᐃᑦ ᑖᒪᓇ.

ᐊᓗᕈᑎ: ᑎᒍᓗᒍ, ᑎᒍᑲᕈᒃ . . .

ᐊᓗᕈᑎ ᓇᐸᕈᑎ ᑎᒍᓇᔪᐊᖅᔪᓂᐅᒃ ᐆᓇᐃᑦᑐᓇᓗᖖᒍᑦ ᐃᒪᕐᒍᑦ ᑭᕕᓕᕐᒪᑦ. ᐱᓂᕐᓗ ᐃᑲᔦᕋᔪᐊᓕᕐᔪ ᖃᐃᒪᑎ ᑲᑕᐃᓪᓚᒃᔨᓐᓇᖅᑖ ᐊᒡᓗᒍᑦ ᑕᐅᖖᒍᓄᖕᒐ ᑭᕕᕐᓗᓂ.

ᐱᓂᖅ: ᔪᕐᑯᑕᐅᙵᑦᑐᑉᑲᓇᓇᔪᕐᔪᒃ!

ᐳᐊᓗᒃᔨᒪᕐᓗᓂ ᖃᐃᒪᑎ ᑎᒍᕐᓗᓂᐅᒃ ᐃᒪᕐᒥᑦ, ᐊᓗᕈᑎᓗ ᓇᐸᕈᑕᕐᒥᒃ ᑎᒍᕐᓗᓂ. ᐱᓂᕐᓗ ᔨᖕᖁᕋᔪᐊᖅᔪᓂᐅᒃ ᖃᐃᒪᑎ ᖅᑲᐅᔨᖅᑐᓇᓘᕐᒪᑦ.

ᐱᓂᖅ: ᐊᕐᓄᕌᖅᑯᑦ ᖅᑲᐅᔨᖅᑐᓇᓘᕐᒪᑕᓗ.

ᐃᔨᖅᑑᒃ ᐊᕐᑯᑎᕐᔪᐊᕐᓗ ᖃᖖᔭᓇᓗᒡᓗ, ᕿᓂᖅᑎᑦ ᖅᑲᑉᓗᓈᑦ ᐊᕐᓅᖅᔨᒪᑦᑎᐊᖅᔪᑎᒃ ᐃᓂᕐᑯᓇᖅᖃᐅᑎᕐᑲᖅᔪᑎᒃ ᕿᑉᓕᖅᑐᓂᒃ, ᑖᒪᓇ ᑲᑑᑦ ᒪᓕᒃᔪᓂ, ᐊᔫᓪᓗ ᐊᒡᕙᖅᔪᑎᒃ ᕿᔪᑯᑎᒥᒃ. ᐊᕐᑯᑎᕐᔪᐊᖅ ᑖᒪᓇ ᑲᐅᑦᑐᐊᕐᒥᐊᕐᒥᓂᒃ ᐅᑉᓗᖅᔨᐅᑎᓐᓄᐊᕐᒥᓂᒃ ᑕᑯᖃᖅᐸᒃᔪᓂ, ᑕᑯᖃᕋᔪᐊᖖᒋᓐᓇᖅᐸᕐᒪᑦ.

ᐊᕐᑯᑎᕐᔪᐊᖅ: ᖃᕕᖖᒐ ᐅᓇ ᐊᑐᑦᑎᐊᕈᐃᖅᐸᓕᓪᓕᐊᓕᕐᒪᑦ ᐅᒥᐊᕐᔪᐊᑉᑕ ᖃᕕᐊᓂᑦ ᐅᖖᒐᔨᒃᔨᖕᓪᓕᐊᕐᓗᑕ.

ᖃᖖᔭᓇᓗᒃ: ᐊᑐᑦᑎᐊᕈᐃᖅᐹᓪᓕᕐᓂᐊᖅᑰᖅᑐᕐᓕ ᐊᖅᓵᕐᓂᕐᓄᑦ.

ᐊᕐᑯᑎᕐᔪᐊᖅ: ᑎᑎᕋᓕᕈᒃ, ᖃᔪᔭᓇᓗᒃ.

ᖃᖖᔭᓇᓗᒃ ᐅᓇᐊᖅᔪᓂ ᑎᑎᕋᐅᑎᐊᑕ ᐃᒪᕐᑲᕐᕕᐊᓄᑦ.

ᖃᖖᔭᓇᓗᒃ: ᐄ, ᐊᑕᓂᕐᔪᐊᖅ.

BEAN: Yes, sir.

FRANKLIN: By God it's cold—note sixteen degrees below zero.

HOLLOWAY: Yes, sir—enough to freeze my ink.

FRANKLIN checks his chronometer.

FRANKLIN: Gentlemen, let us bow our heads . . . "O Lord, we pray that this evening may be holy, good, and peaceful."

ALL: "WE PRAY TO YOU, O LORD."

FRANKLIN: "That your angels may lead us in the paths of peace and goodwill."

ALL: "WE PRAY TO YOU, O LORD."

FRANKLIN: "That we may be pardoned and forgiven for our sins and offences."

ALL: "WE PRAY TO YOU, O LORD."

FRANKLIN: "Let us commend ourselves to the mercy and in your spirit we hope to safely continue our voyage, for You made the mountains and the oceans and You are here with us tonight in this raw, relentless land because You created each sliver of ice, each snowflake . . . "

HOLLOWAY notices ANGU'ŘUAQ and UKUANNUAQ in the distance. She is standing up on her hind legs and ANGU'ŘUAQ is down on all fours, clutching something between his jaws.

" . . . You come down to us through the icebergs and shine through the waves. You blanket us with snow, push us with wind, and—"

HOLLOWAY: Sir—possible enemy sighting to your south-southwest. Man and a big dog—very big dog, sir—very big man, sir.

ᐊᕐᑯᑎᕐᔪᐊᖅ: ᐊᓗᕈᑎᓗ ᐱᓂᕐᓗ—ᖃᐃᒪᑎᓇᓗᒃ ᓇᑉᐸᕆᐊᖅᔪᐅᒃ!

ᐊᓗᕈᑎ: ᐄ, ᐊᑕᓂᕐᔪᐊᖅ.

ᐱᓂᖅ: ᐄ, ᐊᑕᓂᕐᔪᐊᖅ.

ᐊᕐᑯᑎᕐᔪᐊᖅ: ᐆᓇᐃᑦᑐᓇᓗᕐᓗᒃ—ᑎᑎᕋᕈᒃ 16-ᓂᒨᖅ ᐊᑖᓃᑎᕆᔪᖅ.

ᖃᖑᔭᓇᓗᒃ: ᐄ, ᐊᑕᓂᕐᔪᐊᖅ—ᑎᑎᕋᐅᑎᒪ ᐃᒪᕐᓗᐊ ᕿᕿᔪᓇᓗᕐᓗᒃᑕᐅᖅ.

ᐊᕐᑯᑎᕐᔪᐊᖅ ᑲᐅᑦᑐᐊᕐᒥᐊᕐᒥᓄᑦ ᑕᑯᖃᖅᓗᓂ.

ᐊᕐᑯᑎᕐᔪᐊᖅ: ᐊᖑᑕᐅᖅᑲᑎᑦᑲ, ᓂᐊᕐᑯᕗᑦ ᔪᑭᖓᑎᓚᕗᑦ . . . "ᐆ ᐊᑕᓂᖅ, ᑐᒃᔪᐊᖅᑯᒍᑦ ᐅᓐᓄᒃ ᒪᓐᓇ ᓂᖅᔪᖅᑕᐅᓂᖅᑯ'ᓗᑕ, ᐅᓐᓄᖅᑲᑦᑎᐊᕐᓗᑕ, ᖃᐃᒪᓂᖅᑲᕐᓗᑕᓗ."

ᑕᒪᕐᒥᒃ: "ᑐᒃᔪᐊᖅᑯᒍᑦ ᐃᓕ'ᓄᑦ, ᐆ ᐊᑕᓂᖅ."

ᐊᕐᑯᑎᕐᔪᐊᖅ: "ᐊᐃᖏᑦᑕᓇᔭᕐᓂᑦ ᐃᑲᔪᖅᑕᐅᖅᑯ'ᓗᑕ ᐊᑉᕐᑯᑎᒃᓴᑉᑎ'ᓄᑦ ᖃᐃᒪᓂᖅᑲᕐᓗᑕ ᐱᑦᑎᐊᕐᓗᑕᓗ."

ᑕᒪᕐᒥᒃ: "ᑐᒃᔪᐊᖅᑯᒍᑦ ᐃᓕ'ᓄᑦ, ᐆ ᐊᑕᓂᖅ."

ᐊᕐᑯᑎᕐᔪᐊᖅ: "ᐃᔪᒪᕆᔭᖕᓇᐃᕐᕕᐅ'ᔭᐅᓗᑕ ᐱᑦᑎᐊᖖᕆᓐᓂᑉᑎ'ᓄᑦ ᓈᒻᒪᖖᕆᑦᑐᑕᓂᑉᑎ'ᓄᑦᓗ."

ᑕᒪᕐᒥᒃ: "ᑐᒃᔪᐊᖅᑯᒍᑦ ᐃᓕ'ᓄᑦ, ᐆ ᐊᑕᓂᖅ."

ᐊᕐᑯᑎᕐᔪᐊᖅ: "ᒍᓇᓄᔮᐅᓗᑕ ᐊᓂᕐᓃᑦ ᐱ'ᓗᒍ ᐃᓗᐊᖅᑐᑦᑯᑦ ᐃᖕᕆᔮᕋᓗᑕ ᖃᓇᒐᕕᕆᑦ ᑭᖖᒐᑦ, ᑕᓄᐅᕐᓗ, ᑕᖃᒪᓃᖅᑲᑎᕆᔭᑉᑎᒍᑦᓗ ᐅᓐᓄᒃ ᑕᖃᑉᔪᒪᓂ ᓄᓇᒥ ᔪᑕᖅᑲᖖᕆᑦᑐᒥᒃ ᐅᓇᕐᒥᓇᐃᑦᑐᒥ, ᑭᔪᐊᓂᒃ ᐅᑯᐊ ᖃᓇᕚᒃᑲᕕᕆᑦ ᕐᑯᒃᔪᐃᑦ ᕐᑯᑊᓗᐊᕐᓂᓪᓗ ᔪᑯᑦ ᐊᐳᓪᓗ . . . "

ᖃᖑᔭᓇᓗᒃ ᐅᔾᔭᕆᔮᕆᒃ ᐊᖑ'ᔪᐊᕐᓗ ᐅᑯᐊᓐᓄᐊᕐᓗ ᐅᖓᔪᕗᔮᑐᒥ. ᐅᑯᐊᓐᓄᐊᖅ ᓇᖏᖅᑐᖅ ᐊᖑ'ᔪᐊᕐᓗ ᐊᕐᑯᕗᖁ'ᓗᓂ, ᔫᓇᒥᒃᑭᐊᖅ ᑭᖖᒥᐊᖅᑐᖅ.

ᐊᕐᑯᑎᕐᔪᐊᖅ: *(ᑲᔪᔪ'ᓗᓂ ᑕᑯᖖᕆ'ᓇᒥ)* " . . . ᕐᑲᐃᕙᒃᑲᕕᑦ ᐱᕐᑲᓗᔭᒃᑯᑦ, ᒪᓪᓕᖅᑐᒃᑯᓪᓗ ᕐᑲᐅᒪᓃᑦ ᑕᑯᒃᓴᐅ'ᒪᑦ, ᐊᐳ'ᒧᑦ ᐅᓕᒃᔪᒪᕙᑉᑎᒍᑦ, ᐊᓄᓇᒃᑯᓪᓗ ᐃᓅᔪᒃᑯᑦ ᔪᒐ'ᒧᐊᖅᑎᑉᐸᑉᑎᒍᓪᓗ—"

FRANKLIN: Likely *Esquimaux.* We'll call them over. *(calls, mangling the language) Oo-noo-coot [Good evening]?*

The creatures do not move.

Sometimes they come just to stare at us—Ross told me of the time a woman Esquimaux walked sixty miles with her newborn baby just to catch a glimpse of him. *(calls) Qey-gwid [Come here]?*

HOLLOWAY: Should we approach them?

UKUANNUAQ growls.

FRANKLIN: *(realizing)* No, God in Heaven, no—don't move!

The bears walk towards the men.

(whispers) No sudden movements, men—freeze—FREEZE.

The men freeze. UKUANNUAQ sniffs the men.

HOLLOWAY: *(whispers)* Sir, we can shoot—

FRANKLIN: Quiet! Make mental observations—height, width, characteristics.

ANGU'ŘUAQ stops in front of BEAN and offers him the dead seal.

BEAN: . . . What's that?

FRANKLIN: *Pusa hispida*, I think.

BEAN: Sorry, sir—what?

WICKERS: Ringed seal.

HOLLOWAY: Probably his dinner.

BEAN: . . . Why is he looking at me?

ᕵᖑᕷᓇᓗᒃ: ᐊᑕᓂᕐᕶᐊᖅ—ᐅᓇᑕᖅᑕᐅᕸᓐᖑᒐᑉᑕ ᐅᓇᑕᖅᑎᓂᑦ. ᐊᖑᑦᓗ ᖅᑭ'ᒥᐸᓇᓗᒡᓗ—ᖅᑭ'ᒥᔅᔪᒃ ᐊᖏᕶᕌᓗᒃ. ᐊᑕᓂᕐᕶᐊᖅ—ᐃᓄᒃᐸᒡᕶᔅᔪᒃ, ᐊᑕᓂᕐᕶᐊᖅ.

ᐊᖁᑎᕐᕶᐊᖅ: ᐃᔅᑭ'ᒎ'ᔭᕶᑦ? ᖃᐃᑦᖁᓚᕗᑦ. (ᑐᖅᔪᓚ'ᓗᓂ) ᐆᓅᑰᑦ (ᐃᓅᒃᑐᑦ ᐅᖅᑲᑎᐊᖅᐸᙱ'ᒪᑦ ᑯᑕᒃᑐᖅ).

ᑖᕙᑉᑯᐊᒃ ᕶᙱᑦᒎᒃ ᐃᖑᙱᒻᒪᕆᒃᑐᒃ.

ᐊᖁᑎᕐᕶᐊᖅ: (ᐃᓅᓇᕶᒥ'ᒪᒥᑦ ᕶᓕ) ᐃᓛ'ᓂ ᐅᑯᐊᑦ ᖃᐃᑦᖃᑦᑕᖅᑐᑦ ᐃᕷᒋᒃᑭᖅᑐᖅᑮᓘ'ᓗᑎᒃ ᐅᕙᐸᑎ'ᓂᒃ—ᐅᒥᐊᕐᕶᖅᑐᖅᑎ ᐅᖅᑲᖅᓴᒃᕸᒪᓕᖅᑐᖅ ᐊᖅᓇᕉᖅ ᓄᑕᖅᑖᓕᕵᖅᔪᓂ ᐅᖓᕸᒃᑐᒧᑦ ᐱᕶᒃᕸᒪᓕᖅᑐᖅ ᖃᑉᓗᓅᓂᒃ ᑕᑯᓇᕶᐊᕈᒪ'ᓗᓂ. (ᑐᖅᔪᓚ'ᓗᓂ) ᑮᒍᐃᓐ (ᖃᐃᒍᐃᑦ-ᓚᓇᕶᐊᖅᔪᓂ).

ᕵᖑᕷᓇᓗᒃ: ᐅᕐᓂᒡᓚᕗᑦ?

ᐅᑯᐊᓐᓄᐊᖅ ᓇᖅᕸᖕᒐᔮᖅᔪᓂ ᖃᑎᒡᕙᓛᓕᖅᑐᖅ.

ᐊᖁᑎᕐᕶᐊᖅ: (ᑐᑭᕸᓕᑕᐃᓐᓇᓕᖅᔪᓂ ᓇᓅ'ᒪᓂᒃ) ᐄᖅᑭ ᓄᓇᓕᐅᑎ, ᐄᖅᑭ, ᐃᖅᕸᓇᖅᑐᓇᓘᒃ ᐃᖑᑦᑕᐃᓕᑐᕸ.

ᓇᓅᒃ ᐃᓄᖕᓄᙳᒐᐅᕙᓪᓕᐊᕶᒃ.

ᐊᖁᑎᕐᕶᐊᖅ: (ᐃᕸᑉᕶᒃᔪᓂ) ᐃᖑᑳᓪᓚᒃᑕᐃᓕᑐᕸ—ᓄᑦᖃᖕᒐᓗᕸ—ᓄᑦᖃᖕᒐᑦᑎᐊᒻᒪᕆᒡᓗᕸ.

ᓄᑦᖃᖕᒐᑦᑎᐊᒻᒪᕆᒃᔪᑎᒃ. ᐅᑯᐊᓐᓄᐊᑉ ᓇᐃᒪᓕᖅᐸᐃᑦ.

ᕵᖑᕷᓇᓗᒃ: (ᐃᕸᑉᕶᒃᔪᓂ) ᐊᑕᓂᕐᕶᐊᖅ, ᕸᖅᑯᑎᓚᕗᒃ—

ᐊᖁᑎᕐᕶᐊᖅ: ᓂᐸᐃᓗᕸ! ᐃᑦᖃᖅᕵ'ᔮᕗᕸᓗ—ᑕᒃᑎᒋᓂᖕᒋᒃ, ᕸᓕᒃᑎᒋᓂᖕᒋᒃ, ᖃᓄᓇᑦᑑᓃ'ᓂᒃ ᑎᑎᕋ'ᔭᕙᖅᓯᐅᒃ.

ᐊᖑ'ᕶᐊᖅ ᐱᓂᖑᒍᙵᒐᐅᕶᖅ ᑐᓂ'ᓗᓂᐅᒃ ᓇᑦᑎᖅᑕᕆᔮᖃᓗᐊᓂ.

ᐱᓂᖅ: . . . ᐅᓇ ᕶᓇ?

ᐊᖁᑎᕐᕶᐊᖅ: ᓇᓘᔮᕈᖕᓇᖅᑐᖅ ᕶᓇᓇᓗᑭᐊᖅ.

ᐱᓂᖅ: ᕶᓇᒎᖅ?

HOLLOWAY: I suppose he thinks you're the commander of this expedition.

CARTER: He's not familiar with the ranks of the Royal Navy.

BEAN: Do I . . . do I take it, sir?

FRANKLIN: Not if I were you—he's liable to bite off your arm.

HOLLOWAY: Let's shoot him, sir.

FRANKLIN: Everyone stay still—he'll likely give up and leave or eat it himself. Note the behaviour, Holloway.

WICKERS: Why would he want to give us a seal, sir?

FRANKLIN: Perhaps it's an offering of sorts.

HOLLOWAY: *(to the bear)* Over here, boy, over here.

FRANKLIN: *(to HOLLOWAY)* He's not a dog.

CARTER: Might be a trap, sir.

HOLLOWAY: A trap—how so?

CARTER: To get a person positioned between the two of them.

FRANKLIN: Where's the other bear?

WICKERS turns around.

WICKERS: Around behind us.

WICKERS is right. UKUANNUAQ is watching the proceedings from behind.

BEAN: Bloody hell—sorry, sir.

FRANKLIN: Easy, Bean—no sudden moves.

ᐊᓗᕈᑎ: ᓇᑦᑎᖅ.

ᓴᖑᐳᓇᓗᒃ: ᓇ'ᒥᓂᖅ ᓂᖅᑲᐅᑎᒃᓵ.

ᐱᓂᖅ: . . . ᔭ'ᒪᓪᓕ ᐃᐳᒋᕚᖕᖓ?

ᓴᖑᐳᓇᓗᒃ: ᐅᕚᑉᑎ'ᓂᒃ ᐊᑕᓂᖅᔪᐊᖄᓘᓇᔭᒋᓐᓂ'ᒪᑎᐅ'ᓯᔪᖅ.

ᑲᑑᑦ: ᑐᑭᓯᙱᑦᑎ'ᓇᒥᐅ'ᓯᔪᖅ ᐊᑕᓂᓇᕗᐅᔪᓂᒃ ᓴᓇᐳᑐᐃᓐᓇᐅᔪᓂᒡᓗ.

ᐱᓂᖅ: ᖃᓄᖅᓕᐅᖅᑯᔭ'ᒪ, ᓂᖅᑭ ᑎᒍᓚᒎ?

ᐊᖅᑯᑎᖅᔭᐊᖅ: ᐄᖅᑭ—ᑕᓖᑦ ᑮᓂᐊᕚᒃᐹ ᐊᔪᕚᒻᒪᓇᒡᓗᓂᐅᒃ.

ᓴᖑᐳᓇᓗᒃ: ᔪᖅᑯᖅᑎᓚᕗᑦ ᑐᖅᑯᓴᖅᑐᒍ.

ᐊᖅᑯᑎᖅᔭᐊᖅ: ᓄᑦᖅᑲᖓᑦᑎᐊᖅᑐᔪ—ᓴᐱᓕᖅᓂᐊᖅᑐᖅ, ᐊᐅᓪᓚᖅᑐᓂ, ᐃᖕᒥᓂᓘᓐᓃᑦ ᓂᓇᓗᓂᐅᒃ ᓂᖅᑭ. ᓴᖑᐳᓇᓗᒃ, ᖃᓄᖅᓕᐅᖅᓂᖓᓂᒃ ᑎᑎᕋᖅᑐᑦ.

ᐊᓗᕈᑎ: ᔭ'ᒪᓪᓕᑭᐊᖅ ᑐᓂᓇᔭᐊᖅᐹᑎᒍᑦ ᓇᑦᑎᖅᒥᒃ?

ᐊᖅᑯᑎᖅᔭᐊᖅ: ᓇᑯᕈᔪᖅᑑᑎᒋᓐᓂ'ᒪᒍᓘᓐᓃᑦ.

ᓴᖑᐳᓇᓗᒃ: *(ᓇᓄᖅᒍᑦ)* ᐊᑕᐃ ᖃᐃᓗᑎᑦ, ᑕᓴᒧᖕᖓ. *(ᖃ'ᒪᖅᑐᖅᓗᓂ)*

ᐊᖅᑯᑎᖅᔭᐊᖅ: *(ᓴᖑᐳᓇᓗᖕᒧᑦ)* ᖅᑭ'ᒥᐅᙱᑦᑐᖅ ᐅᓇ.

ᑲᑑᑦ: ᓴᒡᓗᓇᔭᐊᖅᑑ'ᓯᔪᖅᔫᓐᓃᑦ.

ᓴᖑᐳᓇᓗᒃ: ᓴᒡᓗᓇᔭᐊᖅᑐᖅᓕ ᔭ'ᒪᑦᑕᐅᖅ, ᖃᓄᖅᓕ?

ᑲᑑᑦ: ᐊᑯᓂᖕᒋ'ᓄᙵᐅᓂᐊᖃᑉᑕ.

ᐊᖅᑯᑎᖅᔭᐊᖅ: ᐊᐃᑉᐹ ᓇᐅᒃ?

ᐊᓗᕈᑎ ᑐᓄ'ᓗᓂ.

ᐊᓗᕈᑎ: ᑭᖑᓂᑉᑎ'ᓂ.

ᐊᓗᕈᑎ ᔭᓕᔪᖅ. ᐅᑯᐊᓐᓄᐊᑉ ᖁᓐᖕᒋᐊ'ᒪᒋᑦ ᑭᖑᓂᖕᒋᑦᑎᒍᑦ.

ANGU'ŘUAQ pushes the seal at BEAN.

Perhaps you best take the seal and be done with it.

BEAN: Just . . . just take it from its mouth, sir?

FRANKLIN: Yes, though I'd take it rather gently if I were you.

BEAN: . . . What do I do with the seal?

HOLLOWAY: Eat it.

CARTER: I'd have to be terrible hungry to eat that stinking thing.

FRANKLIN: As you well know, in '19 I charted 340 miles of coastline east of the Coppermine River and lost ten men to starvation on the journey back to Hudson's Bay—a seal like this might have saved a life or two or three.

BEAN leans closer.

BEAN: . . . The bear's skin is black there under his fur.

FRANKLIN leans closer.

FRANKLIN: . . . By golly it is, black as pitch. Make a note.

HOLLOWAY: Be careful . . .

A huge display of vivid colours erupts across the sky. The men strain to not look up and risk distracting the bears.

UKUANNUAQ growls, scaring everyone.

Let's shoot them both, sir.

FRANKLIN: Shut up and pray they do not hurt us. Bean!

BEAN: Yes, sir.

ᐱᓂᖅ: ᖄ ᔮᖁᑕᐅᖕᖏᑦᑐᑉᑲᓇᓇᓗᕐᔪᒃ—ᖅᑮᔭᓇᓗᒃ.

ᐊᖁᑎᖅᔦᐊᖅ: ᐱᓂᖅ—ᐃᖑᑦᑕᐃᓕᑦᑎᐊᓇᑦ.

ᐊᖑ'ᔦᐊᑉ ᓇᑦᑎᖅ ᐱᓂᕐᒍᙳᐅᑎᓐᓇᔮᐊᓕᖅᔪᓂᐅᒃ.

ᐊᖁᑎᖅᔦᐊᖅ: ᐊᑕᐃᕐᔫᓐᓃᖅ ᐱᑐᐃᓐᓇᕐᓗᒍ ᐃᔪᕐᓇᓂᐊ'ᒪᑦ.

ᐱᓂᖅ: ᐄᖅ . . . ᐃᖅ, ᔫᒡᒍᐊ'ᓂᑦ ᑎᒍᔫᓐᓇᕐᓗᒎ?.

ᐊᖁᑎᖅᔦᐊᖅ: ᐄ, ᔮᒃᑲᐃᓇᔮᐊᕐᓗᑎᐅᒐᓗᐊᖅ.

ᐱᓂᖅ: . . . ᔮᓇᔮᐊᕐᓗᒍᓗ ᓇᑦᑎᖅ ᐅᓇ.

ᔭᖑᔫᓇᓗᒃ: ᓂᓇᓗᒍ.

ᑲᑑᑦ: ᑳᒡᓗᐊᕹᒃᑯᒪ ᑭᔫᐊᓂᒃ ᓂᓇᓂᐊᕋᓗᐊᖅᑕᕋ ᐅᓇ ᒪᒪᐃᑦᑐᓇᓗᒃ.

ᐊᖁᑎᖅᔦᐊᖅ: ᖃᐅᔫᒪᔦᑎᑦ, 1919-ᖑᑎ'ᓗᒍ ᖁᕐᓗᖅᑐᒥ ᓄᓇᓐᖑᐊᓕᐅᖅᑎᑦᑎᒐᓗᐊᕋᒪ ᔭᓇᔫᕚᑦ ᖁᓕᑦ ᑐᖁ'ᓗᑎᒃ ᑳᖕᓂᕐᒧᑦ ᐅᑎᓕᖅᑎ'ᓗᑕ—ᓇᑦᑎᖅᑐᖅᑲᑦᑕᕋᓗᐊᕈᑎᒃ ᑐᖁᓇᔾᙲᑦᑲᓗᐊ'ᒪᑕᓕ.

ᐱᓂᐅᑉ ᖃᒡᓕᒋᐊᕋᓐᓂᖅᔪᒍ ᓇᓄᖅ.

ᐱᓂᖅ: . . . ᒪᒥᖕᒐ ᖅᑭᕐᓇᓇᒃᑐᐸᓇᓗᒃ ᒥᑦᖁᐊᑕ ᐊᑖᓃᑦᑐᖅ.

ᐊᖁᑎᖅᔦᐊᑉ ᖃᒡᓕᒋᐊᕋᓐᓂᖅᔪᓂᐅᒃ ᓇᓄᖅ.

ᐊᖁᑎᖅᔦᐊᖅ: . . . ᔮᓇᐅᕝᕙ ᖅᑭᕐᓂᖅᑐᐸᓇᓗᕐᔪᒃ. ᐊᑕᐃ ᑎᑎᕋ'ᒥᓗᒍ ᖃᓄᓇᓐᓂᐊ.

ᔭᖑᔫᓇᓗᒃ: ᐅᖦᔫᓇᑦᑎᐊᖅᔫᐅᒃ . . .

ᖅᑭᓚᒃ ᐊᖅᓵᓚᖅᑭᔦᐊᓗᒃ ᑕᖅᓵᑦ ᐃᓂᕐᑯᓇᖅᑐᕌᓘᓕ'ᒪᑕ ᐃᑯᒫ'ᓗᑎᒃ ᓂᕹᖕᒐᔦᔾᔭᖅᔫᖅᑐᓪᓗ ᑕᑦᐹᓂ. ᖅᑭᓂᖅᑎᑦ ᑕᑯᔭᖅᑕᐃᓕᓇᔮᐊᖅᑐᑦ ᑕᑦᐸᐅᖕᒐ ᖅᑭᓚᖕᒍᑦ ᖁ'ᒍᑦ, ᓇᓅᒃ ᖃᓄᕐᓕᐅᕐᓂᐊᓇᐊᒃᓵᑕ ᓇᓗᒐᒥᒋᒃ ᐅᖦᔫᓇᕙᓪᓗᓕᖅᒡᑖᒋᒃ.

ᐅᑯᐊᓐᓄᐊᖅ ᖃᑎᒡᕙᔈᓕᖅᑐᖅ, ᐊᖑᑎᑦ ᐃᖅᔫᓕᖅᑐᐃᓐᓇᐅ'ᓗᑎᒃ.

FRANKLIN: Take the damn seal.

BEAN: But, sir, you said—

FRANKLIN: That's an order.

BEAN: Yes, sir.

But BEAN doesn't move.

WICKERS: He's looking at you funny—take it before he changes his mind.

With trepidation, BEAN reaches out and gently takes the dead seal from the bear.

FRANKLIN: Good man.

ANGU'ŘUAQ does not move and continues to stare intently at BEAN.

BEAN: Oh God—what does it want now?

FRANKLIN: It's waiting for something . . . what? Make mental observations, Holloway.

WICKERS: . . . Maybe pretend you're eating the seal.

BEAN: . . . Eating it?

WICKERS: Pretending to.

FRANKLIN: Yes, of course, as a courtesy.

CARTER: . . . mmm . . .

Some of the men giggle.

FRANKLIN: Quiet! Go on, Bean.

HOLLOWAY: I say we shoot them both now, sir.

ᔭᖑᔮᓇᓗᒃ: ᔪᖅᑯᖅᑎᓚᕗᑦ ᑕᒪᑦᑮᒃ.

ᐊᕐᑯᑎᕐᔪᐊᖅ: ᐅᖅᑲᒪᔪᐃᓇᑦᑎ ᑐᒃᔨᐊᕐᑐᔨᑐ ᐱᕗᐅᕐᑯᖏ'ᑐᑕ. ᐱᓂᖅ!

ᐱᓂᖅ: ᐄ, ᐊᑕᓂᕐᔪᐊᖅ.

ᐊᕐᑯᑎᕐᔪᐊᖅ: ᑎᒍᓪᓚᕝᕗᕐᑐᒍ ᓇᑦᑎᕝᕈᒃ ᐃᕗᒡᑐᑎᑦ.

ᐱᓂᖅ: ᐱᑦᕐᑯᖏᑕᕋᑐᐊ'ᒪᓕ—

ᐊᕐᑯᑎᕐᔪᐊᖅ: ᐱᑦᕐᑯᔮᓕᖅᐸᒋᑦ.

ᐱᓂᖅ: ᐄ, ᐊᑕᓂᕐᔪᐊᖅ.

ᑭᔨᐊᓂᒃ ᐱᓂᖅ ᐃᖑᖏᒻᒪᓇᒃᑐᖅ.

ᐊᓗᕈᑎ: ᑕᒃᑰᓇᓗᒃ ᑕᐅᑐᒡᓗᐊᓕᖅᐹᑎᑦ, ᐊᑕᐃ ᑎᒍᓪᓚᕝᕗᕈᒃ ᓄᑦᕐᑲᖓᓂᐊ'ᓂᒃ.

ᐃᖅᔪᔨᐸᓚᓘ'ᑐᓂ, ᐱᓂᖅ ᑖᒪᓇ ᐃᕗᒃᕈᓂ ᔨᒃᑲᐃᑦᑐᑉᔨᓐᓄᐊᕉ'ᓂ ᑎᑐᒋᐊᖅᐹ ᓂᕐᑭ ᓇᓄᕐᒥᑦ.

ᐊᕐᑯᑎᕐᔪᐊᖅ: ᐊᖑᑎᑦᑎᐊᕙᒃ.

ᑭᔨᐊᓂᒃ ᐊᖑ'ᔪᐊᖅ ᐃᖑᖏᒻᒪᓇᒃᑐᖅ. ᑕᐅᑐᒡᓗᐊᖅᔨᓐᓇᖅᑯᑐ ᔪᓕ ᐱᓂᖅ ᑖᒪᓇ.

ᐱᓂᖅ: ᖅᑲᓄᓇᓗᒃ—ᔪᓇᒥᒃ ᐱᔪᒪᓕᖅᐸᑭᐊᖅ?

ᐊᕐᑯᑎᕐᔪᐊᖅ: ᐅᑕᖅᑭᔪᖅ ᔪᓇᒥᒃᑭᐊᖅ . . . ᔪᓇᓕ? ᐅᕝᔮᓇᕗ'ᓂᒃ ᑎᑎᕋᖅᑕᒃᓴᓕᐅᓕᓇᑦ, ᔭᖑᔮᓇᓗᒃ.

ᐊᓗᕈᑎ: . . . ᓂᓇᖑᐊᕋᔪᐊᕐᑐᒍᓕᑭᐊᖅ ᓇᑦᑎᕝᕈᒃ.

ᐱᓂᖅ: . . . ᓂᓇᑐᒎ?

ᐊᓗᕈᑎ: ᓂᓇᖑᐊᖅᔪᓐᓇᕐᑐᒍ.

ᐊᕐᑯᑎᕐᔪᐊᖅ: ᐊᔪᐅ, ᕐᑯᓴᒋᔭᐅᓂᖓ ᐃᒃᐱᒋᓂᐊ'ᒪᒍ.

BEAN touches the dead seal to his mouth . . . then lays it down on the ground.

ANGU'ŘUAQ continues to stare intently at him.

BEAN: (*to ANGU'ŘUAQ*) . . . please don't stare at me like . . . what do you want?

Not sure what else to do, BEAN reaches out his shaking hand and pats the bear on the head like he would a dog.

You're a good bear . . . good bear.

Satisfied, ANGU'ŘUAQ turns and walks away. UKUANNUAQ follows and they head out in the opposite direction from which they came.

FRANKLIN: Well done, Bean, my boy!

WICKERS: Way to go, Bean!

HOLLOWAY: Grand—thought he'd bite your hand off, but grand.

FRANKLIN bows his head and prays.

FRANKLIN: Dear Lord, thank You for sparing us . . . Lighten our darkness, and in Your great mercy defend us from all the dangers of this night. Amen. Say "amen," boys.

ALL: AMEN.

FRANKLIN checks his chronometer.

FRANKLIN: Make a note—two polar bears sighted at twenty-three forty-four—one rather large, the other smaller—no harm done—left behind a dead *Pusa hispida*. Note the particulars of their exchange with Bean.

HOLLOWAY: We could have taken them down, sir.

ᑳᑦ: . . . ᒻᒻᒻ . . .

ᐃᓚᐃᑦ ᑎᑉᔪᒍᔮᓕᕐᓗᑎᒃ.

ᐊᕐᑯᑎᕐᔮᐊᖅ: ᓂᐸᐃᕐᓗᑲᓐᑎᓕ! ᐊᑕᐃ, ᐱᓂᖅ.

ᓴᓐᖑᔮᓇᓗᒃ: ᐊᑕᓂᕐᔮᐊᖅ, ᐊᑕᐃ ᑕᒪᒃᑮᒃ ᔪᖅᑯᖅᑎᑦᑯᒃ.

ᐱᓂᖅ ᐅᓇ ᓇᑦᑎᖅ ᐊᒃᑐᖅᓗᓂᐅᒃ ᑲᓂᕐᒥᓄᑦ,
ᓂᓇᖖᒍᐊᖅᓗᓂᐅᒃ . . . ᒪᓂᕋᕐᒍᑦ ᐃᓚᑉᔪᐊᖅᓗᓂᐅᒃ.

ᐊᖑ'ᔮᐊᑉ ᑕᐅᑐᖕᓗᐊᕋᓐᓂᓕᖅᐹ ᐱᓂᖅ.

ᐱᓂᖅ: (ᐊᖑ'ᔮᐊᕐᒧᑦ) . . . ᑕᐅᑐᖕᓗᐊᙱᓗᙵᓕ . . . ᔮᓇᒥᒃ ᐱᔨᒪᕙᑦ?

ᖃᓄᕐᓕᐅᓇᐊᒃᓵᖅ ᓇᓗᑦᑎᐊᕋᒥ, ᐱᓂᖅ ᑖᒻᓇ ᐃᓭᒃᓗᓂ
ᓴᔪᒃᑐᐸᓇᓘᖓᓗᐊᖅᓗᓂ ᐊᒃᑐᖅᐹ ᓇᓄᖅ ᓂᐊᕐᑯᖖᒍᑦ, ᔮᕐᓗ
ᕿ'ᒥᕐᒥᒃ ᓴᐃᒻᒪᖅᓵᐃᔮᑐᑦ.

ᐱᓂᖅ: ᓇᓄᑦᑎᐊᓪᓗᔮᑎᑦ . . . ᓇᓄᑦᑎᐊᓪᓗᒃ.

ᓈᒻᒪᒋᔫᕋᒥᒋᑦ ᐊᖑ'ᔮᐊᖅ ᑖᒻᓇ ᑐᓄ'ᓗᓂ ᐊᔪᐊᓄᙳᐅᓕᖅᑐᖅ.
ᐅᑯᐊᓐᓄᐊᑉ ᒪᓕᒃᓗᓂᐅᒃ, ᖃᐃᕝᕕᒋᔮᐃᑕ ᐊᑉᑯᑎᒋᔮᐃᑕ
ᐊᔪᐊᒍᓪᓗᓚᖅ ᑐᕌᓕᖅᓗᑎᒃ ᐊᐅᓪᓚᖅᑑᒃ.

ᐊᕐᑯᑎᕐᔮᐊᖅ: ᐃᓗᐊᖅᔪᕗᖅ, ᐱᓂᖅ, ᕐᑯᓯᓇᖅᑯᑎᑦ!

ᐊᓗᕈᑎ: ᐊᔨᒍᐃᑦᑐᓇᓗᒃ ᐱᓂᖅ!

ᓴᓐᖑᔮᓇᓗᒃ: ᐱᑦᑕᐅᔮᖅ—ᑭᔪᐊᓂᒃ ᐊᔾᒍᐃᖅᑕᐅᓂᐊᕋᔮᕆᒍᓗᐊᖅᐸᕆᑦ,
ᐃᓗᐊᖅᔪᕗᖅ.

ᐊᕐᑯᑎᕐᔮᐊᖅ ᔪᑭᖕᒎ'ᓗᓂ ᑐᒃᔪᐊᖅᑐᖅ.

ᐊᕐᑯᑎᕐᔮᐊᖅ: ᐊᑕᓂᖅ ᓄᓇᓕᐅᖅᑎ, ᕐᑯᓯᕆᕚᑉᑎᕆᑦ ᑐᕐᑯᑕᐅᙱ'ᓇᑉᑕ
. . . ᖃᐅᒻᒪᖅᑎᓕᕈᒃ ᑖᖅᑐᖅ, ᓂᑲᒍᔮᖕᓂᖃᕋᕙᑦ ᓴᐳ'ᒥᑎᒍᑦ ᑖᖅᑐᒥ
ᐅᓗᓇᐊᓇᖅᑐᒥ ᑕᓴᒪᓂ ᐅᓐᓄᖕᒥ. ᐊᐃᒥ. ᐊᑕᐃ ᐊᐃᒦ-ᓚᒍᐃᑦᑎ ᑕᒪᑉᔪ.

ᑕᒪᐃᑕ: ᐊᐃᒦ.

FRANKLIN: They're magnificent creatures—the Esquimaux call them *Na-nook*.

HOLLOWAY looks up.

HOLLOWAY: The heavens are exploding . . .

All the men stare up at the dazzling green and yellow curtains of light. BEAN and WICKERS are particularly in awe.

FRANKLIN looks up using his telescope.

FRANKLIN: Yes, but their coruscations are concealing stars of the finest magnitude. Holloway, I'd like to make celestial observations once we finish the official bits, for I always have two masters to serve—God and Science.

HOLLOWAY: Yes, sir.

FRANKLIN: Hoist the flag, Bean, before you fall over backwards.

BEAN: Yes, sir. Bit stiff, sir—sorry.

WICKERS fastens the flag to the rope then raises it. Taking FRANKLIN's lead, they all salute the flag.

FRANKLIN checks his chronometer.

FRANKLIN: Note—flag's up at twenty-three fifty.

HOLLOWAY: Yes, sir.

FRANKLIN: Gentlemen, look west . . . imagine the delicate temple rooftops of Cathay shimmering, rising up, beckoning us onwards. Imagination is all we have to cling to, and so we must imagine our dreams into existence.

HOLLOWAY: Remember Ross and the shimmering he saw in the distance?

FRANKLIN: Yes, a Fata Morgana—a mirage one can sometimes see in the distance, in the narrow band right above the horizon.

ᐊᖁᑎᖅᔪᐊᖅ ᑲᐅᑦᑐᐊᕐᒥᐊᓂ ᑕᑯᓴᓕᖅᓱᓂᐅᒃ.

ᐊᖁᑎᖅᔪᐊᖅ: ᑎᑎᕋᖅᑕᐅᓕ—ᓇᓅᒃ ᒪᔅᖀᒃ ᑕᑯᔭᐅᓚᒥᒃ ᐅᑉᑐᖅᔨᐅᑦ ᐅᕗᖕᒐᖅᑎ'ᑐᒍ 23:44—ᐊᐃᑉᐹ ᐊᖏᑦᕿᔭᖅ ᐊᐃᑉᐹᒍ ᒥᑭᑦᕿᔭᖅ—ᐋ'ᓂᖅᑕᐅᔪᖅᑲᙱᖅᑐᖅ—ᕿᒪᐃ'ᑐᑎᒃ ᓂᕿᒥᒃ ᓇᑦᑎᕐᒥᒃ. ᑎᑎᕋᖅᔨᐅᒃ ᖃᓄᕐᓕᐅᓇᐊᒃᓯᐃᑕᒍ ᐱᓂᕐᒧᑦ.

ᓴᖑᔭᓇᓗᒃ: ᑐᖁᓴᕈᖕᓇᖅᑕᕋᓗᐊᖅᑯᓪᓕ.

ᐊᖁᑎᖅᔪᐊᖅ: ᐱᑦᑕᐅᔪᕌᒍᐃᑦ ᐅᑯᐊ ᐆᒪᔪᑦ—ᐃᓅᒃᑐᑦ ᑕᐃᔭᐅᔪᑦ ᓇᓅᕐᓂᒃ.

ᓴᖑᔭᓇᓗᒃ ᖁ'ᒧᑦ ᑕᑯᓴᓕᖅᓱᓂ.

ᓴᖑᔭᓇᓗᒃ: ᕿᓚᒃ ᔨᓚᓗ ᐃᓂᖁᓇᖅᑐᕌᓗᒃ ᐊᖅᓯᓚᕿᔪᐊᓗᒃ . . .

ᐊᖑᑎᑦ ᖁ'ᒧᑦ ᐋᖅᑐᖕᖓᓕᖅᑐᑦ ᑕᐅᑐᒃᓱᑎᒃ ᐃᑯᒪᓂᒃ ᑐᖑᖅᑐᓂᒃ ᖁᖅᓱᖅᑐᓂᓪᓗ. ᐱᓂᖅᓗ ᐊᓗᕈᑎᓗ ᑕᑯᖃᓐᓂᕈᔪᖕᓂᖅᓯᐃᑑ'ᑐᑎᒃ.

ᐊᖁᑎᖅᔪᐊᖅ ᖁ'ᒧᑦ ᑕᑯᓴᓕᖅᓱᓂ ᕿᓐᖑᑎᒥᒍᑦ.

ᐊᖁᑎᖅᔪᐊᖅ: ᐄᖑᒐᓗᐊᖅ ᑕᓕᖕᖓᑎᑦᑎᔪᐊᓘ'ᒪᑕᓕ ᐅᑉᑐᓇᐊᑦᑎᐊᕙᓇᓗᖕᓂᒃ. ᓴᖑᔭᓇᓗᒃ, ᑕᓴᑉᑯᐊᑦ ᑭᔨᐊᓂᒃ ᓴᓇᑖᕈᑉᑕ ᑎᑎᕋᖅᑕᐅᖁᔭᕋᓗᐊᑦᑲᓕ—ᒪᔅᖀ'ᒪᓂᒃ ᑲᒪᒋᔭᒃᓯᖅᑲᕋᒪ—ᒎᑎᑉ ᐲ'ᓂᒃ ᖃᐅᔭᓴᖅᑎᓪᓗ ᐲ'ᓂᒃ.

ᓴᖑᔭᓇᓗᒃ: ᐊᔨᐅ, ᐊᑕᓂᖅᔪᐊᖅ.

ᐊᖁᑎᖅᔪᐊᖅ: ᐊᑕᐃ ᐱᓂᖅ, ᓇᑉᐸᓇᐊᕈᑦ ᓴᐃᒪᑎ, ᓂᕕᖅᔨᓐᖑᔅᕿᓕᕋᕕᑦ.

ᐱᓂᖅ: ᐄ, ᖄ, ᐊᑕᓂᖅᔪᐊᖅ, ᑎᒥᒐ ᔭᑲᖕᒐᕝᔭᒃᑐᔅᓲ'ᒪᑦ.

ᐊᓗᕈᑎ ᑖᑉᓱᒥᖕᒐ ᓴᐃᒪᑎᒥᒃ ᕿᓚᒃᓱᓂ ᓇᐸᕈᑎᒧᑦ ᖁ'ᒧᓇᐊᖅᑎᑦᐹ. ᑕᒪᐃᑕ ᒪᓕᒃᓱᔅᔪᒃ ᐊᖁᑎᖅᔪᐊᖅ ᓂᖅᓱᕈᑎᒃᓯᓕᐅᖅᑐᑦ ᐊᔅᑲ'ᒥᒍᑦ.

ᐊᖁᑎᖅᔪᐊᖅ ᑲᐅᑦᑐᐊᕐᒥᐊᓂ ᑕᑯᓴᖅᑳᖅᓱᓂᐅᒃ.

ᐊᖁᑎᖅᔪᐊᖅ: ᑎᑎᕋᖅᑕᐅᓕ—ᓴᐃᒪᑎ ᓇᑉᐸᖅᑎᑕᐅ'ᒪᑦ 23:50-ᒥ.

ᓴᖑᔭᓇᓗᒃ: ᐄ, ᐊᑕᓂᖅᔪᐊᖅ.

HOLLOWAY: Sir John Ross saw the passage in front of him, but also thought he saw mountains blocking the way, so he turned around and returned to England—to his eternal shame—

FRANKLIN: No need to go on about it—break open a bottle, Carter.

CARTER opens the case of spirits and passes bottles around—the first to FRANKLIN.

HOLLOWAY: *(to FRANKLIN)* Shouldn't we wait for Crozier and his crew, sir?

FRANKLIN: They'll be along soon—we'll save them a mouthful or two.

CARTER: Cheers, sir.

FRANKLIN: Cheers . . . *(takes a drink, then to HOLLOWAY)* I'd like my tea now, and have someone set up the daguerreotype apparatus.

FRANKLIN snaps his finger at CREW #1 and #2.

HOLLOWAY: Bring his tea, and you—the daguerreotype.

CREW #1 & #2: Yes, sir.

CREW #1 and #2 exit, racing back to the ship. The men pass the bottle. The bell on the Erebus *begins to ring. It rings on the half-hour.*

FRANKLIN: Midnight . . . *(checks his chronometer)* and holding steady. What's keeping Morshead?

HOLLOWAY: He's checking the draught, sir. Flag's up now, shall we head back to the ship and wait for the *Terror*?

FRANKLIN: It'll be along shortly. Keep the men warm with a hornpipe.

HOLLOWAY pulls out a pennywhistle from his jacket.

HOLLOWAY: Yes, sir. *(calls)* Men, a hornpipe is in order—spread out. Give yourselves room.

ᐊᕐᑯᑎᕐᕋᐊᖅ: ᐊᑕᐃ ᓴᓇᔨᑦᑲᑦ, ᐅᐊᖕᓇᕐᒧᑦ ᑕᑯᓗᔪ . . . ᑕᐅᑐᖅᑰᙳᐊᕐᓗᒍ ᐃᒡᓗᕐᕋᐊᑦᑎᐊᕙᒃ ᕿᐸᓕᖅᑐᒥᒃ ᖁᓛᓕᒃ, ᔪᕗᓂᕐᒧᑦ ᑕᐃᑯᖕᒐ ᑎᑭᑦᑎᐊᕈᒥᓇᖅᑐᖅ. ᐃᓯᒪᙳᐊᕐᓂᖅ ᑕᓴᒻᒪ ᐊᑑᑎᒃᓴᑐᐊᓇᒐᑉᑎᒍᑦ, ᐃᓯᒪᙳᐊᕐᓗᑕ ᓴᑦᕿᓇᓯᐊᓇᐊᕐᑲᖅᑐᒍᑦ ᐃᓱᐊᓇᔭᑉᑎ'ᓂᒃ.

ᓴᖑᔨᓇᓗᒃ: ᑕᐃᒻᓇᕕᓂᕐᓕ ᕿᓂᖅᑎᕕᓂᖅ ᑕᑯᖅᑰᕐᑲᑦᑕᖅᔪᒪᓕᕐᓗᐊ'ᒪᑦ ᕿᐸᓕᖅᑰᖅᑐᒥᒃ ᒪᓕᖕᓇᓯᐊᓕᖅᓱᓂᐅᒃ.

ᐊᕐᑯᑎᕐᕋᐊᖅ: ᐋ, ᖃᐅᔨᒪᔭᐅᕋᑦ ᑕᓴᐸᑯᐊᑦ ᐅᖕᒐᔪᒃᑐᒥ ᑕᐅᑐᖕᓇᓕᖅᑲᑦᑕᖅᑐᑦ ᕿᐸᓕᖅᑰᖅᓱᑎᒃ. ᑖᕙᓂ ᓄᓇᐅᑉ ᑭᒡᓕᐊᓂ.

ᓴᖑᔨᓇᓗᒃ: ᑕᐃᒻᓇᓕ ᐊᑉᕐᑯᑎᒃᓴᖅᔪᐅᖅᑐᕕᓂᖅ, ᓇᓂᔪᒐᓗᐊᖅᓱᓂᒎᖅ, ᐅᐃᕝᕙᖅᑕᒃᓴᖅᑲᕋᓗᐊ'ᒪᑦ ᑭᓐᖓᕐᓂᒃ, ᑕᒻᒪᕐᓂᖅᓱᓂ ᐅᑎᑐᐃᓐᓇᕋᓗᐊ'ᒪᑦ ᑯᐃᓐ ᓄᓈ'ᓄᑦ—ᐅᒡᒍᐊᕐᓗᐊᖅᑐᒃᓴᐅᓐᓂᖅᑯᖅ ᑕᐃᒪ—

ᐊᕐᑯᑎᕐᕋᐊᖅ: ᐅᖃᐅᔪᒃᓴᐅᙱᑦᑐᖅ ᑕᓴᒻᒪ, ᐊᑕᐃ ᐊᖕᒪᖅᔪᒍᐃᑦ ᔪᑯᓕᐊᕐᒦᑦᑐᒥᒃ ᐃᒥᕐᓗᖕᒥᒃ, ᑲᑑᑦ.

> ᑲᑑᑦ ᐊᖕᒪᐃ'ᒪᑦ ᕿᕋᕐᑯᑎᓐᓄᐊᒥᒃ ᔪᑯᓕᐊᖃᖅᑐᒥᒃ ᐃᒥᕐᓗᓕᖕᓂᒃ, ᑐᓂᐅᖅᑲᓕᖅᓱᓂᒋᑦ ᐊᖑᑎᓄᑦ—ᐊᕐᑯᑎᕐᕋᐊᖅ ᔪᕗᑦᓕᐅᑎ'ᓗᓂᐅᒃ.

ᓴᖑᔨᓇᓗᒃ: (ᐊᕐᑯᑎᕐᕋᐊᕐᒧᑦ) ᐅᑕᖅᑭᔮᖅᑲᙱᑦᑲᓗᐊᖅᐱᑎᒍᑦ ᐃᑉᑯᐊᑦ ᑳᐱᑕᐃᔭ ᐊᐃᑉᐹ ᓴᓇᔨᖕᒋᓪᓗ?

ᐊᕐᑯᑎᕐᕋᐊᖅ: ᖃᐃᓯᖕᒐᕐᓂᐊᖅᑐᔅᓱᐃᑦ ᐃᑉᑯᐊᑦ ᖃᐃᓐᓇᓇᓐᓂᐊᔅᓱᐃᑦ—ᒥᑭᕋᒥᒃ ᓂᐅᖅᑕᒃᓴᐃ'ᓂᒃ ᔭᓂᕙᐃᓂᐊᖅᑯᒍᑦ.

ᑲᑑᑦ: ᖁᕕᐊᓱᖕᓂᕐᒧᑦ, ᐊᑕᓂᕐᕋᐊᖅ.

ᐊᕐᑯᑎᕐᕋᐊᖅ: ᖁᕕᐊᓱᖕᓂᕐᒧᑦ . . . (ᓂᐅᖅᔪᔅᓵᖅᓱᓂ, ᓴᖑᔨᓇᓗᖕᒧᑦ ᐅᖃᖅᓱᓂ) ᑏᑐᕈᒪᓕᖅᑯᖕᒐᓕ ᐊ'ᔨᓕᐅᑎᑦᑎᐊᕙᓗᒃᑕᐅᖅ ᐃᓪᓗᐊᖅᓴᖅᑕᐅᕐᑯᓕᕐᓕ ᐊᑐᕐᓂᐊᕋᑉᑎᒍᑦ.

> ᐊᕐᑯᑎᕐᕋᐊᖅ ᑯᑉᓗᓂ ᕿᑎᖅᓯᓂᓗ ᔪᖅᑯᖅᑕᖅᑎᑦᑎ'ᓗᓂᒋᒃ ᖃᐃᑦᖁᔮᐃᑦ ᐃᑉᑯᐊᒃ ᓴᓇᔨᒃ ᒪᔅᓯᒃ.

ᓴᖑᔨᓇᓗᒃ: ᑏᑐᖅᑎᒍᒃ, ᐃᔅᕙᓪᓗ—ᐊ'ᔨᓕᐅᑎᑦᑎᐊᕙᕐᑯᑎᒃᑯᑦ ᐊᐃᒃᓯᑲᔪᐅᒃ.

ᓴᓇᕐᕙᓗᒃᑎᒃ ᒪᔅᓯᒃ: ᐋ ᐊᑕᓂᕐᕋᐊᖅ.

The men spread out in a square formation with space between them, then HOLLOWAY *starts to play a hornpipe on his pennywhistle and the men begin their movements, slipping and sliding on the ice, sometimes laughing.*

They are well into the dance when HOLLOWAY *notices two figures appear in the distance.*

HOLLOWAY *abruptly stops playing.*

Bears again, sir! To the northwest! This time let's shoot them dead.

FRANKLIN: Perhaps they want their seal back.

The men draw back, rifles at the ready.

What the devil are they pulling?

CARTER: Looks like a sledge, sir.

HOLLOWAY: By God—those aren't bears.

FRANKLIN *checks his chronometer.*

FRANKLIN: Note, Holloway: sighted two Esquimaux at triple aught three. I shall invite them to join our celebration.

HOLLOWAY *raises his gun.*

HOLLOWAY: Be careful, sir—they're armed.

FRANKLIN: It's the courteous thing to do . . . I'll wish them good evening. *(calls) Oo-noo-coot. Oo-noo-coot. [Good evening?]*

Two Inuit hunters, AĂGIAQ *and* PANINGAJAK, *enter with harpoons.* PANINGAJAK *is frightened and hangs back.* AĂGIAQ *is curious.*

PANINGAJAK: *(to* AĂGIAQ*) Nukaq [younger brother]* . . . don't get any closer to them—no.

ᖨᖅᑭᐃᖅᑯᑎᒃ ᖃᓇᖬᒃ ᑐᐊᕕᐅᖅᑯᑎᒃ ᐅᑎᖅᑐᒃ ᐅᒥᐊᕐᖪᐊᕐᒧᑦ.
ᐊᖕᒍᑎᑦ ᖬᑯᓚᐊᖅ ᓂᐅᖅᖬᕝᕕᒋ’ᓗᕐᖪᒃ ᐊᒥᖅᑳᖅᑐᑦ.
ᐅᒥᐊᕐᖪᐊᑉ ᖬᕙᓂᕿᑖ ᖬᕙᓂᓚᖅᑯᓂ ᖬᕙᓂᖅᐸ’ᒪᑦ ᐃᑳᕐᓂᐅᑉ
ᓇᑉᐹ’ᓄᖖᒐᖄᖕᒐᑦ ᐅᑉᐳᖅᖬᐅᑦ.

ᐊᕐᑯᑎᕐᖪᐊᖅ: ᕐᑯᑖᓄᖖᒐᖅᑐᖅ ᐅᓐᓄᒃᑯᑦ . . . (ᑲᐅᑦᑐᐊᕐᒥᐊᓂ
ᑕᑯᖃᖅᑯᓂᐅᒃ) . . . ᓇᓚᐅᑦᑎᐊᖅᑐᓐᓄᐊᖅ. ᓇᐅᒡᓚ ᓇᐅᑦᑎᖅᑐᖅᑎᕐᒍᒃ.

ᓴᖕᒍᖬᓇᓗᒃ: ᐃᒪᐅᑉ ᐃᑎᓂᐊᓂᒃ ᓇᓗᓇᐃᖅᖬᓇᖨᐊᖅᑐᖅ. ᖨᐃᒪᑎ
ᓇᑉᐸᖕᒐᓚᖅᑐᖅ, ᐅᒥᐊᕐᖪᐊᕐᒧᑦ ᐅᑎᖅᑐᒃᓴᐅᓚᖅᐱᑕ ᐅᑕᖅᑭᓗᒍ
ᐅᒥᐊᕐᖪᐊᑉ ᐊᐃᑉᐹ?

ᐊᕐᑯᑎᕐᖪᐊᖅ: ᖅᑲᐃᖨᖖᒐᕐᓂᐊᕐᓗᒃ. ᐆᓇᐃᖨᓚᕐᑯᓇᒋᑦ
ᐅᕕᓐᖏᐊᕋᓐᓄᐊᑦᑯᑦ ᑐᖃᕐᓈᕐᕕᒋᓚᑦᑭᑦ.

ᓴᖕᒍᖬᓇᓗᒃ ᐅᕕᓐᖏᐊᕐᑯᑎᓂ ᐊᒧ’ᓗᓂᐅᒃ ᑲᐅᑦᑐᐊᕐᒥᓂᑦ ᐊᑎᓖᓂᑦ.

ᓴᖕᒍᖬᓇᓗᒃ: ᐋ, ᐊᑕᐃ. (ᑐᖅᑯᓛᓗᓂ) ᑕᒪᑉᖬ, ᑐᖃᕐᓇᖅᑐᓚᐅᕐᓂᐊᕋᒪ—
ᑲᓂᒌᒃᐸᓪᓛᖖᒋᓪᓗᖬ ᐊᑕᐃ ᑕᖃᒧᖕᒐ.

ᐃᓪᓗᐊᖅᖬᑦᑎᐊᖅᑯᑎᒃ ᐅᖕᒐᖬᒌᕝᕙᒃᑯᑎᒃ ᓴᖕᒍᖬᓇᓗᒃ ᑕᐃᒪ
ᒧᒥᕆᑎᒃᓴᐃ’ᓂᒃ ᐊᑐᓚᖅᑯᓂ ᐅᕕᓐᖏᐊᕆᑎᒥᓄᑦ. ᐊᖕᒍᑎᑦ
ᒧᒥᓚᖅᑯᑎᒃ ᕐᑯᐊᕗᕐᑭ’ᑯᑎᒃ ᖬᑯᒦ’ᓇᒥᒃ, ᐃᒡᓚᓚᖅᐸᒃᑯᑎᒃ.

ᒧᒥᖅᑐᐊᑑᓚᖅᑎ’ᑯᒋᑦ ᓴᖕᒍᖬᓇᓗᒃ ᐅᖬᓇᖬᖅᑲᓚ’ᒪᑦ ᐅᖕᒐᖬᒃᑐᒥ
ᖨᓇᓂᒃᑭᐊᖅ ᒪᕝᑭᒃ ᑕᐅᑐᖕᓇᔮᓚᖅᑐᒃ.

ᓴᖕᒍᖬᓇᓗᒃ ᓄᑦᖅᑲᑳᓪᓚᒃᑯᓂ.

ᓴᖕᒍᖬᓇᓗᒃ: ᓇᓅᒃ ᖨᓚ ᑕᐃᒪ, ᐊᑕᓂᕐᖪᐊᖅ! ᐅᐊᖕᓈᓂ ᑕᐃᑲ!

ᖬᖅᑯᖅᑎ’ᕝᖬᕝᕗᑦ ᑐᕐᑯᖃᕐᑐᕆᒃ ᐅᑯᐊᕐᖪᒃ, ᑐᕐᑯᖃᕐᓚᕝᕗᒃ ᑕᐃᒪ.

ᐊᕐᑯᑎᕐᖪᐊᖅ: ᓇᑦᑎᕐᒥ’ᓂᒃ ᐱᖬᒪᖬ’ᔭᖬᒃ.

ᐊᖕᒍᑎᑦ ᖬᖅᑯᖅᑎᕝᖬᑎᒥ’ᓂᒃ ᐃᓗᐊᖅᖬᕆᐊᖅᑯᑎᒃ.

ᐊᕐᑯᑎᕐᖪᐊᖅ: ᖨᓇᓇᓗᖕᒥᒃ ᐅᓂᐊᖅᑐᕐᓘᒃ ᐅᑯᐊᒃ?

ᑲᑑᑦ: ᖅᑲᒧᑎᐅᕝᑰᖅᑐᕐᓗᖕᒥᒃ.

AĞGIAQ: *(to PANINGAJAK)* He's trying to say you should have a good time in the evening. Why, I wonder?

PANINGAJAK: *(to AĞGIAQ)* They're not real humans—they speak very strangely.

FRANKLIN takes a step towards the hunters.

FRANKLIN: Come join our celebration.

HOLLOWAY: Careful, sir, one cannot ascertain their intentions.

FRANKLIN stops.

PANINGAJAK: *(to AĞGIAQ)* . . . Maybe they are malicious spirits trying to hurt us.

AĞGIAQ stops.

AĞGIAQ: *(to FRANKLIN) Tuunngauvihiluunniit inuuvihiluunniit? [Are you spirits or are you human beings?]*

FRANKLIN: *(to HOLLOWAY)* I wish I could make out their gibberish—where's Morshead?

HOLLOWAY: He'll be along momentarily, sir.

AĞGIAQ: *(to PANINGAJAK)* Maybe they are some form of humans . . . touch one—go ahead, touch one.

PANINGAJAK: *(to AĞGIAQ)* No, nukaq—you touch.

FRANKLIN: *(to AĞGIAQ)* Welcome.

AĞGIAQ: *(to PANINGAJAK)* Maybe they're Ross's men from my father's stories.

PANINGAJAK: *(to AĞGIAQ)* I think they are malicious spirits.

HOLLOWAY looks at the hunters' polar-bear fur pants.

ᓴᖑᔮᓇᓗᒃ: ᐃᑉᑯᐊᕐᓘᒃ—ᓇᓅᖕᒥᒻᒪᓂᒃᑑᒡᓕ.

ᐊᖁᑎᕐᔪᐊᖅ ᑲᐅᑦᑐᐊᕐᒥᐊᓂ ᑕᑯᓴᖅᓗᒍ.

ᐊᖁᑎᕐᔪᐊᖅ: ᑎᑎᕋᓕᖃᒃ ᓴᖑᔮᓇᓗᒃ: ᑕᑯᒐᑉᑕ ᐃᓄᒻᒪᓂᖓᓂᒃ ᒫᖃᖕᓂᒃ ᐱᖓᔪᓄᖕᖓᐅᓂᐊᕙᖅᑎ’ᓗᒍ ᐅᑉᓗᖅᔨᐅᑦ. ᖃᐃᑦᕋᓂᐊᓕᖅᐸᑦᑲᒃ ᑐᓐᖓᔪᒃᑎᓗᒋᒃ.

ᓴᖑᔮᓇᓗᒃ ᔨᖅᑯᖅᑎᕝᔪᑎᓂ ᐊᑐᕋᔪᐊᓕᖅᓗᓂᐅᒃ.

ᓴᖑᔮᓇᓗᒃ: ᐅᕝᔮᖅᑐᑦᑎᐊᓂᑦ—ᐃᑉᑯᐊᒃ ᔨᖅᑯᑎᕝᔪᑎᖅᑲᖅᑐᒃᓵᐅᕚᒃ.

ᐊᖁᑎᕐᔪᐊᖅ: ᑐᓐᖓᓇᕋᔪᐊᓂᐊᖅᑲᕋᑉᑕᓕ . . . (ᑐᖅᓗᓚ’ᓗᓂ) ᖃᐃᒍᐃᑦᑎᒃ ᖁᕕᐊᔪᖅᑲᑎᒥᑎᒍᑦ. ᐆ-ᓅ-ᖂᑦ (ᐅᖃᑦᑎᐊᖕᒥᒻᒪᑦ ᐃᓄᒃᑐᑦ ᑯᑕᒡᓗᐊᖅᑐᖅ) ᐆ-ᓅ-ᖂᑦ.

ᐃᔨᖅᑑᒃ ᐃᓅᒃ ᐊᖑᑏᒃ ᐊᖑᓇᔪᐊᖅᑎᒃ, ᐊᕝᕆᐊᕐᓗ ᐸᓂᖓᔭᒡᓗ, ᐅᓈᓕᕝᕙᖅᓗᑎᒃ. ᐸᓂᖓᔭᒃ ᐃᖅᔨᖓᒥ ᖃᒡᓕᑦᑕᐃᔪᖅ. ᐊᕝᕆᐊᕐᓕ ᑲᒪᔪᖕᒥᑦᑐᖅ ᖃᐅᔮᒪᓇᔪᐊᖅᑐᖅ.

ᐸᓂᖓᔭᒃ: (ᐊᕝᕆᐊᕐᒍᑦ) ᓄᑲᖅ . . . ᖃᒡᓕᕆᐊᕋᓐᓂᖕᒥᓗᕆᑦ—ᐋᕿ.

ᐊᕝᕆᐊᖅ: (ᐸᓂᖓᔭᖕᒍᑦ) ᐅᖃᕋᔪᐊᖅᑐᖅ ᐅᓐᓄᒃᐸᓐᖔ ᖁᕕᐊᔪ’ᕝᕗᒍᒃ—ᔪ’ᒪᒃᓕᑭᐊᖅ?

ᐸᓂᖓᔭᒃ: (ᐊᕝᕆᐊᕐᒍᑦ) ᐃᓅᖕᒥᒻᒪᓂᒃᑐᑦ—ᐅᖃᐅᔮᑦ ᑐᑭᔨᓇᐃᑦᑐᕌᓗᕐᓗᐃᑦ.

ᐊᖁᑎᕐᔪᐊᖅ ᐊᑉᓗᕋᓇᐊᖅᓗᓂ ᐊᖑᓇᔪᐊᖅᑎᓄᑦ.

ᐊᖁᑎᕐᔪᐊᖅ: ᖁᕕᐊᔪᖅᑲᑎᒥᑎᒍᑦ ᐊᑕᐃ.

ᓴᖑᔮᓇᓗᒃ: ᐅᕝᔮᖅᑐᑦᑎᐊᓂᑦ, ᖃᐅᔮᒪᖕᒥ’ᓇᕙᑦ ᖃᓄᓂᑦᑑᔭᖕᒥ’ᓂᒃ ᐅᑯᐊᒃ.

ᐊᖁᑎᕐᔪᐊᖅ ᓄᑦᖃᖅᑐᖅ.

ᐸᓂᖓᔭᒃ: (ᐊᕝᕆᐊᕐᒍᑦ) . . . ᑑᓐᖓᓇᓘ’ᔭᔪᑦ ᐅᑯᐊᑦ ᐱᓂᕐᓗᒃᑕᐅᓇᔪᐊᖅᑐᒃᓴᕌᓘᔪᒍᑦ.

ᐊᕝᕆᐊᖅ ᓄᑦᖃᖅᑐᖅ.

HOLLOWAY: Those are funny looking trousers—pantaloons.

CARTER: Maybe the French got here ahead of us.

There's laughter from the crew, then ARĞIAQ laughs, but PANINGAJAK does not.

PANINGAJAK: *(to ARĞIAQ)* They're scary . . . let's go back.

ARĞIAQ: *(to PANINGAJAK) Angajuk [older brother]*, stay here. They have no harpoons.

WICKERS: *(to HOLLOWAY)* Should we offer them something to eat?

HOLLOWAY: Just keep your eyes on their harpoons, Wickers.

ARĞIAQ takes a few tentative steps towards FRANKLIN.

ARĞIAQ: *Tuunngauvihi . . . ? [Are you spirits . . . ?]*

FRANKLIN: *(to ARĞIAQ)* Welcome. *Oo-noo-coot.*

ARĞIAQ stops in front of FRANKLIN, then slowly extends his hand and touches FRANKLIN—and everyone jumps at the same time. HOLLOWAY points his rifle, steps in front of FRANKLIN, fires a warning shot into the air, and the two hunters either cover their ears and run, or duck, or scream or all three.

HOLLOWAY: STEP BACK—

FRANKLIN: RELIEVE THEM OF THEIR WEAPONS—

HOLLOWAY: SHOOT THEM—

CARTER tries to get their harpoons but misses. ARĞIAQ and PANINGAJAK run, then stop.

ARĞIAQ: *(to PANINGAJAK)* THEY'RE NOT SPIRITS APPARENTLY—

PANINGAJAK: *(to ARĞIAQ)* KEEP RUNNING—

ᐊᔾᒋᐊᖅ: (ᐊᕐᑯᑎᕐᔪᐊᕐᒧᑦ) ᑑᓐᖕᒐᐅᕙᔪᓘᓐᓃᑦ ᐃᓅᕙᔪᓘᓐᓃᑦ?

ᐊᕐᑯᑎᕐᔪᐊᖅ: (ᖃᖕᒍᔮᓇᓗᖕᒧᑦ) ᑐᑭᔪᔪᒪᖕᒃᐸᑦᑲ ᐅᑯᐊᒃ
ᑐᑭᔪᓇᐃᑦᑐᓇᓗᐃᑦ. ᓇᐅᒡᓕ ᓇᐅᑦᑎᖅᑐᖅᑎ?

ᖃᖕᒍᔮᓇᓗᒃ: ᖅᑲᐃᔭᖕᒐᕐᓂᐊᕐᔫᒐᓗᐊᖅ ᐃᒻᓇ.

ᐊᔾᒋᐊᖅ: (ᐸᓂᖕᒐᔭᖕᒧᑦ) ᐃᓄᓇᓘ’ᔭᔪᒃ . . .ᐊᑕᐃ ᐊᒃᑐᔪᒡᒍᐃᑦ, ᐊᑕᐃ.

ᐸᓂᖕᒐᔭᒃ: (ᐊᔾᒋᐊᕐᒧᑦ) ᐄᕐᑭ ᓄᑲᕐᔪᒃ—ᐃᔾᕙᕈᓪᓗ.

ᐊᕐᑯᑎᕐᔪᐊᖅ: (ᐊᔾᒋᐊᕐᒧᑦ) ᑐᓐᖕᒐᔮᒡᓗᔪᒃ.

ᐊᔾᒋᐊᖅ: (ᐸᓂᖕᒐᔭᖕᒧᑦ) ᐊᑖᑕᒪ ᐅᓂᑉᑲᐅᔪᓇᔪᒪᔮᐃᑦ ᐅᑯᐊᑦ, ᔮᓇᐅᕈᕈ.

ᐸᓂᖕᒐᔭᒃ: (ᐊᔾᒋᐊᕐᒧᑦ) ᑑᓐᖕᒐᓇᓘ’ᔭᔪᑦ ᐱᑦᑕᐅᙱᑦᑐᒃᓯᕚᓗᐃᑦ.

ᖃᖕᒍᔮᓇᓗᒃ ᐱ’ᓗᒋᒃ ᐊᖕᒍᓇᔮᐊᖅᑎᑉ ᖅᑲᕐᓕᕙᖕᒋᒃ.

ᖃᖕᒍᔮᓇᓗᒃ: ᐅᑯᐊᒃ ᖅᑲᕐᓕᕚᒃ ᑕᑯᕐᓐᓂᙱᑦᑐᕖᓘᒃ ᐊᖕᒋᔪᓇᓗᕐᔫᒃ.

ᑲᑑᑦ: ᐅᐃᕚᓂᑦ ᑎᑭᑕᐅᖅᑳᖅᑑ’ᔭᔪᑦ ᐅᐃᕚᔪᐅᑎᖅᐸᓗᒃᑐᕐᔫ’ᒪᓂᒃ
ᖅᑲᕐᓕᕙᕐᔫᒃ ᐅᑯᐊᒃ.

ᖅᑲᑉᓗᓈᑦ ᐃᒡᓚᓕᖅᔪᑎᒃ, ᐊᔾᒋᐊᖅ ᐃᒡᓚᖅᑕᐅᓕᖅᔪᓂ
ᐸᓂᖕᒐᔭᒡᓕ ᐃᒡᓚᙱᑦᑐᐱᑑ’ᓗᓂ.

ᐸᓂᖕᒐᔭᒃ: (ᐊᔾᒋᐊᕐᒧᑦ) ᐃᖅᔪᓇᖅᑐᑦ . . .ᐅᑎᓕᕐᓗᒃ.

ᐊᔾᒋᐊᖅ: (ᐸᓂᖕᒐᔭᖕᒧᑦ) ᐊᖕᒐᔪᒃ, ᖃᒪᓃᔪᐅᓇᑦ. ᐅᓈᖅᑲᙱᑦᑐᕐᔪᐃᑦ.

ᐊᓗᕈᑎ: (ᖃᖕᒍᔮᓇᓗᖕᒧᑦ) ᓂᓇᑦᑯᔮᓕᕐᓚᑯᑦ?

ᖃᖕᒍᔮᓇᓗᒃ: ᐅᓈᒋᒃ ᑕᐅᑐᐃᓐᓇᑦᑎᐊᕋᔮᐊᕐᓗᒋᒃ ᖅᑲᐅᔮᖃᕐᓗᒋᒃ
ᑭᔪᐊᓂᒃ, ᐊᓗᕈᑎ.

ᐊᔾᒋᐊᖅ ᐱᔮᒃᐸᓪᓕᐊᔪᖅ ᐊᑕᓂᕐᔪᐊᖕᒋ’ᓄᑦ.

ᐊᔾᒋᐊᖅ: ᑑᓐᖕᒐᐅᕙᔫ . . .

HOLLOWAY: SHOOT THEM—

CARTER: DON'T FUCKING MOVE!

AȒGIAQ: *(to PANINGAJAK)* I TOUCHED ONE!

FRANKLIN: *(to CARTER)* THERE WILL BE NO SWEARING!

PANINGAJAK: *(to AȒGIAQ)* Don't touch!

CARTER: Sorry, sir.

FRANKLIN: This isn't Waterloo—leave them their weapons. If they attack, we'll shoot, but for now be friendly.

AȒGIAQ: *(to PANINGAJAK, re: FRANKLIN's epaulettes)* Look at those shiny things.

PANINGAJAK: *(to AȒGIAQ)* They are dangerous—don't go any closer—

FRANKLIN: *(calls to AȒGIAQ) Oo-noo-coot.*

AȒGIAQ takes a reluctant step towards FRANKLIN.

AȒGIAQ: *(to PANINGAJAK)* They are puny humans, just like us.

FRANKLIN takes another step towards AȒGIAQ.

FRANKLIN: We are a peaceful people.

PANINGAJAK: *(to AȒGIAQ)* These people are not our people—they are very pale and they stink.

HOLLOWAY: Are you sure they're friendly?

FRANKLIN: We'll find out if you don't blow them to kingdom come first.

HOLLOWAY: If they don't kill us with their stink first, sir.

ᐊᕐᑯᑎᕐᕿᐊᖅ: (ᐊᕝᒋᐊᕐᒧᑦ) ᑐᓐᖓᓯᑦᓗᔮᒃ. ᐆ-ᓅ-ᑰᑦ (ᐅᕐᑲᑦᑎᐊᙱᓯᒪᒍ ᐅᓐᓄᕐᑲᑦᑎᐊᑯᔮᓗᓂᕆᒃ ᑯᑕᒃᑲᒥ).

ᐊᕝᒋᐊᖅ ᓄᑦᕐᑲᖅᓗᓂ ᐊᕐᑯᑎᕐᕿᐊᐸ ᓵᖓᓂ, ᐃᓴᒃᓗᓂᓗ ᓯᒃᑲᐃᑦᑐᐸᓯᓐᓄᐊᕐᒥᒃ ᐊᒃᑐᕋᓯᐊᓕᖅᓗᓂᐅᒃ ᑖᒪ ᐊᕐᑯᑎᕐᕿᐊᖅ—ᑕᒪᐃᑕᓗ ᐊᑕᐅᑦᑎᑦᑰᑦ ᕐᑯᓪᓗᓪᓗᐊᖅᓗᑎᒃ ᕐᑭᕝᕆᖅᑐᑦ. ᓴᖑᔫᓇᓗᒃ ᔮᖅᑯᖅᑎᕝᕿᑎᒥᓂᒃ ᔮᖅᑯᖅᔮᕿᖅ ᕐᑯ'ᒧᒃᓗᒍ ᐊᕐᑯᑎᕐᕿᐊᕐᒥᒃ ᓴᐳ'ᔫᓇᓯᐊᖅᓗᓂ, ᐊᖑᓇᓯᐊᖅᑏᒃ ᕐᑯᓪᓗᓪᓗᐊᖅᓗᑎᒃ, ᕐᑯᑭᕐᓇᖅᑐᒃᓵ'ᒪᑦ ᐳᓚ'ᓗᑎᓪᓗ ᐃᓚᐊᓛᖅᑑᒃ.

ᓴᖑᔫᓇᓗᒃ: ᐅᑎᒧᑦ—

ᐊᕐᑯᑎᕐᕿᐊᖅ: ᐅᓈᕆᒃ ᑎᒍᓪᓚᔅᓴᓇᐊᑦᑭᒃ—

ᓴᖑᔫᓇᓗᒃ: ᔮᖅᑯᖅᑎᔮᓐᓇᕐᓗᕆᓪᓕ—

ᕐᑲᑑᑦ ᐅᓈᖏᓐᓂᒃ ᐱᓇᓯᐊᖅᓗᓂ ᐱᙱ'ᓇᒥ, ᐊᕝᒋᐊᕐᓗ ᐸᓂᖓᔭᓪᓗ ᐅ'ᓚᖅᑳᖅᓗᑎᒃ ᓄᑦᕐᑲᓪᓚᒃᔮᓐᓇᖅᑯᒃ.

ᐊᕝᒋᐊᖅ: (ᐸᓂᖓᔭᖑᑦ) ᑑᓐᖓᐅᙱᓐᓂᖅᑐᔅᓗᐃᑦ ᐃᐸᑯᐊᑦ—

ᐸᓂᖓᔭᒃ: (ᐊᕝᒋᐊᕐᒧᑦ) ᐅ'ᓚᓪᓗᐊᕋᓐᓂᓇᑦ—

ᓴᖑᔫᓇᓗᒃ: ᔮᖅᑯᖅᑎᔮᓐᓇᕐᓗᕆᒃ—

ᑲᑑᑦ: ᓄᑦᕐᑲᖓᔅᓗᓪᓗᔮ!

ᐊᕝᒋᐊᖅ: (ᐸᓂᖓᔭᖑᑦ) ᐊᒃᑐᖅᔮᖂᖓ ᐊᑕᐅᔮᕐᒥᒃ!

ᐊᕐᑯᑎᕐᕿᐊᖅ: (ᑲᑑ'ᒧᑦ) ᓂᙵᓪᓗᔮ ᐅᕐᑲᓇᐊᕐᑲᙱᑦᑐᔮ!

ᐸᓂᖓᔭᒃ: (ᐊᕝᒋᐊᕐᒧᑦ) ᐊᒃᑐᖅᑕᐃᓕᑦᑭᑦ!

ᑲᑑᑦ: ᕐᑳ, ᒪᒥᐊᑦᑐᖓ.

ᐊᕐᑯᑎᕐᕿᐊᖅ: ᐅᓇᑕᕖᓪᕿᐊᖅᑐᒦᙱᑦᑐᒍᓪᓕ—ᐅᓈᕆᒃ ᑲᒪᙱᓗᕆᒃ. ᓇᐅᓕᓱᔅᓱᐊᕈᑎᒃ ᔮᖅᑯᖅᑎᓂᐊᖅᑕᑦᑯᒃ, ᑕᕝᕙᓕ ᐱᑦᑎᐊᖑᐊᕐᓗᑕ.

ᐊᕝᒋᐊᖅ: (ᐸᓂᖓᔭᖑᑦ ᐱ'ᓗᕆᑦ ᐊᕐᑯᑎᕐᕿᐊᐸ ᑐᐃᒥᐊᕈᑕᐃᑦ ᐃᓂᕐᑯᓇᖅᓵᐅᑕᐃᑦ) ᑕᒃᑰᒃ ᕐᑭᐸᓕᖅᑐᑦᑎᐊᕙᓇᓗᐃᑦ ᐅᑯᐊᑦ.

AĞGIAQ: *(to* FRANKLIN*) Qilau'mut mumiqpakpihi? [Do you drum dance?]*

FRANKLIN: *(to the crew)* Lay down your weapons.

PANINGAJAK: *(to* AĞGIAQ*)* They don't drum dance like we do to create harmony between people . . . don't get any closer to them.

HOLLOWAY: Lay down our—but sir—

FRANKLIN: That's an order!

The men reluctantly lay down their rifles, then FRANKLIN *greets* AĞGIAQ *with a handshake.*

PANINGAJAK: *(to* AĞGIAQ*)* Don't touch him.

FRANKLIN: Welcome— *Too-naa-hoo-geet-check . . . ? [Welcome to you both?]*

PANINGAJAK: *(to* AĞGIAQ*)* Sounds like he said *tunngahugittik*—that we two should feel the ground beneath us. Yikes, does this mean he might push us over?

AĞGIAQ: *(to* PANINGAJAK*)* I think he is trying to say we should lie down to feel the ground, but I'm not sure why.

AĞGIAQ *returns the handshake in his fashion while* PANINGAJAK*, still uncertain, stands back.* FRANKLIN *points to himself.*

FRANKLIN: My name is John Franklin. I'm commander of this expedition. We consist of the HMS *Erebus* and *Terror*, and I am properly addressed as "sir." This is Officer James Holloway, second in command.

HOLLOWAY *is not keen on shaking hands.*

FRANKLIN *points to* AĞGIAQ.

You, your name uh . . . *hoo-now-root-tin—hooo-vet?*

AĞGIAQ: Ağgiaq . . . *(points to* PANINGAJAK*)* Paningajak.

ᐸᓂᖕᒐᔭᒃ: (ᐊᔅᓯᐊᕐᒧᑦ) ᐅᓗᕆᐊᓇᖅᑐᐊᓗᐃᑦ ᐅᑯᐊᑦ
ᖃᒡᓕᒐᓐᓂᕆᐊᖃᙱᑦᑐᔅᓱᐃᑦ.

ᐊᕐᑯᑎᕐᔪᐊᖅ: (ᑐᖅᓱᓚᔪᖅ ᐊᔅᓯᐊᕐᒧᑦ) ᐆ-ᓅ-ᑰᑦ (ᑯᑕᒃᓱᓂ).

ᐊᔅᓯᐊᖅ ᐱᔪᒪᙱᑦᑲᓗᐊᖅᓱᓂ ᐱᔮᒃᐸᓪᓕᐊᔪᖅ ᔮᒃᑲᐃᑦᑐᒥᒃ
ᐊᕐᑯᑎᕐᔪᐊᕐᒧᑦ.

ᐊᔅᓯᐊᖅ: (ᐸᓂᖕᒐᔭᖕᒧᑦ) ᐃᓄᑐᐃᓐᓇᑦ ᐅᑯᐊᑦ ᐅᕙᑦᑐᑦ.

ᐊᕐᑯᑎᕐᔪᐊᖅ ᐊᐸᓗᕆᐊᖅᓱᓂ ᐊᔅᓯᐊᕐᒧᑦ.

ᐊᕐᑯᑎᕐᔪᐊᖅ: ᐅᓇᑕᖅᑎᐅᙱᑦᑐᒍᑦ.

ᐸᓂᖕᒐᔭᒃ: (ᐊᔅᓯᐊᕐᒧᑦ) ᐃᓄᕐᑯᑎᒋᓵᒃᓴᐅᙱᑦᑐᑦ—ᐊᐅᖃᑦᑎᐊᖅᑰᙱ'ᒪᑕ
ᒪᒪᐃᑦᑐᓇᓘ'ᓗᑎᒃ.

ᓴᖖᔫᓇᓗᒃ: ᐱᑦᑎᐊᖅᑐᓇᓘ'ᔭᔪᒃ ᐅᑯᐊᒃ.

ᐊᕐᑯᑎᕐᔪᐊᖅ: ᖃᐅᔫᓂᐊᖅᑯᒧᑦ ᔨᖅᑯᖅᑎᓪᓚᔅᖀᓗᙱᑦᑯᕕᒥᒃ.

ᓴᖖᔫᓇᓗᒃ: ᑐᕐᑯᑦᖄᙱᑦᑯᐸᑕᓕ ᒪᒪᐃᓃ'ᓄᑦ.

ᐊᔅᓯᐊᖅ: (ᐊᕐᑯᑎᕐᔪᐊᕐᒧᑦ) ᕿᓚᐅ'ᒧᑦ ᒧᒥᖅᐸᒃᐱᔪ?

ᐊᕐᑯᑎᕐᔪᐊᖅ: (ᓴᓇᔫᓄᑦ) ᔪᖅᑯᖅᑎᔅᔪᑎᔪ ᓴᐸᑯᓗᓯᑦ ᑕᐅᓄᖕᒐ ᐃᓕᓗᓯᑦ.

ᐸᓂᖕᒐᔭᒃ: (ᐊᔅᓯᐊᕐᒧᑦ) ᔮᕐᑯᓚᓇᔮᐊᖃᑦᑕᖅᑰᙱᑦᑐᔅᓱᐃᑦ ᐅᕙᑦᑐᑦ
ᐃᓚᕖᑦᑎᐊᕋᔮᐊᖅᓱᑎᒃ ᔮᕐᑯᓚᓂᑦᑯᑦ . . . ᖃᒡᓕᒐᓐᓂᙱᓗᑎᑦ.

ᓴᖖᔫᓇᓗᒃ: ᔮᕚ, ᓴᐸᑯᓗᓯᑦ ᑕᐅᓄᖕᒐ—ᐲ—

ᐊᕐᑯᑎᕐᔪᐊᖅ: ᐱᑦᖁᔮᕙᓯᑦ ᔮᓚᔪᒥᒃ!

ᐱᔪᒪᙱᑦᑲᓗᐊᖅᓱᑎᒃ ᑕᐅᓄᖕᒐ ᐃᓚᔮᐃᑦ ᔪᖅᑯᖅᑎᔅᔪᑎᑎᒃ,
ᐊᕐᑯᑎᕐᔪᐊᕐᓗ ᐊᔅᔮᓯᐊᕐᒧᑦ ᑎᑰᑎᔅᖅᑐᖅᓱᓂ.

ᐸᓂᖕᒐᔭᒃ: (ᐊᔅᓯᐊᕐᒧᑦ) ᐊᒃᑐᖅᑕᐃᓕᒍᒃ.

ᐊᕐᑯᑎᕐᔪᐊᖅ: ᑑ-ᓇ-ᔮ-ᒋᑦ-ᑎ-ᒃ (ᐅᖃᑦᑎᐊᙱ'ᓇᒥᐅᒃ ᓇᓗᒐᒥ ᐃᓄᒃᑐᑦ).

PANINGAJAK: *(to* ARĞIAQ*)* Ask them if they happened to have seen two bears passing through here.

FRANKLIN: *(to* ARĞIAQ *and* PANINGAJAK*)* . . . And what's your business, *Ud-yuck* and *Panny-guy-yak* . . . *(to* HOLLOWAY*)* How do you say "what's your business"?

HOLLOWAY: I don't know their words.

ARĞIAQ: *(to* FRANKLIN*) Takugaluaqpigit nanuuk mařruk tahamunngauřuk? [Did you happen to see two bears passing through here?]*

FRANKLIN: I wish Morshead would get here—he picked up some of their language working with Parry in '25 when they lost the *Fury*.

> *CREW #1 enters carrying a tray with a porcelain teapot, two cups, two saucers, and sugar. He pours a steaming cup of tea each for FRANKLIN and HOLLOWAY. CREW #2 hauls in the bulky daguerreotype.*

HOLLOWAY: Ah, tea—"Tea is the cup of life."

> *PANINGAJAK points to the* Erebus *in the distance.*

PANINGAJAK: *(to* ARĞIAQ*)* Look at that big boat.

ARĞIAQ: *(to* FRANKLIN*) Umiarřuanaluk angiřualuk pigiřaqhi? [That big boat. Is it yours?]*

> *FRANKLIN points to the* Erebus *in the distance.*

FRANKLIN: I think that word *"oom-yuck"* means boat.

ARĞIAQ: *(to* PANINGAJAK*)* Maybe these men are the whale hunters my grandfather spoke about.

PANINGAJAK: *(to* ARĞIAQ*)* Ask him.

CARTER: They seem keen on our ship.

ᐸᓂᖓᔭᒃ: (ᐊᕐᒋᐊᕐᒧᑦ) ᐅᖃᕋᔭᐊᖅᑐᖅ ᑐᓐᖓᕙᑉᐱᑎ'ᓂᒃ ᐅᕐᓵᓇᓗᑕ,
ᐊᕐᒃᓱᓇᔭᐊᕐᓂᐊᒃᓵᓗᐃᑦ ᐅᑯᐊᑦ?

ᐊᕐᒋᐊᖅ: (ᐸᓂᖓᔭᖕᒧᑦ) ᐅᖃᖅᑰᕋᓗᐊ'ᒪᑦ ᐸᑦᑐᖕᖓᓗᓄᒃ ᒪᓂᕋᕐᓂᒧᑦ,
ᔭ'ᒪᑦᑭᐊᖅ.

*ᐊᕐᒋᐊᖅ ᑎᒍᑎᓕᕋᔭᐊᖅᓗᓂᐅᒃ ᑲᒪᔭᙱ'ᒪᑦ, ᐸᓂᖓᔭᒡᓕ ᐃᖅᓱᖓᒥ
ᔭᓕ ᖃᑦᓕᒋᐊᙱᑦᑐᖅ. ᐊᕐᑯᑎᕐᕙᐊᖅ ᐃᖕᒥᓄᑦ ᑎᑦᑯᐊᖅᓗᓂ.*

ᐊᕐᑯᑎᕐᕙᐊᖅ: ᐊᑎᕋ ᔮᓪ ᕗᕌᒃᓚᓐ. ᐊᑕᓂᓇᔾᐅᕙᖓ ᕿᓂᖅᑎᓂᒃ ᐅᑯᓇᓂᒃ.
ᒫᕐᐹᓐᓂᒃ ᐅᒥᐊᕐᕙᐊᕐᑲᖅᑐᒧᑦ ᐃᓅᐸᔅ-ᓗ ᑎᐅᐲ-ᓗ, ᑐᖅᓗᕋᖅᑕᐅᕚᒃᑐᖓ
ᐊᑕᓂᕐᕙᐊᕐᒥᒃ ᐊᕐᑯᑎᕐᕙᐊᕐᒥᒃ. ᐅᓇᓗ ᔾᐃᒥᔪ ᕷᓗᕖ ᕼᖑᓵᓇᓗᒃ, ᑐᒡᓕᓇᕚᖓ.

ᕼᖑᓵᓇᓗᒃ ᑎᒍᑎᕙᒪᙱᑦᑐᖅ.

ᐊᕐᑯᑎᕐᕙᐊᖅ ᑎᑦᑯᐊᖅᑐᖅ ᐊᕐᒋᐊᕐᒧᑦ.

ᐊᕐᑯᑎᕐᕙᐊᖅ: ᐃᕙᑦ, ᐊᑏᑦ ᐲ . . . ᔭ-ᓇᐅ-ᕙ-ᑎᑦ—ᐲ, ᔮ-ᕙᑦ?
(ᐃᓄᒃᑑᕋᔭᐊᖅᓗᓂ).

ᐊᕐᒋᐊᖅ: ᐊᕐᒋᐊᖑᕚᖓ . . . *(ᑎᑦᑯᐊᖅᓗᓂ ᐸᓂᖓᔭᖕᒧᑦ)* ᐅᓇ
ᐸᓂᖓᔭᒃ.

ᐸᓂᖓᔭᒃ: *(ᐊᕐᒋᐊᕐᒧᑦ)* ᐊᐱᓇᓗᒋᑦ ᒫᕐᐹᓐᓂᒃ ᓇᓅᓐᓂᒃ
ᑕᑯᓚᓗᐊᓇᐊᒃᓴᐃᑕ ᑕᕼᒧᙳᐅᕚᓐᓂᒃ.

ᐊᕐᑯᑎᕐᕙᐊᖅ: *(ᐊᕐᒋᐊᕐᒧᑦ ᐸᓂᖓᔭᖕᒧᑦᓗ)* . . . ᔭᓇᔭᐊᕋᐸᑎᒡᓕ ᐊᒡ-ᔭᒃ
ᐸ-ᓂ-ᖓ-ᔭᒡ-ᓗ . . . *(ᕼᖑᓵᓇᓗᖕᒧᑦ)* ᖃᓄᖅ ᐅᖃᐅᔭᓇᑦᑎᐊᕋᔭᖅᑕᕋ
"ᔭᓇᔭᐊᖅᐱᔭᒃ"?

ᕼᖑᓵᓇᓗᒃ: ᐅᖃᐅᔫᑕ ᐅᑯᐊ ᖃᐅᓵᒪᙱᑕᑦᑲ.

ᐊᕐᒋᐊᖅ: *(ᐊᕐᑯᑎᕐᕙᐊᕐᒧᑦ)* ᑕᑯᓚᓗᐊᖅᐱᒋᒃ ᓇᓅᒃ ᒫᕐᐻᒃ ᑕᕼᒧᙳᐅᕚᒃ?

ᐊᕐᑯᑎᕐᕙᐊᖅ: ᓇᐅᑦᑎᖅᑐᖅᑎᕐᓗᒃ ᔭᖃᙱ'ᒪᑦ—ᐃᓄᒃᑐᑦ ᐅᖃᒪᕗᖕᓇᓄᐊ'ᒪᑦ
ᐃᓕᕼᖅᔭᒪᑲᒥ 1825-ᖑᑎ'ᓗᒍ ᐅᒥᐊᕐᕙᐊᑦᑰᖃᑕᐅᑲᓗᐊ'ᒪᑦ ᑕᕼᒧᙳ.

*ᕼᓇᓵ ᐃᔭᖅᓗᓂ ᔭᒡᕹᕐᒥᒃ ᑎᒍᒥᐊᖅᑐᖅ ᑏᓕᐅᑎᖃᖅᑐᒥᒃ,
ᖃᑦᑐᑎᓂᒡᓗ, ᔭᒡᕿᓐᓄᐊᕐᓂᒡᓗ, ᐊᐅᒃᔭᓇᐊᕐᒥᒡᓗ.*

PANINGAJAK: *(to* ARĞIAQ*)* Let's go to that boat!

ARĞIAQ: *(to* FRANKLIN*)* You . . . *Arviqhiuqti? [Are you a whaler?]*

CREW #1: *(to* FRANKLIN*)* Your tea, sir.

FRANKLIN: Thank you. *(to* ARĞIAQ*)* Pardon?

ARĞIAQ: *(to* FRANKLIN*)* You . . . Arviqhiuqti?

FRANKLIN: *(to* HOLLOWAY*)* What's he trying to say?

CREW #1: *(to* FRANKLIN*)* Sugar, sir.

HOLLOWAY: He's saying "you"—"you" as in "you."

FRANKLIN points to his teacup.

FRANKLIN: *(to* ARĞIAQ*)* Tea, gentlemen?

ARĞIAQ: *(to* FRANKLIN*)* You . . . *(pointing to the* Erebus *in the distance) Arviqhiurutikšaqhi? [Is that a whaling boat?]*

FRANKLIN: *(to* ARĞIAQ*)* Will you have a cup of tea?

PANINGAJAK: *(to* ARĞIAQ*)* They don't understand.

HOLLOWAY: *(to* FRANKLIN*)* They don't understand, sir.

CREW #1: I'll get more cups and saucers.

CREW #1 exits.

ARĞIAQ pantomimes a whale swimming with his hands and body.

ARĞIAQ: *(to* FRANKLIN*)* YOU.

FRANKLIN: Me . . . my hands . . . swimming. Dear Lord—your hands swimming—

ᑏᑐᖅᑎᓐᓂᐊ'ᒪᒋᒃ ᐊᕐᑯᑎᕐᔦᐊᕐᓗ ᕋᖑᔫᓇᓗᒡᓗ. ᕋᓇᔫᑉ ᐊᐃᑉᐹ
ᐊᒡᕚᖅᔪᔦᖅ ᐊ'ᔫᓚᐅᑎᓇᓗᖕᒥᒃ ᐱᑐᕐᑲᖅᔪᐅᑎᒥᒃ.

ᕋᖑᔫᓇᓗᒃ: ᑏᑦᑎᐊᕙᒃ—"ᑏᓇᓗᒃ ᐃᓃᕝᔦᑎᒻᒪᓄᓇᓗᒃ."

ᐸᓂᖕᖓᔾᔭᒃ ᑎᑦᑯᐊᖅᓘᓂ ᐅᒥᐊᕐᔦᐊᕐᒧᑦ ᐅᖕᖓᔪᒃᑐᒧᑦ.

ᐸᓂᖕᖓᔾᔭᒃ: *(ᐊᕝᕆᐊᕐᒧᑦ)* ᑕᒃᑰᒃ ᐅᒥᐊᕐᔦᐊᖀᓗᒃ.

ᐊᕝᕆᐊᖅ: *(ᐊᕐᑯᑎᕐᔦᐊᕐᒧᑦ)* ᐅᒥᐊᕐᔦᐊᓇᓗᒃ ᐊᖕᕆᔦᐊᓗᒃ, ᐱᕆᕚᖅᔪ?

ᐊᕐᑯᑎᕐᔦᐊᖅ ᑎᑦᑯᐊᖅᓘᓂᐅᒃ ᐅᒥᐊᕐᔦᐊᖅ ᑖᕙᓃᑦᑐᖅ.

ᐊᕐᑯᑎᕐᔦᐊᖅ: ᐅᕐᑲᐅᔪᖅ ᑖᒻᓇ "ᐅᒻᔭᖅ" ᐅᕐᑲᑦᑎᐊᕿᓗᐊᖅᐸᕿ?

ᐊᕝᕆᐊᖅ: *(ᐸᓂᖕᖓᔾᔭᖕᒧᑦ)* ᐅᑯᐊᓪᓚ ᐊᕐᕕᖅᔪᐅᖅᑎᐅ'ᔾᔦᑦ ᐃᑦᑐᕐᒪ ᐅᕐᑲᐅᔪᓄᕐᑲᑦᑕᖅᔪᒪᕚᐃᑦ.

ᐸᓂᖕᖓᔾᔭᒃ: *(ᐊᕝᕆᐊᕐᒧᑦ)* ᐊᐱᓄᒡᒎᒃ.

ᑳᑑᑦ: ᐅᒥᐊᕐᔦᐊᑉᑎ'ᓂᒃ ᑕᑯᔭᒪᓪᓗᐊᖅᑑᒃ.

ᐸᓂᖕᖓᔾᔭᒃ: *(ᐊᕝᕆᐊᕐᒧᑦ)* ᐅᒥᐊᕐᔦᐊᕐᒧᙱᑐᐅᓗᒃ!

ᐊᕝᕆᐊᖅ: *(ᐊᕐᑯᑎᕐᔦᐊᕐᒧᑦ)* ᐃᕝᕕᑦ . . . ᐊᕐᕕᖅᔪᐅᖅᑎ?

ᕋᓇᔫ: *(ᐊᕐᑯᑎᕐᔦᐊᕐᒧᑦ)* ᐅᕝᕙ ᑏᒃᓯᑦ, ᐊᑕᓂᕐᔦᐊᖅ.

ᐊᕐᑯᑎᕐᔦᐊᖅ: ᕐᑯᔭᓇᖅᑯᑎᑦ *(ᐊᕝᕆᐊᕐᒧᑦ)* ᔦᕚ?

ᐊᕝᕆᐊᖅ: *(ᐊᕐᑯᑎᕐᔦᐊᕐᒧᑦ)* ᔫ . . . ᐊᕐᕕᖅᔪᐅᖅᑎ?

ᐊᕐᑯᑎᕐᔦᐊᖅ: *(ᕋᖑᔫᓇᓗᖕᒧᑦ)* ᑲᓅᕐᓚᐊᕿᔦᐊᖅᑐᑭᐊᖅ ᐅᓇ ᔦᕙᒎᖅ?

ᕋᓇᔫ: *(ᐊᕐᑯᑎᕐᔦᐊᕐᒧᑦ)* ᐊᐅᔪᓄᐊᕐᒥᒃ?

ᕋᖑᔫᓇᓗᒃ: ᔫ-ᓚᔦᖅ ᕐᑲᑉᓗᓅᑐᑦ ᐅᕐᑲᕿᓗᐊᖅᓘᓂ ᐃᕝᕕᒎᖅ.

ᐊᕐᑯᑎᕐᔦᐊᖅ ᑎᑦᑯᐊᖅᓘᒍ ᕐᑲᓪᓗᑦ.

CARTER: FISH.

HOLLOWAY: Fish, yes! I think he means fish, sir—wonders if we want to fish?

FRANKLIN: No, Ağgiaq, my work is not fishing—my work is discovery and observation, for I am at heart a scientist.

AĞGIAQ reaches out and points to FRANKLIN's Knight Commander badge that hangs around his neck as a collared chain.

AĞGIAQ: *(in PANINGAJAK's direction)* This is shiny.

HOLLOWAY swats AĞGIAQ's hand away.

HOLLOWAY: Don't touch!

PANINGAJAK is inclined to take a swing at HOLLOWAY.

FRANKLIN: No need for that—enough!

AĞGIAQ: *(to PANINGAJAK)* Angajuk, no no.

PANINGAJAK: *(to AĞGIAQ)* Don't touch them.

FRANKLIN: *(to AĞGIAQ)* This is of the Royal Hanoverian Guelphic Order, a knighthood bestowed upon me in '33—Carter, give these fellows some trinkets.

CARTER: Here, fellas . . .

CARTER takes a box from the trunk, flips it open, and holds it out to the two hunters.

. . . help yourselves.

AĞGIAQ: *(to CARTER) Hungauřat. [Beads.]*

AĞGIAQ and PANINGAJAK help themselves to the trinkets in the wooden box.

ᐊᕐᑯᑎᕐᔪᐊᖅ: (ᐊᖑᓇᔪᐊᖅᑎᖏᑦ) ᑏᑐᖃᑕᐅᔪᒪᕙᔫᒃ.

ᐊᔾᕆᐊᖅ: (ᐊᕐᑯᑎᕐᔪᐊᕐᒧᑦ) "ᔫ" (ᑎᑦᑯᐊᖅᑯᒍ ᐅᒥᐊᕐᔪᐊᖅ ᑖᕝᕙᓐᓇ ᖃᑉᓗᓈᑐᑦ ᐃᔾᕚᓚᓇᔪᐊᖅᑐᖅ) ᐊᕐᕙᖅᔪᐅᕈᑎᒃᓴᖅᔪ?

ᐊᕐᑯᑎᕐᔪᐊᖅ: (ᐊᔾᕆᐊᕐᒧᑦ) ᑏᑐᕈᒪᒐᓗᐊᖅᐱᑦ?

ᐸᓂᖕᒐᕗᒃ: (ᐊᔾᕆᐊᕐᒧᑦ) ᑐᑭᔪᙱᓪᒪᖏᒃᑐᓇᓗᐃᑦ ᐅᑯᐊᑦ.

ᓴᖑᔭᓇᓗᒃ: (ᐊᕐᑯᑎᕐᔪᐊᕐᒧᑦ) ᑐᑭᔪᙱᓪᒪᖏᒃᑐᓇᓘᒃ ᐅᑯᐊᒃ, ᐊᑕᓂᕐᔪᐊᖅ.

ᓴᓇᔭ: ᐊᐃᒃᓵᕐᓂᐊᕋᒪ ᖃᑦᑐᑎᓂᒃ ᔪᒡᔫᓐᓄᐊᕐᓂᒡᓗ.

ᓴᓇᔭ ᐊᓂ'ᓗᓂ.

ᐊᔾᕆᐊᖅ, ᐊᕐᕙᖑᙳᐊᖅᑯᓂ ᐳᐃᔪᒥᒃ ᑕᕆᐅᕐᒥ.

ᐊᔾᕆᐊᖅ: (ᐊᕐᑯᑎᕐᔪᐊᕐᒧᑦ) ᔫ. (ᖃᑉᓗᓈᑐᑦ ᐃᔾᕚᓚᓇᔪᐊᖅᑯᓂ)

ᐊᕐᑯᑎᕐᔪᐊᖅ: ᐅᕙᖕᒐ . . . ᐊᔾᒐᑦᑲᒃ . . . ᓇᓅᔭᖅᑐᖕᒐ . . . ᔨᔭᕐᑯᒃ ᓇᓗᓇᖅᑐᕌᓗᒃ—

ᑲᑑᑦ: ᐃᖃᓗᒃ.

ᓴᖑᔭᓇᓗᒃ: ᐄ, ᐃᖃᓗᒃᓴᐅᕗᖅ! ᐃᖃᓗᖕᒥᒃ ᐅᖃᐅᔪᖃᖅᑰᖅᑐᖅ— ᐃᖃᓗᒃᑐᕈᒪᔫᒃᓴᐸᑎ'ᓂᒃ?

ᐊᕐᑯᑎᕐᔪᐊᖅ: ᐄᕿ, ᐊᔾᕆᐊᖅ, ᓴᓈᓇᔭᕋ ᐃᖃᓗᒃᔪᐅᕐᓂᐅᙱᑦᑐᖅ— ᕿᓂᖅᑎᐅᔪᖕᒐ ᑕᑯᔭᒻᓂᒃ ᑎᑎᕋᖅᐸᒃᑯᖕᒐ ᖃᐅᔭᓴᖅᑎᐅᒐᒪ.

ᐊᔾᕆᐊᖅ, ᐃᓴᒃᑯᓂ ᑎᑦᑯᐊᖅᑐᖅ ᐊᕐᑯᑎᕐᔪᐊᑉ ᓇᓗᓇᐃᑉᑯᑖᖑᑦ ᐃᓕᑕᕆᔭᐅᔾᔪᑎᐊᖑᑦ ᓂᕕᙵᓗᔪᖅ ᐅᔭᒥᕆ'ᓗᓂᐅᒃ.

ᐊᔾᕆᐊᖅ: (ᐸᓂᖕᒐᕗᒃ ᓵ'ᓗᒍ) ᐅᓇ ᕿᐸᓕᖅᑐᓇᓗᒃ.

ᓴᖑᔭᓇᓗᒃ ᐊᔾᕆᐊᐸ ᐊᔾᓛ'ᓂ ᐸᑎᒃᔪᔪᖅ ᑎᒍᕐᑯᙱ'ᓗᓂᐅᒃ.

ᓴᖑᔭᓇᓗᒃ: ᐊᒃᑐᖅᔪᑦᑕᐃᓖᑦ!

ᐸᓂᖕᒐᕗᒃ ᑐᓪᓗᒃᑐᕈᒪᓕᖅᐸ ᓴᖑᔭᓇᓗᒃ ᑖᒻᓇ.

PANINGAJAK: *(to ARĞIAQ)* Let's bag what we can! Stuff our pockets!

CARTER: *(to PANINGAJAK)* Hey—only one handful each!

FRANKLIN: They are worthless trinkets, Carter.

ARĞIAQ: *(to PANINGAJAK)* Our wives will like these—they are like the shimmering surface of fish eggs.

PANINGAJAK: *(to ARĞIAQ)* Maybe they have a bowhead whale in their boat.

FRANKLIN: *Oom-yuck* means boat, doesn't it? *(to ARĞIAQ and PANINGAJAK)* Yes, that's an *oom-yuck*—the *Erebus*—a Hecla-class bomb vessel built by the Royal Navy.

PANINGAJAK: *(to ARĞIAQ)* Let's go to the boat and get harvested whale meat.

ARĞIAQ and PANINGAJAK start to leave.

FRANKLIN: Yes, that's our *oom-yuck*—370 tons, armed with two mortars and ten—Arğiaq, where are you— *(to HOLLOWAY)* Where are they going?

HOLLOWAY: *(to the hunters)* Excuse me, sir.

PANINGAJAK: *(to ARĞIAQ)* I'll go get our sledge.

CARTER: Whoa there, buddy— *(stops ARĞIAQ)* Don't walk away when Sir John Franklin is addressing you—

PANINGAJAK spies the dead seal.

PANINGAJAK: A seal!

ARĞIAQ: Seal!

PANINGAJAK: *(to ARĞIAQ)* Nukaq, this is freshly caught, very fresh.

The two hunters kneel beside the seal as ARĞIAQ uses his small bone knife to expertly slit open the abdomen and cut out a choice part he hands to PANINGAJAK, who eats it.

ᐊᖅᑯᑎᖅᔨᐊᖅ: ᐅᐃᒻᒪᙱᓗᔪ—ᑕᐃᒫᓇ!

ᐊᔅᓯᐊᖅ: (*ᐸᓂᖕᖓᔭᖕᖑᑦ*) ᐄᖅᑭ ᐊᖕᖓᔭᒃ, ᐄᖅᑭ.

ᐸᓂᖕᖓᔭᒃ: (*ᐊᔅᓯᐊᖑᑦ*) ᐊᒃᑐᖅᑕᐃᓕᖅᑭᑦ.

ᐊᖅᑯᑎᖅᔨᐊᖅ: (*ᐊᔅᓯᐊᖑᑦ*) ᐅᓇ ᐃᓕᑕᕆᔭᐅᔅᔨᑎᔪᐊᕆᔭᖅ 1833-ᖑᑎ'ᓗᒍ—ᑲᑑᑦ, ᐅᑯᐊᒃ ᑐᓂᓕᖅᑭᒃ ᐱᖅᑯᑎᓐᓄᐊᖅᓂᒃ.

ᑲᑑᑦ: ᐅᕝᕗ . . .

ᑲᑑᑦ ᑎᒍᔪ'ᓗᓂ ᐆᖅᒥᒃ ᖅᑭᖁᑕᔨᒥᒃ ᖅᑭᔨᖅᑯᑎᒦᑦᑲᓗᐊᖅᑐᒥᒃ, ᒪᑐᐃᖅᓱᒍ ᐃᓗᓕᖕᖏᑦ ᑐᒍᔭᒃᓴᐅᑎ'ᓗᓂᖏᑦ ᐊᖑᓇᓴᐊᖅᑎᓄᑦ.

ᑲᑑᑦ: ᐃᓴᒪᐃᓐᓇᖅ ᐱᒡᒍᐃᑦᑎ.

ᐊᔅᓯᐊᖅ: (*ᑲᑑ'ᒍᑦ*) ᓴᖕᖓᐅᔭᑦ.

ᐃᓴᒪᐃᓐᓇᖅ ᑎᒍᔪᓕᖅᓱᑎᒃ ᐊᔅᓯᐊᖅᑐ ᐸᓂᖕᖓᔭᒡᓗ.

ᐸᓂᖕᖓᔭᒃ: (*ᐊᔅᓯᐊᖑᑦ*) ᐆᖅᔪᓪᓕᔅᔭᓗᒡᓗᒃ! ᖅᑲᐅᑦᑐᐊᕗᒃ ᑕᑕᑎᑦᑎᐊᖅᑐᕆᑦ!

ᑲᑑᑦ: (*ᐸᓂᖕᖓᔭᖕᖑᑦ*) ᐊᐃ—ᐃᒃᑭᑦᑐᓐᓄᐊᔅᓱᖕᓂᒡᓕ ᐱᕗᓪᓛ'ᓇᒃ!

ᐊᖅᑯᑎᖅᔨᐊᖅ: ᐱᖅᑯᑎᑉᓴᐅᔅᓱᐃᑦ ᐃᑉᑯᐊ ᓴᓇᐅᙱᑦᑐᔅᓱᐃᑦ ᐊᑭᖅᑲᙱᑦᑐᑦ, ᖅᑲᑑᑦ.

ᐊᔅᓯᐊᖅ: (*ᐸᓂᖕᖓᔭᖕᖑᑦ*) ᓄᓕᐊᕗᒃ ᐱᑦᑕᐅᕆᓂᐊᖅᑕᐃᑦ ᐅᑯᐊᑦ—ᓴᕗᒃᑐᑦ ᖅᑭᐸᓕᖅᑐᕕᓚᓗᔅᓱᐃᑦ.

ᐸᓂᖕᖓᔭᒃ: (*ᐊᔅᓯᐊᖑᑦ*) ᐊᖅᕕᖅᑲᖅᑑ'ᔭᔪᑦ ᐅᒥᐊᖅᒥ'ᓂ.

ᐊᖅᑯᑎᖅᔨᐊᖅ: ᐅᒻ-ᔭᖅ ᑖᒻᓇ (*ᐊᔅᓯᐊᖑᑦ ᐸᓂᖕᖓᔭᖕᖑᓪᓗ ᑕᐃᑦᑎᐊᙱ'ᒪᒍ*) ᐄ ᐅᒻᔭᖅ—ᐃᖁᐸᔅ-ᒥᒃ ᑕᐃᔭᐅᔪᖅ ᐅᓇᑕᖅᑎᒃᓴᓂᑦ ᔮᓇᔭᐅᔪᖅ ᔮᓐᖕᖏᔪᐊᓗᒃ ᑖᒻᓇ.

ᐸᓂᖕᖓᔭᒃ: (*ᐊᔅᓯᐊᖑᑦ*) ᐅᒥᐊᖅᔪᐊᖑᙵᐅᓗᒃ ᐊᖅᕕᖅᑕᕆᔭᐅᔪᒥᑦ ᓂᖅᑭᒥᒃ ᐊᐃᒃᑯᖅᓗᓄᒃ.

ᐊᔅᓯᐊᖅᑐ ᐸᓂᖕᖓᔭᒡᓗ ᐊᐃᒃᑯᓕᖅᓴᐊᖅᓱᑎᒃ.

FRANKLIN: A bear brought that to us as a . . . well, a gift—don't mention that in your observations, Holloway—readers will think we'd a bit too much to drink.

HOLLOWAY: You'd think they'd have the decency to cook it first.

AĂGIAQ offers the tastiest bits of the seal to everyone.

WICKERS: No thank you.

AĂGIAQ: *(to FRANKLIN) Tinguk mamaqtupanaluk. [The liver is very tasty.]*

BEAN: Thank you, no.

PANINGAJAK: *(to AĂGIAQ)* How can he resist the tastiest part!

FRANKLIN: Perhaps later.

CARTER: I'll pass.

PANINGAJAK: *(to AĂGIAQ)* Only fools refuse the most delectable part.

PANINGAJAK uses a wound pin on the seal to prevent more bleeding.

HOLLOWAY: What—are they going to sew up the seal? Savages, sir—right ungodly savages.

Some of the men are getting cold—rubbing their hands and jumping on the spot.

FRANKLIN: When we were starving in '19, the Dene people took us in and fed us as if we were their own children, so don't make assumptions about these fellows, Holloway—perhaps they haven't eaten for a few days.

HOLLOWAY: I understand, sir, but they eat blood and smell like dirty babies—

FRANKLIN: We all smell like dirty babies—it's not important. What's important is that we *endure*!

ᐊᕐᑯᑎᕐᕿᐊᖅ: ᐄ ᐅᒥᐊᕐᕿᐊᓇᔭᕗᑦ ᑖᒻᓇ—ᐅ-ᒥ-ᐊ-ᖅ, ᐃᒃᑕᓇᒃᑐᓇᓗᕐᓗᒃ ᕿᓇᕐᑲᑦᑎᐊᖅᑐᕐᓗᒃ—ᐊᔾᔨᐊᖅ ᕿᒦᑦᐱᑦ—(ᔭᖑᔾᔮᓇᓗᖑᒍᑦ) ᕿᒪᖖᒐᐅᓇᕿᐊᖅᑑᒃ ᐃᐸᑯᐊᒃ?

ᔭᖑᔾᔮᓇᓗᒃ: (ᐊᖑᓇᕿᐊᖅᑎᓄᑦ) ᕿᓗᔫᖅ?

ᐸᓂᖕᒐᔮᒃ: (ᐊᔾᔨᐊᕐᒧᑦ) ᕐᑲᒧᑎᐸᑎ'ᓂᒃ ᐱᔮᖅᑐᕐᓂᐊᖅᑯᖕᒐ.

ᑳᑰᑦ: ᐄᕐᕿᕐᓘᒃ—(ᐊᔾᔨᐊᕐᒥᒃ ᓄᑦᕐᑲᖅᑎᑎ'ᓗᓂ) ᐃᕿᒪᖅᕿᑐᐃᓐᓇᓚᐃᑦᑐᑎᑦ ᐊᑕᓂᕐᕿᐊᓇᓗᒃ ᐅᕐᑲᕐᕝᕆᑎ'ᓗᓂᑎᑦ—

ᐸᓂᖕᒐᔮᒃ ᓇᑦᑎᖅᑕᓇᔭᐅᕿᒥᒃ ᑕᑯᒐᒥ.

ᐊᔾᔨᐊᖅ: ᓇᑦᑎᖅ!

ᐸᓂᖕᒐᔮᒃ: (ᐊᔾᔨᐊᕐᒧᑦ) ᓄᑲᖅ, ᐅᓇ ᓇᑦᑎᖅᑕᓇᔮᐅᔮᖅᑐᖅ, ᓄᑖᑦᑎᐊᕙᓇᓗᒃ.

ᐊᖑᓇᕿᐊᖅᑎᒃ ᓫᔫᑦᕐᑯᖅᑐᕐᓗᑎᒃ ᓇᑦᑎᐅᑉ ᔭᓂᐊᓂ, ᐊᔾᔨᐊᖅ ᐱᓚᐅᑎᒥᓂᒃ ᐊᑐᖅᑐᕐᓂ ᔭᐅᓂᕐᒧᑦ ᔭᓇᓫᒪᕿᒧᑦ ᐱᓚᒃᑐᕐᒍ ᓇᑦᑎᖅ ᓂᕐᕿᑦᑎᐊᕙᓐᓄᐊᕐᒥᒃ ᐊᒧᓫ'ᓗᓂ ᑐᓂ'ᓗᓂᐅᒃ ᐸᓂᖕᒐᔮᖑᒧᑦ.

ᐊᕐᑯᑎᕐᕿᐊᖅ: ᓇᓄᕐᒥᑦ ᑐᓂᔾᔨᓫᐊᓇᓫᒪᔭᕗᑦ ᕿᓇᐅᖏ
. . . ᔭᖑᔾᔮᓇᓗᒃ—ᑎᑎᕋᖅᑕᐃᓕᓗᑎᑦ ᑕᔭᐸᕿᒥᖕᒐᑦ—ᐅᕐᑲᓕᒫᖅᑕᐅᒃᐸᑦ ᐃᕿᒪᐃᕈᑎᓇᕿᔨᔭᐅᑐᐃᓐᓇᕐᓂᐊᖅᑐᒍᑦ ᕿᓕᑦᕐᑰᖖᒋᒻᒪᓇᒡᓗᑕ.

ᔭᖑᔾᔮᓇᓗᒃ: ᐅᑯᐊᒃ ᐃᒐᓇᕿᐊᖖᒋᒻᒪᓇᒃᑕᐃᑦ ᓂᕐᕿᕐᓘᒃ ᒥᑭᒐᐃᓐᓇᒻᒪᓇᓗᒃ.

ᐊᔾᔨᐊᖅ ᓇᑦᑎᐅᑉ ᒪᒪᑖᖑᓂᖕᒋ'ᓂᒃ ᑐᓂᐅᕐᑲᐃᔦᖅ ᑕᒪᐃ'ᓄᑦ ᑕᒧᐊᔭᒃᓴᓐᓄᐊᕐᓂᒃ.

ᐊᓗᕈᑎ: ᐄᕐᕿ ᐱᔦᒪᖖᒋᑦᑐᖕᒐ.

ᐊᔾᔨᐊᖅ: (ᐊᕐᑯᑎᕐᕿᐊᕐᒧᑦ) ᑎᖑᒃ ᒪᒪᖅᑐᐸᓇᓗᒃ.

ᐱᓂᖅ: ᕐᑯᔭᓇᕋᓗᐊᖅᑯᓫ ᑭᓫᐊᓂᒃ ᐱᔦᒪᖖᒋᑦᑐᖕᒐ.

ᐸᓂᖕᒐᔮᒃ: (ᐊᔾᔨᐊᕐᒧᑦ) ᒪᒪᕐᓂᖅᓴᐃᑦᑐᒥᒃ ᓇᕐᕈᕆᔭᕐᑲᖅᑐᓇᓗᒃ!

ᐊᕐᑯᑎᕐᕿᐊᖅ: ᐅᕝᕕᑦᑎᐊᒍᔫᓐᓃᑦ.

CREW #1 enters with more cups and saucers.

HOLLOWAY: Yes, sir . . . but the men are getting cold.

FRANKLIN: I've eaten rotten deerskin, boiled lichen, even my boots, and I admit that being called "the man who ate his boots" is not an affectionate term, but one must endure at all costs.

HOLLOWAY: What's that on their sled over there—are those blankets . . . ?

HOLLOWAY exits.

CREW #1: *(to AĂGIAQ)* Tea, sir?

CREW #1 offers AĂGIAQ and PANINGAJAK cups and saucers—which they take. They use the cups to pour their beads into. CREW #1 is unsure what to do.

FRANKLIN: *(to CREW #2)* Set up the daguerreotype here and capture an image of us with the Esquimaux.

CREW #2: Yes, sir.

CREW #1: *(to the hunters)* The cup sits on the saucer like this . . .

CREW #1 pours the beads out of the cups—much to the hunters' consternation—then pours tea for AĂGIAQ and PANINGAJAK and tries to help them hold their cups and saucers correctly as CREW #2 gets under the blacks of the camera set up. Through the commotion, AĂGIAQ and PANINGAJAK do not see CREW #2 go under the blacks. It becomes quite a knockabout.

HOLLOWAY enters with two caribou pelts.

HOLLOWAY: These will be useful to the men, sir, if they can tolerate the smell.

FRANKLIN: They look quite fine indeed—arrange a trade.

ᑲᑑᑦ: ᐱᙱᓗᖕᒐᐅᓐᓈᑦ.

ᐸᓂᖕᒐᔭᒃ: (ᐊᔾᑎᐊᕐᒧᑦ) ᔦᕐᑯᑕᐅᙱᑦᑐᕐᓗᐃᑦ ᑕᕙᑉᑯᐊᑦ ᒪᒪᖀᖑᓂᐊ'ᓂᒃ ᓇᕐᑯᔭᕋᔦᐊᖅᑐᑦ.

ᐸᓂᖕᒐᔭᒃ ᑐᐳᑦᑎᖅᓱᒍ ᓇᑦᑎᖅ ᐊᐅᓇᖀᖅᐸᓪᖀᕐᓂᐊᙱ'ᒪᑦ.

ᑲᓘᔩᓇᓗᒃ: ᒥᖅᓱᕋᔦᐊᖅᑕᓇᓗᖕᒋᑦᑭᐊᖅᑕᐅᖅ ᔦ'ᒪᑦ? ᑐᑭᔨᓇᐃᑦᑐᓇᓗᐃᑦ ᐃᓅᒪᓅᒃ ᐅᑯᐊᒃ ᐅᒃᐱᓂᕖᖅᑳᖅᑰᙱᑦᑐᑦ.

ᐃᓚᐃᑦ ᐊᖑᑎᑦ ᐆᓇᐃᔦᓕ'ᒪᑕ—ᐊᔾᒐᐃᔨᓪᓗᐊᕚᒃᑲᒥᒃ ᕐᑯᒦᙳᖅᑐᑦ ᕐᑭᔾᒋᖅᑕᕋᔦᐊᖅᓱᑎᒃ ᐆᓇᐃᔦᒃᐸᓪᓛᕿᐃᕐᓂᐊ'ᒪᑕ.

ᐊᕐᑯᑎᕐᔪᐊᖅ: ᑳᒃᑐᐊᓘᑎ'ᓗᑕ 1919-ᒥ, ᐃᑦᑭᓕᕐᓂᑦ ᑲᒪᒋᔮᐅᒐᓗᐊᕋᑉᑕ ᓄᑕᕋᖠᔮᐅᔪᑐᑦ, ᐅᑯᐊᓪᓕ ᐃᔦᒪᒋᑦᑎᐊᕋᔦᐊᖠᐊᖅᑲᖅᑕᖅᔨ, ᑲᓘᔩᓇᓗᒃ—ᑕᒃᑰᒃ ᓂᖠᓇᔦᐊᖅᑐᒃᓴᐅᕗᑦ ᐅᑉᓗᓂᒃ ᐊᒥᔦᓂᒃ ᑳᒃᑐᒃᓴᐅᒐᓗᐊ'ᒪᑕ.

ᑲᓘᔩᓇᓗᒃ: ᐋᖑᒐᓗᐊᕐᓕ, ᐊᐅᖕᒥᒃ ᓂᖠᔪᐊᓘᒃ ᒪᐃᒪᐃ'ᓗᑎᒃ ᓄᑕᕐᓐᓄᐊᖅᑐᑦ—

ᐊᕐᑯᑎᕐᔪᐊᖅ: ᑕᒪᑉᑕ ᒪᒪᐃᑦᑐᒍᑦ ᓄᑕᕐᓐᓄᐊᖅᑐᑦ—ᑲᒪᓇᙱᑦᑐᖅ. ᑲᒪᒋᔮᕐᑲᕋᔦᐊᖅᐸᓪᓗᖠᐊᕐᑳᖅᑐᒍᑦ ᑲᐱᓕᖅᑕᐃᓕᓂᒃᓴᑉᑎ'ᓂᒃ!

ᐃᔨᖅᓱᓂ ᑲᓇᔩ ᐃᔨᖅᔨ'ᓗᓂ ᖃᓪᓗᑎᓂᒃ.

ᑲᓘᔩᓇᓗᒃ: ᐋᖑᒐᓗᐊᕐᓕ . . . ᐆᓇᐃᔦᓕ'ᒪᑕ ᐊᖑᑎᑦ.

ᐊᕐᑯᑎᕐᔪᐊᖅ: ᓂᖠᔨᒪᓕᕋᒪ ᑐᒃᑑᔮᑉ ᐊᒥᐊ'ᓂ ᐃᒍᓇᐅᑎ'ᓗᒍ, ᕐᑯᐊᔭᐅᑎᓪᓗ ᖃᓚᔨᒪᑎ'ᓗᒋᑦ ᐃᒪᕐᒥ, ᑲᒫᓘᒃᑲᓪᓘᓐᓈᑦ ᓂᖠᔨᒪᓚᐸᒃ, ᑲᓐᖑᓇᐅᒐᓗᐊᖅᑕᐅᖅ ᐊᑎᕐᑲᖅᑎᑕᐅᒪᖠᒃᑲᓗᐊᕋᒪ ᖃᒫᓘᒃᑐᖅᑐᕚᓂᕐᒥᒃ, ᑭᔨᐊᓂᓪᓕ ᐃᔦᒪ'ᓇᙱᑦᑐᖅ ᑲᐱᓕᖅᑕᐃᓕᓂᖅ ᐃᔦᒪᒋᔮᒃᓴᑐᐊᖑᔪᖅ.

ᑲᓘᔩᓇᓗᒃ: ᔦᓇᓇᓗᐃᑦᑭᐊᖅ ᖃᒨᑎᖕᒋ'ᓈᑦᑐᑦ—ᕐᑭᐱᐅ'ᔭᔪᓪᓘᓐᓈᑦ . . . ?

ᑲᓘᔩᓇᓗᒃ ᐊᓂ'ᓗᓂ.

ᑲᓇᔩ: (ᐊᔾᑎᐊᕐᒧᑦ) ᑏᑐᕈᒪᕚᑦ?

ᑲᓇᔩᑉ ᑐᓂ'ᓗᓂᒥᒃ ᐊᔾᑎᐊᕐᒧ ᐸᓂᖕᒐᔭᓪᓗ ᖃᓪᓗᑎᖕᓂᒃ ᔨᓪᔮᓐᓄᐊᖕᓂᓪᓗ—ᑎᒍ'ᒪᒥᒃ ᖃᓪᓗᑏᒃ ᔽᖠᓇᔦᐊᓕᖅᐸᒥᒃ ᔦᖕᒐᐅᔮᕐᓄᑦ. ᑲᓇᔩ ᓇᓗᓕᖅᑐᐊᓗᒃ.

HOLLOWAY: Here, Carter, you take one. Wickers, give them some salted pork for their trouble.

WICKERS: Yes, sir.

CARTER grabs one of the pelts from HOLLOWAY. PANINGAJAK and AŘGIAQ watch, puzzled.

PANINGAJAK: *(to AŘGIAQ)* Nukaq, they're taking our pelts.

AŘGIAQ: *(to PANINGAJAK)* Maybe they're cold.

HOLLOWAY wraps one of the pelts around himself as WICKERS gets two chunks of salted pork from a trunk and hands them to the hunters.

WICKERS: Here—in exchange for the skins. Pig meat—rather tasty.

AŘGIAQ and PANINGAJAK drop their cups and saucers to take a bite of pork.

CREW #1 is aghast at the dropped cups.

CREW #1: Be careful—those are porcelain cups!

FRANKLIN: When we've got the image, I want you to return to the ship to see if you can spy the *Terror* coming—it should have been here by now.

AŘGIAQ is aghast at the salted pork.

AŘGIAQ: *(to PANINGAJAK)* It's disgusting, really terrible!

HOLLOWAY: Yes, sir.

PANINGAJAK: *(to AŘGIAQ)* It's old meat with no blood—what kind of catch is this?

HOLLOWAY: *(to AŘGIAQ and PANINGAJAK)* Settle down—both of you.

AŘGIAQ: *(to HOLLOWAY) Qanurittuq una anngutikšaq? [What kind of catch is this?]*

ᐊᕐᑯᑎᕐᔪᐊᖅ: (ᓴᓇᔨᑉ ᐊᐃᑉᐹ'ᓄᑦ) ᑕᐃᒻᓇ ᐊ'ᔨᓕᐅᑎᑦᑎᐊᕙᒃ ᐅᕙᖕᒐᓂᐊᕈᒃ ᐃᑦᑐᐊᖅᓯᕆᐊᕐᑐᒍ ᐊ'ᔨᓕᐅᓂᐊᖅᑎᒍᑦᑐ ᐃᓄᒻᒪᕇᑦᑐ.

ᓴᓇᔨᑉ ᐊᐃᑉᐹ: ᐄ ᐊᑕᓂᕐᔪᐊᖅ.

ᓴᓇᔨ: (ᐊᖑᓇᓯᐊᖅᑎᓄᑦ) ᖃᑦᑐᑎᑦ ᓴᑉᑯᐊᑦ ᐃᒪ'ᓇ ᐊᑐᓂᐊᓕᑦ ᐃᓕᕙᒃᑐᕆᑦ ᑐᓐᖕᒐᕙᒃᓴᐃ'ᓄᑦ ᓯᒃᔫᓐᓄᐊᕐᒍᑦ.

ᓈᕚ'ᑐᓂᕆᑦ ᓯᖕᒐᐅᔮᑦ ᖃᑦᑐᑎᓂᑦ—ᐊᖑᓇᓯᐊᖅᑎᒃ ᐃᓗᐃᕝᕂᑎᕆᔮᑦ—ᑏᒃᓴᐃ'ᓂᒃᑐ ᑯᕙᓯᓕᖅᓗᓂ ᖃᑦᑐᑏᖕᓄᑦ, ᐊᔪᓇᖅᓱᕐᓯᐊᖅᓗᕆᒃ ᖃᓄᖅ ᖃᑦᑐᑎᑦᑐ ᓯ'ᒃᔫᓐᓄᐊᑦᑐ ᐊᑐᖅᑕᐅᔩᖃᕐᓃ'ᓂᒃ. ᓴᓇᔨᑉ ᐊᐃᑉᐹᑦᑐ ᐊ'ᔨᓕᐅ'ᒥᒃ ᐃᓗᐊᖅᓴᕐᓯᐊᖅᓗᓂ ᑖᖅᑎᑦᑎᕝᕂᑎᒥᒃ ᕿᐱᕐᑲᖅᓗᓂ ᐅᓕᕆ'ᑐᓂᐅᒃ ᐊ'ᔨᓕᐅᕐᓂᐊ'ᒪᑦ. ᐅᐃᒪᓇᖅᑯᓕᖅᑐᖅ. ᐊᕝᕆᐊᕐᑐ ᐸᓂᖕᒐᔭᒃᑐ ᑕᑯᖕᒋᑕᐃᑦ ᓴᓇᔨᑉ ᐊᐃᑉᐹ ᕿᐱᐅᑉ ᐊᑖᓃ'ᒪᑦ ᑖᖅᑎᑦᑎᕝᕂᑎᒥ.

ᓴᖑᔨᓇᓗᒃ ᐃᓱᖅᑐᖅ ᒪᕝᕈᖕᓂᒃ ᑐᒃᑑᑉ ᐊᒦ'ᓂᒃ ᑎᒍᒥᐊᖅᓗᓂ.

ᓴᖑᔨᓇᓗᒃ: ᐅᑯᐊᒃ ᐊᑑᑎᖅᑲᕐᓂᐊᖅᑑᒐᓗᐊᒃ ᓴᓇᔨᓄᑦ ᒪᒪᐃᕆᓕᑦᓚᖕᒋᓐᓂᕈᓂᕆᒃ.

ᐊᕐᑯᑎᕐᔪᐊᖅ: ᐱᑦᑕᐅᕝᕉᖅᑐᒃ ᐅᑯᐊᒃ—ᓯᓇᒥᒃ ᕿᐆᑎᖅᑲᕐᓯᐊᕐᑐᑎᑦ ᐃᓄᖕᓄᑦ ᑐᓂᔮᒃᓴᓐᓄᐊᕐᒥᒃ.

ᓴᖑᔨᓇᓗᒃ: ᐅᕖ ᑳᑦ, ᐊᑕᐅᓯᕐᒥᒃ ᐱᒡᒍᐃᑦ. ᐊᓗᕈᑎ, ᑐᓂᓕᕐᑭᑦ ᓂᕿᓐᓄᐊᕐᒥᒃ ᑕᓇᐅᓕᖅᓯᒪᔪᒥᒃ ᐆᖅᓯᒪᔪᒥᒃ.

ᐊᓗᕈᑎ: ᐄ, ᐊᑕᓂᕐᔪᐊᖅ.

ᑳᑦ ᑎᒍᓯ'ᒪᑦ ᐊᑕᐅᓯᕐᒥᒃ ᐊᒥᕐᒥᒃ ᓴᖑᔨᓇᓗᖕᒥᑦ. ᐸᓂᖕᒐᔭᒃᑐ ᐊᕝᕆᐊᕐᑐ ᑕᐅᑐᒃᑕᐃᑦ, ᓇᓗ'ᑐᑎᒃ.

ᐸᓂᖕᒐᔭᒃ: (ᐊᕝᕆᐊᕐᒧᑦ) ᓄᑲᖅ, ᐅᑯᐊᑦ ᐊᒥᕐᑯᑎᑉᑎ'ᓂᒃ ᑎᒍᓯᔪᐊᓗᐃᑦ.

ᐊᕝᕆᐊᖅ: (ᐸᓂᖕᒐᔭᖕᒧᑦ) ᐆᓇᐃᓯᒃᑐᓇᓘ'ᔫᒐᒥᒃ.

ᓴᖑᔨᓇᓗᒃ ᐅᓕᕆᓕᖅᓗᓂᐅᒃ ᐊᑕᐅᓯᖅ, ᐊᓗᕈᑎᓗ ᒪᕝᕈᖕᓂᒃ ᓂᕿᓐᓄᐊᕐᓂᒃ ᐊᑯᖅᓯᒪᔪᓂᒃ ᕿᔪᕈᑎᒥᑦ ᐊᒧᓯ'ᑐᓂ ᑐᓂ'ᑐᓂᕆᒃ ᐊᖑᓇᓯᐊᖅᑏᖕᓄᑦ.

FRANKLIN: *(to the hunters)* You're going to get your resemblance captured on the daguerreotype— *(to CREW #2)* Are you ready under there?

CREW #2: *(from under the blacks)* ALMOST, SIR!

PANINGAJAK and AǦGIAQ are spooked by the voice from under the blacks.

PANINGAJAK: *(to CARTER) Tuunngait ataaniittut. [There are spirits under there.]*

CARTER: *(to PANINGAJAK)* I've no idea what you're saying to me.

AǦGIAQ has spied bear tracks.

CREW #2: *(from under the blacks)* Look this way . . . look this way, sir.

HOLLOWAY: *(to the hunters)* Come now, fellows, look sharp.

HOLLOWAY positions AǦGIAQ and PANINGAJAK in front of the box-like daguerreotype.

PANINGAJAK: *(to AǦGIAQ)* I'm frightened, nukaq—let's get away from these men. They are frantic.

AǦGIAQ points down.

AǦGIAQ: *(to PANINGAJAK)* Two bears came through here—look, angajuk, two sets of tracks.

HOLLOWAY: *(to AǦGIAQ and PANINGAJAK)* Stay still—stop wiggling.

CREW #2: *(from under the blacks)* . . . Lovely, look straight ahead now, and—

MORSHEAD: *(off stage)* THE *TERROR*'S GOING ON AHEAD.

FRANKLIN: What?

MORSHEAD enters, terribly winded.

ᐊᓗᓯᑎ: ᐅᖕᕗ—ᑭᐴᑎᒃᓴᖅᑯᑦ ᐊᒥᕐᓄᑦ. ᑰᑰᔪᐅᑉ ᓂᕿᖕᒐ—ᒪᒪᖅᑐᖅ.

ᐊᔅᒋᐊᕐᓗ ᐸᓂᖕᒐᔭᓪᓗ ᖃᓪᓗᑎᓂᒃ ᔪᓪᔮᓐᓄᐊᕐᓂᓪᓗ ᑲᑕᐃ'ᓗᑎᒃ ᑕᒧᐊᓐᓄᐊᕋᔪᐊᓕᖅᓱᑎᒃ ᓂᕿᒥᒃ ᑖᑉᓱᒥᖕᒐᑦ.

ᔭᓇᔫ ᖁᐊᖅᔮᖅᑐᖅ ᖃᓪᓗᑎᑦᑎᐊᖒᒃ ᑲᑕᐃᒐᒥᒋᒃ.

ᔭᓇᔫ: ᐅᔅᔫᖅᑐᑦᑎᐊᕆᑦᑎᒃ ᔭᑉᑯᐊᑦ ᖃᓪᓗᑎᑦ ᐊᑭᑐᔪᓇᓗᐃᑦ!

ᐊᕐᑯᑎᕐᔪᐊᖅ: ᐊ'ᔮᓕᐅᖅᑖᓯᕚᑦ ᐅᑎᕐᑯᔮᓯᑦ ᐅᒥᐊᕐᔪᐊᕐᒧᑦ ᑕᑯᓇᕆᐊᕐᓗᑎᑦ ᐅᒥᐊᕐᔪᐊᑉ ᐊᐃᑉᐹ ᑕᐃᒻᓇ ᖃᐃᕗᓪᓚᐊᓚᕆᐊᒃᓴᖅ—ᑎᑭᑦᑐᒃᓴᓯᓚᕋᓗᐊ'ᒪᑦ.

ᐊᔅᒋᐊᖅ ᓂᕿ ᐃᐳᐃᑦᑐᒦᑦᑐᖅ ᑕᕆᐅᓚᓇᓗᒃ ᑕᑯᕋᓐᓃᒥᔮ.

ᐊᔅᒋᐊᖅ: *(ᐸᓂᖕᒐᔭᖕᒧᑦ)* ᓇᕐᑯᔭᔅᓇᖅᑐᕌᓗᒃ, ᔪᔮᔅᓗᒃ ᑕᔭᒻᒪ!

ᔭᖑᔮᓇᓗᒃ: ᐄ, ᐊᑕᓂᕐᔪᐊᖅ.

ᐸᓂᖕᒐᔭᒃ: *(ᐊᔅᒋᐊᕐᒧᑦ)* ᐱᑐᖃᔅᓗᒃ ᐊᐅᖅᑲᖖᒋᑦᑐᓇᓗᒃ—ᖃᓄᕆᑦᑐᑭᐊᖅ ᐅᓇ ᐊᓐᖑᑎᒃᓴᖅ?

ᔭᖑᔮᓇᓗᒃ: *(ᐊᔅᒋᐊᕐᒧᑦ ᐸᓂᖕᒐᔭᖕᒧᓪᓗ)* ᐅᐃᒪᔪᐃᕆᑦᑎᒃ—ᑕᒪᑉᑎᒃ.

ᐊᔅᒋᐊᖅ: *(ᔭᖑᔮᓇᓗᖕᒧᑦ)* ᖃᓄᕆᑦᑐᖅ ᐅᓇ ᐊᓐᖑᑎᒃᓴᖅ?

ᐊᕐᑯᑎᕐᔪᐊᖅ: *(ᐊᖑᓇᔪᐊᖅᑎᓄᑦ)* ᐊ'ᔮᓕᐅᖅᑕᐅᓂᐊᓯᑉᔪᒃ ᐊ'ᔮᓕᐅᑎᑦᑎᐊᕗᑎᒍᑦ—*(ᔭᓇᔫᑉ ᐊᐃᑉᐹ'ᓄᑦ)* ᐃᓪᓗᐊᖅᔪᑦᑎᐊᖅᓕᖅᐱᑦ?

ᔭᓇᔫᑉ ᐊᐃᑉᐹ: *(ᕿᐱᐅᑉ ᐊᑖᓂᑦ ᑭᐅᓇᔪᐊᖅᓱᓂ)* ᐃᓪᓗᐊᖅᔪᔅᓰᓕᖅᑐᖓ, ᐊᑕᓂᕐᔪᐊᖅ!

ᐸᓂᖕᒐᔭᓪᓗ ᐊᔅᒋᐊᕐᓗ ᖁᓪᓗᒃᑰᒃ ᓂᐱᒥᒃ ᑐᔭᕋᒥᒃ ᕿᐱᑉ ᐊᑖᓂᑦ.

ᐸᓂᖕᒐᔭᒃ: *(ᑲᑑ'ᒧᑦ)* ᑑᖖᒐᐃᑦ ᐊᑖᓃᑦᑐᑦ.

ᑲᑑᑦ: *(ᐸᓂᖕᒐᔭᖕᒧᑦ)* ᑐᔮᖖᒋᒻᒪᕆᒃᑲᑉᑭᑦ.

ᐊᔅᒋᐊᖅ ᑕᑯ'ᒪᑦ ᓇᓄᐃᑦ ᑐᒦ'ᓂᒃ.

MORSHEAD: Crozier's continuing north on the *Terror*—there's too much drift ice coming up behind.

CREW #2: *(from under the blacks)* . . . Please don't move—stay still, for I must capture two plates—STAY STILL!

FRANKLIN: Jumping foxholes— *(to HOLLOWAY)* Bring me the map!

CREW #2: *(from under the blacks)* . . . I almost had it.

MORSHEAD: *(re: AǦGIAQ and PANINGAJAK)* Are these our new guides?

CREW #2 comes out from under the blacks.

CREW #2: Dog's bottom—I almost had it!

FRANKLIN: No, they're traders of sorts, though we should ask them to be our guides. *Ud-yuck* and *Panny-guy-yuck*—this is Oliver Morshead, Engineer and Ice Master— *(to MORSHEAD)* Why in Heaven's name is Crozier barrelling on ahead?

MORSHEAD: The *Erebus* could be ice-bound by morning—rammed in tight on account the wind's up, south-southwest, sir, heading right for us.

AǦGIAQ: *(to PANINGAJAK)* Let's follow the bear's tracks—he might have another seal.

PANINGAJAK: *(to AǦGIAQ)* If these men are whalers, there must be a whale in that big boat.

MORSHEAD: Crozier's heading northwest—he'll wait for us in the open water.

FRANKLIN: No he will not—go signal Crozier to remain where he is!

MORSHEAD: Sir, with all due respect, I gave him the signal that we'd follow.

FRANKLIN: We'd follow—follow where?

AǦGIAQ: *(to PANINGAJAK)* Maybe they haven't got a whale yet—you ask them first.

ᓴᓇᔭᑉ ᐊᐃᑉᐹ: *(ᕿᐱᐅᑉ ᐅᓕᐅᑉ ᐊᑖᓂᑦ)* ᐅᕗᖓ
ᕿᕕᐊᓕᕆᑦᑎ . . . ᐅᕗᖓ ᐊᑕᐃ, ᐊᑕᓂᕐᔪᐊᖅ.

ᓴᖑᔭᓇᓗᒃ: *(ᐊᖑᓇᔪᐊᖅᑏᖕᖑᑦ)* ᐊᑕᐃ, ᐊ'ᔭᓕᐅᖅᑕᐅᑦᑎᐊᕋᔪᐊᕆᑦᑎᒃ.

*ᓴᖑᔭᓇᓗᒃ ᐃᖢᐊᖅᓴᕆᐊᖅᖢᒥᒃ ᐊᔅᒥᐊᕐᓗ ᐸᓂᖕᖓᓯᖕᓗ
ᐊ'ᔭᓕᐅᑎᐅᑉ ᓵᖕᖓᓄᑦ.*

ᐸᓂᖕᖓᓯᒃ: *(ᐊᔅᒥᐊᕐᒧᑦ)* ᐃᖅᔪᖕᖓ ᓄᑲᖅ—ᕿᒪᒃᑎᒍᑦ ᐅᑯᐊᑦ. ᐅᐃᒻᒪᐅᒪᔪᑦ.

ᐊᔅᒥᐊᖅ ᑎᑦᑯᐊᖅᖢᓂ ᑕᐅᓄᖕᖓ.

ᐊᔅᒥᐊᖅ: *(ᐸᓂᖕᖓᓯᖕᒧᑦ)* ᑕᒃᑰᒃ ᐊᖕᖓᔪᒃ—ᓇᓅᒃ ᑕᓴᒨᖓᖅᑐᒃ, ᑐᒥᓇᓗᐃᑦ.

ᓴᖑᔭᓇᓗᒃ: *(ᐊᔅᒥᐊᕐᒧᑦ ᐸᓂᖕᖓᓯᖕᒧᑦᓗ)* ᓄᑦᕐᑲᖕᖓᑦᑎᐊᕐᓗᔦᒃ—
ᐊᐅᓚᖕᖏᒪᕆᒃᓗᔦᒃᓕ ᐊ'ᔭᓕᐅᖅᑕᐅᑦᑎᐊᕐᓂᐊᕋᑉᔦᒃ.

ᓴᓇᔭᑉ ᐊᐃᑉᐹ: *(ᕿᐱᐅᑉ ᐅᓕᐅᑉ ᐊᑖᓂᑦ)* . . . ᑕᔅᓯᑦᑎᐊᓯᒃ, ᐊᑕᐃ
ᑕᓴᒧᖕᖓ ᑕᐅᑐᒃᓗᔦ ᐃᒪ'ᓇ—

ᓇᐅᑦᑎᖅᑐᖅᑎ: *(ᐊᓯ'ᖕᖓᑦ)* ᐅᒥᐊᕐᔪᐊᑉ ᐊᐃᑉᐹ ᑕᐃᒪ ᖄᖕᖏᐅᑎᓕᖅᑐᖅ.

ᐊᕐᑯᑎᕐᔪᐊᖅ: ᔪᓰ?

ᓇᐅᑦᑎᖅᑐᖅᑎ ᐃᔦᖅᖢᓂ ᐃ'ᔾᖖᒍᖅᑰᖅᖢᓂ.

ᓇᐅᑦᑎᖅᑐᖅᑎ: ᐃᒪ ᐅᒥᐊᕐᔪᐊᑉ ᐊᐃᑉᐹ ᑕᑉᐸᐅᖓᓯᑦᓗᖅ ᑐᓵᖅᑐᖅ—
ᑕᓴᒪᓂ ᔦᑯᕐᑲᖅᐸᑦᑖ'ᒪᑦ ᐊᔭᖅᔦᕙᕕᓯᔭᒪᖖᒋᑕᐃᑦ.

ᓴᓇᔭᑉ ᐊᐃᑉᐹ: *(ᕿᐱᐅᑉ ᐅᓕᐅᑉ ᐊᑖᓂᑦ)* . . . ᐃᖑᑦᑕᐃᓕᓇᓱᐊᕆᑦᑎᓕ
—ᓄᑦᕐᑲᖕᖓᑦᑎᐊᒻᒪᕆᒃᓗᔦ ᒪᔅᓴᖕᓂᒃ ᐱᓇᓱᐊᕆᐊᖅᑲᕐᒪ—ᓄᑦᕐᑲᖕᖓᑦᑎᐊᕐᓗᔦ!

ᐊᕐᑯᑎᕐᔪᐊᖅ: ᓱᕐᑯᑕᐅᖖᒋᑦᑐᓇᓗᖕᓗᒃ *(ᓴᖑᔭᓇᓗᖕᒧᑦ)* ᐃᒪ ᓄᓇᖖᒍᐊᖅ
ᖃᐃᑲᐅᒃ!

ᓴᓇᔭᑉ ᐊᐃᑉᐹ: *(ᕿᐱᐅᑉ ᐅᓕᐅᑉ ᐊᑖᓂᑦ)* . . . ᐱᔅᓴᓯᖅᐸᕋ.

ᓇᐅᑦᑎᖅᑐᖅᑎ: *(ᐱ'ᓗᒋᒃ ᐊᔅᒥᐊᕐᓗ ᐸᓂᖕᖓᓯᖕᓗ)* ᐅᑯᐊᒃ
ᐅᓐᓂᖅᑰ'ᔭᒃᓴᕆᓕᖅᐱᑎᒍᒃ?

MORSHEAD: He's going up about eighteen nautical miles, sir—northwest.

PANINGAJAK: *(to AŘGIAQ)* You ask— *(points to MORSHEAD)* Ask this one here.

FRANKLIN: On whose authority did you signal him that the *Erebus* would follow?

AŘGIAQ: *(to MORSHEAD) Arviqtaqaqpa taavani umiaphi'ni? [Is there a whale in your boat over there?]*

MORSHEAD: Well, sir, I assumed that you—

FRANKLIN: ASSUMED? It takes all of four minutes to disembark, come to me, state the situation, take my orders back to the *Erebus*, and give *my* orders to Crozier on the *Terror*—not your *assumption* of what my orders might be.

AŘGIAQ: *(to MORSHEAD)* Arviqtaqaqpa taavani umiaphi'ni? *[Is there a whale in your boat over there?]*

MORSHEAD: Yes, I know, sir, but I fear we're too heavy and the draught—

FRANKLIN: We are *not* too heavy—

MORSHEAD: I already spoke to you about this matter in Greenhithe, sir—

PANINGAJAK: *(to MORSHEAD)* Arviqtaqaqpa taavani umiaphi'ni? *[Is there a whale in your boat over there?]*

FRANKLIN: Balderdash—we're carrying eight thousand cans of preserved meat, nine thousand pounds of lemon juice, three thousand books—all *necessities.*

MORSHEAD: Books!

FRANKLIN: Yes, books—we can't sail halfway round the world without *books*—where are you from— *(to HOLLOWAY)* Where did we pick up this blockhead?

ᓴᓇᔨᑉ ᐊᐃᑉᐹ ᕿᐱᐅᑉ ᐅᓕᐅᑉ ᐊᑖᓂᑦ ᓴᑦᕿᑦᓴᖑᔭᖅᓱᓂ.

ᓴᓇᔨᑉ ᐊᐃᑉᐹ: ᐃᑎᑉᔪᐅᕐᓱᐃᑦ—ᐱᔾᖃᓯᖅᑕᓇᓱᒐ!

ᐊᕐᑯᑎᕐᔪᐊᖅ: ᐄᕿᑉ, ᐱᕐᑯᑎᒃᓵᖅᔪᔮᐅ'ᓯᔪᑉ, ᐊᐱᕆᓇᓯᖅᑕᕗᓪᓕ ᐃᑲᔪᕈᓐᓇᕆᐊᒃᓴᐃᑕ. ᐊᔾᔨᐊᖅ ᐸᓂᖓᓯᒡᓗ ᐅᓇ ᐋᓕᕙ ᓇᐅᑦᑎᖅᑐᖅᑎ, ᓇᐅᑦᑎᖅᑐᖅᑎᐅ'ᒪᑦ ᔪᑯᑦᑯᑦ ᐃᓐᖏᕐᑯᑎᓕᕆᔮᐅ'ᓱᓂ—(*ᓇᐅᑦᑎᖅᑐᖅᑎᒧᑦ*) ᔨ'ᒪᓇᓱᒃ ᐃᒻᓇ ᑳᐱᑕᐃᓯ ᑖᕗᙳᖅᐸᓪᓕᐊᓕᖃᓱᐊᖅᐸᓕ ᓴᒧᙳᙵᕆ'ᓱᓂ?

ᓇᐅᑦᑎᖅᑐᖅᑎ: ᐅᒥᐊᕐᔪᐊᖅᑯᓪᓕ ᔪᑯᒧᑦ ᐊᔪᖅᔪᔪᒪᓂᐊᓕᖅᑰ'ᒪᑦ ᖃᐅᙱᓂᐊ'ᓂᒃ—ᐊᔪᖅᔪᔪᒪᑦᑎᐊᕈᓐᓇᖅᑐᖅ ᐱ'ᓱᒍ ᐊᓄᕆᓇᓱᒃ ᓂᕿᒥ'ᙶᓕᖅᑐᕐᓱᒃ ᐊᓄᖅᓯᐅᒪᓪᓚᕐᔳᓱᙵᓂᐊᖅᑐᖅ.

ᐊᔾᔨᐊᖅ: (*ᐸᓂᖓᓯᖓᒧᑦ*) ᒪᓕᒃᑎᒍᒃ ᑐᒥᖓᕆᑦ—ᓇᑦᑎᖅᑐᒃᓴᕈ'ᒥ'ᒪᑦ.

ᐸᓂᖓᓯᒃ: (*ᐊᔾᔨᐊᕐᒧᑦ*) ᐅᑯᐊᑦ ᐊᕐᕕᖅᔭᐅᖅᑎᐅᒍᑎᒃ ᐊᕐᕕᖅᑲᖅᑐᒃᓵᕐᓱᐃᑦ ᐅᒥᐊᕐᔪᐊᕐᒥ'ᓂ.

ᓇᐅᑦᑎᖅᑐᖅᑎ: ᐅᐊᖓᓇᕐᒧᑦ ᑐᕌᖅᑐᖅ ᑕᐃᒪ ᑳᐱᑕᐃᓯ—ᐅᑕᖅᑭᓂᐊᖅᑖᑎᒍᑦ ᔪᑯᖃᙱᓐᓂᕐᒥ.

ᐊᕐᑯᑎᕐᔪᐊᖅ: ᐅᑕᖅᑭᓚᐃᑦᑐᕐᓱᒃ ᐃᒻᓇ—ᐊᒃᐱᐅᑎᓯᖅᑐᓕᑉ ᓄᑦᑲᖓᑦᑯ'ᓱᒍ!

ᓇᐅᑦᑎᖅᑐᖅᑎ: ᐊᑕᓂᕐᔪᐊᖅ, ᐃᓕ'ᓄᑦ ᑭᐅᒪᓇᔨᐊᙱᑦᑐᖓᐅᒐᓱᐊᖅ, ᑭᔪᐊᓂᒃ ᐊᒃᐱᐅᑎᑖᖅᑕᖃᓱᐊᖃ ᒪᓕᒍᒫᖃᑉᑕᑰᖅ.

ᐊᕐᑯᑎᕐᔪᐊᖅ: ᒪᓕᒍᒫᖃᑉᑕᑰᖅ—ᔨᒧᑦ?

ᐊᔾᔨᐊᖅ: (*ᐸᓂᖓᓯᖓᒧᑦ*) ᐊᕐᕕᖅᑕᙱᑦᑐᒃᓴᕐᓱᐃᑦ ᔨᓕ—ᐊᐱᕆᖅᑳᕐᓱᕆᓪᓕ.

ᓇᐅᑦᑎᖅᑐᖅᑎ: ᑕᑉᐅᖓᐅᓇᔨᐊᖅᑐᖅ ᖃᓂᒃᑐᒧᑦ 18 ᒪᐃᓕᓂᒃ ᐅᖓᔪᒃᑎᕆᔪᒧᑦ.

ᐸᓂᖓᓯᒃ: (*ᐊᔾᔨᐊᕐᒧᑦ*) ᐊᐱᕆᓱᒍ ᐅᓇ—(*ᑎᑦᑯᐊᖅᓱᓂ ᓇᐅᑦᑎᖅᑐᖅᑎᒧᑦ*) ᐅᓇ ᐊᐱᕆᓱᒍ.

ᐊᕐᑯᑎᕐᔪᐊᖅ: ᐃᔨᒪᒃᔫᖅᔪᓐᓇᖅᓱᑎᑦ ᐊᒃᐱᐅᑎᕕᐅᒃ ᒪᓕᖕᓂᐊᖅᑐᕆ'ᓱᑕ?

ᐊᔾᔨᐊᖅ: (*ᓇᐅᑦᑎᖅᑐᖅᑎᒧᑦ*) ᐊᕐᕕᖅᑕᖅᑲᑉ ᑖᕙᓂ ᐅᒥᐊᑉᔪ'ᓂ—

AŘGIAQ: *(to* FRANKLIN*) Arviqtaqaqpihili iluani— [Do you have a whale inside your—]*

FRANKLIN: *(to* AŘGIAQ*)* Do shut up, will you—

HOLLOWAY: *(to* FRANKLIN*)* Bristol, sir—he's very experienced.

MORSHEAD: All I'm saying is that the extra weight of the iron plating on the bow and the steam locomotive engine makes us vulnerable to—

FRANKLIN: By God, man—we'll survive a bit of drifting ice because it is our sworn duty as members of the Royal Navy to navigate the passage!

MORSHEAD: Notions of duty must be flexible in such an unpredictable landscape—this landscape obeys nothing and no one—not you, not me, not the Royal Navy, not the queen—

FRANKLIN: I've had just about enough of your podsnappery!

AŘGIAQ: *(to* MORSHEAD*) ARVIQTAQAQPA UMIARŘUANALUNGMI? [IS THERE A WHALE IN YOUR BIG BOAT OVER THERE?]*

MORSHEAD: *(to* PANINGAJAK*) UCK-VEK-TAH-COCK-KEY-YAIT-CHOOK OOM-YUCK-RUP-TIT-NEE—KEY-NECK-TIO-GAP-TALLY.* NO, THERE'S NO DAMN WHALES IN OUR SHIP—WE'RE EXPLORERS!

PANINGAJAK: *(to* AŘGIAQ*)* They have no whales—they're explorers.

FRANKLIN: What are they saying?

MORSHEAD: *(to* FRANKLIN*)* They think we're whalers, sir.

PANINGAJAK: *(to* AŘGIAQ*)* I think these explorers are about to punch each other out—come on, let's run.

AŘGIAQ: *(to* PANINGAJAK*)* Grab the pelts.

> *AŘGIAQ reaches over and takes the pelt off HOLLOWAY, and PANINGAJAK takes the pelt from CARTER.*

ᓇᐅᑦᑎᖅᑐᖅᑎ: ᐊᑕᓂᕐᔪᐊᖅ, ᐃᔨᒪᒐᓗᐊᕋᒪ ᐃᕝᕕᑦ ᑕᐃᒪ'ᓇ ᐱᑦᖁᔭᓇᓴᕋᓗᐊᕋ'ᓂ—

ᐊᖁᑎᕐᔪᐊᖅ: (ᔨᐊᒃᑐᕐᓗᐊᓕᖅᓱᐅᒃ) ᐃᔨᒪᔭᓐᓇᖅᓱᑎᑦ? ᐊᐱᕆᕙᕇᕈᖕᓇᕋᔭᖅᑕᕋᓗᐊ'ᒪ ᐅᕙᒻᒥᖕᒐᐅᔪᖕᓇᕋᔭᖅᓱᑎᑦ ᐊᐱᕆᓗ'ᒪ ᖃᓄᕐᓕᐅᓇᐊᒃᓴ'ᓂᒃ ᐅᕕᑦᑎᐊᖕᒋᓐᓇᓐᓄᐊᕐᓗ ᐅᑎᕐᓗᑎᑦ ᐅᒥᐊᕐᔪᐊᕐᒧᑦ ᐊᒃᐱᐅᑎᑦᑎᐊᕐᓗᒍᓗ ᑳᐱᑕᐃᓴ—ᑭᔭᐊᓂᒃ ᐃᔨᒪᖅᓱᕋᔨᐊᖅᔭᓐᓇᓕᖅᓱᑎᑦ ᓇ'ᒥᓂᖅ ᐱᕙᓪᓗᕋᕕᑦ.

ᐊᕝᒋᐊᖅ: (ᓇᐅᑦᑎᖅᑐᖅᑎᒧᑦ) ᐊᕐᕕᖅᑕᖃᐸ ᑖᕙᓂ ᐅᒥᐊᑉᔭ'ᓂ—

ᓇᐅᑦᑎᖅᑐᖅᑎ: ᐄᕝᒍᒐᓗᐊᖅ, ᐊᑕᓂᕐᔪᐊᖅ ᐃᒃᑕᕆᒃᐸᓪᓛ'ᒪᑦ ᐅᒥᐊᕐᔪᐊᕗᑦ ᐊᓄᕆᓇᓗᒃᓗ—

ᐊᖁᑎᕐᔪᐊᖅ: ᐃᒃᑕᕆᒃᐸᓪᓛᖕᒋᓪᒪᕆᒃᑐᒍᓪᓕ—

ᓇᐅᑦᑎᖅᑐᖅᑎ: ᐊᒃᐱᐅᑎᑖᖅᑕᕋᓗᐊᑉᑭᑦ ᑕᓴᑉᓱᒥᖕᒐ ᑕᕆᐅᑉ ᐊᑭᐊᓃᑎ'ᓗᑕ, ᐊᑕᓂᕐᔪᐊᖅ—

ᐸᓂᖕᒐᔭᒃ: (ᓇᐅᑦᑎᖅᑐᖅᑎᒧᑦ) ᐊᕐᕕᖅᑕᖃᐸ ᑖᕙᓂ ᐅᒥᐊᕐᔪᐊᕐᒥ—

ᐊᖁᑎᕐᔪᐊᖅ: ᓴᓪᓗᔪᑎᑦ—ᓂᖃᐅᑎᖃᕋᑉᑕ 8000 ᐃᐳᐃᑦᑐᓂᒃ ᓂᕿᓕᖕᓂᒃ; 9000 ᐸᐅᓐ-ᓂᒃ ᔫᕐᓇᖅᑐᑦ ᐃᒥᒐᐃ'ᓂᒃ; 3000 ᐅᖃᓕᒫᒐᕐᓂᒃ—ᑕᒪᐃᑕ ᐊᑐᖅᑐᐊᓗᐃᑦ ᐅᑯᐊᑦ ᑕᒪᐃᑕ ᐊᑐᖅᑕᒃᓴᕗᑦ.

ᓇᐅᑦᑎᖅᑐᖅᑎ: ᐅᖃᓕᒫᒐᓇᓗᐃᑦ!

ᐊᖁᑎᕐᔪᐊᖅ: ᐄ, ᐅᖃᓕᒫᒐᓇᓗᖕᓂᒃ—ᐅᖕᒐᔮᒃᑐᐊᓗᖕᒧᑦ ᐃᖕᒋᕝᕋᓚᐃᑦᑐᒧᑦ ᐅᖃᓕᒫᒐᒃᓴᖃᑦᑎᐊᙱᓗᑕ—ᔨᒥᐅᑕᐅᕕᓪᓕ—(ᓴᖑᔭᓇᓗᖕᒧᑦ) ᔨᒥᑦ ᐅᓇ ᓴᓇᔭᑖᕆᔮᕐᓱᒃᑯᓪᓕ ᔨᖁᑕᐅᙱᑦᑐᓇᓗᒃ ᔨᓕᓚᐃᑦᑐᑉᑲᕆᓇᓗᕐᓱᒃ.

ᐊᕝᒋᐊᖅ: (ᐊᖁᑎᕐᔪᐊᕐᒧᑦ) ᐊᕐᕕᖅᑕᖅᐱᔭ ᐃᓗᐊᓂ—

ᐊᖁᑎᕐᔪᐊᖅ: (ᐊᕝᒋᐊᕐᒧᑦ) ᓂᐸᐃᕐᓱᒃᓗᑎᓪᓕ—

ᓴᖑᔭᓇᓗᒃ: (ᐊᖁᑎᕐᔪᐊᕐᒧᑦ) ᓴᓇᔭᑖᕆᔮᕗᑦ ᐅᓇ ᐊᑭᐊᓂᕐᒥᐅᑕᖅ ᑯᐃᓐ ᒧᓈᓂ—ᐊᔪᒐᐃᑦᖂᖅᑑᒐᓗᐊᕐᓕ.

ᓇᐅᑦᑎᖅᑐᖅᑎ: ᑐᑭᓕᐅᕋᔨᐊᖅᔭᓐᓇᖅᑐᕐᔫᔪᖕᒐᓕ ᐃᒃᑕᕆᒃᑐᓈᒪᑦ ᓴᕕᒃ ᐅᒥᐊᕐᔪᐊᑉ ᔭᕗᓂᐊᓃᑦᑐᖅ ᐃᓐᖏᖁᑎᓪᓗ ᑕᓴᑉᑯᐊᑦ ᐃᒃᑕᕆᒃᑐᖄ'ᒪᑕ—

HOLLOWAY: I beg your pardon—that's *mine*!

HOLLOWAY grabs the pelt back from AŘGIAQ.

AŘGIAQ: *(to HOLLOWAY) Utiphiatkit amiqqut! [Give us back our pelts!]*

AŘGIAQ tries to yank the pelt from HOLLOWAY's grasp.

MORSHEAD: *(to HOLLOWAY)* He says those skins belongs to them.

HOLLOWAY: It's mine, thank you very much.

AŘGIAQ: *(to HOLLOWAY) Tunihiguvit—pitaarumařutit—tunihiluni—pitaara-huaqtuq. [Give—take—give—take.] (to PANINGAJAK)* These ones have the minds of children. *(to HOLLOWAY) Amiqqut utiqtitkit! [Give back our pelts!]*

MORSHEAD: *(to HOLLOWAY)* He wants you to give back the skins.

FRANKLIN: By rights we should return them because they didn't like the pork.

HOLLOWAY: They took handfuls of beads—it's a fair trade.

FRANKLIN: That's an order, Holloway!

MORSHEAD: *(to AŘGIAQ and PANINGAJAK) Peen-yuck-tuck-hee. [You will get them back.]*

HOLLOWAY and CARTER all but throw the pelts back at AŘGIAQ and PANINGAJAK.

PANINGAJAK: *(to AŘGIAQ)* Why are they angry? If they are cold, we will give them a pelt. We are not angry men. *(to CARTER) Ninngaluřuunngittugulli ang-utau'luta. [We are men that don't give into anger easily.]*

MORSHEAD: *(to AŘGIAQ and PANINGAJAK) Angoo-tow-ngeet-chew-hee-gook—hoo-lee-ngeet-chew-hee-loo. [They don't think you're men—they think you're foolish.]*

ᐊᕐᑯᑎᕐᖪᐊᖅ: ᐅᓇᕐᔪᒃ—ᔑᑯᑎᒍᑦ ᐊᔪᖅᔑᓚᐃᑦᑐᓇᓘᖪᒍᓪᓕ
ᐅᒥᐊᕐᖪᐊᖅᑐᖅᑎᐸᓇᓘᒐᑉᑕ ᐊᑉᕐᑯᑎᒃᓵᖅᔑᐅᕐᑯᖬᐅ'ᓗᑕᓗ ᐃᒪᑦᑯᑦ ᑕᓇᐅᒃᑯᑦ!

ᓇᐅᑦᑎᖅᑐᖅᑎ: ᐋᖑᒐᓗᐊᕐᓕ ᑕᕐᒪᓂ ᖃᐅᔾᒪᖕᒋ'ᓇᑉᑎᒍᑦ ᐊᕚᑎᖕᒐ
ᐊ'ᓚᖖᒍᖅᑕᖅᑑ'ᒪᓪᓗ—ᓄᓇ ᑕᕐᒪ ᐊᑕᓂᖃᖖᒋᑦᑐᖅ ᐃᖨᒪᒃᓱᖅᑐᑐᐊᖑᕗᖅ—
ᓈᓚᓚᐃᑖᑎᑦ, ᓈᓚᓚᐃᑖᖕᒐᓘᓐᓃᑦ, ᐅᒥᐊᕐᖪᐊᖅᑐᖅᑐᓕᓇᔾᓂᒡᓘᓐᓃᑦ,
ᑯᐃᓐᒥᒡᓘᓐᓃᑦ ᓈᓚᓚᐃᑦᑐᖅ ᕐᒪ ᐅᑭᐅᖅᑕᖅᑑᑉ ᔑᓛ—

ᐊᕐᑯᑎᕐᖪᐊᖅ: ᑎᑉᖨᐅᕐᔪᐃᑦ, ᑑᕐᖕᒍᖅᑕᐸᓇᓗᒋᓕᖅᐸᒋᑦ!

ᐊᕆᐊᖅ: *(ᓇᐅᑦᑎᖅᑐᖅᑎᒧᑦ)* ᐊᕐᕚᖅᑕᖅᑲᖅᐸ ᐅᒥᐊᕐᖪᐊᓇᓗᖕᒥ—

ᓇᐅᑦᑎᖅᑐᖅᑎ: *(ᐸᓂᖕᒐᔭᖕᒧᑦ)* ᐊᕐᕚᖅᑕᖅᑲᖅᑲᔭᐃᑦᑐᖅ
ᐅᒥᐊᕐᖪᐊᑉᑎ'ᓂ—ᕿᓂᖅᑎᐅᒐᑉᑕᓕ!

*ᖃᐅᔾᒪᔾᐅᓕ: ᓇᐅᑦᑎᖅᑐᖅᑎ ᐃᓄᒃᑑᑦᑎᐊᓚᐃᑦᑑᒐᓗᐊᖅ
ᐊᕐᑯᑎᕐᖪᐊᕐᒥᐅᖕᒐᓂᑦ ᐅᖅᑲᑎᐊᑦᕿᔾᐅᓐᓄᐊᖅᑐᖅ ᖨᓕ ᑯᑕᒃᔪᓂ.*

ᐸᓂᖕᒐᔭᒃ: *(ᐊᕆᐊᕐᒧᑦ)* ᐊᕐᕚᖅᑕᖅᑲᖅᑲᔭᐃᑦᑐᑦ—ᕿᓂᖅᑎᐅᒐᒥᓐᖑᔫᖅ.

ᐊᕐᑯᑎᕐᖪᐊᖅ: ᖃᓄᕐᓕᐅᖅᑐᒃ ᐅᑯᐊᒃ.

ᓇᐅᑦᑎᖅᑐᖅᑎ: *(ᐊᕐᑯᑎᕐᖪᐊᕐᒧᑦ)* ᐊᕐᕚᖅᔑᐅᖅᑎᐅᓇᖨᒋᔾᑎᒍᑦ.

ᐸᓂᖕᒐᔭᒃ: *(ᐊᕆᐊᕐᒧᑦ)* ᐅᑯᐊᑦ ᕿᓂᖅᑎᑦ ᑎᓐᓘᑎᖅᑲᑦᑕᐅᑎᓕᕐᓂᐊᕚ'ᒪᑕ—
ᐊᑕᐃ ᐅ'ᓚᒡᓗ.

ᐊᕆᐊᖅ: *(ᐸᓂᖕᒐᔭᖕᒧᑦ)* ᑎᒍᑦᑭᑦ ᐊᒦᑦ.

*ᐊᕆᐊᖅ ᐃᕐᑲᒃᓗᓂ ᐊᒥᖅ ᑎᒎᔾ ᕐᖑᖨᓇᓗᖕᒥᑦ, ᐸᓂᖕᒐᔭᒡᓗ
ᑎᒍ'ᓗᓂᐅᒃ ᑲᑰ'ᒥᑦ.*

ᕐᖑᖨᓇᓗᒃ: ᖨᖪᓇᓘᖪᑎ—ᐅᓇ ᐱᒐ!

ᕐᖑᖨᓇᓗᒃ ᑎᒍᓪᓚᕐᕐᖅᔪᓗᓂᐅᒃ ᐊᕆᐊᕐᒥᑦ.

ᐊᕆᐊᖅ: *(ᕐᖑᖨᓇᓗᖕᒧᑦ)* ᐅᑎᑉᔑᐊᑦᑭᑦ ᐊᒥᖅᑯᑦ.

ᐊᕆᐊᖅ ᑎᒍᓇᖨᐊᓕᖅᔪᓂᐅᒃ ᕐᖑᖨᓇᓗᒥᑦ.

PANINGAJAK and AŘGIAQ are taken aback, then they bluster and smile, dropping their arms down between their legs to suggest their mighty powers.

FRANKLIN: *(to MORSHEAD)* What did you say to them?

MORSHEAD: I said we don't think they're men—we think they're foolish.

PANINGAJAK: *(to FRANKLIN and his crew) Uvagut angutauřugut hanngiřualuuřugut angunahuaqtiuřugut. (akuarminik titkuaqłuni) Igřuqquqtunaluuřugut. [As men we are strong and we are hunters. (indicating his crotch) We have fantastically huge testicles.]*

AŘGIAQ: *(to FRANKLIN and his crew) Pingahunik niuqaqtugut atauhirlu angiřuraaluk. [Yes, we have three legs and one is very huge.]*

FRANKLIN: *(to MORSHEAD)* Whatever they are inferring—tell them to stop it right now!

MORSHEAD: They say they possess stupendous genitalia, sir.

FRANKLIN: Tell them that our genitals are twice as big as theirs.

MORSHEAD: *(to AŘGIAQ and PANINGAJAK) Eeg-rook-koodlee ee-lee-fint-new-ngaw-nit ah-ngeet-key-yow-yoot [Our testicles are twice as big as yours—so stuff it.]*

PANINGAJAK: . . . Twice as big . . . *(laughs)* Whoaaa, they must be humongous if they are bigger than ours.

Tension is released as all the men find some common ground to laugh about—penis size. FRANKLIN cracks a smile.

FRANKLIN: Morshead, ask them if they would consider being our guides.

MORSHEAD: *(to AŘGIAQ) Oo-neck-toot-rhiggy-yong-nak-peetee-geek? [Would you be our guides?]*

ᓇᐅᑦᑎᖅᑐᖅᑎ: *(ᖃᖑᔮᓇᓗᖕᒧᑦ)* ᓱ'ᒪᓪᓚ ᐱᕆᓇᓱᕆᔭᐃᑦ ᐅᑯᐊᒃ ᐊᒦᒃ?

ᖃᖑᔮᓇᓗᒃ: ᐅᕙᖓ, ᐱᒐᓚ, ᖁᔭᓇᕐᓗᐊᖅᑯᑎᑦ.

ᐊᓯᐊᖅ: *(ᖃᖑᔮᓇᓗᖕᒧᑦ)* ᑐᓂᔪᒍᕕᑦ ᐱᑖᕈᒪᔪᑎᑦ—ᑐᓂᔪᓗᓂ ᐱᑖᕋᓱᐊᖅᑐᖅ *(ᐸᓂᖕᒐᓯᖕᒧᑦ)* ᐅᑯᐊᑦ ᓄᑕᕋᓐᓄᐊᖅᑐᑦ ᐃᓱᒪᖅᑰᒻᒪᕆ'ᒪᑕ *(ᖃᖑᔮᓇᓗᖕᒧᑦ)* ᐊᒥᖅᑯᑦ ᐅᑎᖅᑎᑦᑭᑦ.

ᓇᐅᑦᑎᖅᑐᖅᑎ: *(ᖃᖑᔮᓇᓗᖕᒧᑦ)* ᐅᑎᖅᑎᖅᑯᔮ'ᒪᑦ ᐊᒥᖅᓂᒃ.

ᐊᖅᑯᑎᖅᓯᐊᖅ: ᐄᒃᓴᐅᓯᖅ ᑎᖅᑎᓲᖅᑲᖅᐸᕗᑦ ᓂᖅᑭᑉᑎ'ᓂᒃ ᐱᔪᒪᙱᑦᑲᓗᐊ'ᒪᑕ.

ᖃᖑᔮᓇᓗᒃ: ᓯᖕᒐᐅᖃᖅᓂᒃ ᑎᒍᔪᔫᒐᓗᐊᒃ—ᐅᑎᖅᑎᓲᖅᑲᙱᑦᑐᑦ ᐅᑯᐊᒃ ᐊᒦᒃ.

ᐊᖅᑯᑎᖅᓯᐊᖅ: ᐅᑎᖅᑎᓲᖅᑲᖅᑕᑎᑦ, ᖃᖑᔮᓇᓗᒃ!

ᓇᐅᑦᑎᖅᑐᖅᑎ: *(ᐊᓯᐊᕐᒧᑦ ᐸᓂᖕᒐᓯᖕᒧᓪᓗ)* ᐱᓐᓯᒃᑕᒃᓯ *(ᐅᖅᑲᑦᑎᐊᙵᕆ'ᒪᒍ, "ᐱᓂᐊᖅᑕᖅᓯ").*

ᓇᐅᑦᑎᖅᑐᖅᑎ ᑲᔫᓪᓗ ᐃᒥᖅᓴᔭᖅᑖᒃ ᐊᒦᒃ ᐊᓯᐊᕐᒧᑦ ᐸᓂᖕᒐᓯᖕᒧᓪᓗ.

ᐸᓂᖕᒐᓯᒃ: *(ᐊᓯᐊᕐᒧᑦ)* ᓱ'ᒪᑦ ᓂᙱᐅᒪᓕᖅᐸᑦ? ᐆᓇᐃᓱᑦᑯᑎᒃ ᑐᓂᔪᖕᓇᖅᑕᕋᓗᐊᖅᑯᓪᓕ. *(ᑲᔫ'ᒧᑦ)* ᓂᙱᓚᔫᙱᑦᑐᒧᓪᓕ ᐊᖑᑕᐅ'ᓗᑕ.

ᓇᐅᑦᑎᖅᑐᖅᑎ: ᐊᖑᑕᐅᔫᖄᙱᑦᑐᓇᖄᔪ—ᓱᓕᙱᑦᑐᓇᖄᔪ.

ᐸᓂᖕᒐᓯᒃᓗ ᐊᓯᐊᖅᓗ ᓂᙱᓕᖅᓗᑎᒃ ᐱᔫᓇᓕᖅᑕᐃᑦ ᖁᖕᒑ'ᓗᑎᒃᓗ, ᑕᓕᖅᑎᒃᓗ ᐊᑯᐊᖅᒥ'ᓄᑦ ᐆᒃᑐᕐᙳᐊᖅᓗᔾᔪᒃ ᐃᓪᔪᖅᑯᖅᑐᓇᓘᔪᓐ'ᓗᑎᒃ.

ᐊᖅᑯᑎᖅᓯᐊᖅ: *(ᓇᐅᑦᑎᖅᑐᖅᑎᒧᑦ)* ᖃᓄᖅᑕᕕᑦ?

ᓇᐅᑦᑎᖅᑐᖅᑎ: ᐊᒃᐱᐅ'ᔪᖅᑕᑦᑲᒃ ᐊᖑᑕᐅᔫᖄᙱᑦᑐᓇ'ᓗᒥᒃ —ᓱᓕᙱᑦᑐᓇᓘᓇᓯᕆᖄᖅᑯᓐᖑᖅ.

ᐸᓂᖕᒐᓯᒃ: *(ᐊᖅᑯᑎᖅᓯᐊᕐᒧᑦ ᖃᖑᔮᓇᓗᖕᒧᓪᓗ)* ᐅᕙᒍᑦ ᐊᖑᑕᐅᔪᒍᑦ ᖃᙵᓯᐊᓘᔪᒍᑦ ᐊᖑᓇᓱᐊᖅᑎᐅᔪᒍᑦ—*(ᐊᑯᐊᖅᒥᓄᑦ ᑎᑦᑯᐊᖅᓗᓂ)* ᐃᓪᔪᖅᑯᖅᑐᓇᓘᔪᒍᑦ.

ᐊᓯᐊᖅ: *(ᐊᖅᑯᑎᖅᓯᐊᕐᒧᑦ ᖃᖑᔮᓇᓗᖕᒧᓪᓗ)* ᐱᖕᒐᓱᓂᒃ ᓂᐅᖅᑲᖅᑐᒧᑦ ᐊᑕᐅᓯᖅᓗ ᐊᖕᒋᔪᕌᓗᒃ.

AŘGIAQ: *Qanurliurlutaguuq? [Guides? What do we guide?] (to* PANINGAJAK*)* He wants us to be their guides.

MORSHEAD: *(to* AŘGIAQ*) Oom-yuck-rock-moongow-loohee ikey-yok-loohee-goot hoo-moon-gaow-gyak-suck naloo-gapta. [Come aboard the ship and help us.]*

PANINGAJAK points.

PANINGAJAK: *Takkuuk, nanuq [Look, nanuq.]*

PANINGAJAK and AŘGIAQ have spotted ANGU'ŘUAQ and UKUANNUAQ in the distance.

FRANKLIN: Dear God, those bears have returned.

AŘGIAQ and PANINGAJAK quickly gather their pelts and head off in the same direction the bears have gone.

(to AŘGIAQ and PANINGAJAK) Wait, where are you— *(to MORSHEAD)* Where are they going?

MORSHEAD: *Hoo-moong-ow-lek-pee-hick? [Where are you going?]*

AŘGIAQ: *Malingniaqtaqqut nanuuk. [We are following the two bears.]*

PANINGAJAK: *Nanuttiavak taamna, pittiaqtuq nanuq. [He's a good bear, a kind bear.]*

MORSHEAD: *Taa-hama-nee-loohee eka-yook-tee-goot ooneck-too-teetee-goot hoo-moo-tween-nak. Ah-ke-lick-tow-chiak-neck-too-hee. [Stay and be our guides—help us navigate the area. You'll be well compensated.]*

AŘGIAQ: *Uvapti'ni ikajuqtaujaaqanngittuhili . . . tuhaanahuaqhinnaluhi avatiphi'niittunik. Uřřinahuarlugit nunamiittut, uumařut . . . qilangmut takuh-aqattarluhi nalunairlugu. [You don't need help from us . . . just listen to what is in our environment. Observe carefully what is in the land, the living creatures . . . look up to the sky and gauge what is happening.]*

ᐊᖁᑎᖅᔭᐊᖅ: (ᓇᐅᑦᑎᖅᑐᖅᑎᒧᑦ) ᖃᓄᖅᓕᐅᕋᔭᐊᕋᓗᐊᕈᑎᒃ—ᐅᑯᐊᒃ ᐱᔭᐃᑦᖅᑯᓕᑦᑭᒃ!

ᓇᐅᑦᑎᖅᑐᖅᑎ: ᐊᑕᓂᖅᔭᐊᖅ, ᐅᖅᑲᕋᔭᐊᖅᑐᒃ ᐅᑯᐊᒃ ᐃᒡᔭᖅᑯᖅᑐᔭᓇᓘᒐᒥᖕᖒ.

ᐊᖁᑎᖅᔭᐊᖅ: ᐊᒃᐱᐅᑎᓕᑦᑭᑦ ᐅᕙᒍᕙᓪᓗᖅ ᐊᖕᒋᑦᑭᔭᐸᓇᓗᖅᑲᖅᑐᒍᖕᖒᖅ.

ᓇᐅᑦᑎᖅᑐᖅᑎ: (ᐊᕐᒋᐊᖑᒧᑦ ᐸᓂᖕᒐᔪᖕᒧᓪᓗ) ᐃᒡᔭᒃᑯᓪᓕ
ᐃᓕᐸᔪ'ᓂᐅᖕᒐᓂᑦ ᐊᖕᒋᑦᑭᔭᐸᓇᓗᐃᑦ—ᑖ'ᓇᐃᖅᓗᒡᓕ.

ᐸᓂᖕᒐᔪᒃ: . . . ᐊᖕᒋᑦᑭᔭᐅᔭᓇᓘ'ᔭᔭᑦ . . . (ᐃᒡᓚᖅᓗᑎᒃ)
. . . ᔭᓇᐅᕝᕙ ᐊᖕᒋᔭᕌᓘᒃᓴᐅᕚᑦ ᐅᕙᐸᑎ'ᓂᐅᖕᒐᓂᑦ ᐊᖕᒋᑦᑭᔭᐅᒍᑎᒃ.

ᓂᙵᐅᒪᔭᐃᑳᓪᓚᖕᓂᖅᓗᑎᒃ ᐃᒡᓚᖅᑲᑎᑭᓕ'ᒪᑕ—ᔭᓇᐅᕝᕙ
ᐃᒡᔭᒃᑎᒃ ᐊᖕᒋᓅ'ᓂᒃ ᐃᒡᓚᖅᑲᑎᑭᒍᑎᖅᑲᓕ'ᒪᑕ ᔭᐃᒻᒪᖅᓂᖅᑯᑦ.
ᐊᖁᑎᖅᔭᐊᖅᓘᓐᓅᑦ ᑎᖅᑎᑦᑕᐃᓕᓇᔭᐊᖅᓗᓂ.

ᐊᖁᑎᖅᔭᐊᖅ: ᓇᐅᑦᑎᖅᑐᖅᑎ, ᐊᐱᕆᓕᑦᑭᒃ ᐅᓐᓂᖅᑑ'ᔮᕆᔪᖕᓇᕆᐊᒃᓴᐃᑎᒋᒃ.

ᓇᐅᑦᑎᖅᑐᖅᑎ: ᐅᓐᓂᖅᑑ'ᔮᕆᔪᖕᓇᖅᐱᑎᒋᒃ?

ᐊᕐᒋᐊᖅ: ᖃᓄᖅᓕᐅᖅᓗᑕᔫᖅ? (ᐸᓂᖕᒐᔪᖕᒧᑦ) ᐃᑲᔪᖅᑕᐅᔪᒪᔭᑦ
ᐃᑲᔪᖅᑯᔮᑎᒍᒃ ᓄᓇᓂᒃ ᓇᓗᒐᒥᒃ.

ᓇᐅᑦᑎᖅᑐᖅᑎ: ᐅᒥᐊᖅᔭᐊᖑᖕᒐᖅᓗᔪ ᐃᑲᔪᖅᓗᔪᒧᑦ ᔭᒧᖕᒐᐅᒋᐊᒃᓴᖅ
ᓇᓗᒐᐸᑕ.

ᐸᓂᖕᒐᔪᒃ ᑎᑦᑯᐊᖅᑐᖅᓗᓂ.

ᐸᓂᖕᒐᔪᒃ: ᑕᒃᑰᒃ—ᓇᓄᖅ.

ᐊᕐᒋᐊᖅᓗ ᐸᓂᖕᒐᔪᒡᓗ ᑕᑯᑳᓪᓚᒃᑲᒥᒃ ᐊᖖᒍ'ᔭᐊᖅᒥᒃ
ᐅᑯᐊᓐᓄᐊᖅᒥᒡᓗ ᐅᖕᒐᔪᒃᑐᒥ.

ᐊᖁᑎᖅᔭᐊᖅ: ᔭᕚᓇᓗᒃ ᐃᐸᑯᐊᒃ ᐅᑎᖅᓂᖅᑯᒃ.

ᐊᕐᒋᐊᖅᓗ ᐸᓂᖕᒐᔪᒡᓗ ᑎᒧᓪᓚᓭᖅᓗᓂᒋᑦ ᐊᒥᖅᑎᒃ ᒪᓕᓕᖅᐳᒃ
ᓇᓅᖕᓂᒃ.

ARGIAQ and PANINGAJAK begin to leave.

MORSHEAD: *(to ARGIAQ) Hoo-moongow-nyak-too-tet? [Where are you going?]*

FRANKLIN: What did he say?

ARGIAQ and PANINGAJAK exit.

MORSHEAD: He says we do not need guides—we need only to listen to what is around us. Be alert to the land and the animals and the sky.

FRANKLIN: We shall endeavour to take their counsel—and I will take yours, too, Morshead, because I have no damn choice, but if you ever again *assume* what my orders might be and act upon said assumption, I will have you slapped, bound, gagged, shamed, flogged, and court-martialled—do I make myself clear?

MORSHEAD: Yes, sir.

FRANKLIN: Now, gentlemen . . . *(checks his chronometer)* the *Erebus* will pull up anchor at double aught forty and head northwest. If we're chased by drift ice, we'll place her in deep water, then shut her down without dropping anchor. If the wind holds, she'll drift north and we'll meet up with the *Terror*.

MORSHEAD: Don't give the ice any chance to take hold—we'd best just cut and run—push under full steam power due north to Beechey—

FRANKLIN: Get back to the ship, Morshead, and calm down before you infect us with your tragic, trembling forecasts of doom—

MORSHEAD: But, sir—

FRANKLIN: The North has my heart and perhaps even my soul—but it will not have my bones, nor anyone else's under my command!

MORSHEAD exits as the bells of the ship ring out the half-hour.

ᐊᕐᑯᑎᕐᔪᐊᖅ: (ᐊᔅᒋᐊᕐᒧᑦ ᐸᓂᖕᒐᔭᖕᒧᓪᓗ) ᐅᑕᖅᑭᒍᐃᑦᑎᒃ, ᔪᒦᑉᐱᔭᒃ—
(ᓇᐅᑦᑎᖅᑐᖅᑎᒧᑦ) ᔪᒨᒐᐅᓇᔪᐊᖅᑐᒃ ᐅᑯᐊᒃ?

ᓇᐅᑦᑎᖅᑐᖅᑎ: ᔪᒨᒐᐅᓚᖅᐱᔭᒃ?

ᐊᔅᒋᐊᖅ: ᒪᓚᖕᓂᐊᖅᑕᖅᑯᒃ ᓇᓅᒃ.

ᐸᓂᖕᒐᔭᒃ: ᓇᓄᑦᑎᐊᕙᒃ ᑖᒪ, ᐱᑦᑎᐊᖅᑐᖅ ᓇᓄᖅ.

ᓇᐅᑦᑎᖅᑐᖅᑎ: ᑕᔮᒪᓃᔭᐅᕐᓗᔭ ᐃᑲᔪᖅᑎᒍᑦ, ᐅᓐᓂᖅᑑᑎᑎᒍᑦ
ᔪᒧᑐᐃᓐᓇᖅ. ᐊᑭᓚᖅᑕᐅᑦᑎᐊᕐᓂᐊᖅᑐᔭ.

ᐊᔅᒋᐊᖅ: ᐅᕙᑎ'ᓂᑦ ᐃᑲᔪᖅᑕᐅᔾᔮᖅᑲᖕᒋᑦᑐᔭᓚ
. . . ᑐᔮᓇᔪᐊᖅᔭᓐᓇᕐᓗᔭ ᐊᕙᑎᑉᑎ'ᓃᑦᑐᓂᒃ. ᐅᔾᔮᕆᓇᔪᐊᕐᓗᒋᑦ
ᓄᓇᒦᑦᑐᑦ, ᐆᒪᔫᑦ . . . ᕿᓚᖕᒧᑦ ᑕᑯᔮᖅᑲᑦᑕᕐᓗᔭ ᓇᓗᓇᐃᕐᓗᒍ.

ᐊᔅᒋᐊᕐᓗ ᐸᓂᖕᒐᔭᓪᓗ ᐊᐅᓚᕆᐊᓕᖅᓗᑎᒃ.

ᓇᐅᑦᑎᖅᑐᖅᑎ: (ᐊᔅᒋᐊᕐᒧᑦ) ᔪᒨᒐᐅᓂᐊᖅᑐᑎᑦ?

ᐊᕐᑯᑎᕐᔪᐊᖅ: ᖃᓄᕐᓚᕙ?

ᐊᓂ'ᓗᑎᒃ ᐊᔅᒋᐊᕐᓗ ᐸᓂᖕᒐᔭᓪᓗ.

ᓇᐅᑦᑎᖅᑐᖅᑎ: ᐅᖄᓪᓚᒃᑐᖅ ᐃᑲᔪᖅᑎᖅᑲᕆᐊᖅᑲᖕᒋ'ᓇᑉᑕᔫᖅ—
ᓈᓚᒐᔪᐊᖅᔭᓐᓇᕐᓗᑕ ᐊᕙᑎᑉᑎ'ᓃᑦᑐᓂᒃ. ᐅᔾᔮᕆᓗᒍ ᓄᓇ, ᐆᒪᔫᑦ ᕿᓚᒡᓗ.

ᐊᕐᑯᑎᕐᔪᐊᖅ: ᓈᓚᒐᔪᐊᕐᓂᐊᖅᐸᕗᑦ—ᐃᔾᕙᓪᓗ ᓈᓚᔅᓗᒃᑳ'ᒥᓂᐊᖅᑕᕆᑦ
ᓇᐅᑦᑎᖅᑐᖅᑎ, ᐊᔭᕐᓇᓚ'ᒪᑦ, ᑭᔭᐊᓂᒃ ᐃᔪᒪᖅᔪᑐᐃᓐᓇᓚ'ᒥᒍᕕᑦ
ᐅᖃᐅ'ᔮᒍᕕᑦ ᐅᕙᒻᓂᖕᒐᖅᑐᕆ'ᓗᒍ ᐸᑎᒃᑕᐅᑎᓂᐊᖅᑕᕆᑦ, ᕿᓚᒃᑕᐅᓗᑎᓪᓗ,
ᖃᓅᑦ ᐃᓗᓪᓚᖅᑐᕐᓗᒍ, ᐃᓂᖅᑎᖅᑕᐅᓪᓗᐊᕐᓗᑎᑦ, ᐊᓇᐅᔾᔮᐅᓗᑎᓪᓗ,
ᐃᑦᖃᖅᑐᖅᑕᐅᓗᑎᓪᓗ—ᑑᑦᑎᐊᕋᓗᐊᖅᐱᖕᒑ? (ᔪᐊᒃᑐᕐᓗᐊᓚ'ᒪᒍ)

ᓇᐅᑦᑎᖅᑐᖅᑎ: ᐄ, ᐊᑕᓂᕐᔪᐊᖅ.

ᐊᕐᑯᑎᕐᔪᐊᖅ: ᐊᑕ, ᑕᐃᒪ ᔮᓇᔾᔮᑦᑲ . . . (ᑕᑯᔮᖅᓗᒍ ᐅᑉᓗᖅᔭᐅᑎᓐᓄᐊᓂ
ᑲᐅᑦᑐᐊᕐᒥᐊᓂ) . . . ᐅᒥᐊᕐᔪᐊᕗᑦ ᖃᐃᔪᖖᒐᕐᓂᐊᖅᑐᖅ ᑭᔮᖅᔭᒪᑦᖄᕐᓗᓂ
ᑲᓇᖕᓇᕐᒧᑦ ᑲᔪᔭᓗᓂ. ᔭᑯᓄᑦ ᔭᖃᓚᔭᒪᔪᓄᑦ ᒪᓚᒃᑕᐅᒍᑉᑕ,
ᐃᑎᔪᒨᒐᐅᓂᐊᖅᑐᒍᑦ ᐅᒥᐊᕐᔪᐊᖅ ᓄᑦᖃᖕᒐᑎᔭᓐᓇᕐᓗᒍ ᑭᔮᖕᒋᓪᓗᒍ.

(checks his chronometer) It's double aught thirty, gentlemen—get cracking.

CARTER, HOLLOWAY, CREW #1, and CREW #2, pick up trunks and anything else lying about.

Wickers and Bean—reinforce the flagstaff!

WICKERS: Yes, sir.

BEAN: Yes, sir.

FRANKLIN: . . . And, Holloway, put a note in a cylinder with our particulars and where we're heading.

HOLLOWAY is already scribbling.

HOLLOWAY: Yes, sir—and where are we heading, sir?

FRANKLIN: *(recites)* "Far, far, how far? From o'er the gates of birth,
The faint horizons, all the bounds of earth,
Far-far-away?"

HOLLOWAY has no idea what to do with this information.

(to HOLLOWAY) A bit from a poem by my cousin, Alfred Tennyson—take this down, "As Sir John Franklin prepared to embark, the night sky was alight with energy and the men's spirits were high with adventure."

HOLLOWAY scribbles and hands a note to WICKERS, who puts it into a cylinder and tucks the cylinder near the breathing hole.

All but WICKERS and BEAN exit.

BEAN: Bloody frigging hell—me hands, I can't feel 'em—are they frostbit?

WICKERS checks BEAN's hands.

WICKERS: . . . No, not yet—keep wiggling them.

ᐊᓄᓇᑦᑎᐊᖅᐸᑦ ᐅᒥᐊᕐᔪᐊᖅ ᐃᖏᔾᕋᔪᖕᓇ'ᒪᑦ ᑕᐃᑯᖓ ᐅᒥᐊᕐᔪᐊᑉ ᐊᐃᑉᐹᑕ ᓇᔪᖅᑖᓄᑦ.

ᓇᐅᑦᑎᖅᑐᖅᑎ: ᐊᖑᔭᐅᑦᑕᐃᓕᓇᓱᐊᕆᐊᖅᑲᖅᑐᒍᑦ ᓯᑯᒧᑦ—ᐊᕗᖓ ᐃᖏᔾᕋᑲᐅᑎᒋᓇᓱᐊᖅᐸᓪᓗᖅᑐᒃᓴᐅᕗᒍᑦ—ᐃᓐᖏᕐᑯᑎᑦ ᐊᐅᓚᑦᑎᐊᕐᓗᒋᑦ ᑕᐃᑯᖓ ᑐᕌᑦᑎᐊᑐᐃᓐᓇᕐᓗᑕᓕ—

ᐊᕐᑯᑎᕐᔪᐊᖅ: ᓇᐅᑦᑎᖅᑐᖅᑎᔅᖢᒃ, ᐅᑎᓕᓇᑦ ᐅᒥᐊᕐᔪᐊᕐᒍᑦ, ᐅᐃᒪᓇᓱᐊᕈᐃᕐᓗᑎᑦ ᕐᑯᕕᓱᓱᐃᖅᑎᓐᓂᐊᕕᒃᑕᑉᑎᒍᑦ ᐅᕐᑳᓚᕐᑲᑦᑕᕐᓂ'ᓄᑦ ᐃᓯᒫᓗᒋᕐᑲᑦᑕᖅᑕᔅᖢᒋᔭ'ᓂᒃ—

ᓇᐅᑦᑎᖅᑐᖅᑎ: ᑭᓯᐊᓂᒃ—

ᐊᕐᑯᑎᕐᔪᐊᖅ: ᐅᑭᐅᖅᑕᖅᑐᖅ ᑕᓴᒻᒪ ᐆᒪᑎᒻᓃᓕᖅᑐᖅ, ᑕᕐᓂᒻᓂᓪᓘᓐᓃᑦ ᑎᒍᒥᐊᖅᑐᖅ—ᑭᓯᐊᓂᒃ ᓴᐅᓂᑦᑲ ᓴᓇᔨᑦᑲᓗ ᓴᐅᓃ'ᓂᒃ ᐱᔮᖃᖕᒋᒻᒪᕆᒃᑕᐃ!

ᓇᐅᑦᑎᖅᑐᖅᑎ ᐊᓂ'ᓗᓂ ᐅᒥᐊᕐᔪᐊᑉ ᓯᕗᔭᐅᑕᐃᑦ ᐃᑳᕐᓂᐅᑉ ᓇᑉᐹᓂ ᓯᕗᔭᖅᑎ'ᓗᒋᑦ.

ᐊᕐᑯᑎᕐᔪᐊᖅ: (ᐅᑉᓗᖅᓯᐅᑎᓂ ᑲᐅᑦᑐᐊᕐᒥᐊᓂ ᑕᑯᓴᖅᖢᒍ) ᑭᖑᕙᓯᓐᖑᔾᑮᓕᖅᑐᒍᑦ, ᓴᓇᔨᑦᑲ—ᐊᑕᐃ ᓴᓇᕐᑭᒍᐃᑦᑎ.

ᑲᑑᑦ, ᓴᖑᔨᓇᓗᓪᓗ, ᓴᓇᔨᒃ ᒪᔾᑭᒃ ᕐᑭᔪᕐᑯᑎᓂᒃ, ᐱᕐᑯᑎᕋᓗᖕᓂᓪᓗ ᑎᒍᓯ'ᓗᑎᒃ.

ᐊᕐᑯᑎᕐᔪᐊᖅ: ᐊᓗᕈᑎ ᐱᓂᕐᓗ ᓴᐃᒪᑎᑉ ᓇᐸᕈᑖ ᐃᖢᐊᖅᓴᕐᓐᓂᑲᖅᓯᐅᒃ.

ᐊᓗᕈᑎ: ᐄ, ᐊᑕᓂᕐᔪᐊᖅ.

ᐱᓂᖅ: ᐄ, ᐊᑕᓂᕐᔪᐊᖅ.

ᐊᕐᑯᑎᕐᔪᐊᖅ: . . . ᓴᖑᔨᓇᓗᓪᓗ ᑎᑎᖅᑲᒥᒃ ᐴᖅᓯᓗᑎᑦ ᐅᕐᑯᓚᐃᑦᑐᒧᑦ ᖃᐅᓯᓚᐃᖅᑐᒧᑦ ᑭᓂᐅᑎᓚᐃᑦᑐᒧᑦ ᐴᕐᓗᒍ ᑎᑎᕋᕐᓗᑎᑦ ᓯᓇᐅᔮᒃᓴᑉᑎ'ᓂᒃ ᔭᒧᖕᒐᐅᓇᔭᐊᓇᐊᒃᓴᑉᑎ'ᓂᓪᓗ.

ᓴᖑᔨᓇᓗᒃ ᑎᑎᕌᑦᓚᒃᓯᓐᓇᓕᖅᖢᓂ.

ᓴᖑᔨᓇᓗᒃ: ᐄ, ᐊᑕᓂᕐᔪᐊᖅ. ᔭᒧᓐᖒᖅ ᑐᕌᖅᐱᑕᓕ?

They reinforce the flagstaff.

BEAN: Wickers, did you see—that bear come right up to *me*.

WICKERS: Yes, and you never showed your fear, even though you pissed yourself—I saw.

BEAN: Did anyone else see, you think?

WICKERS: Nah.

BEAN: Wait till I tell me ma—she'll be some proud of me with that bear.

WICKERS: That should hold for a while . . . what's this?

WICKERS pulls something up from the ice near the flagstaff. One side has been chewed up, but it is HUMMIKTUQ's iřgak—from long ago.

BEAN: Looks like a spoon.

WICKERS: Why would a spoon have holes in the middle?

BEAN: Let's see . . . *(examines the object)* Got nice engravings on it. *(puts it in his mouth and bites)* Made of bone probably.

WICKERS: Don't— *(takes it back)* I'm keeping it as a memento—c'mon . . .

But BEAN remains absolutely still . . . staring at something just out of view.

C'mon, Bean . . . c'mon . . . BEAN.

BEAN: Shhh . . . I . . .

WICKERS: . . . What?

BEAN: Shhh—I see a *Youruss mariannus*.

WICKERS: A *what*?

ᐊᕐᑎᕐᔪᐊᖅ: (ᐅᕐᑲᓕᒫᒐᕐᒥ'ᖖᒑᖅᑐᒥᒃ ᑕᐃᔨᓕᖅᓱᓂ ᐃᑦᕐᑲᐅᒪᔭᒥᓂᒃ)
“ᐅᖓᔨᒃᑐᒍᑦ, ᐅᖓᔨᒃᑐᒍᑦ, ᕐᑲᓄᖅ ᐅᖓᔨᒃᑎᒋᕚ? ᕐᑳᖏᐅᑎᓗᒋᑦ ᐃᔨᕐᕕᑦ ᐃᓅᓕᕐᕕᑦ, ᐅᖓᔨᒃᑐᒥ ᑕᐅᑐᖕᓇᕝᔭᒃᑐᑦ, ᓄᓇᑦ ᑭᒡᓕᓇᓗᖏᑦ ᐅᖓᔨᒃᑐᒃᓴᐅᒐᓗᐊᖅᑯᑦ.”

ᓴᖕᒍᔫᓇᓗᒃ ᓇᓗᓕ'ᒪᑦ ᑭᐅᔭᐅᔫᒃᓴᒥᓂᒃ.

ᐊᕐᑎᕐᔪᐊᖅ: (ᓴᖕᒍᔫᓇᓗᖕᒍᑦ) ᐃᓪᓗᕐᒪ ᐱᔨᐊ'ᓂᒃ ᑕᐃᔨᒐᓗᐊᕋᒪ, ᐊᑎᐊ ᐋᓪᕗᕋᑦ ᑕᓂᓴᓐ—ᐅᕝᕙ ᐅᓇ ᑎᑎᕋᓕᕈᒃ, “ᐊᕐᑎᕐᔪᐊᖅ ᐃᓪᓗᐊᖅᓴᖅᐸᕆᖅᑎ'ᓗᒍ ᐊᐅᓪᓚᕐᓂᐊᖅᓱᑎᒃ ᓴᓇᖅᓯ'ᒪᑦ, ᐅᓐᓄᒃ ᕐᑲᐅᒪᔮᔭᖅᔪᖅᓱᓂ ᓴᓇᔮᓪᓗ ᕐᑯᕕᐊᔪᒃᓱᑎᒃ ᓂᕆᐅᒃᑲᒥᒃ ᓄᑖᕐᒍᓐᖓᐅᑎᒋᐊᒃᓴᖅ.”

ᑎᑎᕋᖅᑕᐅᕐᑯᔭᐅᔪᓂᒃ ᑎᑎᕋᖅᓱᓂ ᑎᑎᖅᑲᖅ ᑐᓂ'ᓗᓂᐅᒃ ᐊᓗᕈᑎᒍᑦ, ᐆᕐᒍᑦ ᐃᓕ'ᓗᓂᐅᒃ ᕐᑲᐅᔨᓚᐃᑦᑐᒍᑦ ᐆᖅᓱᒍ ᐊᒡᒎᑉ ᕐᑲᓂᑖᓄᑦ ᐃᓕ'ᓗᒍᓗ.

ᐊᓂ'ᓗᑎᒃ ᑕᑯᒃᓴᐅᔪᐱᑐᐊᓕᖅᑐᒃ ᐊᓗᕈᑎᓗ ᐱᓂᕐᓗ ᑕᓴᒪᓂ ᓇᔪᖅᑑᒃ ᔪᓕ.

ᐱᓂᖅ: ᔪᕐᑯᑕᐅᖖᒋᑦᑐᑉᑲᓇᓇᓗᔅᓱᒃ—ᐊᔅᒐᒃᑲᒃ ᐃᒃᐱᓇᕈᐃᑦᑐᒃ—ᕿᕿᔫ'ᓯᔪᒃ?

ᐊᓗᕈᑎ ᐱᓂᐅᑉ ᐊᔅᒐᐃ'ᓄᑦ ᑕᑯᒥᐊᖅᑐᖅ.

ᐊᓗᕈᑎ: . . . ᐄᕐᑭᔅᓱᒃ, ᕐᑭᕐᑭᒻᒪᓇᖖᒋᑦᑑᒃ—ᐊᑕᐃ ᑎᑭᖅᑎᑦ ᐊᐅᓚᓐᓇᓯᐊᕐᓗᒋᑦ ᐃᔫᑦᑕᕐᓗᒋᑦ.

ᐃᓱᐊᖅᓴᕐᓐᓂᖅᑕᐃᑦ ᓴᐃᒪᑎᑉ ᓇᐸᕿᑖ.

ᐱᓂᖅ: ᐊᓗᕈᑎ, ᑕᐃᒻᓇ ᓇᓄᖅ ᑕᑯᒐᓗᐊᖅᐱᐅᒃ ᐅᕙᒻᓄᖖᒐᐅᑐᐃᓐᓇᖅᑎ'ᓗᒍ?

ᐊᓗᕈᑎ: ᐄ, ᐃᖅᔨᔮᖖᒋᒻᒪᓇᒃᑲᓗᐊᕐᕕᑦ ᕐᑯᐊᖅᓵᕐᓗᐊᕐᕕᓪᓗᓐᓃᑦ ᐊᖑᓪᓚᔅᓵᓗᒃᑲᓗᐊᖅᑎ'ᓗᑎᓪᓗ—ᐄ ᑕᑯᔪᒋᑦ.

ᐱᓂᖅ: ᐊᔨ'ᓂᒃ ᑕᑯᖅᑲᑕᐅᔪᖅᑲᕋᓗᐊᖅᐸ?

ᐊᓗᕈᑎ: ᐄᕐᑭᔅᓱᒃ.

ᐱᓂᖅ: ᐊᓈᓇᒐ ᐊᒃᐱᐅᑎᒍᑉᑯ ᓴᓇᒪᒋᓂᐊᖅᑖᖖᒐ ᓇᓄᕐᒍᑦ ᐱᔮᐅᖖᒋ'ᓇᒪ.

BEAN: Black nose, wee black eyes . . .

WICKERS: O my Lord Jesus God, not again—where?

BEAN: *(hard whisper)* Don't turn around—it's right behind you.

WICKERS, freaked, whirls around.

WICKERS: RUN, MAN, RUN . . .

WICKERS and BEAN run wildly in circles, screaming, until . . .

WHERE IS IT . . .

BEAN: It's a *fatta morana*—a FATTA MORANA, A FATTA MORANA . . .

WICKERS: . . . A what?

BEAN: Fooled you! I FOOLED YOU!

WICKERS: You're in so much trouble now, boyo . . . I'M GOING TO WASH YOUR FACE WITH ICE!

WICKERS topples BEAN as they laugh and wrestle.

ANGU'ŘUAQ enters, followed by UKUANNUAQ, heading straight towards the men . . . but when WICKERS notices the bears, he and BEAN both jump to their feet screaming and laughing . . . and start running.

WICKERS and BEAN exit . . . but the bears remain. They sniff the Union Jack, inadvertently knocking over the flagstaff . . . and it slips into the breathing hole.

ᐊᓗᕈᑎ: ᔮᕆᒪᒋᔾᐅᑦᑎᐊᕐᓂᐊᖅᑐᒃᓴᐅᕗᑎᑦ ᑖᕗᖕᒐ . . . ᖁᓇᓕ ᐅᓇ?

ᔮᐃᒪᑎᑉ ᓇᐸᕈᑖᑕ ᖃᓂᒋᔾ'ᓂ ᐊᒧᔪ'ᒪᑦ ᔪᑯᒦᑦᑐᖅ ᖁᓇᒥᒃᑭᐊᖅ. ᓄᕗᐊ ᐃᓚᖕᒐᖅᑕᐅᔫᒐᓗᐊᖅ ᐆᒪᔫᒧᑦ ᖃᖅᑯᖅᑕᐅᓂᑯ ᖁᓇᐅᓐᓀ ᖁᒻᒥᒃᑐᕕᓂᐅᑉ ᐃᔾᒐᖕᒐ—ᐱᑐᖄᐸᓗᕐᓘᓐᓂᖅ.

ᐱᓂᖅ: ᐊᓘᑎᖅᐸᓗᖅᑐᖅ ᐅᓇ ᖁᓇᑭᐊᖅ.

ᐊᓗᕈᑎ: ᖁ'ᒪᑦᓕᑭᐊᖅ ᐊᓘᑎ ᐳᑐᖄᕐᓂᐊᕋᓗᐊ'ᒪᑦᓕ?

ᐱᓂᖅ: ᑕᑯᓚᒍ..(ᕿᒥᔾᕈ'ᓗᓂᐅᒃ) ᑎᑎᕋᐅᔾᖅᔪᒪᑦᑎᐊᖅᑐᓇᓗᒃ. (ᖄᓂᕐᒥᓄᖕᒐᖅᑎ'ᓗᓂᐅᒃ ᑮᒃᓗᒍ) ᔮᐅᓂᕐᒧᑦ ᔮᓇᔪᒪᑦᕐᑰᖅᑐᕐᓕ.

ᐊᓗᕈᑎ: ᐋᕐᑭ—(ᑎᒍ'ᓗᓂᐅᒃ) ᐱᒋᓂᐊᖅᑕᕋᓕ ᐱᖁᐃᕈᒃ . . .

ᑭᔪᐊᓂᒃ ᐱᓂᖅ ᓄᑦᖄᖕᒐᑦᑎᐊᒻᒪᕆᒃᓗᓂ ᖁᓇᒥᒃᑭᐊᖅ ᑕᑯᒐᒥ ᐅᖕᒐᔪᒃᑐᒥ.

ᐊᓗᕈᑎ: ᐊᑕᐃ, ᐱᓂᖅ . . . ᐊᑕᐃ . . . ᐱᓂᖅ!

ᐱᓂᖅ: ᓂᐸᐃᕐᓗᑎᑦ . . . ᐱ . . .

ᐊᓗᕈᑎ: . . . ᖁᐒ?

ᐱᓂᖅ: ᓂᐸᐃᕐᓗᑎᑦ—ᖁᓇᓇᓗᖕᒥᒃ ᑕᑯᒐᒪ.

ᐊᓗᕈᑎ: ᖁᓇᒨᖅ?

ᐱᓂᖅ: ᕿᕐᓇᕆᒃᑐᒥᒃ ᕿᖕᒐᓕᒃ, ᐃᓃᒥᒃ ᕿᕐᓇᕆᒃᓗᑎᒃ . . .

ᐊᓗᕈᑎ: ᖁᕐᑯᑕᐅᖕᒋᑦᑐᑉᑲᕆᓇᓗᒃ ᐅᑎᕐᔮᖑᔾᕐᓂᖅᐸ ᓇᓗᕐᓗᒃ—ᓇᐅᒃ?

ᐱᓂᖅ: (ᓂᐱᑭᓐᓇᖁᐊᖅᓗᓂ) ᑐᓄᑦᑕᐃᓕᒍᐃᑦ—ᑐᓄ'ᓃ'ᒪᑦ.

ᐊᓗᕈᑎ ᕐᑯᐊᖅᔮᖅᓗᓂ, ᐅᐃᒻᒪᒃᑐᖅ.

ᐊᓗᕈᑎ: ᐅ'ᓚᒡᓗᒃ, ᐅ'ᓚᒡᓗᒃ, ᐅ'ᓚᒡᓗ—

ᐊᓗᕈᑎᓗ ᐱᓂᕐᓗ ᐅ'ᓚᐅᒪᖃᒃ ᐅᐃᒻᒪᑦᑎᐊᖅᓗᑎᒃ ᐃᕆᐊᑳᖅᓗᑎᒡᓗ, ᑕᔾᓀ . . .

ᐊᓗᕆᑎ: ᔭᒦᑦᐸ . . .

ᐱᓂᖅ: ᔭᓇᑭᐊᖅ—ᔭᓇᓕᑭᐊᖅ, ᔭᓇᓇᓗᑭᐊᖅ, ᔭᓇᕐᓱᑭᐊᖅ . . .

ᐊᓗᕆᑎ: . . . ᔭᕚ?

ᐱᓂᖅ: ᑎᑉᔭᕐᓱᐃᑦ! ᐱᔮᓇᓴᒥᑦ!

ᐊᓗᕆᑎ: ᔭᕐᑯᑕᐅᖕᒋᑦᑐᑉᑲᓄᓇᓗᕐᓱᒃ ᐅᓇᑉᔭᐅᕐᓱᒃ ᐊᑭᓂᐊᖅᑕᓇᓗᒥᕙᒥᑦ . . . ᑮᓇᐃᑦ ᐅᐊᕐᓂᐊᖅᑕᕋ ᓯᑯᓇᓗᖕᒍᑦ!

ᐊᓗᕆᑎ ᐱᒋᐊᖅᓱᓂᐅᒃ ᐃᓪᓚᓕᖅᑑᒃ ᓂᖕᒐᐅᑎᙳᐊᖅᓱᑎᒃ.

ᑕᔅᕙᓗ ᐃᓯᕐᓚᖑᓴᕐᓂᖅᓱᓂ ᐊᖑ'ᔭᐊᖅ ᐅᑯᐊᓐᓄᐊᕐᓗ ᒪᓕᒃᓱᓂᐅᒃ, ᑐᕌᑦᑎᐊᖅᓱᑎᒃ ᖃᑉᑐᓈᕐᓄᑦ . . . ᐊᓗᕆᑎ ᐅᔅᓯᓇᓕᕋᒥᒥᒃ ᐱᓂᕐᓗ ᑕᐃᒪ ᒪᑭ'ᓗᑎᒃ ᐃᓇᐊᑖᖅᓱᑎᒃ ᐃᓪᓚᖅᓱᑎᒃ ᔭᓕ . . . ᐅ'ᓚᓕᖅᓱᑎᒃ.

ᖁᓐᖏᐊᖅᕕᕐᒥᑦ ᐊᓂ'ᒪᓂᒃ ᐊᓗᕆᑎᓗ ᐱᓂᕐᓗ . . . ᓇᓅᒃ ᔭᓕ ᑕᐃᑲᓃᑦᑑᒃ. ᓇᐃᒪᓇᔭᐊᖅᑕᐃᑦ ᓴᐃᒪᑎ ᐱᒋᐊᖕᒋᒃᑲᓗᐊᖅᓱᑎᒃ ᓇᐸᕆᑖ ᐅᔅᕆᑎ'ᑐᓂᒥᒃ . . . ᑕᐅᓄᖓ ᐊᒡᑐᒧᑦ ᑭᕙᔮᓐᓂᖅ.

INTERMISSION

NUTQANGAKANNUAQQAARLUTIK

ᓄᑦᖅᑲᖕᒐᑲᓐᓄᐊᖅᑳᕐᓗᑎᒃ

SCENE TWO

Almost two years later. It is June and the midnight sun sparkles along the ridge of the glacial hill in the distance. The ground is dotted with the odd flower.

UKUANNUAQ rests on the land. After a moment, ANGU'ŘUAQ lumbers in, a weaned seal pup in his mouth. He puts it down and is about to eat it when he smells something and raises his head to see figures staggering out of the brightness . . .

CARTER, HOLLOWAY, CREW #1, and FRANKLIN enter. The shreds of their uniforms and rotting pelts are draped over their bodies with rags covering their eyes against the sun as they stumble along, sick and starving.

CARTER plucks a flower then tosses it.

CARTER: These pitiful things cannot be called flowers.

HOLLOWAY: We'll soon see real English flowers again.

CARTER: Yes.

HOLLOWAY: Geraniums and daffodils.

CARTER: Beautiful.

HOLLOWAY: Day lilies.

CREW #1 inhales.

CREW #1: . . . The scent of sweet williams.

ᖃᓄᓇᑦᑑᓂᐊ ᑭᖑᓂᐊᓂ

ᐅᑭᐅᒃ ᒪᔾᕈᒃ ᓈᔪᒪᓕ’ᒪᓂᒃ. ᐊᐅᔭᐅᑎ’ᓗᒍ ᑕᑦᕿᐊ ᓄᕐᓇᕕᐅ’ᓗᓂ ᔪᓚ ᑕᑯᕋᓐᓂᖅᑐᐸᓇᓗᒃ ᔪᕿᓂᕐᓗ ᑖᕝᕙᓂ ᐊᐅᔨᐃᑦᑐᒥ ᖃᐅᒻᒪᒃᓴᐃ’ᒪᑦ ᐳᖅᑐᔨᒥ. ᓄᓇ ᑕᑯ’ᓗᒍ ᓄᓇᕋᓐᓄᐊᖅᑕᖅᑲᖅᑐᖅ ᔨᓚ.

ᐅᑯᐊᓐᓄᐊᖅ ᑕᖃᐃᖅᔪᖅᑐᖅ ᓄᓇᒥ. ᑭᖑᓂᓐᓄᐊᒍᑦ ᐊᖑ’ᔨᐊᖅ ᐃᔪᖅᑐᖅ, ᔪᒡᒍᕐᒥᒍᑦ ᑭᕐᒥᐊᖅᑐᖅ ᓇᑦᑎᐊᖅᑕᓇᔭᒥᓂᒃ. ᑕᐅᓄᕐᒐ ᐃᓕ’ᒪᒍ ᓂᓇᓂᐊᓕ’ᒪᒋᒃ, ᑭᔪᐊᓂᒃ ᔨᓇᒥᒃ ᓇᐃᒪᔾᕉᓕᕋᒥ ᐋᕐᓗᒃᑐᖅ ᑕᑯᒥᐊᖅᕈᓂ ᔨᓇᐅᕝᕙ ᖃᑉᓗᓈᑦ ᖃᐅᒪᔨᒥ’ᖖᒑᖅᑐᑦ ᐱᔨᑦᑎᐊᖖᒋᑦᑐᓇᓗᐃᑦ . . .

ᐃᔪᖅᑯᑦ ᑲᑑᑦ, ᔭᖑᔫᓇᓗᒃ, ᔭᓇᔫ, ᐊᕐᑯᑎᕐᔨᐊᕐᓗ. ᐊ’ᓄᕌᖕᒋᑦ ᔨᕈᖕᒐᑦᑎᐊᖅᕈᑎᒃ ᐅᓕᒃᔪᒪᓇᔨᐊᖅᑐᑦ ᐊᒥᕕᓂᓇᓗᖕᓄᑦ, ᐃᔫᖕᒋᑦ ᑕᓗᔪᒪᓇᔨᐊᖅᕈᓂᒋᑦ ᖃᑉᓗᓈᖅᑕᓐᓄᐊᕐᒍᑦ ᔪᕿᓂᐅᑉ ᖃᐅᒪᓂᐊ ᐱ’ᓗᒍ. ᐋᓐᓂᐊᖅᑐᑦ, ᑳᒃᑐᑦ ᐊᕿᐊᕈᐊᓕᖅᕈᑎᒃ.

ᑖᒻᓇ ᑲᑑᑦ ᓄᓇᕐᓐᓄᐊᕐᒥᒃ ᓄᓇᒥᑦ ᑎᒍᔪ’ᓗᓂ ᐃᒋᔅᔭᖅᔪᓐᓇᖅᕈᓂᐅᒃ.

ᑲᑑᑦ: ᐅᑯᐊᓇᓗᐃᑦ ᓄᓇᕐᒪᓇᐅᖕᒋᑦᑐᓇᓗᕐᓗᐃᑦ.

ᔭᖑᔫᓇᓗᒃ: ᓄᓇᑉᑎ’ᓂ ᑖᕝᕙᓂ ᐊᑭᐊᓂ ᑕᑯᔮᕐᒐᕐᓂᐊᕐᓗᐊᖅᑐᒍᑦ ᓄᓇᕐᒪᓇᕐᓂᒃ.

ᑲᑑᑦ: ᐄ.

ᔭᖑᔫᓇᓗᒃ: ᐊᐅᐸᔫᖅᑕᑦ ᖁᖅᓱᖅᑕᑦᓗ.

ᑲᑑᑦ: ᖁᕕᐊᓇᕐᓂᐊᕐᓗᐊᖅᑯᖅ.

ᔭᖑᔫᓇᓗᒃ: ᖃᑯᖅᑕᑦᓗ.

ᔭᓇᔫ ᓇᐃᒪᖕᒍᐊᖅᕈᓂ.

HOLLOWAY: Sweet williams are edible.

CREW #1: The forget-me-nots will be in bloom.

CARTER: My wife's got nasturtiums in her garden.

CREW #1: We got poppies in our field.

WICKERS enters, struggling to hold up BEAN, who is dying. BEAN's head wobbles and he can barely stand, let alone walk.

WICKERS: Don't forget roses and primroses—right, Bean?

BEAN: *(with difficulty breathing)* . . . roses . . . primroses . . . my favourite.

WICKERS: God, yes—beautiful peonies.

CREW #1: Snowdrops.

HOLLOWAY: No, no snowdrops.

CREW #1: Sorry—

HOLLOWAY: Kill snowdrops—*murder* anything that starts with the word "snow."

CREW #1: Sorry, sir. Violets. Purple violets.

HOLLOWAY: Bears, sir . . . at your south-southwest.

Everyone comes to a halt. ANGU'ŘUAQ picks up the seal and walks towards them.

I'll eat that seal, boys.

CARTER: I'll eat that bear.

FRANKLIN: *(to HOLLOWAY)* My rifle.

CARTER: Let me take a crack at them, sir.

ᔭᓇᔨ: . . . ᑎᐱᑦᑎᐊᕙᖏᑦ ᐊᐅᐸᓵᖅᑐᓐᓄᐊᑦ.

ᔭᖑᔨᓇᓗᒃ: ᐊᐅᐸᓵᖅᑐᓐᓄᐊᑦ ᑕᐃᑯᐊᑦ ᓂᕆᔭᒃᓴᐅᔪᑦ.

ᔭᓇᔨ: ᑐᖑᔪᖅᑕᓐᓄᐊᓪᓗ ᐳᐃᒍᕐᓇᐃᑦᑐᑦ ᔭᑦᕿᐅᒪᓂᐊᕋᓗᐊ'ᒥᔪᑦᑕᐅᖅ.

ᑲᑑᑦ: ᓄᓕᐊᕋ ᓄᓇᕋᑦᑎᐊᕙᖏᓂᒃ ᐱᕈᖅᔭᐃᕙᒃᑐᖅ.

ᔭᓇᔨ: ᐅᕙᒍᓪᓕ ᖃᓂᒋᔭᑉᑎ'ᓂ ᐊᐅᐸᓛᖅᑐᕐᑯᑎᖃᖅᑐᒍᑦ ᐱᕈᖅᑐᓂᒃ ᐊᖏᔾᕋᑉᑎ'ᓂ.

> ᐊᓗᕈᑎ ᔭᑦᕿ'ᓗᓂ, ᐱᔪᒃᑎᓐᓇᔪᐊᖅᑯᓂᐅᒃ ᐱᓂᖅ
> ᑐᕐᑯᕙᓪᓕᐊ'ᓗᓂ ᑖᒻᓇ ᐱᓂᖅ. ᓂᐊᕐᑯᓂ ᐃᒃᑕᕆᒍᔪᒃᑐᖅ
> ᔪᑭᖕᒐᓵᖅᑯᓂ ᒪᑭᑦᑎᐊᓚᐃ'ᓗᓂ ᐱᔪᓚᐃᑦᑐᖅ.

ᐊᓗᕈᑎ: ᐳᐃᒍᖅᑕᐃᓕᓗᒋᑦ ᔭᑉᑯᐊᑦᑕᐅᖅ ᓄᓇᕋᑦ ᕉᔾᔫᑦ ᐊ'ᓚᒋᔭᐃᓪᓗ ᑕᔭᑉᑯᐊᑦ—ᐊᔪᐅ ᐱᓂᖅ?

ᐱᓂᖅ: (ᐊᓂᖅᔮᑦᑎᐊᖅᓯᓇᖏ'ᓗᓂ) . . . ᕉᔾᔫᑦ ᑕᔭᑉᑯᐊᑦ ᐊ'ᓚᒋᔭᐃᓪᓗ ᐱᑦᑕᐅᒥᓂᖅᓯᐃᑦᑑᒥᔭᑦᑲᓕ.

ᐊᓗᕈᑎ: ᐊ'ᓚᐃᑦᑕᐅᖅ ᑕᐃᑯᐊᑦ ᐊᖏᔪᓇᓗᐃᑦ—ᐳᕕᖅᔪᒪᔫᔭᖅᑐᑦ ᓄᓇᕋᐃᑦ.

ᔭᓇᔨ: ᒥᑭᔪᑉᔪᑖᓐᓄᐊᓇᓗᐃᑦᑕᐅᖅ ᖃᖅᑯᖅᑕᓐᓄᐃᑦ ᐊᐳᑎᖅᐸᓗᒃᑐᑦ ᖃᓂᖅᐸᓗᒃᑐᑦ.

ᔭᖑᔨᓇᓗᒃ: ᐄᖁ ᑕ'ᓇᐃᑦᑑᖖᒋᑦᑐᓂᒃ ᐊᐳᑎᖃᕈᒪᔪᐃᖅᑐᖓ.

ᔭᓇᔨ: ᖄ—

ᔭᖑᔨᓇᓗᒃ: ᑕ'ᓇᐃᑦᑐᑦ ᓄᖑᔭᕐᓗᒋᑦ ᖃᒃᑯᓱᒃᑑᓃ'ᓄᒃ ᐊᐳᑎᖅᐸᓗᒃᑐᕐᓗᐃᑦ, ᓄᓇᒃᑯᓪᓕ ᐊᐱᓚᐃᑦᑑ'ᒪᑦ ᐊᐱᓚᐃᒃᑐᒻᒪᓱᒃ ᓄᓇᒻᒪᓱᓇᓗᒃᑯᓪᓕ.

ᔭᓇᔨ: ᖄ. ᒪᒥᐊᓇᖅ, ᐊᐅᐸᕐᕙᔪᒃᑐᓂᓪᓕᑭᐊᖅ, ᐊᑕᐃ ᔭᑉᑯᐊᑦ ᐱᑦᑕᐅᔪᑦ.

ᔭᖑᔨᓇᓗᒃ: ᐊᑕᓂᕐᔪᐋᖅ . . . ᑕᒃᑰᒃ ᓇᓄᓇᓅᒃ ᑖᕙᓂ.

> ᓄᑦᖃᖕᒐᑦᑎᐊᓕᖅᑯᑎᒃ ᑕᒪᐃᑕ. ᐊᖑ'ᔪᐊᕐᓗ ᓇᑦᑎᐊᖅ ᐱ'ᓗᓂᐅᒃ
> ᐱᔪᒻᕕᒥᓕᖅᐸᐃᑦ ᐊᖑᑎᑦ.

FRANKLIN: Thank you, Carter, but I'll handle it.

WICKERS: We have a bit of flint for a fire, sir.

CREW #1: Oh, imagine a hot roast.

CARTER: Roast bear with gravy.

CREW #1: Mmm . . . delicious.

HOLLOWAY: This is our last bullet, sir.

FRANKLIN holds the rifle.

FRANKLIN: Thank you, Holloway. I'll aim for the big one.

ANGU'ŘUAQ and UKUANNUAQ watch . . . ANGU'ŘUAQ takes another step towards the men. It seems he may again offer them a seal.

WICKERS: You're sweating, sir—let Carter take the shot.

FRANKLIN: If I were home, Jane would have doctors attaching leeches, but I'm fine.

CARTER: Shoot at the heart, sir.

CREW #1: In the head is best.

WICKERS: Shhh . . .

CARTER: Better not miss.

FRANKLIN prays.

FRANKLIN: Dear Lord of the tundra, give me the strength and steadiness to . . .

FRANKLIN fires and misses, scaring the bears. They turn and run.

CREW #1: Ahhhh.

ᖃᖑᔮᓇᓗᒃ: ᓇᑦᑎᖅ ᑖᒪ ᓂᕆᓂᐊᖅᑕᕋ.

ᑲᑑᑦ: ᓇᓄᖅ ᑖᒪ ᓂᕆᔪᖕᓇᖅᑕᕋ.

ᐊᕐᑯᑎᕐᔪᐊᖅ: (ᖃᖑᔮᓇᓗᖑᑦ) ᓯᖅᑯᖅᑎᔾᔪᑎᓚ ᓇᐅᒃ.

ᑲᑑᑦ: ᐱᓇᓱᐊᓕᕐᓚᑦᑲᒃ, ᐊᑕᓂᕐᔪᐊᖅ.

ᐊᕐᑯᑎᕐᔪᐊᖅ: ᓈᒻᒪᒃᑐᖅ, ᑲᑑᑦ ᐱᓂᐊᖅᐸᑦᑲᒃ.

ᐊᓗᑭᑎ: ᐃ'ᓂᒃᓴᓐᓄᐊᕐᑲᕋᓗᐊᖅᑯᒍᑦ ᐃᓚᖏᓕᐅᕿᒪᒍᑉᑕ.

ᖃᓇᔮ: ᒪᒪᕿᒥᓇᖅᑐᓇᓗᒃ ᓂᕐᑭ ᐃᓚᓯᒪᔪᑦᑎᐊᕙᐅᒃᐸᑦ.

ᑲᑑᑦ: ᓇᓄᑉ ᓂᕐᑳ ᐃᓚᓯᒪᔪᑦᑎᐊᕙᐅ'ᓗᓂ ᒪᒪᖅᖃᐅᑎᓕᖅᓯᒪ'ᓗᓂ.

ᖃᓇᔮ: ᒻ-ᒻ-ᒻ-ᒻ . . . ᒪᒪᖅᑐᓇᓗᒃᓴᐅᒐᖅ.

ᖃᖑᔮᓇᓗᒃ: ᖅᑲᕐᔪᖅ ᐅᓇ ᐊᑕᐅᓯᓐᓄᐊᖅ ᑕᔾᕙᐱᑐᐊᑦᑎᐊᖑᓕ'ᒪᑦ ᓄᖑᑦᑐᑦ.

ᐊᕐᑯᑎᕐᔪᐊᖅ ᓯᖅᑯᖅᑎᔾᔪᑎ ᑎᒍ'ᓗᓂᐅᒃ.

ᐊᕐᑯᑎᕐᔪᐊᖅ: ᐊᓯᐅᕐᓗᒃ, ᐊᖏᑦᕐᑭᔭᖅ ᐱᓇᓱᐊᕐᓂᐊᖅᐸᕋ.

ᐊᖑ'ᔪᐊᕐᓗ ᐅᑯᐊᓐᓄᐊᕐᓗ ᑕᐅᑐᒃᑑᒃ . . . ᐊᖑ'ᔪᐊᖅ ᐊᑉᓗᕆᐊᖅᓗᓂ ᐊᖑᑎᓄᑦ. ᓱᓕ ᑐᓂᓇᓱᐊᕐᓂ'ᒪᒋᑦ ᓇᑦᑎᐊᕐᒥᒃ ᓂᕆᔭᒃᓴᐃ'ᓂᒃ ᑕᒧᐊᔭᒃᓴᐃ'ᓂᒃ.

ᐊᓗᑭᑎ: ᑭᓂᐅᑎᓕᕋᕕᑦ ᑭᐊᒃᐸᓪᓚᓕᕋᕕᑦ, ᐊᑕᓂᕐᔪᐊᖅ, ᑲᑑᑎᑉᓕ ᐱᓕᐅᒃ.

ᐊᕐᑯᑎᕐᔪᐊᖅ: ᐊᖏᔾᕋᖅᓯᒪᓚᓗᐊᕿᒪ ᓄᓕᐊᕐᒪ ᑲᒪᒋᓇᔭᖅᑖᖓ, ᐃᓗᐊᖅᖃᐃᔮᓂᑦ ᑕᑯᔾᐅᓂᐊᕋᓗᐊᖅᑐᖓᓗ, ᖅᑲᓄᓇᑦᕐᑰᖕᖏᑦᑐᖓ ᓈᒻᒪᒃᑐᓗᔪᖓ.

ᑲᑑᑦ: ᓯᖅᑯᕋᓱᐊᕐᓗᒍ ᐆᒪᑖᒍᑦ, ᐊᑕᓂᕐᔪᐊᖅ.

ᖃᓇᔮ: ᓂᐊᕐᑯᑦᑯᑦ ᐱᑦᑕᐅᑉᕐᑭᔭᐅᔪᕐᓕ.

ᐊᓗᑭᑎ: ᓂᐸᐃᓗᕐᓯ . . .

FRANKLIN: Very sorry, gentlemen.

CREW #1: Not even a moving target—sorry, sir, but ahhhh . . .

CARTER charges to where the bears were and falls upon a bit of seal blood on the ground, shoving the blood and snow into his mouth.

CARTER: Seal blood—warm seal blood!

FRANKLIN: CARTER!

CARTER: . . . Mmmm . . . there's a bit left over—any takers?

FRANKLIN: You'll get ill eating that, Carter.

CARTER: I'm getting ill from *not* eating, sir.

FRANKLIN: *(to WICKERS)* Where's Morshead?

HOLLOWAY: Hunting, sir—he took a few men with him.

FRANKLIN: He's too sick with fever to be hunting.

HOLLOWAY: He insisted, sir.

FRANKLIN: What's our current situation?

HOLLOWAY tries to unroll the tattered map.

HOLLOWAY: There's approximately two hundred and fifty miles left to navigate between Barrow Strait and the mainland, that should connect the passage—

FRANKLIN: I mean our situation *now*—where are we *now*?

HOLLOWAY struggles with the map as he tries to find out.

HOLLOWAY: One moment . . .

ᑲᑑᑦ: ᐊᓐᓇᐃᑦᑕᐃᓕᒍᐃᑦ.

ᐊᕐᑯᑎᕐᖠᐊᖅ ᑐᒃᖠᐊᖅᓱᓂ.

ᐊᕐᑯᑎᕐᖠᐊᖅ: ᓄᓇᓕᐅᖅᑎ ᐅᑭᐅᖅᑕᖅᑐᒥ ᐃᑲᔪᖖᒐ ᓴᔪᒃᐸᓪᓛᕈᐃᖅᑎᖖᒐ . . .

ᐊᕐᑯᑎᕐᖠᐊᖅ ᖠᖅᑯᓇᐊ'ᒪᒍ ᐊᓐᓇᐃ'ᓗᓂ, ᓇᓅᒃ ᖁᓪᓗ'ᒪᓂᓪᓗ ᕿᒫᓪᓚᒃᖠᓐᓇᖅᑯᒃ.

ᓴᓇᖤ: ᐋᐊᐊᐊ.

ᐊᕐᑯᑎᕐᖠᐊᖅ: ᒪᒥᐊᓇᖅ.

ᓴᓇᖤ: ᐊᐅᓚᖖᒋᓪᒪᕆᒃᑐᒥᒃ ᐱᖖᒋᕐᓱᕐᓂᕋᕕᑦ—ᖀᓴᑉᖤᐅᕐᓱᒃ ᐋᐊᐊᐊ . . .

ᑲᑑᑦ ᐹᓪᓚᒃᑲᒥ ᓇᓅᒃ ᓇᖠᖅᑕᕋᓗᐊᖕᒋ'ᓄᑦ ᐊᐳ'ᒦᑦᑐᒥᒃ ᓇᑦᑎᐅᑉ ᐊᐅᖕᒐᓂᒃ ᓂᕆᓇᖠᐊᓕᖅᓱᓂ.

ᑲᑑᑦ: ᓇᑦᑎᐅᑉ ᐊᐅᖓ, ᐆᓇᖤᒃᑐᑦᑎᐊᕙᒃ!

ᐊᕐᑯᑎᕐᖠᐊᖅ: ᑲᑑᑎᕐᓱᒃ!

ᑲᑑᑦ: . . . ᒻᒻᒻᒻ . . . ᒪᒪᖅᑐᖅ ᐊᒥᐊᑦᑯᓕᒃ ᐱᔪᒪᖠᖅᑲᖅᐹ?

ᐊᕐᑯᑎᕐᖠᐊᖅ: ᐋᓐᓂᐊᓕᕐᓂᐊᖅᑐᑎᑦ ᓂᕆᒍᕕᐅᒃ, ᑲᑑᑦ.

ᑲᑑᑦ: ᓂᕆᖖᒋᑦᐸᓪᓛᕐᓂᒻᓄᑦ ᐋᓐᓂᐊᓕᖅᑐᖓ.

ᐊᕐᑯᑎᕐᖠᐊᖅ: (ᐊᓗᕈᑎᒧᑦ) ᓇᐅᓪᓕ ᓇᐅᑦᑎᖅᑐᖅᑎ?

ᓴᖑᖤᓇᓗᒃ: ᐊᓐᖑᑎᒃᓵᖅᖠᐅᖅᑐᖅ—ᓴᓇᖥᑦ ᐃᓚᐃᑦ ᐃᓚᐅ'ᓗᑎᒃ.

ᐊᕐᑯᑎᕐᖠᐊᖅ: ᐋᓐᓂᐊᖅᐸᓪᓛᖅᑐᖅ ᐃᒻᓇ ᐊᓐᖑᑎᒃᓵᖅᖠᐅᓇᐊᖅᑲᖖᒋᑦᑑᒐᓗᐊᖅ.

ᓴᖑᖤᓇᓗᒃ: ᐱᔪᒪᒻᒪᓇᒃᑲᓗᐊ'ᒪᑦ.

ᐊᕐᑯᑎᕐᖠᐊᖅ: ᖠᒦᓕᖅᐱᑕᓕ?

ᓴᖑᖤᓇᓗᒃ ᐃᖤᕕᒋᐊᖅᓱᒍ ᓄᓇᖖᒍᐊᖅ ᐊᓕᒃᑐᖅᖤᒪᐅᖅᑐᖅ.

FRANKLIN: We'll connect the passage, by God we will, but it's altogether a useless, impractical, stupid idea because of that damn eternal ice.

CARTER: Useless—now you tell us, two years in—

WICKERS: *(firmly)* Carter.

FRANKLIN pulls out his chronometer.

FRANKLIN: What's more important to the world is the theory of terrestrial magnetism—how the pull of the earth operates and how . . .

FRANKLIN falls over. HOLLOWAY helps FRANKLIN to his feet.

HOLLOWAY: John, sir—get to your feet, dear man.

FRANKLIN: Spot of dizziness is all . . . thank you . . . now, our coordinates . . . *(fiddles with his chronometer)* longitude is, let's see . . .

CARTER: We're lost.

BEAN seems to fall against WICKERS, who lowers him gently to the ground.

WICKERS: Rest for a little while, Bean.

FRANKLIN: We are never lost with the Lord.

CARTER: I doubt the Lord even knows we're here.

HOLLOWAY: That's enough, Carter.

FRANKLIN shakes his chronometer.

FRANKLIN: These ridiculous chronometers—substandard mechanisms at best—the compass needle hasn't moved for days! We shall follow the sun—it's a far more reliable instrument.

ᓴᖑᔮᓇᓗᒃ: ᐅᖓᓯᒃᑎᒥᓂᖅᑲᖅᑐᖅ 250 ᒪᐃᓕᓂᒃ ᐃᑭᖃᓴᒃᑯᑦ ᑕᐃᑯᖓ ᓄᓇᐃᓐᓇᖅᒍᑦ. ᑕᐃᑰᓇ ᖅᑭᓂᖅᑕᕗᑦ ᐃᑳᖅᕕᓇᓗᒃ ᓇᓂᓂᐊᖅᑕᒃᓯᓇᔭᕗᑦ—

ᐊᖅᑯᑎᖅᓯᐊᖅ: ᐄᖅᑭ ᐊᐱᕆᓇᓯᐊᖅᑐᖓ ᓯᒦᑦᑖᒃᓯᑉᑎ'ᓂ ᑕᔅᓚᓯᑕᕆ.

ᓴᖑᔮᓇᓗᒃ ᓄᓇᙳᐊᖅ ᑕᑯᑦᑎᐊᖃᓯᐊᖅᑐᕐᓂᐅᒃ ᑭᓯᐊᓂᒃ ᐃᒧᑦᑐᖅᑲᖅᐸᑦᑖᓕ'ᒪᑦ ᐃᓯᕕᑦᑎᐊᓚᐃᑦᑐᓇᓗᒃ.

ᓴᖑᔮᓇᓗᒃ: ᐅᕕᑦᑎᐊᕈᒃ . . .

ᐊᖅᑯᑎᖅᓯᐊᖅ: ᓯᑯᐃᓚᐃᑦᑐᒥ ᐃᖓᔅᖃᕕᒃᓯᖅ ᐃᒪᒃᑯᑦ ᑕᐃᓪᓇ ᖅᑭᓂᖅᑕᕗᑦ ᓇᓂᓂᐊᖅᐸᕗᑦ ᓯᓕᓯᒥᒃ, ᑭᓯᐊᓂᒃ ᓯᔮᓇᓗᕐᒍᒃᑕᐅᖅ ᓇᓂᓯᓇᓯᐊᖅᑐᒍᑦ ᓯᑯᕐᒎᖑᒍᑦ ᐱᔭᐅᕙᓪᓛᖅᑐᐊᓘᑎ'ᓗᑕᓗ.

ᑲᒎᑦ: ᖅᑭᓂᖃᓯᐊᖅᑕᒃᓯᐅᖕᖏᓐᓂᖅᑕᖅᑯᑦ ᓯᓇᐅᕙᕙᓕ—ᐊᒃᐱᐅ'ᓯᓕᑕᐃᓐᓇᓕᖅᐱᑎᒍᑦ ᑕᔅᕙ ᐅᑭᐅᖕᓂᒃ ᒫᔅᑭᓇᓗᖕᓂᒃ ᖅᑭᓂᖅᑐᓇᓘᓕᖅᑎ'ᓗᑕ—

ᐊᓗᑭᑎ: (ᐊᑦᖅᑯᓇᖅᑐᓂ) ᑲᒎᑦ ᐱᓯᐃᑲᐃᑦ.

ᐊᖅᑯᑎᖅᓯᐊᖅ ᐅᐸᓗᖅᓯᐅᑎᓂ ᓯᓚᓯᐅᑎᓂ ᐊᒧ'ᓗᓂᐅᒃ.

ᐊᖅᑯᑎᖅᓯᐊᖅ: ᓯᓚᖅᓯᐊᖅᒥᓕ ᑐᑭᓯᑉᐅᑦᓕᖃᓯᐊᖅᑐᑦᑕᐅᖅ ᓯᓚᐅᑉ ᐊᕙᑎᐅᑉ ᐊᐅᓚᓂᐊ'ᓂᒃ—ᖅᑲᓄᕆᑦᑑᓂᐊ'ᓂ ᐊᐅᓚᓂᐊ, ᑲᓄᖅᓗ . . .

ᐊᖅᑯᑎᖅᓯᐊᖅ ᐅᔅᑭ'ᓗᓂ. ᓴᖑᔮᓇᓘᑉ ᐃᑲᔪᖅᑐᓂᐅᒃ ᒪᑭᑎᓐᓇᓯᐊᖅᑐᒍ.

ᓴᖑᔮᓇᓗᒃ: ᔫᓐ ᐊᑕᓂᖅᓯᐊᖅ, ᐊᑕᐃ ᒪᑭᓕᕆᑦ.

ᐊᖅᑯᑎᖅᓯᐊᖅ: ᐅᐃᐸᔅᙳᒐᖅᓯᓐᓇᓐᓄᐊᖃᓗᐊᖃᒪ . . . ᖅᑲᓄᕆᙱᑦᑐᖓ . . . ᐊᑕᐃᔫᖅ ᓯᒦᑦᐱᑕ . . . (ᓯᓚᓯᐅᑎᓂ ᑲᒪᒋᓇᓯᐊᖅᑐᓂᐅᒃ) . . . ᓯᒥᔫᖅ . . .

ᑲᒎᑦ: ᐊᓯᐅᑦᑎᐊᖅᑐᒍᑦ.

ᐱᓂᖅ ᓇᓚᓯᓐᖑᓕ'ᒪᑦ ᐊᓗᑭᑎ ᑕᐅᓄᖓ ᓇᓚᑎ'ᓗᓂᐅᒃ.

ᐊᓗᑭᑎ: ᐱᓂᖅ ᑕᖅᑲᐃᖅᓯᑲᓐᓄᐊᕆᑦ ᑕᓴᒪᓂ.

WICKERS picks up the flower that CARTER tossed away and gives it to BEAN . . .

WICKERS: It's hardly a primrose, but it's . . . *(looks closer at BEAN)* Bean . . .

. . . but BEAN is dead.

FRANKLIN: *(to CARTER)* What time is it?

CARTER: Seventeen aught six, sir.

WICKERS: *(to FRANKLIN)* Bean's gone, sir—he's gone.

FRANKLIN: Very sorry, Wickers.

WICKERS: But he was talking a moment ago . . .

WICKERS holds him in his arms.

HOLLOWAY: I fear soon we'll all be lying down on the breast of our Saviour.

FRANKLIN: Buck up, Holloway—learn to endure.

HOLLOWAY: I am learning, sir.

FRANKLIN: Wickers, let him go. We must press on and find provisions.

WICKERS is crying.

WICKERS: I can't leave him here all alone, sir. I'll carry him back to the ship.

FRANKLIN: Don't cry, Officer Wickers. Crying is a kind of defeat, a failure of nerve.

But WICKERS continues to clutch BEAN, then he snuggles his head into BEAN's neck. Everyone goes quiet with the tension around hunger and death.

WICKERS stares at BEAN's neck, riveted.

ᐊᖁᑎᕐᔪᐊᖅ: ᐊᔭᐅᓕᐃᑦᑐᒍᑦ ᓄᓇᓕᐅᖅᑎᒥᒃ ᒪᓕᒃᑯᐸᑕ.

ᑲᑑᑦ: ᓄᓇᓕᐅᖅᑎᐸ ᖃᐅᔨᒪᙱᓪᒪᕆᒃᑕᒃᓴᕆᔾᑎᒍᑦ ᔪᒦᑦᑖᒃᓴᐸᑎ'ᓂᒃ.

ᓴᖑᔨᓇᓗᒃ: ᑲᑑᑦ, ᐱᔪᐃᓇᑦ.

ᐊᖁᑎᕐᔪᐊᖅ ᔭᓕᔭᐅᑎᓂ ᐊᐅᓕᔾᔭᓕᖅᓱᓂᐅᒃ.

ᐊᖁᑎᕐᔪᐊᖅ: ᐅᑯᐊᕐᓱᐃᑦ ᔭᓕᔭᐅᑎᓇᓗᕐᓱᐃᑦ ᔪᖁᑕᐅᙱᑦᑐᓇᓗᐃᑦ—ᑎᑦᑯᐊᓯᑎᓇᓗᕐᓱᐊᑦ ᐃᖑᙱᓪᒪᕆᒃᔭᒪᓕ'ᒪᑦ ᐅᐸᑐᕐᓂᒃ ᖃᐸᔭᓇᓗᖕᓂᒃ! ᔭᕿᓂᖅ ᒪᓕᒃᐸᓪᓗᓕᕐᓕᕗᑦ ᑕᒻᒪᓈᑦᑯᑎᒻᒪᕆᐅ'ᒪᑦ.

ᐊᓗᓯᑎ ᑎᒍ'ᓗᓂᐅᒃ ᓄᓇᓴᓐᓄᐊᖅ ᑲᑑᑎᐸ ᐃᒥᑕᓴᓗᐊᖕᒐ,
ᐱᓂᕐᒍᑦ ᑐᓂ'ᓗᓂᐅᒃ . . .

ᐊᓗᓯᑎ: ᔪᖕᒋᐅᓇᙱᑦᑑᒐᓗᐊᕐᓕ ᑭᔭᐊᓂᒃ ᐱᑦᑕᐅᔪᓐᓄᐊᖅ . . . *(ᑕᑯᑦᑎᐊᓇᐊᖅᓱᓂ ᐱᓂᕐᒍᑦ)* ᐱᓂᖅ . . .

. . . ᑭᔭᐊᓂᒃ ᐱᓂᖅ ᐃᓅᔪᐃᖅᑑᓐᓂᖅ.

ᐊᖁᑎᕐᔪᐊᖅ: *(ᑲᑑ'ᒧᑦ)* ᔪᒧᙵᓕᖅᐸ ᐅᐸᑐᖅᔭᐅᑦ?

ᑲᑑᑦ: ᐅᓐᓅᓕᖅᑐᖅ.

ᐊᓗᓯᑎ: *(ᐊᖁᑎᕐᔪᐊᕐᒧᑦ)* ᐱᓂᖅ ᑐᖁᔪᖅ, ᐊᑕᓂᕐᔪᐊᖅ—ᐅᓇ ᑐᖁᔪᖅ.

ᐊᖁᑎᕐᔪᐊᖅ: ᐊᔪᕐᓇ'ᒪᑦ, ᐊᓗᓯᑎ.

ᐊᓗᓯᑎ: ᐅᕕᑦᑎᐊᓐᓄᐊᖅ ᐅᕐᑳᓪᓕᒃᑲᓗᐊ'ᒪᑦ ᔪᕐᑲᓯᐃᑳᓪᓕᒃᓱᓂᓗ . . .

ᐊᓗᓯᑎᐸ ᐃᕿ'ᓗᓂᐅᒃ ᐱᓂᕕᓂᖅ.

ᓴᖑᔨᓇᓗᒃ: ᑕᒪᐸᑕ ᓇᓕᖕᓂᐊᖅᑐᒍᑦ ᑐᖁᓗᑕ ᑕ'ᓇ ᐱᐅᓕᔨᐸᑕ ᓵᖕᒐᓂ.

ᐊᖁᑎᕐᔪᐊᖅ: ᖁᓕᙱᓗᑎᑦ ᓴᖑᔨᓇᓗᒃ—ᓴᐱᓕᖅᑖᐃᓕᓇᔪᐊᕆᐊᖅᑲᖅᑐᑎᑦ.

ᓴᖑᔨᓇᓗᒃ: ᐄᖑᒐᓗᐊᕐᓕ, ᐊᑕᓂᕐᔪᐊᖅ.

ᐊᖁᑎᕐᔪᐊᖅ: ᐊᓗᓯᑎ ᐅᓇ ᓴᐸᑯᓕᓯᒃ. ᐃᖕᒋᔾᓴᓴᔪᐊᕆᐊᖅᑲᖅᑐᒍᑦ ᓂᕿᒃᓴᖅᔭᐅᓴᔪᐊᕐᓗᑕ.

Let him go, Wickers.

WICKERS: Sir . . . I can't.

FRANKLIN: Touch him and I will have to kill you.

WICKERS: Please—

FRANKLIN: Better to starve to death. Do you understand, Officer Wickers?

Silence.

DO YOU UNDERSTAND?

WICKERS: Yes, sir, I understand.

FRANKLIN: We'll bury him at sea—slide him into the water through that opening.

WICKERS: I'll go mad if I do not eat.

FRANKLIN: You'll go mad both ways, but you'll shame the admiralty and burn in eternal hellfire if you lay one finger on Bean, a man who was your dear and trusted friend.

CARTER snickers, as does CREW #1.

(to CARTER and CREW #1) QUIET! Stand up, Wickers!

WICKERS gets to his feet, then picks up BEAN and carries him to the breathing hole.

Carter, sing a hymn.

CARTER: Sir, I'm not in the mood—hunger is affecting my singing apparatus.

FRANKLIN: If you cannot honour our dead, then I give you permission to walk out into the tundra and see what kind of a mood you'll be in when that bear finds you—attracted, no doubt, by the smell of seal blood in your

ᐊᓗᕆᑎ ᕿᐊᓕᕋᒥ.

ᐊᓗᕆᑎ: ᑕᓴᒧᖕᖓᐃᓐᓇᖅ ᕿᒪᑐᐃᓐᓇᓚᐃᑕᕋ ᐊᒃᔭᕐᓂᐊᖅᐸᕋ ᐅᒥᐊᕐᔪᐊᑉᑎ'ᓄᑦ.

ᐊᖁᑎᕐᔪᐊᖅ: ᐊᓗᕆᑎ ᕿᐊᑦᑕᐃᓕᓗᑎᑦ. ᕿᐊᔪᑦ ᓵᓚᐅᓯᒪ'ᒪᑕ, ᓴᖖᒋᑦᑎᐊᖖᒋ'ᓇᒥᒃ.

ᑭᓯᐊᓂᒃ ᐊᓗᕆᑎ ᔭᓕ ᑎᒍᒥᐊᖕᒋᓐᓇᖅᖢᓂᐅᒃ ᐱᓂᖅ ᐃᕿ'ᓗᓂᐅᒃ ᖁᕝᕗᓯᐊᒍᑦ ᑯᓂᒃᖢᓂᐅᒃ. ᑕᒪᐃᑕ ᓂᐸᐃᓕᖅᑐᑦ ᑐᖁᔪᖅᑲᕐᓂᖕᖓᓄᑦ ᑳᖕᓃ'ᓄᑦᓗ.

ᐊᓗᕆᑎ ᑕᐅᑐᐃᓐᓇᓕᖅᖢᓂ ᐱᓂᐅᑉ ᖁᕝᕗᓯᐊᓄᑦ ᑳᖕᓂᕐᒥᓂᒃ ᐃᒃᐱᒋᓪᓗᐊᓕᖅᖢᓂᐅᒃ.

ᐊᖁᑎᕐᔪᐊᖅ: ᐊᓗᕆᑎ ᐱᔭᐃᕆᒃ.

ᐊᓗᕆᑎ: ᐄᕿ . . . ᐱᓂᐊᑕᖅᕋ.

ᐊᖁᑎᕐᔪᐊᖅ: ᓂᕆᓇᔭᐊᕆᕕᐅᒃ ᑕᒧᐊᕝᕕᕆᒍᕕᐅᒃ ᑐᖁᓴᕐᓂᐊᖅᑕᕆᑦ.

ᐊᓗᕆᑎ: ᐱᓚᖕᖓ—

ᐊᖁᑎᕐᔪᐊᖅ: ᐊᕿᐊᕆᐊᕐᓂᕐᒧᑦ ᑐᖁᒍᕕᑦ ᐱᑦᑕᐅᑦᕿᔭᐅᔪᖅ. ᑐᑭᓯᕕᖕᖔ, ᐊᓗᕆᑎ?

ᓂᐸᐃᓕᒃᑐᖅᑐᑦ.

ᐊᖁᑎᕐᔪᐊᖅ: ᑐᑭᓯᒐᓗᐊᖅᐱᖕᖔ?

ᐊᓗᕆᑎ: ᐄ, ᑐᑭᓯᕗᖕᖓ.

ᐊᖁᑎᕐᔪᐊᖅ: ᑎᒥᖕᖓ ᐃᓕᓂᐊᖅᐸᕗᑦ ᑕᕆᐅᕐᒧᑦ ᑕᐃᑰᓇ ᐊᖕᒪᓂᒃᑯᑦ ᐃᒪᕐᒧᖖᖓᖅᑎᓗᒍ ᑕᐅᓄᖕᖓ.

ᐊᓗᕆᑎ: ᐃᔭᒪᐃᕆᑎᓂᐊᖅᑐᖕᖓ ᓂᕆᖖᒋᑦᑯᒪ.

ᐊᖁᑎᕐᔪᐊᖅ: ᐃᔭᒪᐃᕆᑎᓂᐊᖅᑐᑎᑦ ᓂᕆᒍ'ᓂᓗ, ᐸᓯᔭᒃᓴᐅᑎᑦᑎᓂᐊᖅᑕᑉᑎᒋᑦ ᐃᑯᐊᓚᒍᒫᕐᓗᑎᑦᓘᓐᓃᑦ ᐃᔭᖅᑲᖖᒋᑦᑐᒥ ᐱᑐᐊᕆ'ᓂ ᑖᒻᓇ ᐱᓂᖅ, ᐃᓚᓐᓇᓂᔭᕋᓗᐃᑦ ᐃᑲᔪᖅᑎᒋᓯᒪᔭᐃᑦᓗ.

ᑲᑑᑦ ᒪᖕᖓᓗᒃᓯᔫᖅᑐᖅ ᐃᔅᓂᒋᔮ, ᓴᓇᔮᓗ.

mouth and your mad belief that you—or any one of us—could survive out here alone!

CARTER sings Mendelssohn's "O for the Wings of a Dove" as FRANKLIN helps WICKERS slide BEAN's body into the hole and push it under.

CARTER: *(sings)* O' for the wings, for the wings of a dove
Far away, far away I would rove.
O' for the wings, for the wings of a . . .

CREW #1 spots a cylinder and picks it up.

CREW #1: Look—

CREW #1 pops open the cylinder and pulls out a paper.

What's this?

HOLLOWAY: Give that to me.

CREW #1 hands it to HOLLOWAY, who reads it then passes it to FRANKLIN, who reads it and rips it up.

CARTER: *(re: the hill in the distance)* I thought this place looked familiar.

FRANKLIN: *(to HOLLOWAY)* Where's the map?

CREW #1: Are we lost?

HOLLOWAY gives a tattered map to FRANKLIN.

FRANKLIN: One day you'll urge your grandchildren to sail the oceans and see the world— *(to HOLLOWAY)* This is the wrong map!

CARTER: Right now I'd rather see English flowers.

FRANKLIN: *These* are your flowers, Carter—the ice, the snow are your flowers now because *this* is your country! That goes for all of you—*this* is your country and *this* is your future—and Officer Wickers!

ᐊᕐᑯᑎᕐᔪᐊᖅ: (ᑳᑑ'ᒧᑦ ᖃᓇᔾᒧᓪᓗ) ᑲᒪᒋᔪᐃᖅᔪᐅᒃ! ᒪᑭᓪᓗᑎᑦ ᐊᓗᕈᑦ!

ᐊᓗᕈᑎ ᒪᑭ'ᓗᓂ ᐱᓂᕐᒥᒃ ᑎᒍ'ᓗᓂ ᐊᒃᖃᓕᖅᓗᓂᐅᒃ ᐊᒡᓗᒧᑦ.

ᐊᕐᑯᑎᕐᔪᐊᖅ: ᑳᑑᑦ ᐱᔭᕐᒥᒃ ᐃᖏᐅᓇ.

ᑳᑑᑦ: ᐃᖕᒋᐅᓚᐃᑦᑐᖕᒐ—ᑳᖕᓂᕐᒍᑦ ᐃᒡᒋᐊᕋ ᐃᓘᕐᓇᑦᑎᐊᖕᒋ'ᒪᑦ.

ᐊᕐᑯᑎᕐᔪᐊᖅ: ᑐᕐᑯᔪᒧᑦ ᐃᖏᐅᓚᐃᑦᑯᕖᑦ ᐊᑕᐃ ᐱᔪᒡᓗᑎᑦ ᓄᓇᒧᑦ ᓇᓂᖃᐅᓗᑎᓪᓗ ᓇᓄᕐᒧᑦ, ᓇᐃᒪᓂᐊ'ᒪᑦ ᐊᐅᒃᑐᖅᑕᕋᓗᐊ'ᓂᒃ ᓇᑦᑎᕐᒥᑦ, ᐅᒃᐱᓇᖃᕐᑲᕐᓂᕋᕖᓪᓗ ᐃᓅᔪᖕᓇᕐᓂᐸᑎ'ᓂᒃ ᑕᖃᒪᓂ ᐃᑲᔪᖅᑕᐅᖖᒋᓗᑕ!

ᑳᑑᑦ ᐃᖏᐅᓕᖅᓗᓂ ᐱᔭᕐᒥᒃ ᑐᒃᔪᐅᑎᒥᒃ, ᐊᕐᑯᑎᕐᔪᐊᕐᓗ ᐊᓗᕈᑎᒥᒃ ᐃᑲᔪᖅᓗᓂ ᑕᐅᓄᖕᖓ ᐱᓂᐅᑉ ᑎᒥᐊ ᑭᕖᑎ'ᓗᒍ ᐊᖕᒪᓂᑦᑯᑦ.

ᑳᑑᑦ: (ᐃᖏᐅᖅᓗᓂ) ᐃᖃᕈᕐᑲᕈᒪ, ᑎᖕᒥᐊᑉ ᐃᖃᕈᐃ'ᓂᒃ ᐅᖓᔪᒃᑐᒨᖓᐅᓇᔭᖅᑐᖓ, ᐃᖃᕈᕐᑲᕈᒪ, ᐃᖃᕈ . . .

ᖃᓇᔾ ᐆᖅᔪᒪᔪᒥᒃ ᑕᑯᖓᒥ ᑎᒍ'ᓗᓂᐅᒃ.

ᖃᓇᔾ: ᑦᑯᒃ—ᔪᓇ ᐅᓇ?

ᖃᓇᔾ ᐊᖕᒪᖅᓗᒍ ᐆᖅ ᐊᓕᓚᔪᒥᒃ ᐊᒧᔪ'ᓗᓂ.

ᖃᖑᔾᓇᓗᒃ: ᖄᐃᑲᐅᒃ ᐅᓇ.

ᖃᓇᔾ ᖃᖑᔾᓇᓗᖕᒧᑦ ᑐᓂ'ᒪᒍ ᐅᖄᓚᒦᖅᓗᓂᐅᒃ ᑐᓂ'ᓗᒍ ᐊᕐᑯᑎᕐᔪᐊᕐᒧᑦ ᐅᖄᓚᒦ'ᒪᒍ ᐅᕈᔪᓚᖅᓗᓂ ᐊᓚᒃᑐᓚᖅᐹ, ᔪᓇᐅᕝᕙ ᓇ'ᒥᓂᖅ ᑎᑎᕋᖅᑕᕖᓃ'ᓂᒃ ᓇᓂᔪᔪᑦ ᐱᒋᐊᕐᕕᒋᖃᐃᑦ ᓄᓇ ᐅᑎᕐᕕᒋᓐᓂ'ᒪᒋᑦ.

ᑳᑑᑦ: (ᐱ'ᓗᒍ ᑭᙵ ᑖᕙᓂ ᑕᐅᑐᖕᓇᖅᑐᖅ) ᔪᓇᐅᕝᕙ ᖃᒪᓅᔪᐅᖅᑖᕐᓂᖅᑯᒍᑦ ᐃᓕᑕ'ᓇᖅᔪᒍᖅ.

ᐊᕐᑯᑎᕐᔪᐊᖅ: (ᖃᖑᔾᓇᓗᖕᒧᑦ) ᓇᐅᒡᓕ ᓄᓇᙳᐊᖅ?

ᖃᓇᔾ: ᐊᔪᐅᕕᑖ?

ᖃᖑᔾᓇᓗᒃ ᑐᓂ'ᓗᓂᐅᒃ ᓄᓇᙳᐊᖅ ᐊᕐᑯᑎᕐᔪᐊᕐᒧᑦ.

WICKERS: Yes, sir?

CARTER: *(to FRANKLIN)* The only future we have is the one in your imagination.

FRANKLIN: *(to WICKERS)* These are *your* men—look after them—I didn't promote you so you could stand around consumed by sorrow. Men die here—women and children die here—and Carter, you're right . . .

AĞGIAQ: *(off stage)* Hell-o.

FRANKLIN: . . . the only future we have is our belief in it.

AĞGIAQ: *(off stage)* Hell-o.

FRANKLIN: *(calls out)* HELLO—WELCOME.

AĞGIAQ and PANINGAJAK enter carrying shiny new rifles. AĞGIAQ speaks English.

Ah, familiar faces. We haven't seen you two for a long time.

AĞGIAQ: You're still alive. We heard shooting.

HOLLOWAY: Franklin scared off a bear.

FRANKLIN: *(to AĞGIAQ)* Where did you learn to speak English?

AĞGIAQ: From Agluukkaq.

FRANKLIN: Who?

AĞGIAQ: Rae . . . John Rae.

PANINGAJAK has not learned how to speak English.

PANINGAJAK: *(lowers his voice, to AĞGIAQ)* Nukaq, they seem to have a smell of really sick people.

FRANKLIN: *(to AĞGIAQ)* Where did you see Rae? Maybe he can help us.

ᐊᖁᑎᕐᔪᐊᖅ: ᖃᑯᒍᑭᐊᖅ ᐃᓐᖑᑕ'ᓂᒃ ᐅᒥᐊᖅᑐᖁᔪᒫᖅᑕᑎᑦ
ᑕᓯᐅᕐᔪᐊᒃᑯᑦ ᓄᓇᕐᔪᐊᑦ ᐊ'ᓚᑦᖀᑦ ᑕᑯᓇᕆᐊᕐᑐᓂᒋᑦ—(ᓵᖑᔮᓇᓗᖕᒍᑦ)
ᐅᓇᐅᖖᒋᒃᑐᕐᓗ ᐊᐃᑉᐸᕙᓗᐊ!

ᑲᑑᑦ: ᑕᕝᕙᓚ ᑕᑯᔪᒪᑦᓗᐊᖅᑐᖕᒐ ᐊᑭᐊᓂᕐᒥᐅᑕᕐᓂᒃ ᓄᓇᕋᑦᑎᐊᕙᓐᓄᐊᕐᓂᒃ.

ᐊᖁᑎᕐᔪᐊᖅ: ᐅᕝᕙ ᐅᑯᐊᑦ ᓄᓇᕋᖁᑎᒋᔭᑎᑦ, ᑲᑑᑦ—ᔨᑯ, ᐊᐳᑦ,
ᓄᓇᕋᖁᑎᒋᓚᖅᐸᑎᑦ ᐅᓇ ᓄᓇᒥᓚᕋᕕᐅᒃ! ᑕᒪᑉᔨᓗ—ᐅᓇ
ᓄᓇᒥᓚᖅᑕᖅᔨ ᐅᓇ ᔨᕗᓂᓯᔭᖅᔨ—ᐃᕝᕕᑦᓗ ᐊᓗᕈᑎ!

ᐊᓗᕈᑎ: ᔭᕚ, ᐊᑕᓂᕐᔪᐊᖅ?

ᑲᑑᑦ: (ᐊᖁᑎᕐᔪᐊᕐᒍᑦ) ᐃᓅᔨᑉᑎ'ᓂ ᔨᕗᓂᒃᓵᖅᑰᖖᒋᒻᒪᓇᒃᑐᒍᑦ
ᑭᔨᐊᓂᒃ ᐃᕝᕕᑦ ᑕᐅᑐᖖᒍᐊᖅᑕ'ᓂᒃ.

ᐊᖁᑎᕐᔪᐊᖅ: (ᐊᓗᕈᑎᒍᑦ) ᐅᑯᐊᑦ ᓴᓇᔫᒋᒐᕕᒋᑦ ᑲᒪᒋᑦᑎᐊᕐᓗᒋᑦ—
ᐃᑲᔪᖅᑎᒋᓇᕆᐊᖅᑕᕋᓗᐊᑉᑭᑦ ᑭᔨᐊᓂᒃ ᕿᐊᕆᓐᖑᐃᓐᓇᖅᑰᓚᕋᕕᑦ. ᐊᖑᑎᑦ
ᑕᓵᒪᓂ ᑐᖁᕚᒃᑐᑦ—ᐊᕐᓇᐃᓪᓗ ᓄᑕᖅᑲᓪᓗ ᑐᖁᕚ'ᒪᑕ—ᐊᔨᐅᒻᒪᓇᒃ . . .

ᐊᕝᒋᐊᖅ: (ᐊᕙ'ᖕᒐᑦ) ᐊ-ᓘ.

ᐊᖁᑎᕐᔪᐊᖅ: . . . ᔨᕗᓂᒃᓴᒥᒃ ᐅᒃᐱᓯᔭᖃᕐᑐᑕ ᔨᕗᓂᒃᓴᖃᕐᓂᐊᖅᑐᒍᑦ.

ᐊᕝᒋᐊᖅ: (ᐊᕙ'ᖕᒐᑦ) ᐊ-ᓘ.

ᐊᖁᑎᕐᔪᐊᖅ: (ᑐᖅᓱᓚ'ᓗᓂ) ᐊ-ᓘ—ᑐᓐᖓᕆᑦᑎᐊᓯᑦᑎ.

ᐃᔨᖅᓱᑎᒃ ᐊᕝᒋᐊᕐᓗ ᐸᓂᖕᒐᔭᒡᓗ ᑎᒍᒥᐊᖅᓱᑎᒃ ᔨᖅᑯᖅᑎᕝᕆᑎᓂᒃ
ᓄᑖᕐᓂᒃ ᕿᑉᓚᖅᑐᓂᒃ. ᐊᕝᒋᐊᖅ ᖃᑉᓗᓈᑐᑦ ᐅᖃᒪᔪᖕᓇᓚᖅᑐᖅ.

ᐊᖁᑎᕐᔪᐊᖅ: ᐃᓚᑕ'ᓇᖅᑐᕌᓘᒃ. ᑕᑯᖖᒋᒃᔩᕐᓗᐊᖅᐸᑉᔨᒃ.

ᐊᕝᒋᐊᖅ: ᐃᓅᔪᔨ ᔭᓚ. ᔨᖅᑯᖅᑎᓐᓇᕆᐊᖅᑐᒥᒃ ᑐᓵᕐᓇᖅᑐᖃᕋᓗᐊ'ᒪᑦ.

ᓵᖑᔮᓇᓗᒃ: ᐊᖁᑎᕐᔪᐊᑉ ᔨᖅᑯᑎᓐᓇᕆᐊᕋᓗᐊ'ᒪᒍ ᓇᓄᕐᓗᒃ.

ᐊᖁᑎᕐᔪᐊᖅ: (ᐊᕝᒋᐊᕐᒍᑦ) ᖃᓄᖅ ᐃᓚᑦᐱᑦ ᖃᑉᓗᓈᑐᑦ ᐅᖃᒪᔪᖕᓇᓚᕋᕕᑦ.

ᐊᕝᒋᐊᖅ: ᐊᒡᓘᒃᑲᕐᒥᑦ.

AŘGIAQ: He is gone. He asked me to help him make things called snowshoes so he could walk back to Montreal.

HOLLOWAY: He *walked* to Montreal—good God—

FRANKLIN: Well he's a Scotsman—they're half wild to begin with.

PANINGAJAK: *(to AŘGIAQ)* They seem to have a smell of sick people.

AŘGIAQ: *(to PANINGAJAK)* I know, angajuk—I can smell it as I also have a nose!

FRANKLIN: We need provisions to take back to our ships—seals, birds—where can we find them?

AŘGIAQ: *(to FRANKLIN)* There are very few seals now . . . our families are starving. *(to PANINGAJAK)* Show him the knives.

PANINGAJAK pulls out a number of cheap knives and offers them to FRANKLIN.

We will give you knives—you give us bullets.

FRANKLIN: We have knives, but those are useless—they're just trinkets.

PANINGAJAK: *(to AŘGIAQ)* We need to have bullets.

AŘGIAQ: *(to FRANKLIN)* Get bullets from your big boat.

FRANKLIN: We have no bullets left either. Our ship's not here, it's up near Victory Point. Crozier and I took our men and split up so we could cover more ground to forage. We had ice all last summer, now more ice again, but July is coming and it will melt so it's imperative to find food and get back to our ships.

AŘGIAQ: Ice is melting very slowly this year—winter ice remains.

FRANKLIN falls again—WICKERS and HOLLOWAY help him up.

HOLLOWAY: Sir, perhaps you'd best sit down.

FRANKLIN pushes him away.

ᐊᕐᑯᑎᕐᔪᐊᖅ: ᔪᒥᑦ?

ᐊᔾᒋᐊᖅ: ᕋᐃ . . . ᔮᓐ ᕋᐃ.

ᐸᓂᖕᒐᓴᒃ ᔪᓚ ᐅᖃᓇᐅᒃᓴᙱᖅᑐᖅ ᖃᑉᓗᓈᑐᑦ.

ᐸᓂᖕᒐᓴᒃ: (*ᐃᔪᑉᔪᒃᓗᓂ ᐊᔾᒋᐊᕐᒧᑦ*) ᓄᑲᖅ, ᐅᑯᐊᑦ ᐋᓐᓂᐊᖅᑐᑐᑦ ᑎᐱᖃᖅᑰ'ᒪᑕ.

ᐊᕐᑯᑎᕐᔪᐊᖅ: (*ᐊᔾᒋᐊᕐᒧᑦ*) ᔪᒥ ᕋᐃ ᑕᑯᒐᓗᐊᕋ'ᓂ? ᐃᑲᔪᕈᖕᓇᖅᑕᒃᓴᓇᕚᑎᒍᑦ.

ᐊᔾᒋᐊᖅ: ᐊᐅᓪᓚᖅᑐᖅ. ᐃᑲᔪᖅᑕᕋᓗᐊᕋ ᓴᓇᔪᒪᒪᒐᓗᐊᕋᒥ ᒪᐅᓴᓈᑦᑯᑎᓂᒃ ᐱᔫᑎᒃᓴᓂᒃ ᐱᔪᒧᒪ'ᒪᓐᖕᒎᖅ ᒫᓐᑐᓇᐊᓚᒧᑦ.

ᓴᖕᒍᐳᓇᓗᒃ: ᐱᔪᓪᓚᔅᓵᓗᖕᓂᖅᐸ ᒫᓐᑐᓇᐊᓚᒧᑦ—ᔪᐳᕌᓗᔅᓘᓐᓂᖅ—

ᐊᕐᑯᑎᕐᔪᐊᖅ: ᔪᒃᑲᑎᒥᐅᑕᐅ'ᒪᑦ—ᑕᐃᑉᑯᐊᑦ ᐅᓇᖕᒥᓇᐃᑦᑐᓇᓗᐃᑦ.

ᐸᓂᖕᒐᓴᒃ: (*ᐊᔾᒋᐊᕐᒧᑦ*) ᐅᑯᐊᑦ ᐋᓐᓂᐊᖅᑐᑐᑦ ᑎᐱᖃᖅᑰ'ᒪᑕ.

ᐊᔾᒋᐊᖅ: (*ᐸᓂᖕᒐᓴᖕᒧᑦ*) ᐋ ᖃᐅᐳᒪᕗᖕᒐ, ᐊᖕᒐᔪᒃ—ᓇᐃᒪᓴᖕᓇᖅᑐᖕᒐ ᕿᖕᒐᖃ'ᒥᒐᒪᓚ!

ᐊᕐᑯᑎᕐᔪᐊᖅ: ᓂᕿᒃᓴᖅᔪᓇᔪᐊᓇᐊᖃᖅᑐᒍᑦ ᐊᒡᓴᕐᓗᒋᑦ ᐅᒥᐊᕐᔪᐊᑉᑎ'ᓄᑦ—ᓇᑦᑎᑦ, ᑎᖕᒥᐊᑦ—ᔪᒥᑦ ᐱᔪᖕᓇᖅᐱᑕ?

ᐊᔾᒋᐊᖅ: ᓇᑦᑎᖅᑦᑎᐊᕈᐃ'ᒪᑦ . . . ᐃᓚᕗᑦ ᑳᒃᑐᐊᓗᐃᑦᑕᐅᖅ. (*ᐸᓂᖕᒐᓴᖕᒧᑦ*) ᐱᓚᐅᑎᓂᒃ ᑕᑯᑎᓚᕈᒃ.

ᐸᓂᖕᒐᓴᒃ ᓵᑦᖁᒻᒥᖅᓗᓂ ᐱᓚᐅᑎᓂᒃ ᐊᑭᑭᑦᖂᖅᑐᓂᒃ ᐊᕐᑯᑎᕐᔪᐊᕐᒧᑦ ᑐᓂ'ᓗᒋᑦ.

ᐊᔾᒋᐊᖅ: ᐱᓚᐅᑎᓂᒃ ᑐᓂᓂᐊᖅᑕᑉᔪ—ᖃᕐᔪᕐᓂᒃ ᐱᔪᒪᒐᒻᓄᒃ.

ᐊᕐᑯᑎᕐᔪᐊᖅ: ᐱᓚᐅᑎᖃᖅᑐᒍᑦ ᐅᑯᐊᑦ ᔪᓇᐅᙱᒻᒪᓇᒃᑐᑦ—ᐱᕐᑯᑎᕐᓗᐃᑦ.

ᐸᓂᖕᒐᓴᒃ: (*ᐊᔾᒋᐊᕐᒧᑦ*) ᖃᕐᔪᖃᓇᐊᖅᑐᒍᑦᑕ.

ᐊᔾᒋᐊᖅ: (*ᐊᕐᑯᑎᕐᔪᐊᕐᒧᑦ*) ᖃᕐᔪᓂᒃ ᐊᐃᒃᓯᕐᓗᔪ ᐅᒥᐊᕐᔪᐊᑉᔪ'ᓂᑦ.

FRANKLIN: Stop fussing—Wickers, get us sorted out on the map.

AȞGIAQ: *(to FRANKLIN)* You are really sick.

FRANKLIN: No, just a touch of weariness—

CREW #1: Bears at your southwest, sir!

ANGU'ȞUAQ enters. He stops, perhaps uncertain.

FRANKLIN: Where's the other one—there's usually two.

WICKERS swiftly turns and looks behind himself. No bear.

WICKERS: All clear, sir.

FRANKLIN: Carter, take the rifle and shoot the bugger.

CARTER: No bullets left, sir.

FRANKLIN: GIVE ME THAT!

CARTER: But there are no bullets—

FRANKLIN grabs the rifle by its muzzle from whomever has it, and raises it over his head as he runs screaming towards ANGU'ȞUAQ . . .

FRANKLIN: I WILL EAT YOU, DO YOU UNDERSTAND—I WILL TEAR YOUR HEART OUT OF YOUR CHEST WITH MY BARE HANDS AND I WILL EAT AND EAT AND EAT UNTIL THERE'S NOTHING LEFT OF YOU BUT TEETH AND BONES THEN I WILL SMASH YOUR TEETH AND CRUSH YOUR BONES AND I WILL BOIL THEM AND SUP ON THEM AND PISS THEM OUT ONTO THIS GODFORSAKEN TUNDRA!

WICKERS: SIR, STOP—SIR!

CARTER: He's mad as hops!

ᐊᕐᑯᑎᕐᓴᐊᖅ: ᔪᑕᖅᑲᐳᐃᖅᑐᒍᑦ. ᓄᖑᑦᑎᓚᑉᑕ. ᐅᒥᐊᕐᓴᐊᕚᑦ ᓴᒪᓃᖕᖏᑦᑐᖅ ᐅᖓᓯᒃᑐᒦᑕᖅᑐᖅ. ᑕᒪᑉᐱᐅᒪᑦᖄᖅᑯᑕ ᐊᕙᓗᔪᐊᖅᑐᒍᑦ ᖅᑭᓂᑦᑎᐊᕈᖕᓇᕐᑯᑦᑐᑕ ᓂᓚᔮᒃᓴᓂᒃ. ᐊᐅᔭᐅᓚᑐᐊᖅᑐᒥ ᓯᑯᖅᑲᐃᓐᓇᕋᑐᐊ'ᒪᑦ ᑕᔾᕿᑐ ᓯᑯᐃᓐᓇᓪᒪᓚᒃ, ᑭᓯᐊᓂᒃ ᐊᐅᔭᐅᔪᖕᖓᕐᓂᐊ'ᒥ'ᒪᑦ ᓯᑯᐃᑦᑕᐃᓐᓇᕐᓂᐊ'ᒪᑦ ᓂᕐᑭᒃᓵᖅᓯᔾᕈᕐᑐᑕ ᐅᑎᓚᐊᖅᑲᖅᑐᒍᑦ ᐅᒥᐊᕐᓴᐊᐸᑎ'ᓄᑦ.

ᐊᔾᕆᐊᖅ: ᓯᑯ ᐊᐅᑦᑎᐊᖕᖏᓪᒪᓚ'ᒪᑦ—ᔪᑕ ᐅᑭᐅᖅᓯᐅᑎᓇᓗᒃ ᓯᑯ.

ᐊᕐᑯᑎᕐᓴᐊᖅ ᐹᓪᓚ'ᒥ'ᒪᑦ ᐊᓗᐱᑎᓗ ᓵᖑᓲᓇᓗᒡᓗ ᐃᑲᔪᑕᖅᐹᒃ.

ᓵᖑᓲᓇᓗᒃ: ᐊᑕᓂᕐᓴᐊᖅ, ᐃᖏᓐᓇᔪᐊᕐᓗᑎᑦᑕ.

ᐊᕐᑯᑎᕐᓴᐊᖅ ᐊᔮᒃᑯᓂᐅᒃ.

ᐊᕐᑯᑎᕐᓴᐊᖅ: ᐱᔪᐃᖕᖓ—ᐊᓗᐱᑎ, ᓄᓇᖑᐊᑕᓇᔪᐊᖅᐸᑦᑐᑕᕐᑐᑎᑦ.

ᐊᔾᕆᐊᖅ: *(ᐊᕐᑯᑎᕐᓴᐊᕐᒧᑦ)* ᐋᓐᓂᐊᖅᑐᐊᓗᓴᑎᑦ.

ᐊᕐᑯᑎᕐᓴᐊᖅ: ᐄᕐᑭᕐᓗᒃ, ᖅᑭᑐᔪᒃᓯᓐᓇᖅᑐᖓ—

ᓵᓇᓲ: ᑕᐃᑲ ᓇᓅᒃ, ᐊᑕᓂᕐᓴᐊᖅ!

ᐊᖑ'ᓴᐊᖅ ᐃᓯᖅᑯᖅ. ᓄᑦᖃᖓᑲᓐᓄᐊᖅᑯᓂ ᓇᓗᔾᐴᑕᕋᒥᒃ.

ᐊᕐᑯᑎᕐᓴᐊᖅ: ᓇᐅᓪᑕ ᐊᐃᐸᐹ—ᒪᔾᐴᖅᑳᑦᑕᕋᓗᐊ'ᒪᓂᒃ.

ᐊᓗᐱᑎ ᑐᓄ'ᓗᓂ ᑕᑯ'ᓗᓂ. ᓇᓄᖅᑲᖅᑲᔭᐃᑦᑐᖅ.

ᐊᓗᐱᑎ: ᔪᓇᖅᑲᖕᖏᑦᑐᖅ, ᐊᑕᓂᕐᓴᐊᖅ.

ᐊᕐᑯᑎᕐᓴᐊᖅ: ᑳᑑᑦ, ᓯᖅᑯᖅᑎᔾᓴᑎᕐᓗᑦ ᑎᒍᑲᐳᒃ ᓯᖅᑯᓪᓚᕐᓵᓗᒡᓗᒍ.

ᑳᑑᑦ: ᖅᑲᕐᓴᖅᑕᖅᑲᖅᑲᔭᐃᑐᖅ, ᐊᑕᓂᕐᓴᐊᖅ.

ᐊᕐᑯᑎᕐᓴᐊᖅ: ᖅᑲᐃᕐᓗᑲᐳᒃ ᐃᒪ!

ᑳᑑᑦ: ᖅᑲᕐᓴᖅᑲᕙᐊᓐᓄᐊᖕᖏ'ᒪᓪᓚ—

ᐊᕐᑯᑎᕐᓴᐊᖅ ᑎᒍᑲᖅᑯᓂᐅᒃ ᓯᖅᑯᖅᑎᔾᓴᑎ,
ᐊᓇᐅᑎᒋᓵᔭᖅᑯᓂᐅᒃ ᐊᖑ'ᓴᐊᕐᒥᒃ ᐱᒋᐊᕋᔪᐊᑕᖅᑐᖅ . . .

ANGU'ŘUAQ rears up on his hind legs and roars back at FRANKLIN, who tries to hit the bear with the butt of his rifle.

HOLLOWAY: JOHN FRANKLIN, SIR!

CREW #1: He's gone right bats.

WICKERS: JOHN FRANKLIN—STOP! THAT'S AN ORDER!

FRANKLIN stops.

ANGU'ŘUAQ exits.

FRANKLIN: *(to the men)* My apologies for such an outburst of . . . dear God.

HOLLOWAY: *(to FRANKLIN)* Sir, perhaps you should sit down and rest.

AŘGIAQ: *(to FRANKLIN)* It is dangerous to anger a bear.

FRANKLIN: *(exhausted)* Yes, I'm very sorry—entirely stupid of me.

PANINGAJAK: *(to FRANKLIN) Pittianngitanaluit taamna nanuq. [You disrespected the bear.]*

AŘGIAQ: *(to FRANKLIN)* When you see an animal, do not scream at them. Ask them to give you their life. Ask gently.

FRANKLIN: I will ask gently next time, thank you.

AŘGIAQ: But do not ask for the life of this bear.

PANINGAJAK: *(to AŘGIAQ)* There's no food here and no bullets . . . let's go look for fish.

AŘGIAQ: Eeeee . . .

AŘGIAQ begins to walk away, followed by PANINGAJAK.

FRANKLIN: Where—excuse me—where are you going?

ᐊᕐᑯᑎᕐᔑᐊᖅ: *(ᓂᙵᒐᒡᓗᐊᓕᖅᓱᓂ ᑳᖕᓂᕐᒧᑦ ᓇᓄᕐᒧᑦ ᐅᕐᑲᖅᑐᖅ)* ᓂᕆᓂᐊᖅᑕᕆᑦ, ᑐᑭᔑᕙᑦ—ᐆᒪᑎᑦ ᐊᒧᓂᐊᖅᑕᕋ ᖅᑲᒪ’ᖕᒐᑦ ᐊᔾᒐᑉᑯᑦ ᓂᕆᓂᐊᖅᑐᖕᒐᓗ ᓂᕇᓐᓇᑦᑎᐊᓕᕐᓗᖕᒐ ᓂᕆᓗᖕᒐ ᓂᕆᓗᖕᒐ ᓂᕆᓗᖕᒐ ᔕᓇᖅᑲᕈᐃᑦᑎᐊᖅᑎ’ᓗᑎᑦ ᑭᔑᐊᓂᒃ ᑭᒍᑏᓐᓇᖅᑎᑦ ᖃᐅᓂᖅᑎᓪᓗ. ᑭᒍᑎᑎᑦ ᖃᐅᓂᖅᑎᓪᓗ ᔑᖅᑲᓪᓕᓂᐊᖅᑕᓇᓗᑦᑲ ᖅᑲᔭᓕᐅᕈᑎᓗᕆᑦ ᓂᐅᕐᓗᒍᓗ ᖅᑲᔭᖅ ᖅᑯᐃᓂᐊᖅᑐᐊᓘᔑᖕᒐ ᓄᓇᔅᓱᖕᒧᑦ ᑕᓴᑉᔑᒧᖕᒐ!

ᐊᓗᕈᑎ: ᐊᑕᓂᕐᔑᐊᖅ, ᐱᔑᐃᕆᑦ—ᐊᑕᓂᕐᔑᐊᖅ!

ᑲᑑᑦ: ᐃᔓᒪᐃᕈᑎᑦᑎᐊᒻᒪᕆᒃᑐᖅ ᐃᒥᖕᒐᔑᑐᑦ!

ᐊᖑ’ᔑᐊᖅ ᓇᖏᖅᓱᓂ ᓇᖅᔑᖕᒐ’ᓗᓂ ᖅᑲᑎᒡᕙᓛᖅᓱᓂ ᐊᖅᑯᑎᕐᔑᐊᕐᒧᑦ, ᐊᖅᑯᑎᕐᔑᐊᕐᓗ ᐊᓇᐅᓐᓇᔑᐊᓕᖅᓱᓂᐅᒃ ᔑᖅᑯᖅᑎᕝᔑᑎᑉ ᖅᑭᔑᑖᒍᑦ ᑲᖏᐊᒍᑦ.

ᓴᖑᔨᓇᓗᒃ: ᐊᖅᑯᑎᕐᔑᐊᖅ, ᐊᑕᓂᕐᔑᐊᖅ!

ᓴᓇᔨ: ᐃᔓᒪᐃᕈᑎᑦᑎᐊᖅᑐᖅ ᐅᓇ.

ᐊᓗᕈᑎ: ᐊᖅᑯᑎᕐᔑᐊᖅ—ᑕᐃᒪ’ᓇ! ᓄᑦᖅᑲᖅᑯᕗᐅᔑᑎᑦ ᐊᔑᐅ!

ᐊᖅᑯᑎᕐᔑᐊᖅ ᓄᑦᖅᑲᖅᑐᖅ.

ᐊᖑ’ᔑᐊᖅ ᐊᓂ’ᓗᓂ.

ᐊᖅᑯᑎᕐᔑᐊᖅ: *(ᐊᖑᑎᓄᑦ)* ᐅᒡᒍᐊᖅᑯᖕᒐ ᐅᐃᒻᒪᒃᑲᓗᐊᕋᒪ . . . ᐆᖃᕐᓘᓐᓂᖅ.

ᓴᖑᔨᓇᓗᒃ: *(ᐊᖅᑯᑎᕐᔑᐊᕐᒧᑦ)* ᐊᑕᓂᕐᔑᐊᖅ ᐊᑕᐃ ᐃᖏᑲᓐᓄᐊᕋᔑᐊᕐᓗᑎᑦ ᑕᖅᑲᐃᖅᔑᕐᓗᑎᓪᓗ.

ᐊᔾᒥᐊᖅ: *(ᐊᖅᑯᑎᕐᔑᐊᕐᒧᑦ)* ᐅᓗᕆᐊᓇᖅᑐᓇᓗᐃᑦ ᓇᓄᐃᑦ ᓂᙵᒃᑎᓐᓇᔑᐊᕆᐊᖅᑲᙱᑕᕗᑦ.

ᐊᖅᑯᑎᕐᔑᐊᖅ: *(ᖅᑭᑐᔑᒡᓗᐊᖅᑐᖅ)* ᐄ, ᖅᑳ, ᐅᒡᒍᐊᖅᑯᖕᒐ—ᐃᔓᒪᑭᑦᑐᖅᓲᓐᓂᕋᒪ.

ᐸᓂᖕᒐᔭᒃ: *(ᐊᖅᑯᑎᕐᔑᐊᕐᒧᑦ)* ᐱᑦᑎᐊᙱᑕᓇᓗᐃᑦ ᑖᒻᓇ ᓇᓄᖅ.

ᐊᔾᒥᐊᖅ: *(ᐊᖅᑯᑎᕐᔑᐊᕐᒧᑦ)* ᐆᒪᔑᒥᒃ ᑕᑯᒍᕚᑦ, ᐃᕆᐊᑖᕐᕚᒥᙱᑐᒥᑦ. ᐊᐱᕆᑐᒥᑦ ᐊᓐᖑᑕᕆᕗᐅᔭᖕᓇᕆᐊᒃᔅᐃᑕ. ᐊᐱᕆᑦᑎᐊᕐᑐᒥᑦ.

AŘGIAQ: We are going to find fish. Char.

CARTER: *(to AŘGIAQ)* Here . . . take my knife and take these hooks and catch some for us, too. When we get back to our ship, we'll give you bullets and steel knives.

FRANKLIN: Very good plan, Carter.

AŘGIAQ: *(to FRANKLIN)* Bullets?

FRANKLIN: Yes, Ařgiaq, as many as we can spare. Will you join us as guides . . . hunters and guides?

AŘGIAQ: *(to PANINGAJAK)* If we hunt for them, they will give us some bullets.

PANINGAJAK: *(to AŘGIAQ)* Nukaq, these strange humans are going to shout at the bear. They are not honest—leave them be.

AŘGIAQ: *(to PANINGAJAK)* Some of them seem honest—like Rae.

PANINGAJAK: *(to AŘGIAQ)* These humans are sick—they stink of starvation.

AŘGIAQ: *(to PANINGAJAK)* We just can't leave them, they are hungry.

PANINGAJAK: *(to AŘGIAQ)* Our relatives are hungry, too. If we hunt for these ones our relatives will have nothing!

AŘGIAQ: *(to PANINGAJAK)* If we use their bullets our relatives will not be hungry!

PANINGAJAK: *(to AŘGIAQ)* If we use our harpoons our relatives will also not be hungry!

CARTER: *(to AŘGIAQ)* Help us, help us.

AŘGIAQ: *(to PANINGAJAK)* These men will surely starve—they are lost!

PANINGAJAK: *(to AŘGIAQ)* What should we do, nukaq?

ᐊᕐᑯᑎᕐᔪᐊᖅ: ᐆ, ᐊᐱᕆᑦᑎᐊᖅᐸᖕᓂᐊᖅᑯᖕᒪ, ᕐᑯᓴᓇᖅᑯᑎᑦ.

ᐊᔾᒋᐊᖅ: ᑭᔭᐊᓂᒃ ᐆᒥᖕᒪ ᓇᓄᕐᒥᒃ ᐊᓐᖑᑕᕆᔾᒪᔪᕆᒋᐊᖅᑲᖏᑦᑐᑎᑦ.

ᐸᓂᖕᒐᓴᒃ: *(ᐊᔾᒋᐊᕐᒧᑦ)* ᓴᒪᓂ ᓂᑭᖅᑲᖏ’ᒪᑦ ᖅᑲᕐᔪᖅᑲᖏ’ᒪᑦᑐ . . . ᐃᖅᑲᓗᒃᔭᐅᓇᐊᖅᑐᕐᓗᒃ.

ᐊᔾᒋᐊᖅ: ᐆᐃᐃᐃᐃ.

ᐊᔾᒋᐊᖅ ᐊᔭᐊᓄᑦ ᐱᔮᖅᑐᖅ ᐸᓂᖕᒐᓴᒡᓗ ᒪᓚᖅᔪᓂᐅᒃ.

ᐊᕐᑯᑎᕐᔪᐊᖅ: ᔮᑦ—ᔮᕖ—ᔮᖖᒐᐅᕝᔭᒡᓚ?

ᐊᔾᒋᐊᖅ: ᐃᖅᑲᓗᒃᔭᐅᕋᔮᐊᕐᓂᐊᖅᑐᒍᒃ. ᐃᖅᑲᓗᒃᐱᖕᓂᒃ ᑕᕆᐅᕐᒥᐅᑕᕐᓂᒃ.

ᑳᑑᑦ: *(ᐊᔾᒋᐊᕐᒧᑦ)* ᐅᕚ . . . ᐅᑦᑯᑕᕋ ᐱᒎᒃ ᐅᑯᐊᒡᓗ ᖅᑲᕐᔪᖅᓴᑦ ᐃᖅᑲᓗᒃᑕᕆᔾᐸᔭ’ᓂᒃ ᑐᓂ’ᔾᐅ’ᓴᕗᒍᒡᓗ. ᐅᒥᐊᕐᔪᐊᐸᑎ’ᓄᑦ ᐅᑎᕈᐸᑕ ᑐᓂᕐᔫᖅᐸᐸᔭᒃ ᖅᑲᕐᔪᖕᓂᒃ ᐱᓚᐅᑎᑦᑎᐊᕙᓇᓗᖕᓂᒡᓗ.

ᐊᕐᑯᑎᕐᔪᐊᖅ: ᐃᔮᒪᑦᑎᐊᖅᑐᑎᑦ, ᑳᑑᑦ.

ᐊᔾᒋᐊᖅ: *(ᐊᕐᑯᑎᕐᔪᐊᕐᒧᑦ)* ᖅᑲᕐᔪᖕᓂᒃ?

ᐊᕐᑯᑎᕐᔪᐊᖅ: ᐆ, ᐊᔾᒋᐊᖅ, ᐊᑐᖏᑕᐸᑎ’ᓂᒃ ᑕᒪᐃ’ᓂᒃ. ᐃᓚᐅᓕᕐᑐᔭ ᐅᕙᐸᑎ’ᓄᑦ ᐊᔭᐅ . . . ᐊᖑᓇᔮᐊᖅᑎᕆᓂᐊᖅᐸᐸᔭᒃ ᐅᓐᓂᖅᑑ’ᔾᕆᑐᔭᓗ.

ᐊᔾᒋᐊᖅ: *(ᐸᓂᖕᒐᓴᖕᒧᑦ)* ᐊᓐᖑᑎᒃᓴᖅᔭᒍᐸᑎᒍᑦ ᑐᓂᓂᐊᖅᑖᑎᒍᑦ ᖅᑲᕐᔪᕐᓂᒃ.

ᐸᓂᖕᒐᓴᒃ: *(ᐊᔾᒋᐊᕐᒧᑦ)* ᓄᑲᖅ, ᐅᑯᐊᑦ ᐃᓄᕐᓗᐃᑦ ᐃᓇᐊᑖᕐᕝᕆᓂᐊ’ᒥᔾᐃᑦ ᓇᓄᖅ, ᔮᓚᖏᑦᑐᐸᔭᐅᕐᓗᐃᑦ ᐅᑯᐊᑦ—ᑲᒪᒋᔮᐃᑦᑭᑦ.

ᐊᔾᒋᐊᖅ: *(ᐸᓂᖕᒐᓴᖕᒧᑦ)* ᐃᓚᐃᑦ ᐅᑯᐊᑦ ᔮᓚᑦᕐᑰᕋᓗᐊᖅᑐᑦ—ᔮᓚᕐᔪᕐᓚ ᕋᐃ ᑕᐃᒪ.

ᐸᓂᖕᒐᓴᒃ: *(ᐊᔾᒋᐊᕐᒧᑦ)* ᐅᑯᐊᑦ ᐃᓄᕐᓗᐃᑦ ᐋᓐᓂᐊᖅᑐᑦ—ᐊᑭᐊᐳᐊᖅᑐᑐᑦ ᑎᐱᖅᑲ’ᒪᑕ.

ᐊᔾᒋᐊᖅ: *(ᐸᓂᖕᒐᓴᖕᒧᑦ)* ᕐᑭᒪᒃᔭᓐᓇᓚᐃᑕᕗᑦ ᑳᒃᑐᐊᓗᐃᑦ.

ᐸᓂᖕᒐᓴᒃ: *(ᐊᔾᒋᐊᕐᒧᑦ)* ᐃᓚᕗᑦ ᑳᒃᑐᑦᑕᐅᖅ. ᐅᑯᐊᑦ ᐊᓐᖑᑎᒃᓴᖅᔭᒍᐸᑎᒍᑦ ᐃᓚᕗᑦ ᐱᖅᑲᓚᐃᑦᑐᑦ!

AĞGIAQ: *(to PANINGAJAK)* So terrible, so terrible . . . but how about . . . *(to FRANKLIN)* We must get food for our relatives, but if two of you follow us and we catch fish, we will give you two some to bring back here.

CARTER: *(to FRANKLIN)* I'll go with them, sir.

FRANKLIN: No, no—what if you get lost?

AĞGIAQ: *(to FRANKLIN)* He'll be with us—my brother and I know this land. This is where we are from.

FRANKLIN: *(to AĞGIAQ)* I can't afford to lose more men. I'd rather you two stayed with us.

AĞGIAQ: Life is life. We cannot stay.

FRANKLIN: We need your expertise.

HOLLOWAY: *(to AĞGIAQ)* Sir, sir—please, dear God in Heaven, we beg you stay with us.

PANINGAJAK: *(to AĞGIAQ)* They're so powerful with their big boats, but they are completely incapable on the land.

AĞGIAQ: *(to FRANKLIN)* You . . . come with us. All of you . . . come with us.

AĞGIAQ and PANINGAJAK exit.

CARTER: I'm going with them.

WICKERS: Wait—I think I've found a reliable route to—

CARTER: You couldn't find your finger if it were stuck up your rectal situation—

WICKERS: THAT WILL DO, CARTER—

CARTER: I'm going with them—going to get me some fish—

WICKERS: Desertion is punishable by death—

ᐊᔅᒋᐊᖅ: *(ᐸᓂᖕᒐᔭᖕᒧᑦ)* ᖅᑲᖅᔪᐃ’ᓂᒃ ᐊᑐᖅᓗᑕ ᐃᓚᕗᑦ ᑳᓚᐃᑦᑐᑦ!

ᐸᓂᖕᒐᔭᒃ: *(ᐊᔅᒋᐊᕐᒧᑦ)* ᐅᓈᑉᑎ’ᓂᓕ ᐊᑐᖅᓗᑕ ᐃᓚᕗᑦ ᑳᓚᐃ’ᒥᔪᑦ!

ᑲᑑᑦ: *(ᐊᔅᒋᐊᕐᒧᑦ)* ᐃᑲᔪᖅᑕᐅᔪᒪᔪᒍᑦ, ᐃᑲᔪᖅᑕᐅᔪᒪᔪᒍᑦ.

ᐊᔅᒋᐊᖅ: *(ᐸᓂᖕᒐᔭᖕᒧᑦ)* ᐅᑯᐊᑦ ᐊᖕᒍᑎᑦ ᐊᕐᑭᐊᕆᐊᕐᓂᐊᖅᑐᓇᓗᐃᑦ—ᐊᔪᐅᔪᒪᔪᑦ!

ᐸᓂᖕᒐᔭᒃ: *(ᐊᔅᒋᐊᕐᒧᑦ)* ᖅᑲᓄᕐᓕᐅᕐᑐᓄᓪᓕ ᓄᑲᖅ?

ᐊᔅᒋᐊᖅ: *(ᐸᓂᖕᒐᔭᖕᒧᑦ)* ᐱᑦᑕᐅᙱᑦᑐᔅᓲᓗᐊᖅ ᐱᑦᑕᐅᙱᑦᑐᔅᓱᒃ
. . . ᐃᒪ’ᓇᓕᑭᐊᖅ . . . *(ᐊᖅᑯᑎᖅᔪᐊᕐᒧᑦ)* ᐃᓚᕗᑦ ᓂᖅᑭᒃᓵᖅᔪᒋᐊᖅᑲᕐᐸᑎᒍᑦ,
ᒪᔅᑭᖕᓂᑦ ᒪᓕᒃᑕᐅᒍᒻᓄᒃ ᐃᖅᑲᓗᒃᑯᐸᑕᓗ ᓇ’ᒥᓂᖅ ᑕᓴᒧᖕᒐ ᐊᒃᓴᑭᖕᓇᖅᓂᐊᖅᑕᖅᔪ.

ᑲᑑᑦ: *(ᐊᖅᑯᑎᖅᔪᐊᕐᒧᑦ)* ᐃᖅᑲᑎᒋᓂᐊᖅᑕᑦᑲ, ᐊᑕᓂᖅᔪᐊᖅ.

ᐊᖅᑯᑎᖅᔪᐊᖅ: ᐄᖅᑭ ᐄᖅᑭ—ᐊᔪᐅᒍᕕᓪᓕ?

ᐊᔅᒋᐊᖅ: *(ᐊᖅᑯᑎᖅᔪᐊᕐᒧᑦ)* ᐅᕙᑉᑎ’ᓃᓂᐊ’ᒪᑦ—ᐊᖕᒐᔪᒐᓗ
ᖅᑲᐅᔭᒪᑦᑎᐊᖅᑕᕗᒃ ᓄᓇ ᑕᓴᒻᒪ. ᓴᒪᓂᖅᒥᐅᑕᒻᒪᓇᐅᔪᒍᓪᓕ.

ᐊᖅᑯᑎᖅᔪᐊᖅ: *(ᐊᔅᒋᐊᕐᒧᑦ)* ᓴᓇᔭᖅᑲᕆᐃᖅᓂᐊᕕᒃᑲᒪ. ᐃᓕᑉᔪᓪᓕᑭᐊᖅ
ᓴᒪᓃᖅᑲᑕᐅᕙᓪᓗᓕᖅᓗᔪᓪᓕ.

ᐊᔅᒋᐊᖅ: ᐃᓅᔪᖅ ᑕ’ᓇᐃ’ᒪᑦ. ᓴᒪᓃᔪᐅᓚᐃᑦᑐᒍᑦ.

ᐊᖅᑯᑎᖅᔪᐊᖅ: ᐃᑲᔪᖅᑎᒋᔪᒪᕙᑉᔪᒃ.

ᓴᖕᒎᔭᓇᓗᒃ: *(ᐊᖕᒎᓇᔭᐊᖅᐲᖕᓄᑦ)* ᐊᖕᒍᑎᒃ—ᖅᑭᓄᒡᕕᒥᕙᑉᑎᒥᒃ
ᓴᒪᓃᔪᐅᖅᑯ’ᓗᔪᒃ ᓇᔪᖅᑎᒍᑦ ᑕᓴᒪᓂ.

ᐸᓂᖕᒐᔭᒃ: *(ᐊᔅᒋᐊᕐᒧᑦ)* ᐊᔪᒐᐃᑦᑑᓴᖅᑐᑦ ᐅᑯᐊᑦ ᐅᒥᐊᖅᔪᐊᖅᑲᖅᒥᒃ,
ᑭᔪᐊᓂᒃ ᓄᓇᒥ ᐊᔪᖅᑐᓇᓗᐃᑦ.

ᐊᔅᒋᐊᖅ: *(ᐊᖅᑯᑎᖅᔪᐊᕐᒧᑦ)* ᐃᔅᕕᑦ . . . ᐃᓚᐅᓗᑎᑦ. ᑕᒪᑉᔪ
. . . ᐃᓚᐅᓗᔪ ᐅᕙᑉᑎ’ᓂ.

ᐊᔅᒋᐊᖅᓗ ᐸᓂᖕᒐᔭᒡᓗ ᐊᓂ’ᓗᑎᒃ.

ᑲᑑᑦ: ᐃᖅᑲᑎᒋᓂᐊᖅᑕᑦᑲᒃ.

CARTER: If we all leave together it's not desertion—it's survival—

HOLLOWAY: We must all return to the *Erebus*.

CARTER: There's nothing left on the ship—let's follow them—they know their way around without a map and they can kill a seal with their bare hands, unlike this lot of stumbling turkeys—

FRANKLIN: They're not dragging two ships behind them as well as the responsibility for a hundred and ten sick, hungry, *impatient* men—

CARTER: We don't have two ships—we barely have one, and she's been locked in the ice for two fucking years, and now we're lost and Crozier and his crew are probably lost—

FRANKLIN: WE SHALL PRESS ON, SIR—

CARTER: HOW SHALL WE PRESS ON, SIR—TELL ME HOW?

Ramrod straight in his rotting pelts, FRANKLIN *moves towards the water and stares out.*

FRANKLIN: We will be alert and listen for the animals and the spirits.

HOLLOWAY: I wouldn't pay any mind to that hocus pocus, sir.

FRANKLIN: Quiet! Listen . . .

Silence as FRANKLIN *listens.*

WICKERS: Sir, we should try to find a trading post—head for Chantrey Inlet then go inland up to the Great Fish River and . . .

Voices can be heard in the distance, faintly at first.

FRANKLIN: . . . Voices . . . voices on the wind . . . spirits . . .

CARTER: Someone's coming!

MORSHEAD: *(off stage)* VICTORY . . .

ᐊᓗᕈᑎ: ᐅᑕᖅᑭᒍᐃᑦᑎ—ᓇᓂᔦᔾᕉᑐᖕᒐ ᐊᑉᕐᑯᑎᒃᓴᐅᓇᔭᖅᑐᒥᒃ ᑕᓇᐅᑦᑯᑎᒍᑦ—

ᑲᑑᑦ: ᓇᓂᔦᓚᐃᑦᑐᑦᑎᐊᖑᒐᕕᓪᓕ ᑎᑦᑯᐊᓇᓚᐃᑕᐃᓪᓘᓐᓃᑦ ᐃᑏᑦ—

ᐊᓗᕈᑎ: ᑕ'ᓇᐃᓕᐅᕈᐃᓇᑦ ᐱᓯᐃᖖᒐ, ᑲᑑᑦ—

ᑲᑑᑦ: ᐃᕐᑲᑎᒋᓂᐊᖅᑕᑦᑲᒃ ᒪᓕᖕᓂᐊᖅᑕᑦᑲᒃ ᐃᕐᑲᓗᒃᔦᐅᕐᓗᖕᒐ—

ᐊᓗᕈᑎ: ᐃᓯᒪᖅᓯᑐᐃᓐᓇᕈᕕᑦ ᒪᓕᒐᑦᑯᑦ ᑐᕐᑯᓵᖅᑕᐅᕐᑯᔮᐅᔪᖕᓇᖅᑐᑎᑦ
ᓈᓚᖖᒋᓐᓂ'ᓄᑦ—

ᑲᑑᑦ: ᑕᒪᑦᑭᐅᒪᓗᑕ ᐊᐅᓪᓚᕈᑉᑕ
ᐃᓯᒪᖅᓯᑐᐃᓐᓇᕐᓂᐅᖖᒋᒻᒪᓇᒃᑐᖅ—ᐊᓐᓇᐅᒪᓂᐅᔦᕐᓕ—

ᓵᖕᒍᔾᓇᓗᒃ: ᑕᒪᑉᑕ ᐅᑎᓇᐊᖅᑲᓕᖅᑐᒍᑦ ᐅᒥᐊᕐᔦᐊᑉᑎ'ᓄᑦ.

ᑲᑑᑦ: ᐅᒥᐊᕐᔦᐊᕐᒥ ᓯᑕᖅᑲᖖᒋᒻᒪᓇ'ᒪᑦ—ᒪᓕᒃᑎᒍᑦ ᐅᑯᐊᒃ—
ᖅᑲᐅᔾᒪᔦᒃ ᓄᓇᖔᐊᖅᑲᖖᒋᑦᑲᓗᐊᖅᓗᑎᒡᓘᓐᓃᑦ ᓇᑦᑎᕈᖕᓇᖅᑐᒡᓘᓐᓃᑦ
ᐊᔾᒐᐃᑎᒍᑐᐃᓐᓇᖅ, ᐅᕙᒍᑉᓯᐅᕐᓗᒡᓕ ᐊᕐᑭᔾᒋᕐᔦᐊᓇᓗᒃᑐᑦ
ᐊᑉᓗᕐᑦᑎᐊᕈᐃᖅᑐᕐᓘᑎ'ᓗᑕ—

ᐊᕐᑯᑎᕐᔦᐊᖅ: ᐃᑉᑯᐊᒡᓕ ᐅᒥᐊᕐᔦᐊᕐᓂᒃ ᒫᕈᓇᓗᖕᓂᒃ
ᑲᒪᒋᔾᒃᓴᖅᑲᖖᒋ'ᒪᓂᒃ ᐅᕙᑉᑐᑦ ᐊᕙᑎᓂᒃ ᑕᓪᓕᒪᓂᒃ ᐅᖕᒐᑖᓂ
ᓵᓇᔾᖅᑲᖖᒋᑦᑐᒃ ᑳᒃᑐᐊᓗᖕᓂᒃ ᐊᕐᑭᐊᕈᐊᖅᐸᓪᓕᐊᔦᓂᒃ
ᕐᑭᓄᔦᐊᓘᓕᖅᑐᓂᒃ ᐃᓄᕐᑯᑎᖅᑲᖖᒋᑦᑐᒃ ᐃᑉᑯᐊᒃ ᐅᕙᑉᑐᑦ—

ᑲᑑᑦ: ᒫᕈᖕᓂᒃ ᐅᒥᐊᕐᔦᐊᕐᑲᕈᐃᕐᑉᑕ ᑖᕙ ᐊᑕᐅᔾᔪᓐᓇᕐᓗᖕᒥᒃ ᐱᕐᑲᖅᓗᑕ
ᔦᑯᒥ ᐊᔦᖅᔦᔦᑐᕐᑲᕐᓗᖕᒥᒃ ᐅᑭᐅᖕᓂᒃ ᒫᕈᓇᓗᖕᓂᒃ ᐊᔦᖅᔦᔦᒪᓪᓕᕐᔅᓗ'ᒪᑦ,
ᐊᔦᐅᒪᓕᕐᑉᑕᓗ ᐅᒥᐊᕐᔦᐊᑉ ᐊᐃᑉᐹ ᓵᓇᔾᖕᒋᓪᓗ ᐊᔦᐅᔦᒪᔦᒃᓴᐅ'ᒥᒐᒥᒃ—

ᐊᕐᑯᑎᕐᔦᐊᖅ: ᑲᔦᔦᓂᐊᖅᑐᒍᑦ ᓯᓕᔦᒥᒃ—

ᑲᑑᑦ: ᖅᑲᓄᕐᓕ ᑲᔦᔦᓂᐊᕐᑲᓗᐊᖅᐱᑕ—ᖅᑲᓄᓇᓗᒃᑕᐅᖅ?

ᐊᕐᑯᑎᕐᔦᐊᖅ ᒪᑭᒪᑦᑎᐊᖑᐊᕐᑲᓯᐊᖅᓗᓂ ᐱᓯᑦᑎᐊᖑᐊᕐᑲᓯᐊᖅᓗᓂ
ᓯᕈᖅᐸᓪᓕᐊᔦᓂᒃ ᐊᒥᕐᓂᒃ ᐅᓕᒃᔦᒪ'ᓗᓂ ᕐᑯᓕᒃᑕᖅᑲᖖᒋ'ᓇᒥ.
ᐊᕐᑯᑎᕐᔦᐊᖅ ᐱᓯᒃᑐᖅ ᐃᒪᕐᒍᑦ ᑐᕐᑳᖅᓗᓂ ᑖᕗᖕᒐ ᑕᐅᑑᒪᔦᖅ
ᐃᓯᒪᒃᓴᖅᔦᐅᖅᓗᓂ.

FRANKLIN prays.

FRANKLIN: Dear Lord, thank You. You come down through the icebergs, Your great power pours out of the sun—

CREW #1: It's Morshead, sir.

MORSHEAD enters, naked and waving around the gold-tipped flagstaff and carrying a chunk of bloody meat under his arm.

MORSHEAD: Victory, boys, VICTORY! We've got dinner!

FRANKLIN: Good God, Morshead—cover yourself!

MORSHEAD: Sir, I'm happy to report I no longer feel the cold—in fact, I feel quite warm.

FRANKLIN: You're suffering from fever, man—cover yourself!

CREW #2 enters covered with furs and clutching bloody chunks of meat.

CARTER: Food . . . FOOD . . . fresh, beautiful meat . . .

And just like that, CARTER yanks the chunk of meat from MORSHEAD and starts ripping it apart and stuffing it into his mouth.

MORSHEAD: . . . No, that's mine!

FRANKLIN: Easy, men—EASY!

CREW #1: I want some—

CREW #2: It's mine, it's fucking mine MINE—

The smell of hot blood has ignited the starving men and the brutal punching and screaming and eating begins. FRANKLIN watches in horror while WICKERS is still too stunned with his own sorrow to take much in.

HOLLOWAY: I'll take that bit—

ᐊᕐᑯᑎᕐᖪᐊᖅ: ᐅᖮᖬᖅᑐᑦᑎᐊᕋᖠᐊᕐᓂᐊᖅᑐᒍᑦ ᓈᓚᒐᖠᐊᕐᓗᒋᑦ ᐆᒪᖪᑦ
ᐃᑲᖬᖅᑎᓪᓗ ᐆᓐᖓᒐᑦ.

ᖤᖑᖬᓇᓗᒃ: ᐃᖠᒪᒋᒋᐊᖅᑲᖕᒋᑕᑎᑦ ᖤᑉᑯᐊᓇᓗᐃᑦ ᐊᖕᒐᑦᑯᖮᖪᖬᑦ.

ᐊᕐᑯᑎᕐᖪᐊᖅ: ᐊᑕ! ᓈᓚᒡᓗᑎᑦ . . .

ᓂᐸᐃ'ᓗᑎᒃ ᐊᕐᑯᑎᕐᖪᐊᖅ ᓈᓚᒃᓱᓂ.

ᐊᓗᕆᑎ: ᐊᑕᓂᕐᖪᐊᖅ ᕐᑭᓂᒡᓱᑲᖅᑕ ᓂᐅᕕᕐᕕᓇᓗᖕᒥᒃ—
ᑕᓇᐅᓐᓄᐊᕐᒍᖖᒐᐅᖮᖂᕐᓗᑕ ᐅᑦᑯᖪᒃᓴᓕᖕᒍᒡᓗ ᑕᐃᒪ . . .

ᐅᖅᑲᒪᖪᑦ ᑐᖤᕐᓇᖅᐸᒡᓕᐊᓕᖅᑐᑦ ᐅᖕᒐᖪᒃᑐᒥᑦ.

ᐊᕐᑯᑎᕐᖪᐊᖅ: . . . ᐅᖅᑲᒪᖪᑦ . . . ᐊᓄᓇᑉ ᓂᐱᕆᖭ . . . ᐆᓐᖓᐃᑦ
ᐃᑲᖬᖅᑎᑦ ᓂᐲᑦ ᑕᖮᕙ . . .

ᑲᑑᑦ: ᖅᑲᐃᖪᖅᑲᓕᖅᑑᓐᓂᖅ!

ᓇᐅᑦᑎᖅᑐᖅᑎ: (ᐊᕙ'ᖖᒐᑦ) ᖭᓚᖅᑲᕐᓂᖅᑯᒍᑦ . . .

ᐊᕐᑯᑎᕐᖪᐊᖅ ᑐᒃᖪᐊᖅᓱᓂ.

ᐊᕐᑯᑎᕐᖪᐊᖅ: ᐊᑕᓂᖅ ᕐᑯᔭᓇᖅᑯᑎᑦ. ᖅᑲᐃᒐᕕᑦ ᐱᖅᑲᓗᖬᖅᑎᔫᖅᓱᑎᑦ,
ᐊᔪᒐᖅᑲᖖᒋᓐᓃᑦ ᐱᔪᖕᓇᕐᓂᕐᖪᐊᓇᖬᐃᑦ ᖤᑦᕐᑭᐅᒪᓕ'ᒪᑦ ᖬᕐᑭᓂᕐᒥᒡᓗ—

ᖤᓇᖬ: ᓇᐅᑦᑎᖅᑐᖅᑎᐅᖪᕐᓕ.

ᓇᐅᑦᑎᖅᑐᖅᑎ ᐃᖬᕐᖤᖑᖬᖅᓱᓂ, ᐅᖬᓐᖓᒐᖪᓇᓗᒃ ᖤᐃᒪᑎᑉ
ᓇᐸᕆᑖ'ᓂᒃ ᑎᒍᒥᐊᖅᓱᓂ ᐊᐅᓛ'ᓗᒍ ᑕᓕᐊᑕᓗ ᐊᐃᑉᐸᒎᑦ
ᑎᒍᒥᐊᖅᓱᓂ ᓂᕐᑭᒥᒃ ᐊᐅᓕᖕᒥᒃ ᕐᑯᑦᑐᒃᑐᒥᒃ.

ᓇᐅᑦᑎᖅᑐᖅᑎ: ᖭᓚᖅᑲᖅᑐᒍᑦ, ᐊᖑᑎᑦ, ᑕᒃᑰᒃ ᓂᓇᖭᒃᓴᖅᑲᓕᖅᑯᒍᑦ!

ᐊᕐᑯᑎᕐᖪᐊᖅ: ᐃᓱᐃᑦᑐᕐᕌᓗᒃ ᐅᓇ, ᓇᐅᑦᑎᖅᑐᖅᑎ—ᐊ'ᓄᕌᖅᑐᓕᓇᑦ!

ᓇᐅᑦᑎᖅᑐᖅᑎ: ᐊᑕᓂᕐᖪᐊᖅ, ᐃᓱᕐᓇᕗᖕᒐ ᐆᓇᐃᖠᖖᒥᓪᒪᓇᓕᖅᑐᖕᒐᓕ—
ᑎᒥᒐ ᐃᓱᕐᓇᑦᑎᐊᖅᑐᖅ.

ᐊᕐᑯᑎᕐᖪᐊᖅ: ᐋᓐᓂᐊᕋᕕᑦ ᐆᓐᓇᒃᑐᑎᑦ—ᐊ'ᓄᕌᖅᑐᓕᓇᑦ!

CREW #2: That's my bit, MY BIT—

MORSHEAD: Fuckin' stealer—I killed it—it's MINE—

CREW #2: Selfish fuckin' bastard, give it give it—

CREW #1: Gimme that, ya fuckin' nothing—

HOLLOWAY: That's my pudding—

CARTER: Mine—my sausages, MINE.

HOLLOWAY: That's my fucking pudding—

MORSHEAD: It's mine MINE, ya bleeding whore—

CARTER: MINE, YA COCKSUCKING MAGPIE—

HOLLOWAY: MY PUDDING MINE—

CREW #1: GIVE IT HERE, SCAG FUCKER—

> *MORSHEAD goes after CARTER with the flagstaff.*

MORSHEAD: I'LL BATTY-FANG YOUR ARSE—

FRANKLIN: MORSHEAD!

> *CARTER is crying, so happy for the taste of food in his mouth. Others are licking up the blood on the ground or licking blood from their fingers.*

(*to MORSHEAD*) Thank you for finding food for the men.

CREW #2: We saw a fox, sir, and Morshead tried to spear it with the flagstaff—we found a rock for him to sharpen the end of it.

MORSHEAD: Then, there in the distance, I saw a bear looking at us.

CREW #2: We daren't move but Morshead walked towards it, praying softly.

ᐃᓯᖅᑯᖅ ᓴᓇᔩᑉ ᐊᐃᑉᐹ ᐅᓕᑲᑦᑕᖅᓯᒪ'ᓗᓂ ᐊᒥᕐᓂᒃ
ᑎᑐᒥᐊᖅᑰᓂᓗ ᓂᕿᓂᒃ ᐊᐅᓕᖕᓂᒃ.

ᑳᑦ: ᓂᕿ . . . ᓂᕿᑦᑎᐊᓇᓗᒃ . . . ᐱᑕᕆᔭᐅᔮᖅᑐᑦᑎᐊᖓᓇᓗᒃ . . .

ᑳᑦ ᑳᓪᓗᐊᕙᒃᑲᒥ ᓂᕿᒥᒃ ᐋᖅᓵᖅᓯᓪᓕᕐᔮᕈᒃᑐᖅ
ᓇᐅᑦᑎᖅᑐᖅᑎᒥᑦ ᐊᓕᒃᑐᖅᑰᓂᐅᒃ ᓂᕆᔪᐸᓈᓕᖅᑐᖅ.

ᓇᐅᑦᑎᖅᑐᖅᑎ: . . . ᐄᕿ, ᐱᒐ ᑖᒻᓇ!

ᐊᕐᑯᑎᕐᔪᐊᖅ: ᐱᔪᐃᓇᑦᑎᒃ—ᐱᔪᐃᕐᓗᓯᒃ!

ᓴᓇᔩ: ᐱᔅᒪᔪᖕᒐ—

ᓴᓇᔩᑉ ᐊᐃᑉᐹ: ᐄᕿ ᐅᖓᖕᒐᖓᓪᓗᕐᓕ ᐱᕐᕈᒐ ᐅᓇ—

ᐊᐅᑉ ᑎᐱᐊᓘᑦ ᐊᓐᖑᑎᑦ ᑳᒃᑐᑦ ᓂᖕᒐᐅᑎᔪᐊᓘᓕᕆᐊᖅᑰᑎᒃ
ᑎᓪᓘᑎᓕᖅᑰᑎᒃ ᐃᕆᐊᓚᖅᑰᑎᓪᓗ ᑳᒃᐸᓪᓚᕐᓃ'ᓃᑦ ᓂᕆᔪᐊᓘᓕᖅᑰᑎᓪᓗ
ᓂᖕᒐᐅᑎ'ᓗᑎᒃ. ᐊᕐᑯᑎᕐᔪᐊᖅ ᑕᐅᑐᒃᑕᐃᑦ ᓇᓗᒋ'ᓗᓂᒋᑦ ᔪ'ᒪᑦ
ᑕ'ᓇᐃᓕᐅᕆᐊᒃᓯᐃᑕ, ᐊᓗᐱᑎᓗ ᔪᖖᒋᓪᒪᕆᒃᑐᖅ ᖅᑭᒃᓰᐱᑎᖅᑲᖅᐸᓪᓛᕐᒥ.

ᓴᖖᔪᓇᓗᒃ: ᓴᒪ ᐱᑕᑐ—

ᓴᓇᔩᑉ ᐊᐃᑉᐹ: ᐱᕐᕈᒐ ᐅᓇ ᐱᔪᐃᖅᑲᐅᒃ—

ᓇᐅᑦᑎᖅᑐᖅᑎ: ᑎᓪᓕᒃᑎᐅᔪᑎᑦ—ᐊᓐᖑᑕᕋᓕ—ᐱᒋᔭᕋ ᓇ'ᒥᓂᕋ—

ᓴᓇᔩᑉ ᐊᐃᑉᐹ: ᐸᓚᐃᑦᑐᕐᕈᓐᓂᖅᑯᑎᑦ ᖃᐃᓪᔫᒃ, ᖃᐃᕐᕈᑲᐳᒃ—

ᓴᓇᔩ: ᐅᖓᖕᒐᖓᓪᓗᕐᓕ ᔪᖅᑯᑕᐅᖖᒋᑉᑐᑉᑲᓇᓇᓗᕐᕈᒃ ᐅᓇ—

ᓴᖖᔪᓇᓗᒃ: ᓂᓇᔭᒃᓴᕋ ᐅᓇ—

ᑳᑦ: ᐅᖓᖕᒐ—ᓂᕿᑦᑎᐊᖓᓇᓗᒃᓴᕋ ᐅᓇ ᖃᐃᕐᕈᒃᑲᒪᒥᐅᒃ.

ᓴᖖᔪᓇᓗᒃ: ᓂᓇᔭᒃᓴᕐᕈᒐ ᐅᓇ—

ᓇᐅᑦᑎᖅᑐᖅᑎ: ᐅᖓᖕᒐ ᐱᒐ ᓇ'ᒥᓂᕋ ᔪᔩᓇᓗᕐᓅ'ᔭᒐᕚᑦ—

ᑳᑦ: ᐅᖓᖕᒐᖓᓪᓗᕐᕈᒃ ᔪᖅᑯᑕᐅᖖᒋᑦᑐᑉᑲᓇᓇᓅᔪᑎᑦ—

MORSHEAD: "Please, dearest Lord in Heaven, don't let this bear move" . . . but I began coughing and the animal started to move away. My arm was trembling—

CREW #2: Trembling like this . . . *(madly shakes his arm)* Then he calmed himself—the great hunter calmed himself.

MORSHEAD: I took hold of the flagstaff, sir, and prayed, "Lord, give me strength," then with my whole being I threw it at the bear and skewered it right through its middle. A flagstaff makes a potent weapon, sir— *(demonstrates)* Like a sword—"Have at you . . . "

With that MORSHEAD spears something and lifts up UKUANNUAQ's bloody head.

TO THE VICTOR . . . go . . . the . . . spoi . . .

He falls down, done in by fever. CREW #2 grabs the flagstaff with UKUANNUAQ's head on it and pumps it into the air.

CREW #2 keeps repeating:

CREW #2: TO THE VICTOR GO THE SPOILS. TO THE VICTOR GO THE SPOILS.

No one notices that ANGU'ŘUAQ has entered and is watching. He looks up at UKUANNUAQ's head, confused at seeing her head but not her body.

ANGU'ŘUAQ exits.

Everyone joins in chanting except FRANKLIN and WICKERS.

ALL: TO THE VICTOR GO THE SPOILS. TO THE VICTOR GO THE SPOILS.

CARTER brings a chunk of bloody meat over to FRANKLIN.

CARTER: Sir.

FRANKLIN: . . . No thank you, Carter. What time is it?

ᔮᖂᔩᓇᓗᒃ: ᓂᕆᔮᒃᓴᕋ ᐅᓇ ᐱᒐ—

ᔮᓇᔩ: ᖃᐃᕐᓱᑲᕈᒃ ᐊᑕᐃ—

ᓇᐅᑦᑎᖅᑐᖅᑎ ᐊᓇᐅᔪᓇᔾᐊᓕᖅᓱᓂ ᑲᑑ'ᒥᒃ ᔮᐃᒪᑎᑉ ᓇᐸᕈᑖ'ᒍᑦ.

ᓇᐅᑦᑎᖅᑐᖅᑎ: ᐅᒃᐸᑏᒃᑭᒃ ᐊᓇᐅᓂᐊᖅᑕᓇᓗᑦᑲᒃ—

ᐊᕐᑯᑎᕐᔦᐊᖅ: ᓇᐅᑦᑎᖅᑐᖅᑎ!

ᑲᑑᑦ ᕐᑯᕕᐊᔾᔪᑦ ᕿᐊᒻᒪᕆᓕᖅᑐᖅ ᓂᕆᓕᑕᐃᓐᓇᓕᕋᒥ. ᐊᔫᑕᓗ ᐊᓗᒃᑐᖅᑐᐊᓗᐃᑦ ᐊᐅᖖᒥᒃ ᒪᓂᕋᕐᒥᑦ ᑎᑭᖅᑎᓪᓗ ᐊᓗᒃᑐᖅᓱᓂᒋᑦ ᒪᒪᕈᔾᓪᓗᐊᖅᓱᑎᒃ.

ᐊᕐᑯᑎᕐᔦᐊᖅ: (ᓇᐅᑦᑎᖅᑐᖅᑎᒧᑦ) ᕐᑯᓯᓇᖅᑯᑎᑦ ᓇᓂᔪᒐᕕᑦ ᓂᕐᑭᒃᓴᐃ'ᓂᒃ ᐅᑯᐊᑦ.

ᔮᓇᔩᑉ ᐊᐃᑉᐹ: ᑎᕆᒐᓐᓂᐊᕐᒥᒃ ᑕᑯᒐᑉᑕ ᓇᐅᑦᑎᖅᑐᖅᑎᓗ ᔮᐃᒪᑎᑉ ᓇᐸᕈᑖ ᐃᐱᒃᓴᖅᑳᖅᓱᒍ ᐅᓯᕋᕐᔪᑦ ᓇᐅᓕᒍᑎᕆᓕᖅᓱᓂᐅᒃ.

ᓇᐅᑦᑎᖅᑐᖅᑎ: ᑕᐃᑲᓂ ᐅᖕᒐᔪᒃᑐᒥ ᑕᑯ'ᓗᖕᒐ ᓇᓄᕐᒥᒃ ᐅᕚᑉᑎ'ᓂᒃ ᑕᐅᑐᒃᑐᐸᓇᓗᒃ ᐃᔩᕆᓪᓗᐊᖅᑖᑎᒍᒃ.

ᔮᓇᔩᑉ ᐊᐃᑉᐹ: ᓄᑦᖃᖕᒐ'ᓗᓄᒃ ᐃᖂᖖᕆᑦᑐᒍᒃ ᑭᔪᐊᓂᒃ ᓇᐅᑦᑎᖅᑐᖅᑎ ᔾᑲᐃᑦᑐᒥᒃ ᐱᔾᓪᕕᕆᓕᖅᐹ, ᑐᒃᔪᐊᖅᓱᓂ ᓂᐱᑭᑦᑐᒥᒃ.

ᓇᐅᑦᑎᖅᑐᖅᑎ: "ᐊᑕᓂᖅ ᕿᓚᖕᒥ, ᓇᓄᖅ ᐅᓇ ᐊᐅᓚᓚᐃᖅᑐᒍᒃ" . . . ᑭᔪᐊᓂᒃ ᕐᑯᐃᖅᑐᓪᓚᕐᔮᖅᔪᓐᓇᓕᕋᒪ ᓇᓄᕐᓱᒃ ᐊᔪᐊᓅᖖᒐᐅᓕᑲᖅᓱᓂ. ᑕᓕᕋ ᔮᔾᒃᑐᐸᓇᓘ'ᓗᓂ—

ᔮᓇᔩᑉ ᐊᐃᑉᐹ: ᐃᒪ'ᓇ ᔮᔾᒃᑐᖅ . . . (ᔮᔾᓪᓗᐊᖖᑯᐊᖅᑎ'ᓗᓂᐅᒃ ᑕᓕᕐᓂ) ᔮᐃᒻᒪᓕᖅᓱᓂ—ᐊᖂᓇᔾᐊᖅᑎᑦᑎᐊᕙᓇᓘᒐᒥ ᐃᖕᒥᓂᒃ ᔮᐃᒻᒪᖅᑎᑦᑐᖅ.

ᓇᐅᑦᑎᖅᑐᖅᑎ: ᑎᒍᒥᐊᑦᑎᐊᖅᓱᒍ ᓇᐸᕈᑕᓕᒃ, ᑐᒃᔪᐊᖅᓱᖕᒐᓗ, "ᓄᓇᓕᐅᖅᑎ, ᔮᖖᕆᓂᖅᑳᓚᖕᒐ" ᑕᐃᒪ ᓇᐅᓕᒃᓱᒍ ᕿᑦᖄᓄᖖᒐᐅᑦᑎᐊᖅᓱᓂ ᖃᐱᑦᑎᐊᖅᑕᕋ. ᔮᐃᒪᑎᑉ ᓇᐸᕈᑎᑐᐃᓐᓈ ᐊᖂᓇᔾᑎᐅᔪᖕᓇᕐᓂ'ᒪᑦ, (ᐆᒃᑐᕋᖅᓱᓂ ᖃᓄᖅ)— ᐅᓇᑕᕈᑎᑐᑦᑕᐅᖅ "ᐱᕆᐊᕐᓚᕆᑦ . . . "

ᓇᐅᑦᑎᖅᑐᖅᑎ ᑕ'ᓇᐃᓕᒐᒥ ᓇᐅᓕᖖᒍᐊᖅᓱᓂ ᔾᓇᒥᒃ—ᔾᓇᐅᐤᐧ ᐅᑯᐊᓐᓄᐊᑉ ᓂᐊᕐᑯᐊ ᐊᐅᖕᕆᓐᓇᓇᓗᒃ ᑲᐳᒻᒥᔮ'ᒪᒍ ᖃᖕᒐᑦᑕᖅᑎ'ᓗᓂᐅᒃ ᓇᐸᕈᑎᒧᑦ.

CARTER checks the chronometer.

CARTER: Seventeen-thirty.

FRANKLIN: Holloway, take a note: "Franklin and his crew left on June 5, 1847, to return overland to the *Erebus*. The sky was bright as the hungry men feasted on the fresh meat of a sea bear."

HOLLOWAY: Yes, sir.

CREW #2: *(to WICKERS)* Morshead won't get up, sir.

CARTER: *(to MORSHEAD)* Get up— *(kicks him)* Get up, man.

WICKERS: Have two men carry him . . . and watch they do nothing shameful.

CARTER: In which direction shall he be carried, Wickers, sir?

WICKERS looks up at the sun, then points.

WICKERS: Northwest, by the sun.

CARTER: *(to CREW #1 and #2)* C'mon, you lazy slimers.

Faces and hands covered in blood and drunk with having something warm in their bellies, the men stumble, carrying chunks of meat, with CREW #2 holding high UKUANNUAQ's head on the flagstaff. CREW #1 starts to sing and others join in . . .

CREW #2: *(sings)* "God save our gracious Queen,
Long live our noble Queen,
God Save the Queen . . .

Send her victorious,
Happy and Glorious,
Long may she reign over us,
God Save our Queen . . . "

All but FRANKLIN and WICKERS exit.

ᓇᐅᑦᑎᖅᑐᖅᑎ: ᓵᓚᖅᑲᖅᑐᒧᑦ . . . ᐱᕆᓴᐅ . . . ᓂᐊ . . .

ᐋᓐᓂᐊᕐᓂᖕᒐᓄᑦ ᑕᐅᓄᖕᒐ ᐹᓪᓚᖕᓂᖅᑐᓂ. ᓴᓇᔩᑉ ᐊᐃᑉᐹ ᑎᒍ’ᓗᓂᐅᒃ ᑖᒻᓇ ᐅᑯᐊᓐᓄᐊᑉ ᓂᐊᖅᑯᐊ’ᓂ ᑲᐳᒻᒥᓴᖅᓯᒪᔪᖅ ᖅᑯ’ᒧᒃᑕᖅᑎᕆᐊᓕᖅᑐᓂᐅᒃ.

ᓴᓇᔩᑉ ᐊᐃᑉᐹ ᐅᖅᑲᓪᓚᐃᓐᓇᖅᑐᓂ.

ᓴᓇᔩᑉ ᐊᐃᑉᐹ: ᓵᓚᖅᑲᖅᑐᒧᑦ ᐱᕆᓴᐅᓂᐊᖅᑐᖅ. ᓵᓚᖅᑲᖅᑐᒧᑦ ᐱᕆᓴᐅᓂᐊᖅᑐᖅ.

ᓂᐸᐃᓯᓐᓇᖅᑐᓂ ᐊᖕᒍ’ᓯᐊᖅ ᐃᓯᖅᑐᖅ ᑕᐅᑐᓕᖅᑐᓂᓗ. ᓄᓕᐊᖕᒐᑕ ᐅᑯᐊᓐᓄᐊᑉ ᓂᐊᖅᑯᐊ’ᓄᑦ ᑕᑯ’ᓗᓂ ᓇᓗ’ᓗᓂᓗ ᓯ’ᒪᑦ ᑎᒥᖅᑲᖖᒋᑦᑖᒃᓵ.

ᐊᓂ’ᓗᓂ ᐊᖕᒍ’ᓯᐊᖅ.

ᑕᐃᒪᑕ ᑕ’ᓇᐃᓕᐅᓕᖅᑐᑦ ᓵᓚᖅᑲᖅᑐᑰᖅ ᐱᕆᓵ, ᑭᓯᐊᓂᒃ ᐊᖅᑯᑎᖅᓯᐊᖅᓗ ᐊᓗᒋᑎᓗ ᑕ’ᓇᐃᓕᐅᖖᒋᑦᑐᐱᑐᐊᒃ.

ᑕᒪᐃᑕ: ᓵᓚᖅᑲᖅᑐᒧᑦ ᐱᕆᓴᐅᓂᐊᖅᑐᖅ. ᓵᓚᖅᑲᖅᑐᒧᑦ ᐱᕆᓴᐅᓂᐊᖅᑐᖅ.

ᑲᑑᑦ ᐊᖅᑯᑎᖅᓯᐊᖅᒍᖖᒐᖅᓗᓂ ᑕᒧᐊᒃᓵ’ᓂᒃ ᑐᓂ’ᓗᓂᐅᒃ.

ᑲᑑᑦ: ᐊᑕᓂᖅᓯᐊᖅ.

ᐊᖅᑯᑎᖅᓯᐊᖅ: . . . ᐄᖅᑭ ᐱᔪᒪᖖᒋᑦᑐᖕᒐ, ᑲᑑᑦ. ᐅᑉᓗᖅᓯᐅᑦ ᓯᒧᖖᒐᓕᖅᐸ?

ᑲᑑᑦ ᐅᑉᓗᖅᓯᐅᑎᒧᑦ ᑕᑯᓴᓕᖅᑐᓂ.

ᑲᑑᑦ: ᐅᓐᓅᓕᖅᑐᖅ.

ᐊᖅᑯᑎᖅᓯᐊᖅ: ᓴᖕᒍᔮᓇᓗᒃ ᑎᑎᕋᓕᓇᑦ: “ᐊᖅᑯᑎᖅᓯᐊᖅ ᓴᓇᔩᕆᓴᐃᑦᑐ ᑕᑦᖅᑭᐊᓂ ᓄᖅᓇᕕᕐᒥ, ᐅᑉᓗᐊ’ᓂ 5-ᒥ, ᐊᕝᕚᒍᐊ 1847-ᖕᒍᑎ’ᓗᒍ ᓄᓇᒃᑰᖅᑐᑎᒃ ᐊᐅᓪᓚᖅᑐᑦ ᐅᒥᐊᖅᓯᐊᖅᒥ’ᓄᑦ ᐅᑎᓕᖅᑐᑎᒃ. ᓯᓚ ᖅᑭᓚᒃ ᖅᑲᐅᒫ’ᓗᓂ ᐊᖕᒍᑎᑦ ᑳᒃᑐᑦ ᓂᓇᖅᑲᑎᕉᒃᓗᑎᒃ ᓇᓐᓄᒃᑕᓇᓴᐅᔩᑉ ᓂᖅᑳ’ᓂᒃ.”

ᓴᖕᒍᔮᓇᓗᒃ: ᐄ, ᐊᑕᓂᖅᓯᐊᖅ.

ᓴᓇᔩᑉ ᐊᐃᑉᐹ: *(ᐊᓗᒋᑎᒧᑦ)* ᓇᐅᑦᑎᖅᑐᖅᑎ ᒪᑭᓚᐃᑦᑐᖅ.

ᑲᑑᑦ: *(ᓇᐅᑦᑎᖅᑐᖅᑎᒧᑦ)* ᒪᑭᓕᓇᑦ—*(ᑐᒃᑲᖅᑐᒍ)* . . . ᐊᑕᐃ ᒪᑭᒡᒍᐃᑦ.

WICKERS: Sir, we best not fall behind . . .

FRANKLIN: I promised I would never again lead men into desolation, but my heart is incautious because there's always something just beyond the next hill—a rock, a river, an observation—there's a world beyond us, beyond even what we can imagine.

WICKERS: Hurry, sir, before we lose them.

FRANKLIN points.

FRANKLIN: Look . . . look out there . . . what is that?

WICKERS looks.

WICKERS: Likely a Fata Morgana—in this light.

FRANKLIN puts his hands over his eyes against the sun.

FRANKLIN: . . . It's the city of Cathay . . .

WICKERS looks.

WICKERS: . . . No it's not, it's a . . . actually, it looks like a . . . a . . .

FRANKLIN: Lend me your spectacles.

WICKERS pulls out the iřgak—HUMMIKTUQ's bone sun goggles—and hands them to FRANKLIN, who puts them on.

Yes, it is—it's Cathay, lit with a thousand resplendent lights.

FRANKLIN shakily hands the iřgak back to WICKERS, who puts them on and tries to make out the letters in the distance.

WICKERS reads.

WICKERS: Cir Cum Polar Oil Plate Farm. Circumpolar Oil Platform.

FRANKLIN: No, it's Cathay . . .

ᐊᓗᑭᑎ: ᒪᔾᑭᖕᓄᑦ ᐅᓇ ᐊᒡᔭᖅᑕᐅᓕ . . . ᖄᐅᓲᔭᕐᓗᒥᒃ ᐱᑦᑎᐊᕆᐊᒃᓴᐃᑕ.

ᑲᑑᑦ: ᓱᒧᑦ ᑐᕌᖅᑯᕕᒥᒃ ᐊᒡᔭᖅᓯᓗᑎᒃ, ᐊᓗᑭᑎ?

ᐊᓗᑭᑎ ᓯᖅᑭᓂᕐᒧᑦ ᑕᑯᔭᖅᑳᖅᖢᓂ, ᑎᑦᑯᐊᖅᖢᓂᓗ.

ᐊᓗᑭᑎ: ᑕᐃᑰᓇ, ᓯᖅᑭᓂᖅ ᒪᓕᒡᓗᒍ.

ᑲᑑᑦ: *(ᖃᓇᓲᖕᓄᑦ)* ᐊᑕᐃ ᓯᕚᑐᐃᑦᑐᓇᓘᔨᓯᒃ.

ᑮᓇᐃᑦ ᐊᔾᒐᐃᒡᓗ ᐊᐅᖕᒋᓐᓇᐅ'ᓗᑎᒃ ᓂᕆᓕᑕᐃᓐᓇᖁᒥᒡᓗ ᐃᒥᖕᒐᓱᑐᑦ ᐱᓱᒃᑐᑦ ᓂᖅᑭᓂᒃ ᑎᒍᒥᐊᖅᖢᑎᒃ, ᖃᓇᓲᑉ ᐊᐃᑉᐹᓗ ᓇᐸᑭᑕᕐᒥᒃ ᐅᑯᐊᓐᓄᐊᑉ ᓂᐊᖅᑯᐊ'ᓂᒃ ᑲᐳᒻᒥᖃᖅᓯᒪᔪᒥᒃ ᑎᒍᒥᐊᖅᖢᓂ. ᖃᓇᓲ ᐃᖕᒋᐅᖅᑐᖅᖄᓗᓕ'ᒪᑦ ᐊᓲᑦ ᐃᖕᒋᐅᖅᑲᑕᐅᓕᖅᖢᑎᒃ . . .

ᖃᓇᓲᑉ ᐊᐃᑉᐹ: *(ᐃᖕᒋᐅᖅᖢᓂ)* ᒎᑎᑉ ᑯᐃᓐ ᐱᐅᓕᕚ, ᐃᓅᑦᑎᐊᖅᑎᓗᒍ . . . ᒎᑎᑉ ᐱᓕᐅᒃ . . .

ᖄᓕᖅᑲᖅᑎᓗᒍ, ᖁᕕᐊᓱᒃᑎᓗᒍ, ᐊᑕᓂᐅᓗᓂ, ᒎᑎᑉ ᐱᓕᐅᒃ . . .

ᐊᒥᓲᓂᖕᒋᑦ ᐊᓂ'ᓗᑎᒃ ᑭᓱᐊᓂᒃ ᐊᖅᑯᑎᖅᓱᐊᖅ ᐊᓗᑭᑎᓗ ᐊᓂᖖᒋᑦᑐᒃ.

ᐊᓗᑭᑎ: ᖅᑭᒪᒃᑕᐅᑦᑕᐃᓕᒋᐊᖅᑲᖅᑐᒍᓪᓕ . . .

ᐊᖅᑯᑎᖅᓱᐊᖅ: ᐅᖅᑲᖅᓯᒪᓕᖁᓗᐊᖁᒪ ᐊᓯᐅᑎᑦᑎᓂᐊᕐᒋᑦᑐᓇ'ᓗᖕᒐ ᖃᓇᓲᓪᓂᒃ, ᐆᒪᑎᓪᓂᒃ ᐃᖢᐃᓕᖁᒪ ᓱᓇᑐᐃᓐᓇᐃᑦ ᓇᓗᓇᖅᓂ'ᒪᑕ ᓂᕆᐅᒋᙱᑕᑉᐱ'ᓂᒃ ᖃᑦᖅᑭᒃᑐᖅᑲᖅᐸᖕᓂ'ᒪᑦ ᓲᖅᓗ ᑕᐃᑰᓇ ᑭᙵᐅᑉ ᐅᖕᒑᑐᑦ—ᐅᔭᖁᓱᓪᓱᒃᑕᖅᑲᑭᖕᓇ'ᒪᑦ, ᑰᒐᓇᓗᖕᒥᒡᓘᓐᓃᑦ, ᑕᑯᔮᒃᓴᓇᓗᖕᒥᒡᓘᓐᓃᑦ ᓱᓇᒥᒃ—ᑕᐅᑐᙱᑕᑉᐱ'ᓂᒃ ᐱᖅᑲ'ᒪᑦ, ᐊᓗᑭᑎ, ᓱᔾᔪᓇᓗᖅᖢᒃ ᐃᓱᒪᒋᙱᑕᑉᐱ'ᓂᒡᓘᓐᓃᑦ ᐱᖅᑲ'ᒪᑦ ᓇᓗᓇᖅᑐᖄᓗᒃ.

ᐊᓗᑭᑎ: ᑐᐊᕕᓕᕆᑦ ᖅᑭᒪᒃᑕᐅᓂᐊᕕᒃᑲᒻᓄᒃ.

ᐊᖅᑯᑎᖅᓱᐊᖅ ᑎᑦᑯᐊᖅᖢᓂ.

ᐊᖅᑯᑎᖅᓱᐊᖅ: ᑕᒃᑰᒃ . . . ᓱᓇᓇᓗ . . . ᑖᕙᓂ?

ᐊᓗᑭᑎ ᑕᑯ'ᓗᓂ.

ᐊᓗᑭᑎ: ᑕᑯᖅᑰᖅᓯᓐᓇᓕᖅᑐᑎᑦ ᓯᓚ ᖃᒻᒪ ᖅᑲᓄᓇᓐᓂᐊ ᐱ'ᓗᒍ.

FRANKLIN falls but WICKERS grabs him, accidentally dropping the iřgak, and the two explorers vanish into the mists of time.

What FRANKLIN thought was Cathay is actually a forty thousand ton, four hundred–foot tall drilling platform in the twenty-first century, rising out of the waters of the Northwest Passage.

We hear a low drone punctuated by a pumping sound, transitioning into the twenty-first century.

ᐊᕐᑯᑎᕐᔪᐊᖅ ᐊᔾᓛᒥᒃ ᑕᓗᒥᓇᔪᐊᖅᓱᒥᒃ ᔭᕐᑭᓂᐅᑉ ᖃᐅᒪᓂᐊ’ᓄᑦ.

ᐊᕐᑯᑎᕐᔪᐊᖅ: . . . ᐅᖕᑲᔭᒃᑐᕐᔪᐊᖅ ᐃᓄᒋᐊᒃᑐᕐᔪᐊᖅ . . .

ᐊᓗᕿᑎ ᑕᑯ’ᓗᓂ.

ᐊᓗᕿᑎ: . . . ᐄᕐᑭ, ᑕ’ᓇᐅᖖᒋᑦᑐᖅ ᔪᓇᖅᐸᓗᒃᑐᓇᓗᑭᐊᖅ. . . .

ᐊᕐᑯᑎᕐᔪᐊᖅ: ᐃᔾᑲᒃ ᐊᑐᕐᓚᒍ.

ᐊᓗᕿᑎ ᑲᐅᑦᑐᐊᕐᒥᓂᑦ ᐊᒍᔭ’ᓗᓂ ᐃᔾᑲᖕᒥᒃ, ᔪᒻᒥᒃᑐᑲᓘᑉ ᐃᔾᑲᕙᓂᑐᕐᑲᓇᓗᐊ, ᑐᓂ’ᓗᓂᐅᒃ ᐊᕐᑯᑎᕐᔪᐊᕐᒍᑦ, ᐊᑎ’ᓗᓂᐅᒃ.

ᐊᕐᑯᑎᕐᔪᐊᖅ: ᐄ ᑕᔾᕙ—ᐃᓄᒋᐊᒃᑐᕐᔪᐊᖕᒍᓐᓂᖅᑯᖅ ᐃᑯᒪᕐᑲᑦᑎᐊᖅᓱᓂ ᐃᓂᕐᑯᓇᖅᑐᕌᓗᐃᑦ ᐃᑯᒪᐃᑦ.

ᐊᕐᑯᑎᕐᔪᐊᑉ ᑐᓂ’ᓗᓂᐅᒃ ᐃᔾᑲᒃ ᐊᓗᕿᑎᒧᑦ ᐊᑎ’ᓗᓂᐅᒃ ᐅᕐᑲᓚᓛᕋᔪᐊᓚᖅᑯᖅ ᔪᓇᒥᒃᑭᐊᖅ ᑕᑯᔾᒥᓂᒃ.

ᐊᓗᕿᑎ ᐅᕐᑲᓚᓛᕋᔪᐊᖅᖅᑐᖅ.

ᐊᓗᕿᑎ: ᐅ-ᑭ-ᐅᖅ-ᑕᖅ-ᑐ-ᒥ ᐅᖅ-ᓱᕐ-ᔪ-ᐊ-ᓚ-ᓇ-ᔮᑦ ᑐᓐᖕᑲ-ᕙ-ᐊᑦ ᐅᑭᐅᖅᑕᖅᑐᒥ ᐅᖅᓱᕐᔪᐊᓚᓇᔮᑦ ᑐᓐᖕᑲᕙᐊᓐᖕᒎᖅ.

ᐊᕐᑯᑎᕐᔪᐊᖅ: ᐄᕐᑭᕐᓱᒃ ᐃᓄᒋᐊᒃᑐᕐᔪᐊᖖᒍᔪᖅ ᕿᓂᖅᑕᕋᓗᐊᖅᑯᑦ ᐅᖕᑲᔭᒃᑐᖅ ᓇᓂᔾᖅᑯᑦ . . .

ᐊᕐᑯᑎᕐᔪᐊᖅ ᐹᓪᓚᒃᓱᓂ ᐊᓗᕿᑎᑉ ᑎᒍᔾ, ᑲᑕᐃ’ᓗᓂᐅᒃ ᐃᔾᑲᒃ, ᒪᔾᕈᒃ ᔪᕐᑲᕈᐃᖅᐸᓪᓚᐊᔪᒃ ᑕᑯᒃᓴᐅᔪᐃᖅᓱᑎᒃ.

ᐊᕐᑯᑎᕐᔪᐊᑉ ᐃᓄᒋᐊᒃᑐᕐᔪᐊᖖᒍᓇᔪᒋᔾᕋᓗᐊᖕᑲ ᔪᓇᐅᕙ ᔭᕗᓂᒻᒪᓇᐊᓄᑦ ᑕᐅᑐᖕᓂ’ᒪᑦ ᐅᖅᔪᕐᔪᐊᓚᓇᔮᕐᑲᕈᓛᕐᓂᖕᑲᓄᑦ ᐅᑭᐅᖅᑕᖅᑐᒥ. ᑐᓐᖕᑲᕙᐊᑦ ᐊᖕᒋᔪᐸᓇᓗᒃ ᑕᓇᐅᕐᒦᑦᑐᖅ ᐃᒃᑕᓇᒃᑐᐸᓇᓗᒃ ᑕᑭᔪᕌᓗᒃ ᕿᓂᖅᑎᑦ ᕿᓂᖅᑕᕋᓗᐊᖕᒋᑦᑕ ᐊᑉᕐᑯᑎᒃᓴᐅᑉ ᒥᒃᓵᒍᑦ.

ᑐᔾᕐᓇᖅᑐᕐᑲᖅᓱᓂ ᖅᑲᑕᐃᑦᑐᒥᒃ ᐸᐸᐸᐸ-ᓚᔪᒥᒃᓗ ᐅᑭᐅᖖᔪᓛᖅᑐᓄᑦ ᐊᑉᓗᓇᐊᖖᒍᐊᓚᖅᓱᑎᒃ ᔭᕗᓂᕌᓗᖕᒎᑦ.

2031

BREATH

Every breath is a sacrament, an affirmation of our connection with all other living things, a renewal of our link with our ancestors and a contribution to generations yet to come. Our breath is a part of life's breath, the ocean of air that envelopes the earth.

—David Suzuki, *The Sacred Balance: Rediscovering Our Place in Nature*

2031-ᒥ

ᐊᓂᖅᖀᖅᑐᖅᓂᖅ

ᐊᓂᖅᖀᖅᑐᖅᑎ’ᓗᑕ ᓵᕐᓗ ᑐᒃᓯᐊᖅᑐᒍᑦ, ᐆᒪᖅᑲᑎᒌᖕᓂᖅᑲᕋᑉᑕ
ᓵᓇᑐᐃᓐᓇᕐᓂᒃ ᐆᒪᔪᓂᒃ, ᐊᑕᔾᕕᒋ’ᓗᒋᓪᓗ ᓯᕗᓕᑐᖅᑲᕗᑦ,
ᑭᖑᓪᓕᐅᔪᒫᖅᑐᓄᓪᓗ ᐊᒃᑐᐊᙵᓂᖅᑲ’ᒪᑦ. ᐊᓂᖅᖀᖅᑐᖅᓂᕗᑦ ᐃᓚᒋᔭᐅᔪᖅ
ᐃᓅᓯᑉ ᐊᓂᕐᓂᐊ’ᓄᑦ, ᓄᓇᕐᔪᐊᕌᓘᑉ ᓯᓚᕆᔮᓄᑦ ᐊᓂᕐᓂᐊᓄᑦ.

—ᑎᑎᕋᖅᓯᒪᔫ ᑕᐃᕕᑎ ᓴᔩᑭᑉ, ᐅᖅᑲᓕᒫᒐᓕᐊᖕᒐᓃᑦᑐᖅ ᓄᓇᕐᔪᐊᕐᒥ
ᐃᓂᒋᔭᑉᑕ ᒥᒃᓵᓄᑦ

ACT III

SCENE ONE

It is a cloudy day in March, 2031. The glacial hill in the distance is gone and the ground is slush. The Circumpolar Oil platform is offshore and cannot be seen, but the sound—a constant low thumping—can be heard.

ANGU'ŘUAQ enters. Old, hungry, his fur yellowing, he walks around what was once the breathing hole, though in this temperature it is more "slush" than "hole." He walks in circles then smells something—humans. He looks up then, with some difficulty, he hurries off.

MR. and MRS. GRIFFITH-THOMSON and AINSWORTH enter, all dressed in fashionable northern wear, but with jackets open, no hats or mitts. It is warm here.

AINSWORTH: Our dog walker says Coco's friendly in the park, but she'd rather be around people than other dogs.

MRS. GRIFFITH-THOMSON: Bogart thinks he's a person.

MR. GRIFFITH-THOMSON: (*to MRS. GRIFFITH-THOMSON*) That's coz you keep feeding him ice cream.

MRS. GRIFFITH-THOMSON: I know, but every time I open the freezer he comes running, wagging his tail, pretending to be very good. Bogart knows I'll surrender and give him *crème glacée*.

AINSWORTH: *The Seafarer* cruise ship has an indoor dog run built right around their weather deck.

ᖁᓐᖏᐊᖅᑕᐅ𑪲ᒃᓴᖅ ᑭᖑᓪᓖᖅᑐᖅ

ᖃᓗᓯᑦᑑᓂᐊ ᐱᒋᐊᕐᓂᐊᓂ

𑪰ᓚ ᓄᕗᔭ𑪲ᖅ ᐅᐱᓐᖖᒑᑦᑯᑦ ᐊᕗᓐᓂᕙᖕᒥ 2031-ᖑᑎ'ᑐᒍ. ᐊᐅᔪᐃᑦᑐᕙᓂᖅ ᐊᐅᔪᐃᑦᑑ𑪰ᒪᓕᖅᑐᖅ ᐊᐅᒃ𑪰ᒪ'ᑐᓂ ᒪᓂᕋᕐᑐ ᒪᐅᔭᕐᓇᖅᑐᖅ. ᐅᖅᓱᕐ𑪲ᐊᓕᓯ𑪸ᑦ ᑐᓐᖓᒐᕙᖃᖅᑐᑦ ᑕᓯᐅᕐᒥ ᐃᒪᕐᒥ ᑭ𑪴ᖅ𑪰ᒪ𑪲ᒥᒃ ᑕᑯᒃᓴᐅᖖᒋᑦᑲᓗᐊᖅᓗᓂ ᑐ𑪴ᕐᓇᖅᑐᖅ—ᖃᑎᑐ𑪲ᖅ ᐸᑉᐸᑉᐸᑉ-ᓚ𑪲ᖅ.

ᐃ𑪰ᖅᓗᓂ ᐊᖑ'𑪲ᐊᖅ. ᐊᖑ'𑪲ᐊᑐᖃᐸᓇᓘᓕᖅᑐᖅ, ᑳᒃᑐᕐᓗ, ᐱᕐᓚᓂᓇᓘ'ᓗᓂ ᖁᖅᓱᖅᑐᐸᓇᓘᓕᖅᑐᖅ, 𑪰ᑯᖃᑦᑎᐊᖃᐃᔭᐃᑦᑑᓕᖅᑐᖅ 𑪰ᓚ ᐆᓇᔪᓕᕐᓂᖑᓄᑦ ᐊᒡᓗᖃᑦᑎᐊᕈᐃ'ᒪᑦ. ᐱ𑪻ᒪ𑪲ᖅ ᓇᐃᒪᐅᖅᑐᕐ𑪵ᓗᓕᖅᓗᓂ 𑪺ᓇᒥᒡᓕᑭᐊᖅ—𑪺ᓇᐅᕝᕙ ᐃᓄᖕᓂᒃ—ᑕᑯᒐᒥᒥᑦ ᐊᐅᓚᑦᑎᐊᓚᐃ'ᓗᓂ ᕿᒫᓇ𑪺ᐊᓕᖅᑐᖅ.

ᐃ𑪰ᖅᓗᑎᒃ ᓄᓕᐊᓰᒃ ᖃᑉᓗᓈᒃ ᒍᓯᕙᔅ-ᑖᒻᓴᓐ ᑕᐃᒪᑐ ᐊᐃᓐᔨᕗᐊᑦ, ᐊ'ᓄᕌᖅ𑪰ᒪᑦᑎᐊᖅᓗᑎᒃ ᐅᑭᐅᖅᑕᖅᑐᒥ ᓴᓇᔭᐅ𑪲ᓂᒃ ᑭ𑪰ᐊᓂᒃ ᐆᓇᕐᓂᖑᓄᑦ 𑪰ᓚ ᐊᓕᒃᑕᖅᑐᖕᒋᑦ 𑪱ᒃ𑪰ᒪᖖᒋᑦᑐᑦ ᓇ𑪴ᖅ𑪰ᒪᖖᒋᑦᑑᒃ ᐳᐊᓗᒃ𑪰ᒪᖖᒋᑦᑐᒡᓗ.

ᐊᐃᓐᔨᕗᐊᑦ: ᕿ'ᒥᖁᑎᑉᑎ'ᓂᒃ ᐱᖃᐃᓕ𑪴ᖅᑎᑦᑎ𑪸ᒋᔭᕗᑦ ᐅᖃᖃᑦᑕᖅᑐᖅ ᕿ'ᒥᕗᓐᖒᖅ, ᑯᑯᖕᒥᒃ ᑕᐃᒪ ᐊᑎᓕᒃ, ᐱᑦᑎᐊᖃᑦᑕᖅᑑᒐᓗᐊᖅ ᕿ'ᒥᐅᖃᑎᒥᓂᒃ ᑕᑯᒑᖕᒐᒥᒃ ᑭ𑪰ᐊᓂᒃ ᐃᓄᖕᓃᑦᑐᒪᓂᖅᓴᐅᕗ'ᒪᑦ.

ᐊᕐᓇᐅᑦᕿᔭᖅ ᒍᓯᕙᔅ-ᑖᒻᓴᓐ (ᒌ-ᑏ): ᐃᓅᓇ𑪺ᒋ𑪲ᖅᑕᐅᖅ ᕿ'ᒥᕗᑦ.

ᐊᖑᑕᐅᑦᕿᔭᖅ ᒍᓯᕙᔅ-ᑖᒻᓴᓐ (ᒌ-ᑏ): *(ᓄᓕᐊᕐᒥᓄᑦ)* ᐊᐃ𑪰ᑯᓰᖅᑐᖅᑎᖃᑦᑕᕋ'ᓂ ᑕ'ᓇᐃᑕᐅ𑪲ᑦᑐᒃ ᐃᓅᓇ𑪺ᒋᓕᖅᐸ'ᒪᑕ.

MRS. GRIFFITH-THOMSON: Bogart would love that, wouldn't he?

AINSWORTH: I purchased three condos on *The Seafarer*—one each for my son and daughter and their families, and one for me.

MR. GRIFFITH-THOMSON: We bought a bolthole property in New Zealand, near Queenstown. It's got good elevation. No dog run though—instead I'll be putting Bogart in the freezer.

MRS. GRIFFITH-THOMSON: *(smiling)* You will not.

AINSWORTH: Living on the water is the safest place to live now.

MR. GRIFFITH-THOMSON: Yes and no—New Zealand is— *(points)* What the hell is that . . .

AINSWORTH: The Circumpolar Oil platform.

MR. GRIFFITH-THOMSON: People aren't going to pay money to look out their very expensive stateroom windows and see drilling platforms like that giant piece of shit. This ain't the face of ecotourism.

MRS. GRIFFITH-THOMSON: Matson said hundreds of companies are up here drilling. Half aren't even legitimate.

AINSWORTH: It's a damn shame but—

Pings emit from the tracking devices on their wristbands.

We've reached the longitude and latitude. Now we wait.

MR. GRIFFITH-THOMSON looks out.

MR. GRIFFITH-THOMSON: I see some folks coming . . .

They wait.

MRS. GRIFFITH-THOMSON: Close your eyes and imagine a sleek ship weaving through four thousand years of history—Inuit ceremonial grounds, the graveyards of Ross and Franklin . . . it's so beautiful . . . so tranquil.

ᐊᕐᓇᐅᑦᕐᑭᔭᖅ ᕇ-ᑏ: ᐋᖑᒐᓗᐊᕐᓕ ᕐᑯᐊᖅᔫᕙᒃ ᐅᒃᑯᐃᕌᖕᒐᑉᑯ ᖃᐃᑲᐅᑎᕆᖅᑲᑦᑕᖅᑐᖅ ᑐᒃᔪᖅᑐᖅᓱᓂ ᐱᑦᑎᐊᙳᐊᖅᑐᓇᑑ’ᑐᓂ. ᖃᐅᔮᒪᒐᒥ ᕐᑭᓄᐃᓐᓇᖅᐸᑦ ᐊᐃᓯᕐᑯᓈᖅᑐᖅᑎᓕᐊᕐᓂᐊᕋᑉᑯ.

ᐊᐃᓐᓯᕗᐊᑦ: ᐃᒻᓇ ᐅᒥᐊᕐᔪᐊᓇᓗᒃ ᐸᓚᕋᖅᑐᖅᔪᐅᑎᓇᓗᒃᑕᐅᖅ ᐃᖃᐃᓕᖓᕐᕙᖃᒻᒪᓇᒃᑐᖅ ᕐᑭ’ᒥᓄᑦ.

ᐊᕐᓇᐅᑦᕐᑭᔭᖅ ᕇ-ᑏ: ᕐᑭ’ᒥᕗᓪᓕ ᐱᑦᑕᐅᕆᓇᔭᖅᑖ ᑖᒻᓇ, ᐊᔪᐅ?

ᐊᐃᓐᓯᕗᐊᑦ: ᑖᑉᕕᒪᓂ ᐅᒥᐊᕐᔪᐊᕐᒥ ᓂᐅᕙᖅᑑᒐᓗᐊᖅᑐᖕᒐ ᐱᖕᒐᓯᒻᒪᓇᖕᓂᒃ ᐃᓂᒃᓴᓕᐅᖅᑕᐅᔪᒪᔪᓂᒃ ᐃᓪᓗᑑ’ᑐᑎᒃ ᐅᒥᐊᕐᔪᐊᑉ ᐃᓗᐊᓂ—ᐃᕐᓂᒻᓄᑦ, ᐸᓂᒻᓄᑦ, ᐃᓚᒋᔭᐃ’ᓄᑦᑐ, ᐊᑕᐅᔪᕐᑐ ᐅᕙᒻᓄᑦ.

ᐊᖑᑕᐅᑦᕐᑭᔭᖅ ᕇ-ᑏ: ᐅᕙᒍᓪᓕ ᓂᐅᕙᖅᑐᒍᒃ ᑖᕙᓂ ᓂᐅ-ᔫᓚᓐᒥ ᓄᓇᒥ ᐳᖅᑐᔨᑦᑐᒥᒃ ᐃᔮᖅᔪᒨᕙᕆᔪᖕᓇᖅᑕᑉᑎ’ᓂᒃ ᖃᓄᕐᓕᐅᖅᑐᕐᑲᑳᑦᓚᖕᓂᖅᐸᑦ. ᕐᑭ’ᒥᕐᔪᑦ ᐱᕐᑲᐃᓕᕵᕐᕙᖅᑲᕆᑦᑑᒐᓗᐊᕐᓕ—ᕐᑭ’ᒥᕐᓱᒃ ᕐᑯᐊᖅᔫᕙᖕᔪᖕᒐᖅᑎᑐᐃᓐᓇᕐᓂᐊᖅᑕᕐᑕᓕ. *(ᓄᓕᐊᓂ ᐱᔩᓇ’ᑐᓂᐅᒃ)*

ᐊᕐᓇᐅᑦᕐᑭᔭᖅ ᕇ-ᑏ: *(ᕐᑯᖕᒐ’ᑐᓂ)* ᐱᓂᐊᖕᖏᑦᑐᑎᑦ ᔨᔭᓇᓗᖅᓱᒃ.

ᐊᐃᓐᓯᕗᐊᑦ: ᓛ’ᓇᐅᓕᖅᑐᖅ ᐅᒥᐊᕐᔪᐊᕐᒥ ᐊᑦᑕᓇᖕᖏᓐᓂᖅᓴᐃᑑᔨᓇᔭᐅᔪᖅ ᔨᒥᑐᐃᓐᓇᖅ ᐃᓅᕙᖃᕐᓗᓂᒍᖅ ᔪᓚᕐᔪᐊᕐᒥ.

ᐊᖑᑕᐅᑦᕐᑭᔭᖅ ᕇ-ᑏ: ᐋᖑᒐᓗᐊᕐᓕ ᔨᓕ—ᓂᐅ-ᔫᓚᓐᒥᑦᑕᐅᖅ—*(ᑎᑦᑯᐊᓪᓚᒃᔪᓐᓇᖅᓱᓂ)* ᔨᓇᓇᓗᒃ ᐃᒻᓇ . . .

ᐊᐃᓐᓯᕗᐊᑦ: ᐅᑭᐅᖅᑐᖅᑐᒥ ᐅᖅᓱᕐᔪᐊᓕᓇᔫᑦ ᑐᓐᖓᕙᓇᓗᐊᑦ.

ᐊᖑᑕᐅᑦᕐᑭᔭᖅ ᕇ-ᑏ: ᐸᓚᕋᖅᑎᑦ ᑮᓇᐅᔭᕐᒥ’ᓂᒃ ᐊᑐᕐᓂᐊᖕᖏᑦᑐᖅ ᐅᒥᐊᕐᔪᐊᑦᑰᓇᐊᒃᓴᕐᒥ’ᓂᒃ ᐅᒥᐊᕐᔪᐊᒦᓐᓇᔨᐊᓇᐊᒃᓴᖅ ᐊᑭᑐᔪᒥ ᑕᑯᓂᐊᕈᒥᒃ ᐃᒪ’ᓇᑦᑐᓇᕗᕐᕗᖕᓂᒃ ᐅᖅᓱᕐᔪᐊᓕᓇᔫᑦ ᐱᐊ’ᓂᒃ. ᐊᕙᑎᒥᒃ ᔨᔭᐅᖕᖏᑦᑐᒥᒃ ᑕᑯᓇᔨᐊᕈᒪᓂᐊ’ᒪᑕᓕ. ᐅᑯᐊᑉᔨᕐᕗᐃᑦ ᐅᖅᓱᕐᔪᐊᓕᓇᔫᑦ ᐅᕈᓗᔨᖕᖑᓇᖅᑐᖌᓗᕐᕗᐃᑦ.

ᐊᕐᓇᐅᑦᕐᑭᔭᖅ ᕇ-ᑏ: ᒪᑉᓴᑳᖅ ᐅᕐᑲᓪᓚᒃᑑᒐᓗᐊᖅ ᐊᒥᕝᕋᖅᑐᐸᓇᑑᓕ’ᒪᑕᔫᖅ ᐅᖅᓱᕐᔪᐊᖅᔪᐅᖅᑎᑦ ᓇ’ᒥᓂᓘᑦ ᐅᑭᐅᖅᑕᖅᑐᒍᖕᒐᐅᔪᑦ, ᓇᑉᐸᓪᓗᐊᖕᖏᓪᓗᔫᖅ ᐱᔪᖕᓇᐅᑎᑖᖅᑎᑕᐅᖕᖏᒻᒪᓇᒃᕗᑎᒃ.

ᐊᐃᓐᓯᕗᐊᑦ: ᐃ ᐅᒡᒍᐊᕐᓇᖅᑑᒐᓗᐊᕐᓕ—

MR. GRIFFITH-THOMSON: Except for that ugly piece of shit.

MRS. GRIFFITH-THOMSON: This morning I thought about names—*Polar Star* or *Polaris*. We could create a brand image using the North Star: "Winter Solstice Under the North Star."

MR. GRIFFITH-THOMSON: Come to think of it, I probably got stock in Circumpolar—got stock in everything else.

AINSWORTH: New Years is more familiar to people in the south than winter solstice. How about something like: "New Year's Under the Aurora Borealis."

MRS. GRIFFITH-THOMSON: Solstice carries more meaning up here because it's the beginning of the slow turning towards the sun.

MR. GRIFFITH-THOMSON: Hon, let the pros look after branding and you concentrate on finding investors, coz we're 4.3 million short.

AINSWORTH: I'm not worried. People are keen to see the Arctic.

MATSON: *(off stage)* Is that the spot?

MRS. GRIFFITH-THOMSON: Yes.

> *MATSON enters with DUFORT and RIVERA . . . their pings going off after arriving.*

MATSON: I was just telling these two that we could launch from Montreal on the solstice, then sail to Saguenay—Gaspé, Nuuk in Greenland, Disko Bay—

RIVERA: It's astonishing.

MATSON: What?

> *LEE enters.*

RIVERA: Sorry, didn't mean to interrupt, but no photograph can capture how it feels to be out here. I am exposed and insignificant—I am really nothing here

ᐊᕐᒐᐅ'ᒥᐊᖅᑎᒃ ᖃᓇᑕᐅᔭᓐᓄᐊᖅᑎᒃ ᓂ'ᓕᓕ'ᒪᑕ ᑐᔭᕐᓇᓕᖅᑯᑦ.

ᐊᐃᓐᓯᕗᐊᑦ: ᑎᑭᓐᓇᔪᐊᖅᑕᑉᑎ'ᓄᑦ ᑎᑭᓐᓂᖅᑯᒍᑦ. ᔭᒪᓂ ᐅᑕᖅᑭᔪᓐᓇᓇᐊᖅᑲᓕᖅᑐᒍᑦ.

ᐊᖑᑕᐅᑦᕿᔭᖅ ᑮ-ᑏ ᑕᑯᒥᐊᖅᓱᓂ.

ᐊᖑᑕᐅᑦᕿᔭᖅ ᑮ-ᑏ: ᐃᓄᖕᓂᒃ ᖃᐃᕙᓪᓕᐊᔪᖅᑲᓕᖅᑰ'ᒪᑦ . . .

ᐅᑕᖅᑭᔪᑦ.

ᐊᕐᓇᐅᑦᕿᔭᖅ ᑮ-ᑏ: ᔪᑯᖕᒥᕐᓗᔪ ᑕᐅᑐᖕᒍᐊᕐᓗᔪᓗ ᐅᒥᐊᕐᔭᐊᑐᖃᕕᓂᕐᒥᒃ ᓴᒧᖕᒐᐅᔭᕕᓂᕐᒥᒃ ᐃᓄᐃᑦ ᓄᓇᒥᔭᐃ'ᓄᑦ ᓇᔪᖅᑖ'ᒧᑦ ᐅᑭᐅᑦ 4000 ᐅᖓᑖᓂ ᓄᓇᒥᔭᐃᑎᒨᖅᓱᑎᒃ ᑕᐃᑉᑯᐊᑦ, ᐃᓗᕕᖅᑕᐅ'ᓗᑎᒡᓗ ᔭᒪᓂ ᕿᓂᖅᑎᕕᓂᑦ ᑕᐃᑉᑯᐊᑦ . . . ᓄᓇ ᑕᑯᕋᓐᓂᖅᑐᑉᐸᓇᓗᒃ . . . ᔭᐃᒪᓇᖅᑐᖅ.

ᐊᖑᑕᐅᑦᕿᔭᖅ ᑮ-ᑏ: ᑕᑯᕋᓐᓃᑦᑐᓇᓘᒐᓗᐊᖅᓱᓂ ᐅᖅᔪᕐᔭᐊᖅᔪᐅᖅᑎᕐᓱᐃᑦ ᐱᐊᑦ ᐅᓇ.

ᐊᕐᓇᐅᑦᕿᔭᖅ ᑮ-ᑏ: ᐅᑉᓛᖅ ᐃᔨᒪᔩᒐᓗᐊᖅᑐᖓ ᐊᑎᒃᓴᓂᒃ ᐸᓚᕋᖅᑎᔪᐅᑎᐅᓇᔭᖅᑐᒧᑦ—ᐅᑉᓗᓇᐊᕐᔪᐊᖅ ᐅᑉᓗᓇᐊᓇᔭᒡᒎᓐᓃᑦ. ᖃᐅᔫᑉᑲᐃᔾᔭᑎᒃᓴᓚᐅᕈᖕᓇᖅᑐᒍᓪᓗ ᐅᑉᓗᓇᐊᙳᐊᖅᑲᖅᑐᓂᒃ. ᔫᕐᓗ: ᐅᑭᐅᑦᑯᑦ ᐅᑉᓗᑭᑦᑑᓂᖓᓄᑦ ᐸᓚᕋᓇᐊᓇᑦ ᐅᑉᓗᓇᐊᕐᓂᒃ ᖃᐅᒪᔪᓂᒃ ᑕᑯᓐᓇᔭᐊᕐᓗᑎᑦ.

ᐊᖑᑕᐅᑦᕿᔭᖅ ᑮ-ᑏ: ᐃᑉᑯᓂᖓᓕ ᐅᖅᔪᕐᔭᐊᓕᓇᔪᑦᑯ'ᓂᒃ ᑮᓇᐅᔭᓕᐅᖃᑕᐅᔪᒃᓴᐅᖅᑰᕋᒪᓕ—ᑕᔪᑉᑯᓇᓂᒃ ᑮᓇᐅᔭᓕᐅᕐᕕᖃᖅᑐᐊᓘᒐᒪᒪ ᐊᒥᔾᕋᖅᑐᑉᐸᓇᓗᖕᓂᒃ ᐋ'ᓚᑦᖀᒃᑐᓂᒃ ᑎᒥᐅᔪᓂᒃ.

ᐊᐃᓐᓯᕗᐊᑦ: ᐅᑉᓗᑭᑦᑐᒥᒃ ᑐᑭᔪᖅᑰᖕᒥ'ᒪᑕ ᑕᐃᑉᑯᐊᑦ ᐆᓇᖅᑐᒥ ᓄᓇᑖᑦ, ᐊᔾᓵᒍᑦ ᓄᑖᕐᒥᒃ ᑐᔭᐅᒪᓂᖅᓴᐅᓚᓗᐊ'ᒪᑕ, ᐃᒪ'ᓇᓕᑭᐊᖅ: "ᐊᔾᓵᒍᑦ ᓄᑖᕐᒥ ᖁᕕᐊᓱᖃᑕᐅᒡᒍᐃᑦᑎ ᐊᖅᓯᓚᕿᔪᒥ ᐅᑭᐅᖅᑕᖅᑐᒥ."

ᐊᕐᓇᐅᑦᕿᔭᖅ ᑮ-ᑏ: ᐅᑉᓗᑭᑦᑐᖅ ᔭᒪᓂ ᐊᑐᖅᑕᐅᓂᖅᓴᐅᓚᓗᐊ'ᒪᑦ ᔪᕿᓂᐅᑉ ᐅᑎᖅᐸᓪᓕᐊᓂᖓᓂᒃ ᐊᑐ'ᒪᑦ ᓂᓇᐅᒥᔭᐅᕙ'ᒪᑦ.

ᐊᖑᑕᐅᑦᕿᔭᖅ ᑮ-ᑏ: ᐃᓱᒪᒋᖕᒋᓗᒋᑦ ᔭᑉᑯᐊᑦ ᕿᓂᖅᑳᓇᐊᖃᕋᑉᑕ ᑮᓇᐅᔭᓂᒃ ᐊᒥᒐᖅᓯᖅᑐᓇᓘᒐᑉᑕ 4.3 ᒥᓕᐊᓂᒃ ᕿᓂᓇᐊᖃᕐᓂᐊᖅᑐᑎᓪᓕ.

ᐊᐃᓐᓯᕗᐊᑦ: ᐃᓱᒫᓗᖕᒋᑦᑐᖓ. ᐊᒥᓱᓇᓗᐃᑦ ᐅᑭᐅᖅᑕᖅᑐᒧᖕᒐᐅᓇᓱᐊᕈᒪᔪᖃ'ᒪᑦ ᐸᓚᕋᖅᑎᓂᒃ.

. . . yet also I feel how tremendously the land is holding me and how the light is like a canopy of fire . . .

MATSON: Yes, it is gorgeous . . . so where was I—Disko Bay, across Davis Strait to Pond—

LEE's ping goes off.

LEE: God, this thing—I hate being tracked.

MATSON: It's internal tracking, Lee, and it's off now—to Pond Inlet, then along Croker Bay past Beechey, down into Victoria Strait—that's eleven days.

DUFORT: Nine.

MATSON: Nine's perfect—right on time for New Year's Eve, then on to Cambridge Bay, Kuglugtuk, and Alaska.

RIVERA: My wife, Adelina, she can't wait to see Alaska. We discovered we have relatives in Fairbanks . . . *(cocks his ear)* What's that noise . . .

AINSWORTH: Beechey's where Franklin and his boys wintered in 1845. Poor bastard got caught in the middle of the Little Ice Age.

RIVERA notices Circumpolar Oil.

RIVERA: Ah . . . a drilling platform.

MR. GRIFFITH-THOMSON: Welcome to eco-fucking-tourism 2031.

DUFORT: It is what it is . . . same everywhere. Point is we're going to rise above it—this venture will transcend reality and offer a glimpse of "how it used to be."

MATSON: Well said. Dream big.

AINSWORTH: *(to DUFORT)* You should be the one writing the brochure—not me.

ᒪᑉᓴᑳᖅᑐᖅ: *(ᐊᕙ'ᖓᑦ)* ᐅᕙᓂᐅᒐᓗᐊᖅ?

ᐊᕐᓇᐅᑦᕿᔭᖅ ᑮ-ᑏ: ᐃᔾᔭ.

ᐃᓯᖅᖢᑎᒃ ᒪᑉᓴᑳᖅ ᑑᕗᐊᕐᓪᓗ ᓇᕕᐊᕋᓗ . . . ᖃᓇᑕᐅᔭᓐᓄᐊᖅᑎᓪᓗ ᓂ'ᓚᐅᒪᔪᑦ ᑐᓴᕐᓇᖅᑐᑦ.

ᒪᑉᓴᑳᖅ: ᐅᑯᐊᒃ ᐊᒃᐱᐅᑎᓵᖅᑕᕋᓗᐊᑦᑲᒃ ᐊᐅᓪᓚᖅᑐᒃᓴᐅᒐᑉᑕ ᐅᑉᓗᑭᓐᓂᐊᓂᒃ ᐅᒥᐅᕐᔪᐊᑦᑯᑦ ᐃᖏᔾᕋᓗᑕ ᒫᓐᑐᓇᐊᓚᒥᑦ—ᑕᓇᐅᕐᔪᐊᕐᒍᙱᒐᐅᓗᑕ, ᓅᖑᓪᓗ ᑲᓛᓛᑦ ᓄᓅ'ᓄᑦ ᖃᒪᓂᕐᔪᐊᕐᒧᑦ ᑕᐃᑲᓂ—

ᓇᕕᐊᕋ: ᓱᓯᕌᓗᒃᑕᐅᖅ.

ᒪᑉᓴᑳᖅ: ᓱᓇ?

ᑖ ᐃᓯᖅᑐᖅ.

ᓇᕕᐊᕋ: ᖄ, ᐅᖃᒪᑎ'ᓗᔪ ᓄᑦᖃᖅᑎᓇᓯᐊᙳᕆᑦᑲᓗᐊᖅᐸᑉᔪ ᑭᔪᐊᓂᒃ ᑕᒃᑰᓇᓗᒃ—ᓄᓇᑦᑎᐊᕙᐸᓇᓗᒃ ᐃᒃᐱᖕᓇᕐᓗᐊᖅᑐᖅ ᐃᓄᑉᓯᕐᔫᓂᕋ ᐃᒃᐱᒋᓪᓗᐊᖅᑕᕋ ᓯᓇᐅᙱᑦᑐᕐᔫᓯᖓ, ᔪᓚ ᓄᓇ ᐊᕙᑎ ᐊᖏᓯᐊᔫ'ᒪᑦ ᑕᓴᒪᓂ . . . ᑎᒍᒥᐊᖅᑕᐅᓯᔭᕋᒪ ᓄᓇᒥᑦ ᐃᑯᒪᓗ ᑕᓴᒻᒪ ᐃᓂᖁᓇᖅᑐᕌᔫ'ᒪᑦ . . .

ᒪᑉᓴᑳᖅ: ᐄ, ᐱᑦᑕᐅᔾᔫᖅᑐᖅ . . . ᖃᓄᕐᓚᐅᕋᓗᐊᕋᒪᓚ ᐳᐃᒍᖅᑲᔭᕋᒪ—ᐄ ᖃᒪᓂᕐᒥᑦ ᑕᐃᑰᖓ ᐃᑭᕋᓴᒃᑯᑦ ᒥᑦᑎᒪᑕᓚᖕᒧᑦ ᑕᐃᒪ—

ᑖᑉ ᐊᔾᒐᐅᒻᒥᐊᓐᓄᐊᖓ ᓂ'ᓚ'ᒪᑦ ᓇᓪᓚᖅᖢᓂ.

ᑖ: ᐅᓇᔅᖢᒃ ᐃᖢᐃᑦᑐᕌᓗᒃ ᖃᐅᔫᓴᖅᑕᐅᕙᒃᑲᒪ—ᒪᓚᒃᑕᐅᒐᒪ ᔪᒨᒐᐅᒐᓗᐊᕌᖓᒐᒪ.

ᒪᑉᓴᑳᖅ: ᖃᐅᔫᓴᖅᑕᐅᙳᕆᑦᑐᑎᑦ ᐊᕙ'ᖓᑦ, ᑖ, ᓴᒪᓃᓐᓇᔅᖢᓪᓚ ᖃᐅᔫᓴᖅᑕᐅᒐᕕᑦ, ᑕᔾᕙᓚ ᖃᒥᓐᖓᒐᓚᖅᑐᖅ—ᐲ, ᒥᑦᑎᒪᑕᓚᖕᒧᑦ ᑕᐅᓄᖓ ᕿᑭᖅᑕᕐᔪᐊᑦᑯᑦ ᐃᑭᕋᓴᖕᒧᑦ—ᐅᐸᓗᑦ ᑕᔾᕙ 11-ᖑᓇᓴᖅᑐᑦ.

ᑑᕗᐊᕐᑦ: ᖁᓚᐅᙱᓐᓄᐊᖅᑐᑦ ᐅᐸᓗᑦ.

ᒪᑉᓴᑳᖅ: ᐄ, ᐅᐸᓗᑦ ᖁᓚᐅᙱᓐᓄᐊᖅᑐᑦ ᓈᒻᒪᖕᓂᐊᖅᑐᑦ ᑎᑭᐅᑎᓗᑕ ᐅᖅᔪᖅᑑᕐᒧᑦ ᐊᔾᖄᒍᑦ ᓄᑖᕐᒥ ᑭᖑᓂᐊᒍᑦ ᑲᔪᓯᒥᐊᕐᓗᑕ ᐃᖅᑲᓗᒃᑑᑦᑎᐊᕐᒧᑦ, ᖁᕐᓗᖅᑐᒧᑦ, ᑕᐃᑯᖕᒐᓗ ᐊᓛᔅᑲᒧᑦ.

DUFORT: I'm just the translator.

MATSON: For our maiden voyage we can invite media, even the prime minister if she's still in power. She seems at ease in the north, and barring an uncontrollable methane release, we could attract loads of coverage.

LEE: Methane's always uncontrollable.

MATSON: Let's not go there, Lee—I'm just citing an example of competing news stories—

MRS. GRIFFITH-THOMSON: But she's right. With permafrost thawing there's no way to control the CO_2 being released by the microbes—

MR. GRIFFITH-THOMSON: You talk about turning towards the sun, so look on the bright side for a—hon, everyone knows this crap—don't bore us with it.

DUFORT: We've been in a feedback loop for years—are we dead yet? No.

LEE: I had the worst dream last night.

AINSWORTH: I didn't sleep much either.

LEE: It was one of those dreams that don't feel like a dream because in the dream you wake up in your own bedroom.

DUFORT: They call that a "false awakening."

LEE: But it felt so real. Emilie and I were sleeping. Michael's crib is in our bedroom, and when I heard him crying I got up to bring him into the bed so Emilie could nurse him but . . . when I looked in the crib, I saw a bear cub . . . the cub was dead and I was relieved . . . but where was the baby? I tried to lift up the bear to get at the baby, but the baby was gone . . . there was nothing left but a bit of blood.

MRS. GRIFFITH-THOMSON: Awful dream . . .

LEE: I panicked—"Where did the baby go?"

ᕆᕕᐊᕋ: ᓄᓕᐊᕋ ᐋᑕᓛᓇ ᑕᑯᔪᒪᓪᓗᐊᖅᑐᖅ ᐊᓛᔅᑲᒥᒃ. ᓱᓇᐅᕝᕙᒡᒍᖅ ᐃᓚᖃᕐᓂᕋᒻᓄᒃ ᑕᐃᑲᓂ . . . (*ᓱᓇᒥᒃ ᑐᓴᕋᓱᐊᓕᖅᑐᖅ*) . . . ᓱᓇᑦᑕᐅᖅ ᑐᓴᕐᓇᓕᖅᑐᖅ . . .

ᐊᐃᓐᓯᕗᐊᑦ: ᐅᕙᓂ ᐊᕐᑯᑎᕐᔪᐊᕐᓗ ᓴᓇᔨᖕᒋᓪᓗ ᐊᔪᖅᓯᓯᒪᓕᖅᑐᑦ 1845-ᖑᑎ'ᓗᒍ. ᑕᐃᑉᓱᒪᓂ ᐆᓇᐃᑦᑐᐊᓘᑎ'ᓗᒍ ᐃ'ᔨᓇᓗᖕᒦᓯᐅᕋᓗᐊ'ᒪᑕ ᐅᑭᐅᕌᓗᑦᑯᑦ ᐊᔪᖅᓯᓯᒪ'ᓗᑎᒃ.

ᕆᕕᐊᕋ ᐅᖅᓱᕐᔪᐊᓕᕆᔨᑦᑯᑦ ᑐᓐᖓᕕᐊᑦ ᐃᒪᕐᒥ ᐅᔾᔨᕆ'ᒪᒍ.

ᕆᕕᐊᕋ: ᐅᖅᓱᕐᔪᐊᖅᓯᐅᖅᑎᑦᑯᑦ ᑐᓐᖓᕕᓇᓗᐊᑦ ᐃᑰᑕᕐᕕᐊᑦ.

ᐊᖑᑕᐅᑦᕿᓴᖅ ᑮ-ᑏ: ᐅᕈᓗᓱᓐᖑᓇᖅᑐᑉᑲᕆᓇᓗᔅᓗᒃᑕᐅᖅ ᐳᓚᕋᕋᓱᐊᖅᓗᓂ 2031-ᒥ ᓱᓇᖃᖕᒋᑦᑐᒧᑦ ᓱᓇᐅᕝᕙ ᐊᕙᑎᒥᒃ ᐊᓯᕈᖅᑎᖃᖅᓂᐊᖅᓂᖅᓗᓂ.

ᑑᕗᐊᕐᑦ: ᐋᖑᒐᓗᐊᖅᑕᐅᖅ ᐊᔪᕐᓇ'ᒪᑦ ᓱᒥᑐᐃᓐᓇᖅ ᓯᓚᕐᔪᐊᕐᒥ ᑕᐃ'ᓇᐃᑦᑑᓕ'ᒪᑦ. ᓴᐱᓕᖕᒋᓗᑕ ᐱᓂᐊᖅᑐᒍᑦ—ᓇ'ᒥᓂᕆᓇᓱᐊᖅᑕᑉᑯᓪᓕ ᑕᑯᒃᓴᐅᓂᐊᖕᒋᑦᑐᑦ ᓴᑉᑯᐊᑦ ᐱᔪᒥᓇᐃᑦᑐᑦ, ᖃᐅᔨᑉᑲᐃᓂᐊᕋᑉᑕ "ᖃᓄᕆᑦᑑᓯᒪᓕᕋᓗᐊᕐᓂᐊ'ᓂᒃ ᑕ'ᓇᐃᑦᑐᖃᖕᒋᑎ'ᓗᒍ ᑕᐃᑉᓱᒪᓂ." ᐅᑉᓗᒥᐅᓯᖅ ᐱᑦᑕᐅᖕᒋᑦᑐᑦ ᑕᓴᑉᑯᐊᑦ ᑐᑯᒃᓴᐅᑎᓚᐃᑕᕗᑦ.

ᒪᑉᓴᑳᖅ: ᐅᖃᑦᑎᐊᖅᑯᑎᑦ. ᓴᐱᓕᖕᒋᒻᒪᕆᒃᓗᑕ.

ᐊᐃᓐᓯᕗᐊᑦ: (*ᑑᕗᐊᕐᑦᒧᑦ*) ᐃᔅᕕᕙᓪᓗᖅ ᖃᐅᔨᑉᑲᐃᔅᓯᑎᒃᓴᒥᒃ ᑎᑎᕋᖅᐸᓪᓗᖅᑐᒃᓴᐅᒐᓗᐊᖅᑯᑎᑦ.

ᑑᕗᐊᕐᑦ: ᑐᑭᓕᐅᕋᓱᐊᖅᓯᓐᓇᖅᑐᕐᔫᓯᖓ.

ᒪᑉᓴᑳᖅ: ᓯᕗᓪᓕᕐᒥ ᐊᐅᓪᓚᕐᓂᐊᕐᓗᑕ ᐳᓚᕋᖅᑎᑦᑎᓗᑕ, ᖃᐅᔨᑉᑲᐃᖅᑳᕈᖕᓇᖅᑐᒧᑦ ᑐᓴᒃᓴᓕᕆᔨᓂᒃ ᑐᓴᖅᑎᑦᑎᔅᓯᑎᒃᓴᐃ'ᓂᒃ ᑐᓂᓗᒋᑦ, ᑲᕙᒪᕐᔪᐊᑦᑯᓗ ᐊᑕᓂᒻᒪᕆᐊᑦ ᑕᐃᒻᓇ ᓱᓕ ᐊᑕᓂᕆᔭᐅᒍᓂ ᐃᓚᐅᔪᖕᓇᔅᓴ'ᔭᕗᖅ. ᑕᐃᒻᓇ ᖁᕕᐊᓲᑎᖃᖅᑲᑦᑕᖅᑐᖅ ᐅᑭᐅᖅᑕᖅᑐᒥᒃ, ᐊᑖᓂ'ᖔᖅᑐᓂᒃ ᐳᑉᓚᐃᖅᑐᖃᖕᒋᓐᓂᕈᓂᓕ ᒪᓂᕋᕐᒥᑦ, ᑐᓴᒐᒃᓴᒃᑯᑦ ᖃᐅᔨᑉᑲᐃᑦᑎᐊᕈᖕᓇᕐᓂᐊᖅᑐᒍᑦ ᓇ'ᒥᓂᑉᑎ'ᓂᒃ ᓴᓇᓴᑉᑎ'ᓂᒃ.

ᓛ: ᐊᑖᓂ'ᖔᖅᑐᑦ ᐳᑉᓚᐃᑦ ᓇᓗᓇᖃᑦᑕ'ᒪᑕ ᐸᑉᓚᐃᑳᓪᓚᒃᓯᓐᓇᖅᐸ'ᒪᑕ ᖁᓴᒋᓐᓇᖅ.

ᒪᑉᓴᑳᖅ: ᐃᓱᒪᒋᖕᒋᑦᓗᒋᑦ ᑕᓴᑉᑯᐊᑦ—ᖃᐅᔨᑎᓐᓇᓱᐊᖅᓯᓐᓇᖅᑕᑉᓯ ᖃᓄᖅ ᐊ'ᔨᒌᖕᒋᑦᑐᖅᑕᖃᕆᐊᒃᓴᖅ ᑐᓴᒐᒃᓴᒃᑯᑦ ᐊᑕᐅᑦᑎᒃᑰᖃᑦᑕᖅᑐᓂᒃ—

MRS. GRIFFITH-THOMSON: Dreams never make sense.

MR. GRIFFITH-THOMSON: Can't take them seriously.

LEE: The bear cub weighed a ton.

DUFORT: Maybe the stress of this trip is weighing on you because you're away from your baby. The trip is weighing on me, too, but we'll be back in Ottawa tonight.

MATSON: The company jet is in Gjoa Haven waiting to meet our helicopter, which should be here like . . . now.

Suddenly MRS. GRIFFITH-THOMSON *steps into the hole in the slush and nearly sinks up to her waist before she can stop herself.*

MRS. GRIFFITH-THOMSON: Ohhh . . . OHHH . . .

Everyone instantly gives her a hand.

MATSON: Mrs. Thomson—

MR. GRIFFITH-THOMSON: Lori, hon—

MRS. GRIFFITH-THOMSON: I'm all right—

MR. GRIFFITH-THOMSON: You okay—

RIVERA: Take my arm—

MRS. GRIFFITH-THOMSON: I'm fine, just . . . surprised.

AINSWORTH: *(looking out)* Is that Larkin and Roy?

RIVERA: *(looking out)* . . . Hard to tell.

MATSON: *(looking out)* Maybe they're folks from the rig.

AINSWORTH: *(looking out)* I left my gun on the chopper.

ᐊᕐᓇᐅᑦᕿᔭᖅ ᕇ-ᑏ: ᑕᓕᔭᕐᓕ. ᓄᓇ ᕿᕿᓴᒪᐃᓐᓇᖅᑐᕕᓂᖅ
ᐊᐅᒃᐸᓪᓕᐊᓂᐊ’ᓄᑦ ᓄᓇ ᐳᑉᓚᐃᑦᖃᑕᓕ’ᒪᑦ ᓇᓗᓇᖅᓱᓂᓗ—

ᐊᖑᑕᐅᑦᕿᔭᖅ ᕇ-ᑏ: ᓴᕿᓂᖅᓴᐅᕈᒪᐃᓐᓇᖅᐸᒃᑲᕕᑦ ᐊᑕᐃ
ᖁᕕᐊᓇᑦᕿᔪᓂᒃ ᐃᑕᒪᖃᕋᑕᐊᓕᓇᑦ—ᐊᐃ, ᐳᑉᓚᕐᓱᐃᑦ
ᖃᐅᔨᒪᔭᐅᑦᑎᐊᖅᑐᑦ—ᐅᖃᐅᓯᓇᔮᖅᑲᖕᒥᑦᑕᑎᑦ.

ᑑᕗᐊᕐᑦ: ᖃᐅᔨᒪᔭᐅᔦᑐᖃᕐᓱᐃᑦ ᐊᑯᓂᓇᓗᒃ ᑐᔮᐅᒪᓕᖅᑕᖅᑯᑦ—
ᑕᔮᑉᑯᓄᖕᒐᑦ ᑐᖁᑕᐅᒐᓗᐊᖅᐱᑖ? ᐄᕿᕐᓱᒃ.

ᓛ: ᐃᖅᓴᓇᖅᑐᒥᒃ ᓴᓐᓇᒃᑑᒪᕆᔭᖅᑲᕋᓗᐊᕐᒪ ᐅᓐᓄᐊᖅ.

ᐊᐃᓐᓯᕗᐊᑦ: ᓴᓂᑦᑎᐊᙱᒻᒪᒃᓇᒃᑐᖕᒐᓗ.

ᓛ: ᓴᓐᓇᒃᑑᒪᑎ’ᓗᖕᒐ ᑐᐸᙳᐊᖅᓴᓐᓇᕋᒪ ᑕᓕ ᓴᓐᓇᒃᑑᒪᓐᓂᕋᒪ
ᖃᐅᔨᙱ’ᓗᖕᒐ ᓴᓐᓇᒃᑑᒪᑎᔭᕋ ᐱᒻᒪᓇᐅᔮᖅᑐᓇᓘ’ᓗᓂ
ᐃᒡᓗᐊᒻᓃᑦᑲᓗᐊᕋᒪᓗ ᑕᓕᒻᒪᓇᒃᑐᑐᑦ ᐃᑦᖁᒪᔭᑐᑦ.

ᑑᕗᐊᕐᑦ: ᑐᐸᐅᒪᙳᐊᖅᓴᒪᐃᓐᓇᕋᓗᐊᕋᕕᐅ’ᔪᔭᕐᓘᓐᓃᑦ.

ᓛ: ᐱᒻᒪᓇᓇᓘᔮᖅᓱᓂᓗ. ᓄᓕᐊᕋᓗ ᓴᓂᒃᑲᒻᓄᒃ. ᐅᑕᕋᓐᓄᐊᑉᑕ
ᐃᒡᓕᐊ ᐃᒡᓗᐊᑉᑎ’ᓃ’ᒪᑦ, ᕿᐊᓕ’ᒪᓪᓗ ᑐᔮᕐᓇᖅᑐᖅ ᑎᒧᒥᐊᕋᓗᐊᕋᑉᑯ
ᓄᓕᐊᕐᒪ ᐊᒫᒪᒃᑎᓐᓂᐊ’ᒪᒧ . . . ᑭᓴᐊᓂᒃ ᐃᒡᓕᓐᓄᐊᖕᒐᓄᑦ ᑕᑯᒐᒪ
ᓇᓄᐊᓐᓄᐊᖑᓐᓂᖅ . . . ᑐᖁᖕᒐ’ᒪᓪᓗ ᐃᖅᓴᑕᐃᖅᑐᖕᒐ . . . ᑭᓴᐊᓂᒃ ᓇᐅᒃ
ᐅᑕᕋᕗᒃ? ᓇᓄᐊᓐᓄᐊᖅ ᑐᖁᖕᒐᔭᖅ ᑎᒧᔭᕋᓗᐊᕋ ᐅᑕᕋᕗᒃ ᐊᑖᓃᓇᑕᒥ’ᓗᒧ,
ᑭᓴᐊᓂᒃ ᐅᑕᕋᕗᒃ ᑕᖃᙱᒻᒪᓄ’ᒪᑦ . . . ᐊᐅᖃᖅᓱᓂ ᐊ’ᓕᓂᐊᓂ.

ᐊᕐᓇᐅᑦᕿᔭᖅ ᕇ-ᑏ: ᐱᔪᒥᓇᐃᓪᓗᐊᖅᑐᓇᓗᕐᓱᒃ . . .

ᓛ: ᐅᐃᒻᒪᒡᓗᐊᓕᖅᓱᖕᒐ “ᓇᐅᒃ ᐅᑕᕋᕋ ᑕᒧᖕᒐᐅᔭᖅ?”

ᐊᕐᓇᐅᑦᕿᔭᖅ ᕇ-ᑏ: ᓴᓐᓇᒃᑐᕐᓂᖅ ᑐᑭᖃᑦᑎᐊᖅᐸᙱ’ᒪᑦ ᑕ’ᓇᐃᑦᑐᕐᓕ.

ᐊᖑᑕᐅᑦᕿᔭᖅ ᕇ-ᑏ: ᐃᑕᒪᕆᕙᓪᓛᓇᐊᖃᙱᑕᖅᑯᑦ.

ᓛ: ᐃᒃᑕᓇᒃᑐᓇᓘᒐᓗᐊ’ᒪᑦ ᓇᓄᐊᓐᓄᐊᖅ ᑕᐃᓪᓇ.

ᑑᕗᐊᕐᑦ: ᐅᑕᕋᓐᓄᐊᖅᓯ ᐅᖕᒐᒥ’ᓗᒨᒃᓴᐅᔭᖅ ᕿᑐᑕᓕᕋᕕᓪᓗ
ᐊᐅᓪᓚᖅᓴᒪᒃᓵᕐᓂ’ᓄᑦ. ᐅᕙᖕᒐᓕ ᕿᑐᑕᒃᑐᐊᓘ’ᒥᔭᖕᒐ ᑭᓴᐊᓂᒃ ᐋᑐᕚᒧᑦ
ᐅᑎᖅᓴᒪᓂᐊᕋᒪ ᐅᓐᓄᒃᐸᑦ.

MATSON: So did I—dumb of me—Larkin and Roy should be here by now—I told them thirteen hundred sharp.

AINSWORTH: Are you sure these are the correct coordinates?

MATSON checks her device.

MATSON: Positive.

MRS. GRIFFITH-THOMSON: Brrrr . . . that water's cold.

MR. GRIFFITH-THOMSON takes off his jacket.

MR. GRIFFITH-THOMSON: Here, hon—wrap this round your legs.

MRS. GRIFFITH-THOMSON: I'm fine, hon.

LEE: *(looking out)* . . . Did you see that? The person dropped something in the snow—no, they're picking something up.

DUFORT: You call this snow—my feet are soaked.

MATSON: *(re: her boots)* You should get a pair of these—great in cold, great in wet. I got them in Ottawa.

MR. GRIFFITH-THOMSON: *(looking out)* Look, there's another person following behind them.

MRS. GRIFFITH-THOMSON: *(to MATSON)* I think I'll get a pair of those boots next time.

MATSON: They're the best, Lori . . . *(looking out, lowering her voice)* I hope that's not a gun they're carrying.

MATSON steps forwards to greet the yet unseen intruder.

Hello. I'm Matson Da—

QI'NGAQTUQ: *(off stage)* DON'T MOVE!

ᒪᑉᓵᑳᖅ: ᓇ'ᒥᓂᐸᑕ ᑎᖕᒥᔩᕐᔦᐊᖕᒐᑦ ᐅᖅᓱᖅᑑᕐᒦ'ᒪᑦ ᐅᑕᖅᑭ'ᑐᑎᒃ ᕐᑯᓕᒥᒨᓕᐸᑎ'ᓂᒃ, ᓇᐅᑭᐊᖅ ᕐᑯᓕᒥᒨᓕᕐᓗᒃ . . . ᑭᖑᕙᖅᑐᕐᓗᒃ.

ᐊᕐᓇᐅᑦᕐᑭᔾᔭᖅ ᕿ-ᑏ ᔫᑯᒥ ᐊᖕᒪᓂᕐᒍᑦ ᑐᑎᓪᓚᕐᔮᓗ'ᒪᑦ ᑭᕙ'ᓗᓂ ᐃᒪᕐᒍᑦ ᐃᒻᒪᒃᑐᐊᓘ'ᓗᓂ ᐃᒫᕐᑲᔭᖅᓗᓂ ᐃᒫᖖᒋᑦᑐᖅ.

ᐊᕐᓇᐅᑦᕐᑭᔾᔭᖅ ᕿ-ᑏ: ᐆᐅᐅ . . . ᐆᐅᐅ . . .

ᑕᒪᐃᑕ ᐃᑲᔪᓕᖅᐸᐃᑦ.

ᒪᑉᓵᑳᖅ: ᖃᓄᓇᖖᒋᑦᑐᑎᐅᒐᓗᐊᖅ—

ᐊᖑᑕᐅᑦᕐᑭᔾᔭᖅ ᕿ-ᑏ: ᓄᓕᐊᓐᓄᐊᖅ—

ᐊᕐᓇᐅᑦᕐᑭᔾᔭᖅ ᕿ-ᑏ: ᖃᓄᓇᖖᒋᑦᑐᖕᒐ—

ᐊᖑᑕᐅᑦᕐᑭᔾᔭᖅ ᕿ-ᑏ: ᖃᓄᓇᑦᑕᐃᓕ—

ᓇᕙᐊᕋ: ᑕᓕᕋ ᑎᒍᓗᒍ—

ᐊᕐᓇᐅᑦᕐᑭᔾᔭᖅ ᕿ-ᑏ: ᖃᓄᓇᖖᒋᑦᑐᖕᒐ . . . ᐃᔨᒪᒋᖖᒋᕐᓘᒃᑲᐸᑯ.

ᐊᐃᓐᓯᕗᐊᑦ: *(ᑖᕗᖕᒐ ᑕᑯ'ᓗᓂ)* ᐃᐸᑯᐊᒡᓕ ᓛᑲᓐᓗ ᐳᐃᓘ'ᓯᔦᒃ.

ᓇᕙᐊᕋ: *(ᑖᕗᖕᒐ ᑕᑯ'ᓗᓂ)* . . . ᓇᓗᓇᖅᑐᕌᓗᒃ.

ᒪᑉᓵᑳᖅ: *(ᑖᕗᖕᒐ ᑕᑯ'ᓗᓂ)* ᐅᖅᓱᕐᔦᐊᖅᔫᖅᑎᓂ'ᖖᒑᔫᒪᔦ'ᓯᔦᒃ ᑐᓐᖕᒐᕙᐊ'ᓂᑦ.

ᐊᐃᓐᓯᕗᐊᑦ: *(ᑖᕗᖕᒐ ᑕᑯ'ᓗᓂ)* ᔫᖅᑯᖅᑎᕝᔦᑎᕐᓗᒐ ᕿᒪᕐᓘᒃᓘᒍᓗ ᕐᑯᓕᒥᒨᓕᖕᒥ.

ᒪᑉᓵᑳᖅ: ᐅᕙᖕᒐᓗ—ᕗᕐᑯᑕᐅᖖᒋᑦᑐᓇᓗᒃ—ᐃᐸᑯᐊᒃ ᓛᑲᓐᓗ ᐳᐃᓗ ᖃᐃᕗᖖᒐᖅᑐᒃᓴᐅᒐᓗᐊᖅᑯᒃ ᕗᖅᑲᖖᒋ'ᓗᑎᒃ—ᖃᐃᑦᕐᑯᓯᕋᓗᐊᑦᑲᒃ ᐅᐸᓗᐳᒥᑕᕐᕙᒃ ᐊᓂᒍᓂᐊ'ᓂ ᖃᐃᓐᓇᓇᑦᑯ'ᓗᒋᒃ ᕗᖅᑲᖖᒋᒻᒪᓇᒃᑑᒃ.

ᐊᐃᓐᓯᕗᐊᑦ: ᑕᒻᒪᖖᒋᑦᑲᓗᐊᖅᑯᓪᓕ ᐅᑯᐊᑦ ᑕᒻᒪᓈᑦᑯᑎᔫᑎᑦ?

ᒪᑉᓵᑳᖅ ᖃᐅᔮᓴᖅᓗᓂᐅᒃ ᖃᓇᑕᐅᔾᔭᓐᓄᐊᓂ.

ᒪᑉᓵᑳᖅ: ᐋ ᑕᒻᒪᖖᒋᑦᑐᑦ.

No one is sure whether to put up their hands in surrender or what to do.

QI'NGAQTUQ enters carrying some lightweight equipment . . . and walking very carefully.

AINSWORTH: We didn't do anything.

QI'NGAQTUQ: *(to MATSON)* You might be stepping on tracks.

AINSWORTH: *(looking down)* Tracks?

QI'NGAQTUQ: Bear tracks . . .

MR. GRIFFITH-THOMSON: Who are you?

QI'NGAQTUQ: . . . are hard to see if you're not looking for them and harder to see in this melt . . . *(to MATSON)* Yep, you're stepping on one.

MATSON looks down.

MATSON: Oh yeah, I—

QI'NGAQTUQ: DON'T MOVE. NOBODY MOVE.

MATSON: Sorry.

MR. GRIFFITH-THOMSON: Who are you?

QI'NGAQTUQ: *(to MATSON)* Very carefully lift your left foot up and move towards your left—watch you don't step on another track . . . then lift your right foot . . .

MATSON carefully moves her feet as QI'NGAQTUQ examines the track.

. . . I'm searching for a pattern in this bear's trajectory . . .

Using a small scoop, QI'NGAQTUQ scoops up the slush that forms the bear's paw track and drops it into a sterile sample bag.

DUFORT: Is there a bear around here?

ᐊᕐᓇᐅᑦᕿᔦᖅ ᒋ-ᑎ: ᐆᓇᐃᑦᑐᕌᓗᒃ ᐃᒪᖅ ᑕᔭᒻᒪ.

ᐊᖑᑕᐅᑦᕿᔦᖅ ᒋ-ᑎ ᒪᑦᑕᖅᑲᓂ.

ᐊᖑᑕᐅᑦᕿᔦᖅ ᒋ-ᑎ: ᐅᕝᕙ ᐅᓇ ᓂᐅ'ᓄᑦ ᕿᐱᒃᓴᖅ.

ᐊᕐᓇᐅᑦᕿᔦᖅ ᒋ-ᑎ: ᐊᐃᔫᖅ ᖃᓄᓇᙵᕆᑦᑐᖓ.

ᓚ: *(ᐊᒍᖓ ᑕᐅᑐᒃᑲᓂ)* . . . ᐃᒻᓇ ᐃᓄᒃ ᑕᑯᒐᓗᐊᖅᐱᐅᒃ? ᑲᑕᐃᔦᖅ ᐊᐳ'ᒨᑦ—ᐄᕿ, ᔦᓇᒥᒃ ᑎᒎᔦᓐᓂ'ᒪᑦ.

ᑑᒍᐊᕐᑦ: ᐊᐳᑕᐅᔦᓇᔭᐃᑦ ᔭᒻᒪ ᐊᐳᑕᐅᔾᑉᐸᙵᕆᑦᑐᖅ—ᑲᒫᓘᑦᑲᒃ ᐃᒻᒪᒃᔦᒪᑦᑎᐊᖅᑐᒃ.

ᒪᐸᔭᑳᖅ: *(ᑲᒫᓘᕆᒃ ᐱ'ᓗᕆᒃ)* ᐃᒪ'ᓇᐃᑦᑐᖅᑖᖅᑐᒃᓴᐅᒐᓗᐊᖅᑯᑎᑦ—ᐆᓇᐃᑦᑐᒥ ᐱᑦᑕᐅᔦᑦ, ᖃᐅᔦᖅᑐᒥ ᐱᑦᑕᐅᔦᑦ ᑭᐊᒃᐸᓪᓚᓚᐃ'ᓗᑎᒃ, ᐱᑖᓇᔾᑲ ᐋᑐᕚᒥ.

ᐊᖑᑕᐅᑦᕿᔦᖅ ᒋ-ᑎ: ᑕᒃᑰᒃ ᑕᐃᒻᓇ ᐊᐃᐸᐹ'ᓄᑦ ᒪᓕᒃᑕᐅ'ᒪᑦ.

ᐊᕐᓇᐅᑦᕿᔦᖅ ᒋ-ᑎ: *(ᒪᐸᓴᑳᕐᒧᑦ)* ᑕ'ᓇᐃᑦᑐᖅᑖᖅᑐᒃᓴᐅᒐᓗᐊᖅᑐᖓ ᖃᑯᒍᕿᐊᖅ.

ᒪᐸᔭᑳᖅ: ᐱᑦᑕᐅᓂᖅᓴᐃᑦᑑᔪᑦ ᐅᑯᐊᑦ . . . *(ᐊᒍᖓ ᑕᑯ'ᓗᓂ, ᓂᐱᕿᑦᑐᒥᒃ ᐅᕐᑲᒪᓕᖅᑐᖅ)* ᔦᖅᑯᖅᑎᔾᔦᑎᖅᑲᙵᕆᑦᑑ'ᔭᔦᖅ ᐃᒻᓇ.

ᒪᐸᔭᑳᖅ ᐊᐸᓗᓇᐊᖅᑐᖅ ᑐᕌᖅᑲᔪ ᑕᐃᒻᓇ ᖃᐃᕙᓪᓕᐊᔦᖅ.

ᒪᐸᔭᑳᖅ: ᐊᐃ, ᒪᐸᓴᑳᖑᔦᖓ—

ᕿ'ᖓᖅᑐᖅ: . . . *(ᐊᕙ'ᖓᑦ)* ᐃᖑᑦᑕᐃᓕᓗᑎᑦ ᓄᑦᕿᖓᑦᑎᐊᒻᒪᓇᓪᓗᑎᑦ.

ᐅᓇᑕᖅᑕᐅᓕᓇᐊᒃᓵᒥ'ᓂᒃ ᓇᓗᔦᐊᓘ'ᒪᑕ ᖃᓄᕐᓕᐅᓇᐊᒃᓴᖅ ᓇᓗ'ᓗᑎᒃ.

ᐃᔦᖅᑲᓂ ᕿ'ᖓᖅᑐᖅ ᑎᒎᒥᐊᖅᑲᓂ ᔭᓇᔾᐳᑎᓂᒃ . . . ᖃᐅᔦᔭᑦᑎᐊᖅᑲᓂ ᔦᒃᑲᐃᑦᑐᐸᔦᓐᓄᐊᕐᒥᒃ ᐱᔦᒃᑐᖅ.

ᐊᐃᓐᓯᒍᐊᑦ: ᔦᙵᕆᒻᒪᓇᒃᑐᒎᓚ.

ᕿ'ᖓᖅᑐᖅ: *(ᒪᐸᓴᑳᕐᒧᑦ)* ᑐᑎᑦᑕᐃᓕᓗᕆᑦ ᐅᑯᐊᑦ ᑐᒥᑦ.

QI'NGAQTUQ: Yep.

LEE: Oh my god, WHERE?

QI'NGAQTUQ holds up the sterile bag.

QI'NGAQTUQ: . . . In here.

LEE: You had me there for a second.

QI'NGAQTUQ: Paw tracks leave behind minute amounts of DNA on the snow. The lab's analysis will tell us more about this bear. I prefer blood samples but there's a ban on invasive procedures—a ban I helped put in place.

RIVERA: Are you a veterinarian?

QI'NGAQTUQ: Biologist. Qi'ngaqtuq Donoghue.

MATSON: Matson Day—hello. This is Ainsworth, Mr. and Mrs. Griffith-Thomson, Lee, Dufort, and Rivera. We're a group of entrepreneurs—Oceanus Adventures—you may have heard of us.

QI'NGAQTUQ: Nope—never.

AINSWORTH: We're building a cruise ship, a fully stabilized, highly strengthened, ice-class Polar Code PC5. The ship's eco-sustainable, whale-safe, and boasts 93% of its services as wholly recyclable—

LEE: You sound like a walking brochure.

AINSWORTH: I know—I'm writing the bloody thing!

QI'NGAQTUQ: Too many cruise ships here—they're bumping into each other.

MRS. GRIFFITH-THOMSON: We're also developing ice replacement, huge floating white solar reflectors to deflect the sun's rays from the water—

ᐊᐃᓐᓯᕗᐊᑦ: *(ᑕᐅᓄᖕᒐ ᑕᑯ'ᓗᓂ)* ᑐᒥᕐᑲ'ᒪᑦ?

ᖅᑭ'ᖕᒐᖅᑐᖅ: ᓇᓄᐃᑦ ᑐᒦᑦ . . .

ᐊᖑᑕᐅᑦᕿᔭᖅ ᒌ-ᑏ: ᔪᓇᐅᔪᑎᑦ?

ᖅᑭ'ᖕᒐᖅᑐᖅ: . . . ᑕᐅᑐᖕᓇᑦᑎᐊᖅᐸᖕᖏ'ᒪᑕ ᑐᒥᑦ ᐊᐳᓪᓗ ᓴᒻᒪ
ᐊᐅᒃᑐᐊᓘᓂᖕᒐᓄᑦ ᑕᒃᑯᒃᓴᐅᑦᑎᐊᕈᐃᖅᑐᑦ . . . *(ᒪᑉᓵᕐᔫᑦ)* ᐄ,
ᑐᑎᕝᕕᒥᔭᐃᑦ ᑐᒥ ᑕᕝᕙ.

ᒪᑉᓵᖅ ᑕᐅᓄᖕᒐ ᑕᑯ'ᓗᓂ.

ᒪᑉᓵᖅ: ᖅᑮᓴᓇᓗᒃᑕᐅᖅ—

ᖅᑭ'ᖕᒐᖅᑐᖅ: ᓄᑦᖃᖕᒐᑦᑎᐊᒻᒪᓂᒡᓗᔪ, ᐊᐳᖁᖅᑕᐃᑎᔪᐃᑦᑎ.

ᒪᑉᓵᖅ: ᖄ.

ᐊᖑᑕᐅᑦᕿᔭᖅ ᒌ-ᑏ: ᔪᓇᐅᒐᕙᑦ?

ᖅᑭ'ᖕᒐᖅᑐᖅ: *(ᒪᑉᓵᕐᔫᑦ)* ᐃᔪᒐᒃᐱᑦ ᓴᐅᒥᖅᓯᐊ ᖃᖕᒐᑦᑕᖅᑎᓗᒍ
ᔪᒃᑲᐃᓗᑎᑦ ᓅᒥᐊᕐᓗᑎᓪᓗ ᓴᐅᒥ'ᓄᑦ—ᖃᐅᔮᓴᓂᑦ ᑐᑎᒥᐊᒃᓴ'ᓂᒃ ᓇᓅᑉ
ᑐᒦ'ᓄᑦ . . . ᑕᐃᒪᓗ ᐃᔪᒐᒃᐱᑦ ᑕᓯᖅᐱᖅᓯᐊ ᖁ'ᒍᒃᑎᒥᐊᕐᓗᒍ ᑕ'ᓇ
ᐊᐳᓂᐊᖅᐸᒡᓗᑎᑦ . . .

*ᒪᑉᓵᖅ ᔪᒃᑲᐃᑦᑐᐸᔪᓐᓄᐊᕐᓱᖕᒥᒃ ᐊᐳᖁᖁᔪᐊᓯᖅᓱᓂ
ᖅᑭ'ᖕᒐᖅᑐᕐᓗ ᖃᐅᔮᓴᓯᖅᓱᓂᒥᑦ ᓇᓅᑉ ᑐᒥᖕᒥᑦ.*

ᖅᑭ'ᖕᒐᖅᑐᖅ: . . . ᖃᓂᖅᑐᖕᒐ ᖃᓄᕐᓯᖕᒐᔫᒃᓴᐃᑕ ᑐᒥᖕᒥᑦ
ᔪᒦᓐᓇᔭᓂᐊᒃᓴᐃ'ᓂᒃ ᓇᓗᓇᐃᔭᖁᔪᐊᖅᓱᖕᒐ . . .

*ᓴᓪᓚᖅᓴᖅᔪᒪᕙᒌᑦᑎᐊᖅᑐᒥᒃ ᐆᕐᒥᒃ ᐊᑐᖅᓱᓂ ᖅᑭ'ᖕᒐᖅᑐᖅ ᐆᔪ'ᒪᑦ
ᓇᓅᑉ ᑐᒥᐊ'ᓂᒃ, ᐊᐳᑕᐅ'ᓗᓂ ᐃᓗᐃᑦᑑᑎ'ᓗᓂᐅᒃ ᐃᑎᔮ ᐆᕐᔪᑦ.*

ᑑᕗᐊᕐᑦ: ᓇᓄᖅᑲᕐᓂ'ᒪᑦ ᑕᓴᒪᓂ?

ᖅᑭ'ᖕᒐᖅᑐᖅ: ᐃᕝᔭᒻᒪᓂᒃ.

ᑖ: ᔪᓇᐅᕝᕙᑎ ᔪᒥ?

QI'NGAQTUQ: Fake ice?

DUFORT: Yeah, the reflectors can be remodelled or remotely folded up in the event of severe weather—that's the theory—and we're also—

TUUTALIK: *(off stage)* SECURITY.

QI'NGAQTUQ: *(very gently mocking)* Security.

MR. GRIFFITH-THOMSON: Getting mighty crowded in this part of the world.

TUUTALIK, a security guard enters, fully loaded.

TUUTALIK: What's your business here?

MR. GRIFFITH-THOMSON: Who are you?

MATSON: Oceanus Adventures—we're just waiting for our colleagues to finish up a shoot.

TUUTALIK: Shooting what—caribou? Bears?

MATSON: No, an ad—a photograph for our investment brochure.

TUUTALIK: How'd you get up here?

MATSON: Chopper. It should be arriving any—

TUUTALIK: What make?

MATSON: Pardon me?

TUUTALIK: The chopper.

AINSWORTH: Airbus—H230, I think—why?

LEE: Has there been an accident?

ᕐᑭ'ᖕᒐᖅᑐᖅ ᐹᖅᓯᒪᔪᖅ ᑐᒥ ᔭᑦᕐᑭ'ᑐᓂᐅᒃ.

ᕐᑭ'ᖕᒐᖅᑐᖅ: . . . ᐅᕙᓂ, ᐃᓗᐊᓂ.

ᓛ: . . . ᔨᔩᖅᓱᒃ.

ᕐᑭ'ᖕᒐᖅᑐᖅ: ᐃᔨᒎᑕ ᒪᒥᐊ'ᓂᑦ ᐊᒥᕐᕙᓛᓐᓄᐊᕐᓂᒃ ᑎᒍᔭᓇᔪᐊᖅᑐᖕᒐ. ᕐᑲᐅᔩᔭᕐᓴᔨᐊᖅᓗᒥᑦ ᑕᔭᑉᑯᐊᑦ ᐊᔪᕐᓇᖅᑐᕐᓴᓗᐃᑦ ᒥᑭᕙᓪᓛ'ᒪᑕ ᐊᐳ'ᒧᓪᓗ ᐊᑦᑕᑕᖅᔨᒪ'ᓗᑎᒃ ᒥᑭ'ᒪᑕ ᑐᒥᑦ. ᐊᐅᖕᒋᑦ ᕐᑲᐅᔩᔭᖅᓗᒋᑦ ᐱᑦᑕᐅᑉᕐᑭᔭᐅᔫᒐᓗᐊᖅ ᑭᔨᐊᓂᒃ ᐱᑦᕐᑯᔭᐅᔨᐃ'ᒪᑦ ᒪᓕᒐᑎᒍᑦ— ᒪᓕᒐᕐᒥᒃ ᑖᑉᓱᒪᓂᒃ ᔭᓇᕐᑲᑕᐅᒐᓗᐊᖅᑐᖕᒐᓕ.

ᓂᕕᐊᕋ: ᐆᒪᔪᓄᑦ ᐃᓗᐊᖅᓴᐃᔩᐅᕕᑦ?

ᕐᑭ'ᖕᒐᖅᑐᖅ: ᐃᓗᐊᖅᓴᐃᔩᐅᖖᒋᑦᑐᖕᒐ ᐆᒪᔪᓕᕆᔩᑐᐃᓐᓇᐅᔪᖕᒐᓕ. ᐊᑎᕐᑲᖅᑐᖕᒐ ᕐᑭ'ᖕᒐᖅᑐᖅ ᑖᓇᔪᐅᒥᒃ.

ᒪᑉᔭᑳᖅ: ᐅᕙᖕᒐᓕ ᒪᑉᔭᑳᖅ ᑕᐃ-ᒥᒃ ᐊᑎᕐᑲᖅᑐᖕᒐ. ᐅᓇᓗ ᐊᐃᓐᓯᕗᐊᑦ, ᐅᑯᐊᓪᓗ ᓄᓕᐊᕇᒃ ᒍᕆᕕᔅ-ᑖᓪᓴᓐ, ᐅᓇᓗ ᓛ, ᐅᓇᑉᑕᐅᖅ ᑑᕗᐊᕐᑦ ᐅᓇᓗ ᓂᕕᐊᕋ. ᓇ'ᒥᓂᕐᑲᖅᑎᐅᔪᒍᑦ—ᐳᓚᕋᖅᑐᓕᕆ'ᓗᑕ ᑕᕆᐅᑦᑯᑎᒍᑦ ᐅᒥᐊᕐᔪᐊᑦᑯᑦ—ᐅᕙᑉᑎ'ᓂᒃ ᑐᔭᐅᒪᔪᒃᓴᐅᕗᑎᑦ.

ᕐᑭ'ᖕᒐᖅᑐᖅ: ᑐᔭᐅᒪᔫᕐᓴᐃᑦᑐᖕᒐ ᐃᓕᑉᓯ'ᓂᒃ.

ᐊᐃᓐᓯᕗᐊᑦ: ᐳᓚᕋᖅᑐᖅᔪᐅᑎᓕᐅᓕᖅᑐᒍᑦ ᐅᒥᐊᕐᔪᐊᓇᓗᖕᒥᒃ, ᐃᒃᑕᕆᒃᑐᕌᓗᖕᒥᒃ, ᐊᔨᕈᓚᐃᑦᑐᑦᑎᐊᕙᖕᒥᒃ, ᔨᑯᔨᐅᑕᐅᔪᑦᑎᐊᕙᓇᓗᖕᒥᒃ. ᐊᕙᑎᒥᒃ ᔨᕈᖅᑎᓚᐃ'ᓗᓂ, ᕐᑭᓇᓗᒃᑲᓄᑦ ᐊᑦᑕᓇᖖᒋᑦᑐᖅ ᐊᒃᑕᑯᒃᓴᓕᐅᖖᒋᑎᒋᓂᖕᒐ 93%-ᖖᒍᒻᒪᕆ'ᒪᓪᓗ—

ᓛ: ᔭᕆᒻᒪᔅᔮᑲᔅᔭ ᐅᓇ ᕐᑲᐅᔩᑉᑲᐃᔩᑐᑦ.

ᐊᐃᓐᓯᕗᐊᑦ: ᕐᑲᐅᔩᑉᑲᐃᔩᒋᔭᐅᔪᖕᒐᓕ—ᔭᓃᕆᔭᕋ!

ᕐᑭ'ᖕᒐᖅᑐᖅ: ᐳᓚᕋᖅᑐᖅᔨᐅᑎᓂᒃ ᐅᒥᐊᕐᔪᐊᕐᑲᖅᐸᓪᓛᓕ'ᒪ ᑕᔭᒪᓂ ᐊᐳᖅᑕᓕᖅᑐᓪᓘᓐᓃᑦ ᑲᔨᒃᑕᓕᖅᓗᑎᒃ ᐊᒥᔾᕋᖅᐸᓪᓛᕐᓃ'ᓄᑦ.

ᐊᕐᓇᐅᑦᕐᑭᔮᖅ ᑮ-ᑏ: ᔭᓇᔪᒍᓪᓗ ᔪᑯᖖᒍᐊᕐᓂᒃ, ᐊᖕᒋᔪᓇᓗᖕᓂᒃ ᕐᑲᒃᑯᕆᒃᑐᓂᒃ ᐳᒃᑕᔪᓂᒃ ᔨᕐᑭᓂᐅᑉ ᕐᑲᐅᒪᓂᐊ ᐆᓇᖅᐸᓪᓛᕐᑯᖖᒋ'ᓗᒍ—

ᕐᑭ'ᖕᒐᖅᑐᖅ: ᔪᑯᖖᒍᐊᕐᓂᒃ?

TUUTALIK: No, just checking. I hear that line a lot—"Chopper's coming to pick us up." There's lots of illegal hunting up here, illegal drilling—folks getting up to all kinds of mischief. I need to see some ID.

MATSON hands TUUTALIK some ID.

Matson Day?

MATSON: Yes.

TUUTALIK: *(to MR. GRIFFITH-THOMSON)* And you?

Everyone hands TUUTALIK a piece of ID except QI'NGAQTUQ.

(to QI'NGAQTUQ) You with them?

QI'NGAQTUQ: No.

TUUTALIK: *(to QI'NGAQTUQ)* ID.

QI'NGAQTUQ: Why do we have to show you our ID?

TUUTALIK begins handing back the IDs to their owners.

TUUTALIK: *(to QI'NGAQTUQ)* Because I work for Circumpolar Oil and you're standing inside the outside perimeter of the fence—Dufort Bonnière?

DUFORT: *Oui.*

QI'NGAQTUQ: We're not inside the fence.

TUUTALIK: No, but you're too close to the perimeter fence—Lori Griffith-Thomson?

MRS. GRIFFITH-THOMSON: That's me—thank you.

AINSWORTH: The fence is way over there.

TUUTALIK: For safety and security reasons, Circumpolar Oil established a thirty-metre perimeter around the *outside* of the fence—Rivera Garcia.

ᑑᕗᐊᕐᑦ: ᐋ, ᑕᕵᑉᑯᐊᑦ ᐳᒃᑕᖤᑦ ᓈᑕᐅᔪᖕᓇᖅᑐᑦ ᖠᓚᑦᑕᐅᙱᓐᓂᖅᐸᑦ ᒪᓪᓕᖅᐸᑦ ᐴᖅᑕᐅᔪᖕᓇᕐᓂᐊ’ᒪᑕ ᐅᖕᒐᖠᒃᑐᒥᑦ ᖃᓇᑕᐅᕷᒃᑯᑦ—ᕵᓇᕷᐅᑦᑎᐊᕋᓗᐊᕈᑎᒃ ᑕ’ᓇᐃᓂᐊᖅᑐᒃᓴᐅᕗᑦ, ᑕᐃᒪᓗ—

ᑑᑕᓕᒃ: (*ᐊᕙ’ᖕᒐᑦ ᓂᐱᑐᖤᒥᒃ*) ᐱᓕᐅᖠᒪᑦ!

ᕿ’ᖕᒐᖅᑐᖅ: (*ᐃᓪᓚᐅᑎᑦᓯᕝᐆᖅᓗᓂᐅᒃ ᐲᕵᓇ’ᓗᒍ*) ᐱᓕᐅᖠᒪᓇᓗᒃ.

ᐊᖑᑕᐅᑦᕿᕷᖅ ᑮ-ᑏ: ᐃᓄᐃᓚᒦᓇᖤᒥᓇᕋᓗᐊᖅᑐᒍᓪᓚ.

ᑑᑕᓕᒃ ᐃᖠᖅᓗᓂ ᐱᓕᐅᖠᒪᙳᐊᖑ’ᓗᓂ—ᖠᖅᑯᑎᕝᖤᑎᖅᑲᖅᓗᓂ.

ᑑᑕᓕᒃ: ᕵᒪᓂ ᖤᒐᑉᖠ?

ᐊᖑᑕᐅᑦᕿᕷᖅ ᑮ-ᑏ: ᖤᓇᐅᖤᑎᓪᓚ?

ᒪᑉᕵᑳᖅ: ᐳᓚᕋᖅᑐᓕᓈᐅᖤᒍᑦ ᐅᒥᐊᕐᖤᐊᑦᑯᑦ ᑕᓇᐅᕐᒥ—ᐅᑕᖅᑭᖠᓐᓇᖅᑐᒍᑦ ᕵᓇᖅᑲᑎᑉᑎ’ᓂᒃ ᖤᓐᓇᖤᐊᖅᑐᓂᒃ.

ᑑᑕᓕᒃ: ᖤᓐᓇᖤᐊ’ᒪᑕ—ᑐᒃᑐᖠᐅᖅᑐᖅ? ᓇᓄᖅᖠᐅᖅᑐᖅ?

ᒪᑉᕵᑳᖅ: ᐋᖅᑭ, ᓇ’ᒥᓂᑉᑎ’ᓄᑦ ᖃᐅᖡᑉᑲᐃᕝᖤᑎᓕᐅᖅᑐᑦ—ᐊ’ᖡᓕᐅᕋᖤᐊᖅᓗᑎᒃ ᖃᐅᖡᑉᑲᐃᕝᖤᑎᒧᑦ ᐃᓕᕷᐅᖤᒃᓴᓂᒃ.

ᑑᑕᓕᒃ: ᖃᓄᕐᓕ ᑕᕵᒨᖕᒐᐅᕙᖠ?

ᒪᑉᕵᑳᖅ: ᖁᓕᒥᒎᓕᑦᑯᑦ. ᖃᐃᖤᖕᒐᕐᓂᐊᓕᖅᑐᒃᓴᐅ—

ᑑᑕᓕᒃ: ᖃᓄᓇᑦᑐᖅ?

ᒪᑉᕵᑳᖅ: ᖤᕚ?

ᑑᑕᓕᒃ: ᖁᓕᒥᒎᓕᒃ ᖃᓄᓇᑦᑐᖅ.

ᐊᐃᓐᓯᕗᐊᑦ: H230-ᖑᖅᑰᖅᑐᖅ, ᖤ’ᒪᓪᓕ?

ᓖ: ᑲᑉᖠᒪᖤᖅᑲᕋᓗᐊ’ᒪᑦ ᑕ’ᓇᐃᑦᑐᒥᒃ?

ᑑᑕᓕᒃ: ᐋᖅᑭ. ᑐᕵᖅᐸᒃᑲᒪ ᑕ’ᓇ ᖁᓕᒥᒎᓕᒃ ᖃᐃᖤᖕᒐᕐᓂᐊᖅᑑᓚ’ᓗᑎᒃ ᖃᐃᓂᐊᙱᓪᒪᓇᒃᑎ’ᓗᒍ ᕵᓪᓗᖅᑲᑦᑕ’ᒪᑕ, ᐊᒥᖤᓇᓗᐃᑦ ᐱᓂᕐᓗᒃᑐᑦ

RIVERA: Yes.

TUUTALIK: Ryan Griffith-Thomson?

MR. GRIFFITH-THOMSON: None other.

TUUTALIK: *(to everyone)* Move six feet to your left and you're good. *(to QI'NGAQTUQ)* Can I see your ID?

QI'NGAQTUQ: There's no signage here that says there's an outside perimeter.

TUUTALIK: Guess you could say I'm the signage.

QI'NGAQTUQ: . . . I know you. Your mom is Ibřuq.

TUUTALIK: I need all of you to step further to your left.

The following dialogue between QI'NGAQTUQ and TUUTALIK can be spoken in Nattilingmiut or in a combination of English and Nattilingmiut.

QI'NGAQTUQ: *Anaanait Ibřurmik atiqaqtuq? [Is your mother's name Ibřuq?]*

TUUTALIK: *Ningiumnik uqauhiqaqquuqtutit. Anaanaga atiqaqtuqtauq Ibřurmik, amaupta ningiunganit. [Perhaps you mean my grandmother. But my mom is also named after Ibřuq our great grandmother's grandmother.]*

QI'NGAQTUQ: *Ii itqaumattiaqtara ningiut—tiphinaqturaaluu'luni quvian-aqpakhimařuq, ingiuqtinaluu'luni. Tuutaliunniravit . . . [Yes, I remember your grandmother—she was comical and she was such a great singer! You must be Tuutalik.]*

TUUTALIK: *Ii Tuutaliuřunga. [Yes, I am Tuutalik.]*

MR. GRIFFITH-THOMSON: *(to DUFORT)* We need a translator.

DUFORT: For sure. Auto-translate.

ᐆᒪᖀᖅᔪᐅᖅᑐᑎᒃ, ᐅᖅᓱᕐᖀᐊᖅᔪᐅᖅᑐᑎᒡᑐ—ᒪᓕᕆᕐᓂᒃ ᔨᕋᐃᖠᑦ. ᑕᑯᓚᑦᑲ ᓇᑐᓇᐃᑉᑯᑕᓇᔮᖅᔪ.

ᒪᑉᔮᑳᖅ ᓇᑐᓇᐃᑉᑯᑎᓂ ᐊᑎᕐᑲᕐᕕᕆᔮᓂ ᒪᓂ'ᑐᓂᐅᒃ.

ᑑᑕᓕᒃ: ᐊᑏᑦ ᒪᑉᔮᑳᖅ ᑕᐃ?

ᒪᑉᔮᑳᖅ: ᐄ.

ᑑᑕᓕᒃ: *(ᐊᖑᑕᐅᑦᕿᔮᖅ ᑮ-ᑏᒍᑦ) ᐃᔮᕕᓪᓕ?*

ᑕᒪᐃᑕ ᓇᑐᓇᐃᑉᑯᑕᓇᔮᐃ'ᓂᒃ ᐊᑎᕐᑲᕐᕕᕆᔮᐃ'ᓂᒃ ᑐᓂᔪᔪᒪᓕ'ᒪᑕ ᑑᑕᓕᖕᒍᑦ ᑭᔪᐊᓂᒃ ᕿ'ᖕᒐᖅᑐᖅ ᐱᙱᑦᑐᖅ.

ᑑᑕᓕᒃ: *(ᕿ'ᖕᒐᖅᑐᒍᑦ)* ᐅᑯᓇᓅᕐᑲᑕᐅᖀᑎᑦ?

ᕿ'ᖕᒐᖅᑐᖅ: ᐄᕿ.

ᑑᑕᓕᒃ: *(ᕿ'ᖕᒐᖅᑐᒍᑦ)* ᐊᑕᐃ ᓇᑐᓇᐃᑉᑯᑦ ᑕᑯᓚᒎ.

ᕿ'ᖕᒐᖅᑐᖅ: ᔨ'ᒪᓪᓕ ᓴᑦᕐᑯᒻᒥᓇᐊᕐᑲᖅᐱᑕ ᓇᑐᓇᐃᑉᑯᑕᑉᑎ'ᓂᒃ?

ᑑᑕᓕᒃ ᐅᑎᖅᑎᑦᑎᕙᓪᓕᐊᖀᖅ ᓇᑐᓇᐃᑉᑯᑕᕐᓂᒃ.

ᑑᑕᓕᒃ: *(ᕿ'ᖕᒐᖅᑐᒍᑦ)* ᐅᖅᓱᕐᖀᐊᓕᓇᔮᕐᖀᐊᓂ ᓵᓇᔮᐅᒐᒪ ᐱᖀᖓᐅᑎᕐᑲᕐᕕᕆᔮᑉᑕᑐ ᐃᑐᐊᓅᑦᑲᕕᑦ ᑭᒡᓕᐊ ᑕᐃᑲ—ᑑᕗᐊᕐᑦ ᐸᓂᐊᓇ? *(ᑐᖅᑐᓚ'ᑐᒍ)*

ᑑᕗᐊᕐᑦ: *(ᐅᐃᕚᑐᑦ ᑭᐅ'ᑐᓂ)* ᐄ.

ᕿ'ᖕᒐᖅᑐᖅ: ᑭᒡᓕᐊᑕ ᐃᑐᐊᓅᙱᒻᒪᓇᒃᑐᒍᑦ.

ᑑᑕᓕᒃ: ᖃᓂᒋᕙᓪᓖᕋᕕᐅᒃ ᐅᓇ ᑭᒡᓕ ᔪᓚᓪᓕᖅᓓᐅᖀᖅ—ᑐᐊᓇ ᒍᓇᕙᔅ-ᑖᒻᓴᓐ *(ᐊᕐᓇᐅᑦᕿᓴᕐᒍᑦ ᑐᖅᑐᓚ'ᑐᓂ)*

ᐊᕐᓇᐅᑦᕿᔮᖅ ᑮ-ᑏ: ᐅᕙᖓ ᐄ ᔨᕙᔫᖅ.

ᐊᐃᓐᓱᕗᐊᑦ: ᐅᖓᓯᒃᑐᓇᑐᒃ ᑕᐃᒪ ᑭᒡᓕ ᑖᕙᓂᕌᑑ'ᒪᑦ ᔮᒪᓅᙱᒻᒪᓇᒃᑐᖅ.

QI'NGAQTUQ: *Ilannarigaluara'ni aniga Paningajak. [You were friends with my brother, Paningajak.]*

TUUTALIK: *Ii tuharaluarama hana'mat Iqalungni. [Yes, I had heard he was working in Iqaluit.]*

QI'NGAQTUQ: *Ii. Ilihairiuřuq, ilihaiva'mat Inuktut. [Yes. He's a teacher, teaches Inuktut.]*

TUUTALIK: *Hunauvva. Atai avunngarannirit. [Good for him. Now move over.]*

QI'NGAQTUQ: *Hu'malli ukunani hanavit? [Why are you working for this company?]*

TUUTALIK: *Akłuřut atqunariaqa'mata annaumařřutikšatuinnarnut akłuittullu ihumakšurniqšau'mata. [The poor are forced to compromise for their basic needs, while the rich have choices.]*

QI'NGAQTUQ: *Paningajak uqaallakhimařuq, "Tuutalik ajugailaanguřuq ihihaqatigiini." [Paningajak once said, "Tuutalik is the smartest person in my class."]*

TUUTALIK: *Paningajagli ta'na ihumagikpanga qujana. Una hanaariřara pittauřuq. Akiliqtauttiarama tujurmiviqaqtitau'lunga akiqanngittumik hannavimni. [It's Paningajak's business if he believes that, but this is a good job. Good pay. They even give me accommodation on site—for free.]*

QI'NGAQTUQ: *Nutaarmik iliharviqaliqtuq Uqšuqtuurmi, hanaakšaqaqłunilu qauřihaqtinut, kihianiktauq miřvingmi piliuhimannguaqšanik qiniqtut. [There's a new school in Gjoa Haven, and job openings, mostly in science, but they need security guards at the airport.]*

TUUTALIK: *Hu'malli akpiutinnahuaqpinga qauřimanngittuuřaaqhiqtutut—makimařunga taipšumanituunngittunga. [Why do you speak to me like I don't know what I'm doing—I know what I'm doing. I'm not like I was five years ago.]*

LEE: This is so weird.

ᑑᑕᓕᒃ: ᐱᓂᕐᓗᒃᑕᐅᕐᑯᖕᒋ'ᓗᑕ ᐱ'ᓂᕐᓗᒃᑐᕐᑲᕐᑯᓇᒍᓗ ᑭᒡᓕᓕᐅᖅᓯᒪᒐᑉᑕ 30 ᒦᑕᓂᒃ ᓯᓚᓪᓕᖅᓱᐅᔪᒥᒃ ᑭᒡᓕᒻᒪᓇᖕᒥᑦ—ᓇᕕᐊᖅ ᒫᓰᔅ. *(ᑐᖅᓴᓚ'ᓗᒍ)*

ᓇᕕᐊᖅ: ᐄ.

ᑑᑕᓕᒃ: ᖃᐃᓴᓐ ᒍᓇᕙᔅ-ᑖᒻᓴᓐ? *(ᐊᖑᑕᐅᑦᕿᓴᕐᒧᑦ ᑐᖅᓴᓚ'ᓗᓂ)*

ᐊᖑᑕᐅᑦᕿᔭᖅ ᒋ-ᑎ: ᐅᕙᖕᖓ ᑕᔅᕙ.

ᑑᑕᓕᒃ: *(ᑕᒪᐃ'ᓄᑦ)* ᑕᒻᐸᔪ ᐊᑯᖕᖓᖃᓐᓂᑲᕈᐸᔪ ᔅᐅᒥᐸᔪ'ᓄᑦ ᐱᔦᐃᕐᓂᐊᖅᑕᐸᔪ. *(ᕿ'ᖕᖓᖅᑐᒧᑦ)* ᐊᑕᐃ ᓇᓗᓇᐃᐸᑯᑕᓇᔭᐃᑦ ᑕᑯᓚᒍ.

ᕿ'ᖕᖓᖅᑐᖅ: ᑎᑎᖃᖅᔪᒪᔪᕐᑲᖕᒋᒻᒪᓇ'ᒪᑦ ᓯᓚᓪᓕᖅᓱᐅᔪᒥᒃ ᑭᒡᓕᕐᑲᐸᔪᐊᕐᓂᐊ'ᓂᒃ.

ᑑᑕᓕᒃ: ᑐᔅᐅᒪᑎᑦᑎᔮᐅᔪᖕᖓᓕ.

ᕿ'ᖕᖓᖅᑐᖅ: . . . ᕐᑲᐅᔮᒪᔭᒋᑦ. ᐊᓅᓇᐃᑦ ᐃᐸᔪᕐᒥᒃ ᐊᑎᑲᖅᑐᖅ.

ᑑᑕᓕᒃ: ᑕᒻᐸᔪ ᐊᑯᖕᖓᖃᓐᓂᕐᑯᓴᐸᔪ ᔅᐅᒥᐸᔪ'ᓄᑦ.

ᑕᐃᒪᓗ ᕿ'ᖕᖓᖅᑐᕐᓗ ᑑᑕᓕᒡᓗ ᐃᓅᖓᒥ ᐅᕐᑲᒪᕐᑲᑎᒌᓕᖅᑐᒃ ᓇᑦᑎᓕᖕᒥᐅᑐᑦ ᐃᓛ'ᓂ ᕐᑲᐸᓗᓇᐅᔭᖅᐸᒃᑭ'ᓗᑎᒃ.

ᕿ'ᖕᖓᖅᑐᖅ: ᐊᓅᓇᐃᑦ ᐃᐸᔪᕐᒥᒃ ᐊᑎᑲᖅᑐᖅ?

ᑑᑕᓕᒃ: ᓂᖕᒋᐊᒻᓂᒃ ᐅᕐᑲᐅᔦᕐᑲᖅᑰᖅᑐᑎᑦ. ᐊᓅᓇᖓᐸᑕᐅᖅ ᐊᑎᕐᑲ'ᒥᔪᖅ ᐃᐸᔪᕐᒥᒃ ᐊᒪᐅᐸᑕ ᓂᖕᒋᐅᖕᖓᓂᑦ.

ᕿ'ᖕᖓᖅᑐᖅ: ᐄ ᐃᑦᕐᑲᐅᒪᑦᑎᐊᖅᑕᖅ ᓂᒋᐅᑦ—ᑎᐸᔦᓇᖅᑐᖅᓘ'ᓗᓂ ᕐᑯᕕᐊᓇᖅᐸᒃᔦᒪᔪᖅ, ᐃᖕᒋᐅᖅᑎᓇᓘ'ᓗᓂ! ᑑᑕᓕᐅᓐᓂᖃᕕᑦ . . .

ᑑᑕᓕᒃ: ᐄ ᑑᑕᓕᐅᔪᖕᖓ.

ᐊᖑᑕᐅᑦᕿᔭᖅ ᒋ-ᑎ: ᑐᔅᔮᕐᑲᓇᐊᕐᑲᖅᑯᓕᖅᑐᒍᑦ.

ᑑᕗᐊᕐᑦ: ᐊᑕᐃ . . .ᕐᑲᓇᑕᐅᔭᒃᑯᑦ.

ᕿ'ᖕᖓᖅᑐᖅ: ᐃᓚᓐᓇᓇᖓᓗᐊᖅ'ᓂ ᐊᓂᖓ, ᐸᓂᖕᖓᓴᒃ.

ᑑᑕᓕᒃ: ᐄ, ᑐᔅᖃᓗᐊᖅᑐᖕᖓ ᔅᓇ'ᒪᑦ ᐃᕐᑲᓗᖕᓂ.

QI'NGAQTUQ: *(kindly) Pittauřumik aturahugiřutit kihianik tammaumařutit. Inuuhikšammari'nik hagviqtukšaruravit. [Tuutalik, you may think you have found something, but you have lost something again—perhaps you've lost yourself.]*

TUUTALIK: *Inuuhipkut tammaumanngittungali—una hanaakšapituałługa! Avunngarannikait—ataị! [I'm not lost—this job is the only choice I have! Move now—go away!]*

QI'NGAQTUQ: *Ilagiřatit niqikšai'nik pijaaqaraluaqtutit kihianik qanurliuriakša'nik ihumanahuariaqaravit ili'nut pittaupqiřaqaqtukšauvuq. [I know you have to feed your family, but think of what you're doing. There must be a better way.]*

TUUTALIK: *Kamagihuinnga ima'naaqtuqtaujumanngittunga. [Look, this is not your business.] (in English to* QI'NGAQTUQ*)* You have to move NOW— *(to the others)* ALL OF YOU!

MR. GRIFFITH-THOMSON: Hey, take it easy—we're waiting for our helicopter.

QI'NGAQTUQ: I have a right to stand on the same land the animals stand on, Tuutalik.

TUUTALIK: I know, but there's an *outside* perimeter for thirty metres beyond the fence and my job is to make sure no one trespasses, so if you want do your business *inside* the *outside* perimeter and don't want to show me ID, then I'll have to see a letter from whomever you're working for.

QI'NGAQTUQ: I can't know ahead of time if a bear's going to wander into the *inside* of your *outside* perimeter—animals don't recognize borders—and you're standing on one of the tracks!

TUUTALIK: And you're standing on company property!

QI'NGAQTUQ: When I finish examining the damn track *you're standing on*, I'll move six feet to my damn left.

TUUTALIK: I'll be watching to see that you damn well do.

ᕿ’ᖕᒐᖅᑐᖅ: ᐄ. ᐃᓕᓴᐃᔨᐅᔪᖅ, ᐃᓕᓴᐃᕙ’ᒪᑦ ᐃᓄᒃᑐᑦ.

ᑑᑕᓕᒃ: ᔭᓇᐅᕝᕙ. ᐊᑕᐃ ᐊᕗᙳᒐᕋᓐᓂᓕᖏᑦ.

ᕿ’ᖕᒐᖅᑐᖅ: ᔭ’ᒪᓪᓕ ᐅᑯᓇᓂ ᓴᓇᕕᑦ?

ᑑᑕᓕᒃ: ᐊᒃᓱᔪᑦ ᐊᑦᕐᑯᓇᓇᐊᖅᑲ’ᒪᑕ ᐊᓐᓇᐅᒪᔾᔪᑎᒃᓴᑐᐃᓐᓇᕐᓄᑦ
ᐊᒃᓱᐃᑦᑐᓪᓗ ᐃᔭᒪᔪᕐᓂᖅᓴᐅ’ᒪᑕ.

ᕿ’ᖕᒐᖅᑐᖅ: ᐸᓂᖕᒐᔭᒃ ᐅᖄᓪᓚᒃᔭᒪᔪᖅ, “ᑑᑕᓕᒃ ᐊᔪᒐᐃᓛᙳᔪᖅ
ᐃᓕᓴᖃᑎᖏᓂ.”

ᑑᑕᓕᒃ: ᐸᓂᖕᒐᔭᒡᓕ ᑕ’ᓇ ᐃᔭᒪᕆᒃᐸᖕᒐ ᖁᔭᓇ, ᐅᓇ ᓴᓈᓇᔾᔪᖃ ᐱᑦᑕᐅᔪᖅ.
ᐊᑭᓕᖅᑕᐅᑦᑎᐊᖃᒪ ᑐᔪᕐᒥᕙᖅᑲᖅᑎᑕᐅ’ᓗᖓ ᐊᑭᖅᑲᙱᑦᑐᒥᒃ ᓴᓇᕕᓪᓂ.

ᕿ’ᖕᒐᖅᑐᖅ: ᓄᑖᕐᒥᒃ ᐃᓕᓴᕐᕕᖅᓕᖅᑐᖅ ᐅᖅᓱᖅᑑᕐᒥ, ᓯᓈᒃᓴᖅᑲᖅᓗᓂᓗ
ᖃᐅᔨᓴᖅᑎᓄᑦ, ᑭᔭᐊᓂᒃᑕᐅᖅ ᒥᕝᕕᖕᒥ ᐱᓕᐅᔭᒪᙳᐊᖅᓯᓂᒃ ᕿᓂᖅᑐᑦ.

ᑑᑕᓕᒃ: ᔭ’ᒪᓪᓕ ᐊᒃᐱᐅᑎᓇᔭᐊᖅᐱᖕᒐ ᖃᐅᔨᒪᙱᑦᑑᔭᖅᔪᖅᑐᑐᑦ—
ᒪᑭᒪᔭᖕᒐ. ᑕᐃᑉᓯᒪᓂᑑᙱᑦᑐᖕᒐ.

ᓛ: ᔭᔨᖀᓗᕐᓗᒃ ᓇᓗᓇᖅᑐᖀᓗᒃ.

ᕿ’ᖕᒐᖅᑐᖅ: (ᐱᑦᑎᐊᖅᓗᓂ) ᑑᑕᓕᒃ, ᐱᑦᑕᐅᔭᒥᒃ ᐊᑐᕋᔭᕆᔭᑎᑦ ᑭᔭᐊᓂᒃ
ᑕᒻᒪᐅᒪᔭᑎᑦ—ᐃᓅᔭᒃᓵᒻᒪᓇ’ᓂᒃ ᓴᓪᕖᔭᒃᓴᕈᕋᕕᑦ.

ᑑᑕᓕᒃ: ᐃᓅᔭᑉᑯᑦ ᑕᒻᒪᐅᒪᙱᑦᑐᖕᒐᓕ—ᐅᓇ ᓴᓈᒃᓴᐱᐊᕐᓗᒐ!
ᐊᕗᙳᒐᕋᓐᓂᑲᐃᑦ—ᐊᑕᐃ!

ᕿ’ᖕᒐᖅᑐᖅ: ᐃᓚᒥᔭᑎᑦ ᓂᕿᒃᓴᐃ’ᓂᒃ ᐱᔮᖅᑲᕋᓗᐊᖅᑐᑎᑦ
ᑭᔭᐊᓂᒃ ᖃᓄᕐᓕᐅᕆᐊᒃᓴ’ᓂᒃ ᐃᔭᒪᓇᔭᐊᕆᐊᖅᑲᕋᕕᑦ. ᐃᓕ’ᓄᑦ
ᐱᑦᑕᐅᑉᕿᔭᖅᑲᖅᑐᒃᓴᐅᕗᖅ.

ᑑᑕᓕᒃ: ᑲᒪᕆᔭᐃᙵ ᐃ’ᒪᓈᖅᑐᖅᑕᐅᔭᒪᙱᑦᑐᖕᒐ. (*ᕿ’ᖕᒐᖅᑐᒍᑦ
ᖃᑉᓄᓈᑑᖅᓗᓂ*) ᐊᕗᙳᒐᕋᓐᓂᓇᐊᖅᑲᖅᑐᑎᑦ ᐊᑕᐃ (ᐊᔫ’ᓄᑦ) ᑕᒪᑉᔭ ᐊᑕᐃ!

ᐊᙳᑕᐅᑦᕿᔭᖅ ᖀ-ᑏ: ᐱᔭᐃᓇᑦ—ᐅᑕᖅᑭᔭᒍᑦ ᖁᓕᒥᒎᓕᑉᑎ’ᓂᒃ.

ᕿ’ᖕᒐᖅᑐᖅ: ᓄᓇᒥ ᓇᖕᒋᖅᔪᔪᖕᓇᖅᑐᖕᒐ ᐆᒪᔭᑦ ᓄᓇᒋᔭᐃ’ᓂᒃᑕᐅᖅ, ᑑᑕᓕᒃ.

QI'NGAQTUQ: I bet you will—watching through Circumpolar's damn satellite surveillance.

TUUTALIK: I hope you find your bear.

QI'NGAQTUQ: It's not *my* bear—bears belong to everyone and to no one, and they have souls—*arnirniq*—or have you forgotten?

TUUTALIK: Please, everyone respect the perimeter . . . *(to QI'NGAQTUQ)* And you know something—my mom's happy I got this job because now she can eat good.

TUUTALIK exits. QI'NGAQTUQ goes back to examining tracks.

RIVERA: *(to QI'NGAQTUQ)* Small world.

QI'NGAQTUQ: Very small and very large.

MATSON: *(to QI'NGAQTUQ)* Did I hear you say bears have souls?

QI'NGAQTUQ: *(to MATSON)* Yes. Their souls are as alive as my skin, as this water, as your face. Do you have a problem with that?

MATSON: . . . No, not at all.

DUFORT: I'm agnostic myself, so I'm fine with humans having souls, but not animals.

QI'NGAQTUQ: Bears stand and walk on their hind legs, just like we do. In many of our stories they remove their fur coats and become humans then put their fur coats back on and become bears again. Humans and bears did not exist without the other.

MR. GRIFFITH-THOMSON: You're a scientist—a biologist—don't tell me you believe that stuff?

QI'NGAQTUQ: It's biological truth.

AINSWORTH: To each their own.

ᑑᑕᓕᒃ: ᐄᖑᒐᓗᐊᖅ, ᑭᓱᐊᓂᒃ ᓱᓚᓪᓕᖅᓯᕐᒥᒃ ᑭᒡᓕᖅᑳ’ᒪᑦ ᖄᖏᖅᑕᐅᑦᑕᐃᓕᑎᕆᐊᖅᑲᖅᑕᒻᓂᒃ ᓴᓈᓇᒐᑉᑯ. ᔪᓐᓇᔪᐊᕈᒪᒍᕕᑦ ᑕᕝᕙᓂ ᓱᓚᓪᓕᖅᓯᕐᒥ ᑐᓂᓵᖅᑲᕐᓂᐊᖅᑕ’ᒪ ᓇᑐᓇᐃᑉᑯᑕᕐᒥᒃ ᑎᑎᖅᑲᒥᒡᓗ ᐊᑕᓂᓇᓯᑉᓱ’ᓂᑦ.

ᕿ’ᖕᒐᖅᑐᖅ: ᖃᐅᔾᔨᒪᕙᑮᓚᐃᑦᑐᖕᒐ ᓇᓄᖅ ᔪᑯᑦᑎᐊᒍᑦ ᓄᓇᒥ ᐱᔪᖕᓂᐊᓇᐊᒃᓵ ᑭᒡᓕᑉ ᐃᓗᐊᒍᑦ ᔪᑯᑦᑎᐊᒍᓪᓘᓐᓃᑦ—ᐆᒪᔾᔪᑦ ᑲᒪᔪᙱ’ᒪᑕ ᑭᒡᓕᕐᕆᖕᓂᒃ—ᑐᒦ’ᓂᒃ ᖄᖕᒐᓃᑦᑲᕕᑦ ᑕᒃᑰᒃ ᑕᕝᕙ!

ᑑᑕᓕᒃ: ᓄᓇᒥᔾᔭᒻᓂᓗ ᐃ’ᓇᕕᑦ!

ᕿ’ᖕᒐᖅᑐᖅ: ᑐᒥᐊ ᑖᒻᓇ ᖃᐅᔾᔮᖅᑖᑭᑉᑯ ᑐᑎᔪᐃᑭ’ᓂ ᐊᕗᙵᕋᓐᓂᕐᓂᐊᖅᑯᖕᒐ ᔮᐅᒥᒻᓄᑦ.

ᑑᑕᓕᒃ: ᑕᐅᑐᖕᓂᐊᖅᐸᕆᑦ ᐊᕗᙵᕋᓐᓂᓇᐊᒃᓵ’ᓂᒃ ᑕ’ᓇ.

ᕿ’ᖕᒐᖅᑐᖅ: ᑕᐅᑐᖕᓂᐊᖅᑐᒃᓴᐅᕙᑎᑦ ᐅᖅᓱᕐᕙᐊᓕᓇᖑᑦᑯᑦ ᐊ’ᖑᓕᐅᑭᑎᐊᒍᑦ ᖁ’ᒨᒃᑕᐅᓱᒪᕙᑎᒍᑦ ᐊᓂᕐᓂᖅᑲᙱᑦᑐᒦᑦᑐᖅ ᕿᓚᖕᒥ ᑕᐃᒻᓇ.

ᑑᑕᓕᒃ: ᓇᓂᕐᓴ’ᓯᕙᐃᑦ ᐃᒻᓇ ᓇᓄᕐᓗᒃ ᕿᓂᖅᑕᕐᓗᒥᔾᔭᑦ.

ᕿ’ᖕᒐᖅᑐᖅ: ᐱᒥᙱᑕᕋᓕ—ᐱᒥᔾᔭᐅᒐᓗᐊᖅᓗᑎᒃ ᑕᒪᐃ’ᓄᑦ ᐱᒥᔾᔭᐅᙱᒻᒪᓇᒃᑭᓪᓗᑎᒃ, ᐊᓂᕐᓂᖅᑲᖅᓗᑎᒡᓗ—ᐳᐃᒍ’ᓱᒐᕕᓪᓘᓐᓃᑦ.

ᑑᑕᓕᒃ: ᑲᒪᒋᑦᑎᐊᖅᓱᐅᒃ ᐅᓇ ᑭᒡᓕ ᖄᖏᐅᑎᙱᓗᒍ . . . *(ᕿ’ᖕᒐᖅᑐᒧᑦ)*—ᖃᐅᔾᔨᒪᕐᑯᔾᔨᕙᕆᑦᑕᐅᖅ ᐊᓈᓇᒐ ᖁᕕᐊᔪᑦᑎᐊᖅᑐᖅ ᐆᒥᖕᒐᑦ ᓴᓈᖅᑲᓕᕋᒪ ᓂᓇᑦᑎᐊᖅᐸᓕ’ᒪᓐᖘᖅ.

ᑑᑕᓕᒃ ᐊᓂ’ᓗᓂ. ᕿ’ᖕᒐᖅᑐᕐᓗ ᔪᓕ ᖃᐅᔾᔭᐃᕙᖅ ᓇᓄᑦ ᑐᒦ’ᓂᒃ.

ᓇᕕᐊᒐ: *(ᕿ’ᖕᒐᖅᑐᒧᑦ)* ᔪᓇᐅᐤᕙ ᖃᐅᔾᔨᒪᔾᕙᑎᕙᓱᒃ.

ᕿ’ᖕᒐᖅᑐᖅ: ᓱᓚᕐᕙᐊᖅ ᒥᑭ’ᓗᓂᓗ ᐊᖏᕙᐊᓘ’ᓗᓂᓗ.

ᒪᑉᓭᑳᖅ: *(ᕿ’ᖕᒐᖅᑐᒧᑦ)* ᐅᖅᑲᕐᓗᐊᖅᐱᑦ ᓇᓄᐃᑦ ᐊᓂᕐᓂᖅᑲ’ᒪᑕ?

ᕿ’ᖕᒐᖅᑐᖅ: *(ᒪᑉᓯᑳᒧᑦ)* ᐄ. ᐊᓂᕐᓂᐊᒎᖅ ᐆᒪᔪᖅ ᐱᓪᒪᓇᓇᓗᒃ ᐅᕙᑉᑐᑦ ᓴᑉᑯᐊᖄᓗᐃᑦᑕᐅᖅ ᐱᓪᒪᓇᐅᓂᖏᑐᑦ ᐊᓂᕐᓂᐊᑦ ᑕ’ᓇ ᐱᓪᒪᓇᒃ. ᐃᓗᐃᔾᔪᑎᒋᕕᐅᒃ?

MRS. GRIFFITH-THOMSON: Culturally very intriguing, but Ms. Donoghue—

QI'NGAQTUQ points to a track.

QI'NGAQTUQ: Look—there's a bit of fur in this track.

LEE: Is there a real polar bear in this area?

QI'NGAQTUQ carefully scoops up the track.

QI'NGAQTUQ: I'm tracking him. This is a very old bear that has never been tagged. We have satellite imagery of him returning to this area a lot, but no real data beyond stuff like "he has only one ear"—look . . . tracks on top of tracks, like he was walking in circles.

DUFORT notices something in the slush.

DUFORT: . . . What's this?

DUFORT picks up HUMMIKTUQ's iřgak that WICKERS once had in his possession. Although they are badly chewed on one side, they have survived across time.

Looks like a . . . spoon.

QI'NGAQTUQ: Let's see. An iřgak. (*places it on her eyes*) From long ago.

MRS. GRIFFITH-THOMSON: . . . So exquisite. May I try it on?

QI'NGAQTUQ hands the iřgak to MRS. GRIFFTH-THOMSON, who puts them on.

MR. GRIFFITH-THOMSON: Bet that's worth a lot of money.

MRS. GRIFFITH-THOMSON: How old do you think they—

QI'NGAQTUQ swiftly puts up her hand.

ᒪᐸᓴ̵ᑳᖅ: ᐄᕿ . . . ᓈᒻᒪᒃᑐᖅ.

ᑑᕗᐊᕐᑦ: ᐅᕙᖓᓕ ᐅᒃᐱᙱᑦᑐᖓ, ᐃᓄᐃᓪᓕ ᐊᓂᕐᓂᖃᕈᖕᓇᖅᑐᑦ ᑕᕐᓂᖃᕐᓗᑎᒃ ᑭᔨ̵ᐊᓂᒃ ᐆᒪᓯ̵ᑦ ᐱᖃᓚᐃᑦᑑᓇᓯ̵ᒋᔭᑦᑲ.

ᕿ'ᖓᖅᑐᖅ: ᓇᓄᐃᑦ ᑭᖑᓪᓕᕐᒥ'ᓄᑦ ᓇᖏᖅᔨ̵ᔭᖕᓇᖅᑐᑦ ᐱᔪ̵ᒍᖕᓇᖅᑐᓪᓗ ᐅᕙᑉᑐᑦ. ᐅᓂᑉᑳᖅᑐᐊᑉᑎ'ᓂ ᑐᓴ̵ᐅᒪᓐᓇᖅᑐᖅ ᐊᒥᕐᒥ'ᓂᒃ ᐊᔨ̵ᕙᐃᔭᖕᓇ'ᒪᑕ ᐃᓄᙳᕐᓗᑎᒃ ᓇᓅᑉᔨ̵ᐊᕈᖕᓇᓇ'ᓗᑎᒃ ᑕ'ᓇᐃ'ᒪᑕᒎᖅ. ᐃᓄᐃᓪᓗ ᓇᓄᐃᓪᓗ ᐱᙳᖅᑎᑕᐅᔨ̵ᒪᓯ̵ᕕᓃᙴᖅ ᐊᑕᐅᑦᑎᑦᑯᑦ.

ᐊᖑᑕᐅᑦᕿᓴ̵ᖅ ᒌ-ᑏ: ᖃᐅᔨ̵ᓴ̵ᖅᑎᐅᓯ̵ᑎᑦ ᐆᒪᓯ̵ᑕᓇᔨ̵ᐅᓯ̵ᑎᑦ ᓯ̵ᑕᓯ̵ᒥᒃ ᓴ̵ᑉᑯᐊᑦ ᐅᒃᐱᓇᒐᓗᐊᖅᐱᒋᑦ?

ᕿ'ᖓᖅᑐᖅ: ᓯ̵ᑕᓯ̵ᖅ ᑕ'ᓇᐃᑦᑐᖅ.

ᐊᐃᓐᓯᕗᐊᑦ: ᐅᒃᐱᕈᒪᒍᓂ ᐅᒃᐱᕐᓚ.

ᐊᕐᓇᐅᑦᕿᓴ̵ᖅ ᒌ-ᑏ: ᐃᓚᑦᖁᓯᕐᒍᐊᖑ'ᓗᓂ ᑐᓴ̵ᕐᓂᖅᑐᖅ ᑭᔨ̵ᐊᓂᒃ ᓯ̵ᑕᓇᓯ̵ᒋ'ᔭᑲᕕᒋᑦ ᕿ'ᖓᖅᑐᖅ—

ᕿ'ᖓᖅᑐᖅ ᑎᑦᑯᐊᖅᓗᓂ ᑐᒥᒍᑦ.

ᕿ'ᖓᖅᑐᖅ: ᑕᒃᑯᒃ—ᐅᓇ ᑐᒥ ᒥᑦᖁᖃᖅᑐᖅ ᒥᑭᓯ̵ᓐᓄᐊᕐᒥᒃ.

ᑖ: ᓯ̵ᑕᓯ̵ᒥᒃ ᑕᓴ̵ᒪᓂ ᓇᓄᒻᒪᓇᒃᑕᖃᖅᑑᓐᓂ'ᒪᑦ?

ᕿ'ᖓᖅᑐᖅ ᓯ̵ᒃᑲᐃ'ᓗᓂ ᑎᒍᔫ ᐊᐳᑦ ᑐᒥᖃᖅᑐᖅ ᖃᓗᕋᖅᓗᒍ.

ᕿ'ᖓᖅᑐᖅ: ᒪᓕᒃᐸᒃᑕᕋ ᐅᓇ. ᐱᑐᖃᐸᓇᑑᓕᖅᑐᖅ ᓇᓄᑐᖃᓇᓗᒃ ᓇᓗᓇᐃᑉᑯᑕᓕᖅᑕᐅᔨ̵ᒪᓕᙱᒻᒪᓇᒃᑐᕐᑑᓐᓂᑦ. ᐊ'ᔮᓕᐅᑎᑎᒍᑦ ᑕᑯᒃᓴᐅᕙᒃᑑᒐᓗᐊᖅ ᑕᓴ̵ᒧᙵᓗᐅᓖᖓᓕᒥ, ᑭᔨ̵ᐊᓂᒃ ᖃᐅᔨ̵ᒪᙱᒻᒪᓇᒃᑕᕗᑦ ᖃᓄᓇᑦᑑᔫᒃᓭ ᖃᐅᔨ̵ᒪᒐᓗᐊᖅᓗᒍ ᐊᑕᐅᓯ̵ᓐᓇᕐᒥᒃ ᓯ̵ᐅᑎᖃᕐᓂ'ᒪᑦ—ᑕᒃᑯᒃ . . . ᑐᒥᑦ ᑐᒥᖃ'ᒥᓯ̵ᑦ ᐊᑖᒍᑦ, ᓰ̵ᕐᓗ ᐱᓯ̵ᐃᓐᓇ'ᒪᑦ ᐱᓯ̵ᒡᕕᒋᒐᓗᐊᖅᑕᒥᒍᑦ.

ᑑᕗᐊᕐᑦ ᐅᔅᔮᓇᓯ̵ᖃᓚ'ᒪᑦ ᓯ̵ᓇᒥᒃᑭᐊᖅ ᒪᓴ̵ᖕᒦᑦᑐᖅ).

ᑑᕗᐊᕐᑦ: . . . ᓯ̵ᓇᑉᑕᐅᖅ ᐅᓇ?

QI'NGAQTUQ: *Ata . . . [Listen . . .]*

DUFORT: What? *(sees something approaching, suddenly afraid) Ah câlisse!*

MATSON: *(suddenly afraid)* Oh my god, it's a . . . oh my god no . . . no, it's . . . *(laughs)* Oh my god, that's— *(calls and waves)* ROY!

Two polar bears enter, one on all fours with a fish in its mouth, one standing on its hind legs carrying camera equipment, a tripod, and a folded up plastic "ice floe."

LARKIN: Hey, sorry we're late—Roy kept losing his fish.

MATSON: You two are doing such an amazing job—for a second I thought you were *real*!

ROY: The fish kept sliding out of my mouth—the material's too slippery.

LARKIN: *(to ROY)* You've got to practise clenching those jaws.

LEE: *(to ROY)* You totally have the walk down.

ROY: Yeah, it's all in the motion of the bum, the neck, and the feet.

MATSON: *(to ROY and LARKIN)* Better get out of your suits—chopper will be here any minute . . . in fact, I think I hear it . . .

ROY and LARKIN take off their bear heads. ROY gets out of his bear suit as LARKIN fusses with the camera.

The sound of a distant chopper can be heard . . . faintly at first.

AINSWORTH: Larkin, did you get good shots?

LARKIN: Oh yeah, great stuff—tons of options, wait till you see these . . .

MATSON: Larkin, meet Qi'ngaqtuq, she's a biologist . . . *(to QI'NGAQTUQ)* . . . Larkin's a fabulous photographer—this is Roy—he's an animal movement trainer.

ᑑᕗᐊᕐᑦ ᓇᒡᕚᕋᒥ ᓱᒻᒥᒃᑐᕋᓘᑉ ᐃᔅᒐᖕᒐᓂᒃ ᐊᓗᕈᑎᑉ ᐱᓯᒪᓕᕋᓗᐊᖅᑖ'ᓂᒃ. ᓄᕗᐊᒍᑦ ᓱᕈᖅᑕᐅᓯᒪᓐᓄᐊᖅᑐᖅ ᑭᓯᐊᓂᒃ ᓱᓕ ᐱᑦᑕᐅᔅᐴᖅᑐᖅ ᐱᑐᖅᑲᐸᓚᓘᒐᓗᐊᖅᖢᓂ.

ᑑᕗᐊᕐᑦ: ᓱᓇᖅᐸᓗᒃᑐᖅ ᐅᓇ . . . ᐊᓘᑎᐅ'ᔭᔪᕐᓘᓐᓃᑦ.

ᖅᑭ'ᖕᒐᖅᑐᖅ: ᑕᑯᓚᒍ. ᐃᔅᒐᒃ ᐅᓇ *(ᐊᑎ'ᓗᓂᐅᒃ)* . . . ᑕᐃᑉᓱᒪᓂᑕᐅᔪᖅ.

ᐊᕐᓇᐅᑦᖅᑭᓴᖅ ᒌ-ᑏ: . . . ᑕᑯᕋᓐᓂᖅᑐᐸᓇᓗᒃ. ᐆᒃᑐᕐᓚᒍᓕ?

ᖅᑭ'ᖕᒐᖅᑐᖅ ᑐᓂ'ᓗᓂᐅᒃ ᐃᔅᒐᒃ ᐊᕐᓇᐅᑦᖅᑭᓴᕐᒧᑦ, ᐊᑎ'ᓗᓂᐅᒃ.

ᐊᖑᑕᐅᑦᖅᑭᓴᖅ ᒌ-ᑏ: ᐊᑭᑐᔪᒃᓴᐅᕗᖅ.

ᐊᕐᓇᐅᑦᖅᑭᓴᖅ ᒌ-ᑏ: ᖅᑲᓄᖅ ᐱᑐᖅᑲᐅᑎᒥᓇᓱᒥᕕᐅᒃ ᐅᓇ—

ᖅᑭ'ᖕᒐᖅᑐᖅ ᐊᔅᒐᓂ ᖅᑯ'ᒧᒃᑎ'ᓇᒥᐅᒃ.

ᖅᑭ'ᖕᒐᖅᑐᖅ: . . . ᐊᑕ . . .

ᑑᕗᐊᕐᑦ: ᓱᕚ? *(ᓱᓇᒥᒃ ᑕᑯᒐᒥ ᖅᑲᐃᕙᑦᓕᐊᓕᖅᑐᒥᒃ ᐃᖅᓯᓕᖅᖢᓂ)* ᐳᓚᓗᑕ!

ᒪᑉᓴᑳᖅ: ᓱᕚ? *(ᐃᖅᓯᓕᕋᒥᓗ)* ᓱᓇᓇᓗᒃ, ᓱᓇᓇᓗᒃᑕᐅᑭᐊᖅ . . . ᖅᑮ, ᓱᓇᐅᕝᕙ . . . *(ᐃᒡᓚᖅᖢᓂ)* ᓱᓇᐅᕝᕙᓕ—*(ᑐᖅᖢᓚ'ᓗᒍ, ᓄᓗᕋᕐᕕᒥᕚ)* ᕈᐃ!

ᐃᓯᖅᖢᑎᒃ ᒪᔅᕈᒃ ᓇᓄᙳᐊᒃ, ᐊᐃᑉᐹ ᓇᓄᖅᑐᑦ ᐱᓱᒃᑐᖅ ᐊᐃᑉᐹᓗ ᐊᑉᓗᕋᖅᖢᓂ ᐱᓱᒃᑐᖅ ᐃᓄᒃᑐᑦ ᑎᒍᒥᐊᖅᖢᓂ ᐊ'ᔩᓕᐅᑎᒥᒃ ᓯᑯᙳᐊᕐᒥᒡᓗ.

ᓚᑭᓐ: ᖅᑳ ᑭᙳᕙᕋᒻᓄᒃ—ᕈᐃ ᓇᓄᙳᐊᖅᓯᐅᑎᒥᓂᒃ ᐊᑐᖅᖢᓂ ᑲᑕᐃᖅᑲᑦᑕᕋᓗᐊ'ᒪᑦ ᐃᖅᑲᓗᙳᐊᕐᒥᓂᒃ.

ᒪᑉᓴᑳᖅ: ᐃᓕᑉᑎᒃ ᓇᓄᙳᐊᑦᑎᐊᕙᓇᓘᔭᓯᒃ—ᑕᑯᓴᕋᒪ ᓇᓄᒻᒪᑎᓇᓘᓇᓱᒋᓴᕋᓗᐊᑉᓯᒃ!

ᕈᐃ: ᐃᖅᑲᓗᙳᐊᖅᑯᑎᓚ ᐅᓇ ᐱᐊᒃᐸᒡᓛ'ᒪᑦ ᑲᑕᐃᖅᑲᑦᑕᖅᑕᓇᓗᒋᓚᓗᐊᕋᑉᑯ.

ᓚᑭᓐ: *(ᕈᐃᒧᑦ)* ᐆᒃᑐᕋᕋᓱᐊᖅᑲᑦᑕᓇᐊᖅᑲᖅᑐᑎᑦ ᑭᖕᒥᐊᑦᑎᐊᕋᓐᓂᕋᓱᐊᖅᑲᑦᑕᕋᓗᒍ.

LARKIN: Nice to meet you, Qi'ngaqtuq.

ROY: Hello.

QI'NGAQTUQ: Hello.

LARKIN picks up her camera.

LARKIN: Take a look . . . here's Roy on the ice floe . . .

Everyone stomps all over the slush as they gather around LARKIN to look at the photographs on her camera. Impressed by what they see, they ooh and aah.

MATSON: *(to QI'NGAQTUQ)* We're putting together investment packages, thus the "human" bears. Fares will be astronomical so passengers will want a guarantee of sighting polar bears.

QI'NGAQTUQ: The idea of "human bears" is a very dangerous proposition.

MATSON: No, not human—we plan to build remote-controlled robotic bears—a mother and two cubs—then position them on ice-replacement sectionals.

LARKIN: Matson, take a look at these. I think they really express the tone you're after.

MATSON takes the camera from LARKIN and everyone keeps looking at the photos as LARKIN begins to get out of her bear suit.

MATSON: Wow . . . brilliant.

AINSWORTH: Beautiful . . .

MRS. GRIFFITH-THOMSON: Lovely . . .

MR. GRIFFITH-THOMSON: Where's that chopper—I need a drink.

MRS. GRIFFITH-THOMSON: Patience, hon.

ᓛ: (ᕈᐃᒧᑦ) ᓇᓄᖅᑐᑦ ᐱᓯᖅᑲᑦᑕᑦᑎᐊᓕᖅᑐᑎᑦ.

ᕈᐃ: ᐄ, ᐊᐅᓚᓂᖕᒋᑦᑎᒍᑦ ᓄᓘᒃ, ᖅᑯᖕᒍᔭᖅ, ᐃᔭᒃᑲᓪᓗ.

ᒪᑉᔭᑳᖅ: (ᕈᐃᒧᑦ ᓛᑲᓐᒧᓪᓗ) ᓇᓄᙲᐊᖅᔭᐅᑎᔭᒃ ᐊᔭᕙᕆᐊᖅᓗᒋᒃ—ᖅᑲᐃᓯᖕᒐᖅᓂᐊᓕ'ᒪᑦ ᖅᑯᓕᒥᒎᓕᒃ . . . ᐊᑕ, ᖅᑲᐃᔨᒃᓴᐅᓕᖅᑯᖅᓕ . . .

ᕈᐃᓗ ᓛᑲᓐᓗ ᓂᐊᖅᑯᙲᐊᖅᑎᒃ ᐊᔭᕙᕆᐊᖅᓱᒋᒃ. ᕈᐃᓗ ᑎᒥᔭᐅᑎᓂ ᐊᔭᕙᖅᓱᓂᐅᒃ ᓛᑲᓐᓗ ᐊ'ᔨᓕᐅᑎᒥᓂᒃ ᐃᓪᓗᐊᖅᔭᖅᓯᐊᖅᑐᖅ.

ᖅᑯᓕᒥᒎᓕᒃ ᑐᓴᖅᓇᖅᐸᓪᓕᐊᓕᖅᑐᖅ ᐅᖕᒐᓯᒃᑐᒥᑦ . . . ᓂᐱᑭᑦᖅᑰᖅᑳᖅᓱᓂ.

ᐊᐃᓐᓯᕗᐊᑦ: ᓛᑲᓐ ᐊ'ᔨᓕᐅᑦᑎᐊᕋᓗᐊᖅᐱᑦ ᐊᑐᒐᒃᓴᑉᑎ'ᓂᒃ?

ᓚᑭᓐ: ᐃᔾᔭ, ᐊ'ᔨᓕᐅᒪᑦᑎᐊᕋᒪ—ᐊᒥᔾᕋᖅᑐᐸᓇᓗᖕᓂᒃ, ᑕᑯᔪᒫᖅᐸᑎᑦ ᐅᑯᐊᑦ ᑕᑯᕋᓐᓂᖅᑐᓇᓗᐃᑦ . . .

ᒪᑉᔭᑳᖅ: ᓛᑭᓐ, ᐅᓇ ᖅᑭ'ᖕᒐᖅᑐᖅ, ᐆᒪᔪᓕᕆᔨᐅᔪᖅ . . . (ᖅᑭ'ᖕᒐᖅᑐᒧᑦ) . . . ᓛᑲᓐ ᐅᓇ ᐊ'ᔨᓕᐅᖅᑎᐅᔪᖅ ᓯᒥᑐᐃᓐᓇᖅ ᖅᑲᐅᔨᒪᔭᐅᔪᖅ—ᐅᓇᓗ ᕈᐃ—ᐆᒪᔪᙲᐊᖑᓂᖅᒥᒃ ᐃᓕᓴᐃᔨᐅᔪᖅ.

ᓚᑭᓐ: ᐊᔭᐅ, ᖅᑭ'ᖕᒐᖅᑑᔪᑎᑦ.

ᕈᐃ: ᐊᐃ.

ᖅᑭ'ᖕᒐᖅᑐᖅ: ᐊᐃ.

ᓚᑭᓐ ᐊ'ᔨᓕᐅᑎᓂ ᑎᒍ'ᑐᓂᐅᒃ.

ᓚᑭᓐ: ᑕᒃᑰᒃ . . . ᐅᓇ ᕈᐃ ᔭᑯᙲᐊᖅᒦᑎ'ᑐᓂ ᐊ'ᔨᓕᐅᖅᑕᕋᓗᐊᕋ . . .

ᐊᒡᓗᙲᐊᑦᑯᑦ ᑐ'ᒥᕋᕋᓗᒃᑐᐊᓗᐃᑦ ᑲᑎ'ᑐᑎᒃ ᓛᑲᓐ ᒥᒃᓵᒍᑦ ᐊ'ᔨᓕᐅᑖᓄᑦ ᑕᑯᖅᑲᑕᐅᓇᓯᐊᖅᓱᑎᒃ, ᑕᑯᕋᓐᓂᕈᓯᒃᓱᑎᒃ ᐆ-ᓚᔨᑦ ᐋ-ᓚ'ᑐᑎᒃ.

ᒪᑉᔭᑳᖅ: (ᖅᑭ'ᖕᒐᖅᑐᒧᑦ) ᖅᑲᐅᔨᑉᑲᐃᔾᔨᑎᒃᓯᓂᒃ ᓴᓇᒐᑉᑕ ᐊᑐᖅᑐᒍᑦ ᓇᓄᙲᐊᖅᓂᒃ. ᐳᓚᕋᖅᑎᑦ ᐊᑭᓅᓇᓗᖕᒥᒃ ᓂᐅᕕᖅᓂᐊ'ᒪᑕ ᑕᑯᔪᒪᒻᒪᕆᒃᑲᓗᐊ'ᒪᑕ ᓇᓄᖅᓂᒃ.

QI'NGAQTUQ: I'd like to collect more data, but you're stomping down the tracks and walking all over them.

RIVERA moves.

RIVERA: Sorry.

MRS. GRIFFITH-THOMSON: Sorry.

MATSON: These are perfect, Rivera, look . . .

DUFORT gently puts the iřgak into his jacket as he looks through the camera.

QI'NGAQTUQ: *(to DUFORT)* You cannot legally take the iřgak. Put it back where you found it.

DUFORT: . . . Yes, for sure . . . *(looks through the camera again)* In a second.

LARKIN glances up and something in the distance catches her eye. LEE peers at photographs in the camera.

LEE: The one where she's looking over her shoulder is cute.

LARKIN: *(looking out)* . . . Hey . . . hey, Roy . . .

ROY: *(absently)* Yeah?

LARKIN: *(looking out)* HEY, GET AWAY, MOVE—

MATSON: *(looking out)* Oh my god—

Everyone screams.

QI'NGAQTUQ: *(looking in LARKIN's direction)* Back. Away. Very. Slowly.

DUFORT: *(looking in LARKIN's direction)* Larkin.

ROY: *(looking in LARKIN's direction)* Oh shit oh shit oh shit . . .

ᕿ’ᖕᒐᖅᑐᖅ: ᓇᓄᙳᐊᖅᑲᕐᓗᔪ ᐱᑦᑕᐅᙱᑦᑐᖅ.

ᒪᑉᓴᑳᖅ: ᐳᓚᕋᖅᑎᖅᑲᓕᖅᐸᑦ ᐊᑐᕐᓂᐊᖅᑐᒍᑦ ᐃᓄᖕᓂᒃ ᐃᓗᐊᓃᑦᑐᖅᑲᙱᑦᑐᓂᒃ ᖃᓇᑕᐅᔭᑦᑰᖅᑎᓐᓂᐊᖅᑕᕗᓪᓕ ᐊᐅᓚᑎᓐᓂᐊᕐᓗᒋᑦ ᓴᒫᙵᑦ—ᓇᓄᙳᐊᕐᒥᒃ ᐊᑎᖅᑕᕐᑲᖅᑐᒥᒃ ᒫᔪᖕᓂᒃ, ᐃᑖᔨᓂᐊᖅᑐᒍᑦ ᔪᑰᙳᐊᕐᒍᑦ.

ᓚᑭᓐ: ᒪᑉᓴᑳᖅ, ᐅᑯᐊᑦ ᑕᑯᑦᑭᑦ. ᑕᑯᕋᓐᓂᓇᑦᑎᐊᕐᓂᐊᖅᑕᒃᓴᓇᔭᑎᑦ.

ᒪᑉᓴᑳᖅ ᐊ’ᔩᓕᐅᑦ ᑎᒍ’ᒪᒍ ᑖᑲᓐᒥᑦ ᑕᒪᐃᑕ ᔮᓕ ᑕᑯᓇᔮᐊᖅᕈᑎᒃ ᐊ’ᔩᓕᐅ’ᒧᑦ ᑖᑲᓐᓗ ᐊᔪᕆᓕᖅᕈᓂᐅᒃ ᓇᓄᙳᐊᖕᖑᔾᔪᑎᓂ.

ᒪᑉᓴᑳᖅ: ᐱᑦᑕᐅᔮᕋᓗᒃ . . . ᑕᑯᕋᓐᓂᖅᑐᑦ.

ᐊᐃᓐᓯᒍᐊᑦ: ᑕᑯᕋᓐᓂᕐᓗᐊᖅᑐᖅ . . .

ᐊᕐᓇᐅᑦᕿᔮᖅ ᒋ-ᑎ: ᑕᑯᕋᓐᓂᖅᑐᐸᓇᓗᐃᑦ . . .

ᐊᖑᑕᐅᑦᕿᔮᖅ ᒋ-ᑎ: ᓇᐅᓪᓕᑭᐊᖅ ᖁᓕᒥᑰᓕᕐᕈᒃ—ᐃᒥᕐᓗᒃᑐᕈᒪᓕᕋᒪᓕ.

ᐊᕐᓇᐅᑦᕿᔮᖅ ᒋ-ᑎ: ᓴᐃᒪᓇᔾᔭᐊᕐᓗᑎᓪᓕ.

ᕿ’ᖕᒐᖅᑐᖅ: ᑲᑎᖅᔾᔭᐃᖑᕝᕕᓕᕈᒪᒐᓗᐊᖅᑐᖕᒐ ᖃᐅᔩᓴᖅᑕᒃᓯᒪᓂᒃ ᑭᔪᐊᓂᒃ ᑐᒥᑦ ᐅᑯᐊᑦ ᑐ’ᒥᕋᕋᐸᔪᒋᑦ ᐅᖑᒐᓘᓐᓃᑦ ᑐᑎᕝᕕᒋᑦᑲᑦᑕᓕᖅᑕ’ᒪ.

ᓇᕕᐊᕋ ᐊᒍᖕᒐᕋᓐᓂᖅᕈᓂ.

ᓇᕕᐊᕋ: ᖄ.

ᐊᕐᓇᐅᑦᕿᔮᖅ ᒋ-ᑎ: ᖄ.

ᒪᑉᓴᑳᖅ: ᐅᑯᐊᑦ ᐱᑦᑕᐅᔭᓇᓗᐃᑦ, ᓇᕕᐊᕋ, ᑕᒃᑰᒃ . . .

ᑑᒍᐊᕐᑦ ᐃᔾᔨᒐᒃ ᖃᐅᑦᑐᐊᕐᒥᓄᖕᒐᖅᕈᓂᐅᒃ ᑕᑯᓇᔮᖅᑎ’ᓗᓂ ᐊ’ᔩᓕᐅᑎᒧᑦ.

ᕿ’ᖕᒐᖅᑐᖅ: *(ᑑᒍᐊᕐᑦᒧᑦ)* ᐃᔾᔨᒐᒃ ᑖᓪᓇ ᐱᑖᓇᓚᐃᑕᐃᑦ ᒪᓕᒐᑎᒍᑦ ᐱᑦᕋᑯᔭᐅᙱᑦᑐᖅ. ᐅᑎᖅᑎᓵᖅᑲᖅᑕᐃᑦ ᓄᓇᒧᑦ ᓇᔾᔫᕐᕕᒋᔭ’ᓄᑦ.

ᑑᒍᐊᕐᑦ: . . . ᐄᖑᒐᓗᐊᖅ, ᐊᔪᐅ . . . *(ᐊ’ᔩᓕᐅ’ᒧᑦ ᑕᑯᒋᐊᑉᓵᖅᕈᓂ)* ᐅᕝᕕᑦᑎᐊᒍᓕ.

QI'NGAQTUQ: *(calmly, in LARKIN's direction)* Do. Not. Run. Back away one step at a—no, don't . . .

ROY hurries towards LARKIN and pushes LARKIN out of the way of the approaching bear . . . then he just stands there, petrified.

MATSON: Roy—back away . . . god, I can't believe I left my fucking gun on the . . . god . . .

ANGU'ŘUAQ enters. He lumbers in, sinking ankle deep in the slush, then faces ROY, who suddenly raises his bag or "bear head" or whatever is handy and takes a swipe at the bear . . . but he misses . . .

QI'NGAQTUQ: Don't—

. . . ANGU'ŘUAQ raises his giant paw and knocks ROY over. It happens so fast that for a moment no one knows what to do.

(to ROY) Don't look directly at the bear . . .

ANGU'ŘUAQ puts his big paw on ROY's chest, ready to attack.

(to ANGU'ŘUAQ) Be wise. Do not harm the man. Even though you are hungry, be wiser than your hunger. Back away.

ANGU'ŘUAQ stops, turns, stares at QI'NGATUQ, then, driven by his nature and his hunger, he lunges and with his big jaws he grabs ROY's head, ripping his face.

Everyone screams.

ROY: MY EYES EYES EEEIIIIIII . . .

QI'NGAQTUQ: *(to ANGU'ŘUAQ) IHUMATTIARIT. A'NIQTAILULUGU TAAMNA. KAAKTUALUUGALUARUVIT. TAMUAHUNGNIIT ATUNNGILUGU. MANIMMIQTURIARIT. [BE WISE. DO NOT HARM THE MAN. EVEN THOUGH YOU ARE HUNGRY, BE WISER THAN YOUR HUNGER. BACK AWAY . . .]*

ᓛᑲᓐ ᐅᖓᓯᒃᑐᒧᑦ ᑕᑯᖃᓕᕋᒥ ᔪᓇᒥᒃᑭᐊᖅ ᑕᑯᔾᔩᕋᒥ.
ᐊ'ᔫᓕᐅ'ᒧᑦ ᑕᑯᒥᐊᖅᑐᓂ ᐊ'ᔫᙳᐊᕐᒥᒃ.

ᓛ: ᐊ'ᔫᙳᐊᕐᓕ ᐅᓇ ᓇᓄᙳᐊᕐᑲᖅᑐᖅ ᖅᑭᕕᐊᖅᑎ'ᑐᒍ ᑕᑯᕋᓐᓂᖅᑐᖅ.

ᓚᑭᓐ: *(ᐊᕗᖓ ᑕᐅᑐᒃᑐᓂ)* . . . ᔪᔫᓇᓗᒃ, ᔪᔫᓇᓗᒃ . . . ᕈᐃ . . .

ᕈᐃ: *(ᐅᔾᔫᓇᑦᑎᐊᙱ'ᑐᓂ)* ᔪᕙᔫ?

ᓚᑭᓐ: *(ᐊᕗᖓ ᑕᐅᑐᒃᑐᓂ)* ᐊᕗᙵᓇᑦ ᐊᕗᙵᓕᓇᑦ—

ᒪᑉᓴᑳᖅ: *(ᐊᕗᖓ ᑕᐅᑐᒃᑐᓂ)* ᐃᖅᔨᓇᖅᑐᓇᓗᒃ—

ᑕᒪᐃᑕ ᐃᓄᐊᓛᓕᖅᑐᑦ.

ᖅᑭ'ᖓᖅᑐᖅ: *(ᓛᑲᓐᒧᑦ ᖄ'ᑐᓂ)* ᑭᖑᑉᐱᖅᑕᖅᑐᓕᖅᑐᑎᑦ ᔪᒃᑲᐃᑦᑐᑉᔪᓐᓄᐊᕐᒥᒃ.

ᑑᒍᐊᕐᑦ: *(ᓛᑲᓐᒧᑦ ᖄ'ᑐᓂ)* ᓛᑲᓐ.

ᕈᐃ: *(ᓛᑲᓐᒧᑦ ᖄ'ᑐᓂ)* ᖅᑮᓴᓇᓗᒃ ᖅᑮᓴᓇᓗᒃ ᖅᑮᓴᓇᓗᒃ.

ᖅᑭ'ᖓᖅᑐᖅ: *(ᓛᑲᓐᒧᑦ ᖄ'ᑐᓂ ᐅᐃᒪᙱᑦᑎᐊᖅᑐᓂ)* ᐅ'ᓚᙱᑐᑎᑦ.
ᑭᖑᑉᐱᐊᖅᑐᑎᑦ ᔪᒃᑲᐃᑦᑐᒥ—ᐄᖅᑭ ᑕ'ᓇᐅ . . .

ᕈᐃ ᓛᑲᓐᒧᙵᖅᑐᓂ ᐊᓯᒃᑐᓂᐅᒃ ᓇᓄᒻᒪᓂᓇᓗᖕᒧᑦ
ᐱᔪᐅᓂᐊᙱ'ᒪᑦ . . . ᕈᐃᑐ ᓇᓄᖅ ᖄ'ᑐᒍ ᐃᖅᔨᔪᐸᓇᓗᒃ.

ᒪᑉᓴᑳᖅ: ᕈᐃ ᑭᖑ'ᒧᑦ ᐱᓯᒡᓗᑎᑦ . . . ᔨᖅᑯᖅᑎᔾᔪᑎᓇᓗᖅᑐᓚ
ᖅᑭᒪᓪᓚᔅᓵᓗᒃᑲᑉᑯ ᐅᒥᐊᕐᔪᐊᕐᒥ . . . ᔪᖅᑯᑕᐅᙱᑦᑐᑉᑲᓇᓇᓗᒃ . . .

ᐊᖑ'ᔪᐊᖅ ᑕᐃᒪ ᐃᔨᖅᓴᖑᕙᖅᑯᖅ. ᒪᐅᓯᖅᓇᖅᑐᒥ ᐱᔪᒃᑐᖅ
ᒪᓴᔅᓴᖅᑐᖅ, ᕈᐃᒧᑦ ᑐᕌᖅᑐᓂ ᕈᐃ ᐊᓇᐅᓇᔪᐊᖅᔨᓐᓇᓕᖅᐹ
ᐆᕐᒥᓄᑦ ᓂᐊᖅᑯᙳᐊᕐᒥᓄᑦᑑᓐᓃᑦ ᔪᓇᒧᑦ
ᐊᓇᐅᓇᔪᐊᓕ'ᒪᒍ . . . ᐊᓐᓇᐃᖐ . . .

ᖅᑭ'ᖓᖅᑐᖅ: ᐱᙱᓪᓗᒍ ᑕ'ᓇᐅᙱᑦᑐᖅ—

. . . ᐊᖑ'ᔪᐊᖅ ᐃᓵᒃᑐᓂ ᐊᓯᓪᓚᔅᓴᖑᕙᖅᑐᓂᐅᒃ ᕈᐃ. ᑕᒪᐃᑕ
ᖃᓄᖅᓕᐅᓇᐊᒃᓴᖅ ᓇᓗ'ᒪᑕ ᐃᖅᔨ'ᑐᑎᓪᓗ.

ANGU'ŘUAQ looks at QI'NGAQTUQ then back at ROY then back at QI'NGAQTUQ again . . . then he lets ROY drop. The bear backs away. Maybe it was QI'NGAQTUQ's words, or the ancient feeling of affection that HUMMIKTUQ once stirred in the bear.

QI'NGAQTUQ holds her hand in front of ANGU'ŘUAQ as if to reassure him.

(to everyone) Hurry—I'll keep the bear back—be quick.

Everyone hurries to help ROY, who has passed out. QI'NGAQTUQ watches ANGU'ŘUAQ.

MATSON: Roy, are you breathing, are you breathing—HE'S NOT BREATHING—

AINSWORTH: . . . Yes he is—he's breathing—

MATSON: Thank god, thank Jesus, Lord Buddha, thank you—where's the fucking chopper?

DUFORT: He's bleeding very badly.

LARKIN: I'm scared, I'm scared—

MR. GRIFFITH-THOMSON: I need a drink.

LEE: I know CPR.

MATSON: Let's get him to the rig, to Circumpolar—that security guy—he'll help us. *(calls)* HELP.

QI'NGAQTUQ calls very loud without looking away from the bear.

QI'NGAQTUQ: TUUTALIK!

LARKIN: HELP HELP.

TUUTALIK enters, his gun pointed at the bear.

ᕿ’ᖕᖓᖅᑐᖅ: (ᐱᐅᒧᑦ) ᓇᓄᖅ ᐃᖨᕆᖖᕆᓪᓗᒍᑕ . . .

ᐊᖑ’ᖬᐊᖅ ᑐᑎᓕ’ᒪᒍ ᐱᐅ ᖃᑎᓛᒍᑦ, ᐅᕆᐊᕐᓂᐊᓕᕐᒥᐅᒃ.

ᕿ’ᖕᖓᖅᑐᖅ: (ᐊᖑ’ᖬᐊᕐᒧᑦ) ᐃᖨᒪᑦᑎᐊᓇᑦ. ᐊ’ᓂᖅᑕᐃᓕᓗᒍ ᑖᒻᓇ.
ᑳᒃᑐᐊᓅᒐᓗᐊᐱᕕᑦ ᑕᒧᐊᖨᖕᓅᑦ ᐊᑐᖖᕆᓗᒍ. ᒪᓂᒻᒥᖅᑐᓇᐊᓇᑦ.

ᐊᖑ’ᖬᐊᖅ ᓄᑦᖃᖅᖢᓂ, ᕿᕕᐊᖅᖢᒍ ᕿ’ᖕᖓᖅᑐᖅ ᐃᖨᕆ’ᓗᒍᓗ,
ᑭᖨᐊᓂᒃ ᑳᓪᖢᐊᕕᒃᑲᒥ ᐊᔪᓕ’ᒪᑦ ᐱᕆᐊᖅᖨᓐᓇᓕᖅᐹ ᐱᐅ
ᑮᖨᑦᑕᓕᖅᖢᓂᐅᒃ ᑭᓈᓗ ᐊᓕᒃᑐᑦᑎᐊᖅᖢᒍ.

ᑕᒪᐃᑕ ᐃᓇᐊᑖᓕᖅᖢᑎᒃ.

ᐱᐅ: ᐃᔫᒃᑲᒃ ᐃᔫᒃᑲᒃ ᐄᐄᐄᐊᐃᐊᐃᐊᐃᐊᐃ . . .

ᕿ’ᖕᖓᖅᑐᖅ: (ᐊᖑ’ᖬᐊᕐᒧᑦ) ᐃᖨᒪᑦᑎᐊᓇᑦ. ᐊ’ᓂᑕᐃᓕᓗᒍ ᑖᒻᓇ.
ᑳᒃᑐᐊᓅᒐᓗᐊᐱᕕᑦ ᑕᒧᐊᖨᖕᓅᑦ ᐊᑐᖖᕆᓗᒍ. ᒪᓂᒻᒥᖅᑐᓇᐊᓇᑦ.

ᐊᖑ’ᖬᐊᖅ ᕿ’ᖕᖓᖅᑐᒥᒃ ᑕᐅᑐᖅᑳᖅᖢᓂ ᐱᐅᒥᓪᓗ ᑕᑯ’ᓗᓂ
ᕿ’ᖕᖓᖅᑐᕐᓗ ᑕᑯᐸᖨᐊᖅᖢᒍ . . . ᐱᐅᓗ ᐱᖨᐃᓕᕐᓂᖅᖢᓂᐅᒃ.
ᒪᓂᒻᒥᖅᑐᓕᖅᑐᕐᓗ. ᕿ’ᖕᖓᖅᑑᑉ ᐅᖅᑲᐅᖨᐊ’ᓄᓪᓅᓐᓃᑦ
ᐃᒃᐱᒍᖨᓕᖅᑎᑕᐅ’ᒪᑦ ᐅᖕᖏᓗ ᑎᒍᐊᖅᖨᕕᓂᕐᒥᓂᒃ ᖨᒻᒥᒃᑐᕐᒥᒃ
ᐊᐅᓚᔾᓐᓂᕐᒥ ᑐᑭᖨᓕᖅᑐᖅ ᐅᖅᑲᐅᖨᓇᕗᐅᖬᓂᒃ.

ᕿ’ᖕᖓᖅᑐᖅ ᐊᖑ’ᖬᐊᕐᒧᑦ ᐃᖃᒃᖢᓂ ᐱᑦᑎᐊᑎᕆᒐᒥᕆᑦ ᕐᑯᓯᓕᒧᑦ.

ᕿ’ᖕᖓᖅᑐᖅ: (ᑕᒪᐃ’ᓄᑦ) ᑐᐊᕕ—ᑲᒪᕆᓂᐊᖅᐸᕐ—ᐃᑲᔪᓕᖅᖨᐅᒃ ᐊᑕᐃ.

ᑕᒪᐃᑕ ᐃᑲᔪᕐᖨᐊᓕᖅᑐᑦ ᐱᐅᒥᒃ ᖃᐅᔾᒪᖨᐃᖅᖨᒪ’ᒪᑦ. ᕿ’ᖕᖓᖅᑐᕐᓗ
ᑕᐅᑐᐃᓐᓇᖅᖢᓂ ᐊᖑ’ᖬᐊᕐᒥᒃ.

ᒪᐸᕗᖄᖅ: ᐱᐅ, ᐊᓂᖅᕘᖅᑐᖅᐱᑦ ᐊᓂᖅᕘᑦᑐᖅᐱᑦ—ᐊᓂᖅᕘᖅᑐᖖᕆᑦᑐᖅ—

ᐊᐃᓐᓯᕗᐊᑦ: ᐄ ᐊᓂᖅᕘᖅᑐᖅᑐᖅ—

ᒪᐸᕗᖄᖅ: ᒎᑎ ᕐᑯᓯᓕᕚᕗᑦ ᔩᓯᓯᓗ ᑕᒪᐃᑕᓗ ᕐᑯᓯᓇᖅᑯᑦ—ᓇᐅᕐᖢᒃ ᑕᐃᒪ
ᕐᑯᓕᒥᒎᓕᐸᖨᕐᖢᓪᓕ?

ᑑᕗᐊᕐᑦ: ᐊᐅᓇᑖᖅᑐᐊᓗᒃ.

TUUTALIK: Gate's open . . . we got first aid guys inside.

Everyone exits . . . AINSWORTH *and* DUFORT *carry* ROY, *and* MRS. GRIFFITH-THOMSON *is the last to leave. When everyone is gone,* TUUTALIK *takes a step towards* ANGU'ŘUAQ.

Don't come back here anymore or I'll have to shoot you. *Utiphaaqtailiguit. Taavaniigguit. Ungahiktumiigguit!* Don't come back. Stay away. Stay far away!

TUUTALIK *exits.*

ANGU'ŘUAQ *looks to his left, then his right, then straight ahead. There is nowhere else for him to go but here.*

After a moment he sniffs the ground where the breathing hole used to be . . . then he raises his foreleg like he used to do with HUMMIKTUQ *and waits.*

The sound of a helicopter overhead scares him.

ANGU'ŘUAQ *exits.*

As we transition into Scene Two, the following text is heard:

The Aurora Borealis *is a Polar Code* PC5 *(Category* A*) vessel designed to navigate remote polar passages year-round, and safely explore unchartered water, while providing exceptional comfort. It is an expert-led expedition voyage combining rugged adventure and Zodiac landings with rare discovery, extraordinary wildlife, and stunning landscapes few have ever seen. Its* WX-BOW *is key to its design; its powerful wave-slicing action provides an extremely smooth ride in even adverse conditions and reduces spray on deck for superior observation. The ship is eco-sustainable, whale-safe, and boasts 93% of its services as wholly recyclable. Guests enjoy first-class luxury, superb amenities, and scrumptious cuisine like Arctic char in a sea of asparagus and mushroom broth; East Coast oysters with homemade yogurt and fingered citron; venison with red whortleberry gel,*

ᓚᑭᓐ: ᐃᖅᓯᔪᖓ, ᐃᖅᓯᔪᖓ—

ᐊᖑᑕᐅᑦᕿᔮᖅ ᕆ-ᑏ: ᐃᒥᕐᓗᒃᑐᕈᒪᓂᕐᖀᓗᓂ’ᒥᖓᒪ.

ᓃ: ᐊᓂᖅᖂᖅᑐᖅᑎᑦᑎᓂᕐᒥᒃ. ᐃᓕᖃᖅᓱᒪᔪᖓ ᐃᑲᔪᕈᓐᓇᖅᑕᕋ.

ᒪᑉᖃᑳᖅ: ᐅᖅᓱᕐᔪᐊᓕᓇᔾᑦᑯᑦ ᑐᓐᖓᕙᐊᓄᑦ ᐊᓪᔭᕐᓚᕗᑦ—ᐱᓕᐅᔪᒪᙳᐊᖑᔪᒧᑦ ᑕᐃᒪ—ᐃᑲᔪᕈᓐᓇᖅᑖᑎᒍᑦ (ᑐᖅᓱᓚ’ᓗᓂ) ᐃᑲᔪᖅᑕᐅᔪᒪᔪᒍᑦ!

ᖅᑭ’ᖕᖓᖅᑐᖅ ᐃᓇᐊᓛᓕᖅᓱᓂ ᑐᖅᓱᓚ’ᓗᓂ, ᑕᐅᑐᒃᑲᓗᐊᖅᓱᒍ ᔪᓕ ᓇᓄᖅ.

ᖅᑭ’ᖕᖓᖅᑐᖅ: ᑑᑕᓖᒃ!

ᓚᑭᓐ: ᐃᑲᔪᖅᑕᐅᑕ ᐃᑲᔪᖅᑕᐅᑕ.

ᐃᔪᖅᓱᓂ ᑑᑕᓕᒃ ᔪᖅᑯᖅᑎᔾᔪᑎᓂ ᑐᕿᖅᓱᒍ ᓇᓄᕐᒧᑦ.

ᑑᑕᓕᒃ: ᐅᑯᐃᖅᔪᒪᔪᒍᑦ . . . ᐃᓗᐊᓂ ᐃᓘᐊᖅᓴᐃᓈᑕᖅᑲᖅᑐᖅ.

ᑕᐃᒪᐃᑕ ᖁᓐᖏᐊᖅᕕᖕᒥᑦ ᐊᓂ’ᓗᑎᒃ . . . ᐊᐃᓐᓯᕗᐊᓪᓗ ᑑᕗᐊᓪᓗ ᑎᒍᒥᐊᖅᑐᒃ ᕈᐃᒥᒃ, ᐊᕐᓇᐅᑦᕿᔮᖅ ᕆ-ᑏ ᑭᖑᓪᓕᐅ’ᓗᓂ. ᑕᒪᐃᑕ ᔪᖅᑲᕈᐃᓕᖅᑎ’ᓗᕆᑦ ᑑᑕᓕᒃ ᐊᑉᓗᕿᓇᐊᓕᖅᑯᖅ ᐊᖑ’ᔪᐊᕐᒍᑦ.

ᑑᑕᓕᒃ: ᐅᑎᑉᖂᖅᑕᐃᓕᓗᑎᑦ, ᔪᖅᑯᓇᐊᖅᑲᕐᓂᐊᕕᒃᑲᑉᑭᑦ.

ᐊᓂ’ᓗᓂ ᑑᑕᓕᒃ.

ᐊᖑ’ᔪᐊᖅ ᖃᐅᒥᖕᒍᑦ ᖅᑭᕕᐊᖅᓱᓂ ᑕᓕᖅᐱᖕᒍᓪᓗ, ᖂᖕᒥᓄᓪᓗ. ᔪᒍᙵᐅᕕᒃᓴᖅᑲᙱᑦᑎᐊᖅᑑᓐᓂᖅ.

ᐅᑕᖅᑭᔮᖅᓱᓂ, ᓇᐃᒪᓕᖅᑐᖅ ᓄᓇᒥᒃ ᔪᑯᖅᑲᙵᐃ’ᒪᑦ ᔪᑯᖅᑲᕈᐃᒻᒪᓇ’ᒪᑦ ᐊᓪᓗᖅᑲᓚᐃᓕ’ᒪᑦ . . . ᐃᔫᖓᑕ ᔪᕗᓂᐊ ᐃᖃᒃᓱᒍ ᑕᐃᒪ’ᓇᑐᑦ ᔪᒻᒥᒃᑐᖅᑯᑦ ᑎᒍᐊᔪᒥᓄᑦ ᐱᖅᑲᑦᑕᖅᔪᒪᓕᖅᑖᑐᑦ, ᐅᑕᖅᑭ’ᓗᓂᓗ.

ᖅᑯᓕᒥᒎᓕᒃ ᑐᖃᖅᓇᓕ’ᒪᑦ ᖅᑯᓪᓗᒃᓱᓂ.

or brined, roasted quail eggs browned in foamed butter with Jerusalem artichokes. Enjoy luxuriously appointed boutique staterooms with a master bath featuring heated floor, bidet, and a spa flotation tub with an ocean view. Imagine your dreams into existence on the Aurora Borealis.

ᐊᓂ'ᓗᓂ ᐊᖑ'ᖪᐊᖅ.

ᐅᑯᐊᑦ ᐊᑖᓂ ᑎᑎᕋᖅᔑᒪᖪᑦ ᐊᑐᖅᑕᐅᔪᖕᓇᖅᑐᑦ ᖁᓐᖏᐊᖅᕕᖕᒥ ᐊ'ᓚᖖᒍᖅᑎᑦᑎᓇᔑᐊᖅᑎ'ᓗᑎᑦ ᐃᓪᓗᐊᖅᔕᐃᑎ'ᓗᑎᑦ ᖃᓄᓇᑦᑑᓂᐊᖅᑐᒧᑦ ᑭᖑᓂᐊᓂ. ᐊᑐᖖᒋᑦᑲᓗᐊᕐᓗᑎᓪᓘᓐᓃᑦ:

ᐅᒥᐊᕐᖪᐊᖅ ᐊᑎᖅᑲᖅᑐᖅ ᐊᖅᓴᕐᓂᕐᒥᒃ ᐅᑭᐅᖅᑕᖅᑐᖅᔑᐅᑕᐅᕗᖅ ᐊᖮᕌᒍᑉ ᐃᓗᐊᓂ ᖃᖓᑐᐃᓐᓇᖅ ᐃᖏᖮᕋᔪᖕᓇᖅᖢᓂ, ᐃᒪᑦᑰᕈᖕᓇᖅᑐᕐᓗ ᖃᐅᔑᒪᔕᐅᖖᒋᑦᑐᓂ, ᐃᓗᐊᓂᓗ ᐃᖢᐊᖅᑐᐸᓇᓗᖕᓂᖅ ᐃᓂᖅᑲᖅᖢᓂ. ᐳᓚᕋᖅᑐᖅᔑᐅᑕᐅᒐᓗᐊᖅ ᐊᐅᓚᑕᐅ'ᒪᑦ ᖃᐅᔑᒪᔒᑕᒻᒪᓇᐅᔕᓂᑦ ᐳᓚᕋᖅᑎᑦᑎᔪᖕᓇ'ᒪᑕᓗ ᑕᑯᑎᑦᑎᐊᕐᓗᑎᑦ ᐊ'ᔑᒌᖖᒋᑦᑐᓂᒃ ᑕᑯᕋᓐᓂᖅᑐᓂᒃ ᑕᑯᔕᐅᔑᒪᑦᑎᐊᖖᒋᑦᑐᓂᓪᓘᓐᓃᑦ ᐆᒪᔕᕐᓂᒃ ᓄᓇᓂᓪᓗ ᐅᑭᐅᖅᑕᖅᑐᒥ. ᐅᒥᐊᕐᖪᐊᑉ ᔑᕗᓂᐊ ᓴᓇᔑᒪᑦᑎᐊᕐᓂᖕᒐᓄᑦ ᓯᒻᒥᔖᕋᓗᒃ ᒪᑦᓚᖅᑐᓂᓗ ᐃᖑᓚᐃᑦᑐᖅ ᐊᐅᓚᔭᐃᑦᑐᖅ ᒪᓪᓕᖅᑐᐊᓛᑎ'ᓗᒍᓘᓐᓃᑦ ᐃᒪᖅ ᔑᕿᖅᑕᓚᐃ'ᒪᓪᓗ ᐅᒥᐊᕐᖪᐊᑉ ᐃᓗᐊᓄᑦ ᐳᓚᕋᖅᑎᑦ ᑕᐅᑐᒃᕕᒃᓴᖅᑲᑦᑎᐊᑦᕿᔕᐅ'ᓗᑎᒃ. ᐅᒥᐊᕐᖪᐊᕐᓚ ᐊᕙᑎᒥᒃ ᖪᕈᕈᑎᖅᑲᖖᒋᑦᑎᐊᖅᑐᖅ, ᕿᓇᓗᒃᑲᓄᑦ ᐊᑦᑕᓇᖖᒋᑦᑐᖅ ᐊᑐᖅᑕᐃ'ᓂᓪᓗ 93%-ᖏᑦ ᐊᑐᒐᒃᓴᑦ ᐊᑐᖅᑕᐅᑉᔑᐊᕈᖕᓇᖅᑐᑦ ᐃᒋᑕᐅᖖᒋᓗᑎᒃ ᐊᒃᑕᖅᕕᖕᒧᑦ ᐊᒃᑕᑯᒃᓴᓚᐅᖖᒋᓛᖖᒍ'ᓗᓂ. ᐳᓚᕋᖅᑎᑦ ᐃᓪᓗᐊᖅᑲᑦᑎᐊᖅᖢᑎᒃ ᖨᓇᑐᐃᓐᓇᕐᓂᒃ ᐊᑐᒐᒃᓴᖅᑲᑦᑎᐊᖅᖢᑎᒃ ᓂᕿᑦᑎᐊᕙᐸᓇᓗᖕᓂᓪᓗ ᓂᖅᖪᐅᕈ'ᔕᐅᕙᒃᖪᑎᒃ ᐃᖅᑲᓗᒃᐱᖕᒥᒃ ᑕᐃᒪ ᖃᔪᓚᐅᖅᑕᐅ'ᓗᓂ ᑯᐊᓐᓂᓚᖅᑕᐅ'ᓗᓂᓗ; ᐅᕕᓗᕐᓂᓪᓗ ᒪᒪᖅᓯᐅᑎᓚᖅᑕᐅᔑᒪᖪᓂᒃ; ᑐᒃᑑᔕᑉ ᓂᕿᐊᓂᓪᓗ ᐸᐅᓐᖓᕐᓂᒃ ᒪᒪᖅᓯᐅᑎᓚᖅᔑᒪᖪᒥᒃ; ᐊᕿᖮᑭᓐᓄᐊᓪᓗ ᐃᒐᔑᒪᖪᑦ ᐸᔪᓚᖅᑕᐅ'ᓗᑎᒃ ᐱᕈᖅᑐᓚᖅᑕᐅ'ᓗᑎᒃ. ᖁᕕᐊᒋᔭᖕᓇ'ᒥᔕᑎᑦ ᐃᓪᓗᐊᐸᓇᓗᐃᑦ ᐃᓚᐃᑦ ᐊᑭᑐᑦᕿᔕᑦ ᖁᐃᔭᖅᑐᕐᕕᖕᒥᑦ ᓴᓇᔑᒪᑦᑎᐊᖅᖢᑎᒃ ᐆᓇᔪᒃᑐᓂᒃ ᓇᑎᖅᑲᖅᑐᑦ, ᐃᖁᐃᔕᐅᑎᖃᖅᖢᑎᒃ ᑯᕕᔕᓂᒃ, ᐅᐊᕐᕕᖃᒻᒪᓇᒃᖢᑎᓪᓗ ᐊᖏᔕᓂᒃ ᐳᒃᑕᕐᕕᒋᔭᖕᓇᖅᑕᑦ ᑕᐅᑐᒡᓗᒍ ᑕᓇᐅᕐᔕᐊᕌᓗᒃ ᐃᒐᓛᑦᑯᑦ. ᑕᐅᑐᖖᒍᐊᓇᑦ ᐃᔓᒪᒋᓗᒍ ᐱᔪᒪᔕᑎᑦ ᑕᒪᕐᒥᒃ ᔕᑦᕿᐅᒪᑦᑎᐊᖅᑐᑦ ᐅᒥᐊᕐᖪᐊᕐᒥ ᐊᖅᓴᕐᓂᕐᒥᒃ ᑕᐃᔕᐅᖪᒥ.

SCENE TWO

It is four years later, December 31, 2034, and the weather is mild. It's almost midnight on the deck of the Aurora Borealis, *an ultra-modern cruise ship discreetly decorated to reflect the holiday spirit.*

The STEWARD *enters with a buffet overflowing with delicacies and sweets, an ice sculpture of a dancing bear as its centrepiece. The* STEWARD *organizes a tray of champagne and glasses, as well as a basket of colourful cones and tiara party hats and noisemakers.*

Music from a small orchestra drifts up from the deck below . . . as well as voices and laughter.

RIVERA *enters in a tuxedo.*

STEWARD: Champagne, Mr. Garcia?

RIVERA: *Gracias.*

RIVERA *stands at the rail and looks up to the sky.*

LUCY *enters, followed by her grandmother,* MARIANNE. *Both are dressed up.*

LUCY: Grammy, look, a polar bear. It's standing on one foot.

MARIANNE: It's dancing . . . it's a dancing bear.

STEWARD: Champagne?

LUCY: Why is it dancing?

ᖃᓄᓇᑦᑑᓂᐊ ᕿᙵᓂᐊᓂ

ᐅᑭᐅᑦ ᓯᑕᒪᐃᑦ ᓈᓯᒪᓕᖅᑐᒃ, ᓯᕿᓐᖏᓘᑕᐅᔪᖅ ᐅᑉᓗᐊᓗ 31-ᖑᔪᖅ 2034-ᒥ, ᓯᓚ ᐆᓇᐃᙱᑦᑐᖅ. ᐅᓐᓄᑦᑯᑦ ᖁᓘᓄᙷᕐᓂᐊᓕ’ᒪᑦ ᐅᒥᐊᕐᔪᐊᕐᒥ ᐊᖅᓴᕐᓂᕐᒥᒃ ᑕᐃᔭᐅᔪᒥ, ᐅᒥᐊᕐᔪᐊᓇᓗᒃ ᐳᓚᕋᖅᑎᓂᒃ ᐅᓯᖅᑲᖅᑐᖅ, ᖁᕙᐊᓲᒡᕙᒃᓯᐅᑎᓂᒃ ᐃᓂᑯᓇᖅᔭᖅᑕᐅᓯᒪᔪᖅ.

ᐃᓯᖅᖢᓂ ᔭᓇᔨ ᓂᖅᖤᐅᖅᑎ ᓂᕆᔭᒃᓴᓐᓄᐊᕌᓗᓐᓂᒃ ᐊ’ᔩᒦᙱᑦᑐᓂᒃ ᐃᒃᖤᖕᓇᖅᑐᐊᓗᖕᓂᒃ ᒪᒪᖅᑐᕌᓗᖕᓂᒃ ᐃᓯᖅᓯ’ᓗᓂ. ᕿᑦᖄᓃᑦᑐᖅᑲᖅᖢᓂ ᔭᓇᐅᔭᖅᓯᒪᔪᒥᒃ ᓯᑯᒧᑦ ᓇᓄᙵᐊᕐᒥᒃ ᑕᑯᖃᓐᓂᕈᑎᒃᓴᒥᒃ. ᔭᓇᔨ ᐃᑦᑐᐊᖅᔭᕆᐊᖅᖢᓂ ᐃᒪᐅᑎᓂᒃ ᐃᒥᖅᓗᒃᓯᐅᑎᓂᒃ, ᖁᖁᐊᕈᒃᓴᓂᒃ ᓇᓴᙵᐊᖅᓂᓪᓗ ᐊᖅᑰᒧᑦ ᓄᑖᙵᓂᐊ’ᓄᑦ ᖁᕙᐊᓰᑎᒃᓴᓂᒃ.

ᑐᓴᕐᓂᖅᑐᖅᑲᖅᖢᓂ ᑐᓴᕋᓐᓈᖅᑐᑦ ᑕᐅᓇ’ᖓᑦ . . . ᐅᖃᒪᔪᑦᓗ ᐃᓪᓚᖅᑲᑎᒌᒃᖢᑎᒃ.

ᓇᕕᐊᕋ ᐃᓯᖅᖢᓂ ᖃᑉᓗᓈᖅᑕᕐᓂᒃ ᐊ’ᓄᕌᖅᓯᒪᑦᑎᐊᖅᑐᖅ.

ᔭᓇᔨ: ᐅᐊᐃᓂᑐᕈᒪᕕᑦ ᐳᑉᓚᒃᑎᑦᑎᓯᒪᔪᒥᒃ, ᒥᔅᑕ ᓛᓯᐊ?

ᓇᕕᐊᕋ: (ᓯᐹᓂᔅᑐᑦ ᑭᐅ’ᓗᓂ ᖁᔭᓐᓇᒦᖅᖢᓂ) ᒍᕌᓯᐊᔅ.

ᓇᕕᐊᕋ ᐅᒥᐊᕐᔪᐊᑉ ᑭᓪᓕᐊᓂ ᓇᖏᖅᑐᖅ ᑕᑉᐸᐅᖓᓗ ᕿᓚᖑᑦ ᑕᐅᑐᒃᑐᖅ.

ᐃᓯᖅᑐᒃ ᓘᓯᓗ ᓂᖏᐅᓂᓗ ᒪᓇᓐᓄᐊᖅ, ᐊ’ᓄᕌᖅᓯᒪᑦᑎᐊᖅᑐᒃ ᖁᕙᐊᓰᑎᒃᓴᓂᒃ.

ᓘᓯ: ᓂᖏᐅᖅ, ᑕᒃᑰᒃ, ᓇᓄᙵᐊᓇᓗᒃ ᓈ’ᖏᖅᓯᒪᔪᖅ.

MARIANNE: Yes, please. *(to LUCY)* It's dancing because it's happy.

The STEWARD hands LUCY a candy.

STEWARD: Here, Lucy . . . a gold chocolate coin.

LUCY: Thank you . . . *(points to the noisemakers)* Can I please have one of those too?

STEWARD: Pick one . . .

LUCY takes a noisemaker—a spinner.

LUCY: This one. Thank you.

MARIANNE: Don't use it until the clock strikes twelve.

MRS. GRIFFITH-THOMSON enters.

MRS. GRIFFITH-THOMSON: *(to MARIANNE)* It's too bad your daughter couldn't be here after all the work she did.

MARIANNE: Yes, Larkin would love this, but she's on a contract in Moscow . . . luckily she's able to have a hologram visit with Lucy before Lucy goes to bed.

MRS. GRIFFITH-THOMSON: That's nice. *(looks around)* You know, despite everything, it's astonishing at night.

RIVERA: . . . Astonishing, yes, when you can't see the water.

LUCY has started to run around the deck making noise with her noisemaker.

MRS. GRIFFITH-THOMSON: *(to RIVERA)* I can only imagine what you might be feeling.

RIVERA: First New Year's without my wife.

MRS. GRIFFITH-THOMSON: It must be terribly hard.

ᒪᓂᓐᓄᐊᖅ: ᒧᒥᖅᑐᖅ . . . ᒧᒥᖅᑎᐅᓐᓂ'ᒪᑦ.

ᓴᓇᔪ: ᐳᓚᒃᑎᑦᑎᔪᒪᔭᒥᒃ ᐅᐊᐃᓂᑐᓂᑦ?

ᓘᓯ: ᔨ'ᒪᑦ ᒧᒥᖅᐸ?

ᒪᓂᓐᓄᐊᖅ: ᐋ ᐱᓚᖕᒐ. *(ᓘᓯᒧᑦ)* ᒧᒥᖅᑐᕐᓚ ᖁᕕᐊᔨᒃᑲᒥ.

ᓴᓇᔪ ᓘᓯ ᑐᓂ'ᓗᓂᐅᒃ ᑯᑯᖕᒥᒃ.

ᓴᓇᔪ: ᐅᕝᕙ, ᓘᓯ . . . ᑯᑯᒃ ᑆᓇᐅᔭᙳᐊᖅ.

ᓘᓯ: ᖁᔭᓇᖅᑯᑎᑦ . . . *(ᑎᑦᑯᐊᖅᓱᕆᑦ ᓂᐱᖅᑯᖅᑐᔾᔨᑎᑦ ᐅᓚᑉᕿᐅᔭᑦ)* ᑕ'ᓇᐃᑦᑐᒥᒡᓗ ᐱᓚᖕᒐ?

ᓴᓇᔪ: ᓂᕈᐊᕐᓗᑎᑦ ᐊᑕᐃ . . .

ᓘᓯ ᑎᒍᔪ'ᓗᓂ ᐅᓚᑉᕿᐅᔭᓐᓄᐊᕐᒥᒃ—ᑲᐃᑉᔭᐅᑎᓐᓄᐊᖅ ᓂᐱᕐᑲᖅᑐᖅ.

ᓘᓯ: ᐅᓇ. ᖁᔭᓇᖅᑯᑎᑦ.

ᒪᓂᓐᓄᐊᖅ: ᐊᑐᖖᒋᒡᓗᒍ ᑭᔪᐊᓂᒃ ᖁᓛᓄᖖᒐᖅᐸᑦ ᐅᑉᓗᖅᔪᐅᑦ.

ᐃᔪᖅᓱᓂ ᐊᕐᓇᐅᑦᕿᔭᖅ ᕇ-ᑏ.

ᐊᕐᓇᐅᑦᕿᔭᖅ ᕇ-ᑏ: *(ᒪᓂᓐᓄᐊᕐᒧᑦ)* ᐸᓃᑦ ᓴᒧᖖᒐᐅᖅᑲᑕᐅᖖᒋ'ᒪᑦ ᓴᓇᖅᑲᑕᐅᒐᓗᐊᖅᓱᓂ ᐅᑯᓇᓂ ᓴᓇᖅᑲᑕᐅᔨᐸᓇᓘᖅᑳᖅᓱᓂᓗ.

ᒪᓂᓐᓄᐊᖅ: ᐋ, ᓛᑲᓐ ᐃᒻᓇ ᐸᓂᒐ ᖁᕕᐊᕆᓇᔭᖅᑖ ᓴᒪᓂ ᑭᔪᐊᓂᒃ ᓴᓇᔭᒃᓴᖅᑲ'ᒪᑦ ᐅᓛᓴᒥ . . . ᑭᔪᐊᓂᒃ ᖃᓂᑕᐅᔭᒃᑯᑦ ᐅᖕᒐᔪᒃᑐᒥᑦ ᐸᓂᖕᒥᓂᒃ ᓘᓯᒥᒃ ᑕᑯᔪᖕᓇᖅᓂᐊᖅᑑᒐᓗᐊᖅ ᓘᓯ ᐃᓐᓇᓕᖅᔪᒪᖖᒋᓐᓂᐊ'ᓂᒃ ᐅᓐᓄᒃ.

ᐊᕐᓇᐅᑦᕿᔭᖅ ᕇ-ᑏ: ᔪᓇᐅᕝᕙ *(ᑕᑯᓐᓇᔪᐊᖅᑐᖅ ᑕᑯᔭᒃᓴᓂᒃ)* ᑕᓴᒻᒪ ᔪᑕᖅᑲᑦᑎᐊᖖᒋᑦᑲᓗᐊᖅᓱᓂ ᐃᓂᖁᓇᖅᑐᖀᓗᒃ ᐅᓐᓄᑦᑯᑦ.

ᓂᕕᐊᕋ: . . . ᑭᔪᐊᓂᒡᓚ ᐃᒪᖅ ᑕᐅᑐᖕᓇᖕᒋᑎ'ᓗᒍ ᓴᓗᒪᐃᓪᓗᐊᕕ'ᒪᑦ.

ᓘᓯ ᐅ'ᓚᐅᒪᓕᖅᑐᖅ ᐅᓚᑉᕿᐅᔭᓂ ᓂᐸᓗᒃᐸᓪᓚᑯᔨᐊᖅᓱᓂᐅᒃ.

RIVERA: This was our dream. You knew how excited Adelina was about this ship and this . . . anyway.

MRS. GRIFFITH-THOMSON: She was a special person, Rivera.

MARIANNE: Lucy, what did Grammy say about the noise?

LUCY: I'm just practising.

LUCY slows down a little and looks over the railing at the water.

RIVERA: I thought *el viaje*—the voyage would distract my sadness.

MRS. GRIFFITH-THOMSON: Has it?

RIVERA: Oh yes, very much most of the time . . . no, Lori, it's made everything much worse.

MRS. GRIFFITH-THOMSON puts her hand on RIVERA's arm.

MR. GRIFFITH-THOMSON enters in a tux with LEE, who is in a glittering gown. LEE is very pregnant.

MR. GRIFFITH-THOMSON: Ah ha—there's where the champagne's hiding.

LEE: *(to RIVERA)* How do you say happy 2035 in Spanish?

RIVERA: *Feliz Dos Mil Treinta y Cinco.*

LEE: *Feliz Dos Mil Treinta y Cinco.*

RIVERA: Yes, very good.

STEWARD: *(to MR. GRIFFITH-THOMSON)* Champagne?

LEE: *(to STEWARD)* Just the tiniest drop . . . thanks.

MR. GRIFFITH-THOMSON: *(to STEWARD)* I need a full glass for the toast.

MRS. GRIFFITH-THOMSON: *(to MR. GRIFFITH-THOMSON)* Hon, you've had enough—

ᐊᕐᓇᐅᑦᕿᔪᖅ ᒌ-ᑏ: (ᓇᕙᐊᕋᒧᑦ) ᖃᓄᓇᑦᑖᒃᓵ’ᓂᒃ ᑐᑭᔨᕝᕘᖅᑐᖓ ᐃᓚᐃᕋᓗᐊᕋᕙᑦ.

ᓇᕙᐊᕋ: ᐄ, ᐊᕝᕌᒍᑦ ᓄᑖᕐᒦᔨᐅᖅᔨᒪᓕᙱ’ᓇᒪ ᓄᓕᐊᕋ ᔮᖃᙱᑎ’ᑐᒍ.

ᐊᕐᓇᐅᑦᕿᔪᖅ ᒌ-ᑏ: ᐊᑦᕐᑯᓇᕐᓇᖅᑐᒃᓴᐅᕗᖅ.

ᓇᕙᐊᕋ: ᑕᕙᒻᒪ ᓂᓇᐅᓇᔮᐸᓇᓗᒋᒐᓗᐊᕋᐸᑎᑦᑯᒃ. ᐋᑕᑖᓇ ᓄᓕᐊᕋ ᐆᒥᖓ ᐅᒥᐊᕐᔦᐊᕐᒥᒃ ᖁᕙᐊᒋᔮᖃᕋᓗᐊ’ᒪᑦ ᐅᓇᓗ . . . ᐋ ᐊᔦᕐᓇ’ᒪᑦ ᖁᔭᓇ.

ᐊᕐᓇᐅᑦᕿᔪᖅ ᒌ-ᑏ: ᐃᓄᑦᑎᐊᕙᐅᒐᓗᐊ’ᒪᑦ ᓄᓕᐊᑦ.

ᒪᓇᓐᓄᐊᖅ: ᔫᓯ, ᐊᒃᐱᐅᑎᔮᕋᓗᐊᐸᑭᑦ ᓂᐹᖅᐸᑦᑖᕐᑯᙱ’ᑐᑎᑦ ᓈᓚᙱ’ᓇᕙᖕᒑ?

ᔫᓯ: ᐆᒃᑐᕋᕋᔮᐊᖅᔨᓐᓇᖅᑐᖓ.

ᔫᓯ ᔮᒃᑲᐃᓪᓕᒥᐊᖅᑯᓂ ᐅᒥᐊᕐᔦᐊᑉ ᐊᕙᓗᐊᓃ’ᑯᓂ ᑕᐅᑐᒃᑐᖅ ᑕᐅᓄᖓ ᐃᒪᕐᒧᑦ.

ᓇᕙᐊᕋ: ᐃᔮᒪᔩᒐᓗᐊᖅᑐᖓ ᐅᒥᐊᕐᔦᐊᑦᑯᑦ ᐃᓚᐅᒍᒪ ᖁᕙᐊᔮᙱᓐᓂᕋ ᐊᑐᕈᐃᕈᖕᓇᕋᑉᑯ.

ᐊᕐᓇᐅᑦᕿᔪᖅ ᒌ-ᑏ: ᐊᓂᒍᖅᐸ?

ᓇᕙᐊᕋ: ᐄᖑᔦᒃᓵᐅᕗᖅ ᖃᓄᑭᐊᖅ . . . ᐄᕿ, ᔮᓇᑐᐃᓐᓇᑦ ᖃᐱᓕᕐᓇᕐᓂᖅᖃᐸᓇᔫᓕᖅᑐᑦ.

ᐊᕐᓇᐅᑦᕿᔪᖅ ᒌ-ᑏ ᐊᕝᒐᓂ ᐃᓕ’ᑐᓂᐅᒃ ᓇᕙᐊᕋᐅᑉ ᑕᓕᐊᓄᑦ ᔮᕐᑐ ᖃᐃᒻᒪᖅᖃᕋᔮᐊᖅᑯᒍ.

ᐃᔨᖅᑯᑎᒃ ᐊᖑᑕᐅᑦᕿᔪᖅ ᒌ-ᑏ ᐊ’ᓄᖔᖅᔨᒪᑦᑎᐊᖅᑐᖅ ᖃᑉᑐᓈᖅᑕᕐᓂᒃ ᑖᑐ ᕿᑉᓕᖅᑐᒥᒃ ᕿᑕᐅᔮᖅᔨᒪ’ᑐᓂ ᓄᑕᕋᒃᓵᖃᕋᒥ ᓈᖅᑯᖅᑐᐤᔭᒃᑐᕐᑐ.

ᐊᖑᑕᐅᑦᕿᔪᖅ ᒌ-ᑏ: ᐋ—ᐅᑉᐸ ᐃᒥᕐᓗᒃ ᐅᐸᓂ ᐃᔮᖅᑕᐅᔨᒪᔫᓐᓂᖅ.

ᓛ: (ᓇᕙᐊᕋᒧᑦ) ᖃᓄᖅ ᐅᖃᐅᔨᓇᓇᔭᖅᑕᕋᓕ ᓯᐹᓂᒡᑐᑦ ᐃᒪ’ᓇ ᖁᕙᐊᔮᒡᓗᔨ 2035-ᒥ?

MR. GRIFFITH-THOMSON: I need some for the toast— *(to STEWARD)* Fill hers up, too—fill everyone's up to the brim.

AINSWORTH enters wearing the original iřgak, now inlaid with diamonds.

MRS. GRIFFITH-THOMSON: Ainsworth! *I* so wanted to buy that but we missed the auction!

AINSWORTH: Still can't see a damn thing through them—no wonder Dufort didn't want them.

MRS. GRIFFITH-THOMSON: You don't know how to look through them. These slits were made narrow to reduce the amount of light and increase visual clarity and prevent snow blindness. Brilliant design.

AINSWORTH: I'll sell them to you—at a discount.

MRS. GRIFFITH-THOMSON: Let's see . . . oh they're exquisite . . .

He hands the iřgak to her and she examines it before putting it on.

DUFORT enters in a tux, excited.

DUFORT: *(to everyone) Bonne année, mes amis.*

RIVERA: *(to DUFORT) Feliz año nuevo, mi amigo.*

DUFORT: There's a killer whale swimming alongside us on the port side near! Come and see.

LEE: I've seen so many killer whales on this trip I don't ever want to see another one as long as I live.

DUFORT: This one's feisty—right near the surface.

LUCY: Grammy, can I go see the killer whale?

MARIANNE: All right, Lucy—but hold Mr. Bonnière's hand.

STEWARD: We're starting the celebrations soon.

ᓇᕙᐊᕋ: ᐃᒪ'ᓇ: *ᕙᓕᔅ-ᑑᔅ-ᒦᑦ-ᑐᓃᓐᑕ-ᐃ-ᓲᓐᑯ.*

ᓛ: *ᕙᓕᔅ-ᑑᔅ-ᒦᑦ-ᑐᓃᓐᑕ-ᐃ-ᓲᓐᑯ.*

ᓇᕙᐊᕋ: ᐄ, ᑕ'ᓇᒻᒪᓇᒃ.

ᖃᓇᔮ: *(ᐊᖑᑕᐅᑦᕿᔪᖅ ᕇ-ᑏᒧᑦ)* ᐳᓚᒃᑎᑦᑎᔨᒪᔪᒥᒃ ᐅᐊᐃᓂᑐᓃᑦ?

ᓛ: *(ᖃᓇᔮᒧᑦ)* ᐃᒪᑭᑦᑐᑉᔫᓛᓐᓄᐊᕐᒥᒃ ᐱᓚᖓ . . . ᖁᓯᓇᖅᑯᑎᑦ.

ᐊᖑᑕᐅᑦᕿᔪᖅ ᕇ-ᑏ: *(ᖃᓇᔮᒧᑦ)* ᐃᒪᐅᑎᒐ ᑕᑕᕐᑯᔪᕋᓕ ᖁᕙᐊᔫᑎᕆᓂᐊᖅᑕᐸᑎ'ᓄᑦ ᖁᓛᓄᖕᒐᖅᐸᑦ.

ᐊᕐᓇᐅᑦᕿᔪᖅ ᕇ-ᑏ: *(ᐅᐃᒥᓄᑦ)* ᑕᐃᒪ'ᓇ ᐱᕗᓛᓕᕋᕙᑦ—

ᐊᖑᑕᐅᑦᕿᔪᖅ ᕇ-ᑏ: ᐱᕆᐊᖅᑲᕋᒪ ᖁᕙᐊᔫᑎᕆᓂᐊᖅᑕᐸᑎ'ᓄᑦ ᖁᓛᓄᖕᒐᖅᐸᑦ—*(ᖃᓇᔮᒧᑦ)* ᓄᓕᐊᒪᓗ ᐃᒪᐅᑖᑦᑕᐅᖅ ᑕᑕᑎᕆᐊᕐᓗᒍ ᑕᒪᐃᑕᓗ ᐅᑯᐊᑦ.

ᐃᔨᖅᓱᓂ ᐊᐃᓐᓯᕗᐊᑦ ᐃᔾᒐᑐᖅᑲᕐᒥᒃ ᐊᑎᔨᒪᔪᖅ ᑭᔨᐊᓂᒃ ᕿᐸᓕᖅᑐᓂᒃ ᐊᑭᑐᔪᓂᒃ ᑕᐃᒪᓐ-ᑎᓂᒃ ᐃᓂᖁᓇᖅᖃᖅᑕᐅᔨᒪᓕᖅᑐᖅ ᐃᔾᒐᑐᖅᑲᖅ.

ᐊᕐᓇᐅᑦᕿᔪᖅ ᕇ-ᑏ: ᐊᐃᓐᓯᕗᐊᑦ! ᑖᒻᓇ ᓂᐅᕙᕈᒪᔫᕋᓗᐊᕋ ᑭᔨᐊᓂᒃ ᐱᑐᖅᑲᕐᓂᖅ ᓂᐅᕙᖅᑎᑦᑎᑎ'ᓗᕆᑦ ᐃᓚᐅᖕᒋᕝᕙᒃᑲᑕ!

ᐊᐃᓐᓯᕗᐊᑦ: ᑭᔨᐊᓂᒃ ᑕᐅᑐᑦᑎᐊᕐᓇᐃᑦᑐᕌᓗᒃ—ᑑᕗᐊᕐᑦ ᐱᔪᒪᖕᒋᓐᓂᖅᑖ ᑕᐅᑐᖕᓇᐃᑦᑐᓇᓘ'ᒪᑦ.

ᐊᕐᓇᐅᑦᕿᔪᖅ ᕇ-ᑏ: ᐊᑎᑦᑎᐊᖕᒋ'ᓇᕙᐅᒃ. ᐅᓇ ᑕᐅᑐᒡᕙᐊ ᐊᖕᒪᓂᐊ ᓂᕈᑭᑦᑐᓐᓄᐊᖑᔪᖅ ᐃᓪᓗᒃᑎᓂᐊᖕᒋ'ᒪᑦ ᖄᐅᒪᕗᓛᖅᑎ'ᓗᒍ ᐅᐱᓐᖖᑯᑦ. ᖃᓇᔨᒪᑦᑎᐊᖅᑐᑦ ᑕᖃᑯᐊᑦ ᐊᑑᑎᓕᐸᓇᓗᐃᑦ.

ᐊᐃᓐᓯᕗᐊᑦ: ᓂᐅᕙᓕᕈᓪᓕ—ᐊᑭᑭᑦᑐᒥᒃ ᐱᓂᐊᖅᐸᑦ.

ᐊᕐᓇᐅᑦᕿᔪᖅ ᕇ-ᑏ: ᐊᑕᐃ ᑕᓗᓚᒍ . . . .ᐆ ᐱᑦᑕᐅᔪᐸᓇᓗᒃ ᖃᓐᑎᐊᖅᔨᒪᔪᐊᓗᒃ . . .

ᑐᓂ'ᒪᒍ ᕿᒥᕐᕈᓕᖅᓗᓂᐅᒃ ᐊᑎᓂᐊᖄᖅᓗᒍ.

ᑑᕗᐊᕐᑦ ᐃᔨᖅᓱᓂ ᐊ'ᓄᕌᖅᔨᒪᑦᑎᐊᖅᓱᓂ ᖁᕙᐊᔪᒃᑐᖅ.

DUFORT: We'll hurry.

LUCY and DUFORT exit. MRS. GRIFFITH-THOMSON puts the iřgak over her eyes.

STEWARD: Champagne?

AINSWORTH: Please . . .

MRS. GRIFFITH-THOMSON: Ryan, I absolutely must have these. How do I look?

MR. GRIFFITH-THOMSON: . . . Like a cat that just got electrocuted. (*holds his glass out to the STEWARD*) Top it up.

MRS. GRIFFITH-THOMSON: (*to MARIANNE*) He's hopeless.

MARIANNE: (*re: the iřgak*) . . . May I?

MRS. GRIFFITH-THOMSON hands the iřgak to MARIANNE, who tries it on . . .

STEWARD: Who would like champagne?

AINSWORTH: Please . . .

MR. GRIFFITH-THOMSON: Buy 'em if you want, hon. (*to AINSWORTH*) Cheers, pal.

AINSWORTH: Cheers.

MARIANNE tries looking through the iřgak.

MARIANNE: I can't see a thing.

She hands them back to MRS. GRIFFITH-THOMSON just as AINSWORTH spits out his champagne over the side.

AINSWORTH: (*to STEWARD*) There's nothing wrong with serving Dom Pérignon Réserve de L'Abbaye, but it's a poor choice for this occasion.

ᑑᕗᐊᕐᑦ: *(ᑕᒪᐃ’ᓅᑦ ᐅᐃᕖᑑᖅᖁᓂ ᐊᕐᕌᒍᑦ ᓄᑖᕐᒥ ᖁᕕᐊᓱᖁᓴᔭᖅ)* ᐸᓐ-ᐊᓐᓂ-ᒥᔅ-ᐊᒥᔅ.

ᓇᕕᐊᕋ: *(ᑕᒪᐃ’ᓅᑦ ᓯᐹᓂᔅᑑᖅᖁᓂ ᐊᕐᕌᒍᑦ ᓄᑖᕐᒥ ᖁᕕᐊᓱᖁᓴᔭᖅ)* ᕕᓚᔅ-ᐊᓐᔭ-ᓄᐃᒍ-ᒥ-ᐊᒦᒍ.

ᑑᕗᐊᕐᑦ: ᑕᒃᑰᒃ ᐋᕐᓗᒃ ᐃᒪᕐᒥ ᐳᐃᔮᖅ ᖃᓂᒋᔮᑉᑎ’ᓂ! ᖃᐃᒡᒍᐃᑦᑎ ᑕᑯᓇᓱᐊᖅᓱᐅᒃ.

ᑖ: ᐊᒥᓱᓇᓗᖕᓂᒃ ᐋᕐᓗᖕᓂ ᑕᑯᓱᒪᓕᕋᒪ ᕿᒪᓃᓱᐅᖅᑎ’ᓗᑕ ᑕᑯᔭᒪᓯᐃᒻᒪᓇᒃᑐᖕᒐ ᐃᓅᓯᒻᓂ ᑕ’ᓇᑦᑐᓂᒃ.

ᑑᕗᐊᕐᑦ: ᐅᓇ ᐅᓇᖕᒥᓇᐃᑦᕐᑰᖅᑐᖅ—ᐳᐃᑦᑎᐊᖅᑐᐊᓗᒃ.

ᓘᓯ: ᓂᖕᒋᐅᖅ, ᐋᕐᓗᖕᒥᒃ ᑕᑯᖃᑕᐅᔭᖕᓇᖅᑯᖕᒑ?

ᒪᓂᓐᓄᐊᖅ: ᐄᖕᒍᒐᓗᐊᖅ—ᑭᓯᐊᓂᒃ ᑕᓯᐅᕐᓗᒍ ᐊᖕᒍᑦ ᑖᒻᓇ ᐸᓂᐊᓇ.

ᔭᓇᓲ: ᖁᕕᐊᓱᖃᑎᒌᖕᓂᕗᑦ ᐱᒋᐊᑦᑎᐊᕐᓂᐊᓕᖅᑐᖅ ᖁᑖᓄᖖᒐᕐᓂᐊᓕ’ᒪᑦ.

ᑑᕗᐊᕐᑦ: ᑐᐊᕕᐅᕐᓂᐊᖅᑯᒍᒃ.

ᐊᓂ’ᓗᑎᒃ ᓘᓯᓗ ᑑᕗᐊᕐᑦᓗ. ᐊᕐᓇᐅᑦᕿᔮᖅ ᒌ-ᑏ ᐃᕐᒐᒃ ᐊᑎ’ᓗᓂᐅᒃ.

ᔭᓇᓲ: ᐳᑉᓚᒃᑎᑦᑎᓯᒪᔮᒥᒃ ᐅᐊᐃᓂᑐᓈᑦ?

ᐊᐃᓐᓯᕗᐊᑦ: ᐊᑕᐃ . . .

ᐊᕐᓇᐅᑦᕿᔮᖅ ᒌ-ᑏ: ᐅᐃᒃ, ᐅᓇ ᐱᑖᓇᔫᖅᑲᖅᑕᕋ. ᖃᓄᓇᑦᕐᑰᖅᑐᖕᒐᓚ ᐊᑎᒐᑉᑯ ᑕᑯᕋᓐᓂᖅᑯᖕᒑ?

ᐊᖕᒍᑕᐅᑦᕿᔮᖅ ᒌ-ᑏ: . . . ᐳᓯᑳᖕᒍᔫᖅᑐᑎᑦ ᐆᑕᐅᓯᒪᔮᒥᒃ ᐊᕐᕈᔭᕐᒍᑦ. *(ᐃᒪᐅᑎᓂ ᒪᓂᔫ ᔭᓇᓲᒧᑦ)* ᑕᑕᑎᑉᓯᐊᕈᒃ.

ᐊᕐᓇᐅᑦᕿᔮᖅ ᒌ-ᑏ: *(ᒪᓂᓐᓄᐊᕐᒧᑦ)* ᔭᐱᕐᓇᖅᑐᖄᓗᒃ ᐅᓇ.

ᒪᓂᓐᓄᐊᖅ: *(ᐱ’ᓗᒍ ᐃᔮᒃ)* . . . ᐊᑎᓚᒎ?

MR. GRIFFITH-THOMSON: Tastes just fine. I grew up drinking Rondel Brut Cava, so this here is pretty tasty.

LEE holds out her glass.

LEE: *(to STEWARD)* . . . Just a tiny drop more.

AINSWORTH: I need to find something that's actually drinkable.

AINSWORTH exits.

MR. GRIFFITH-THOMSON: He's a big snob.

STEWARD: Who would like more of *this* champagne?

MR. GRIFFITH-THOMSON: I'll have another.

RIVERA: Yes, *gracias.* It's very good.

MRS. GRIFFITH-THOMSON: I've dreamed of ushering in the New Year on top of the world.

RIVERA: Not quite the top—we're still about 2,400 kilometres from the North Pole.

LUCY and DUFORT enter. LUCY starts spinning her noisemaker.

MARIANNE: Did you see the killer whale?

LUCY: No.

DUFORT: It's hard to see anything in the black water—too oily.

The aurora borealis appears . . . but the colours are faded and the overall effect less than dazzling.

LEE: *(to RIVERA)* I can say Happy New Year in Mandarin—*Gong xi fa cai.*

LUCY sees the auroras.

ᐊᖅᓇᐅᑦᖅᑭᔭᖅ ᓰ-ᑏ ᐃᔾᒐᒃ ᑐᓂ'ᓗᓂᐅᒃ ᒪᕆᓐᓄᐊᖅᒧᑦ ᐊᑎᓇᖃᐊᓕᖅᑯᓗᓂᐅᒃ ᒪᕆᓐᓅᑉ . . .

ᓴᓇᕗ: ᖃᓇᓕ ᐳᑉᓚᒃᑎᑦᑎᔪᒪᔭᒥᒃ ᐅᐊᐃᓂᑐᕈᒪᕙ?

ᐊᐃᓐᓯᕗᐊᑦ: ᐊᑕᐃ ᐅᕙᖕᒐ . . .

ᐊᖕᒍᑕᐅᑦᖅᑭᔭᖅ ᓰ-ᑏ: ᓂᐅᕕᖅᓗᒍ ᐱᔪᒪᒍ'ᓂ ᐃᔾᒐᒃ.

(ᐊᐃᓐᓯᕗᐊᖅᒍᑦ) ᖅᑯᕕᐊᖃᖕᓂᖅᒍᑦ ᐃᒥᖅᑐᒍᑦ.

ᐊᐃᓐᓯᕗᐊᑦ: ᖅᑯᕕᐊᖃᖕᓂᖅᒍᑦ.

ᒪᕆᓐᓄᐊᖅ ᑕᑯᓐᓇᖃᐊᖅᑯᓗᓂ ᐃᔾᒐᑦᑯᑦ.

ᒪᕆᓐᓄᐊᖅ: ᑕᐅᑐᖕᓇᖅᑐᖅᑲᕕᐊᓐᓄᐊᙵᒋᑦᑐᖅ.

ᒪᕆᓐᓅᑉ ᐃᔾᒐᒃ ᐅᑎᖅᑎᑖ ᐊᖅᓇᐅᑦᖅᑭᔭᖅ ᓰ-ᑏᒧᑦ ᐊᐃᓐᓯᕗᐊᑦ ᐅᕆᐊᖅᑎ'ᓗᒍ ᐃᒪᖅᒧᑦ ᐃᒥᖅᓗᒃ ᓇᖅᕈᒋ'ᓗᓂᐅᒃ.

ᐊᐃᓐᓯᕗᐊᑦ: (ᓴᓇᕗᒧᑦ) ᑕ'ᓇᐃᑦᑐᓇᓗᒃ ᐳᑉᓚᒃᑎᑦᑎᔪᒪᔭᖅ ᖅᑲᓄᕆᑦᖅᑰᙵᒋᑦᑑᒐᓗᐊᖅ ᑭᔪᐊᓂᒃ ᒪᒪᖅᓂᖅᓴᒥᒃ ᐊᑭᑐᓂᖅᓴᒥᒃ ᐱᔭᒃᓴᐅᒐᓗᐊᖅᑐᑎᑦ ᐊᔾᕌᒍᑦ ᓄᑖᖑ'ᒪᑦ.

ᐊᖕᒍᑕᐅᑦᖅᑭᔭᖅ ᓰ-ᑏ: ᒪᒪᖅᑰᖅᑑᒐᓗᐊᖅ ᐅᓇ, ᑕᒃᑰᒃᑕᐅᖅ ᐃᓅᖃᒃᑎ'ᓗᖕᒐᓕ ᐊᑭᑭᑦᑐᓇᓗᖕᓂᒃ ᐱᖅᑲᑦᑕᖅᔪᒪᒐᐸᑕ ᐅᓇᓕ ᐱᑦᑕᐅᑉᖅᑭᓯᐸᓇᓗᐊ.

ᓛ ᓴᓇᕗᒧᑦ ᐃᒪᐅᑎᓂ ᒪᓂ'ᓗᓂᐅᒃ.

ᓛ: (ᓴᓇᕗᒧᑦ) . . . ᒥᑭᔭᓐᓄᐊᖅᒥᒃ ᖃᓕ.

ᐊᐃᓐᓯᕗᐊᑦ: ᐃᒥᕈᖕᓇᖅᑕᒻᓂᒡᓕ ᖅᑭᓂᕆᐊᖅᑲᕋᒪ.

ᐊᐃᓐᓯᕗᐊᑦ ᐊᓂ'ᓗᓂ.

ᐊᖕᒍᑕᐅᑦᖅᑭᔭᖅ ᓰ-ᑏ: ᓇᖅᕈᑐᔭᓇᓗᒃ ᐃᒻᓇ.

ᓴᓇᕗ: ᖃᓇᓗ ᐆᒪ'ᖕᒐᑦ ᐱᔪᒪᕙ?

ᐊᖕᒍᑕᐅᑦᖅᑭᔭᖅ ᓰ-ᑏ: ᐊᑕᐃ ᐱᑉᔪᐊᖅᓚᖕᒐ.

LUCY: Grammy, look—UP IN THE SKY!

MARIANNE: *(looking up)* Beautiful.

LEE: Emilie's going to kill me for drinking, but my excuse is that I'm drinking to beauty . . .

DUFORT takes photographs of the auroras, as do some of the others. MRS. GRIFFITH-THOMSON looks at the sky through the iřgak.

MR. GRIFFITH-THOMSON: *(looking up)* They sure don't look like the northern lights in our brochure—colours are kind of *faded.*

RIVERA: *(looking up)* . . . They're dazzling . . .

LUCY: *(looking up)* Where do they come from?

MARIANNE: *(looking up)* It's God showing us a glimpse of Heaven.

DUFORT: Well, actually— *(to LUCY)* They occur when gaseous particles in the earth's atmosphere collide with charged particles released from the sun's atmosphere. Different types of gas particles colliding result in different colours.

LUCY: *(to DUFORT)* We studied gas particles in science.

MARIANNE: Lucy's very good at science and English. She writes little poems.

MRS. GRIFFITH-THOMSON: I read somewhere that the Inuit believe the northern lights are their ancestors playing soccer with a walrus head, and if children are playing outside and whistle, the northern lights will come down and cut off their heads!

RIVERA: *Dios mío.*

LEE: In Norse mythology these lights were the spears of warrior women—the Valkyries. They rode on horseback and led fallen soldiers to their final resting place at Valhalla.

ᓇᕕᐊᕋ: ᐄ, ᖁᔭᓇᖅᑯᖅ. ᐱᑦᑕᐅᔪᖅ.

ᐊᕐᓇᐅᑦᕿᔭᖅ ᒌ-ᑏ: ᐊᔾᕌᒍᑦ ᓄᑖᒦᔨᐅᕈᒪᓪᓗᐊᖅᑐᑐᖅᑲᐅᒐᓗᐊᕋᒪ ᐅᑭᐅᖅᑕᖅᑐᒥ ᓄᓇᕐᔪᐊᑉ ᑳᑉᔨᖓᓂ.

ᓇᕕᐊᕋ: ᓄᓇᐅᑉ ᑳᑉᔨᖓᓃᖕᒋᑦᑲᓗᐊᖅᑐᒍᑦ ᔪᓕ ᑕᐃᒪ 2,400 ᑭᓛᒥᑕᐅᔪᖅ ᑎᑭᓐᓇᔪᐊᕐᓗᒍ.

ᐃᔨᖅᑐᖅ ᓘᓯᓗ ᑑᕗᐊᕐᓪᓗ. ᓘᓯ ᐅᓚᑉᕿᐅᔭᕐᑯᑎᒥᒍᑦ ᓂᐸᓗᒃᐸᓪᓚᒃᑐᖅ.

ᒪᓇᓐᓄᐊᖅ: ᑕᑯᒐᓗᐊᖅᐱᐅᒃ ᐋᕐᓗᒃ?

ᓘᓯ: ᐄᖅᑭᔅᓱᒃ.

ᑑᕗᐊᕐᑦ: ᐃᒪᖅ ᐅᖅᔪᕐᔪᐊᖅᑲᖅᐸᓪᓛᕐᓂᐊᓄᑦ—ᑕᐅᑐᖕᓇᖅᑐᖅᑲᑦᑎᐊᖅᑲᔭᐃᑦᑐᖅ.

ᑕᑦᐹᓂ ᐊᖅᓴᕐᓂᑦ ᑕᑯᒃᓴᐅᒐᓗᐊᖅᓱᑎᒃ . . . ᖃᐅᒪᑦᑎᐊᕈᐃᖅᑐᑦ.

ᑖ: *(ᓇᕕᐊᕋᒧᑦ)* ᓴᐃᓂᕈᑐᑦ ᐅᖅᑲᔪᓇᔫᖕᓇᖅᑕᕋ ᐊᔾᕌᒍᑦ ᓄᑖᕐᒥ ᖁᕕᐊᓱᒍᐃᑦᑎ—ᐃ'ᒪᓇ ᒍᖕ-ᔪ-ᕙᑦ-ᑐᐃ.

ᓘᓯ ᐊᖅᓴᕐᓂᑦ ᑕᑯ'ᓗᓂᒋᑦ.

ᓘᓯ: ᓂᖏᐅᖅ ᑕᒃᑰᒃ—ᕿᓚᖕᒥ ᑕᑦᐹᓂ!

ᒪᓇᓐᓄᐊᖅ: *(ᖁ'ᒧᑦ ᑕᑯ'ᓗᓂ)* ᐃᓂᖁᓇᖅᑐᑦ.

ᑖ: ᐃᒥᓕᐅᑉ ᑐᖁᔭᕐᓂᐊᖅᑖᖓ ᐃᒥᕋᒪ, ᑭᔪᐊᓂᒃ ᐃᓂᖁᓇᖅᑐᖅᑲᕐᓂᖓᓄᑦ ᐃᒥᖅᑯᖓ . . .

ᑑᕗᐊᕐᑦ ᐊ'ᔨᓕᐅᒪᔪᖅ ᐊᖅᓴᕐᓂᕐᓂᒃ, ᐊᔫᓪᓗ ᐊ'ᔨᓕᐅᖅᑲᑕᐅ'ᓗᑎᒃ. ᐊᕐᓇᐅᑦᕿᔭᖅ ᒌ-ᑏ ᖁ'ᒧᑦ ᕿᓚᖕᒧᑦ ᑕᑯᓇᔪᐊᖅᓱᓂ ᐃᔾᒐᑦᑯᑦ.

ᐊᖑᑕᐅᑦᕿᔭᖅ ᒌ-ᑏ: *(ᖁ'ᒧᑦ ᑕᑯ'ᓗᓂ)* ᐅᑯᐊᑦ ᐊᖅᓴᕐᓂᑦ ᖃᐅᒪᑦᑎᐊᙱᑦᑐᑦ ᑎᑎᕋᖅᑕᑉᑕ ᖃᐅᔨᑉᑲᐃᔾᔪᑎᑉᑕ ᐊ'ᔨᙳᐊᖏ'ᓂᒃ ᐊ'ᔨᐅᙱᒻᒪᓇᒃᑐᑦ.

ᓇᕕᐊᕋ: *(ᖁ'ᒧᑦ ᑕᑯ'ᓗᓂ)* . . . ᑕᑯᕋᓂᕐᓗᐊᖅᑐᓪᓚ . . .

ᓘᓯ: *(ᖁ'ᒧᑦ ᑕᑯ'ᓗᓂ)* ᔪᒥ'ᖕᒑᖅᑐᓪᓚ ᓴᑉᑯᐊᑦ?

RIVERA: Where's that?

MARIANNE: It's another name for Heaven.

MRS. GRIFFITH-THOMSON: *(to RIVERA)* The Valkyries—they're from the show by . . . what's his name . . . my head's—too much champagne— *(to MR. GRIFFITH-THOMSON)* What's his name, hon?

MR. GRIFFITH-THOMSON: Who?

MRS. GRIFFITH-THOMSON: The German fellow who wrote the show about the Valkyries.

MR. GRIFFITH-THOMSON: I don't know what you're talking 'bout—I never know what you're talking about.

DUFORT: Wagner?

AINSWORTH enters triumphantly waving a bottle of champagne.

AINSWORTH: Krug Grande Cuvée anyone?

LEE holds out her glass.

LEE: Oh my god POUR . . . but just a drop.

MR. GRIFFITH-THOMSON: I'll have some.

MARIANNE: Yes, me too, please.

LUCY wanders around again, peering over the railings.

RIVERA: *(looking up)* They're going away. Will they come out again?

DUFORT: I don't know. They don't come out every night.

RIVERA: But it's New Year's.

ᒪᕆᓐᓄᐊᖅ: *(ᖁ’ᒧᑦ ᑕᑯ’ᓗᓂ)* ᓄᓇᓕᐅᖅᑎᒥ’ᖕᓛᖅᑐᑦ ᑕᑯᑎᑖᑎᒍᑦ ᕿᓚᖕᒥᒃ.

ᑑᕗᐊᕐᑦ: ᐃᒪ’ᓇᓕ— *(ᑑᓯᒧᑦ)* ᔭᑦᕿᖃᑦᑕᖅᑐᓪᓕ ᓄᓇᒥ’ᖕᓛᖅᑐᑦ ᐳᔩᑦ ᑲᑎᑦᑕᕌᖕᒐᑕ ᔪᕿᓂᐅᑉ ᐳᔪᐊ’ᓂᒃ. ᐳᔩᑦ ᐊ’ᕝᕇᖏᑦᑐᑦ ᑲᑎᓕᕌᖕᒐᑕ ᑕᖅᓴᑦ ᐋ’ᓚᑦᖀᑦᖃᑦᑕᖅᑐᑦ ᑕ’ᓇ.

ᑑᓯ: *(ᑑᕗᐊᕐᑦᒧᑦ)* ᐃᓕᔭᕐᕕᖕᒥ ᐃᓕᔭᖅᑑᒐᓗᐊᖅᑐᒍᑦ ᐳᔩᑦ ᒥᒃᓵ’ᓄᑦ ᖃᐅᔨᔭᖅᑐᓕᕆᓂᕐᒥᒃ ᐃᓕᔭᖅᑎ’ᑐᑕ.

ᒪᕆᓐᓄᐊᖅ: ᑑᓯ ᐃᓕᔭᕐᕕᖕᒥ ᐱᑦᑎᐊᖅᐸᒃᑐᖅ ᖃᐅᔨᔭᕐᓂᕐᒥᒡᓗ ᑎᑎᕋᕐᓂᕐᒥᒡᓗ. ᑎᑎᕋᖃᑦᑕᖅᑐᕐᓗ ᐱᓯᓐᓄᐊᕐᓂᒃ.

ᐊᕐᓇᐅᑦᕿᔮᖅ ᕇ-ᑏ: ᐅᖃᓕᒫᖅᓯᒪᓕᖅᑐᖓ ᔮᖅᐸᓂᑭᐊᑦ ᐃᓄᐃᓐᖑᖅ ᐃᓚᐃᑦ ᐅᒃᐱᕆᔭᖃ’ᒪᑕ ᐊᖅᓴᕐᓂᑦ ᒧᖅᐸᖃᑦᑕ’ᒪᑕ ᐊᐃᕕᐅᑉ ᓂᐊᖁᐊ’ᓂᒃ ᒧᖅᐸᖃᖅᓱᑎᒃ ᓄᑕᖃᓪᓗᒎᖅ ᐅᓚᑉᕿᒍᑎᒃ ᐅᓐᓄᑦᑯᑦ ᐊᖅᓴᕐᓂᕐᓄᑦ ᓂᐊᖁᐃᖅᑕᐅᔪᓐᓇ’ᒪᑕᒎᖅ!

ᕆᕕᐊᕋ: *(ᓯᐹᓂᔅᑐᑦ ᐊᖦᕌᒍᑦ ᓄᑖᖅ ᐱ’ᓗᒍ ᐅᖃᐅᓯᑐᖃᖅᒥᒍᑦ)* ᑎᐅᔅ-ᒥᐅ.

ᓖ: ᑕᐃᑉᑯᐊᓪᓕ ᐊᑭᐊᓂᕐᒥᐅᑕᐃᑦ ᓄᐊᕖᑦᓴᓐᒥᐅᑕᐃᑦ ᐅᒃᐱᕆᔮᖃᖅᑐᑦ ᐊᖅᓴᕐᓂᓐᖑᖅ ᔭᑉᑯᐊᑦ ᐊᕐᓇᐃᑦ ᐅᓇᑕᖅᑎᑦ ᓇᐅᓕᒋᔭᐃᑦ ᐊᖅᓴᕐᓂᑦ— ᑕᐃᔭᐅᕙᑦ ᐊᕐᓇᐃᑦ ᕖᑦᑯᓇᔅ-ᓂᒃ. ᕿ’ᒥᕐᕚᐊᑦᑰᖅᐸᒃᓱᑎᒃ ᐅᓐᓂᖅᑑ’ᔨᕚ’ᒪᒋᑦ ᐅᓇᑕᖅᑎᑦ ᐊᖑᑎᑦ ᑐᖅᑯᓐᓂᐊᓕᕌᖕᒐᑕ ᑕᐃᑯᖕᒐᒎᖅ ᕚᓪᔭᓚᒧᑦ.

ᕆᕕᐊᕋ: ᔮᒦᑦᑐᖅ ᐃᒻᓇ ᕚᓪᔭᓚ?

ᒪᕆᓐᓄᐊᖅ: ᕿᓚᖕᒧᓐᖕᒎᖅ ᔭᐃᒪᓇᖅᑐᕕᖕᒧᑦ ᐊᒡᓴᖅᐸᒃᑕᐃᑦ ᐊᖑᑎᑦ.

ᐊᕐᓇᐅᑦᕿᔮᖅ ᕇ-ᑏ: *(ᕆᕕᐊᕋᒧᑦ)* ᕚᓪᔭᓚ ᐃᑉᑯᐊᑦ ᑕᐅᑐᒃᓯᒪᔭᑦᑲᑦ ᑕᕐᓇᔭᐅᑎᑦᑯᑦ ᑕᕐᓇᔭᐅᓯᐅᖅᑎ ᑕᐃᒻᓇ ᔮᓇᒥᒃᑭᐊᖅ ᐊᑎᐊᖃᖅᓱᓂ ᐳᐃᒍᖅᑕᕋ—ᐃᒥᖖᒐᒃᔭᓕᕋᒪ *(ᐅᐃᒥᓄᑦ)*—ᐊᐃ, ᖃᓄᕉᖅ ᐃᒻᓇ ᐊᑎᖃᖅᑐᖅ?

ᐊᖑᑕᐅᑦᕿᔮᖅ ᕇ-ᑏ: ᔭᓇ?

ᐊᕐᓇᐅᑦᕿᔮᖅ ᕇ-ᑏ: ᔩᒪᓂᒥᐅᑕᖅ ᑕᕐᓇᔭᐅᓯᐅᖅᓯᒪᓕᖅᑐᖅ ᕖᑦᑯᓇᔅ ᒥᒃᓵ’ᓄᑦ.

ᐊᖑᑕᐅᑦᕿᔮᖅ ᕇ-ᑏ: ᖃᐅᔨᒪᔾᕋᔭᐃᑕᔅᓱᒐ ᐃᒻᓇ— ᖃᐅᔨᒪᕙᖖᒋ’ᓇᒪᑑᓐᓃᑦ ᐅᖃᐅᔨᕆᓇᔭᐊᖅᐸᒃᑕ’ᓂᒃ.

MR. GRIFFITH-THOMSON: They don't know it's New Year's—how the hell would the northern lights know it was New Year's? *(to STEWARD)* More champagne.

CAPTAIN Matias enters in his smart white uniform. He is flanked on either side by MATSON in a gown and ROY in a tuxedo. Blind, ROY wears dark glasses and clutches MATSON's arm.

CAPTAIN: Ladies and gentlemen, *mesdames et messieurs* . . . please join me in raising a glass to the maiden voyage of the absolutely magnificent *Aurora Borealis*!

Everyone cheers and drinks.

MATSON: Thank you, Captain Matias. Four years ago a few of us stood near these exact coordinates and dreamed about creating something beautiful and functional and sustainable. Today the land and the ice are gone, and so is Circumpolar Oil, though they've left a terrible legacy, but we have achieved our dream . . . and tonight, as we sail through Victoria Strait in Nunavut, the traditional territory of the Netsilik and the graveyard of many explorers, let's toast Larkin and Roy, whose . . .

Everyone begins to cheer.

Wait, wait—HOLD IT . . . Larkin can't be with us, but her mother, Marianne, and her daughter, Lucy, are here on her behalf. Let's raise a glass to Larkin and the brave, unstoppable Roy, whose stunning media campaign has the *Aurora Borealis* booked solid for the next five years.

Everyone cheers and drinks.

And finally, let's raise a glass to each other . . . *(toasts)* "Here's to tall ships, here's to small ships, here's to all the ships at sea, but the best ships are our friendships, here's to you and here's to me."

More cheers and toasts.

AINSWORTH: *(toasts)* "The meek shall inherit the earth—the brave will get the oceans!"

ᑰᕗᐊᕐᑦ: ᐅᕚᒡᓄ-ᒥᒃ ᐊᑎᕐᑲᖅᑐᖅ?

ᐃᓯᖅᑯᓂ ᐊᐃᓐᓯᕗᐊᑦ ᐊᐅᓚᔩᖅᑯᓂ ᐃᒥᕐᑐᖕᒥᒃ ᓯᑯᓕᐊᕐᒥᒃ ᐅᐊᐃᓂᒥᒃ ᓇᓂᔮᒥᓂᒃ.

ᐊᐃᓐᓯᕗᐊᑦ: ᓴᑉᑯᓇᓂᒃ ᐆᒃᑐᕈᒪᔭᕐᑲᖅᐸ?

ᓈ ᐃᒪᐅᑎᓂ ᒪᓂᕆ’ᑐᓂᐅᒃ.

ᓈ: ᐊᑕᐃ . . . ᒥᑭᔭᓐᓄᐊᕐᒥᐅᒐᑐᐊᖅ.

ᐊᖑᑕᐅᑦᕿᔮᖅ ᕇ-ᑏ: ᐊᑕᐃ ᐱᓚᖓ.

ᒪᓇᓐᓄᐊᖅ: ᐅᕙᖓᑐ, ᖁᔭᓇᖅᑯᑎᑦ.

ᑑᓯ ᐊᓯᐊᓄᙵᓕᖅᑯᓂ ᑕᐅᓄᖓ ᐃᒪᕐᒧᑦ ᑕᐅᑐᓕᖅᑯᓂ.

ᓇᕕᐊᕋ: *(ᖁ’ᒧᑦ ᑕᑯᕆᐊ’ᒪᑦ)* ᕿᕐᑲᐱᐃᓕᖅᑐᑦ. ᐅᑎᑉᓯᐊᐱᒫᖅᐸᑦ ᐊᖅᓴᕐᓂᑦ?

ᑰᕗᐊᕐᑦ: ᖃᓄᑭᐊᖅ. ᐅᓐᓄᒃᑕᒫᖑᙱᑦᑐᒃᑯᑦ ᓴᑦᕿᖃᑦᑕ’ᒪᑕ ᑕᓴᑉᑯᐊᑦ.

ᓇᕕᐊᕋ: ᐊᔾᕌᒧᑦ ᓄᑖᖑᒐᑐᐊᕐᓕ.

ᐊᖑᑕᐅᑦᕿᔮᖅ ᕇ-ᑏ: ᖃᐅᔨᒪᙱᑦᑐᕐᑯᐃᑦ ᐊᔾᕌᒧ’ᒥᒃ ᓄᑖᖑᔭᒥᒃ— ᖃᓄᓇᑐᕐᑯᓪᓕ ᐊᖅᓴᕐᓂᑦ ᖃᐅᔨᒪᓇᔭᖅᐸᑦ ᓴᑦᕿᓇᕿᐊᕐᑐᑎᒃ? *(ᓴᓇᔨᒧᑦ)* ᐃᒥᕐᑐᒃᑐᑉᓯᐊᕐᓚᖓ.

ᑳᐱᑕᐃᔮ ᐃᓯᖅᑯᓂ ᐊ’ᓄᕌᖅᓯᒪᔭᖅ ᖃᑯᖅᑕᕐᓂᒃ. ᓴᓂᐊᓂ ᑕᔾᕙ ᒫᓴᑳᖅ ᕿᑕᐅᔮᖅᓯᒪᔭᖅ, ᑕᐃᒪᑐ ᐱᐃ ᐊᖑᑎᓯᐅᑎᒥᒃ ᐱᑦᑕᐅᔭᒥᒃ ᐊᑐᖅᑐᖅ. ᑕᐅᑐᒍᐃᕋᒥ ᐱᐃ ᑖᖅᑐᓂᒃ ᐃᔾᒐᒃᓯᒪᕐᑲᑦᑕᓕᖅᑐᖅ, ᑎᒍᒥᐊᕐᑐᐊᖅᑯᓂᐅᒡᑐ ᒫᓴᑳᑉ ᑕᓕᐊ.

ᑳᐱᑕᐃᔭ: ᐊᕐᓇᐃᑦᑐ ᐊᖑᑎᑦᑐ, *(ᐅᐃᕖᑐᑦ)* ᒥᑕᓪ-ᐃ-ᒥᓰᔅ . . . ᐊᑕᐃ ᐃᒪᐅᑎᓯ ᖁ’ᒧᒃᑎᑐᕆᑦ ᖁᔭᓕᓂᕐᒧᑦ ᐅᒥᐊᕐᔭᐊᑦᑎᐊᕙᓇᑐᒃ ᐅᓇ ᐊᑐᖅᑕᐅᓐᖓᕐᓂᖓᓄᑦ ᐃᖕᕆᔾᕋᔾᔭᑎᕆ’ᔮᐅ’ᑐᓂ.

ᑕᒪᐃᑕ ᖁ’ᒧᒃᓯ’ᑐᑎᒃ ᓂᐅᖅᓯ’ᑐᑎᒡᑐ.

ᒫᓴᑳᖅ: ᖁᔭᓇᖅᑯᑎᑦ, ᑳᐱᑕᐃᔮ. ᐅᑭᐅᑦ ᓯᑕᒪᐃᑦ ᓈᓯᒪᓕᖅᑐᑦ ᑕᔾᕙᓂ ᑲᑎᒪᓂᕆᔮᑉᑎ’ᓂᒃ ᐅᕐᑲᖅᓯᒪᓕᖅᑯᑕᑐ ᓴᓇᔪᒪ’ᑐᑕ

MR. GRIFFITH-THOMSON: Offshore—I'll second that.

CAPTAIN: More champagne!

DUFORT: *Plus de champagne!*

STEWARD: Champagne's on the way.

MARIANNE: Lucy, be careful. Don't lean over the railing.

LUCY: I'm not.

LUCY continues to lean over the railing.

ROY: Matson, tell me the dinner wasn't spectacular.

MATSON: The Quebec lamb and *tomme du kamouraska* sheep's milk cheese, then the quail eggs—exquisite, Roy.

MRS. GRIFFITH-THOMSON: Yes, it's a miracle Ryan ate his quail egg. Usually he just makes fun of little eggs.

LEE: Quails are tiny, perfect beings. Maybe they have souls.

MR. GRIFFITH-THOMSON: I prefer turkeys.

LUCY looks down over the railing.

LUCY: There's a piece of ice down there.

MARIANNE: It's just pretend ice, Lucy.

LUCY: Oh.

MATSON: It's almost time—party hats everyone! *(to the STEWARD)* Pass the basket!

ROY: I want the gold one.

ᐱᑦᑕᐅᔪᒥᒃ, ᐊᑑᑎᖅᑲᑦᑎᐊᖅᑐᒥᒃ, ᐊᕙᑎᒥᒃ ᐱᑦᑕᐅᔨᐃᖅᑎᑦᑎᙱᑦᑐᒥᒃ.
ᐅᐸᓗᒥᐅᔪᖅ ᓄᓇᖅᑲᕈᐃ’ᒪᑦ ᔪᑯᖅᑲᕈᐃ’ᒪᓪᓗ, ᐅᖅᓱᕐᔪᐊᓕᕆᔮᖅᑲᕈᐃᖅᖢᓂᓗ
ᔦᕈᖅᑎᑦᑎᖅᑳᕋᓗᐊᖅᖢᑎᒃ ᐊᕙᑎᒥᒃ, ᑭᔪᐊᓂᒃ ᑕᒃᑯᒃ
ᖤᑦᕿᔪᒪᔭᕋᓗᐊᑉᑎ’ᓂᒃ ᖤᑦᕿᑎᑦᑎᔪᒪᓕᕋᑉᑕ ᑕᔾᕙ . . . ᐅᓐᓄᒃᓗ
ᐃᖏᔾᕋᒐᑉᑕ ᐃᑭᕋᖤᑦᑯᑎᒍᑦ ᓇᑦᑎᓕᖕᒥᐅᑦ ᓄᓇᒋᔾᕋᓗᐊ’ᓂᒃ ᕿᓂᖅᑎᓪᓗ
ᐊᒥᔾᕋᖅᑐᑦ ᐃᓗᕕᖅᔪᒪᕕᒋᔭᐃ’ᓂᒃ, ᖁᔭᓕᓚᒍᒃ ᖄᑲᓐᓗ ᕈᐃᓗ . . .

ᐸᑦᑕᒃᑑᒪᓕᖅᑐᑦ ᖁᕕᐊᔦᒃᖢᑎᒃ.

ᒪᑉᖤᑳᖅ: ᐅᕕᑦᑎᐊᒍ ᐅᕕᑦᑎᐊᒍ—ᐊᑕ . . . ᖄᑲᓐ ᐅᕙᓃᙱᑦᑑᒐᓗᐊᖅ
ᑭᔪᐊᓂᒃ ᐊᓅᓇᖕᒐ ᒪᓇᓐᓄᐊᖅ ᐸᓂᐊᓗ ᓘᔭ ᐃᓚᐅ’ᓗᑎᒃ
ᐃᓇᖕᒋᖅᑎᒋᔭᐃᑦ ᐅᕙᓂ. ᐊᑕᐃ ᐃᒪᐅᑎᖁᑦ ᖁ’ᒍᒃᑎᓚᖁᑦ ᖄᑲᓐ ᐱ’ᓗᒍ
ᐅᓇᓗ ᕈᐃ ᐊᔪᓚᐃᑦᑐᕿᓗᒃ ᖃᐅᔮᑉᑲᐃᑦᑎᐊᕐᓂᖕᒐᓄᑦ ᐅᒥᐊᕐᔪᐊᖅ
ᐅᓇ ᐳᓚᕋᖅᑎᖅᑲᐃᓐᓇᕐᓂᐊᓕ’ᒪᑦ ᐊᑭᓕᖅᐸᖀᖅᔪᒪᔦᓂᒃ ᐅᑭᐅᓂᒃ
ᑕᓪᓕᒪᒻᒪᓇᖕᓂᒃ.

ᑕᒪᐃᑕ ᖁ’ᒍᒃᔪ’ᓗᑎᒃ ᓂᐅᖅᔪᒍᑦ.

ᒪᑉᖤᑳᖅ: ᑕᐃᒪᓗ ᐅᕙᑉᑎ’ᓄᑦ ᐃᒪᐅᑎᑉᑎ’ᓂᒃ ᖁ’ᒍᒃᔪᓕᖅᑕ
. . . *(ᖁ’ᒍᒃᑎ’ᓗᓂᐅᒃ ᐃᒪᐅᑎᓂ)—ᐅᖅᑲᓕᒫᒐᕐᒦᑦᑐᒥᒃ ᑕᐃ’ᓗᓂ:*
“ᐅᕝᕙ ᐅᒥᐊᕐᔪᐊᕐᓄᑦ ᐳᖅᑐᔪᓄᑦ, ᐅᒥᐊᕐᔪᐊᕐᓄᑦ ᒥᑭᑦᕿᔦᓄᑦ, ᑕᒪᐃ’ᓄᑦ
ᐅᒥᐊᕐᔪᐊᕐᓄᑦ ᑕᓇᐅᕐᒦᑦᑐᓄᑦ, ᑭᔪᐊᓂᒃᑕᐅᖅ ᐱᑦᑕᐅᓂᖅᓴᐃᑦᑑᔪᖅ
ᐃᓚᓐᓇᓃᖕᓂᒍᑦ, ᐅᕝᕙ ᐃᓕ’ᓄᑦ ᐅᕝᕙ ᐅᕙᒻᓄᑦ.”

ᖁ’ᒍᒃᔫᑦᖅᑲᑦᑕᖅᖢᑎᒃ ᓂᐅᖅᔪᕙᒃᖢᑎᒃ ᐅᖅᑲᐅᔪᖅᑲᖅᐸᒃᖢᑎᒃ
ᖁᔭᓕᔾᔪᑎᒥ’ᓂᒃ.

ᐊᐃᓐᓯᒍᐊᑦ: *(ᖁ’ᒍᒃᑎ’ᓗᓂᐅᒃ ᐃᒪᐅᑎᓂ) “ᐱᑦᑎᐊᖅᑐᑦ ᓄᓇᕐᔪᐊᕐᒥᒃ*
ᑐᓂᔭᐅᓂᐊᖅᑐᑦ—ᐃᖅᔪᓚᐃᑦᑐᓪᓗ ᑕᕆᐅᕐᔪᐊᕐᓂᒃ ᑐᓂᔭᐅᕙᓪᓗᖅᑐᒃᓴᑦ!”

ᐊᖑᑕᐅᑦᕿᔭᖅ ᕇ-ᑏ: ᑕᕆᐅᕐᒥ ᐃᒪᕐᒥ—ᐄ ᐊᔪᐅ.

ᑳᐱᑕᐃᔭ: ᐃᒥᕐᓗᖕᒥᒃ ᔦᓕ ᐱᑉᔪᐊᕐᓚᖕᒐ!

ᑑᒍᐊᕐᑦ: *(ᐅᐃᕖᑑᖅᖢᓂ)* ᐃᒥᕐᓗᖕᒥᒃ ᔦᓕ ᐱᑉᔪᐊᕐᓚᖕᒐ!

ᖤᓇᔮ: ᖅᑲᐃᑕᐅᓕᖅᑐᖅ.

ᒪᓇᓐᓄᐊᖅ: ᓘᔭ, ᐅᔾᔮᖅᑐᕐᓗᑎᑦ. ᐊᕙᓗᑉ ᐅᖕᒐᑖᓄᙵᒐᖅᑕᐃᓕᓗᑎᑦ
ᖄᖕᒋᙱᑦᓗᒍ.

The STEWARD quickly hands around the basket and people pick out a party hat and put it on. They chatter among themselves. MATSON hands ROY the gold one.

LUCY: I wish I could see a big whale.

MATSON: If we're lucky we might see some polar bears.

LUCY: Really?

CAPTAIN: Ladies and gentlemen, raise your glasses and . . . *(checks his device)* Ten!

ALL: Nine, eight, seven, six, five, four, three, two, one—HAPPY NEW YEAR! *Bonne Année!* HAPPY 2035 . . .

The following actions happen fast and overlap.

Fireworks, lights, and sounds explode from the ship as passengers blow their horns and spin their noisemakers repeating "Happy New Year," kissing each other and guzzling champagne. The CAPTAIN shakes hands with passengers as LEE kisses DUFORT, AINSWORTH kisses MARIANNE, MR. GRIFFITH-THOMSON and MRS. GRIFFITH-THOMSON kiss, then MR. GRIFFITH-THOMSON turns and kisses LEE. MRS. GRIFFITH-THOMSON kisses RIVERA . . . then LUCY sees something in the water . . .

LUCY calls to something in the water.

LUCY: HELLO . . . *(to the adults)* Granny, I see a whale.

MRS. GRIFFITH-THOMSON: *(to RIVERA)* Happy New Year.

RIVERA: *(to MRS. GRIFFITH-THOMSON) Feliz año.*

LUCY continues walking alongside the railing towards the stern, still watching something in the water.

LUCY calls to whatever she sees in the water.

LUCY: HELLO . . .

ᓘᓯ: ᐱᖕᒋᑦᑐᖓ.

ᓘᓯ ᐊᕙᓗ ᔪᓕ ᖄᓐᖏᔪᓐᖑᕌ.

ᕈᐃ: ᒪᑉᓴᑳᖅ, ᓂᕆᕕᕐᔦᐊᕐᓂᕗᑦ ᒪᒪᖅᑐᕋ̇ᓘᕆᓗᐊᖅ ᐊᔪᐅ?

ᒪᑉᓴᑳᖅ: ᐊᔪᐅ, ᑯᐸᐃᒃᔪᐅᑎ ᓂᕐᑭ, ᔫᓯᓕᐅᖅᔪᒪᔦᕐᓗ, ᐊᕐᑭᔾᒋᓐᓄᐊᑦ ᒪᓐᓂᓐᓄᐊᖕᒋᓪᓗ—ᒪᒪᖅᑐᐸᓇᓗᐃᑦ—ᐊᔪᐅ, ᕈᐃ.

ᐊᕐᓇᐅᑦᕐᑭᓴᖅ ᕇ-ᑏ: ᐄ, ᐅᐃᓚᓘᓐᓃᑦ ᓂᕆᕐᑲᑕᐅᔦᖅ ᒪᓐᓂᓐᓄᐊᕐᓂᒃ. ᒥᑭᕙᓪᓛᖅᑐᕆᑦᕐᑲᑦᑕᖅᖢᓂᒋᑦ ᓂᕆᕙᖕᒋᑦᑲᓗᐊ'ᒪᒋᑦ ᑕᓴᑉᑯᐊᑦ.

ᓛ: ᐊᕐᑭᔾᒋᓐᓄᐊᑦ ᑕᓴᑉᑯᐊᑦ ᐱᑦᑕᐅᔦᓇᓗᐃᑦ. ᑕᕐᓂᕐᑲᖅᑑ'ᓴᔦᑦ.

ᐊᖑᑕᐅᑦᕐᑭᓴᖅ ᕇ-ᑏ: ᐊᕐᑭᔾᒋᕐᔦᐊᓪᓚ ᒪᒪᑦᕐᑭᓴᐅᓇᔪᒋᓴᑦᑲᑦ.

ᓘᓯ ᑕᐅᓄᖓ ᑕᑯ'ᓗᓂ.

ᓘᓯ: ᑕᒃᑰᒃ ᑕᐅᓇᓂ ᔪᑯᕐᑲᖅᑐᖅ.

ᒪᕆᓐᓄᐊᖅ: ᔪᑯᖕᖑᐊᑐᐃᓐᓇᖅ ᑖᒻᓇ, ᓘᓯ.

ᓘᓯ: ᔪᓇᐅᕝᕙ.

ᒪᑉᓴᑳᖅ: ᕐᑯᓛᓄᖕᖓᕐᓂᐊᓕᖅᑐᖅ—ᓇᓴᖕᖑᐊᖅᔪ ᐊᑎᓕᖅᔪᐅᒃ! (ᓴᓇᔫᒧᑦ) ᑐᓂᐅᑦᕐᑲᐃᓕᕐᓗᑎᑦ ᓇᓴᖕᖑᐊᕐᓂᒃ.

ᕈᐃ: ᕐᑯᖅᓱᖅᑐᑦᑎᐊᕙᓇᓗᒃ ᐱᔦᒪᓴᕋ.

ᓴᓇᔫ ᑐᓂᐅᖅᑲᐃᓕᖅᓗᓂ ᐱᔦᒪᓴᒥ'ᓂᒃ ᑎᒍ'ᓗᑎᒃ ᓇᓴᖅᓗᑎᒡᓗ. ᐅᖅᑲᒪᖅᑲᑎᕇᓕᖅᓗᑎᒃ. ᒪᑉᓴᑳᖅ ᕐᑯᖅᓱᖅᑐᒥᒃ ᐱᔦᒪᓴᕋᓗᐊ'ᓂᒃ ᑐᓂ'ᓗᓂᐅᒃ ᑖᒻᓇ ᕈᐃ.

ᓘᓯ: ᑕᑯᔦᒪᓪᓗᐊᖅᑐᖓ ᐊᖏᔦᒥᒃ ᕐᑭᓇᓗᑲᕐᒥᒃ.

ᒪᑉᓴᑳᖅ: ᓇᓄᕐᓂᒃᓘᓐᓃᑦ ᑕᑯᔦᓖᔅᓴ'ᓴᕗᒍᓪᓚ.

ᓘᓯ: ᔪᓕᔦᒥᒃ?

DUFORT: *Bonne année et bonne santé.*

LEE kisses DUFORT.

LEE: Oh god—say it in French again.

DUFORT: *Bonne année et bonne santé.*

CAPTAIN: I best go below to wish everyone happy New Year there too . . .

CAPTAIN Matias exits.

LUCY calls again to something in the water.

LUCY: Come back . . .

The orchestra on the deck below plays "Auld Lang Syne" as LUCY walks alongside the railing towards the stern, following something in the water.

MATSON: *(sings)* Shall old acquaintance be forgot . . .

ALL: *(sing)* And never brought to mind?

LUCY calls again to something in the water.

LUCY: COME BACK.

ALL: *(sing)* Should old acquaintance be forgot
And auld lang syne?

MRS. GRIFFITH-THOMSON starts to sing robustly and RIVERA joins her . . . LUCY is climbing up the steps to the stern.

LUCY continues calling to something in the water.

LUCY: COME HERE.

ALL: *(sing)* For auld lang syne, my dear,
For auld lang syne,

ᑳᐱᑕᐃᔭ: ᐊᕐᓇᐃᓪᓗ ᐊᖑᑎᓪᓗ ᐊᑕᐃ ᐃᒪᐅᑎᓯ ᖁ'ᒧᒃᑎᓗᒋᑦ . . . (ᖃᕆᑕᐅᔭᕐᒥᓄᑦ ᑕᑯᔭᖅᑐᖅ) ᖁᓕᑦ!

ᑕᐃᒪᐃᑦ: 9, 8, 7, 6, 5, 4, 3, 2, 1—ᐊᔾᖀᒍᑦ ᓄᑖᕐᒧᑦ ᒪᒃᐱᔅᓴᖑᔭ'ᒪᑦ ᖁᔭᓇᖅᑯᖅ! ᖁᕕᐊᓱᑦᑎᐊᕆᑦᑎ 2035-ᒥ . . .

ᐅᐃᒪᐅᒪᔪᑦ ᑕᔾᕙ.

ᖄᖅᑕᖅᑐᑦ ᐃᑯᒪᓪᓗ ᓯᖅᑯᖅᑕᕐᓂᕐᓗ ᑐᓴᕐᓇᖅᑐᖅ ᐅᒥᐊᕐᔪᐊᕐᒥᑦ, ᐅᒥᐊᕐᔪᐊᕐᒦᑦᑐᓪᓗ ᖃᑉᓗᓈᑦ ᖁᖁᐊᕈᑎᒥ'ᓂᒃ ᓯᐱᒪ'ᓗᑎᒃ ᐅᓚᑉᖁᑎᑎᓪᓗ ᑲᐃᕕ'ᓗᒋᑦ ᐃᕆᐊᓛᖅᑐᑎᒃ "ᐊᔾᖀᒍᑦ ᓄᑖᕐᒥ ᖁᕕᐊᓱᒍᐃᑦᑏ-ᓚ'ᓗᑎᒃ, ᑯᓂᖅᑦᑕᐅᑎ'ᓗᑎᒃ ᐃᒥᖅᓗᑎᒃ ᐃᒥᕐᓗᖕᒥᒃ. ᑳᐱᑕᐃᔭᓗ ᑎᒎᑎᔪᖅ ᐳᓚᕋᖅᑎᓂᒃ, ᓛᓗ ᑯᓂᒃᓯᔪᖅ ᑑᕗᐊᕐᑦᒥᒃ, ᐊᐃᓐᓯᕙᐊᑦ ᑯᓂᒃᓯ'ᓗᓂ ᒪᕆᓐᓄᐊᕐᒥᒃ, ᓄᓕᐊᕇᒃ ᒌ-ᑏᑦᑯᒃ ᑯᓂᒃᑑᓪᓗ, ᐊᖑᑕᐅᑦᕿᔭᕐᓗ ᑯᓂᒃᓯ'ᒋᐊᖅᓗᓂ ᓛᒥᒃ. ᓄᓕᐊᖕᒐᓗ ᑯᓂᒃᓯ'ᓗᓂ ᕆᕕᐊᕋᒥᒃ . . . ᓘᓯᓗ ᑕᑯᑳᓪᓚ'ᒪᑦ ᓱᓇᒥᒃᑭᐊᖅ ᑕᕆᐅᕐᒥ ᐃᒪᕐᒥ ᑕᐅᓇᓂ . . .

ᓘᓯ ᐃᒪᕐᒦᑦᑐᒧᑦ ᑐᖅᓱᓚ'ᓗᓂ.

ᓘᓯ: ᐊᐃ . . . (ᐃᓂᕐᓂᕐᓄᓪᓗ) ᓂᖏᐅᖅ, ᑕᑯᒐᒪ ᕿᓇᓗᒐᕐᒥᒃ.

ᐊᕐᓇᐅᑦᕿᔭᖅ ᒌ-ᑏ: (ᕆᕕᐊᕋᒧᑦ) ᐊᔾᖀᒍᑦ ᓄᑖᕐᒥ ᖁᕕᐊᓱᒍᐃᑦ.

ᕆᕕᐊᕋ: (ᐊᕐᓇᐅᑦᕿᔭᖅ ᒌ-ᑏᒧᑦ) (ᓯᐹᓂᔅᑐᑦ ᐅᖃᖅᓗᓂ "ᐊᔾᖀᒍᑦ ᓄᑖᕐᒥ ᖁᕕᐊᓱᒍᐃᑦ") ᕙᓕᔅ ᐋᓐᔪ.

ᓘᓯᓐᓄᐊᖅ ᐱᓱᒃᑐᖅ ᑖᒻᓇᓗ ᐊᕙᓗ ᒪᓕᒃᓗᒍ ᐅᒥᐊᕐᔪᐊᑉ ᓯᕗᓂᐊ'ᓄᑦ, ᑕᐅᑐᐃᓐᓇᖅᓗᓂ ᐃᒪᕐᒧᑦ ᑕᐅᓄᖓ.

ᓘᓯ ᐃᒪᕐᒦᑦᑐᒧᑦ ᑐᖅᓱᓚ'ᓗᓂ.

ᓘᓯ: ᐊᐃ . . .

ᑑᕗᐊᕐᑦ: (ᐅᐃᕖᑐᑦ) ᐸᓐ-ᐊᓐᓂ-ᐃ-ᐸᓐᓵᓐᑎ (ᐊᔾᖀᒍᑦ ᓄᑖᕐᒥ ᖁᕕᐊᓱᒍᐃᑦᑎ ᐃᓅᑦᑎᐊᕐᓗᓯᓗ).

ᓛ ᑑᕗᐊᕐᑦᒥᒃ ᑯᓂᒃᓯ'ᓗᓂ.

ᓛ: ᐅᐃᕖᑐᑦ ᐅᖃᑉᓯᐊᕈᒃ ᑐᓴᕐᓂᖅᑐᖀᓗᒃ.

We'll take a cup of kindness yet,
For auld . . .

By now LUCY *is at the stern looking down at the water—*ANGU'ŘUAQ*'s big paw appears . . . then his head.* LUCY *jumps back.*

LUCY: Grammy—look!

ANGU'ŘUAQ *is old and skeletal . . . but desperate hunger has given him the strength to climb up the rungs of the ship. Painfully he tries to pull himself up onto the deck as the black water pours off of him.*

People scream.

MARIANNE: LUCY, GET AWAY FROM THERE!

MARIANNE *runs and grabs* LUCY *as* ANGU'ŘUAQ *struggles to climb up another rung.*

DUFORT: . . . It's trying to climb into the ship!

MARIANNE: Oh my God—

DUFORT: (*to* ANGU'ŘUAQ) HEY—GET LOST—

STEWARD: Everyone stay back—STAY BACK!

But people are too scared, or too fascinated, to move. LEE *holds her big belly.*

LEE: (*to her belly*) Stay calm, darling, stay calm.

MR. GRIFFITH-THOMSON: It doesn't look like the polar bear in the brochure.

ROY: A bear . . . (*panicking*) . . . no no NO NO NO!

MATSON: (*to* ROY) Come, let's go below—quickly.

ROY: NO NO NO . . .

MATSON *exits with* ROY.

ᑑᕗᐊᕐᑦ: *(ᐅᐃᖄᑐᑦ)* ᐸᓐ-ᐊᓐᓂ-ᐃ-ᐸᓐᓵᓐᑎ (ᐊᕝᖀᒍᑦ ᓄᑖᕐᒥ ᕐᑯᕚᐊᔪᒍᐃᑦᑎ ᐃᓅᑦᑎᐊᕐᑐᔨᑐ).

ᑳᐱᑕᐃᔭ: ᐅᓄᙱᑲᐅᒥᐊᖅᑲᕋᒪ ᑎᒎᑎᔭᖅᑐᕐᓱᒥᑦ ᐳᓚᕿᖅᑎᑦ ᐊᔫᑦ ᐊᕝᖀᒍᑦ ᓄᑖᙳᔪᖅ ᐱ’ᑐᒍ.

ᑳᐱᑕᐃᔭ ᐊᓂ’ᑐᓂ.

ᑑᓯ ᐃᒪᕐᒦᑦᑐᒧᑦ ᑐᖅᓱᓚ’ᑐᓂ.

ᑑᓯ: ᖃᐃᑉᓵᓇᑦ . . .

ᑐᓴᕐᓇᖅᑐᓕᐅᖅᑐᖄ’ᒪᑦ ᑐᓴᕐᓈᖅᑕᐅᔪᑦ ᐅᒥᐊᕐᔪᐊᑉ ᖄᖓᓂ ᐊᕝᖀᒍᑦ ᓄᑖᖅᔨᐅᑎᒥᒃ ᐃᖏᐅᓕᖅᑐᑎᒃ. ᑑᓯᓐᓄᐊᕐᑐ ᔪᓚ ᐱᔪᒃᑐᖅ ᐊᕙᑐ ᒪᓕᒃᑐᒍ ᐅᒥᐊᕐᔪᐊᑉ ᔪᕗᓂᐊ’ᓄᑦ ᔪᓚ ᑕᐅᑐᐃᓐᓇᖅᑐᓂ ᐃᒪᕐᒧᑦ ᑕᐅᓄᖓ.

ᒪᑉᓵᖅ: *(ᐃᖏᐅᓕᖅᑐᖅ)* ᐃᓚᓐᓇᕗᑦ ᐳᐃᒍᖅᑐᒥᑦ . . .

ᑕᒪᐃᑕ: *(ᐃᖏᐅᖅᑐᑦ)* ᐊᐅᓚᔩᔪᐃᕐᑐᒥᑦ?

ᑑᓯ ᐃᒪᕐᒦᑦᑐᒧᑦ ᑐᖅᓱᓚ’ᑐᓂ.

ᑑᓯ: ᐊᑕᐃ ᖃᐃᑉᓵᓇᑦ . . .

ᑕᒪᐃᑕ: *(ᐊᑕᐅᑦᑎᑦᑯᑦ)* ᐃᓚᓐᓇᕗᑦ ᐳᐃᒍᖅᑐᒥᑦ . . . ᑕᐃᒪ’ᖓᓂᑐᖃᖅ?

ᐊᕐᓇᐅᑦᕿᔮᖅ ᓰ-ᑏ ᐃᖏᐅᕐᑐᐊᓕᖅᑐᖅ ᓇᕙᐊᕋᑐ ᐃᖏᐅᕐᑐᐊᖃᑎᒋᓕᖅᑐᓂᐅᒃ . . . ᑑᓯ ᒪᔪᕋᓕᖅᑐᖅ ᐅᒥᐊᕐᔪᐊᑉ ᔪᕗᓂᐊᑕ ᖄᖓᓄᑦ.

ᑑᓯ ᐃᒪᕐᒦᑦᑐᒧᑦ ᑐᖅᓱᓚᒋ’ᑐᓂ.

ᑑᓯ: ᖃᐃᑲᐃᑦ.

ᑕᒪᐃᑕ: *(ᐃᖏᐅᖃᑎᒌᒃᑐᑦ)* ᑕᐃᒪ’ᖓᓂᑐᖃᖅ, ᐊᐃ, ᑕᐃᒪ’ᖓᓂᑐᖃᖅ, ᐱᑦᑎᐊᕐᓂᕐᒥᒃ ᐊᑐᕐᑐᑕ, ᑕᐃᒪᖓ . . .

*ᑑᓯ ᐅᒥᐊᕐᔪᐊᑉ ᑭᖑᐊᓃᓕ’ᒪᑦ ᑕᐅᓄᖓ ᑕᐅᑐᒃᑐᓂ ᔪᓚ—
ᕿᓇᓗᒐᐅᖕᒋᓐᓂ’ᒪᑦ ᑕᕝᕙᒎᖅ ᐊᖑ’ᔪᐊᖅ ᐃᔨᒐᒡᔪᐊᓂ*

STEWARD: Where's the captain— *(calls)* CAPTAIN!

RIVERA: It looks too weak to hurt anyone.

LEE: Maybe it's a giant skunk or something.

AINSWORTH: It's the biggest predator on earth—this guy could eat a car!

They use their noisemakers to try to frighten the bear.

STEWARD: Don't go near the bear.

LUCY: Its paws are so big.

MARIANNE: Hang on to me, Lucy.

LUCY: Are you scared?

MARIANNE: *(terrified)* No. Just stay back.

LEE takes pictures of the bear with her device.

LEE: Emilie is never going to believe I saw a polar bear ON our ship!

MR. GRIFFITH-THOMSON: *(to ANGU'ŘUAQ)* SCRAM—BEAT IT—

STEWARD: Please don't go near the bear while I get the—

The STEWARD exits . . . calling.

(off stage) CAPTAIN MATIAS.

DUFORT: *(to ANGU'ŘUAQ)* GO AWAY . . . SHOO—

RIVERA: He's too old to cause any trouble.

AINSWORTH: *(to ANGU'ŘUAQ)* Hey, old chap—hey, look up here—

AINSWORTH throws his champagne at the bear.

ᐃᔅᒃᓱᓂᐅᒃ . . . ᓂᐊᖁᐊᓗ ᔅᑦᕿᒃᓱᓂ ᐋᕐᓗ'ᒪᑦ. ᓘᓯ ᖁᒡᓗᒃᓱᓂ ᑭᖕᒍ'ᒧᑦ ᕿᔾᔨᖅᑐᖅ.

ᓘᓯ: ᓂᖕᒋᐅᖅ—ᑕᒃᑰᓇᓗᒃ!

ᐊᖕᒍ'ᕙᐊᖅ ᐊᖕᒍ'ᕙᐊᑐᖅᑲᐅᓚ'ᒪᑦ ᔅᐅᓃᓐᓇᐅ'ᓗᓂ . . . ᑭᔭᐊᓂᒃ ᐆᒪᓇᕗᐊᕐᓂᖕᒐ ᔅᖖᒋᓂᐊᓄᑦ ᒪᓯᖃᕈᖕᓇᓐᓄᐊᖅᑐᖅ ᒪᓯᖃᐅᑎᓂᒃ ᐅᒥᐊᕐᕙᐊᑉ ᒪᓯᖃᐅᑕᐃ'ᓂ ᕗᒃᑲᐃᑦᑐᒥᒃ ᒪᓯᖅᓱᓂ ᐊ'ᓂᑭᕗᑦᖁᖅᓱᓂ ᐅᒥᐊᕐᕙᐊᑉ ᖂᖕᒐᓄᖖᒐᖃᕗᐊᖅᓱᓂ ᒪᓯᖅᑐᖅ, ᐃᒪᖅ ᕿᕐᓇᓐᒃᑐᖅ ᒥᑦᖁᐊ'ᓂᑦ ᖁᕚᕙᐊᓘ'ᓗᓂ.

ᐃᓇᐊᓛᒪᕙᐊᓘᓚᖅᑐᑦ.

ᒪᓐᓄᐊᖅ: ᓘᓯ, ᔅᒨᖖᒐᓇᐊᕐᓗᑎᑦ ᑐᐊᕚ!

ᒪᓐᓄᐊᖅ ᐃᓐᖑᑕᕐᒥᓂᒃ ᑎᒍᓪᓚᕐᔅᓗᒃᓱᓂ ᐊᖕᒍ'ᕙᐊᖅ ᒪᓯᖃᖃᕗᐊᖅᑐᓇᓘ'ᒪᑦ.

ᑑᕗᐊᕐᑦ: . . . ᐅᒥᐊᕐᕙᐊᕐᒧᖖᒐᐅᓚᕐᑲᖅᑑᓐᓂᖅ!

ᒪᓐᓄᐊᖅ: ᐃᖅᓯᓇᖅᑐᖄᓗᒃ—

ᑑᕗᐊᕐᑦ: (ᐊᖕᒍ'ᕙᐊᕐᒧᑦ) ᐅᓇᓇᓗᒃ—ᐊᕗᖖᒐᓇᑦ—

ᔅᓇᔮ: ᖃᒡᓚᑦᑕᐃᓚᓗᓯ—ᐊᕝᓃᓗᓯ!

ᐃᖅᓯᓪᓗᐊᕚᒃᑲᒥᒃ ᑕᐅᑐᒡᓗᐊᖅᓱᑎᒡᓗ ᐃᖕᒍᖖᒋᒻᒪᓇᒃᑐᑦ. ᓛ ᓯᖕᒐᐃᒐᒥ ᓈᕐᒥᓂᒃ ᐸᑎᖕᒥᕙᖅ.

ᓛ: (ᓄᑕᖃᒃᓴᒥᓄᑦ) ᔅᐃᒪᓗᑎᑦ, ᐅᓇᓐᓄᐊᖅ.

ᐊᖕᒍᑕᐅᑦᕿᔾᔭᖅ ᑰ-ᑏ: ᓇᓄᖅ ᐅᓇ ᐊ'ᔫᖖᒍᐊᕐᒦᑦᑐᓂᐅᖕᒐᓂᑦ ᐊ'ᔫᖖᒋᑦᑐᓇᓗᒃ.

ᐱᐃ: ᓇᓄᓇᓗᒃ . . . (ᐅᐃᒻᒪᓚᖅᓱᓂ) . . . ᐄᕐᑭ ᐄᕐᑭ ᐄᕐᑭ ᐄᕐᑭ ᐄᕐᑭ!

ᒪᑉᔅᑳᖅ: (ᐱᐃᒧᑦ) ᐊᑕᐃ ᐊᑖᓄᖖᒐᐅᓗᒃ—ᑐᐊᕚ.

ᐱᐃ: ᐄᕐᑭ ᐄᕐᑭ ᐄᕐᑭ . . .

ᐊᓂ'ᓗᑎᒃ ᒪᑉᓴᑳᕐᓗ ᐱᐃᓗ.

MR. GRIFFITH-THOMSON ventures closer, clutching a bottle of champagne.

MRS. GRIFFITH-THOMSON: Hon, be careful—

ANGU'ŘUAQ rises up, his head momentarily visible. LEE screams.

MR. GRIFFITH-THOMSON: . . . It's covered in oil.

LEE: . . . Eeewww.

ANGU'ŘUAQ disappears from view.

MR. GRIFFITH-THOMSON: *(to ANGU'ŘUAQ)* Stay down, boy, down . . .

RIVERA: Hey, people—stop! It's probably starving.

The STEWARD enters.

STEWARD: Captain's on his way—

DUFORT: *(to the STEWARD)* They're throwing things at the bear—

STEWARD: Please—everyone remain calm—

DUFORT: A polar bear's dangerous—a hungry polar bear's even more dangerous—

DUFORT yanks a lifesaver off the railing. The STEWARD tries to take it from him and it's a bit of a tug of war, but DUFORT wins and throws the lifesaver down at the animal.

LUCY: It's getting hurt—they're hurting the bear, Grammy.

MARIANNE: They're helping it to go back into the water.

AINSWORTH: *(to STEWARD)* MORE CHAMPAGNE—BRING MORE BOTTLES.

The STEWARD takes two bottles of champagne from the buffet table, but before the STEWARD has a chance to pour . . .

ᓴᓇᔮ: ᓇᐅᓪᓕ ᑳᐱᑕᐃᔭ—(ᑐᖅᑯᓚᑦᑐᒍ) ᑳᐱᑕᐃᔮ!

ᓂᕕᐊᕋ: ᓴᖏᑦᑐᓇᓗᒃ ᐱᕐᓕᕆᒥ ᐋᓐᓂᖅᔪᓚᐃᑦᑰᖅᑐᖅ.

ᓖ: ᓇᓅᖏᑦᑑᓯᔪᕐᔫᓐᓃᑦ ᔪᓇᓇᓗᒃᑕᐅᑭᐊᖅ ᐅᓇ ᒪᒪᐃᑦᑰᖅᑐᖅ.

ᐊᐃᓐᓯᒍᐊᑦ: ᑕᓴᑉᑯᐊᑦ ᓇᓄᐃᑦ ᐊᖏᓛᖑᒍᑦ ᔪᓚᕐᔪᐊᕐᒥ ᓂᕿᑐᖅᑎᓂᒃ—
ᐅᓇ ᓄᓇᑦᑰᕈᑎᒥᒃ ᓂᓂᔪᖕᓇᒻᒪᓂᑦᑰᖅᑐᖅ!

ᐅᓚᑉᕿᐅᔭᕐᒥᓐᓄᑦ ᓂᐱᑐᔪᑎᒍᑦ ᓇᓄᖅ ᕿᒫᑎᓐᓇᔪᐊᖅᑕᐃᑦ.

ᓴᓇᔮ: ᖃᓪᓕᕆᐊᖏᕆᓗᒍ ᓇᓄᖅ.

ᓘᓯ: ᐃᔪᑲᕆᑦ ᐊᕆᔪᕌᓗᐃᑦ.

ᒪᓂᓐᓄᐊᖅ: ᑎᒍᖕᒐ ᓘᓯ.

ᓘᓯ: ᐃᖅᔪᕕᑦ?

ᒪᓂᓐᓄᐊᖅ: (ᐃᖅᔪᑲᓗᐊᖅᑯᓗᓂ) ᐄᕿ. ᖃᓪᓕᕆᐊᖅᑕᐃᓕᐅᒃ.

ᓖ ᓇᓄᕐᒥᒃ ᐊᔾᔭᓕᐅᒪᔪᖅ ᖃᓂᑕᐅᔮᒍᑦ.

ᓖ: ᐃᓚᓐᓇᑦᑲᓕ ᐅᒃᐱᕐᓂᐊᖏᑦᑐᑦ ᑕᑯᑲᒪ ᓇᓄᕐᒥᒃ ᐅᒥᐊᕐᔪᐊᑉᑕ
ᐃᓗᐊᓂ ᐊᔾᔭᓕᐅᕐᓗᒍ ᑭᔪᐊᓂᒃ!

ᐊᖑᑕᐅᑦᕿᔭᖅ ᕿ-ᑏ: (ᐊᖑᔪᐊᕐᔫᑦ) ᐊᒎᖕᑲᓂᑦ—ᐊᑕᐃ—

ᓴᓇᔮ: ᖃᓪᓕᕆᐊᖏᕆᓗᒍ ᓇᓄᖅ ᖃᐃᑦᑯᓂᐊᖅᑕᕋ ᑳᐱᑕᐃᔭ—

ᐊᓂᑦᑐᓂ ᓴᓇᔮ . . . ᑐᖅᑯᓚᑦᑐᓂ.

ᓴᓇᔮ: (ᐊᕚᖕᑲᑦ) ᑳᐱᑕᐃᔮ.

ᑑᒍᐊᕐᑦ: (ᐊᖑᔪᐊᕐᔫᑦ) ᐊᒎᖕᑲᓂᑦ . . . ᐊᑕᐃ ᐊᒎᖕᑲ—

ᓂᕕᐊᕋ: ᖃᓄᕐᓕᐅᓚᐃᑦᑐᖅ ᓴᖏᑦᑐᓚᓘᑦᒪᑦ ᐊᖑᔪᐊᑐᖅᑲᐅᑲᒥ ᐃᓐᓇᒃᓴᐸᓇᓘᑦᒪᑦ.

ᐊᐃᓐᓯᒍᐊᑦ: (ᐊᖑᔪᐊᕐᔫᑦ) ᐅᓇᓇᓗᒃ ᐅᒍᖕᑲ ᕿᕕᐊᓂᑦ—ᓴᒧᖕᑲ—

Sorry, chap, we need both.

. . . AINSWORTH grabs both bottles from the STEWARD, takes aim, and hurls them down at the bear. DUFORT grabs a deck chair.

STEWARD: *(to AINSWORTH)* No, sir, no . . . don't throw bottles at the bear—

RIVERA: *(to AINSWORTH)* Enough—

DUFORT throws the deck chair down at the bear.

LUCY: *(to AINSWORTH)* STOP—DON'T DO THAT!

MARIANNE: Lucy—

DUFORT lifts up a small table and RIVERA goes after him.

RIVERA: I said enough— *(slams down the table that DUFORT is holding)* THAT'S ENOUGH.

MR. GRIFFITH-THOMSON: *(to RIVERA)* Get the hell out of the way.

AINSWORTH: Hey, this is the same bear—this is the same bear that attacked Roy!

LEE: That would be just too spooky.

DUFORT: That's the one!

AINSWORTH: Look, it's got one ear—IT'S THE SAME FUCKING BEAR!

LEE: Language—there's a child here!

DUFORT: He blinded Roy—I'll blind him.

. . . DUFORT picks up the table again and throws it down at the bear. Sounds come from the bear . . . a half growl, half cry.

MR. GRIFFITH-THOMSON: *(to the bear)* Ugly old bear—hey, you're standing on a section of our ice!

ᐊᐃᓐᓱᖁᐊᑦ ᐃᒪᐅᑎᓂ ᐃᒥᕐᓗᓕᒃ ᐃᒋ'ᓗᓂᐅᒃ ᓇᓄᕐᒧᑦ.

ᐊᖑᑕᐅᑦᕿᓭᖅ ᕆ-ᕆ ᖃᒡᓕᒋᐊᕋᓐᓂᖅᑖ ᑎᒍᒥᐊᕐᓗᐊᖅᑐᓂ
ᐃᒥᕐᓗᖅᑲᐅᑎᒥᒃ ᔦᑯᓕᐊᕐᒥᒃ.

ᐊᕐᓇᐅᑦᕿᓭᖅ ᕆ-ᕆ: ᐊ'ᓂᖅᑕᐃᓕᓗᑎᑦ—

ᐊᖑᕐᔦᐊᖅ ᖄᖕᒐᓄᖖᒐᖅᐸᓪᓕᐊᓕᕋᒥ, ᓂᐊᕐᑯᐊ
ᑕᐅᑐᖕᓇᓐᓄᐊᖅᑐᓂ. ᓖ ᐃᓇᐊᓛᕐᓗᐊᓕᖅᑐᖅ.

ᐊᖑᑕᐅᑦᕿᓭᖅ ᕆ-ᕆ: . . . ᐅᖅᓱᕐᔦᐊᕐᒧᑦ ᒥᖑᐊᖅᔦᒪᑦᑎᐊᖅᑐᑦ ᒥᑦᕐᑯᐃᑦ.

ᓖ: . . . ᐃᖅᔦᓇᖅᑐᖂᓗᒃ ᓭᓗᒪᐃᑦᑐᓇᓗᒃᑕᐅᖅ.

ᐊᖑ'ᔦᐊᖅ ᑕᐅᑐᖕᓇᕈᐃᑲᓐᓄᐊᓕᖅᑐᓂ.

ᐊᖑᑕᐅᑦᕿᓭᖅ ᕆ-ᕆ: (ᐊᖑ'ᔦᐊᕐᒧᑦ) ᐅᓇᓂ, ᐅᓇᓃᓗᑎᑦ, ᑕᐅᓄᖕᒐ, ᐊᑕᐃ . . .

ᓇᕕᐊᕋ: ᑲᒪᒋᔦᐃᖅᔦᐅᒃ—ᑕᐃᒪ'ᓇ! ᑳᒃᑐᐊᓘᔦᒃᓴᐅ'ᒪᑦ ᐱᕐᓕᔦᐸᓇᓗᒃ.

ᓭᓇᔦ ᐃᔦᖅᑐᓂ.

ᓭᓇᔦ: ᑳᐱᑕᐃᓭ ᖃᐃᓕᖅᑐᖅ—

ᔫᖁᐊᕐᑦ: (ᓭᓇᔦᒧᑦ) ᒥᓪᓗᖅᔦᓇᔦᐊᖅᑐᓇᓗᐃᑦ ᓇᓄᕐᒥᒃ—

ᓭᓇᔦ: ᑕᒪᐸᔦ—ᓭᐃᒪᓇᔦᐊᕐᓗᔦ ᐅᐃᒪᔦᐃᓇᑦᑎ—

ᔫᖁᐊᕐᑦ: ᐃᖅᔦᓇᖅᑐᓇᓗᐃᑦ ᓇᓄᐃᑦ ᑳᒃᑎ'ᓗᒋᓪᓗ ᐃᖅᔦᓇᕐᓂᖅᓴᐃᑦᑑ'ᒪᑕ—

ᔫᖁᐊᕐᑦ ᑎᒍᔦᓪᓕᕐᓭ'ᒪᑦ ᐳᒃᑕᑎᒥᒃ. ᓭᓇᔦᓗ ᐋᖅᓭᕋᔦᐊᖅᑐᒍ
ᓄᔦᑎᓕᖅᑑᒃ, ᑭᔦᐊᓂᒃ ᔫᖁᐊᕐᑦ ᐊᑭᒐᒥ ᐳᒃᑕᑎ ᐃᒋ'ᓗᓂᐅᒃ
ᒪᔪᕋᕋᔦᐊᖅᑐᒧᑦ ᓇᓄᕐᒧᑦ ᐊᕚᕋᔦᐊᖅᑐᒍ.

ᔫᓯ: ᓂᖕᒋᐅᖅ, ᐅᓇ ᓇᓄᖅ ᐱᓂᕐᓗᒃᑕᐅᓕᖅᑐᖅ—ᐅᑯᐊᑦ
ᐋ'ᓂᖅᔦᓇᔦᐊᖅᑐᓇᓗᐃᑦ.

ᒪᓇᓐᓄᐊᖅ: ᐃᒪᕐᒧᑦ ᐅᑎᖅᑎᓐᓇᔦᐊᖅᔦᓐᓇᖅᑕᐃᑦ.

ᐊᐃᓐᓱᖁᐊᑦ: (ᓭᓇᔦᒧᑦ) ᐃᒥᕐᓗᒃᑐᐸᔦᐊᖅᑕ—ᔦᑯᓕᐊᕐᓂᒃ ᓭᑦᕐᑯᒻᒥᖅᔦᒋᐊᓇᑦ ᓭᒧᖕᒐ.

AINSWORTH picks up another deck chair but RIVERA grabs it . . .

RIVERA: *(to AINSWORTH)* I said enough!

. . . and RIVERA gives the chair to the STEWARD.

MR. GRIFFITH-THOMSON: *(in the direction of the bear)* GET OFFA OUR ICE.

MRS. GRIFFITH-THOMSON: I can't watch this—I'm going up to the bow to enjoy a bit of peace and quiet.

CAPTAIN Matias enters.

RIVERA: *(to MRS. GRIFFITH-THOMSON)* May I join you?

MRS. GRIFFITH-THOMSON: Yes, please do.

MRS. GRIFFITH-THOMSON and RIVERA exit.

CAPTAIN: Where's the bear now?

AINSWORTH: Clinging to the rungs, Captain—

STEWARD: It's right down there—

LUCY: CAPTAIN—PLEASE SAVE THE BEAR.

MARIANNE: *(to LUCY)* The captain's here now—everything's going to be fine.

The CAPTAIN looks down over the stern.

CAPTAIN: Now there's a sorry looking sight.

MR. GRIFFITH-THOMSON picks up a tray of fancy desserts.

MR. GRIFFITH-THOMSON: Let's give it something to eat.

AINSWORTH: Are you crazy—it's climbing up here to eat us—

MR. GRIFFITH-THOMSON: If it eats something it might leave—

ᓴᓇᖢ ᑎᒍᖢᓪᓚᕐᓴᖅᑐᖅ ᒪᕐᕈᖕᓂᒃ ᖢᑯᓕᐊᕐᓂᒃ ᐃᒃᐸ'ᒦᑑᖕᓂᒃ
ᐃᒪᐅᑎᓄᑦ ᑯᕙᖢᓂᐊᓕᖅᑎ'ᑐᒍᑐ ᓄᑦᖃᖅᑎᑕᐅ'ᒪᑦ . . .

ᐊᐃᓐᓯᖁᐊᑦ: ᐅᑯᐊᒃ ᑕᒪᑦᑰᒃ ᐱᔫᖅᑲᖅᑕᑦᑯᒃ ᖢᑯᓕᐊᒃ.

. . . ᐊᐃᓐᓯᖁᐊᑦ ᑎᒍ'ᑐᓂᒥᑦᑐ ᖢᑯᓕᐊᒃ ᐃᒥ'ᑐᒥᑦᑐ ᑕᐅᓄᖕᒐ
ᓇᓄᕐᔪᑦ ᒪᕙᕋᕋᖢᐊᖅᑐᔪᑦ. ᑑᖁᐊᕐᓪᓗ ᑎᒍᖢᒥᐊᖅᓱᓂ ᐃᒃᖢᕙᐅᑕᕐᒥᒃ.

ᓴᓇᖢ: (ᐊᐃᓐᓯᖁᐊᕐᔪᑦ) ᐋᕐᑭ, ᐋᕐᑭ . . . ᐃᒥᑦᑎᕐᑲᑦᑕᖖᒥᑐᑎᑦ
ᖢᑯᓕᐊᕐᓂᒃ ᓇᓄᕐᔪᑦ—

ᓇᕕᐊᕋ: (ᐊᐃᓐᓯᖁᐊᕐᔪᑦ) ᑕᐃᒪ'ᓇ—

ᑑᖁᐊᕐᓪᓗ ᐃᒃᖢᕙᐅᑕᖅ ᑕᐃᒪ ᐃᒥ'ᑐᓂᐅᒃ ᑕᐅᓄᖕᒐ ᓇᓄᕐᔪᑦ.

ᓘᓯ: (ᐊᐃᓐᓯᖁᐊᕐᔪᑦ) ᐋᕐᑭ—ᑕ'ᓇᐅᖖᒋᑦᑐᖅ!

ᒪᓇᓐᓄᐊᖅ: ᓘᓯ—

ᑑᖁᐊᕐᑦ ᑎᒍᖢ'ᒪᑦ ᐃᒃᐸᑎᓐᓄᐊᕐᒥᒃ ᓇᕕᐊᕋ ᐱᒥᐊᖅᓱᓂᐅᒃ
ᐱᑦᑕᐃᓕᕐᑯ'ᑐᒍ.

ᓇᕕᐊᕋ: ᐅᕐᑳᓪᓚᒃᑲᓗᐊᕋᒪ ᐊᒃᐱᐅᑎᖄᖢ ᑕᐃᒪ'ᓇᒎᖅ—
(ᐸᑎᒃᑐᐊᖅᓱᓂᐅᒃ ᐃᒃᐸᑎ ᑖᒻᓇ ᑑᖁᐊᕐᑦ ᑎᒍᒥᐊᖅᑖ) ᑕᐃᒪ'ᓇᒎᖅ.

ᐊᖕᒍᑕᐅᑦᕿᖄᖅ ᑮ-ᑏ: (ᓇᕕᐊᕋᒍᑦ) ᐊᖁᖖᒐᑲᐃᑦ.

ᐊᐃᓐᓯᖁᐊᑦ: ᐅᓇᓕ ᓇᓄᖅ ᑕᕝᕙ ᕿᐃᒥᒃ ᑮᖢᖢᒪᓕᖅᑐᖅ!

ᓛ: ᐃᓗᐃᑦᑐᕌᓗᕐᓗᒃ ᑖᒻᓇᐅᓐᓂᕿᓂ.

ᑑᖁᐊᕐᑦ: ᑕᕝᕙ ᑖᒻᓇᐅᖢᖅ!

ᐊᐃᓐᓯᖁᐊᑦ: ᑕᒃᑰᒃ ᐊᑕᐅᖢᖕᓇᕐᒥᒃ ᖢᐅᑎᓕᒃ—ᑖᒻᓇᐅᓐᓂᖅᑯᕐᓕ!

ᓛ: ᐱᕗᓪᓛᖖᒋᓪᓗᖢ—ᓄᑕᕋᕐᒥᒃ ᑐᓴᖢᖅᑲ'ᒪᑦ!

ᑑᖁᐊᕐᑦ: ᕿᐃᒥᒃ ᑕᐅᑐᒍᐃᖅᑎᑦᑎ'ᒪᑦ—ᑕᐅᑐᒍᐃᖅᑎᓐᓂᐊᖅᑕᕋᓕ ᓇᓄᕐᔪᒃ.

CAPTAIN: No, don't feed it—

MR. GRIFFITH-THOMSON: But it'll go away if we—

MR. GRIFFITH-THOMSON throws the tray down to the bear.

CAPTAIN: NO, DON'T . . . PLEASE! Let cooler heads prevail. *(to the STEWARD)* We have to manually lower Lifeboat Two. There's no other way.

STEWARD: Yes, sir.

CAPTAIN: *(to AINSWORTH, DUFORT, and MR. GRIFFITH-THOMSON)* Gentlemen, give him a hand—hurry.

The STEWARD exits followed by AINSWORTH, DUFORT, and MR. GRIFFITH-THOMSON. The CAPTAIN looks over the stern again.

LUCY: They're going to rescue the bear, Grammy.

MARIANNE: Yes, yes, I can see that. Let's go below. It's after your bedtime.

LUCY: They're going to put the bear in a lifeboat.

LEE: From now on I'm only drinking ginger ale.

The STEWARD, AINSWORTH, DUFORT, and MR. GRIFFITH-THOMSON enter carrying a lifeboat—two on each side. It's not so much heavy as it is cumbersome. The many glasses of champagne have made the men unsteady on their feet. They improvise small talk as they attempt this feat.

AINSWORTH: We oughta have a photo of this in the brochure.

They laugh.

CAPTAIN: Hurry, gentlemen. It looks like he's going to try again . . .

The CAPTAIN looks over stern, helping the men to guide the boat.

Position it directly above the animal.

. . . ᑑᕗᐊᕐᑦ ᑎᒍᑉᔨᐊᖅᓱᒍ ᐃᒃᐸᑎᓐᓄᐊᖅ ᐃᒥ'ᓗᓂᐅᒃ ᑕᐅᓄᖓ ᒪᔪᕋᕋᔭᐊᖅᑐᒧᑦ. ᓇᓄᕐᓗ ᑐᔭᕐᓇᓕᖅᑐᖅ . . . ᔭᖕᒌᑦᑐᒥᒃ ᖃᑎᒡᕙᓖᖅᓱᓂ ᖁᐊ'ᓗᓂᓗ.

ᐊᖑᑕᐅᑦᕿᔮᖅ ᒌ-ᑏ: (ᓇᓄᕐᒧᑦ) ᐃᓂᕐᑯᓇᐃᑦᑐᓇᓗᒃ ᓇᓄᕐᓱᒃ—ᐄᖅ ᑕᒃᑰᒃ ᔨᑯᖑᐊᑉᑎ'ᓄᖕᖓᐅᔩᑎᑦ!

ᐊᐃᓐᓯᕗᐊᑦ ᑎᒍᔨᓪᓚᕐᔭ'ᒥ'ᒪᑦ ᐃᒃᔨᕙᐅᑕᕐᒥᒃ ᐃᒥᑕᒃᓴᒥᒃ ᑭᔨᐊᓂᒃ ᓇᕕᐊᕋ ᐋᖅᔮᖅᔪ'ᓗᓂ . . .

ᓇᕕᐊᕋ: (ᐊᐃᓐᓯᕗᐊᕐᒧᑦ) ᐅᖄᓪᓚᒃᑲᓗᐊᕋᒪ ᑕᐃᒪ'ᓇᔫᖅ!

. . . ᓇᕕᐊᕋᓗ ᑖᒪᓇ ᐃᒃᔨᕙᐅᑕᖅ ᑐᓂ'ᓗᓂᐅᒃ ᔭᓇᔮᒧᑦ.

ᐊᖑᑕᐅᑦᕿᔮᖅ ᒌ-ᑏ: (ᓇᓄᕐᒧᑦ) ᔨᑯᖑᐊᑉᑎ'ᓂᑦ ᐊᔨᕙᑲᓇᑦ.

ᐊᕐᓇᐅᑦᕿᔮᖅ ᒌ-ᑏ: ᑕᐅᑐᒍᒪᖕᒋᑦᑐᖓ ᑕ'ᓇᐃᓚᐅᖅᑐᓂᒃ—ᐊᔨᐊᓄᖕᖓᐅᓂᐊᕋᒪ ᔭᐃᒪᓇᔮᐊᕐᓗᖓ.

ᑳᐱᑕᐃᔭ ᐃᔨᕐᔭᖑᔭᖅᑯᖅ.

ᓇᕕᐊᕋ: (ᐊᕐᓇᐅᑦᕿᔮᖅ ᒋ-ᑎᒧᑦ) ᒫᓕᒡᓚᖓ?

ᐊᕐᓇᐅᑦᕿᔮᖅ ᒌ-ᑏ: ᐄ, ᐊᑕᐃ.

ᐊᕐᓇᐅᑦᕿᔮᖅ ᒋ-ᑎᓗ ᓇᕕᐊᕋᓗ ᐊᓂ'ᓗᑎᒃ.

ᑳᐱᑕᐃᔅ: ᔮᒦᓕᖅᐸ ᑕᐃᒪ ᓇᓄᖅ?

ᐊᐃᓐᓯᕗᐊᑦ: ᒪᔪᕋᐅᑎᓃᑦᑐᖅ ᑎᒍᒥᐊᕐᓗᐊᖅᑐᖅ—

ᔭᓇᔮ: ᑕᒐᓇᓇᓗᒃ—

ᓘᓯ: ᑳᐱᑕᐃᔅ—ᓇᓄᖅ ᑐᕐᑯᔭᖅᑕᐅᑎᑕᐅᑦᑕᐃᓕ'ᔅᓴᖅᔨ.

ᒪᓇᓐᓄᐊᖅ: (ᓘᓯᒧᑦ) ᑳᐱᑕᐃᔅ ᔭᒪᓃᓕ'ᒪᑦ ᓈᒻᒪᖕᓂᐊᓕᖅᑯᖅ.

ᑳᐱᑕᐃᔅ ᑕᐅᓄᖓ ᑕᑯ'ᓗᓂ.

ᑳᐱᑕᐃᔅ: ᐱᕐᓚᒃᑲᓇᕐᓱᒃ ᐃᒻᓇ.

DUFORT: Here, sir?

CAPTAIN: Come a little farther this way.

MARIANNE: It's bedtime, Lucy. Let's go—

MARIANNE tries to get LUCY away from the situation.

LUCY: Grammy, no, I want to stay . . . I'm staying.

AINSWORTH, DUFORT, and MR. GRIFFITH-THOMSON help the STEWARD position the lifeboat directly over ANGU'ŘUAQ. It's a bit of a dance, moving this way . . . then that way.

STEWARD: Whooaa—watch your fingers—

AINSWORTH: Here, Captain?

CAPTAIN: A little farther to the right, to the right—no, to the left.

DUFORT: Aim for his head.

AINSWORTH: . . . It's trying to get away—

CAPTAIN: Keep going, keep going—no . . . other way, other way—

AINSWORTH: He's a wily bugger . . .

CAPTAIN: Keep it steady . . . keep it high as we can go . . .

They lift up the lifeboat as high as it can go.

. . . and one, two, three—RELEASE!

They hurl the lifeboat over the back of the ship and it lands on top of the bear. A thud is heard, then a high-pitched yelp/squeal . . . then a splash.

Silence.

ᐊᖑᑕᐅᑦᑭᖅᔭᖅ ᒌ-ᑏ ᑎᒍᔪ'ᒪᑦ ᔪᒡᔮᖅᔨᐊᕐᒥᒃ ᓂᓇᖁᓗᒃᑕᒃᓴᖅᑲᐅᖅᑐᒥᒃ ᔭᓇᔪᒪᑦᑎᐊᖅᑐᓂᒃ.

ᐊᖑᑕᐅᑦᑭᖅᔭᖅ ᒌ-ᑏ: ᓂᓇᑎᓚᕗᑦ.

ᐊᐃᓐᓯᕗᐊᑦ: ᐃᔨᒪᖅᑲᖖᕆᑦᑐᑎᑦ—ᒪᔪᖁᖅᑐᖅ ᑕᔭᒧᖕᒐ ᓂᓇᔪᒪ'ᒫᑎᒍᓪᓚ—

ᐊᖑᑕᐅᑦᑭᖅᔭᖅ ᒌ-ᑏ: ᓂᓇᓐᓄᐊᓪᓚᔅᔭᖅᑳᖅᓗᓂᓗᓐᓃᑦ ᐊᔪᐊᓄᖖᒐᐅᔪᖕᓇᖅᑐᖅ—

ᑳᐱᑕᐃᔅ: ᐄᖅᑭ ᖅᑭᒥᓇᖖᕆᓪᓗ—

ᐊᖑᑕᐅᑦᑭᖅᔭᖅ ᒌ-ᑏ: ᐊᔪᐊᓄᖖᒐᐅᓂᐊ'ᒪᓪᓚ ᐱᒍᑉᑕ—

ᐊᖑᑕᐅᑦᑭᖅᔭᖅ ᒌ-ᑏ ᔪᒡᔮᖅᔨᐊᖅ ᓂᖅᑭᓚᒃ ᐃᒋᓪᓚᔅᓴᖅᔪᓐᓇᖅᓱᓂᐅᒃ ᑕᐅᓄᖕᒐ ᓇᓄᖅᒍᑦ.

ᑳᐱᑕᐃᔅ: ᐄᖅᑭ, ᐱᔨᐃᑲᓇᑦ . . . ᐄᖅᑭ! ᐃᔨᒪᑦᑎᐊᖁᔨᐊᖅᓗᑕ ᑭᔪᐊᓂᒃ. (ᔭᓇᔫᒍᑦ) ᐅᒥᐊᓐᓄᐊᖅ ᑎᒻᒧᔾᔨᑎ ᐅᓄᖖᒐᖅᑎᕆᐊᖅᓗᒍ ᐊᔪᐊᒍᑦ ᐱᓚᐃ'ᓇᑉᑕ ᐊᔪᖅᓇᖅᔪ'ᒪᑦ.

ᔭᓇᔫ: ᐄ, ᐊᑕᓂᖅᔪᐊᖅ.

ᑳᐱᑕᐃᔅ: (*ᐊᐃᓐᓯᕗᐊᕐᒧᑦ, ᑑᕗᐊᖅᒧᓪᓗ ᐊᖑᑕᐅᑦᑭᖅᔭᖅ ᒌ-ᑏᒧᓪᓗ*) ᐊᖑᑎᑦ, ᐊᑕᐃ ᐃᑲᔪᓚᖅᔪᐅᒃ—ᑐᐊᕙ.

ᐊᓂ'ᓗᓂ ᔭᓇᔫ ᒪᓚᒃᓗᓂᒋᓪᓗ ᐊᐃᓐᓯᕗᐊᑦ, ᑑᕗᐊᖅᑦ, ᐊᖑᑕᐅᑦᑭᖅᔭᖅ ᒌ-ᑏᓗ. ᑖᒻᓇᓗ ᑳᐱᑕᐃᔅ ᑕᐅᓄᖕᒐ ᑕᑯᒋ'ᓗᓂ.

ᓘᓯ: ᓇᓄᖅᒥᒃ ᐃᑲᔪᖅᓂᐊᓚᖅᑐᑦ, ᓂᖕᒋᐅᖅ.

ᒪᓂᓐᓄᐊᖅ: ᐄ, ᐄ ᓇᓗᓇᕈᐃᖅᑐᖅ, ᐊᑕᐃ ᐅᓄᖖᒐᐅᓗᒃ ᐃᒡᓗᐊᕐᒧᑦ ᐃᓐᓇᓇᐊᖅᑲᓚᖁᕙᑦ.

ᓘᓯ: ᓇᓄᖅ ᐅᒥᐊᓐᓄᐊᕐᒧᑦ ᐃᓚᔭᐅᓂᐊᖅᑐᖅ ᑐᖅᑯᓂᐊᖖᕆ'ᒪᑦ.

ᓛ: ᐅᓐᓄᖕᒥᑦ ᐃᒥᖅᓗᒍᐃᖅᓂᐊᖅᑐᖕᒐ ᐃᒥᒐᐃᓐᓇᖅᓂᒃ ᐃᒥᒐᖅᓂᒃ ᐱᕙᓪᓗᖅᓂᐊᓚᖁᒪ.

ᐃᔪᖅᓗᑎᒃ ᔭᓇᔫ, ᐊᐃᓐᓯᕗᐊᑦ, ᑑᕗᐊᖅᑦ, ᐊᖑᑕᐅᑦᑭᖅᔭᖅ ᒌ-ᑏᓗ ᐊᒡᔭᖅᔨᔪᑦ ᑎᒻᒧᔾᔨᑎᓄᐊᖅᒥᒃ ᐅᒥᐊᖅᔪᐊᑉ ᖃᓴᓐᓄᐊᖕᒐᓂᒃ—ᐃᒡᓗᒃᑐᑦ ᒫᔾᔫ'ᓗᑎᒃ ᐊᒡᔭᖅᑕᐃᑦ ᑎᒻᒧᔾᔨᑎ. ᐃᒃᑕᓇᒃᐸᓪᓛᖖᕆᑦᑑᒐᓗᐊᖅ

The men look over and wait . . . then MR. GRIFFITH-THOMSON *turns around triumphantly.*

MR. GRIFFITH-THOMSON: Bull's eye!

AINSWORTH: Good man, Captain, good man.

DUFORT: It's not going to bother us anymore.

MR. GRIFFITH-THOMSON: Somebody go tell Roy . . .

Some people applaud and some do not. LEE *whoops.* MARIANNE *hugs* LUCY, *but* LUCY *pushes her grandmother away.*

The CAPTAIN *calls up to the bridge.*

CAPTAIN: Forwards full throttle.

Music can again be heard drifting up from the orchestra below deck.

Come along, folks, the night is young—there's lots of food and champagne and dancing until dawn.

LEE: Ainsworth, let's dance.

AINSWORTH: First I need some champagne.

MR. GRIFFITH-THOMSON *holds out a glass.*

MR. GRIFFITH-THOMSON: Me too.

MATSON *enters—excited.*

MATSON: QUICK, EVERYONE—COME TO THE STARBOARD SIDE NEAR THE BOW—THERE'S A MOTHER AND TWO CUBS STANDING ON AN ICE FLOE.

LEE: Lucy, come see the baby cubs.

MARIANNE: Lucy's upset.

ᑭᔨᐊᓂᒃ ᐊᖏᕝᔭᒃᑐᓇᓗᕐᔫ'ᒪᑦ ᑎᒻᒧᕝᔨᑎ ᑖᒻᓇ. ᐃᒥᖓᕝᔭᒃᑯᑎᒃ ᐱᔨᑦᑎᐊᖖᒋᑦᑐᑦ. ᐊᒡᔭᖅᔨᓇᔨᐊᖅᑯᑎᒃ ᐅᖅᑲᒪᖅᑲᑎᒌᒃᑐᒃ ᖁᔭᒋᓐᓇᖅ.

ᐊᐃᓐᓯᕈᐊᑦ: ᖃᓄᕐᓕᐅᕐᓂᕈᑦ ᑕᕝᕙ ᐊ'ᔮᖖᒍᐊᖅᑲᖅᑲᑕᐅᓇᓯ'ᒪᑦ ᖃᐅᔮᑉᑲᐃᕝᔨᑎᑉᑎ'ᓂ ᐳᓚᕋᖅᑐᒃᓴᓄᑦ.

ᑕᒪᕐᒥᒃ ᐃᒡᓚᓕᖅᑯᑎᒃ.

ᑳᐱᑕᐃᓯ: ᑐᐊᕕᐅᕐᑐᔨ, ᒪᔪᕋᕋᔨᐊᕐᓂᐊᓕ'ᒥ'ᒪᑦ . . .

ᑳᐱᑕᐃᔨ ᑕᐅᓄᖓ ᖃᐅᔮᔭᖅᑐᖅ, ᐊᖑᑎᑦ ᐅᒥᐊᓐᓄᐊᕐᒥᒃ ᑎᒻᒧᕝᔨᑎᒥᒃ ᑐᕌᖅᑎᑦᑎᐊᕐᑯ'ᑐᒋᑦ.

ᑳᐱᑕᐃᓯ: ᓇᓅᑉ ᖁᓛᓄᑦ ᑐᕌᖓᑎᑦᑎᐊᕐᓗᔨᐅᒃ.

ᑑᕈᐊᕐᑦ: ᐅᕈᖓ?

ᑳᐱᑕᐃᓯ: ᐊᕈᖖᒐᕋᓐᓂᓐᓄᐊᖅ.

ᒪᓇᓐᓄᐊᖅ: ᐃᓐᓇᓇᐊᖅᑲᓕᕋᕕᑦ ᐊᑕᐃ ᓲᓯ. ᐃᒡᓗᐊᑉᑎ'ᓅᖖᒐᐅᓗᒃ—

ᒪᓇᓐᓄᐊᖅ ᐊᔨᐊᓄᖖᒐᐅᑎᑦᑎᓇᔨᐊᕐᓗᐊᓕᖅᑐᖅ ᓲᓯᒥᒃ ᑕᑯᕐᑯᖖᒋ'ᓗᓂᐅᒃ.

ᓲᓯ: ᐄᖅᑭ ᓂᖏᐅᖅ, ᓴᒪᓃᑦᑐᒪᔪᖓ . . . ᓴᒪᓃᓂᐊᖅᑐᖓᓕ.

ᐊᐃᓐᓯᕈᐊᑦ, ᑑᕈᐊᕐᑦ, ᐊᖑᑕᐅᑦᑭᕝᔭᖅ ᒌ-ᑏᑐ ᐃᑲᔪᓕᖅᑐᑦ ᓴᓇᔨᒥᒃ ᑎᒻᒧᕝᔨᑎ ᓇᓅᑉ ᖁᓛᓄᖖᒐᖅᑎᑦᑎᐊᕋᔨᐊᖅᑯᒍ. ᑎᒻᒧᕝᔨᑎ ᐊᐅᓚᕙᒃᑯᓂ ᐊᕈᖓ ᓴᒍᖓᓗ, ᓄᑦᖃᖓᑎᓐᓇᔨᐊᖅᐸᒃᑯᓂᒋᑦ.

ᓴᓇᔮ: ᐊᓴᐃ—ᑎᑭᖅᑎᑦ ᐅᕝᔮᓇᑦᑭᑦ—

ᐊᐃᓐᓯᕈᐊᑦ: ᐅᕉᓇ, ᑳᐱᑕᐃᔨ?

ᑳᐱᑕᐃᓯ: ᑕᓕᖅᐱᒧᑦ ᓅᒐᓐᓂᓐᓄᐊᕐᑐᒍ, ᑕᓕᖅᐱᒧᑦ—ᐄᖅᑭ, ᓴᐅᒥ'ᓄᕙᑦᑐᖅ.

ᑑᕈᐊᕐᑦ: ᓂᐊᕐᑯᐊ'ᓄᑦ ᑐᕌᑦᑎᐊᕐᑐᑎᑦ.

ᐊᐃᓐᓯᕈᐊᑦ: . . . ᕿᒫᓇᔨᐊᓕᖅᑐᖅ—

MATSON: *(to LUCY)* The little cubs will cheer you up, Lucy. Their fur is pure white, like real snow!

CAPTAIN: LADIES AND GENTLEMEN—A MOTHER BEAR AND TWO CUBS UP NEAR THE BOW.

Everyone else exits with the exception of LUCY and MARIANNE.

LUCY looks over the railing of the boat.

LUCY: Hello. Hello . . .

MARIANNE: No, Lucy, don't look . . . come with me . . .

LEE: *(off stage)* Oh wow, aren't they so cute.

MR. GRIFFITH-THOMSON: *(off stage)* Stand against the railing so I can get you and the bears in the same shot.

AINSWORTH: *(off stage)* Perfect creatures!

LUCY: I can't see him, Grammy . . . where did he go?

MARIANNE: He's sailing away in the lifeboat, Lucy. Safe and sound.

LUCY: Is he, Grammy? Is he really sailing away?

MARIANNE: Yes, Lucy. Now let's go see the cubs.

MARIANNE takes LUCY's hand and they make their way to the bow as the whole ship begins to move out of sight . . .

Then ANGU'ŘUAQ—terribly wounded and shaking—is finally seen in the darkness, gasping for breath, gasping and gasping as he tries to stay afloat in the black, oily water.

He hears something and cocks his one ear, hoping to hear HUMMIKTUQ's voice on the wind . . . then he raises his foreleg as if reaching for help . . . but there is no help.

ᑳᐱᑕᐃᔭ: ᐊᑕᐃ ᐊᑕᐃ ᓴᒨᓇ—ᐋᖅᑭ . . . ᐃᒡᓗᐊᒍᕙᓪᓗᖅ ᐃᒡᓗᐊᒍᓪ—

ᐊᐃᓐᓯᕗᐊᑦ: ᓱᖅᑯᑕᐅᖕᖏᑦᑐᑉᑲᕆᓇᓗᒃ ᐅᓇ ᐊᔨᒪᐃᑦᑐᓇᓗᒃ . . .

ᑳᐱᑕᐃᔭ: ᐃᖑᑎᑦᑕᐃᓕᓗᔪᐅᒃ . . . ᐳᖅᑐᔮᒥᑎᑦᑎᐊᖅᓗᒍᓗ . . .

ᖃᖓᑦᑕᖅᑎᑦᑎᐊᕋᓱᐊᖅᓗᓂᒋᑦ ᑎᒻᒧᔮᑎ ᐅᒥᐊᓐᓄᐊᖅ.

ᑳᐱᑕᐃᔭ: . . . ᐊᑕᐅᔪᖅ, ᒫᕈᒃ, ᐱᖓᓱᑦ—ᐊᑕᐃ ᓴᐳᑲᖅᔪᐅᒃ!

ᓴᐳᑦᓚᖅᓵᓗᒃᔪᓐᓇᖅᐸᐃᑦ ᑎᒻᒧᔮᑎ ᑕᐅᓄᖓ ᓇᓅᑉ ᖄᖓᓄᑦ. ᐊᕚᖅᔪᒐᒥᒃ ᓇᓄᖅ ᐅᓇ ᑐᓴᕐᓇᓕᖅᑐᖅ ᖃᑕᐃᑦᑐᖅ ᕿᐊᔮᑐᑦ . . . ᐃᒪᕐᒧᑦ ᑲᑦᓗᓂ ᑐᓴᕐᓇᖅᑐᖅᓗ ᐃᒪᕐᒧᖕᖓᕋᒥ.

ᑕᐃᒪᓗ ᓂᐱᖃᕈᐃᖅᑐᖅᓵᓗᒃᓗᓂ.

ᐊᖑᑎᑦ ᑕᐅᓄᖓ ᑕᐅᑐᒃᑐᑦ ᐅᑕᖅᑭ'ᓗᑎᒡᓗ . . . ᑕᐃᒪ ᐊᖑᑕᐅᑦᖅᑭᔮᖅ ᒌ-ᑏ ᑐᓄ'ᓗᓂ ᓵᓚᖃᖅᑐᑐᑦ ᖁᕕᐊᓱᑦᖁᖅᓗᓂ ᐃᓵᒃᑕᖅᑐᖅ.

ᐊᖑᑕᐅᑦᖅᑭᔮᖅ ᒌ-ᑏ: ᑐᖅᑦᑎᐊᖅᑐᖅ!

ᐊᐃᓐᓯᕗᐊᑦ: ᐃᓄᑦᑎᐊᕚᒃ, ᑳᐱᑕᐃᔮ, ᐊᖑᑎᑦᑕᐅᔮᑎᑦ.

ᑑᕗᐊᖅᑦ: ᐃᓱᒪᒋᔮᒃᓴᐅᓱᐃᓕᖅᑯᖅᓕ.

ᐊᖑᑕᐅᑦᖅᑭᔮᖅ ᒌ-ᑏ: ᕈᐃ ᐃᒪᓇ ᐊᒃᐱᐅ'ᔮᐅᑲᖅᓕ . . .

ᐃᓚᐃᑦ ᐸᑦᑕᒃᑐᖅᑐᑦ ᐃᓚᐃᑦ ᐸᑦᑕᒃᑐᖕᖏᑦᑐᑦ. ᓛ ᓂ'ᓕᖅᑎᖅᑐᐊᓗᒃ. ᒪᕆᓐᓄᐊᖅ ᔫᓯᒥᒃ ᐃᖅᑭᔪ'ᓗᓂ ᑭᔪᐊᓂᒃ ᔫᓯ ᐃᖅᑭᑕᐅᔮᒪᖕᖏᑦᑐᖅ.

ᑳᐱᑕᐃᔭ ᐊᖅᑯᑎᓄᑦ ᑐᖅᓗᓚ'ᓗᓂ.

ᑳᐱᑕᐃᔭ: ᐊᑕᐃ ᐃᖏᕐᖄᓕᖅᑕ ᓱᑲᔮᒥᒃ.

ᐊᑖᓂᑦ ᑎᑕᒃᑐᓂᒃ ᑐᓴᕐᓇᖅᑐᖃ'ᒪᑦ.

ᑳᐱᑕᐃᔭ: ᐊᑕᐃ ᐅᓐᓄᒃᐸᓪᓛᖕᖏ'ᒪᑦ ᓱᓕ—ᓂᖅᑭᖃᑦᑎᐊᖅᑐᖅ, ᐃᒥᖅᓗᖃᖅᑐᖅ, ᐱᓘᖅᓗᔪ ᒧᒥᕈᓐᓇᖅᑐᔪ ᖁᕕᐊᓱᒡᓗᔪ.

ᓛ: ᐊᐃᓐᓯᕗᐊᑦ, ᒧᒥᖅᓗᒃ.

Gasping mightily for breath, ANGU'ŘUAQ *tries to hold up his head but has no strength left . . . struggling for life, he takes his last breath, and dies. His head falls forwards and for a brief moment he floats . . . then he slips under the water.*

This is the exact vision HUMMIKTUQ *foresaw in her dream five hundred years ago.*

Silence.

The end.

At curtain the madrigal "Weep, O Mine Eyes" by John Bennet blends with drumming by an Inuit artist.

Weep, O mine eyes and cease not,
Alas, these your spring tides methinks increase not.
O when you begin you to swell so high
That I may drown me in you.

ᐊᐃᓐᓯᕗᐊᑦ: ᐃᒥᕐᔪᖅᒥᒃ ᐱᑲᖅᑳᕐᓚᖓᓕ.

ᐊᖑᑕᐅᑦᕿᔭᖅ ᕇ-ᑏ ᐃᒪᐅᑎᓂ ᒪᓂᒋ’ᔪᓂᐅᒃ.

ᐊᖑᑕᐅᑦᕿᔭᖅ ᕇ-ᑏ: ᐅᕙᖓᓗ.

ᒪᑉᔮᖅ ᐃᓯᖅᑯᓂ—ᐅᐃᒻᒪᒃᑐᖅ.

ᒪᑉᔮᖅ: ᖃᐃᑲᓇᑦᑎ—ᔭᔪᖕᖓ ᓯᕗᐊᓄᑦ—ᑕᒃᑯᒃ ᓇᓄᖅ ᐊᑎᖅᑕᓚᒃ ᒪᕐᕈᖕᓂᒃ ᓯᑯᒦᑦᑐᑦ.

ᓛ: ᑕᒃᑯᒃ ᔫᓯ ᐊᑎᖅᑕᓐᓄᐊᒃ ᒪᕐᕈᒃ.

ᒪᓂᓐᓄᐊᖅ: ᔫᓯ ᕿᐊᔪᓐᖑᔪᖅ ᖁᕕᐊᔪᙱᑦᑐᖅ.

ᒪᑉᔮᖅ: *(ᔫᓯᒧᑦ)* ᑕᒃᑯᒃ ᐅᑯᐊᒃ ᖁᕕᐊᓇᖅᑐᓐᓅᒃ, ᔭᐃᒻᒪᕐᓂᐊᖅᑐᑎᑦ ᔫᓯ. ᒥᑦᕐᑯᖕᒋᑦ ᖃᕐᑯᖅᑐᐸᓇᓗᐃᑦ, ᐊᐳᑦᑐᑦ ᖃᑯᖅᑐᑦ!

ᑳᐱᑕᐃᔭ: ᐊᕐᓇᓪᓗ ᐊᖑᑎᓪᓗ—ᑕᑯᔭᒃᓴᑦ ᐅᑯᐊᑦ ᐊᕐᓇᓪᓗᖅ ᓇᓄᖅ ᐊᑎᖅᑕᓚᒃ ᒪᕐᕈᖕᓂᒃ ᐅᒥᐊᕐᔪᐊᑉᑕ ᓯᕗᓂᐊᓂ ᑕᐅᓇᓂ.

ᑕᒪᐃᑕ ᐊᓂ’ᔪᑎᒃ ᑭᓯᒥᒃ ᔫᓯᓗ ᒪᓂᓐᓄᐊᕐᓗ ᐊᓂᙵᕆ’ᒪᓂᒃ.

ᔫᓯ ᑕᐅᓄᖓ ᑕᑯ’ᔪᓂ ᓇᓄᕐᓄᑦ.

ᔫᓯ: ᐊᐃ. ᐊᐃ . . .

ᒪᓂᓐᓄᐊᖅ: ᐄᕐᑭ ᔫᓯ, ᑕᑯᓇᓱᐊᙵᕆᓪᓗᕆᑦ . . . ᒪᓕᙵ.

ᓛ: *(ᐊᕙ’ᙵᓕᑦ)* ᐅᑯᐊᒃ ᓂᕕᐅᕐᓇᖅᑐᕌᔫᒃ ᐊᑎᖅᑕᓐᓄᐊᒃ.

ᐊᖑᑕᐅᑦᕿᔭᖅ ᕇ-ᑏ: *(ᐊᕙ’ᙵᓕᑦ)* ᐊᕗᙵᓕᕐᔪᓯ ᑕᐅᑐᖕᓇᖅᑎᓐᓇᓱᐊᕐᔪᒋᑦ ᓇᓄᐃᑦ ᐊ’ᕚᓚᐅᕐᓂᐊᕐᒪ ᑕᑯᒃᓴᐅᖅᑲᑕᐅᑎ’ᔪᓯ.

ᐊᐃᓐᓯᕗᐊᑦ: *(ᐊᕙ’ᙵᓕᑦ)* ᓇᓄᑦᑎᐊᕙᓇᓗᐃᑦ!

ᔫᓯ: ᐊᖑ’ᔦᐊᖅ ᑕᐅᑐᖕᓇᕈᐃᖅᑐᖅ ᓂᖏᐅᖅ . . . ᓱᒍᙵᓕᐅᕙᓚ ᑕᐃᒪ?

ᒪᓂᓐᓄᐊᖅ: ᑎᒻᒧᔾᔦᑎᒃᑯᑦ ᓱᒍᑭᐊᖅ, ᔫᓯ, ᓈᒻᒪᒃᑐᒦᑦᑐᖅ ᖃᓄᓇᔭᐅᓚᐃᓕᖅᑐᖅ.

ᓘᓯ: ᓂᖏᐅᖅ, ᔭᓕᔪᒥᒃ ᑎᒻᒧᔾᔪᑎᒃᑰᓕᖅᐸ? ᔭᓕᔪᒥᒃ?

ᒪᓂᓐᓄᐊᖅ: ᐄ, ᓘᓯ, ᐊᑕᐃ ᐊᑎᖅᑕᓐᓄᐊᒃ ᑕᑯᓴᖅᑐᖅᑎᑦᑯᒃ.

ᒪᓂᓐᓄᐊᖅ ᐃᓐᖑᑕᓂ ᑕᓯᐅᖅᓗᓂᐅᒃ ᐅᒥᐊᕐᔪᐊᑉ ᔪᕕᓐᖑᓗᓄᑦ ᐱᔭᒃᓗᑎᒃ ᐅᒥᐊᕐᔪᐊᕐᑐ ᑕᐅᑐᖕᓇᕿᐃᖅᐸᓪᓕᐊᓕᖅᓗᓂ . . .

ᑕᐃᒪᑐ ᐊᖑ'ᔪᐊᖅ—ᐋ'ᓂᖅᑕᐅᓯᒪᓪᑐᐊᖅᑐᖅ ᓴᔪᒃᑐᕌᑐᓪᑐ—ᑕᑯᒃᓴᐅᓕᑕᐃᓐᓇᓕᖅᑯᖅ ᑖᖅᑐᒥ, ᐊᓂᖅᓵᖅᑐᕋᔭᐊᖅᑐᖅ, ᐃ'ᓴᖑᔾᔫᖅᑐᖅ ᐃᑐ'ᒍᑦ ᐊᓂᖅᓵᑦᑎᐊᖅᓴᓇᙱᑦᑐᖅ ᓇᓘᔮᕐᑐᐊᖅᓗᓂ ᐃᒪᕐᒥ ᕿᕐᓇᓇᒃᑐᒥ ᐅᖅᔪᕐᔪᐊᓕᓇᑐᖕᒥ.

ᑐᓴᕐᒥᓕ ᔭᓇᒥᒃᑭᐊᖅ ᔨᐅᑎᐱᑐᐊᕐᒥᒍᑦ ᑐᓴᕐᔭᐊᓕᖅᓗᓂ ᑐᓴᕈᒪᒐᒥᓕ ᔭᒻᒥᒃᑰᖅ ᓂᐱᐊ'ᓂᒃ ᐊᓄᓇᑦᑯᑎᒍᑦ . . . ᑕᐃᒪᑐ ᐃᓯᒐᓂ ᐃᓴᒃᓗᒍ ᔮᕐᑐ ᐃᑲᔪᖅᑕᐅᔪᒪᔪᑐᑦ . . . ᑭᓯᐊᓂᒃ ᐃᑲᔪᖅᑕᐅᓇᙱᑦᑐᖅ.

ᐊᓂᖅᓵᕐᔭᐊᖅᑐᕐᑐᐊᓕᖅᓗᓂᑐ ᐊᖑ'ᔪᐊᖅ ᐋᕐᑐᖕᒐᓐᓇᔭᐊᖅᓗᓂ ᓴᖖᕇᓪᑐᐊᕕᓕ'ᒪᑦ ᐊᔪᓕᖅᑐᖅ . . . ᐆᒪᓇᔭᐊᕐᑐᐊᖅᓗᓂ ᐊᔪᓕ'ᒪᑦ ᑕᔾᓭᑐ ᑭᖑᓪᓕᖅᐹᑦᑎᐊᕐᒥᒃ ᐊᓂᖅᓵᖅᑐᖅᐳᖅ ᐊᓂᕐᓂᖅᑲᕈᐃᓕᖅᓗᓂᑐ ᑐᕐᑯ'ᑐᓂᑐ. ᓂᐊᕐᑯᐊᑐ ᔭᑭ'ᑐᓂ ᓯᕕᑭᑦᑐᒥᒡᑐ ᐳᒃᑕᐅᒪᔪᖅ . . . ᑕᐅᓄᖕᒐᑐ ᐃᒪᕐᒍᑦ ᑭᕕᔅᓴᖕᒍᔭᖅᓗᓂ.

ᑕᓴᒻᒪ ᔭᒻᒥᒃᑐᕐᑐᓘᑉ ᑕᐅᑐᒃᐸᕇᖅᔪᒪᔫ ᔪᓐᓇᒃᑑᒪ'ᑐᓂ ᐅᑭᐅᑦ 500 ᑕᐃᑉᓱᒪᓂ.

ᓂᐸᐃᔾᔭᓇᒃᑐᖅ.

ᐃᔭᐊ ᑕᔾᓭ.

ᖃᑉᑐᓈᑦ ᐱᔫᑦ ᑐᓴᕐᓇᓕᖅᓗᓂ ᑕᐃᔭᐅᔪᖅ ᖁᒻᕕᐅᕐᑕᒃ ᐃᔮᑦᑲᒃ, ᔫᓐ ᐸᓇᑦ ᐱᔭᐊ, ᐊᑕᐅᑦᑎᑦᑯᑦ ᐃᓄᐃᑦ ᕿᓚᐅᑕᐃᓪᑐ ᐊᑐᖅᑕᐅᔪᑦ.

ᖁᒻᕕᐅᕐᑕᒃ ᐃᔮᑦᑲᒃ,
ᔭᓇᐅᕝᕙ, ᐅᐱᓐᖕᓛᑦᑯᑦ ᖁᕕᐊᓇᐃᑦᑑᓂ'ᒪᑦ, ᐃᒪᖅᑐᔪᒍᓂ ᑕᐃᒪ ᑕᓇᐅᖅ
ᐅᑯᓂ ᖁᕕᐅᕐᓂᕐᒍᑦ ᐃᒫᕈᒪᐅᓐᓃᑦ.

THE ONE WHO ADOPTED A POLAR BEAR

BY NILAULAAQ AGLUKKAQ, GJOA HAVEN, NUNAVUT

PUBLISHER'S NOTE

This version of "The One Who Adopted a Polar Bear" comes straight from Nattilingmiut oral tradition and has never been written down. Nilaulaaq is one of the few people who currently carry this story from a long line of intergenerational oral transmission. Nilaulaaq, Colleen, and Siobhan are pleased to include this story here, as it helps to document and share the Nattilingmiut version using new technologies for the community and for the readers of the play. Nilaulaaq's recording of this version can also be heard directly at www.tamalik.com. It is important to the community that the oral version remains available along with the written versions.

TRANSLATOR'S NOTE

As a child in her fishing camp at Nattilik Lake and as a student of her language and cultural courses in the winters at Keeveeok School in Taloyoak, Nunavut, I've been enriched by Nilaulaaq's lively stories my whole life. We worked together on this piece so I could explore the underlying impressions of her phrases and expressions to bring you, the reader, a bit closer to the experience of being with her, if only through text. She is a unilingual Elder—we work together in her language. In my effort to bridge her language, the original language of the story, and a version for an English audience, I tried to recreate her masterfully painted scenes by exploring her vivid use of words, intonation, and breath in the oral recorded form. We also had conversations together about different scenes, and so I've enriched the English translation with some of her elaborations from those talks. Nattilingmiut dialect and culture is particularly colourful, flavourful, and nuanced. The English translation is adapted, not

ᑎᒍᐊᖅᑐᕕᓂᖅ ᓇᓄᐊᓐᓄᐊᕐᒥᒃ—ᓂᓚᐅᑖᖅ
ᐊᒡᔫᒃᑲᐅᑉ ᐅᓂᑉᑳᖅᑖ

ᓂᐱᓕᐅᖅᑐᖅ ᑎᑎᕋᖅᓱᓂᐅᒃ ᖅᑲᑉᑐᓅᑑᓕᖅᓱᓂᐅᒃ ᔮᓇᑦ ᑕᒪᓕᒃ ᒪᒍᕋᐅᑉ, ᐅᒥᓕᐅᑉ ᔩᑎᐅᑉ ᐸᓂᐊ ᑕᑐᕐᔪᐊᓂ ᐱᕈᕐᓂᑰᔪᖅ ᐃᓕᓴᐃᔭᖅᑲᖅᓱᓂ ᓂᓚᐅᑖᕐᒥᒃ ᓄᑕᕋᐅ'ᑐᓂ.

ᓂᐱᓕᐅᖅᔪᒪᔪᒥᑦ ᑕᔅᕙ:

ᐅᓇ ᐱᒋᐊᕈᑎᒋᓂᐊᖅᑕᕋ ᔪᕗᓪᓛᑦᑐᒥᒃ ᐆᒃᑐᕐᓂᐊᖅᑕᕋ ᐅᓂᑉᑳᕈ'ᔭᐅ'ᑐᖓ ᔪᓂᓕᖅᐸᔪᒐᒪ ᑕᐃᑉᓱᒪᓂ ᔪᓂᓕᕐᑲᑦᑕᖅᔪᒪᓕᕋᑉᑕ ᐊᖓᔪᒐᑐ. ᑕᓴᑉᑯᓄᖓᑦ ᔪᓐᓇᒃᓴᐅᑎᕐᑲᖅᓱᑕ ᐅᓂᑉᑳᕐᓂᒃ ᔪᓐᓇᒃᓴᖅᑕᐅᕙᔪᒐᑉᑕ ᕐᑯᖏᐊᒐᕐᑲᖏ'ᒪᑦ ᐊᔪᐊᓂᒃ. ᐅᓐᓄᓕᓵᓐᓄᐊᖅᑎ'ᑐᒍᑐ ᑕᐃᒪ ᑕᓴᑉᑯᐊᑦ ᐊᖓᔪᖅᑳᖅᑯᑦ ᓇᑦᓚᕆᐊᕌᖓᑕ ᓇᑦᓚᕐᑯᔪᐅᕙᒃᑲᑉᑕ ᓇᑦᓚᖅᑕᐅᕙᔪ'ᑐᑕ ᐊᓂᕐᑯᔪᐅᖏ'ᑐᑕ ᐅᓐᓄᒃᑯᑦ ᐅᑉᓛᓐᓄᐊᒃᑯᓪᓗ ᑐᐸᕐᑲᔪᕌᖓᑕ ᑐᐸᒃᐸᒃᓱᑕ ᑕᐃᒪ'ᓇ ᐅᑉᓛᓐᓄᐊᒃᑯᑦ ᐃᓕᓴᕐᓇᖏᑦᑑᒐᑐᐊᖅ ᐅᑉᓛᓐᓄᐊᒃᑯᑦ ᑕᒫᓂ ᔪᓚ ᖃᐅᒪᓕᓵᓐᓄᐊᖅᑎ'ᑐᒍ ᐃᑖ'ᓂ ᑖᖅᑎ'ᑐᒍ ᑐᐸᒃᐸᓚᐅᕋᑉᑕ. ᑕᔅᕙ ᔪᓐᓇᒃᓴᖅᑕᐅ'ᑐᑕ ᐃᒪ'ᓇ ᐱᔭᐅᕙᔪᒐᑉᑕ ᐅᓇ ᐅᓂᑉᑳᕐᓂᐊᖅᑕᕋ ᔪᕗᓪᓛᑦᑐᖅ . . . ᓇᐃᑦᑐᓐᓅ'ᒪᑦ.

ᑕᐃᑉᓱᒪᓂ ᓴᒃᑯᐊᑦ ᐱᔭᕐᑲᖅᐸᔪᖏ'ᒪᑕ ᐊᕐᓇᑦᕐᑯᐊᔅᓴᓇᑐᒃᓱᑎᒡᑐ ᑭᔪᐊᓂᒃ ᐃᓅᕙᔪ'ᒪᑕ ᑕᐃᒪ ᐊᕐᓇᑦᕐᑯᐊᖅᑐᖃᔭᐅᖅᑲᑦᑕᖅᑐᑦ ᑕᐃᑉᓱᒪᓂ ᐋᓂᑦᕐᑳᓕᖀᖓᑕ ᑭᔪᐊᓂᒃ. ᐋᓂᑦᕐᑳᓕ'ᒪᙴᖅ ᑕᔅᕙ ᐊᕐᓇᑦᕐᑯᐊᖅᑐᓕᖅᑐᑦ ᓇᑐᔪᐅᔨᐃᖅᐸᒃᑐᑦ ᑎᒫᒍᑦ ᐊᐅᓚᓐᓂᖓᑦ ᖃᐅᔭᒪᔪᐅᓕᖀᖓᒥᒃ. ᐋᓂᑦᕐᑳᓕᕿᒥᒎᖅ ᑕᔅᕙ ᐊᕐᓇᑦᕐᑯᐊᖅᑯᖅ—ᑕ'ᓇᐃᓕᔪᐅᕙᔪᔪᒎᑦ.

ᑖᒻᓇ ᐊᕐᓇᑦᕐᑯᐊᖅᓵᓐᓄᐊᕉᖅ ᐱᔮᕐᑲᖅᑲᖏ'ᑐᓂ ᓄᑕᕋᖅᑲᖏ'ᑐᓂ ᐃ'ᓇᒥ ᓇᓄᐊᓐᓄᐊᕐᒥᒎᖅ ᒥᑭᔪᓐᓄᐊᕐᒥᒃ—ᓇᓐᓄᒃᑐᖅᑲ'ᒥᒐᒥ

literal, as there are so many underlying cultural agreements in Nattilingmiutut that are not available to the English audience. It never deviates from the original content and structure though: only minor explanations are added. It's a real honour to support her life's work of preserving Nattilingmiut dialect and culture. The syllabic transcription of this story utilizes the adapted syllabic system that was developed by Nilaulaaq and Nattilingmiut teachers in Gjoa Haven, Taloyoak, and Kugaaruk, Nunavut.

—Janet Tamalik McGrath

THE ONE WHO ADOPTED A POLAR BEAR

I am going to begin a series with this particular story. Back in the day, I was told many stories while in bed at night, as was the usual routine for my older sister and me. These special times were filled with stories to go to sleep by, and were a child's way to learn many things. So, when it was right at the edge of evening, we'd wait for our parents to arrange themselves on the family bed. Of course, we were also expected to go to bed then too. As children we were not allowed out at night and we were also expected to rise promptly in the early morning along with our parents. We didn't rise early for the purpose of going out to a school, as there was no such thing in my childhood. We'd rise each day with the first signs of light in the morning, and sometimes even while it was still dark out. Storytelling was our way of being prepared for a restful night's sleep. This story is the first in my collection that I'll share, because it is very short.

Back then, there were people who might happen to be alone in life, and therefore without any help, like older women on their own. Yet, they also lived just fine for the most part. At that time, it was customary to call an old woman by the term *arnatquaqšaaq* only when they were clearly elderly, for example, with perhaps a bent-over posture and an unsteady gait. The term was only used for someone with permanent features that were the hallmarks of advanced age: this woman I speak of was a true woman of age—an arnatquaqšaaq. This particular small and old woman had all the features of a very old being. But she was also without a helper, without any children around her. This was her situation.

Then one day, as it happened, there was a tiny little bear cub—as someone had apparently caught a female bear for food and the cub had been orphaned. Because of the woman's situation, the people gave the cub to her to adopt and raise as her own. And so it goes, the woman adopted a little polar bear cub to raise it.

And with this little gift of life, she was very blessed and she treated him exactly like her very own child. She cared for him, nurtured him, and tenderly

ᐊᕐᓇᐃᖅᑕᐅ'ᒪᑦ—ᓇᓄᐊᓐᓄᐊᕐᒥᒨᖅ ᑎᒍᐊᖅᑎᑕᐅᒍᖅ. ᑎᒍᐊᖅᑎᑕᐅᒍᖅ ᓇᓄᓐᓄᐊᕐᒥᒃ ᒥᕐᑭᕆᓐᓄᐊᕐᒥᒃ.

ᑎᒍᐊᖅᑎᑕᐅᒐᒥᒨᖅ ᑕ'ᓇ ᓄᑕᖅᑲᒥᑐᑦᑎᐊᖅ ᓄᑕᖅᑲᑐᑦ ᐸᒥᖅᓴᖅᑖ. ᐸᒥᖅᓴᕐᒥᐅᒃ ᑕᐃᒪ'ᓇ ᐱᕐᑲᑎᕌᓐᓇᖅᓗᒍ ᐃᒡᓗᒥᓃᕐᒥᓐᓇᖅᑎᓕᖅᓗᓂᐅᒡᓗ ᕆᓚᓪᓕᐅᒐᒥ ᐊᕆᖅᑲᖕᒥ'ᓇᒥ. ᑕ'ᓇᒨᖅ ᐱᕐᕿᑎᓕᕐᒥᐅᒃ ᐸᒥᖅᓴᕐᒥᐅᒃ ᓂᓇᑉᑲᖅᐸᒃᓗᒍ ᑕᐃᒪ'ᓇ ᑲᒪᒋᑦᑎᐊᖅᓗᒍ. ᓄᑕᖅᑲᒥᑐᒻᒪᓇᒃ ᑕ'ᓇ ᓇᒡᓕᒋᓕᖅᓗᓂᐅᒃ.

ᑕᕝᕙᒨᖅ ᐱᕈᖅᐸᓪᓕᐊᓂᖕᒐᓂᒃ ᑕᐃᒪ'ᓇ ᐊᔪᕈᐃᖅᓭᖅᐸᓪᓕᐊ'ᓗᒍ ᐃᓕᕐᒥ ᑕᓯᑉᑯᓂᖕᒐᖕᒨᖅ ᐃᓄᖕᓄᑦ ᖃᐅᕆᒪᕗᐅᓕᕐᒥ ᑖᒻᓇᓗ ᐊᕐᓇᑦᕐᑯᐊᖅᑰᖅ ᐃᑲᔪᖅᑐᒐᐅᑳᖅᑐᒃᓴᐅᓐᓂᕐᒥ. ᕋᓕᐊᓇᐊᕌᖕᒐᑕᒨᖅ ᐊᐅᓪᓚᕌᖕᒐᑕ ᑕᐃᒪ'ᓇ ᐊᐅᓪᓚᖅᑎᑕᐅᓐᓄᐊᕐᑲᑦᑕᖅᓗᓂ ᐊᖕᒋᕝᕙᕌᖕᒐᒥᒃ, ᐊᖕᒋᕝᕙᕌᖕᒐᑕ ᐅᔨᕆᓭᐅᕙᒃᑲᒥ ᐱᕋᒃᓗᓂᓗ ᐃᑉᐸᒃᑲᒥ. ᐊᖕᒋᕝᕙᕌᖕᒐᒥᒨᖅ ᑕᕝᕙᖕᒐ ᑎᒍᐊᖅᔨᒥᓄᑦ ᐃᔨᖅᐸᒃᓗᓂ ᑕᐃᒪ'ᓇ. ᐅᒡᓚᕌᖕᒐᓪᓗᒨᖅ ᑎᒍᐊᖅᔨᓂ ᐹᖅᑲᑎᒋᕙᒃᓗᓂᐅᒃ ᑕᐃᒪ'ᓇ ᑕ'ᓇ ᐊᔪᕈᐃᖅᓴᒌ ᔨᕗᓪᓛᑦᑐᒥᒃ.

ᑕᕝᕙ ᑎᒍᐊᕐᒥ ᐱᔪᖕᓇᖅᔨ'ᒪᑦ ᐃᓂ'ᒪᑦ ᐱᕌᒋᓕᖅᓗᓂᐅᒡᓗ ᑕᐃᒪ'ᓇ ᑐᑭᔨᐊᑦᑎᐊᖅᑐᕉᖅ ᐃᓄᐃᑦ ᐅᖅᑲᐅᔨᖕᒋ'ᓂᒃ ᐅᖅᑲᒪᕆᓂᒃ ᑐᑭᔨᐊᑦᑎᐊᖅᑐᖅ ᑭᔨᐊᓂᒃ ᐅᖃᓪᓚᓚᐃᑦᑐᖅ ᐅᖃᓪᓚᓚᐃ'ᓗᓂ ᑕᐃᒪ'ᓇ. ᒪᐅᖅᔫᖅᑲᑕᐅᖅᑲᑦᑕᓕᖅᑯᕉᖅ ᑎᒍᐊᖕᒐ ᑖᒻᓇ ᐃᓂᕐᒥ ᒪᐅᓕᖅᑐᐊᓗᖕᓃᓕᕐᒥ ᑕᓖᓂ ᒪᐅᖅᔫᖅᑲᑕᐅᖅᑲᑦᑕᓕᕐᒥ ᐊᑎᖅᑲᑕᐅ'ᓗᓂ ᑕᐅᓄᖕᒐ ᐅᔨᕆᓭᐅᕋᐃᕐᒥ ᐱᕋᒃᓗᓂ ᑕᐃᒪ'ᓇ ᖃᒧᑎᑦ ᖃᓂᖕᒐ'ᓂᒃ ᒪᓕᒃᓗᓂ ᑕᐃᒪ'ᓇ ᐃᓚᐅᕙᒃᓗᓂ.

ᑕ'ᓇᒨᖅ ᒪᐅᖅᔫᓕᕌᖕᒐᑕ ᓂᒃᐸᓂᕌᖕᒐᑕ ᐊᒡᓗᔨᕝᕆᑎᕙᒃᓗᓂᒋᓪᓗ ᑕᐃᒪ'ᓇ ᐃᓚᐃᑦ ᐊᒡᓗᒥᒃ ᓇᒡᕖᑭᑎᕙᒃᓗᒋᑦ ᓇᓇᐊᖅᐸᒃᑲᒥ. ᑕᕝᕙᒨᖅ ᓂᒃᐸᓕᖅᐸᑕ ᐅᐃᕝᒍᓕᖅᐸᒃᓗᓂᒋᑦ ᑖᕝᕙᖕᒐ. ᐅᐃᕝᒍᖅᑑᖅᑕᐅᕆᑦ ᑕᓭᑉᑯᐊᑦ ᐊᒡᓗᓂᒃ ᕿᓂᖅᓗᑎᒃ ᓇᓂᔩᖕᒐᒥᒃ ᑕᐃᒪᓐᓇ ᖁᑖ ᐊᔪᕝᕙᒃᑲᑦᑕᖅᓗᒍ ᓇᑦᑎᖅᑎᑦᑎᓇᕋᐊᖅᓗᓂ ᑕᓭᑉᑯᓂᖕᒐ ᐃᓄᖕᓂᒃ. ᑕ'ᓇᒨᖅ ᐅᐃᕝᒍᖅᓗᓂ ᓇᑦᑎᖅᑎᖅᑲᑦᑕᖅᑑᒐᒥ ᐅᐃᕝᒍᖅᑲᑎᖅᑲᖅᑐᒃᓴᐅᒐᒥ. ᓇᑦᑎᕌᖕᒐᒥᓐᖕᒨᖅ ᑎᖕᒍᒃᑐᓇᐊᕌᖕᒐᑕᒨᖅ ᑲᑎ'ᓗᑎᒃ ᑕᕝᕙᖕᒐ ᑎᖕᒍᒃᔨᐅᖅᑐᖅᑲᕌᖕᒐᑦ ᓇᑦᑎᖅᑐᖅᑲᕌᖕᒐᑦ. ᑎᖕᒍᒃᑐᓕᕌᖕᒐᑕᒨᖅ ᑎᖕᒍᒃᑐᖅᑲᑕᐅᕙᒃᓗᓂ ᑕᐃᒪ ᓂᓇᖅᑲᑕᐅᕙᒃᓗᓂ.

ᐊᖕᒋᕝᕙᐅᒋᐊᕌᖕᒐᑕ ᑕ'ᓇᒨᖅ ᐅᖅᑲᒪᓕᕌᖕᒐᑕ ᕋᒎᑦ ᐊᒡᓗᒎᖕᒐᐅᓂᐊᕐᒥᒃ ᐅᖅᑲᒪᓕᕌᖕᒐᑕᒨᖅ ᓈᓚᒃᐸᒃᓗᓂ ᑐᓴᕙᒃᓗᓂ ᐃᓚᐅᖅᑲᑦᑕᖕᒋ'ᓗᓂ

watched over him while providing all his needs. She had the little cub by her side always and she kept him inside her home as well, so the two lived alone together in their dwelling. And so it was that she was his mother, and she cared for, fed, and loved the little thing just like he was her very own.

And as time went on, and this cub grew bigger, she began to train and educate him to give him the skills he would need in life. After a while, the people in her camp became accustomed to seeing her adopted bear-child and they accepted him as part of their community. They could see how the bear would potentially be of great support to the aged woman in the long run. With that awareness, when they prepared to go away hunting, they began to include the bear in some ways. At first, one could see him coming home with the hunters from a trip—he'd be proudly perched up on the *qamutik* (dog-team sledge) as he was too young to run or walk all the way at that time, but he did walk a bit even then. And when, on such occasions he returned home, he would enter his adoptive mother's home like his very own home, which of course it was by now. And when she went out and about on visits to the people, she'd bring the bear along, all with the intention of preparing him with a basic understanding of humans and their ways and behaviours.

And so it was, as time passed further, that her adopted son had matured to a responsible stage of life, and sure enough, he became her provider. By then, he could understand all of the human conversations, understanding people very well. The only thing was that he could not utter a word himself, not even a single one. Even with this complete silence, he was a capable and responsible member of the community of hunters. Of course, by this time, he also didn't even need to ride on the qamutik at all. Instead, he powerfully walked right behind it, following it, as he participated as one capable of carrying his own weight.

As a community member, the bear faithfully offered his skills in sniffing out the seal holes. This was a hard task for the hunters on their hunting trips to the sea ice, because the holes are well hidden. These hunting trips require much patience and skill in general, both to find the holes and then to wait—often a long time—for a seal to come up for breath. In this way, the bear helped many to find the seals' breathing holes faster, by using his sensitive sniffer. Each time they were out on the sea ice to hunt for seals, the bear would roam about in a certain pattern to make short the difficult task of locating the breathing holes. When he'd find such a hole, he'd then carefully remove the snow from the opening to prepare it for the hunters' use. And so it was like that. He'd walk over the wide ice plain scanning for signs, and perhaps he had a human friend that he would do this together with. Because of his role, when the hunters caught a seal and they shared in the ritual of eating the fresh liver together, the bear also took part in the special ceremony and ate a morsel just like the others.

ᐅᖃᒪᓚᐃ’ᓇᒥ ᑭᔪᐊᓂᒃ ᐃᓚᐅᔾᔨᕙᒃᑐᑎᑦ. ᐊᖏᕐᖁᐅᒋᐊᖁ̇ᖕᖓᑕᓗᒎᖅ
ᑕᐃᒪ’ᓇ ᐊᖏᕐᖁᐅᖃᑕᐅᕙᒃᑐᓂ.

ᐊᖏᕐᖁᖁ̇ᖕᖓᒥᒎᖅ ᑎᑯᐊᖅᔪᒥᓄᑦ ᑕᕐᕚᖕᖓ ᐃᔪᖅᐸᒃᑐᓂ.
ᓇᑦᑎᖅᑐᖃᖁ̇ᖕᖓᖕᖒᖅ ᑖᒻᓇ ᑎᑯᐊᖅᔪᐊ ᓂᖃᐃᑐᖅᑎᑕᐅᕙᒃᑐᓂ,
ᓂᕿᒥᒃ ᑐᓂᔾᔪᕙᒃᑐᓂ ᐅᖅᓱᐊᓂᒃᑯ ᑕᐃᒪ’ᓇ ᑎᑯᔾᔪᒥ’ᓄᑦ ᐊᓐᓂᐅᒪᔨᖅ
ᓂᖃᐃᑐᖅᑎᑕᐅᕙᒃᑲᒥ ᓂᕆᕙᒃᑲᒥ.

ᑕ’ᓇᒎᖅ ᒪᐅᖅᓱᖅᑐᐊᓘᖕᖓᒥᒃ ᐅᑭᐅᖕᖓ ᑕᕙᒻᓇ.
ᐅᐸᓗᖅᑐᔪᓚᓗᐊᖅᑐᒥᒎᖅ ᓇᑦᑎᖅᓴᖅᑯᐃᖅᑲᕐᕙᓇᓗᒃᔪᓐᓇᖅᑯᑦ
ᓇᑦᑎᖅᓴᖅᑯᐃᖅᑐᐊᓘ’ᒪᑕ ᐅᐸᓗᖅᑐᔨᒥ ᑕ’ᓇᐃᓕᔨᒃᓴᐅᔨᒥ
ᑖᖅᔪ’ᔭᐃᖅᑎ’ᓗᒍ. ᓇᑦᑏᓪᓕᐅᓕᖅᑐᐊᓘᖕᖓᒥᓐᖒᖅ ᑳᓕᖅᑲᕐᕙᓇᓗᒃᔪᓐᓇᖅᑯᑦ
ᑳᓕᖅᑲᕐᕚᓗᒃᑲᒥᓐᖒᖅ ᑖᒻᓇᒎᖅ ᓇᓄᕈ̇ᖅ ᐳᑖᓕᖁ̇ᖕᖓ ᐳᑖᖅᑐᓂ
ᑕᐃᒪ’ᓇ ᓈᓚᒃᐸᒃᑐᖅ ᔮᒧᑦ ᐊᐅᓪᓚᕐᓂᐊᓇᐊᒃᓴᐃᑕ ᐊᖃᒍᙳᒎᖅᐸᑦ. ᑕ’ᓇ
ᓈᓚᒃᐸᒃᑲᒥ ᐃᓚᐅᕙᒃᑲᓗᐊᖅᑐᓂ ᓇᑦᑏᓪᓕᐅᖅᑲᔨᐊᓗᐃᑦ ᑳᓕᖅᑲᔨᑦ
ᔪᓚᓪᓕᓈᑦ ᑖᐸᑯᐊᑦ.

ᓄᓇᓗᒎᖅ ᑕᑦᐸᖕᓇ ᐅᖕᖓᔪᓇᓗᖕᖠ’ᓗᓂ ᑕᐅᑐᖕᓇᖅᑐᓂ ᓄᓇ ᐃᑦᑐᖅ,
ᑕᓄᐅᖕᒋᓐᓇᕐᖢᑦᑐᑦ ᑖᐸᑯᐊᑦ. ᑳᓕᖅᑲᓕᖁᒥᓐᖒᖅ ᓂᖃᐃᔭᒃᔪᐅᓕᖁᒥᒃ
ᐃᑖᓐᖒᖅ ᐅᖄᓪᓚᒃᑯᖅ ᑖᒻᓇ ᓇᓄᖅ ᑐᔪᑎ’ᓇᒍ ᑎᖅᓕᐊᓘᑉᓕᖅᑐᓂ,
“ᑕᑭᒃᓱᒪ ᐊᖅᓇᑦᖁᐊᖅᔮᐸ ᑎᑯᐊᖕᖓ ᑐᖅᑯᔪᖅᓗᒍ ᓂᕈᔾᔭᐅᓚᓗᐊᖅᑯᖅ”
ᑕ’ᓇᓪᓕᐅᖃᑦᑕᓕᖅᑐᑎᓐᖒᖅ ᐅᖄᓚᖃᑦᑕᓕᖅᑐᑦ. ᐊᖅᓇᑦᖁᐊᖅᔮᕈ̇ᖅ
ᐊᒃᐱᐅ’ᔫᐅᒍᖅ ᑖᒻᓇ: ᑎᑯᔾᔫᖕᖒᖅ ᑐᖅᑯᔪᓚᐅᓗᓂ ᓂᕈᔾᔪᐅᔪᒪᔫᓚᓗᐊᖅ
ᐊᒃᐱᐅ’ᔫᐅᒍᖅ.

ᐊᖅᓇᑦᖁᐊᖅᔮᖅᓗ ᑖᒻᓇ ᓄᑕᖅᑲᓂ ᑖᒻᓇ ᑎᑯᐊᓂ ᔫᖅᑲᐃᒻᒪ
ᓄᑕᖅᑲᒥᑐᑦ ᐸᒥᖅᓴᖁᒥᐅᒃ ᐊᓐᓂᓇᓕᖅᓗᓂᐅᒃ ᓇᓪᓕᒋ’ᓗᓕᐅᓪᓗ. ᑕᔾᕗ
ᐊᐃᑉᖄ’ᓗᓂᒎᖅ ᐊᐃᕈᖅ ᑖᒻᓇ ᓇᓄᖅ ᐅᓐᓄᒃᑯᑦ ᔪᓂᖕᓇᖅᔪ’ᒥ’ᒪᑦ
ᐊᐃᕈᖅ ᐳᑖᖅᑳᖅᓗᓂ, ᓇᖏᖅᔪ’ᒪᑦ ᑕᐅᓄᖕᖓ ᐊᒃᐱᐅᑎᕖ ᑎᑯᐊᓂ,
“ᑎᑯᐊᒃ, ᑐᖁᔭᐅᓗᑎᓐᖒᖅ ᓂᕈᔾᔪᐅᔪᒪᓕᖅᑐᑎᑦ” ᐊᒃᐱᐅᑎᕖ. ᓇᓄᕈ̇ᖅ
ᑖᒻᓇ ᔪᑭᓚᒥ ᑕᐅᓄᖕᖓ ᑎᑯᐊᖅᔪᒥᓄᑦ ᔭᖕᖓᓄᙵᖅᓗᓂ. ᖁᔾᕚᔾᒎᖅ
ᑕᐅᓄᖕᖓ ᑲᑕᖓᓕᖅᓗᑎᒃ ᕿᐊᓕᖅᓗᓂ ᓂᐱᖃᙵᒋ’ᓗᓂ.

ᕿᐊᓕ’ᒪᑦ ᐊᒃᐱᐅᑎᕖ ᐅᖃᐅᑎᓕᖅᐹ: ᑎᑯᐊᒃ, ᐅᓐᓄᐊᒍᑦ
ᔪᓂᓕᖅᑲᒃᐸᑕ ᑕᑦᐸᐅᖕᖓ ᓄᓇ ᒥᒃᓵᓄᑦ ᐊᐅᓪᓚᕈᖕᓇᕈᕝᕕᑦ
ᐊᐅᓪᓚᖅᓗᑎᑦ, ᔪᑯ ᑕᕙᒻᓇ ᔪᖁᐸᑎᓕᕐᓂᖅᐸᓪᓘᓐᓃᑦ ᑕᒪᐅᖕᖓ ᓄᓇᐸ
ᔫᓂ ᓇᓗᓇᐃᖅᔪᒪᒋᐊᕈᖕᓇᖅᑰᓚᓗᐊᖅᑐᑎᑦ ᑕᑦᐸᐅᖕᖓ ᐱᔮᓪᓗᖕᖓ
ᓄᓇᒨᖕᖓᐅᓇᔮᐊᖅᓂᐊᖅᑯᙱᖅᓱᓂᒎᖅ ᐆᓇᐃᑦᑐᐃ’ᒪᓐᖒᖅ

And at the end of those hunting trips when they would get ready to leave to go home, the hunters often shared their thoughts with one another about which area they would next search for seal breathing holes. To these conversations, the bear would listen very attentively. He'd hear and understand everything, but never would he speak with them, because indeed he could not speak. And even so, he was a full participant in everything the hunters did. As they would all leave to return to their homes from a hunt, the bear appeared to any onlooker to be just one of the hunters.

And upon arriving back from a hunting trip, the bear would go into his adoptive mother's home, returning to where he belonged. His mother was always given a portion of the catch of the day because her son was part of the successful hunt. She'd be given portions of meat and fat and that food kept her well and alive.

That was how it was in this particular year during the winter of his maturation. As it happened though, in the season of the long day, there was all of a sudden a change, and there were no seals to be found. It happened right at the time when there was no more darkness in the skies. And without a supply of seals, of course, the people became very hungry and close to the point of starvation. The bear in this situation still very dutifully carried out his practice of visiting about and listening to the people talk about where they were going to try and look for food on the next day's hunt. And so it was, he'd be listening for information, but the situation was desperate and there were no seals time after time and the people of the camp were famished.

There was a highland that could be seen up there a far way away in the distance, and the peoples' camp was in the lower sea area. They were all very wretchedly hungry by now and they had no more resources whatsoever to draw upon. At that point one of the people said—of course, when the bear was nowhere around—he said, "That old woman down there has a bear that we can kill and eat!" And then the idea this one proposed began to spread in their midst. Someone heard the idea and went to warn the old woman and said, "Your beloved adopted one is in danger of being killed because the people want to eat."

So the old woman, with regards to hearing this about her bear-child—her adopted beloved one—the one she raised close to her bosom like her own child, she of course reacted with an urge to do something. So that evening, when he had returned home from his visiting about in the camp—as he usually did—and just when he had settled a bit, as it was about time to go to sleep, the small old woman stood up in front of him, to try to be closer to his height. She solemnly looked up at him in the eyes and said, "Listen, my dear one, there are some that are making arrangements to kill you and eat you . . . "

ᓄᓇᒧᖖᖓᐅᓗᖕᖓ ᑕᑦᐸᐅᖕᖓ ᓯᓂᕋᒃᓗᖕᖓ ᓄᓇ ᑕᔭᒻᓇ ᓯᓈᒧᑦ ᐱᓱᒃᓗᖕᖓ ᕿᓂᖅᐸᒧᒫᖅᐸᕆᑦ, ᐊᒃᐱᐅᑎ'ᒪᒍ.

ᐅᓐᓄᐊᕈ'ᒪᓐᖖᖅ ᑖᒻᓇ ᓇᓄᖅ ᔭᐃᒻᒪᒃᑲᒥ ᐅᓐᓄᐊᕈ'ᒪᑦ ᐃᖅᓯᓇᖅᑐᒃᓵᐅ'ᒪᑦ ᐃᖅᓯᖓᒥ. ᐅᓐᓄᐊᕈ'ᒪᓐᖖᖅ ᐊᓂᖓᒥᖖᖅ ᑎᒍᐊᖅᓯᐊᑕ ᐊᐅᓪᓚᕐᑯ'ᒪᒍ ᓄᓇᒧᑦ ᑕᑦᐸᐅᖕᖓ ᐅᓐᓂᖅᑑᑎᑦᑎᐊ'ᒪᒍ ᐊᐅᓪᓚᖅᓗᓂ.

ᐊᕐᓇᑦᕐᑯᐊᖅᓛᕁᖅ ᑖᒻᓇ ᐊᓯᖅᑲᐃᖅᓗᓂ. ᐊᓯᖅᑲᐃᕋᒥ ᐊᐅᓪᓛᖅᑲᓕᔅᔭᓗ'ᒪᑦᑕ ᐃᓄᖅᑲᐃᓕ'ᒪᑕ ᑕᑦᖅᑲᑦᑯᐊᑦ ᐃᒡᓗᕕᒃᑲᑦ.

ᐊᕐᓇᑦᕐᑯᐊᖅᓛᓐᓄᐊᔅᓗᒎᖅ ᑖᒻᓇ ᑎᒻᒧᑦ ᑕᑦᐸᐅᖕᖓ ᐱᓱᕆᐊᔅᔭᖖᒍᔾᔭᖅᑯᖅ. ᐱᓱᒃᑲᒥ ᑕᑦᐸᐅᖕᖓ ᑎᒻᒎᕙᒃᑲᒥ ᓄᓇᒧᓐᖖᖅ ᑕᑦᐸᐅᖕᖓ ᐃᒪᕈᖅᐸᑦᓛᖖᕆᓐᓂᖕᖓᓂᒃ ᑎᒻᒧᒃᑲᒥ.

ᓄᓇᒎᖅ ᑕᔭᒻᓇ ᓯᓂᕋᒃᓗᒍ ᑕᐅᓄᖕᖓ ᐱᓱᒃᐸᓕᖅᑯᖅ ᐱᓱᒃᐸᓕᕋᒥ ᕐᑯᕕᐊᑦᑕᒃᓯᖅᐸᒃᓗᓂ ᓯᓂᒃᐸᒃᓗᓂ ᓄᓇᒥ ᑕᒫᓂ.

ᑕᐅᓇᓂᒎᖅ ᓯᓂᕋᒃᓗᒍ ᐱᓱᓕ'ᒥ'ᒪᑦ ᑕᑲᑦᑯᐊᓐᖖᖅ ᓇᓐᓄᓐᖖᖅ ᑕᐅᓇᓂ ᐱᖕᖓᓱᑦ ᐊᕐᑯᐱᓲᑦ ᓯᑯᐸ ᖄᖕᖓᓂ ᓯᕐᑯᒥᓯᒪᐅᓕ'ᒪᑦ ᑕᔭᒻᓇ ᓯᕐᑯᒥᓯᒪᓲᓂᒎᖅ ᐱᖕᖓᓲ'ᓗᑎᓐᖖᖅ ᓇᓐᓄᓐᖖᖅ ᑕᐅᓇᓂ ᑕᐅᑐᖕᓇᖅᓯ'ᒪᑕ. ᑎᒫᓄᓐᖖᖅ ᑕᒪᐅᖕᖓ ᐱᓱᒃᑲᒥ ᑐᖅᓗᓚᕚᐃᑦ: ᑎᒍᐊᒃ . . . ᑎᒍᐊᒃ . . . ᑎᒍᐊᕋ ᓇᐅᒃ-ᑐᖅᓗᓂᒎᖅ ᑐᖅᓗᓚᐅᓕᖅᑐᖅ. ᑖᖅᑯᐊᓐᖖᖅ ᓇᓐᓄᓐᖖᖅ ᒪᑭ'ᓇᒥᒃ ᑕᐅᓄᖕᖓ ᕿᒪᓯᔅᔭᖖᒍᔾᔭᖅᑯᑦ ᐱᖕᖓᓱᑦ, ᑕᐅᓄᖕᖓ ᑕᓇᐅᒧᑦ. ᕿᒫ'ᒪᑕ ᑎᒍᐊᓂ ᑕᔾᔭᕚᖖᕆᑦᑐᖅ ᓇᓗᓱᐃᕋᒥ.

ᐱᓱᒃᐸᓕᓇᕗᖅ ᑞᕗᖕᖓ ᓯᓂᕋᒃᓗᒍ ᓄᓇ ᑕᔭᒻᓇ ᐱᓱᒃᐸᓕ'ᒥᖓᒥᒍᖅ, ᓇᓐᓄᒃᑕᐅᑦᕈᖅ ᑖᖅᑯᐊᒃ ᑕᐅᓇᓂ ᓯᑯᐸ ᖄᖕᖓᓂ ᐊᕐᑯᐱᓲᒃ ᐊᕐᑯᐱᓲᓐᖖᖅ ᑕᑲᓐᓇ ᑕᑯᕆᕞᕆᒃ ᓇᓐᓄᒃ. ᓱᓕᒎᖅ ᑎᒫᓄᖖᖓᐅᓕᔅᔭᓗ'ᒥᖓᒥ ᑐᖅᓗᓚᐅᓕᓇᕗᖅ: ᑎᒍᐊᒃ . . . ᑎᒍᐊᒃ . . . ᑎᒍᐊᕋᓇᐅᒃ-ᑐᖅᓗᓂᒎᖅ ᑐᖅᓗᓚᐅᓕᖅᑐᖅ. ᑖᒻᓇᒎᖅ ᐊᐃᑉᐹᒎᖅ—ᐊᕐᑯᐱᓲᖓᒥ ᑕᒪᕐᒥᒃ— ᐊᐃᑉᐹᒎᖅ ᓇᖕᕆᖅᓯᖓᒥᒎᖅ ᑕᐅᓇᓂᒎᖅ ᑕᓯᑎᓕᖅᑐᖅ ᑎᒥᓂ ᑕᔭᒻᓇ ᐱᖅᑲᐃᔭᓕᖅᓗᒍ ᑕᔾᔭ'ᖓᖅ ᓇᖕᕆᖅᓯ'ᓗᓂ. ᑖᒻᓇᒎᖅ ᑕ'ᓇᐃᓪᓕᐅᖅᑖᕋᒥ ᑕᐅᓇᓂ ᐱᖅᑲᐃᔭᖅᑖᕋᒥ ᓇᓅᖅᑲᑎᓂᒎᖅ ᐅᕐᓂᒃᐹ ᐊᕐᑯᐱᓲᖅ. ᑕᔾᔭᕗᖖᒎᖅ ᑎᑭ'ᓇᒥᐅᒃ ᒥ'ᖕᕆᔅᔭᖖᒍᔾᔭᖅᐹ ᑕᒪᐅᓇᒎᖅ ᑐᐸᕐᑯᔮᖕᖓᑕ ᓇᑖᒧᑦ ᑮ'ᓗᓂᐅᒃ, ᑮ'ᓗᓂᐅᓐᖖᖅ ᑕᔾᔭᕗᖕᖓ ᑭᖕᒥᖅᑐᖓᓇᓗᕆᓕᕋᒥᐅᒃ ᑐᐸᕐᑯᔮᖕᖓᒍᓐᖖᖅ ᑕᔾᔮᕗᓇ ᑰᖓᒥᐅᒃ ᑐᕐᑯᔭᖅᓗᓂᐅᒃ. ᑐᕐᑯ'ᒪᓐᖖᖅ ᑭᖕᒥᐊᖅᓗᓂᐅᒃ ᑕᔾᔮᕗᓇ ᑕᑦᐸᐅᖕᖓ ᐃᒫᕈᑎᖓᒥᐅᒃ ᑕᑦᐸᐅᖕᖓᒎᖅ ᓇᕿᑎᓕᖅᐹ.

ᓇᕿᑎᓕᕋᒥᐅᒃ ᑎᒍᐊᖅᓯᒥᓄᑦ—ᑎᒍᐊᓇᓐᓂᓚᒎᖅ ᑕᔾᔭᕚ—ᑕᑦᐸᐅᖕᖓ'ᒪᓐᖖᖅ ᑕᒪᐅᖕᖓᒎᖅ ᓇᑯᒃᓗᓂ ᑕᑦᐸᐅᖕᖓᕈᑎᖓᒥᐅᒃ.

The polar bear then dropped his head down slowly in order to meet the height of his human mother and he went face to face with her. Then great, large, wet tears splashed down to the ground from his eyes as he began to cry while looking into her eyes. His cry was of course completely silent, as he could not make any sound, but his sadness was expressed nonetheless.

As the bear stood there weeping, his mother began to speak to him about a plan she had to save him from this situation:

> This evening when we are sure that all of them have gone to sleep, you must go up to the land up there. If you can reach that far highland up there, then you *must*. And then later in this season, when the sea ice begins to break up, as it usually does, you can see where the sea meets the land, and that is the path I will try and take to go up towards the land where you are and look for you. When it is no longer cold out, I will make the trek up inland myself by following the distant shoreline as a reference. I will walk and I will search for you with everything in me.
>
> This is what she said to him.

Then the evening quietude came, and by now the polar bear was solaced by his adoptive mother's words and by her plan, because he had been very afraid with the news he had heard about what the people wanted to do to him. Indeed, it must have been a very frightful situation for them. And so then the bear slipped out, leaving his home, and he made his way up towards the highland, as instructed by his mother. And he listened to exactly how she described the land to be along the way and he followed precisely everything she had explained to him.

Now the old woman was at home alone again. She was all alone as she had been before. But this time, she was truly alone, as even the camp members had moved away in their search for food, so she had no more neighbours around her now either.

By and by, when the weather warmed up, this tiny little old lady began a mighty journey up towards the highlands on foot. She walked further and further up and away from the sea while always keeping the shoreline in view, ascending higher and higher on her trek. She knew she needed to complete the whole journey before the land there got wet and mushy from melt water, as it does at that time of the year.

Then, when the old woman arrived at a certain point, she then began her descent by going parallel to the visible shoreline. As she walked down—she was by now quite exhausted—she did everything she could to keep her attention alive and not give way to drowsiness or lose her balance. When she had

ᑕᔅᕙᓂᒎᖅ ᑎᒻᒧᒃᑲᒥᐅᒃ ᓄᓴᒃᓱᓂᐅᒃ ᓄᓇᓕ’ᑐᓂᐅᒃ ᑖᒻᓇ ᓇᓄᖅ.
ᓄᓇᓕ’ᒪᒍᒎᖅ ᑖᑉᓱᒪᒎᖅ ᐊᕐᓇᑦᕐᑯᐊᒃᓵᑉ ᐱᓚᓕᖅᓱᓂᐅᒃ, ᐱᓚᒃᓱᓂᐅᒡᓗ
ᓇᓄᖅᑑᒪᓕᖅᓱᑎᒃ ᑕᐃᒪ’ᓇ ᓂᕐᑭᒋᕐᓴᖕᖑᓴᖅᐹᒃ ᑕᒫᓂ ᓂᕐᑭᒋᓕᕋᒥᔅᓴᒎᖅ
ᑖᒻᓇᒎᖅ ᑎᒍᐊᕐᒥᓃᓕᖅᓱᓂᓗ ᑕᐃᒪ’ᓇ ᑎᒍᐊᓂᓗ ᑕᐃᒪ’ᓇ
ᓴᓕᐊᖅᑕᕐᑲᑦᑕᓕᖅᓱᓂ ᑕᔅᕙᓂ ᓄᓇᒦᓕᖅᓱᑎᒃ ᑕᔅᕙᓂ.

ᑕᔅᕗᖕᒐᓗ ᓇᓗᓕᕐᓱᒃᓱᒍ ᖃᓄᕐᓕᐅᒻᒪᓇᐊᒃᓂᐊᓵ ᑭᖑᐊᒍᑦ.
ᑎᒍᐊᕐᒥᓃᓕᓇᐊᖕᖑᓂ ᑐᓴᕐᓇᖅᑑᒐᓗᐊᖅ. ᓇᓗᓕᕐᓱᒃᐸᕋ.

walked enough for a time, she'd then lay to sleep right on the open tundra. Each day she walked yet again, in the same fashion, guided by the view of the distant shoreline to keep herself oriented.

After some time of walking like this, one day, all of a sudden, she spotted three bears crouched in a sitting position on all fours on some ice pans down on the ocean's surface. The three bears on the ice pans were a welcomed sight for her indeed. As she headed towards the lowland she cried out in their direction with a heartfelt longing, "Beloved adopted one, beloved adopted one . . . whhhere . . . now . . . is . . . my dearly beloved?" With that, all at once, all three of the bears jumped up and took right off, running away, further down on the sea ice. She could tell by the way they shot off that indeed her beloved bear-child was not amongst them.

She then continued on her path, using the distant shoreline for her orientation. Later, as she walked on, two more bears came into her vision. As before, she headed towards the lowland while crying out to the bears she saw, "Beloved adopted one, beloved adopted one . . . whhhere . . . now . . . is . . . my dearly beloved?" With that, one of the two bears—they had both been down on all fours—stood up straight, took a distance from the other, and then he stretched his body down to energize his muscles. He then stood up again and stretched down once more. Then—all of a sudden, he swiftly charged at the sitting bear, lunging in on it and biting down firmly on its windpipe. He clamped down tightly with his great jaws, killing the bear. And when the bear was fully dead, he dragged it from the ice pans into the water, and he entered into the water with his catch. Then he swam through the water with the bear in his jaws, heading towards the shore to get to the land.

As the old woman watched this scene unfolding, it became apparent to her that the swimming bear was indeed her bear-child, and that he was bringing this gift of food to her. When the bear arrived at the shore, he dragged it up to the land, pulling it with his great jaws. Once the harvest was laid down on the land, the old woman began to skin it and cut up the meat. And there it was that there was food to eat at last! From this time on, the old woman stayed together with her bear-child, living as before, but in a new place on the land. Her bear-child would come and go from that new place from that time on, hunting as he did before, coming and going, providing for the two of them.

And this is the part where the story ends. I don't know what they did after that. What I heard is that whatever happened from there, they were always together. There is regrettably no more that I know about this story myself.

ACKNOWLEDGEMENTS

I am indebted to the following artists and organizations for their support and guidance: the Stratford Festival—Antoni Cimolino, Artistic Director; David Auster, Producer; and Bob White ("follow the bear"), Director of the Foerster Bernstein New Play Development Program—Reneltta Arluk, Director of Indigenous Arts at the Banff Centre; Catherine Banks; Zack Russell; Jillian Keiley, Artistic Director of the National Arts Centre English Theatre; Kevin Loring, Artistic Director of the National Arts Centre Indigenous Theatre; the Writers' Trust of Canada's Berton House Writers' Retreat in Dawson City, Yukon; the Canada Council for the Arts for their generous support; and the following actors who participated in an early reading of the play at the University of Alberta in Edmonton: Barry Bilinsky, Nadien Chu, Alex Donovan, Brian Dooley, Philip Geller, Evan Hall, Emily Howard, Joshua Languedoc, Sandy Nicholls, Sarah Ormandy, Steve Pirot, Jan Selman, Murray Utas, and Kathleen Weiss.

With thanks to the English and Indigenous Theatres at the National Arts Centre for their support of the translation—a significant contribution to this publication, the theatrical production, and to ongoing Inuktut language revitalization and cultural-preservation work in the community.

Thank you to Annie Gibson, Blake Sproule, and Jessica Lewis at Playwrights Canada Press for their excellent care and commitment to this epic publication. Thank you to the Stratford Festival—particularly C.J. Astronomo, David Auster, and Dona Hrabluk—for facilitating and providing support for the photo shoot that led to the cover image, and to Angu'řuaq's designer, Daniela Masellis, and photographer Ann Baggley.

Premiere director Reneltta Arluk was asked to present at the Puppet Power 2020: Puppets Go Existential conference, and created a pre-recorded video with Colleen Murphy, designer Daniela Masellis, and composer Carmen Braden to share their journey, process, and impact on the Stratford production of *The Breathing Hole*. The video she created can be found at https://vimeo.com/418021879/baf27bf883.

Born in Rouyn-Noranda, Quebec, and raised in Northern Ontario, Colleen Murphy won the 2016 and 2007 Governor General's Literary Award for English Language Drama for her plays *Pig Girl* and *The December Man / L'homme de décembre* respectively. Both plays were also awarded a Carol Bolt Award. Other plays included *The Society For The Destitute Presents Titus Bouffonius*, *Armstrong's War*, *The Goodnight Bird*, *The Piper*, and *Beating Heart Cadaver*, which was short-listed for a Governor General's Literary Award. She is also a librettist—*Fantasma* for composer Ian Cusson, *My Mouth On Your Heart* for composer August Murphy-King, and *Oksana G.* for composer Aaron Gervais—and an award-winning filmmaker. She has been Writer-in-Residence at six universities and Playwright-in-Residence at two Canadian theatres as well as at Finborough Theatre in the UK.

Siobhan Arnatsiaq-Murphy has performed traditional Inuit drum dance and has worked as a choreographer for over twenty years. She studied ballet and was in the aboriginal modern dance core at the Banff Centre for the Arts with the Aboriginal Dance Project. In her choreography work, Siobhan melds traditional drum dancing with modern dance. She is a graduate of the University of Victoria where she earned her law degree in 2005. She has worked as a lawyer and also taught drum dancing to youth and children. Siobhan lives in Iqaluit and has three wonderful daughters and a stepson.

Janet Tamalik McGrath grew up in Nattilik culture in the 1970s. Throughout her childhood and early teen years she lived on the land in the summers with Nattilingmiut families, becoming fluent in the dialect and familiar with traditional values and teachings. After high school she became a regional interpreter-translator for the Nattilik area, innovating on audio presentation modes, assisting in the documentation of Nattilik grammar, and supporting script and font amendments to reflect the dialect's unique phonemes. Her M.A. thesis was conducted and documented in Nattilingmiut dialect ("Conversations with Nattilingmiut Elders on Conflict and Change: *Naalattiarahuarnira*" 2004). Currently she works as a language advocate and consultant for Nattilik communities, and was approached by Qaggiavuut Society for assistance with *The Breathing Hole*.

A NOTE FROM QAGGIAVUUT

The 2017 production of The Breathing Hole *at the Stratford Festival was supported by the artists of Qaggiavuut from Iqaluit, Nunavut, facilitated by Exective Director Ellen Hamilton. This note accompanied the original production program.*

Qaggiavuut is a non-profit society dedicated to strengthening the Nunavut performing arts, with a focus on Inuit. In 2017 we begin an international fundraising campaign to build a Nunavut Performing Arts Centre—Nunavut is the only territory/province in Canada without one. We know that a space for the Nunavut performing arts is vitally important so that Nunavut, Canada, and the world can hear the Inuit point of view in our culture, when Inuit artists strengthen traditional practice and create new work.

The partnership between Qaggiavuut and the Stratford Festival was an exciting and challenging part of our drive to include Inuit in Canadian theatre. It began when director Reneltta Arluk reached out to us to hold a reading of *The Breathing Hole* with Inuit actors in Iqaluit, but immediately initiated an intense discussion about cultural authenticity and who can and how to create drama from the Inuit perspective in a post-colonial Canada. It was months of critique and two revisions by playwright Colleen Murphy based on feedback and cultural knowledge from Inuit actors Miali Buscemi, Vincent Karetak, Siobhan Arnatsiaq-Murphy, Annabella Piugattuk, Mary Itorcheak, Alika Komangapik, and Laakkuluk Williamson Bathory, but what it asserts is a genuine concern for authenticity and Indigenous cultural truth.

During the process, we coined a new term—Inuit Cultural Dramaturge—and Qaggiavuut looks forward to a productive and collaborative relationship between Canada's southern and northern theatre communities in the years to come. We urge all who wish to hear the voices of Inuit artists to help us build a Nunavut Performing Arts Centre and shout out "Qaggiavuut! Come into the large iglu that we have built together!"

First edition: November 2020
Printed and bound in Canada by Imprimerie Gauvin, Gatineau

Jacket photo of Angu'řuaq, designed by Daniela Masellis, by Ann Baggley, and provided with the support of the Stratford Festival.

PLAYWRIGHTS CANADA PRESS
202-269 Richmond St. w.
Toronto, ON
M5V 1X1

416.703.0013
info@playwrightscanada.com
www.playwrightscanada.com
@playcanpress

MIX
Paper from responsible sources
FSC® C100212
FSC www.fsc.org